Blood and Concrete

Blood and Concrete

*21st Century Conflict in Urban
Centers and Megacities*

Dave Dilegge, Robert J. Bunker,
John P. Sullivan, and Alma Keshavarz,
Editors

A Small Wars Journal Anthology

Rev. date: 01/12/2019

To order additional copies of this book, contact:
Xlibris
1-888-795-4274
www.Xlibris.com
Orders@Xlibris.com
788027

CONTENTS

Acronyms xv

Preface: to "Blood and Concrete"
           David Kilcullen xxxi

Foreword: Urban Warfare Studies
           John Spencer xxxix

Introduction: Blood and Concrete
           John P. Sullivan, Robert J. Bunker, Alma
           Keshavarz and Dave Dilegge xlvii

Chapter 1   Terrorism and Cities:
           A Target Rich Environment
           Russell W. Glenn 1

Chapter 2   Preparing for Future Joint Urban Operations:
           The Role of Simulations and
           the Urban Resolve Experiment
           Peter W. Wielhouwer 7

Chapter 3   Postcard from Mumbai: Modern Urban Siege
           John P. Sullivan and Adam Elkus 32

Chapter 4   The Future of Terrorism: Mass Hostage Taking
           in Russia and Mumbai
           Luke Allison 54

Chapter 5   London Riots: Decentralized Intelligence
           Collection and Analysis
           Alex Calvo 72

Chapter 6   Command of the Cities: Towards a Theory
             of Urban Strategy
             John P. Sullivan and Adam Elkus 84

Chapter 7   Urban Land Use by Illegal Armed Groups
             in Medellin
             Geoffrey Demarest..102

Chapter 8   The Strategic Challenge of Riots:
             Riot Action and Crowd Power
             John P. Sullivan and Adam Elkus 121

Chapter 9   Somalia 20 Years Later—Lessons
             Learned, Re-learned and Forgotten
             Michael A. Marra and William G. Pierce 136

Chapter 10   Into the Cities: Dark, Dense, and Dangerous
             Frank G. Hoffman...159

Chapter 11   The 'New' Playbook? Urban Siege in Nairobi
             John P. Sullivan and Adam Elkus 165

Chapter 12   Mega Cities, Ungoverned Areas,
             and the Challenge of Army Urban
             Combat Operations in 2030-2040
             David Shunk...173

Chapter 13   Narco-Cities: Mexico and Beyond
             John P. Sullivan...185

Chapter 14   A Proposed Framework for Appreciating
             Megacities: A US Army Perspective
             Michael Bailey, Robert Dixon, Marc Harris,
             Daniel Hendrex, Nicholas Melin and
             Richard Russo..200

Chapter 15   On Megacities
             Geoffrey Demarest..222

Chapter 16   Intelligence Challenges in Urban Operations
               James Howcroft 225

Chapter 17   Employing Armor Against the Islamic State:
               The Inevitable Urban Combined Arms Fight
               Dennis A. Lowe 237

Chapter 18   A Case for Reflection: On the Ground
               in Iraq, Afghanistan, and Detroit
               Kirby Dennis, Kris Karafa and Rebecca Patterson ...257

Chapter 19   Urban Siege in Paris: A Spectrum of Armed Assault
               John P. Sullivan and Adam Elkus 270

Chapter 20   Book Review: The Robin Hood Guerrillas
               Michael L. Burgoyne................................291

Chapter 21   City As a System Analytical Framework:
               A Structured Analytical Approach to
               Understanding and Acting in Urban Environments
               Mark Lomedico and Elizabeth M. Bartels 296

Chapter 22   The Role of CCTV in Terrorist TTPs:
               Camera System Avoidance and Targeting
               Christopher Flaherty................................309

Chapter 23   Operational Environment Implications
               of the Megacity to the US Army
               Darryl Ward.......................................325

Chapter 24   Technical Challenges for Simulation
               and Training in Megacities
               Jon Watkins and Chuck Campbell..........................335

Chapter 25   Megacities: The Good, the Bad, and the Ugly
               Russell W. Glenn 350

Chapter 26   How to Hold or Take a Big City—
               Seven Lines of Effort
               Geoff Demarest.......................................370

Chapter 27   U.S. Army Mega City Operations:
              Enduring Principles and Innovative Technologies
              Frank Prautzsch 382

Chapter 28   Megacities and Dense Urban Environments:
              Obstacle or Opportunity?
              Dawn A. Morrison and Colin D. Wood..................392

Chapter 29   Anticipating Megacity Responses to Shocks:
              Using Urban Integration and
              Connectedness to Assess Resilience
              Shade T. Shutters, Wes Herche and Erin King.........409

Chapter 30   Using the Internet of Things to Gain
              and Maintain Situational Awareness in
              Dense Urban Environments and Mega Cities
              Alfred C. Crane and Richard Peeke.......................420

Chapter 31   It's in There: Rethinking(?)
              Intelligence Preparation of the Battlefield
              in Megacities/Dense Urban Areas
              Richard L. Wolfel, Amy Krakowka Richmond,
              Mark Read and Colin Tansey 425

Chapter 32   An Analytical Framework for Operations
              in Dense Urban Areas
              William Hedges 435

Chapter 33   Assessing Physiological Response to Toxic
              Industrial Chemical Exposure in Megacities
              Danielle L. Ippolito..456

Chapter 34   Atmospheric Impacts and Effects
              Predictions and Applications for Future
              Megacity and Dense Urban Area Operations
              David Knapp, Robb Randall and Jim Staley............474

Chapter 35   Complex IPB
              Tom Pike and Eddie Brown 482

Chapter 36   Megacity Madness
Gustav Otto and A.J. Besik 493

Chapter 37   People, Infrastructure, and Conflict:
Analyzing the Dynamics of Infrastructure
Disruption and Community Response
Natalie Myers, Jeanne Roningen, Ellen
Hartman, Tina Hart, Scott Tweddale and
Patrick Edwards 503

Chapter 38   The Role of Network Science in Analyzing
Slums in Rapidly Growing Urban Areas
Amy Krakowka Richmond, Chris Arney,
Kathryn Coronges and Matthew Simonson 516

Chapter 39   Game Review: Operation Whirlwind—
The Soviet Assault on Budapest, 1956
Michael Peck...528

Chapter 40   On the Likelihood of Large
Urban Conflict in the 21st Century
Sean M. Castilla...533

Chapter 41   Fighting in Megacities—The Army's Next Challenge
Gary Anderson...543

Chapter 42   Enabling Smart City Resilience
Through Center of Gravity Analysis
Victor R. Morris 547

Chapter 43   Complex Cyber Terrain in Hyper-Connected
Urban Areas
Mike Matson 564

Chapter 44   Cyber Operational Considerations
in Dense Urban Terrain
Paul Maxwell, Andrew Hall and Daniel Bennett.....577

Chapter 45   A Flexible Data-Centric Approach for
              Modeling and Analyzing Hyper Connected Megacities
              K. Selçuk Candan, Shade T. Shutters and
              Christian Fortunato 596

Chapter 46   On a Modern Form of Terrorism:
              Small-Scale and Self-Contained
              Kyle R. Brady...602

Chapter 47   Preparing General Purpose Forces for Combat
              in Megacities: How Conventional Units Can
              Best Train for Fighting in Dense Urban Terrain
              Adam Scher 607

Chapter 48   The Tricky Business of Counting the Costs
              of Armed Conflict in Cities
              Robert Muggah..617

Chapter 49   Surrounded, Yet Unaware: Achieving Isolation
              in Future Urban Terrain
              Ryan Orsini 630

Postscript: Cities in the Crossfire:
              The Global Rise of Urban Violence
              Margarita Konaev 647

Afterword: Urban Operations: Meeting Challenges, Seizing
              Opportunities, Improving the Approach
              Russell W. Glenn 653

Recommended Reading 665

Selected References..667

Notes on Contributors..683

ABOUT SMALL WARS JOURNAL
AND FOUNDATION

Small Wars Journal facilitates the exchange of information among practitioners, thought leaders, and students of Small Wars, in order to advance knowledge and capabilities in the field. We hope this, in turn, advances the practice and effectiveness of those forces prosecuting Small Wars in the interest of self-determination, freedom, and prosperity for the population in the area of operations.

We believe that Small Wars are an enduring feature of modern politics. We do not believe that true effectiveness in Small Wars is a 'lesser included capability' of a force tailored for major theater war. And we *never* believed that 'bypass built-up areas' was a tenable position warranting the doctrinal primacy it has held for too long—this site is an evolution of the MOUT Homepage, *Urban Operations Journal*, and urbanoperations. com, all formerly run by the *Small Wars Journal's* Editor-in-Chief.

The characteristics of Small Wars have evolved since the Banana Wars and Gunboat Diplomacy. War is never purely military, but today's Small Wars are even less pure with the greater inter-connectedness of the 21st century. Their conduct typically involves the projection and employment of the full spectrum of national and coalition power by a broad community of practitioners. The military is still generally the biggest part of the pack, but there a lot of other wolves. The strength of the pack is the wolf, and the strength of the wolf is the pack.

The *Small Wars Journal's* founders come from the Marine Corps. Like Marines deserve to be, we are very proud of this; we are also conscious and cautious of it. This site seeks to transcend any viewpoint that is single service, and any that is purely military or naively U.S.-centric. We pursue a comprehensive approach to Small Wars, integrating the full joint, allied, and coalition military with their governments' federal or national agencies, non-governmental agencies, and private organizations. Small Wars are big undertakings, demanding a coordinated effort from a huge community of interest.

We thank our contributors for sharing their knowledge and experience, and hope you will continue to join us as we build a resource for our community of interest to engage in a professional dialog on this painfully relevant topic. Share your thoughts, ideas, successes, and mistakes; make us all stronger.

"…I know it when I see it."

"Small Wars" is an imperfect term used to describe a broad spectrum of spirited continuation of politics by other means, falling somewhere in the middle bit of the continuum between feisty diplomatic words and global thermonuclear war. The *Small Wars Journal* embraces that imperfection.

Just as friendly fire isn't, there isn't necessarily anything small about a Small War.

The term "Small War" either encompasses or overlaps with a number of familiar terms such as counterinsurgency, foreign internal defense, support and stability operations, peacemaking, peacekeeping, and many flavors of intervention. Operations such as noncombatant evacuation, disaster relief, and humanitarian assistance will often either be a part of a Small War, or have a Small Wars feel to them. Small Wars involve a wide spectrum of specialized tactical, technical, social, and cultural skills and expertise, requiring great ingenuity from their practitioners.

The *Small Wars Manual* (a wonderful resource, unfortunately more often referred to than read) notes that:

> *Small Wars demand the highest type of leadership directed by intelligence, resourcefulness, and ingenuity. Small Wars are conceived in uncertainty, are conducted often with precarious responsibility and doubtful authority, under indeterminate orders lacking specific instructions.*

The "three block war" construct employed by General Krulak is exceptionally useful in describing the tactical and operational challenges of a Small War and of many urban operations. Its only shortcoming is that is so useful that it is often mistaken as a definition or as a type of operation.

We'd like to deploy a primer on Small Wars that provides more depth than this brief section. Your suggestions and contributions of content are welcome.

Who Are Those Guys?

Small Wars Journal is NOT a government, official, or big corporate site. It is run by Small Wars Foundation, a non-profit corporation, for the benefit of the Small Wars community of interest. The site principals are Dave Dilegge (Editor-in-Chief) and Bill Nagle (Publisher), and it would not be possible without the support of myriad volunteers as well as authors who care about this field and contribute their original works to the community. We do this in our spare time, because we want to. McDonald's pays more. But we'd rather work to advance our noble profession than watch TV, try to super-size your order, or interest you in a delicious hot apple pie. If and when you're not flipping burgers, please join us.

Acronyms

3D	Third Dimension
4D	Fourth Dimension
5D	Five Dimensional
6LowPAN	Low-Power Wireless Personal Area Network
A2/AD	Anti-Access/Aerial Denial
AAV	Assault Amphibious Vehicle
ABM	Agent Based Model
AChe	Acetylcholinesterase
AFB	Air Force Base
AFV	Armored Fighting Vehicle
AGI	Artificial General Intelligence
AI	Area of Interest
AI	Artificial Intelligence
AICP	American Institute of Certified Planners
Alb	Albumin
ALI	Acute Lung Injury
ALP	Alkaline Phosphatase
ALT	Alanine Aminotransferase
ANG-2	Angiopoitetin-2
AO	Area of Operations
AOC	Army Operating Concept

APC	Armored Personnel Carrier
ARCIC	Army Capabilities Integration Center
ARDS	Acute Respiratory Distress Syndrome
ARL	Army Research Laboratory
ASAP	Advanced Strategic Art Program
ASCOPE	Areas, Structures, Capabilities, Organizations, People and Events
AST	Aspartate Aminotransferase
ASURE	Arizona State University Research Enterprise
AT	Anti-Tank
ATAK	Android Tactical Assault Kit
ATGM/AT	Anti-Tank Guided Missile/Anti-Tank
ATP	Army Techniques Publication
ATSD	Advanced Training and Simulation Division
AUC	Autodefensas Unidas de Colombia (Self Defense Forces of Colombia)
AWG	Asymmetric Warfare Group
AWPO	Army Weather Proponent Office
BACRIM	Bandas Criminales (Criminal Bands)
BBM	Blackberry Messenger
BCT	Brigade Combat Team
BNP	B-Type Natriuretic Protein
BOPE	Batalhão de Operações Policias Especiais (Special Police Operations Battalion)
BPL	Broadband over Power Lines
BUN	Blood Urea Nitrogen
C2	Command and Control
C4ISR	Command, Control, Computers, Communications, Intelligence, Surveillance, Reconnaissance
CA	Capability Approach

CAJIT	Central American Joint Intelligence Team
Cal	Calbindin-D28
CALL	Center for Army Lessons Learned
CAP	Comandos Armados de Pueblo (People's Armed Commandos)
CASCADE	Center for Assured and Scalable Data Engineering
CASI	Center for the Advancement of Sustainability Innovations
CAST	Center for Advanced Study on Terrorism
CBRNE	Chemical, Biological, Radioactive, Nuclear, Explosive
CC	Critical Capability
CC16	Clara Cell 16
CC-CR-CV	Critical Capability-Critical Requirement-Critical Vulnerability
CCTSO	Combatting Terrorism Technical Support Office
CCTT	Close Combat Tactical Trainer
CCTV	Closed Circuit Television
CEVT	Construction Equipment Virtual Trainer
ChAT	Choline Acetyltransferase
ChE	Cholinesterase
CI	Confidence Interval
CIA	Central Intelligence Agency
CK	Cytokeratin
CLA	Civil Liaison Administration
Clu	Clusterin
CNN	Cable News Network
CNS	Central Nervous System
CO	Carbon Monoxide
COA	Course of Action
COG	Center of Gravity
CONUS	Continental United States
COR1A	Coronin 1A

COTS	Commercial Off The Shelf
COX2	Cyclooxygenase Type 2
CPI	City Prosperity Index
CPK	Creatine Kinase
CPS	Cognitive, Physical, and Social
CR	Critical Requirement
CREATE	Cultural Reasoning and Ethnographic Analysis for the Tactical Environment
CROWS	Common Remotely Operated Weapon System
CS	2-Chlorobenzylidene Malononitrile (Riot Control Agent)
CSC	Cyber Support Center
CSO	Conflict and Stabilization Operations
CSO	Cyber Support Officer
CTTSO	Combating Terrorism Technical Support Office
CV	Critical Vulnerability
CVE	Countering Violent Extremism
DARPA	Defense Advanced Research Projects Agency
DC	Direct Current
DESA	Department of Economic and Social Affairs
DHS	Department of Homeland Security
DIA	Defense Intelligence Agency
DIMEFIL	Diplomatic, Information, Military, Economic, Financial, Intelligence, and Law Enforcement
DIY	Do It Yourself
DNA	Deoxyribonucleic Acid
DoD	Department of Defense
DOTMLPF	Doctrine, Organization, Training, Materiel, Leadership, Personnel, and Facilities
DREN	Defense Research and Engineering Network
DTIC	Defense Technical Information Center

DU/Area	Dwelling Units per Area
DUA	Dense Urban Area
DUCT	Dense Urban and Complex Terrain
DUT	Dense Urban Terrain
eCO_2	Exhaled Carbon Dioxide
ECOG	Environmental Center of Gravity
ELN	Ejército de Liberación Nacional (National Liberation Army)
EMON	Emergent Multi-Organizational Network
EMS	Emergency Medical Service
eNO	Exhaled Nitric Oxide
EO/IR	Electro-Optical Infrared
ERDC	Engineer Research Development Center
ESRI	Environmental Systems Research Institute
EUD	End User Device
F_2-IsoP	F_2-Isoprostanes
FAASV	Field Artillery Ammunition Support Vehicle
FAR	Floor Area Ratio
FARC	Fuerzas Armadas Revolucionarias de Colombia (Revolutionary Armed Forces of Colombia)
F-ASCOPE	Foreign-Area, Structures, Capabilities, Organizations, People and Events
FDNY	Fire Department, New York (City)
FIBUA	Fighting In Built Up Areas
FM	Field Manual
FMSO	Foreign Military Studies Office
FSB	Federalnaya Sluzhba Bezopasnosti (Federal Security Service)
FY	Fiscal Year

G	Generation
G2	Military Intelligence (Staff)
Gbps	Gigabytes per second
GCRI	Global Conflict Risk Index
GDP	Gross Domestic Product
GFAP	Glial Fibrillary Acidic Protein
GI	Gastrointestinal
GIGN	Groupe d'intervention de la Gendarmerie nationale (National Gendarmerie Intervention Group)
GIS	Geographic Information Systems
GOVT	Government
GPGPU	General Purpose Graphics Processing Units
GPS	Global Positioning Service
GRIA 1	Glutamate Receptor 1
GSG-9	Grenzschutzgruppe 9 (Border Protection Group 9)
GTD	Global Terrorism Database
GTS	Global Transaction Strategy
HADR	Humanitarian Assistance/Disaster Relief
HAS	Human Serum Albumin
HISA	Human-Infrastructure Systems Analysis
HITL	Human in the Loop
HPX	Hemopexin
HQ	Headquarters
HQDA	Headquarters Department of the Army
HRED	Human Research and Engineering Directorate
HRT	Hostage Rescue Team
HUMINT	Human Intelligence
IAG	Illegal Armed Groups
IBCT	Infantry Brigade Combat Team
IBM	Internal Business Machines

ICAM-1	Intercellular Adhesion Molecule-1
ICoE	Intelligence Center of Excellence
ICRC	International Committee of the Red Cross
ICS	Incident Command System
ICS	Industrial Control Systems
ICT	Information and Communication Technology
ICT	Internet Communications Technology
IDA	Institute for Defense Analyses
IDF	Israeli Defense Force
IDP	Internally Displaced Person
IED	Improvised Explosive Device
IEEE	Institute of Electrical and Electronics Engineers
IGO	Inter-Governmental Organization
IL	Interleukin
IMU	Inertial Measurement Unit
IN3	Internet Interdisciplinary Institute
IoP	Internet of People
IoS	Internet of Services
IoT	Internet of Things
IPB	Intelligence Preparation of the Battlefield
IPO	Intelligence Preparation for Operations
IPOE	Intelligence Preparation of the Operational Environment
IRA	Irish Republican Army
ISI	Islamic State of Iraq
ISIL	Islamic State in Iraq and the Levant
ISIS	Islamic State in Iraq and al-Sham
ISR	Intelligence, Surveillance, and Reconnaissance
IT	Informational Technology
ITAR	International Traffic in Arms Regulations
ITN	Intelligence Transportation Network
ITU	International Telecommunications Union

J9	Joint Experimentation Directorate
JAWP	Joint Advanced Warfighting Program
JCATS	Joint Conflict and Tactical Simulation
JCIDS	Joint Capabilities Integration and Development System
JFCOM	Joint Forces Command
JFE	Joint Forcible Entry
JIIM	Joint, Interagency, Intergovernmental, and Multinational
JMRC	Joint Multinational Readiness Center
JOF	Joint Operations Forces
JP	Joint Publication
JRTC	Joint Readiness Training Center
JSAF	Joint Semi-Automatic Forces
JUO	Joint Urban Operations
K	Kilogram
KIM-1	Kidney Injury Molecule-1
LAV	Light Armored Vehicle
Lcn2	Lipcalin 2
LCV	Live, Constructive, and Virtual
LED	Light Emitting Diode
LeT	Lashkar-e-Taiba (Army of the Righteous)
LG3	Prelecan C-terminal Fragment LG3
LIDAR	Light Detection and Ranging
LOC	Lab on a Chip
LOC	Lines of Communication
LOS	Line of Sight
LPO	Lipid Peroxiation
LSP-1	Lymphocyte Specific Protein-1
LTC	Lieutenant Colonel

LVC	Live, Constructive, Virtual
LysoPC	Lysophosphatidylcholine
LZ	Landing Zones
M	Million
M2M	Machine-to-Machine
MAC	Media Access Control
MAC-TAC	Multi-Assault Counter-Terrorism Action Capabilities
MAGTF	Marine Air-Ground Task Force
MAJ	Major
MANET	Mobile Ad Hoc Network
MBP	Myelin Basic Protein
Mbps	Megabytes per second
MCTP	Marine Corps Tactical Publication
MDI	Methylene Diphenyl Diisocyanate
MDMP	Military Decision-Making Process
MEDVAC	Medical Evacuations
MEF	Marine Expeditionary Force
METT-TC	Mission, Enemy, Terrain and weather, Troops and support available, Time/space/logistics, Civil considerations
MI	Military Intelligence
MIF	Migration Inhibitory Factor
MILES	Multi-Integrated Laser Equipment System
MILSATCOM	Military Satellite Communications
miRNA	micro-Ribonucleic Acid
MITM	Man-in-the-middle (attack)
MK	Mark
MLN	Movimiento de Liberación Nacional (National Liberation Movement)
MMP-9	Matrix Metalloproteinase-9

MOPP	Mission Oriented Protective Posture
MOS	Military Occupational Specialty
MOUT	Military Operations in Urban Terrain
MPO	Myeloperoxidase
M&S	Modeling and Simulation
MS-13	Mara Salvatrucha 13
MUTC	Muscatatuck Urban Training Complex
MVD	Ministerstvo Vnutrennikh Del (Ministry of Interior)
MWE	Men, Weapons, Equipment
NAG	N-Acetyl-ß-D-Glucosaminidase
NASA	National Aeronautics and Space Administration
NATO	North Atlantic Treaty Organization
NDU	National Defense University
NEG	Negative
NFC	Near Field Communications
NFP	Neurofilament Triplet Proteins
NGAL	Neutrophil Gelatinase-associated Lipocalin
NGO	Non-Governmental Organization
NIC	National Intelligence Council
NLOS	Non-Line of Sight
NMP22	Nuclear Matrix Protein-22
NO_2	Nitrogen Dioxide
NRL	Naval Research Laboratory
NSF-REU	National Science Foundation Research Experience for Undergraduates
NYPD	New York (City) Police Department
OBJ	Objective
OCONUS	Outside the Continental United States
ODL	Operational Data Layers
OE	Operational Environment

OIF	Operation Iraqi Freedom
OneSAF	One Semi-Automated Forces
OP	Observation Post
OP	Organophosphate
OPFOR	Opposing Force
OPSEC	Operational Security
OSINT	Open Source Intelligence
P2P	Person-to-Person
PAI-1	Plasminogen Activator Inhibitor-1
PAN	Personal Area Network
PBEF	Pre-B-Cell Colony-Enhancing Factor
PCC	Primeiro Comando da Capital (First Command of the Capital)
PCP III	Procollagen Peptide III
PGM	Precision Guided Munition
PIR	Parachute Infantry Regiment
PIRA	Provisional Irish Republican Army
PKK	Partiya Karkerên Kurdistanê (Kurdistan Workers' Party)
PMESII-PT	Political, Military, Economics, Social, Infrastructure, Information-Physical Terrain
PNS	Peripheral Nervous System
PNT	Position, Navigation, and Timing
POS	Positive
PRCS	Palestinian Red Crescent Society
PRIO	Peace Research Institute Oslo
R2P	Responsibility to Protect
RAGE	Receptor for Advanced Glycation End products
RAID	Recherche, Assistance, Intervention, Dissuasion (Search, Assistance, Intervention, Deterrence)

RAND	Research and Development
RDECOM	Research, Development, and Engineering Command
RECIPE	Restructure, Enable, Connect, Inter-organize, Place, and Extend
RF	Radiofrequency
RFID	Radiofrequency Identification
RIG	Rapid Initiatives Group
RKG-3	Ruchnaya Kumulyativnaya Granata-3 (Handheld Shaped Charge Grenade-3)
RPG	Rocket Propelled Grenade
RPO	Reaktivnyy Pekhotnyy Ognemet (Reactive Infantry Flamethrower)
RSPER	Rio/São Paulo Extended Metropolitan Region
S100B	S100 Calcium-Binding Protein B
SC	Smart City
SCADA	Supervisory Control and Data Acquisition
SCAT	Surprise, Concentration, Audacity, and Tempo
SEDAC	Socioeconomic Data and Applications Center
SIGINT	Signals Intelligence
SIRRA	Sustainable Installations Regional Resource Assessment
SMA	Strategic Multi-Layer Assessment
SMS	Short Message Service
SNA	Somali National Alliance
SNE	Synthetic Natural Environment
SOD	Superoxide Dismutase
SOF	Special Operations Forces
SOSRA	Suppress, Obscure, Secure, Reduce, Assault
SP	Surfactant Protein
SPP	Scalable Parallel Processor

SQL	Structured Query Language
SSA	Strategic Sustainability Assessment
SSG	Strategic Studies Group
START	Study of Terrorism and Responses to Terrorism
S&T	Science and Technology
SWAT	Special Weapons and Tactics
SWEAT-MSO	Sewage, Water, Electricity, Academics, Trash, Medical, Safety, and other Considerations
SWJ	Small Wars Journal
TALOS	Tactical Assault Light Operator Suit
TCE	Trichloroethylene
TCP	Terceiro Comando Puro (Pure Third Command)
TCP	Traffic Control Post
TCP/IP	Transmission Control Protocol/Internet Protocol
TDI	Toulene-2,4-Diisocynate
TEW	Terrorism Early Warning (Group)
TEWG	Terrorism Early Warning Group
TFF3	Trefoil Factor 3
TIC	Toxic Industrial Chemical
TIM	Toxic Industial Material
TNFR	Tumor Necrosis Factor Receptor
TNI	Troponin I
Tp-e	Tpeak-Tend
TRADOC	Training and Doctrine Command
TRC	Terrorism Research Center
TSM	Tactical Scalable MANET (Mobile Ad Hoc Network)
TTP	Tactics, Techniques, and Procedures
UA	Urban Area
UAV	Unmanned Aerial Vehicle

UCDP	Uppsala Conflict Database Program
UGIRH	Urban Generic Information Requirements Handbook
UGV	Unmanned Ground Vehicle
UHF	Ultra High Frequency
UK	United Kingdom
UN	United Nations
UNITAF	United Nations Task Force
UNOSOMI	United Nations Operations in Somalia I
UNOSOMII	United Nations Operations in Somalia II
UNRWA	United Nations Relief and Works Agency
UNTAF	United Nations Task Force
UPP	Unidade de Polícia Pacificadora (Police Pacification Unit)
USACE	United States Army Corps of Engineers
USACEHR	United States Army Center for Environmental Health Research
USECT	Understand, Shape, Engage, Consolidate, and Transition
USG	United States Government
USMC	United States Marine Corps
USN	Ubiquitous Sensor Network
US	United States
USS	United States Ship
VDBP	Vitamin-D-Binding Protein
VEGF	Vascular Endothelial Growth Factor
VHF	Very High Frequency
VR	Virtual Reality
VTOL	Vertical Take Off and Landing
VUCA	Volatility, Uncertainty, Complexity, and Ambiguity
vWF	von Willebrand Factor

W	Watt
WARSIM	War Simulation
WMD	Weapons of Mass Destruction
WWI	World War I
WWII	World War II

Preface

to "Blood and Concrete"

David Kilcullen

Denver, Colorado

August 2018

"The future is not the son of Desert Storm, but the stepchild of Somalia and Chechnya." With this quote from United States Marine Corps General Charles Krulak, the *Urban Operations Journal*—an "online aid for members of United States, allied and coalition military services researching urban operations"—launched its web portal (as such things were quaintly then known) in early 2002.

That original portal was long ago subsumed into the *Small Wars Journal (SWJ)*, which has turned out to be one of the most influential platforms for peer-to-peer debate and knowledge sharing on irregular warfare of the post-9/11 world. But the initial emphasis on complex, messy operations in urbanized terrain, fighting among urban populations, providing humanitarian assistance and stabilization support, and understanding conflict in the world's rapidly-growing (and increasingly-connected) cities has remained a focus for the journal's editors and contributors, many of whom have direct practical experience of urban warfare, ever since.

This anthology reflects the *SWJ* community's long-standing interest in urban operations. It covers everything from high-intensity conventional urban warfare, through irregular warfare, counterinsurgency and stabilization operations, urban terrorism and civilian policing, urban counter-narcotics and gang violence, to methods for managing urban riots and civil unrest. It runs the gamut from intelligence preparation of the urban battlespace, to training, simulation, strategy, tactics (friendly and enemy) and concepts like the urban siege, urban influence operations and the weaponization of cities themselves. It does not neglect bigger-picture questions either—such as how likely, really, are urban operations going to be in the 21st century, whether urban environments are obstacles or opportunities for military forces, and which aspects of urban conflict planners and capability developers are best-advised to select as a focus their efforts. In short, for anyone interested in rapidly gaining a good feel for the state of the art in current thinking across a host of issues within this complex problem set, *Blood and Concrete* is a great place to start.

One of the most valuable aspects of *Blood and Concrete* is that it brings so many leading contemporary thinkers—more than 80 authors, from a wide variety of backgrounds—together in one volume. It's impossible to mention all contributors, though all are insightful and their ideas well worth pondering. Some selected highlights include Robert Muggah's chapter on assessing the costs of urban operations, the several chapters on various aspects of urban siege by Adam Elkus and John Sullivan, and the debate—played out though multiple pieces by several contributors—around conceptual frameworks for understanding and modeling urban environments, and for integrating cyber-operations and the internet of things into urban information maneuver. Valuable long-term context comes from chapters by Russell Glenn, Gary Anderson and Frank Hoffman—all of whom were thinking and writing about urban operations long before the invasion of Iraq thrust conflict in cities into the consciousness of most military commanders. New voices, both from the field and from the increasingly sophisticated analytical community focused on urban operations and urban analysis, add current insights from observation and experience. But literally every chapter deserves to be read by anyone seriously engaged in thinking about, operating in, or planning for urban environments and the operations that increasingly center in them, as the world continues its long-standing megatrend toward urbanization.

Of course, not all the contributors agree—this anthology reflects a robust and ongoing debate over several major issues, which is as it should be. Urban operations are by far the most dynamic and rapidly-changing form of conflict on the planet, and the moment we think we have "cracked the code" on these kinds of operations, when we imagine that the science is settled, the key questions are asked and answered, or the main insights are fixed, when our debate congeals into dogma, will be the moment we open ourselves up to our next humiliating defeat. Indeed, this is such a dynamic and contested field that, to the extent that we agree on anything in the current debate on urban operations, we should probably ask ourselves what we're missing.

One of the most important debates to be found in these pages concerns urban operations in megacities, or what we might call "mega-urban operations." These operations have such different characteristics from normal urban operations—the inability to isolate or "invest" a megacity objective by maneuvering outside the city, the lack of air or sea points of disembarkation unencumbered by urban clutter, or the sheer challenges of scale, mass and concentration of force in developing sufficient force ratios for successful operations—that they are of a different class, and certainly they present a different magnitude of challenge entirely.

When the U.S. Army took a renewed doctrinal interest in urban operations in 2013, one of the key issues—since reflected in a series of Army concepts and discussed in several chapters here—concerned operations in megacities, those with populations of 10 million or more. This partly reflected the available data at the time, which predicted rapid and potentially unsustainable growth in many of the world's megacities. More recent data suggest that while mega-urban operations may indeed become a major challenge over a 20- to 30-year time horizon, the most immediate security challenges and humanitarian concerns are likely to emerge from small- and medium-sized cities, primarily on coastlines in the developing world, which tend to have excessively large rates of population growth compared to their governance capacity, infrastructure and political stability. Mega-urban operations may well be the most demanding future scenario: the examples from Mumbai and Paris in this anthology—as well as the multiple chapters on megacities—suggest that this is likely the case, and show the significant range and diversity of thought being put into this problem. But as the chapters on Nairobi, Mogadishu, Iraq, Afghanistan and other small- and medium-city locations show, a city need not be a megacity to pose an immensely difficult challenge, one that traditional urban operations doctrine (let alone the emerging concepts of mega-urban operations) will be hard-pressed to meet.

A second very significant debate that emerges from these pages concerns the problem of how to model and conceive of urban agglomerations and dense urban terrains as part of an IPB, planning process or operational evaluation. The notion of the "urban triad", still extant in U.S. and allied military doctrine (which considers a city as combining three elements: a built environment comprising terrain constructed by humans, a population of significant size and density, and an urban infrastructure) is increasingly being challenged by the emerging concept of the "urban quad", developed in recent USMC and allied work through NATO's ongoing Urbanization Project and the wargaming and experimentation associated with that program. The urban quad concept suggests that in addition to the three elements of terrain, population and infrastructure, the information layer of urban environments—the degree of connectedness and the speed and density of information flow inside, through and among cities—represents a fourth element, almost a fourth operational maneuver space, in its own right.

This notion is implicit in several chapters in *Blood and Concrete*, including Mike Matson's on complex cyber-terrain in hyper-connected urban areas, the chapter by Candan, Shutters and Fortunato on hyper-connected megacities, and Maxwell, Hall and Bennett's discussion of cyber-operations. Likewise, Mark Lomedico and Ellie Bartels's chapter on the city as a system, and the chapter on network science in urban analysis by Amy Krakowka Richmond and her team, provide useful food for thought on new ways to exploit the density and complexity of urban information flows as a means to understand and analyze urban systems, which are increasingly "self-revealing environments" whose information layer—if read correctly—can help illuminate the other elements of the urban quad. Yet as recent operations in Iraq, Syria and Ukraine suggest—and as the experimental results of NATO's work have demonstrated—this is an area whose potential is only just beginning to be understood.

Another debate centers on whether to enter or avoid urban areas, which is one of the most pressing strategic questions engaging high-level policymakers who think about urban operations. This was a critical consideration in planning for the reconquest of cities occupied by the Islamic State in Iraq and Syria, as well as during the recent extended urban siege of Marawi in the Philippines. It is addressed in several chapters of *Blood and Concrete,* but is likely to remain a concern for the foreseeable future. To the extent that such a diverse set of contributions to this debate can be said to have a theme, one of the main ideas that emerges from this anthology is that however much we might wish to avoid fighting in cities, and whatever clever maneuvers or political negotiations our leaders engage in to avoid those urban fights, when push comes to shove, we as operators have an absolute obligation to be ready to enter, fight and prevail in the urban environment, and to ensure our elected leaders know the unvarnished truth about what it will take, and our fighting men and women have the essential tools to deal with it.

At the same time, however, there are intriguing hints—from Ryan Orsini's chapter on isolating urban areas in megacity operations, Mike Matson's chapter on dealing with hyper-connected urban environments, and John Sullivan and Adam Elkus's notion of "control of the cities"— to suggest that the emergence of hyper-connected urban spaces that are increasingly linked to a global network of communications, financial and information flows, people movement and diaspora populations, will create new opportunities to secure (or disable) cities without ever having to set foot in them.

As this anthology brings together a range material produced over several years, it's no criticism to note that it incorporates relatively little on the implications of the most recent round of urban operations, to include the reconquest of cities controlled by the Islamic State in Iraq and Syria, the increasing urbanization of what was once a primarily rural conflict in Afghanistan, the stunning success (and long-drawn-out defeat) of the Islamic State faction that seized and held the city of Marawi for five months in 2017, and the latest cycle of hybrid urban operations in Ukraine. The U.S. Army's insights and observations from the battles of Mosul and Raqqa are likewise still available only in restricted form, while the lessons learned by our enemies (and by non-Western forces like those of Iran, Hezbollah, Russia and Syria) from those campaigns are yet to be widely disseminated. All of this will be food for thought when it comes time to issue a revised and updated version of *Blood and Concrete,* which I have no doubt will be needed sooner rather than later.

Such an updated anthology would do well to solicit and include a wider variety of material on air operations in urban environments—something our air forces have gained great experience in over recent years, and which has been examined closely by some leading airpower thinkers. Urban operations are joint operations, and the role of piloted aircraft, drones (both small and large), airborne firepower, battlefield airmobility, aeromedical evacuation, airspace control and counter-drone operations (among a host of other air-related issues) is only going to become more critical as time goes on.

Likewise, the role of seapower—of amphibious operations, littoral maneuver, riverine and sealift operations, seaborne logistics and naval surface fires in subduing, protecting or defending a city is hugely relevant when the vast majority of urban populations on the planet continue to cluster on coastlines. Complex coastal hydrography, congested approaches, denied or contested ports and harbors, and the presence of enemies with increasingly capable anti-access and area denial capabilities are all factors that will increase the importance of sea control and seaspace denial for successful future urban operations. Logistics, likewise, generally deserves an expanded focus in future thinking on urban operations, since both supporting our own forces and providing essential needs for massive local populations have proven fiendishly difficult for logisticians in all recent urban operations. Partner forces are a further topic worthy of close attention in future anthologies, given their central importance to our success, as the recent Marawi, Mosul, Raqqa, Kunduz and Ghazni battles have demonstrated all too clearly.

One thing is unarguable: urban operations are here to stay. Not only have the vast majority of major battles and campaigns this century taken place in urban (and often coastal) terrain, but the largest battles of any kind since the Second World War—those of Mosul and Aleppo—took place in cities. Urban warfare, as societies continue to urbanize, will only become more decisive, and although professionals clearly need to be ready and able to fight in any environment at any time, if this anthology—and the history of the *Small Wars Journal* and its oft-forgotten predecessor, the *Urban Operations Journal*—tell us anything, it's that we ignore or forget urban operations at our peril.

Foreword

Urban Warfare Studies

John Spencer

West Point, New York

August 2018

The U.S. military has a long history of conducting urban operations. Be it during the American Civil War, World War II, Somalia, Panama, Bosnia, or Iraq, soldiers and marines have confronted urban warfare. Nevertheless, despite our long history, our military profession spends little time preparing for urban operations. When confronted, we expect soldiers to adapt to urban fighting, and then afterwards refocus on preparing for combat in more ideal environments such as the plains and mountain passes of Eastern Europe. This tendency to adapt, forget, and adapt again to missions in populated urban areas will no longer suffice.

Urban warfare is a soldier's nightmare. The challenges of the physical terrain alone are so daunting that urban fighting is often described as combat in hell.[1] Soldiers would rather be anywhere else than fighting deep in urban canyons of rubble, abandoned vehicles, multi-story buildings, subway and sewer tunnels, and congested streets where every window, dark alley, and corner could hold a waiting gunman, sniper, or ambush. The soldier yearns for the comforting security of cover and concealment but remains visible and a potential target from almost every angle. The experience is as psychologically draining as it is physically demanding, especially when approaches to urban operations often require soldiers clear every street, building, and room.

Urban terrain is the most complex and difficult place to conduct military operations. But the challenges of urban environments aren't just about the physical terrain. In fact, the terrain may be a lesser challenge than the population.

Urban environments exist to support human society. Populations can range from thousands to tens of millions in a single city, which are a collection of neighborhoods, suburban, peri-urban, industrial, and other areas bound together by physical, social, and information networks. These populations will be present in military operations. No matter how much military forces may try to clear residents before and during battle, people always remain. Despite two mandatory evacuations executed by both German and U.S. forces before the Battle of Aachen in 1944, for example, over a thousand civilians refused to leave even as the city was reduced to rubble around them.[2] More recently, the 2008 Battle of Sadr City in Iraq was fought among its 2 million residents, while the battle to dislodge the Islamic State from Mosul also unfolded amongst a population of close to a million.[3] Fighting in the future will be fought among even larger populations.

Throughout history, military theorists as far back as Sun Tzu in the late sixth century BC advised against conducting operations in cities. But most foundational military theories predate the urbanization of the world's population.

The world became more urban than rural over ten years ago. This change happened very rapidly. In 1990, the world population was 43 percent (2.3 billion) urban and by 2015, it had grown to 54 percent (4 billion). By 2030, the global urban ratio is projected to be over 60 percent and by 2050, 70 percent. Much of this increased urban growth is happening in developing countries that struggle to provide services and governance to their existing populations.[4] Under such circumstances, non-state actors increasingly contest political control. These terrorists, insurgents, and revolutionaries leach on the urban environments to take advantage of civil, political, and economic grievances of the population. They chose the urban environment to gain a temporary advantage against technological superior military forces as they hide and operate amongst the complex, dense physical and human terrain.

Warfare has become an urban phenomenon. Crime, conflict, and political violence now occur more often in urban than rural areas.[5] In the past ten years, the majority of the world's most violent conflicts have been fought in cities like Aleppo, Raqqa, Mosul, Marawi, Gaza, Mogadishu, Donetsk, Saana, and many others.[6]

While the rapid growth of the global population and its urbanization are well known by many, the military and broader U.S. national security enterprise has been slow to change. This is despite the influential military leaders that have warned of the present and future urban nature of warfare.[7] One of the most famous and cited is the former Marine Corps Commandant General Charles Krulak who said when asked about the future of warfare:

"Understanding that whatever our [American] interests are going to be, it is going to eventually lead us into what we call the three-block war [where soldier and marines are simultaneously required to conduct humanitarian assistance on one block, peace-keeping on the other, and traditional warfighting the next over]. Why? Because they've watched CNN, the enemy has. They've seen the might of our technology. They're not going to fight us straight up. We're not going to see the son of Desert Storm anymore. You're going to see the stepchild of Chechnya."[8]

General Krulak's predictions have come true and the urban predicament facing modern militaries is even greater than he envisioned because cities have also become much bigger, denser, and more complex. Today, there are over 31 megacities (cities with over 10 million residents), 436 cities with between 1 and 5 million inhabitants, and an additional 551 cities with between 500,000 and 1 million inhabitants.[9]

Indeed, megacities have gained a considerable amount of interest and consideration within the US military. These efforts included a major year-long study in 2014 conducted by the Chief of the Staff of the Army's Strategic Studies Group that concluded the Army is woefully unprepared to operate in megacities.[10] The scale and complexity of megacities exceed current military doctrine, capabilities, and most importantly thinking.

Broadly speaking, the military has two major requirements for preparing for the full range of military operations, from humanitarian assistance and disaster relief to high intensity combat, in dense urban areas: how to understand the environment and how to operate in the environment.

Military organizations are constantly changing. Personnel and leaders turn over frequently as they move to new assignments. The ability to maintain trained and ready formations is a complex process of professional education, training, experience, manning, and much more. The ability to maintain and pass on collective knowledge about fighting rests firmly on the role of doctrine. It feeds the schools and unit training with what and how to prepare for combat missions. But doctrine has its limitations.

A good example of the limitations of doctrine is the experience of Marine Corps Lieutenant Colonel Ernie Cheatham during the 1968 Tet Offensive that took place during the Vietnam War. Cheatham was given less than 24 hours to transition from jungle operations to the biggest urban battle the U.S. military had experienced since World War II, the Battle of Hue. With the limited time he had, he attempted to give himself a crash course in urban warfare by reviewing two military manuals: *Combat in Built-Up Areas* and *An Assault on a Fortified Position*.[11] What Cheatham gained from those manuals, the need for high explosive and penetrating weapons, the need to stay out of the streets and open areas, and the need for combined arms maneuver surely aided in his mission to clear the city of North Vietnamese Army forces. But at what was cost? Cost calculated in U.S. personnel, Vietnamese civilians, and the city? What else did he and the marines fighting in Hue need to know?

The scale and density of the physical terrain, population, and city systems matter in urban operations. Military thinkers have come to understand urban areas as complex systems of systems designed to sustain and support human life. These systems have in puts (water, food, power, fuel) and outputs (sewage, trash, industrial waste) required to sustain life and provide the functions (governance, security, markets, banking, social) that allow concentrated human populations to prosper. Any military operation or action will alter, if not destroy, these systems. Altering or destroying urban systems may be a military necessity, but historically operations have been conducted without a full understanding of the impact of military actions.

Once the scale and density increase to a certain level, the complexity in the environment increases exponentially—i.e. different networks, systems, and functions moving in different directions. Military forces often try to impose order on their environments. They seek to reach a level of control to facilitate the commander's ability to visualize, describe, and direct forces to accomplish their assigned mission. Normal control measures and decision-making frameworks will not work in megacities and major dense urban areas.

Aversion to megacities and dense urban areas is a reasonable response. The difficulty and complexity are hard to imagine. But the world and warfare have changed. There is no option. We must adapt now and not wait until the next mission, emergency, or battle. It comes down to risk.

How much are we willing to risk? How much blood are we willing to spill? The blood not only of the non-combatant residents of the next urban conflict, but the blood of the soldiers not prepared for the urban fight whom we ask to adapt on the fly.

Current military doctrine cannot be our only solution to preparing for the future. Doctrine relies heavily on past experiences and lessons learned. To be sure, there is much we can and should learn from past urban experiences. But there are experiences we just don't have. The US military has never operated in a megacity. Even the major city battles of World War II—Stalingrad, Manila, Berlin—had less than 3 million residents at the start of urban fighting. Even more recent urban operations in Baghdad, Iraq with an estimated population of 6 million residents, does not meet the megacity classification. We need new concepts to address these challenges which through analysis, experimentation, exercises, and actual experience can evolve into a comprehensive urban warfare doctrine.

We need a much broader body of knowledge, lessons, and dialogue on past, present and future operations in dense urban areas and megacities. For over a decade, the *Small Wars Journal* has served as that forum and repository for discussing urban operations. After reading this anthology, students of urban operations and soldiers who could face the mission of fighting in cities will be better prepared. They, possibly you, will have a better understanding of what is known, what is unknown, what are the right questions to ask, and what you should think about. The urban environment becomes more complex with each passing day. Let not another needless drop of blood be spilt on concrete for the wanting of a lesson already learned or a question already asked.

Notes

[1] Russell W. Glenn, *Combat in Hell: A Consideration of Constrained Urban Warfare.* Santa Monica, CA: RAND Corporation, 1996, https://www.rand.org/pubs/monograph_reports/MR780.html.

[2] Christopher R. Gabel, "Knock 'em All Down: The Reduction of Aachen, October 1944" in William G. Robertson, Ed. *Block by Block: The Challenges of Urban Operations.* Fort Leavenworth, Kansas: U.S. Army Command and General Staff College Press, 2003: 85.

[3] David E. Johnson, M. Wade Markel, and Brian Shannon, *The 2008 Battle of Sadr City: Reimagining Urban Combat.* Santa Monica, CA: RAND Corporation, 2013. https://www.rand.org/pubs/research_reports/RR160.html.

[4] *Human Population: Lesson Plans.* Population Reference Bureau. 1 July 2009. http://www.prb.org/Publications/Lesson-Plans/HumanPopulation/Urbanization.aspx.

[5] Wendy MacClinchy, "Violence Today" in *States of Fragility 2016: Understanding Violence.* Paris: OECD, 2016, p. 31-67; and Keith Krause, "From Armed Conflict to Political Violence: Mapping and Explaining Conflict Trends." *Daedalus.* Vol. 145, Issue 4, Fall 2016: 113-126.

[6]   Margarita Konaev and John Spencer, "The Era of Urban Warfare is Already Here." *Foreign Policy Research Institute*, https://www.fpri.org/article/2018/03/the-era-of-urban-warfare-is-already-here/.

[7]   Thomas Ricks, "Army chief: Time to prepare for urban war." *Foreign Policy*. 22 March 2017, https://foreignpolicy.com/2017/03/22/army-chief-time-to-prepare-for-urban-war/.

[8]   Interview with Gen. Charles Krulak, "Semper Fidelis." *Newshour*. Public Broadcasting Service, 25 June 1999, https://www.pbs.org/newshour/spc/bb/military/jan-june99/krulak_6-25.html.

[9]   *The World's Cities in 2016*, United Nations Data Booklet, http://www.un.org/en/development/desa/population/publications/pdf/urbanization/the_worlds_cities_in_2016_data_booklet.pdf.

[10]   Marc Harris et. al. (Megacities Concept Team), *Megacities and the United States Army: Preparing for a Complex and Uncertain Future*. Washington, DC: Chief of Staff of the Army, Strategic Studies Group, June 2014: 1-28, https://www.army.mil/e2/c/downloads/351235.pdf.

[11]   Mark Bowden, *Hue 1968: A Turning Point of the American War in Vietnam*. New York: Atlantic Monthly Press, 2017: 239.

Introduction

Blood and Concrete

John P. Sullivan, Robert J. Bunker, Alma Keshavarz and Dave Dilegge

Los Angeles, California and Largo, Florida

November 2018

Muscatatuck Urban Training Complex (MUTC), Indiana
April 2016 (Image: Robert J. Bunker)

Urban warfare is once again a concern among military operational planners. Indeed, the growing urban nature of the human habitat makes the study of urban warfare and the broader exploration of urban operations—including policing, disaster response, and conflict prevention a pressing concern. The urban nature of current and future conflict will make understanding the urban operational space an imperative for security and civil protection and a core competency for military and security services worldwide.

Conventional wisdom has been to avoid military operations in cities because they are costly and bloody. This axiom becomes harder to accept however when the majority of the world becomes urban. The fact urban settings are becoming the dominant global feature is hard to ignore. Contemporary projections widely assert that the majority of the world—some 55 percent—lives in urban areas. This became the case around 2008. according to UN estimates. This observation is accompanied by a projection that the urban population will increase to 70 percent of the world's total by 2050. Yet, there is evidence that this projection severely undercounts the true urban population load. Using advanced geospatial technology, including high-resolution satellite images, researchers at the European Commission estimate that 84 percent of the world's population, some 6.4 billion people, is urban. Asia and Africa are among the most densely populated.[1]

Two observations immediately come to the surface: 1) understanding urban areas demands study and research of the urban domain, and 2) this understanding demands the development of intelligence frameworks (that integrate geospatial concepts and human dimensions of terrain) for conducting the entire range of urban operations.[2] It has been recognized that the urban domain is fraught with complexity and ushers in new demands for military decision-making and integrating civil-military strategies for population protection.[3] Part of the complexity is driven by unfamiliarity of urban domain by military operators; part by the terrain features and population dynamics of urban settings.[4]

Beyond these dimensions, there is no single archetypal city. Cities range in size and complexity, from small cities—edge cities and suburban clusters—with 'built up terrain' to metropolitan areas to megacities (megapolises) and polycentric mega-city clusters and regions.[5] Added to this must be global cities and global slums.[6] All of these city forms present unique challenges. Differentiating between the tactical, operational, and strategic concerns accompanying each of these distinct (and sometimes converging) conurbations is essential to understanding and preparing for urban operations. Yet, understanding urban combat and conflict demands more. It demands the development of the entire nature of urban space. Is urban space an organism (actual or metaphorically); is it an ecosystem or ecological niche; or is it a unique combination of both.[7] Cities can also be fragile, feral, and connected.[8] The connectivity among cities in the global system and within a nation can be viewed as the interactions between a 'space of flows' and a 'space of place(s).'[9] They can also implode or fall apart.[10]

On Blood and Concrete

This text, *Blood and Concrete*, has its foundation in the exploration of practice in addressing small wars in cities. In 1993, third world conflict in Somalia brought the dynamics of urban warfare and warlordism to the front page of public perception in the book—later movie—*Black Hawk Down*. As the 1990s unfolded, conflict in the former Yugoslavia also brought the horrors of urban warfare to the forefront.[11] The 1992 Los Angeles riots exposed the fault lines of urban unrest. Urban terrorism also punctuated the decade from the 1993 attack on the World Trade Center through the Oklahoma City Bombing, and Tokyo Sarin Attack.[12] Military, police[13], and intelligence services started to explore modern urban conflict. *Small Wars Journal* has been part of this exploration from the onset of urban operations research in the 1990s. Starting as the MOUT Homepage (addressing Military Operations in Urban Terrain), then progressing to *Urban Operations Journal* and urbanoperations.com, *SWJ* Editor Dave Dilegge led the effort to examine and document through research and learned discussion the dynamics found in contemporary and emerging urban warfare, illuminating their prominence in small wars. This text documents that exploration.

The articles included in this anthology range from Russell Glenn's exploration of urban terrorism in "Terrorism and Cities: A Target Rich Environment" (2005) to Robert Muggah's discussion of the complexity of assessing the impact and effects of urban conflict in "The Tricky Business of Counting the Costs of Armed Conflict in Cities" (2018) and Ryan Orsini's discussion of isolation in "Surrounded, Yet Unaware: Achieving Isolation in Future Urban Terrain" (2018). Along the way, a total of 49 substantive chapters address the array of issues faced when 'fighting in built up areas' (FIBUA) or policing urban communities. These topics include tactical operations, intelligence, training and exercising, and political and social dimensions of urban operations. Discussion of riots and terrorism accompany combat focused essays to ensure appreciation of the range of contingencies faced in urban operations.

Riots, for example, are covered by Alex Calvo in "London Riots: Decentralized Intelligence Collection and Analysis" (2011) and by John P. Sullivan and Adam Elkus in "The Strategic Challenge of Riots: Riot Action and Crowd Power" (2012). The concept of urban siege[14] is discussed in "Postcard from Mumbai: Modern Urban Siege" (2009), "The 'New' Playbook? Urban Siege in Nairobi" (2013), and "Urban Siege in Paris: A Spectrum of Armed Assault" (2015) by John P. Sullivan and Adam Elkus while combat in megacities is addressed in 12 essays, including exposes by Russell W. Glenn, David Shunk, Michael Bailey (along with Robert Dixon, Marc Harris, Daniel Hendrex, Nicholas Melin and Richard Russo), Gary Anderson, and Geoffrey Demarest among others. Many of these articles were submitted as part of the collaboration between *SWJ* and the *Mad Scientist Initiative* sponsored by the U.S. Army Training and Doctrine Command (TRADOC). Sullivan and Elkus also outline the need for a strategic understanding and approach to urban conflict in "Command of the Cities: Towards a Theory of Urban Strategy" (2011).

While the majority of the chapters included here were initially published online at *SWJ*, several unique components round out this anthology. In addition to a table of acronyms, the text includes this introductory chapter, a preface by David Kilcullen, a foreword by John Spencer, a postscript by Margarita Konaev, and an afterword by Russell W. Glenn—all specifically written for this collection. These pieces outline the emerging literature on urban operations and urban warfare and conflict and are accompanied by a listing of selected references. Urban conflict is dominated by 'blood' in the terms of casualties and 'concrete' in terms of the built environment (and a means of manipulating that environment).[15] All of the contributions here help illuminate the state of the art in urban warfare studies; several help push the envelope toward a better understanding of the future of the 'blood and concrete' that dominate urban operations.

Leveraging these prior perceptions and introductory insights, questions addressing the following thematic elements related to the successful pursuit of U.S. urban focused operations should be reflected upon when consulting this anthology:

- *Urban Warfare Schools & Training Centers*: How should urban warfare and training centers be organized and at what scale? The 1,000-acre Muscatatuck Urban Training Complex (MUTC) is presently the largest in the U.S. and "contains sixty-eight buildings, a reservoir, tunnel system, and over nine miles of roads" but this pales in comparison to the scale of actual megacities U.S. may one day be expected to operate within.[16] The Army's Asymmetric Warfare Group's (AWG) 300-acre facility is even smaller.[17] Other localized training facilities—including 'combat towns' at Army posts and Marine camps—are equivalent in size to the downtowns of small towns and cities found across the U.S. Further, should the U.S. Army and U.S. Marine Corps each possess their own schools (centers) or should a joint Army-Marine mega-center—spanning thousands of acres and comprised of hundreds of buildings (as well as an extensive tunnel and sewer system)—be developed? On the other hand, the Marines have a three-week urban operations course at Camp Pendleton[18]—could this form the nucleus of a longer USMC Enlisted or Officer level MOS (Military Occupational Specialty) type school? How will naval and coast guard capabilities be integrated into this joint training scheme in order to accommodate urban-littoral interface considerations?[19]

Urban Leaders Course at Camp Pendleton, California, 8 March 2016. (U.S. Marine Corps photo by Lance Cpl. Justin E. Bowles/ Released) [FOR PUBLIC DISTRIBUTION//NO LIMITATIONS ON USE] [20]

- *Dedicated Branch & Publications*: Should the U.S. Army have a dedicated Urban Warfare branch at the combat arms or combat support level or should such a specialty initially be created as a Corps of Engineers sub-specialty? If such a branch existed would its own branch bulletin further our understanding of urban warfare? Presently, urban warfare writings—including new doctrine revisions—can be sporadic in nature and treated at times like a bastard stepchild.[21] Should prizes in military journals and publications such as *Military Review, Parameters, Marine Corps Gazette*, or *Naval War College Review* be established to further our thinking on this topical area? Should TRADOC's *Mad Scientist Initiative* writings related to future urban conflict and the Modern War Institute's *Urban Warfare Project* at West Point be expanded?

- *Urban Warfare Kits:* Years ago (22 to be exact), Ralph Peters wrote a highly prophetic, yet now overlooked piece—"Our Soldiers, Their Cities"—which discussed how the Army needed to reorganize and arm for the coming age of urban conflict.[22] Given the harsh demands and realities of close in city fighting in rubble and debris, soldier gear and hardware would need to be further ruggedized and tailored for such operations and tactical actions. Derived from such recognized needs, should 'Urban Warfare Kits' be developed which would be the corollary of pre-existing US DoD "Non-Lethal Capability Sets"?[23] Such kits would conceivably contain knee and arm pads, protective gloves (e.g. mesh butcher-like), ballistic shields, shotguns, breeching tools, smoke grenades, thermobaric munitions, and related equipment.[24]

- *Dedicated Urban Warfare Units*: At what point does the U.S. military field dedicated urban warfare units on par with the Army's 10th Mountain Division (Light Infantry) or its air assault divisions (e.g. the 101st Airborne and 82nd Airborne)? Given the Army's focus on brigade level units, would this be the natural structure of an experimental urban warfare force? Would an expeditionary bridge equivalent level unit also be the Marine Corps natural experimental urban warfare force size? Would these forces be designated light, medium, or heavy units? Or would components of them—such as weapons or heavy assault companies or battalions—augment them as their heavy elements?[25]

- *Machine and Human Force Structure Mixtures:* As armed robotic systems begin to be fielded by the U.S. military, what is the appropriate force structure mix of these systems and human operatives for urban combat? Will dedicated human, human-machine mixes, and dedicated machine units exist?[26] Do we invest our R&D efforts related to flying and crawling insect swarms, four-legged or flying sized-predators, human size bi-pedal, or tracked/wheeled machine units? The combat descriptions from "Demons in the Tall Grass"—linked to the

U.S. Army TRADOC G2 *Mad Scientist Initiative*'s Future of Warfare 2030-2050 project—related to the performance of the robotic Hyenas and Buffalos suggest that we need to move beyond traditional human-centered perspectives of what armed robotic systems may look like in the decades to come.[27] Of course, determining the appropriate human-machine and machine variability force structure mixes for urban combat would greatly benefit from having dedicated Army and Marine combat branch and school/training center proponents.

Hopefully, this volume can become a foundation for future research, a training resource for much needed preparation for urban operations, and a springboard for future articles addressing the rise of urban conflicts and the incorporation of new weapons including drones, artificial intelligence (AI), the inter-connectedness found in the cyberspace-urban interface, and the risks and challenges presented by climate change, migration, resource (water, food) shortages in the urban domain, population growth in littoral zones (urban-littoral interface), and the challenges they present at *Small Wars Journal* and elsewhere.

Muscatatuck Urban Training Complex (MUTC), Indiana
April 2016 (Image: Robert J. Bunker)

Notes

[1]   Gregory Scruggs, "'Everything we've heard about global urbanization turns out to be wrong' researchers." *Reuters.* 12 July 2018, https://www.reuters.com/article/us-global-cities/everything-weve-heard-about-global-urbanization-turns-out-to-be-wrong-researchers-idUSKBN1K21UU.

[2]   On the need for urban understanding, see David Kilcullen's comments in John Spencer. "MWI Podcast: War Goes To The City, With David Kilcullen." Modern Warfare Institute. 14 November 2018, https://mwi.usma.edu/mwi-podcast-war-goes-city-david-kilcullen/. On urban intelligence preparation (Intelligence preparation of the battlefield or IPB and Intelligence Preparation for Operations or IPO), see Jamison Jo Medby and Russell W. Glenn, *Streetmart: Intelligence Preparation of the Battlefield for Urban Operations.* MR-1287-A. Santa Monica, CA: The Arroyo Center, The RAND Corporation, 2002: 1-165, http://www.rand.org/pubs/monograph_reports/MR1287.html and John P. Sullivan and Alain Bauer, Eds., *Terrorism Early Warning: 10 Years of Achievement in Fighting Terrorism and Crime.* Los Angeles: Los Angeles County Sheriff's Department, October 2008, https://www.academia.edu/1115115/Terrorism_Early_Warning_10_Years_of_Achievement_in_Fighting_Terrorism_and_Crime.

[3]   See John P. Sullivan, "Protecting the Populace: Humanitarian Considerations in Urban Operations." *Stratfor.* 2 June 2018, https://www.stratfor.com/horizons/fellows/dr-john-p-sullivan/26062018-protecting-populace-humanitarian-considerations-urban-operations.

[4]   Cities are inherently complex. This complexity is compounded by multiple interactive factors. Among these issues are: density, vertical and underground spaces. See Russell W. Glenn, *Heavy Matter: Urban Operations' Density of Challenges.* MR-1239-JS/A. Santa Monica, CA: The National Defense Institute—The Arroyo Center, the RAND Corporation, 2000, https://www.rand.org/pubs/monograph_reports/MR1239.html; Stephen Graham,

Vertical: The City from Satellites to Bunkers. London: Verso, 2018; and Daphné Richemond-Barak, *Underground Warfare.* New York: Oxford University Press, 2018.

[5] See John P. Sullivan, "The Urban Imperative: War, Terrorism, and Insecurity in Megacities." *Stratfor.* 13 February 2018, https://worldview.stratfor.com/horizons/fellows/dr-john-p-sullivan/13022018-urban-imperative-war-terrorism-and-insecurity-megacities.

[6] Global cities, global slums, and their connectivity in the network of cities (including integrating the cyber realm into operations) is an emerging facet of urban operations. See for example, Saskia Sassen, *The Global City* and *Cities in a World Economy.* Thousand Oaks, CA: Sage Publications, 2018; Saskia Sassen, *The Global City: New York, London, Tokyo.* Princeton University Press, 2001, https://www.opendemocracy.net/article/the-new-wars-and-cities-after-mumbai-0; and John P. Sullivan, "New Wars in the City: Global Cities—Global Slums." *Stratfor.* 4 July 2018, https://www.stratfor.com/horizons/fellows/dr-john-p-sullivan/04072018-new-wars-city-global-cities-global-slums.

[7] David Kilcullen raises these foundational questions in his interview by John Spencer (see note 2). See also David Kilcullen, *Out of the Mountains: The Coming Age of the Urban Guerrilla.* New York: Oxford University Press, 2013.

[8] On fragility, see Robert Muggah, "Fixing Fragile Cities: Solutions for Urban Violence and Poverty." *Foreign Affairs.* 15 January 2015, https://www.foreignaffairs.com/articles/africa/2015-01-15/fixing-fragile-cities. On fertility, see Richard Norton, "Feral Cities." *Naval War College Review.* Vol. 56, No. 4, Autumn 2003: 97-106, www.nwc.navy.mil/press/Review/2003/Autumn/pdfs/art6-a03.pdf; Robert J. Bunker and John P. Sullivan, "Integrating Feral Cities and Third Phase Cartels/Third Generation Gangs Research: The Rise of Criminal (Narco) City Networks and BlackFor." *Small Wars & Insurgencies.* Vol. 22, No. 5, December 2011: 764-786, DOI: 10.1080/09592318.2011.620804; and Robert J. Bunker, *The Emergence of Feral and Criminal Cities:*

U.S. Military Implications in a Time of Austerity. Land Warfare Paper 99W. Arlington, VA: Association of the United States Army, April 2014, https://scholarship.claremont.edu/cgu_fac_pub/555/. On connectivity, see Manuel Castells, *The Informational City: Economic Restructuring and Urban Development.* Hoboken, NJ: Wiley-Blackwell, 1992: 1-416.

[9]   For Manuel Castells, the 'space of flows' connects distant locals around shared functions, identity, and meaning. This inter-connectedness influences, social, economic, political, and conflict dynamics and helps define the 'space of places' found in urban life. In addition to *The Informational City: Economic Restructuring and Urban Development* (see note 8 above), see Manuel Castells, *Communication Power.* New York: Oxford University Press, 2013: 1-624; and Manuel Castells, *Networks of Outrage and Hope; Social Movements in the Internet Age* (Second Edition). Cambridge: Polity, 2015: 1-328.

[10]   Failed cities are a parallel to failed states. Cities can also be destroyed or severely damaged. See the literature on 'urbicide,' specifically Martin Coward, *Urbicide: The Politics of Urban Destruction.* New York: Routledge, 2008.

[11]   On Mogadishu, see Mark Bowden, *Black Hawk Down: A Story of Modern War.* New York: Atlantic Monthly Press, 1999. On Sarajevo, see David Stanford, Mike Jackson, and Sam Ruppert, "MWI Battlefield Assessment on the Siege of Sarajevo." Modern Warfare Institute. 5 December 2015, https://mwi.usma.edu/mwi-battlefield-assessment-siege-sarajevo/.

[12]   On the Los Angeles riot, see John P. Sullivan, "Critical Pathways: Responding to the 1992 Los Angeles Riot." *Journal of California Law Enforcement.* Vol. 30, No. 1, 1996: 14-18, https://www.academia.edu/1117334/Critical_Pathways_Responding_to_the_1992_Los_Angeles_Riot. The 1993 World Trade Center attack was a wake up call for the US in terms of jihadi terrorism, see "1993 World Trade Center Bombing." 9/11 Memorial & Museum, https://www.911memorial.org/1993-world-trade-center-bombing. A review of the Oklahoma City Bombing is found at "Oklahoma

City Bombing Fast Facts." *CNN*. 25 March 2018, https://www.cnn.com/2013/09/18/us/oklahoma-city-bombing-fast-facts/index.html. On the Tokyo sarin attack, see "March 20, 1995: The sarin attack that turned Tokyo into a war zone." *Straits Times*. 6 July 2018, https://www.straitstimes.com/asia/east-asia/march-20-1995-the-sarin-attack-that-turned-tokyo-into-a-warzone.

[13] On policing and urban operations, see John P. Sullivan, "Policing Urban Conflict: Urban Siege, Terrorism and Insecurity." *Stratfor*. 19 April 2018, https://worldview.stratfor.com/horizons/fellows/dr-john-p-sullivan/30042018-policing-urban-conflict-urban-siege-terrorism-and-insecurity.

[14] Urban siege is a metaphor for distributed swarming attacks that create a perception of being besieged by the population involved. See John P. Sullivan, "Policing Urban Conflict: Urban Siege, Terrorism and Insecurity." *Stratfor*. 19 April 2018, https://worldview.stratfor.com/horizons/fellows/dr-john-p-sullivan/30042018-policing-urban-conflict-urban-siege-terrorism-and-insecurity for a discussion of urban siege and in contrast a discussion of classic siege in John P. Sullivan, "Urban Warfighting and Classic Siege." *Stratfor*. 20 March 2018, https://worldview.stratfor.com/horizons/fellows/dr-john-p-sullivan/20032018-urban-warfighting-and-classic-siege.

[15] On concrete, see John Spencer, "The Most Effective Weapon on the Modern Battlefield is Concrete." Modern War Institute. 14 November 2016, https://mwi.usma.edu/effective-weapon-modern-battlefield-concrete/.

[16] John Spencer, "The Army Needs An Urban Warfare School and It Needs It Soon." Modern War Institute. 5 April 2017, https://mwi.usma.edu/army-needs-urban-warfare-school-needs-soon/.

[17] Ibid.

[18] Justin Bowles, "Urban Leaders Course: The Experts in Urban Warfare." *Marines*. 23 March 2016, https://www.imef.marines.mil/News/News-Article-Display/Article/702352/urban-leaders-course-the-experts-in-urban-warfare/.

[19] The need for service specific and joint urban operations schools demands additional debate since the urban opspace challenges commanders, their subordinate leaders, and operators from the army and all other services, including the navy, coast guard and marines for urban-littoral operations and the air force (and naval and marine air) for close air support. Interacting with allied militaries (and with gendarmerie and police partners) should be a component of these urban operations schools. See John P. Sullivan, "New Wars in the City: Global Cities – Global Slums." *Stratfor.* 4 July 2018, https://worldview.stratfor.com/horizons/fellows/dr-john-p-sullivan/04072018-new-wars-city-global-cities-global-slums.

[20] Justin Bowles, "Urban Leaders Course: The Experts in Urban Warfare." *Marines.* 23 March 2016, https://www.imef.marines.mil/News/News-Article-Display/Article/702352/urban-leaders-course-the-experts-in-urban-warfare/.

[21] U.S. military urban doctrinal thinking, however, to a limited extent is being updated. See Marine Corps Warfighting Publication 3-35.3, *Military Operations on Urban Terrain (MOUT)*. Washington, D.C.: Headquarters U.S. Marine Corps, 26 April 1998, http://www.marines.mil/Portals/59/MCWP%203-35.3.pdf (Superseded by MCRP 12-10B.1, *Military Operations on Urban Terrain (MOUT)*. Washington, D.C.: Headquarters U.S. Marine Corps, 2 May 2016, https://www.marines.mil/Portals/59/Publications/MCRP%2012-10B.1%20(Formerly%20MCWP%203-35.3).pdf?ver=2016-06-27-101305-967) and FM 3-06, *Urban Operations*. Washington, D.C.: Headquarters U.S. Army, 26 October 2006, https://fas.org/irp/doddir/army/fm3-06.pdf. See also ATTP 3-06.11 (FM 3-06.11), Combined Arms Operations in Urban Terrain. Washington, D.C.: Headquarters U.S. Army, June 2011, https://www.globalsecurity.org/military//library/policy/army/attp/attp3-06-11.pdf. For Joint Operations, see Joint Publication 3-06, *Joint Urban Operations*. Washington, D.C.: The Joint Chiefs of Staff, 20 November 2013, http://www.jcs.mil/Portals/36/Documents/Doctrine/pubs/jp3_06.pdf.

[22] Ralph Peters, "Our Soldiers, Their Cities." *Parameters*. Spring 1996: 43-50, http://strategicstudiesinstitute.army.mil/pubs/parameters/articles/96spring/peters.htm.

[23] Non-Lethal Weapons Program, "Non-Lethal Capability Sets / Escalation-of-Force Mission Modules." U.S. Department of Defense. nd, https://jnlwp.defense.gov/Current-Non-Lethal-Weapons/Non-Lethal-Capability-Sets-EoF-Mission-Modules/.

[24] For an urban combat equipment listing, see John Spencer, "A Soldier's Urban Warfare Christmas Wish List." Modern War Institute. 23 November 2018, https://mwi.usma.edu/soldiers-urban-warfare-christmas-wish-list/ (This article was originally published 19 December 2017, https://www.realcleardefense.com/2017/12/19/a_soldierrsquos_urban_warfare_christmas_wish_list_299086.html).

[25] While MOUT (Military Operations in Urban Terrain) capabilities are recognized as needed for both the U.S. Army and Marines, neither service is currently discussing any type of unit reorganization for such dedicated operations. For recent articles related to the need for urban combat operations capabilities, see Robert W. Lamont, "Future Urban Combat Capabilities? What investments are needed?" *Marine Corps Gazette*. January 2017, https://www.mca-marines.org/gazette/2017/01/future-urban-combat-capabilities and Todd Smith, "The future battlefield: Army, Marines prepare for 'massive' fight in megacities." *Military Times*. 6 March 2018, https://www.militarytimes.com/news/your-army/2018/03/06/the-future-battlefield-army-marines-prepare-for-massive-fight-in-megacities/.

[26] For more on the fielding of such weaponry, see Robert J. Bunker, *Armed Robotic Systems Emergence: Weapons Systems Life Cycles Analysis and New Strategic Realities*. Carlisle, PA: Strategic Studies Institute, U.S. Army War College, 14 November 2017, https://ssi.armywarcollege.edu/pubs/display.cfm?pubID=1368.

[27] Mike Matson, "Demons in the Tall Grass." *Small Wars Journal*. 7 July 2017, http://smallwarsjournal.com/jrnl/art/demons-tall-grass.

Chapter 1

Terrorism and Cities:
A Target Rich Environment

Russell W. Glenn

First Published April 2005

It should surprise no one that the North Vietnamese chose to strike Hue and Saigon during their 1968 Tet Offensive; that attacks by Tamil Tiger bombers have focused on the Sri Lankan capital of Colombo; or that New York City and Washington, D.C. were the foci for the aggressions of September 11, 2001. Cities are the richest of terrorist targets. They are rich in significance due to their density of high visibility and politically symbolic features. They are opulent in the attention they bestow on those committing a terrorist assault; television, radio, and print media representatives are inevitably immediately at hand, likely in considerable numbers. There is a wealth of concealment and support for individuals preparing to perpetrate an act, especially in those urban areas of the developed world in which virtually every nationality and demographic group are found in some numbers. The sheer density of activities per unit of time means that a man or woman rarely attracts notable attention unless their behaviors are of a character so unusual as to dramatically contrast with others in the immediate vicinity. This abundance of activity allows perpetrators to enter, exit, or pass through an urban area with relative ease. Familiarity with one's neighbors and the homogeneity of most rural environments mean that a stranger attracts immediate notice. The outsider is in contrast often the norm in large towns or cities, allowing him or her to move about and mingle effectively unnoticed.

Urban areas are also affluent in relevance to the daily lives of much of the world's population. Over half of earth's population resides in built-up areas. Most developed nations are in particular highly urbanized; many developing nations have extraordinary rates of escalating urbanization. Television and motion pictures frequently focus on the lives of individuals residing, working, or seeking new beginnings in cities. An attack on a rural target may be difficult to relate to for those not in the immediate vicinity, especially a strike involving lives in a distant nation. The ubiquity of urbanization, on the other hand, means that images of destruction and descriptions of metropolitan havoc are readily comprehended by city dwellers anywhere. Tragedy among Japanese farmers is likely to stimulate little sympathetic understanding in many parts of the world, not because there is a lack of compassion but rather because the farmers' lives are so alien to most hearing of the event. Contrarily, many residents of New York, London, Moscow, Hong Kong, Cairo, and Calcutta had little trouble envisioning the consequences of the September, 1995 Tokyo subway nerve agent attack.

Cities are rich in the extent of consequences an attack can precipitate. Urban events are far more likely to have local, regional, national, and international impact than is the case in any but the most exceptional rural incidents. The September 11, 2001 strike on the World Trade Center had financial and commercial aftereffects that permeated the most distant economies. While there is some redundancy in world financial and commercial systems, there is also great interdependence, a series of interrelationships that ensures a blow against one point is felt throughout affected economic sectors. In comparison, redundancy in the agricultural sector comes with less interdependence; a strike might well be of considerable magnitude but have only regional or national consequences. Other suppliers readily stepped forward when the British beef industry suffered a bout of foot and mouth disease in 2001.

Surprisingly, perhaps, a terrorist group may find metropolitan areas in developing nations even more lucrative than those in developed countries. A native metropolis frequently offers perpetrators a larger and more secure support base on which to draw. Indigenous terrorists are likely to find a greater proportion of residents sympathetic, or at a minimum apathetic, to their motivations. Predominant demographics can facilitate anonymity. The successful attacks on the *U.S.S. Cole* in Yemen, Khobar Towers in Saudi Arabia, and federal building in Oklahoma City are three instances in which the similarity of terrorist characteristics and those of the indigenous population worked against preemptive detection.

These many factors ensure that cities will continue to attract the attentions of undesirable non-state actors and state-sponsored irregular aggressors. Two elements are especially notable in the battle against urban terrorism. First, any resolution should incorporate all of a state's means of favorably influencing the desired outcome. Success is rarely attainable without an orchestration of appropriate economic, political, diplomatic, and other means in addition to those involving the military. This is particularly true when there are even moderate constraints on the use of force. Second, public preparation linked to an effective response system is crucial. Urban residents must be convinced of the need to support anti-terrorist efforts and told how to assist in countering the threat. Given their willing participation, the public must further be convinced that their cooperation will result in effective action. There is a need to demonstrate to the man or woman on the street who makes a report that justice in dealing with legitimate threats will follow. (There is similarly a requirement to demonstrate that deliberately false reports, whether made for the purpose of settling scores or other reasons, will result in punishment of the accusers.)

Neither of these two elements is unique to urban contingencies, but the character of challenges in a built-up area notably influences the nature of both. The greater density of individuals and groups that must be influenced means that achieving desired objectives will be very demanding of time and resources. The positive effects of density, which include faster transmission of propaganda, are more than offset by the multiple counter influences that such densities provide. The typical urban resident has a broader spectrum of influences on his or her life than is the case with those living in more sparsely populated environs; he or she therefore has more alternative perspectives impacting his or her daily decision-making. Northern Ireland provides an effective example; there multiple groups struggle to support their interests, at times using coercion to ensure compliance amongst the hesitant and those supporting alternative stands. Progress in interdicting support for Unionist and Republican acts of violence has been slow to show itself despite years of orchestrating economic, political, social, and military initiatives. Similar opposing influences will affect the viability of an education campaign elsewhere. Success can mean having to overcome generations of deeply ingrained antipathies. Sometimes little more than an insightful approach is needed to trigger success. In Greece, efforts to "put the black hat on the bad guys" by advertising the horrors suffered by victims of terrorism was fundamental to undermining popular support for the perpetrators and their causes. Officials having to overcome such long-standing prejudices are only rarely so fortunate. Progress is far more likely to demand a long-term, well-orchestrated, and carefully managed dedication of economic and other resources to redress actual and perceived grievances.

Educating citizens domestically would include psychologically preparing them for urban terrorist-related events. Such education would improve national preparedness to detect, counter, and minimize a strike's negative consequences. A more aware public would know to report a parcel left unattended in a public area. Its members would understand how to identify and notify authorities regarding suspicious activities. Ideally, they would become savvy in the ways of the terrorist and thus know how to react should an incident occur in their vicinity (for often a first attack is but a means of flushing a greater number and density of targets into the kill zone of a second). It would be hoped that the educated man or woman would better respond to on-scene authorities' guidance, thereby reducing the incidence of panic, facilitating quarantine procedures should they be necessary, and otherwise causing members of the public to act in the best interests of themselves and others. Specially targeted groups (e.g., police, fire, emergency medical, hospital, and transportation system employees) would receive training tailored to take advantage of their responsibilities and the constant public presence their positions entail.

Education is but a part of what should be a greater program of preparing a public for urban terrorism, whether domestically or abroad. Responses to an attack should be in accordance with standing plans and procedures. Those responses should be rehearsed at multiple echelons by all with relevant responsibilities. Rehearsals should include devil's advocates' input, that from individuals capable of challenging officials with realistic scenarios (such those involving a city's off-duty emergency response personnel voluntarily rushing to a point of attack, their good intentions thereby putting the city's readiness for subsequent strikes and continuous operations in jeopardy). Such challenges must incorporate strategic as well as tactical considerations so as to ensure that post-event decisions act to mitigate negative economic, diplomatic, and other consequences. Effective rehearsals and exercises will therefore require participation by a wide range of parties representing many governmental and private organizations.

That cities offer a wealth of benefits to the terrorist attacker is readily apparent, as is the inevitability of future strikes. Yet there is also abundance available to others seeking more favorable objectives. The collective character of many cities' residents has a richness of which those responsible for combating terrorism should make better use. The residents of London have repeatedly refused to be intimidated by the Irish Republican Army's threats much as they stood fast against World War II aerial bombardment. Oklahoma City did not break despite the sudden loss of 168 citizens on April 19, 1995. The attacks of September 11, 2001 let the world see that New York City is more a community than its aloof reputation would have led many to believe possible. Assaults on London, Oklahoma City, New York, and Washington, D.C. were attributable to those urban areas' political, economic, and symbolic affluence. The notoriety and other consequences of such strikes did resonate worldwide, but the resonations rapidly took on a character counterproductive to the perpetrators' objectives. Ultimately it was the bounteousness of the urban residents' character that came to characterize each of these events. Urban terrorism may never be eliminated, but its probability of success and level of impact can be diminished by initiatives that capitalize on the wealth of support, expertise, and strength of collective character existent in many city populations.

Chapter 2

Preparing for Future Joint Urban Operations: The Role of Simulations and the *Urban Resolve* Experiment

Peter W. Wielhouwer

First Published July 2006

Executive Summary

Operations in urban areas have long perplexed military planners, and military analyses predict extensive urban operations for the foreseeable future. Even analyses of the recent urban operations in Iraq recommend significant revision of future training efforts for the conduct of urban operations, emphasizing the need for improved modeling and simulation of urban terrain. While the historic approach has generally been to avoid cities or wage massive campaigns of attrition, it is clear that urban areas cannot be avoided and that modern sensibilities chafe at wide-spread collateral damage.

This paper discusses recent developments in the area of joint urban operations concept development and experimentation, arguing that initiatives under way at U.S. Joint Forces Command have great potential for improving preparation for urban conflict. The paper first discusses the context for new thinking and doctrine on joint urban operations, including analysis of recent data on patterns of global urbanization and U.S. troop deployment and responses. The strategies being used for assessing urban operations concepts are presented, including preliminary detailed results from the ongoing *Urban Resolve* experiment and its application of cutting-edge modeling and simulation technologies.

Briefly, *Urban Resolve's* breakthrough first phase, completed in October, 2004, convinced senior leaders that its experimental approach and tools could be applied across a wider range of venues to assist the Defense Department with current 'real world' problems. *Urban Resolve* has thus been expanded to assess nascent urban capabilities and to immediately address current challenges, such as the unconventional use of mortars in Iraqi cities. *Urban Resolve* and its associated modeling and simulation capabilities are thus important support elements in the current approach to training and preparing U.S. forces for joint urban operations.

Preparing for Future Joint Urban Operations: The Role of Simulations and the *Urban Resolve* Experiment

Operations in urban areas have perplexed military planners since the advent of the walled city. As early as 1400 B.C., Israelite armies were conducting sieges against the residents of their future Promised Land. One thousand years later, Sun Tzu advised, "The worst policy is to attack cities. Attack cities only when there is no alternative…[T]hose skilled in war…capture his [enemy's] cities without assaulting them and overthrow his state without protracted operations."[1] Very recently, U.S. and Iraqi joint forces were engaged in street-to-street urban combat again in Fallujah, wrestling control of the city from insurgents.

From this and other recent operations ranging from Mogadishu to Kabul to Baghdad, new doctrine and new capability requirements are emerging to enable more effective urban operations. These changes reflect new thinking that is complemented by experiments using state of the art modeling and simulation at U.S. Joint Forces Command's Joint Experimentation directorate. This article argues that Joint Urban Operations concept development and experimentation have great potential for improving preparation for urban conflict. First, the context for new thinking and doctrine on joint urban operations is articulated, including analysis of recent data on patterns of global urbanization and U.S. troop deployment and responses over the last half-century. The strategies being used for assessing urban operations concepts are then discussed, showing the ways in which the *Urban Resolve* experiment applies cutting-edge modeling and simulation technologies to the subject. The conclusions suggest the ways in which these activities support current and future joint force operations.

The U.S. Army's major 'Lessons Learned' document for Operation Iraqi Freedom, *On Point*, made prescient recommendations for future training efforts: "What must be done next is to build a simulation that affords joint commanders the opportunity to plan and execute realistic training in large urban areas that replicate both the urban core and urban sprawl. This task, while daunting, is not out of reach."[2] The present article argues that such a simulation is already in hand.

We Have Seen the Future War, and It Is Urban

When it comes to operations in urban areas, military planners face distinct challenges that de-rive from the city's characteristics, its *urban triad*. These are a complex manmade terrain super-imposed on natural terrain, a large and densely distributed population, and physical and service infrastructures. "These characteristics interact to make each urban area a complex and dynamic system of systems, with a unique physical, political, economic, social, and cultural identity." Joint Urban Operations are the joint operations planned and conducted in these environments.[3] While the ability of Operation Iraqi Freedom (OIF) Phase I coalition forces to adapt and make the way for success in their urban battles is widely praised, future joint forces will benefit from improved doctrine, training, and leadership in the area of urban operations.

It is now clear that this is a matter of extraordinary importance, as all indicators point to extensive urban operations for the foreseeable future. First, the nation's adversaries will continue to move their battles into urban areas, where they believe American asymmetric warfighting advantages may be neutralized. Second, the world's population is relocating to urban areas to a significant degree, including in those regions where U.S. forces were most active in the last two decades. Third, American urban operations will continue to include stability, reconstruction, and humanitarian operations, with important strategic consequences.[4]

Patterns of U.S. Military Deployments and Responses, 1950-2002

Part of this discussion hinges on whether U.S. forces are required to engage extensively in urban areas compared with other areas. We can, for example, assess whether urbanization trends (the propensity for population growth in urban, versus rural, areas) are related to U.S. military activity. We should be concerned if our military is more likely to be deployed or engaged in areas where urbanization is occurring. If military deployments or engagements are not taking place in urbanizing areas, then the concerns about the impact of worldwide urbanization on the U.S. military may be misplaced.

Three sets of data, which to my knowledge have not yet been considered in concert, relate directly to this question. First, the United Nations tracks national populations and publishes urban growth rates by country and region. Second, a new dataset on U.S. military deployment rates was published in late 2004 by the Heritage Foundation, documenting the number of billets assigned to countries for every year from 1950 through 2003. Finally, Thomas Barnett, a Naval War College professor with close ties to the Defense Department's Office of Force Transformation recently collated U.S. military responses to situations worldwide between 1990 and 2002.[5] Although a nation-by-nation analysis of these datasets could be undertaken, here I aggregate the data by region. In this way, we can assess whether there is a first-order relationship between regional urbanization and U.S. military activity.

To test the hypothesis that U.S. deployments are related to urban growth, I compare regional urban growth rates with changes in troop deployment patterns across that time period (see Appendix Table A-1). This measure is developed by taking the mean number of troops deployed to each region in each decade; the 1990s mean is subtracted from the 1950s mean, yielding the change in average regional troop deployments over the four decades. As we would expect, the number of billets varies considerably; compare, for example, the 129,000 troops on average deployed in 1990s Northern and Western Europe with Southern Africa's 32. To make a direct comparison between regions, I convert the troop changes to percentages. In Northern and Western Europe, this produces a 1950s-1990s reduction in U.S. troops of 58.2%: (309,188 - 129,192) ÷ 309,188 = .582.

Table 1 presents regions' 1950-2000 urban growth rates and percentage change in U.S. troops deployed over the same time period. Regions are rank-ordered by urban growth rate. Eastern Africa had the highest urban growth rate, at an average of 5.77% per year, followed by Western Africa (5.33%), Western Asia and Middle Africa (4.41%). The regions with the slowest urban growth were Northern and Western Europe (0.84%), Southern Europe (1.38%), North America (1.59%, excluding the U.S.), and Eastern Europe (1.75%). The world's urban growth rate was 2.68%, with a substantial difference between developed (1.4%) and less-developed regions (3.73%).

Only four regions saw increases U.S. troop levels: Eastern Europe (+1,579%), Western Africa (+779%), Western Asia (+95%), and Eastern Africa (+15%). The massive increase in U.S. troops in Eastern Europe during the '90s is clearly a function of Cold War-Post Cold War adjustments but represents a real change of only 1,282 billets; similarly, Western Africa's increase represents only 91 billets. (The political connotations of the Eastern Europe changes are historically unique, so I drop it from this part of the analysis.) Excluding these two regions, there was typically a 40% reduction in U.S. troops between 1950 and 1999.

Table 2 (see also Appendix Table A-2) shows Barnett's classification of U.S. military responses to different types of situations between 1990 and 2002; regions are ranked by their 1950-2000 urban growth rates. The region with the most U.S. responses is Western Asia, with 35; 69% involved force application, while 31% were humanitarian (including peacekeeping). Southern Europe, which includes the nations of the former Yugoslavia, saw 23 U.S. responses, of which about half were humanitarian (mainly NATO peacekeeping missions). Eastern Africa witnessed 16 responses; although predominantly peacekeeping, Task Force Ranger's October 1993 experience in Mogadishu shows that humanitarian missions can devolve quickly into combat. About 57% of all military responses were humanitarian, and 43% were intended primarily as shows of force, contingency positioning, or combat operations.

There is a strong statistical relationship between urban growth and troop deployments. There is a multiple correlation between urban growth and military deployment changes of 0.62 (on a scale of 0 to 1), and urban growth rate explains 38% of the variation in troop deployment changes. Regions with urban growth rates greater than about four percent in the last half of the twentieth century were likely to see increasing U.S. troop deployments, while regions with lower rates saw troop presence reduced. Additionally, there is reasonably strong relationship between urban growth rates and U.S. military responses. Excluding Southern Europe's NATO mission, the measures have a correlation coefficient of .58, urban growth rate explains 34% of the variation in U.S. responses, and a one percent increase in urban growth produced 3.9 more U.S. military responses. The overall picture that emerges from these data is of increasing American military engagement in rapidly urbanizing areas of the world, confirming the extant assertion of military analysts that calls for improved preparation for combat and humanitarian operations in urban environments.[6]

It should be noted that Barnett has a somewhat different take on the distribution of military activity in the post-Cold War time frame.

He suggests that the U.S. engages in those areas of the world that are excluded from economic globalization's bandwagon. The results in the analysis presented here do not contradict his assertion, because the less developed regions of the world experienced much faster urban growth than developed areas, so American military activity took place in the less developed regions with their high urban growth rates.

The Iraq Example

Operation Iraqi Freedom epitomizes the issues that apply to urban operations. The 1991 Gulf War taught the Iraqi military leadership that fighting the American-led coalition in the wide-open spaces of the Arabian Peninsula was a hopeless undertaking. In the 2003 war, the fighting capacity of the Iraqi armed forces was centered in urban areas, but the regime and most cities fell quickly. The relatively meager combat challenges initially faced by coalition joint forces have left little room for complacency about urban warfare, however. Post-major combat operations (including humanitarian and stability operations) have produced uneven stability on the road to the final transition to Iraqi civilian control, with the most virulent insurgency elements concentrated in cities. The relative calm of Iraq's first election day on January 30, 2005 was a promising harbinger, though the insurgency continues to find support where economic reconstruction is slow.

On Point, while generally positive about joint urban operations in Iraq, notes two "significant deficiencies" in U.S. training on the subject. First, the primary training facilities for U.S. forces are modeled as small towns or villages, rather than major metropolitan areas. Second, legacy computer simulations were insufficiently realistic to adequately prepare joint force commanders or warfighters for urban operations.[7] In summary, while our military is the best funded and equipped in the world, doctrine and training lagged, until recently, when it came to preparation for urban operations. In the last ten years, the challenge of doctrine and concept development was framed by two distinct, yet related questions.

Critical Question 1: How Will We Fight?

*How can we fight in urban terrain against an intelligent,
determined, well-equipped adversary and win quickly
without unacceptable casualties to ourselves or our
allies, unacceptable civilian casualties, or unacceptable
destruction of infrastructure?*[8]

The question itself reframes the debate on urban operations.
Historically, the primary issue was simply how to fight in urban terrain;
collateral damage was of secondary concern. Beginning in 1998 a Joint
Urban Working Group addressed the new question and made several
recommendations for developing an effective new joint doctrine for
urban operations.[9]

The core of the resulting Joint Urban Operations (JUO) concept is
to apply new and innovative thinking regarding joint capabilities and
urban operations, and new technologies to bring the open environment
advantages our military currently enjoys into to urban environments.
Two elements comprise the new thinking: joint (versus service-centric)
operational capabilities and a new conceptual framework for urban
terrain. The JUO concept leverages emerging technologies to conduct
effective urban warfare while explicitly addressing concerns about
friendly casualties and collateral damage. Rather than relegating
planning for action in cities to secondary status, urban operations are
viewed as important opportunities for accelerating the attainment of
strategic goals.

The Strategy: New Thinking and Doctrine

The center of gravity for new, innovative thinking on JUO is U.S.
Joint Forces Command's (JFCOM) Joint Experimentation directorate
(J9), headquartered in Suffolk, Virginia. In 2003 JFCOM was designated
as the Defense Department's Executive Agent for improving capabilities
in joint urban operations, and partners with the Institute for Defense

Analyses (IDA) and its Joint Advanced Warfighting Program (JAWP) for doing so.

The modern framework for conducting JUO is articulated in all of the major documents prompted by the deliberations of the Joint Urban Working Group. In general, the self-conscious end state of JUO is transferring control to a nonmilitary authority after strategic and operational objectives have been achieved. The doctrine is summarized by the acronym USECT.[10] Joint Force Commanders must:

- **Understand**: Evaluate the urban battlespace first, including the urban triad and the threat, to determine the implications for military operations.
- **Shape**: Establish favorable conditions for engagement by influencing the strategic setting and controlling the physical environment.
- **Engage**: Apply diplomatic, informational, military, and economic capabilities to achieve operational objectives, from full-scale combat to humanitarian assistance.
- **Consolidate**: Protect what has been gained and retain the initiative to disorganize the adversary in depth, to maintain operational advantage.
- **Transition**. Return control to civilian authorities; the transfer could be to another military force or international organization.

JUO conceptual innovations have led to several new operational and tactical approaches. In general, they reflect transition *from* operations that use massed confrontation, attrition, contiguous and sequential tactics, *to* operations that are information-based, using discriminate precision force projection, measured effects, and overmatching power. The new urban warfare concepts "offer the prospect of significantly reducing both friendly and civilian casualties, as well as collateral damage, however, they also require greatly improved capabilities for achieving under-standing *before* engaging."[11]

The JUO Joint Integrating Concept currently being developed at JFCOM outlines in more de-tail the conditions and capabilities needed for planning and conducting successful joint urban operations. Because the urban environment is too complex for single-agency or single-service solutions, "generating desired effects and avoiding unintended effects [requires] careful integration of joint forces and interagency supporting capabilities at each point of action and at every level of decision."[12] A significant portion of the directorate's JUO energy is dedicated to this task.

Critical Question 2: How Do We Determine How We Fight?

How can we determine which concepts, matériel, tactics, techniques, and procedures are most effective for fighting in urban terrain?

The approach for addressing this question was articulated in the *National Security Strategy of the United States*, "Innovation within the armed forces will rest on experimentation with new approaches to warfare, strengthening joint operations, exploiting U.S. intelligence advantages, and taking full advantage of science and technology." This echoed congressional language supporting the creation of "an energetic and innovative organization" within the Defense Department for future-oriented experimentation.[13] Most recently, the 2004 Unified Command Plan as-signed to JFCOM responsibility for leading and coordinating joint concept development and experimentation.

The command's strategy is to develop capabilities and concepts that will increase the effectiveness of joint force commanders in the field, through vigorous debate, collaboration, refinement, prototyping, and experimentation. Its Joint Concept Development path generates promising concepts through discovery and concept refinement experimentation. By collaborating with Services, combatant commands, multinational partners, and civilian agencies the pathway assesses concepts' potential for conversion to prototypes and informs future force investments. Concepts with promise for improving near-term warfighting capabilities are refined in the Joint Prototype Pathway to get them into the hands of joint warfighters as quickly as possible.

Four main experimentation methods are used in concept development: war games, experiments in virtual environments, constructive simulations, and live simulations. The stage of concept maturation determines the mix of experimentation methodologies applied. Once new concepts emerge, "born jointly" from exploration, then refinement and assessment occur in a nonlinear and complementary experimentation process. Virtual environment experiments and constructive simulations grow in importance.

Human-In-The-Loop (HITL) experiments are crucial at this point. Blue concept developers play against Red Teams in real time; the mission of the Red team is to challenge, react, and adapt to the Blue team playing according to the parameters of the new concept. Red team does not respond according to pre-programmed algorithms but simulates the response of an aggressive and adaptive enemy. In essence, Red tries to see if they can push the new concept to failure. This permits exploration of the interaction between new concepts and new technologies; assesses real and prototype command-and-control; and controls for human factors, such as cognitive reasoning and training.

The *Urban Resolve* Experiment

The JUO office is currently in the midst of a major multi-year experiment, *Urban Resolve*, involving HITL concept refinement exploring JUO enabling concepts. (Earlier experiments and war games include the *Joint Urban Warrior* series, co-sponsored with the Marine Corps.) As initially conceived, the experiment consisted of three major phases, focused on three key JUO capabilities: achieving a high-level of situational *understanding* via networked sensors; *shaping* (isolating and controlling) the urban battlespace through precision effects; and effectively *engaging* by maneuvering joint forces. The experiment was initially truly future-oriented, attempting to identify capabilities for execution in the 2015-2020 timeframe.

Urban Resolve's overall scenario involves a 2015 invasion of an island nation by a fundamentalist opponent (Red). Red forces are forced by a

U.S.-led Combined Joint Task Force into a major urban center, where Red is preparing for a final defense. Phase 1 included four HITL trials, occurring between June and October, 2004 (although concept and simulation development began in early FY04). Participants in the HITL phases were distributed, located at J9 Facilities (Suffolk, VA), Ft. Belvoir (Northern VA), Wright-Patterson Air Force Base (Dayton, OH), the Space and Naval Warfare Systems Command Support Center (San Diego, CA), and the Maui High Performance Computing Center, (Kihei, HI).

Phase 1 assessed a Joint Force Commander's ability to acquire situational understanding when he has access to a persistent and pervasive intelligence, surveillance, and reconnaissance (ISR) network suited to the urban environment. The ISR assets tested included human intelligence, current unmanned high- and medium-altitude sensors, and future low-altitude sensors (Organic Air Vehicles under development at the Defense Advanced Research Projects Agency [DARPA]). The players were challenged to use sensors to detect and track targets that frequently move in and out of sight; to pick those targets out of dense background clutter; to find very well concealed targets; to distinguish military targets from civilian look-alikes; and to disguise sensors and deploy them in stealthy ways.

Phase 2, tentatively scheduled for July through September 2006, will focus on shaping the battlespace via precision weaponry. Specifically, it will assess the Blue commander's ability to isolate and control the urban environment using standoff precision strike weapons systems. Phase 3 is tentatively scheduled for 2007 and will focus on forces engaging Red through joint maneuvers, adding full ground and special operations forces.

During Phase 1, senior leaders realized that its experimental approach and tools could be applied across a wider range of venues to assist the Defense Department with other vexing challenges. Under their explicit guidance, *Urban Resolve* was expanded to generate a baseline assessment of our overall urban warfighting capabilities and supporting programs, and to immediately address challenges being faced in current urban operations. The two new "real world" applications of Urban Resolve will be (1) quickly adapting its modeling and simulation capability (discussed below) into a mission planning and rehearsal tool for deploying joint forces, and (2) assisting with developing more effective responses to non-traditional mortar attacks now occurring in Iraq. This more comprehensive character expands *Urban Resolve's* charter to investigate a wider range of near and far term urban issues to better support the joint war-fighter.

Simulating the Urban Triad: Joint Semi-Automatic Forces

A central component of *Urban Resolve* is its use of the breakthrough simulation toolkit known as JSAF (Joint Semi-Automatic Forces), an outgrowth of DARPA Synthetic Theater of War initiatives:

> JSAF is a simulation system that generates entity level platforms such as infantrymen, tanks, ships, airplanes, munitions, buildings, and sensors, which interact at the individual level in a robust synthetic natural environment....The synthetic environment is a representation of real world terrain, oceans, and weather conditions that affect the behaviors and capabilities of the synthetic forces...Command and control behaviors and architectures are realistically simulated, as are sensors, logistics, weapons effects, and entities' reaction to various combat stimuli.[14]

The importance of JSAF to the experiment can be understood in terms of the urban triad. The simulation portrayed a complex three-dimensional urban terrain of more than 1.8 million discrete buildings. Of those, about 65,000 had the capacity for greater interaction with Red and Blue forces, such as the ability to enter, fight inside, and view the street from inside a building. The environment was mapped based on two sections of a real city; the buildings, parking lots, and other urban clutter simulated actual physical characteristics, such as being built of wood or concrete. The presence of so many buildings simulated line-of-sight limitations as Blue team members moved through the city.

JSAF also simulated the large, densely distributed urban population. More than 110,000 discrete person-entities were routinely simulated; about 35,000 were active and displaying culturally-appropriate behaviors. (Tests confirmed that one million entities could be generated in the simulation; a significantly higher number seems very likely.) Civilian vehicles and pedestrians were fully integrated into the simulation, controlled by a "Green" team, and Red and Blue teams both had to take civilian presence into account in their play. For example, a roadblock set up by the Red team would adversely affect traffic flow and Red's own movement. The simulated infra-structure reflected the model city. City streets and highways were affected by culturally-specific traffic flows; traffic and civilian presence increased around mosques at the appropriate times for daily prayers.

All the entities and players were affected by the urban triad, including being constrained to act in real time. A human intelligence agent, for instance, might be tasked for information acquisition. If "he" received the task during normal sleeping hours, the mission could not be per-formed until enough time had elapsed for getting up, getting dressed, traveling to the assigned site, observing the desired activity, and establishing communication with the Blue team players.

The Technology

The technical scale of the experiment was unprecedented. The architecture that allowed the distributed simulation to be effective had three elements: JSAF, Scalable Parallel Processors, and the Defense Research Engineering Network.[15] As we have seen, JSAF demonstrated the capacity to integrate very large numbers of entities into the experiment. The experiment's architecture joined JSAF with Scalable Parallel Processor (SPP) clusters to enable these performance levels. An SPP cluster is a group of interconnected processors that work together as a supercomputer. It breaks apart large computational tasks, parcels them out to the processors in the cluster, and reassembles them quickly. These clusters allow greatly increased computational speed without the use of expensive individual high-powered computers. In short, the JSAF-SPP combination vastly improves the training capability of HITL experiments, because the urban terrain, entity behaviors, sensors, weapons platforms and effects, and the civilian population and clutter of a city are more realistically simulated.

Two supercomputer clusters were used in *Urban Resolve*, located in Kehei (Maui), Hawaii and Wright-Patterson AFB. The SPP clusters were linked to the rest of the federation via the Defense Research Engineering Network. This very large and efficient DOD network provided the bandwidth necessary to transmit information from one site to another (up to 140 Mb/s), with no significant data transfer delay. This meant that players distributed across the country could inter-act in real time, on a 24/7 basis.

Results and Achievements

While comprehensive findings of *Urban Resolve* Phase I are being analyzed as this paper is being written, it is clear that its players successfully used JSAF to assess the impact on situational awareness of a pervasive ISR network. Three levels of understanding were assessed: "Where is Red?", "What is Red doing?", and "What is Red going to do in the future?" Between 60% and 70% of Red forces were successfully detected. Even after sensor operators eliminated high- and medium-altitude sensors in later trials, Blue analysts adapted their techniques, tactics, and procedures to accomplish the mission. Red's current activities were correctly identified be-tween 55% and 70% of the time, and 60%-70% of Red's future actions were correctly anticipated. A total of 80%-90% of Red entities were tracked by the sensor network.

Several significant technical achievements are associated with *Urban Resolve* Phase 1. First, J9 built, for this experiment, the largest, most complex, most reliable Virtual Urban Environment in the world to date. On the hardware front, the distributed simulation architecture controlled re-motely over 300 computer nodes on the SPP and on the network; collected and analyzed massive amounts of data—about 100 gigabytes per week; and successfully conducted a large-scale distributed experiment over the DREN. Nearly 1.7 terabytes of data were collected over the experiment's four trials.

The experiment applied, for the first time, SPP supercomputers for interactive, real-time forces modeling. JFCOM was able to use the SPP hardware on a continuous basis, in which the players and simulation operators controlled entities on the supercomputers. This required new levels of cooperation between the JFCOM simulation team, the DREN program office, and the High-Performance Computer Center management teams.

Joint Urban Operations and the Future Joint Warfighter

While urban conflict has always been part of military operations, the transformation in U.S. foreign policy under the Truman Doctrine also opened the door for expanded military engagement in non-combat activities. Operation Iraqi Freedom is a prominent recent example. As noted in early postwar analysis, "urban warfare in Iraq …. highlights the need to see urban warfare in peacemaking and nation-building terms and the need to develop suitable tactics, training, and equipment."[16] This finding is reinforced by analysis of the relationship between urban growth rates, changes in U.S. troop deployment, and military responses. The logical conclusion is that expanded Joint Urban Operations concept and doctrine development, experimentation, modeling and simulation will benefit practitioners of warfare's operational arts.

In light of these considerations, we can identify several specific advantages that seem likely to accrue to joint warfighters from JUO concept development and experimentation. First, they will benefit from commanders' improved understanding of the urban battlespace, obtained through training in constructive simulations and advanced planning capabilities currently being fielded in the combatant commands.[17] Improved ISR has also been shown to vastly improve situational understanding and promise to revolutionize intelligence preparation of the urban battle-space.[18] These technologies will help future warfighters cope with elements unique to the urban triad.

Second, joint forces will be better prepared for the actual battle. By planning, training, and rehearsing for operations via advanced virtual simulations, commanders will gain better under-standing of the impact of civilian population dynamics, urban structures and infrastructure. This will equip them to more effectively shape the battlespace to their own advantage. Smarter engagement with the adversary will result from the improved understanding and shaping process.

Moreover, improved preparations will occur in the near term as *Urban Resolve's* capabilities are applied to planning for and coping with current challenges in Iraq. Although joint experimentation has generally focused on the operational level of war, JSAF and SPP now allow JFCOM to selectively investigate key joint warfighting issues from strategic through operational to tactical, creating the opportunity to better recognize and understand key linkages and relationships in the conduct of joint operations. The initial effort to apply these modeling and simulation capabilities will be focused on improving our ability to deal with the extensive use of mortars and rockets to attack our forces in theater, with a strong possibility of then addressing the challenge posed by improvised explosive devices on the ground in Iraq.

Third, the JUO conceptual framework explicitly includes stability and reconstruction operations (Consolidation) and begins with the end-state in mind (Transition), facilitating more effective planning. Early understanding of the cultural and geographic dimensions of an urban environment, along with precision engagement, eases the movement to stability operations. These increase commanders' awareness of the longer term implications of tactical decisions. By employing maneuver rather than attrition in urban engagement, noncombatant and combatant casualties may be minimized, attenuating post-combat resentment of coalition forces engaged in humanitarian and reconstructive operations. And by employing precision munitions with an awareness of nonmilitary and culturally sensitive urban sites, the joint force may avoid unnecessary collateral damage that undermines domestic and international support.

Despite Sun Tzu's advice, military commanders continue to find that cities are central elements in the logistical and operational landscapes. Future Joint Force Commanders and war-fighters will benefit from the training opportunities afforded by new simulation and modeling initiatives, such as those demonstrated in *Urban Resolve*. Its breakthrough simulation of the urban triad improves prospects for gaining and maintaining information and decision superiority in the urban battlespace. Military planners and forces also have greater prospects for success in urban operations short of combat. Should combat be required, planning tools allow commanders to anticipate the consequences of tactical decisions and improve opportunities for smoother and swifter transitions to civilian control.

Appendix Table A-1. United States Troop Deployments to World Regions, 1950-2003 (Decade Averages)

	Decade Averages						1950s-1990s
Region/Country	1950s	1960s	1970s	1980s	1990s	2000-03	Change
Africa							
Eastern Africa	788	1,620	555	119	908	223	120
Middle Africa	0	59	37	55	43	24	-16
Northern Africa	15,384	7,031	1,009	1,238	1,592	493	-13,792
Southern Africa	35	18	21	19	32	39	-4
Western Africa	12	81	77	102	103	102	91
Americas							
North America (non-US)	22,983	14,777	3,116	2,370	934	278	-22,049
Central America	10,972	10,638	9,998	10,892	8,399	491	-2,573
Caribbean	7,334	4,945	3,505	2,523	4,543	751	-2,792
South America	920	765	427	292	387	526	-534
Asia							
Eastern Asia	318,109	147,040	102,434	91,134	81,298	79,584	-236,811
South Central Asia	568	2,000	850	102	93	6,581	-475
Southeast Asia	15,471	236,398	99,806	15,381	2,787	615	-12,684

Western Asia	6,623	10,729	6,683	6,037	12,939	56,325	6,316
Europe							
Northern and West-ern Europe	309,188	300,095	248,466	287,130	129,192	86,211	-179,996
Southern Europe	21,042	25,657	25,041	28,426	23,457	23,377	2,415
Eastern Europe	81	72	89	121	1,363	271	1,282
Oceania	4,839	2,359	1,794	1,111	778	538	-4,062

Cell entries are the average number of U.S. military billets assigned to countries in each region in each decade, and aggregated. The original data are reported annually by country; regions are as defined by the United Nations. Antarctica, Continental U.S. and U.S. territories outside the continental United States are excluded.

Source: Tim Kane, "Global U.S. Troop Deployment, 1950-2003," Heritage Foundation Center for Data Analysis Report #04-11 (www. heritage.org/Research/NationalSecurity/cda04-11.cfm accessed 18 January 2005).

Appendix Table A-2. U.S. Military Responses to Situations, 1990-2002, by Region.

	Combat	Show of Force	Contingency Positioning or Reconnaissance	Evacuation or Security	Peacekeeping	Total
Africa						
Eastern Africa		1	1	/	7	16
Middle Africa				5	2	7
Northern Africa	1			1		2
Southern Africa					2	2
Western Africa				9	2	11
Americas						
North America (non-US)						0
Central America		1				1
Caribbean		2	2	3	3	10
South America			6			6
Asia						
Eastern Asia		2	1	1		4
South Central Asia	5					5

Southeast Asia			1	3	4	8
Western Asia	7	15	2	9	2	35
Europe						
North and Western Europe					1	1
Southern Europe	3	5	2	5	8	23
Eastern Europe						0
Oceania						0
Totals:	16	26	15	43	31	131

Sources: Military response data are from Thomas P.M. Barnett, "The Pentagon's New Map," *Esquire*, March 2003 (www.thomaspmbarnett.com/published/pentagonsnewmap.htm 28 Jan 2004. Regions are as defined by the United Nations.

Table 1. World Regions, Urban Growth Rates (Ranked) and Changes in U.S. Troop Deployment, 1950-2000

	Rank	1950-2000 Urban Growth Rate	Rank	Troop Deployment (1950s-1990s)
Eastern Africa	1	5.77	4	15.2
Western Africa	2	5.33	2	779.5
Western Asia	3	4.41	3	95.4
Middle Africa	3	4.41	8	-27.4
Southeast Asia	5	4.02	13	-82
Northern Africa	6	3.74	16	-89.7
Central America	7	3.67	7	-23.4
South America	8	3.44	10	-58
South Central Asia	9	3.34	14	-90
Eastern Asia	10	3.25	12	-74.4
Southern Africa	11	3	6	-10.7
Caribbean	12	2.75	9	-38.1
Oceania	13	2.14	15	-83.9
Eastern Europe	14	1.75	1	1,579.10
North America (non-US)	15	1.59	17	-95.9

Southern Europe	16	1.38	5	11.5
North and Western Europe	17	0.84	11	-58.2
World		2.68	Mean	103.2
			Median	-38.1

Mean (without Europe): -40

Median (without Eastern Europe and Western Africa): -58.0

a. Average annual rate at which a region's urban population increased between 1950 and 2000. Source: U.N. Department of Economic and Social Affairs, *World Urbanization Prospects: 2001 Revision*, www.un.org/esa/population/publications/wup2001/WUP2001report.htm accessed 22 September 2004.

b. The difference in the average number of U.S. military billets assigned to countries in each region in each decade (see Appendix Table 1). Original data are reported annually by country; here they are aggregated by U.N. region (see Appendix Table A). Excluded are Antarctica, Continental U.S. and U.S. territories outside the continental United States. Source: Tim Kane, "Global U.S. Troop Deployment, 1950-2003," Heritage Foundation Center for Data Analysis Report #04-11 (http://www.heritage.org/Research/NationalSecurity/cda04-11.cfm accessed 20 January 2005).

Table 2. World Regions and U.S. Military Responses to Situations, 1990-2002.

Region[a] (Ranked by 1950-2000 Urban Growth Rate)		U.S. Military Responses Involving Force[b]		U.S. Military Humanitarian ReSponses		Total U.S. Military Responses
1.	Eastern Africa	2	(-12.5%)	14	(-87.5%)	16
2.	Western Africa	0	(0)	11	(-100)	11
3.	Middle Africa	0	(0)	7	(-100)	7
4.	Western Asia	24	(-68.6)	11	(-31.4)	35
5.	Southeast Asia	1	(-12.5)	7	(-87.5)	8
	Subset Mean:	5.4		10		15.4
6.	Northern Africa	1	(-50)	1	(-50)	2
7.	Central America	1	(-100)	0	(0)	1
8.	South America	6	(-100)	0	(0)	6
9.	South Central Asia	5	(-100)	0	(0)	5
10.	Eastern Asia	3	(-75)	1	(-25)	4
11.	Southern Africa	0	(0)	2	(-100)	2
12.	Caribbean	4	(-40)	6	(-60)	10
13.	Oceania	0	(0)	0	(0)	0
14.	Eastern Europe	0	(0)	0	(0)	0
15.	North America (non-US)	0	(0)	0	(0)	0
16.	Southern Europe	10	(-43.5)	13	(-56.5)	23
17.	North and Western Europe	0	(0)	1	(-100)	1
	Subset Mean	2.5		2.0		4.5
	Totals:	57	(-43.5)	74	(-56.5)	131

a. Regions are as defined by the United Nations. Urban Growth Rate is the average annual rate at which a region's urban population increased between 1950 and 2000. Source: U.N. Department of Economic and Social Affairs, *World Urbanization Prospects: 2001 Revision.*

b. See Appendix Table 2. U.S. Military responses to situations
    data are from Thomas P.M. Barnett, "The Pentagon's New
    Map," *Esquire*, March 2003. Responses Involving Force
    include combat, shows of force, and contingency positioning or
    reconnaissance; Humanitarian Responses include evacuations
    or security and peacekeeping or relief.

Notes

[1] Sun Tzu, *The Art of War*, trans. Samuel B. Griffith (New York,
     Oxford University Press, 1971), 78-79.

[2] *On Point: The United States Army in Operation Iraqi Freedom*
     (Leavenworth, KS: Center for Army Lessons Learned, 2004), 390.

[3] Joint Chiefs of Staff, *Doctrine for Joint Urban Operations* (JP
     3-06, September 2002), chapter I.

[4] National Defense Panel, *Transforming Defense—National Security
     in the 21ˢᵗ Century*, (Arlington, VA, 1997); Christopher J. Bowie, et
     al., "Trends in Future Warfare," *Joint Force Quarterly* (35, 2004),
     129-133; Robert F. Hahn and Bonnie Jezior, "Urban Warfare and
     the Urban Warfighter of 2025," *Parameters* (Summer 1999), 74-
     86. *Doctrine for Joint Urban Operations*; Dept. of the Army, *Urban
     Operations*, Field Manual 3-06, June 2003; North Atlantic Treaty
     Organization, *Urban Operations in The Year 2020*, (NATO RTO
     Technical Report #71) April 2003.

[5] U.N. Department of Economic and Social Affairs, *World
     Urbanization Prospects: 2001 Revision*, (www.un.org/esa/
     population/publications/wup2001/WUP2001report.htm
     accessed 22 September 2004). Tim Kane, "Global U.S. Troop
     Deployment, 1950-2003," Heritage Foundation Center for
     Data Analysis Report #04-11 www.heritage.org/Research/
     NationalSecurity/cda04-11.cfm accessed 20 January 2005).
     Thomas P.M. Barnett, "The Pentagon's New Map," *Esquire*.
     March 2003 (www.thomaspmbarnett.com/published/
     pentagonsnewmap.htm accessed 28 January 2005).

[6]   The equations on which these calculations are:
        Change in Troop Deployment = - 9.6206 + (10.7 * Urban Growth
        Rate2) - (47.9 * Urban Growth Rate)
        U.S. Military Responses = -6.2 + (3.9 * Urban Growth Rate)

[7]   *On Point*, 390.

[8]   The two critical questions are drawn from USJFCOM/J9
        Brief (Unclassified), "Urban Resolve Experiment Update," 21
        September 2004.

[9]   The working group included: Offices of the Secretaries of Defense
        and State, the Commanders-in-Chief, the Services, Joint Staff,
        and representatives of DoD agencies. Later, the Joint Advanced
        Warfighting Program (JAWP) at the Institute for Defense Analysis
        (IDA) became engaged. See LtCol Duane Schattle, "Joint MOUT
        Mission Area Analysis and Mission Need Assessment," In *The
        City's Many Faces*, Ed. Russell W. Glenn (RAND, 2000) and
        Department of Defense, *FY-04 Department of Defense Master
        Plan for Joint Urban Operations,* 1 October 2003, Chapter 1.

[10]   This discussion synthesizes and, at times, closely paraphrases the
        description of the framework in the core JUO documents. USECT
        phases are interdependent, continuous, and simultaneous.

[11]   *DoD JUO Master Plan*, 17. "Taking the 'Revolution in Military
        Affairs' Downtown," *IDA Research Summaries* 9 (Spring/Summer
        2002); BG Robert E. Schmidle and LtCol Frank G. Hoffman,
        "Commanding the Contested Zones," *Proceedings* 130 (Sept
        2004).

[12]   "Joint Urban Operations Integrating Concept," Draft Working
        Paper (version .95), 4 June 2004, 18

[13]   George W. Bush, *National Security Strategy of the United States of
        America*, September 2002, 30. See also 10 U.S.C. § 485 (1998)
        and related notes.

[14]   "Joint Semi-Automated Force (JSAF) Information Paper" (20
        May 2003) www.mstp.quantico.usmc.mil/modssm2/InfoPapers/
        INFOPAPER%20JSAF_files/INFOPAPER_JSAF.htm, accessed
        12 October 2004; Andy Ceranowicz and Mark Torpey, "Adapting
        to Urban Warfare," Paper presented at the Interservice/Industry

Training, Simulation, and Education Conference (December 2004), Orlando, FL. The STOW simulation (renamed JSAF) transitioned to JFCOM in 2000 and is now owned and managed by J9; software is provided free of charge to DOD organizations and projects.

[15] Andy Ceranowicz, Rae W. Dehncke, and Tony Cerri, "Moving Toward a Distributed Continuous Experimentation Environment," Paper presented at the Interservice/Industry Training, Simulation, and Education Conference (I/ITSEC) December, 2003.

[16] *The Iraq War*, 368.

[17] Such as the Standing Joint Force Headquarters (Core Element) and its enabling concepts. See Peter W. Wielhouwer, "Toward Information Superiority: The Contribution of Operational Net Assessment," *Air & Space Power Journal* (forthcoming).

[18] Jamison J. Medby and Russell W. Glenn, *Street Smart: Intelligence Preparation of the Battlefield for Urban Operations* (RAND, 2002).

Chapter 3

Postcard from Mumbai: Modern Urban Siege

John P. Sullivan and Adam Elkus

First Published 16 February 2009

According to many television news reports, the Mumbai terrorist attacks were a "siege." But there were no catapults, cannons, or breaching ladders. Instead, a dozen men with guns paralyzed one of the world's largest cities, killing 173 with barely concealed glee. Sadly, Mumbai heralds a new chapter in the bloody story of war in cities—the siege of the city from within. The *polis* is fast becoming a war zone where criminals, terrorists, and heavily armed paramilitary forces battle—and all can be targeted.[1] All the while, gardens of steel spring up, constricting popular movement and giving way to an evolving architecture of fear. The "feral city" and the military colony battle each other for dominance in the urban siege.

Defending against the urban siege requires bridging the gap between police and military, building a layered defense, and fighting to preserve the right to the city. Despite the terrifying nature of the threat, the ultimate advantage lies with the vibrant modern city and the police, soldiers, and civilians tasked to defend it. The key to success lies in the construction of resilient physical and moral infrastructure.

Cities, Sieges, and the Engine of War

City sieges are as old as cities themselves. Fortifications took the place of soldiers in the field, as walls required no food or supplies to maintain, offered more defensive power, and allowed light infantry the opportunity to savage attackers with projectiles.[2] Military theorists from Sun Tzu onwards counseled armies to avoid fights in cities—those who disregarded their advice often suffered bloody defeat, their soldiers riddled with arrows on the parapets or shot down in narrow streets. Yet the contest between the attacking army and the urban defender was by no means static—technology and social change fueled an arms race between attack and defense.

To break through the fortress, attackers developed new and innovative methods of penetration and increased their artillery's firepower. Castles, once impregnable in the Middle Ages, became death traps with the advent of cannons. The defense, in turn, developed stronger fortifications as well as complex methods of interlocking fire support. The fortification revolution of the 16th century, for example, introduced the system of bastioned defense, with broad and low bastions erected in a circular formation to create flanking fire.[3]

During the urban revolution of the 20th century, blitzkrieg and "deep battle" maneuver operations allowed armies to bypass fortifications and disable and dislocate opposing forces. Commando operations, such as the glider assault on Eben Emael, destroyed fortresses that could have halted the enemy advance. Because traditional fortifications could not halt the enemy, the city itself was turned into a living weapon.[4] The Soviets shredded German armies wholesale through vicious street fighting in the battles of Stalingrad and Leningrad, the Germans returned the favor in Berlin, and the Chinese achieved one of their few conventional victories over the Japanese in the battle of Tai-erh-chaung, slaying up to 16,000 of the invaders.[5]

The decline of conventional great power war, however, changed the nature of external siege. Nuclear weapons, stronger networks of trade and relations, and the bipolarity of the Cold War lessened interstate war, largely putting a stop to conventional external siege. As a result, external sieges increasingly took the form of conventional occupying armies fighting against networked urban insurgents. Insurgents attacked invading conventional armies through a combination of hybrid conventional/irregular partisan defense and urban guerrilla warfare. One frightening example of this dynamic is the 1994 Chechen defense of Grozny against the Russian armed forces. A Russian force comprising 40,000 men suffered losses of 2,805 killed, 10,319 wounded, 393 missing and 133 captured against a Chechen force of 7,000 at most.[6]

A parallel phenomenon of this period is the classical urban insurgency. Urban insurgency, like external siege, is not a new phenomenon. As Anthony James Joes notes in his study *Urban Guerrilla Warfare*, one can find accounts of urban insurgency in Thucydides.[7] The current wave of urban insurgency originated in the wave of 19th century urban anarchist cells in Russia, Europe, and the United States. The immense expansion of urban sprawl that occurred in the 20th century and the growth of subversive left ideologies provoked a string of ideologically motivated urban guerrillas to follow their example.

Unlike classical guerrillas, who stuck mostly to the countryside and engaged in a strategy of protracted ideological war, urban insurgents attempted to incapacitate the government through strategies of sheer violence. They hoped that by doing so, they could raise the consciousness of the people and seize power. Urban guerrillas tended to be small cells of radicalized students and middle-class intellectuals. Many received training and assistance from Soviet bloc nations and Arab insurgent groups. This form of urban warfare was mostly prevalent in Latin America, although left urban insurgent strategy could be seen in the United States and Europe with terrorist groups such as the Symbionese Liberation Army and the Red Army Faction.

Urban guerrilla warfare, for the most part, was a remarkable failure. The expected uprising of the masses did not occur, as the guerrillas made little to no effort to propagandize among the proletariat. They preferred spectacular acts of terrorism that attracted media attention but didn't bother to devise any mechanisms for translating their press success into popular support. The left urban insurgents also alienated the people with their tactics, which were often indistinguishable from common terrorism.[8] Urban guerrilla movements, usually confined to a small cadre of well-off intellectuals, were almost universally crushed by the state. With the formation of special law enforcement counter-terrorist units in the 1970s, left insurgents also lost the tactical advantage they enjoyed against ordinary beat policemen. If the bloody disaster at the 1972 Munich games was the high point of the urban terrorist, the 1977 GSG-9 hostage rescue of Lufthansa Flight 181 spelled the decline of the left urban insurgency.

The most successful urban insurgencies, such as the 1994 bleeding of the Russians in Grozny, the IRA's long-running urban campaign against the British, and the 1950s urban insurgency against the French in Algiers, were all waged against foreign occupiers. Even so, most of them were tactical failures for the insurgent. The Russians eventually occupied Grozny, though they left in disgrace. The IRA, increasingly bereft of public support and riddled with British informers, elected to make peace with the British. The French eventually crushed the urban insurgency in Algiers through the usage of autonomous commando teams, pseudo-operations, and extensive torture. The 1968 spasm of urban violence in Saigon, which was supposed to "liberate" the city from American and South Vietnamese forces, succeeded only in shattering American public opinion. The vast majority of Vietcong commandos and sappers were slaughtered in the American/Vietnamese response.

Back to the Future in Mumbai

Unfortunately, urban siege is back—and the new networked terrorists and criminal insurgents have changed the nature of the game. They exist in what John Robb calls a "bazaar of violence," collaborating in an emergent manner across geographic and factional boundaries.[9] Future insurgents are also likely to cloak themselves within a deception array of defensive information operations designed to make themselves formless to defending intelligence agencies.[10] They mass their forces in cyberspace, coalesce, and then unite for devastating strikes on civilian and military targets.

Terrorism and ideological insurgency are by no means the only threat to the state, as criminal insurgents pose a different—but no less terrifying problem—for public security. Criminal insurgents and militias fight for a small piece of the state, utilizing a reverse inkblot method to generate zones of disorder. Protracted criminal wars are going on in Mexico, Guatemala, and Brazil, where police struggle against increasingly sophisticated cartels and street gangs. In Mexico, cartels have assassinated both beat cop and high-level *federale* alike with frightening efficiency. At the same time, criminal insurgents also attach themselves to the superstructure of the state and co-opt its governing and security arms.[11] Terrorists and criminal insurgents can also corrupt non-state forces such as non- governmental organizations and private military companies for use as kill vehicles against the state.[12]

There are several methods that terrorists and criminal insurgents use to besiege cities from within—pure terror and systems disruption, although the two are often combined together. Both methods are sustained means of besieging a city with a campaign of protracted urban violence. Pure terror is a form of social systems disruption. It is a spasm of violence intended to demonstrate to the public that the authorities cannot help them, and that they are helpless against the power of the gun. In Brazil, the First Capital Command (*Primeiro Comando da Capital* or PCC) launched a massive attack in 2006 to demonstrate its power, detonating car bombs, gunning down law enforcement, destroying banks, and destabilizing transportation systems. They effectively shut down the city of São Paulo, paralyzing it and terrifying its residents.[13]

In his history of the car bomb, *Buda's Wagon*, urbanist Mike Davis also catalogues a terrifying blitz of sustained city sieges that took place in over 20 cities during the 1990s.[14] Perhaps the most grisly urban siege Davis records was the criminal insurgent Pablo Escobar's one-man war against the Colombian government. From the mid-1980s to the mid-90s, Escobar targeted everyone from Colombian politicians to hapless shoppers with lethal car bombs—turning the cities of Medellin and Bogota into death traps. His car bombs and assassinations killed hundreds of law enforcement officials and civilians, and Escobar was only stopped after a government-sponsored death squad eliminated his organization and put him to flight.[15]

Certain urban sieges have more instrumental aims. For example, al-Qaeda in Iraq's targeting of the Adhamniya Mosque ignited an internecine conflict between the Sunnis and Shiites. The 2005 occupation of the Beslan school in Russia by Chechen insurgents and the clumsy attempt to re-take it by Russian special forces operatives created widespread horror and underlined the Chechen ability to strike at Russia's children. Few things are more horrifying than the thought of children being slaughtered wholesale by fanatical terrorists, and this brutal fact made the Chechen operation a resounding success.

There are disturbing possibilities for paramilitary terrorist sieges in America. We are fixated on the possibility of weapons of mass destruction terrorism but ignore the simpler methods of operational swarming and siege in major cities. While the success of the Mumbai terrorists came in large part from the tactical and operational inadequacy of Indian law enforcement response, it is easy to imagine a small group of terrorists creating multiple centers of disorder at the same time within a major American city in same manner. An equally terrifying scenario is a Beslan-type siege in school centers with multiple active shooters. Paramilitary terrorists of this kind would aim for maximum violence, target hardening, and area denial—capabilities that many SWAT units would be hard-pressed to counter.[16]

Unlike pure terror, systems disruption eschews instrumental targeting of civilians and instead focuses on disabling vital nodes that sustain the city. While civilians are often the victims of collateral damage of the attacks, the main targets are the machines. Most modern cities are sustained by a series of complex—and vulnerable—networks of commerce, governance, energy, communications, and water that can be targeted by insurgents. These networks are so tightly coupled together that certain failures in one system can have cascading effects in others.

In the early stages of the Iraqi insurgency, insurgents targeted electrical systems, power plants, oil pipelines, and other centers of sustenance. Insurgents also mounted frequent raids aimed at American logistics. Convoys of basic supplies to American expeditionary civilian and soldiers became dangerous assignments carried out by groups of heavily armed contractors. The disruption of public services paralyzed the city and undermined the faith of the population in the government and Coalition forces.

Other examples of systems disruption have occurred in Nigeria and Mexico, where guerrillas and terrorists have targeted energy utilities and supplies. Granted, the apocalyptic predictions of systems disruption attacks aimed at American utilities have not yet occurred, and it's important to point out that industrial societies have a natural resiliency that terrorism theorists often underrate. But given the importance that al-Qaeda (and other) strategists have placed on bleeding the superpower into submission, they are a possibility that we cannot rule out.

While both urban siege methods have different tactics, techniques, and procedures, they rely on similar operational methods—the decentralized urban assault unit. The Mumbai attack utilized highly mobile autonomous groups that overwhelmed the Indian response capability by striking many different targets at once. These capabilities aren't only found in terrorist groups. Cartels utilize heavily armed paramilitary assault teams (comprised of former Mexican and Guatemalan special forces operatives) for complex tactical operations in Mexico (and within US borders). The end result is a protracted urban war in which the city is besieged from within.

It is too soon to make a definitive statement about this method's success—most urban sieges by non-state forces in the past have been failures. The modern urban insurgent's tactical attacks have served their purpose, but it hard to see how they accomplish strategic objectives. But it has the potential to be a highly effective tool of coercion and disrupting everyday life. Government responses to urban terrorism, however well intentioned, have exacerbated the problem through the usage of urban military special operations forces and the construction of militarized space.

Walking Through Walls and Military Urbanism

In Brazil, an urban war is in progress between military police urban warfare units and drug gangs. The paramilitary police launch all-out war against the drug gangs. These are not law enforcement actions but military operations designed to annihilate the traffickers themselves. The assaults were launched with police, special operations units, and helicopters. There is little distinction made between residents of the *favela* and drug traffickers.[17] Extensive human rights complaints have accumulated against the police actions, with rights groups alleging that the police and soldiers have deliberately killed innocent people.[18] Their violent actions have amassed popular support among the middle and upper classes, which view the urban poor with disdain and hate the violent and sadistic drug traffickers. This support does nothing, however, in the lower-class *favelas*.

The most elite of the Brazilian urban operations units is BOPE, a special operations unit under the command of the Brazilian military police. In a purely tactical sense, BOPE is a success—the BOPE officers are one of the few law enforcement conventional forces who can utilize the city as a weapon against their opponents. Traffickers fear BOPE more than the corrupt regular police. Their symbol is a grinning skull impaled on a sword.[19] But in a strategic sense they—along with the regular police—alienate the poor residents of the *favela* and put the city into a permanent state of war.

Thankfully, the Brazilians seem to be adopting a more reasonable strategy. According to the *Washington Post*, Brazilian police officers are cribbing from American counterinsurgency tactics in Iraq, setting up permanent outposts within the *favelas*, pounding the pavement in search of usable intelligence, and spending government funds on public works.[20] Whether or it succeeds will depend on the overall strategy and the police's support from the government and non-governmental organizations. There are strong reasons to be skeptical, given the immense corruption of the Brazilian civil sector, but the strategy at least represents an evolutionary step from the raiding mentality represented by BOPE.

The Israeli Defense Force (IDF)'s operations against Palestinian urban insurgents also have failed to stamp out urban insurgency. Beginning in early 2000, the Israelis utilized a combination of targeted airstrikes from air and naval platforms combined with Special Forces raids into the interior. Beginning with Operation Defense Shield and Operation Determined Path, the IDF utilized swarming tactics designed at collapsing terrorist infrastructure. Many small units backed up by micro UAVs and helicopters converged from many different directions simultaneously, operating out of contact with the enemy. These tactics avoided the enemy's area of strength, surprising, confusing, and deceiving them.[21]

As Israeli architect Eyal Weizmann noted in an article for *Frieze* magazine, the IDF's thought reconceptualized the city as not just the site but also a *medium* of war. Urban special operations units turned the city into a death trap for insurgents, surprising them by blasting through walls and floors. Such operations use the post-structuralist philosopher Gilles Deleuze's concept of the *rhizome*, a decentralized unit of organization. While such operations may be tactically and operationally brilliant, the theoretical insights in them mean little to the scared Palestinian family at the other end of the wall that an IDF trooper blasts through while executing a rhizome maneuver.[22]

The most recent Israeli operations have not matched the tactical brilliance exhibited by Shimon Naveh's rhizome maneuvers. The current Gaza operation to put it bluntly, a pure raid, as Israelis made little effort to reach out to those inundated by their artillery fires.[23] As of the writing of this essay, major ground operations have ceased, but Hamas' organization remains intact. Rocket fire continues against Israeli targets and periodic Israeli operations continue against Hamas positions within the ruined urban zone.

While BOPE officers and IDF special operations forces may be masters at manipulating the city as fluid operational space, they have an overly materialist conception of the city—it is not just buildings but also people. They ignore the *social spaces* in their strategies, which center overwhelmingly on manipulating material forces to their advantage. The net effect is to reify the concept of the city as a protracted battleground instead of gaining the support of the population and developing resilient security infrastructure.

Some nations choose to employ militias as primary security forces against non-state urban forces. The murderous government-sponsored "Los Pepes" death squad ground Pablo Escobar's gang down with a series of brutal operations aimed at his organization and associates.[24] The Colombian AUC also was employed as a counter-guerrilla force that extensively targeted leftist organizers and labor unions as well as FARC guerrillas in a variety of environments. While these forces can create enough controlled chaos to counter the insurgents, they also destroy government legitimacy. They lack real public support themselves, only generating respect through fear and violence.

In order to better understand the dynamics of modern urban siege, it is also important to understand two trends in modern politico-urban theory—the feral city and military urbanism.

Failed Communities, Feral Cities, and Military Urbanism

The feral city is an area in which state power is nonexistent, the architecture consists entirely of slums, and power is a complex process negotiated through violence by differing factions. As Richard Norton notes in the *Naval War College Review*, the feral city is wracked with disease, poverty, and pollution, and cannibalized by graft.[25] But intercity, national, and even international economic and political processes occur—the city is a strategic actor interacting with the outside world. The feral city is an extreme endpoint of failed communities. Decaying megapolises provide fertile ground for non- state groups to contest control from the state.

After the end of European colonialism, the independent governments that rose from the ashes of the colonial state tried to modernize and consolidate, cracking down on ethnic, regional, and religious movements that contested state control and attempting to provide patronage in the form of employment, health care, and education. Yet this was ultimately unsustainable, as the pressure to cut costs to attract investors led many governments to cut back public services, and much of the developing world simply ran out of resources. Globalization also created huge skews in income, adding to the chaos. In many areas of the developing world, the government is functionally absent.[26] And as military historian Martin van Creveld noted, "A community which cannot safeguard the lives of its members...is unlikely to command their loyalty or survive for very long. The opposite is also correct: any community able and... willing to exert itself to protect its members will be able to call on those members' loyalty."[27] This is where the criminal insurgent comes in.

Generally, transnational organized crime groups benefited from the existence of a stable state order. While traditional criminal enterprises exploited the seams between states, they did not seek to challenge the state; rather they used corruption and political manipulation to further their enterprises. This is changing, as a new species of global gangsters create parallel states to exploit the absence of effective states, endemic corruption, and grey or shadow economies.[28]

Louise Shelley, director of American University's Transnational Crime and Corruption Center observes that, "the newer crime groups most often linked to terrorism have no interest in a secure state."[29] They promote and exploit grievances at local levels and through the globalization of conflict to secure the maneuver room to capture profit. The embedded nature of network crime structures in local communities and the inability of both domestic and international militaries, as well as law enforcement agencies, to control their activities make these new criminal soldiers a growing danger.

These terrorist-insurgent-criminal interactions are particularly virulent in "global cities" and the slums of mega-cities, including sub-national or cross-border enclaves or "lawless zones." Lawless zones and criminal enclaves are areas (ranging from neighborhoods to entire cities—feral cities—to regions, to states, and cross-border zones), where gangs, criminal enterprises, insurgents, or warlords dominate social life and erode the bonds of effective security and the rule of law. The interactions of technology, networks, "global cities," and non-state actors and contested enclaves set the stage for the urban sieges of the future.[30]

Criminal netwarriors (soldiers) have altered the nature of crime and war, thereby altering the operational space within which the police, security services, and military function. Modern warfare is distinguished by the ability of insurgents to carry out omnidirectional spatial maneuver. Non-state actors have the power to rapidly shift between material, cyber, social, and political spaces. They do not recognize front and rear lines. They have the power to enter forbidden spaces that the state cannot recognize. This is their chief challenge to state power in an era where state power either is declining or in the midst of a painful transformation. This phenomenon finds it mirror in the proliferation of non-state organizations, viral "smart mobs," state-within-states, quasi-feudal criminal empires, and virtual states—all spaces beyond the reach of state power.

What the "feral city" chiefly represents is a giant challenge to state power. It is an emergent process, driven by a hive-mind intelligence that is the sum of a deviant social ecosystem composed of diffuse, bickering, but interacting factions that form a hidden order. Each "feral city" or "failed neighborhood" can serve as a pivot point in a giant network that is fast becoming a postmodern criminal empire that grows like a cancer within the interior space of the state. This is not an empire that has a unified base—it is the sum of a mass of economic, political, legal, and cultural processes that interact to form networks of power distributed within each individual citizen.[31] This criminal empire, slowly emerging, is the sum of the political-legal-cultural processes of the illicit economy. It is a global form of neo-feudalism linked together by cyberspace, globalization, and a series of concrete ungoverned zones.

This is truly what the anarchist Hakim Bey meant when he analogized the now commonly-cited "Temporary Autonomous Zones" to the medieval Assassins that "founded a 'State' which consisted of a network of remote mountain valleys and castles, separated by thousands of miles, strategically invulnerable to invasion, connected by the information flow of secret agents, at war with all governments." Bey connects the dots when he states "technology—freed from all political control—could make possible an entire world of autonomous zones."[32]

The state's response to the feral city is military urbanism. Cities undergoing urban sieges transform into gardens of steel. Concrete bunkers, "steel rings" designed to stop car bombs, checkpoints, blast walls, towers, barbed-wire fences, fortifications, and other military architecture slowly colonize the city. Security cameras, heavily armed guards, gated communities, private soldiers, and protected areas spring up. This constricts civilian movement and psychologically suggests a permanent state of war. As urban threats increase, many modern cities throughout industrial states are at risk of becoming military colonies.

On a tactical and operational level, the military colony attempts to deny spatial movement to the insurgent and terrorist by enclosing the open commons within rings of steel, barbed wire, and blast walls. Often times, military operations in feral cities are a process of strategic terraforming, slowly transforming selected elements of the feral city into a military colony.

In counterterrorism focusing solely on target hardening has a mixed record at best. Unless, in the case of Israel, the city is completely walled off from the source of disorder, the enemy finds a way to seep through cracks in conventional defenses. Granted, many of these responses (such as the blast wall in Baghdad) were responses to desperate circumstances. But the city, the *polis*, is the root of democratic political participation since the days of Athens. Military architecture erodes space for politics and culture, which has never flourished in a state of existential warfare. Perhaps the most important aspect of the current decline in violence in Iraq is the gradual erosion of such architecture in Baghdad. Although some urbanists (chief among them the philosopher Paul Virilio) see the city as designed expressively for and as a result of war, the city as war machine is model that cannot be sustained.[33]

Law Enforcement Responses to Urban Siege

Violence on its own can rarely generate lasting power—hence the importance of "clear, hold, and build" in modern counterinsurgency. Global and local defense against urban terror and feralization should be based on three principles—fighting for *social* as well as material space, hybridization of police-military response, and the right to the city. Little of what we are about to recommend is new or particularly novel, but the failure to embrace many of these solutions suggests that we ought to repeat them for effect.

Because the real battles of urban insurgency take place inside in social spaces, military and police forces cannot concede these battlespaces to the opponent. Entering social spaces requires prolonged contact with the population, the maintenance of political legitimacy, and the enlistment of the populace in the defense of the city. Prolonged contact with the populace is a process of establishing neighborhood headquarters, police stations, and other zones where social exchange occurs in tandem with a political counterinsurgency strategy.

In order for such an exchange to be most successful, the conventional force obviously must maintain political legitimacy by avoiding the targeting of civilians and utilizing strategic non-military projects. Communication of shared objectives is extremely important—hence the importance of police officers and soldiers being strong presences in neighborhood meetings and other social spaces.

Building popular defense networks is a process of building psychological as well as physical resilience. A network of human sensors—if properly processed through co- production of intelligence—can be ultimately more successful in the defense of a city than a thousand security cameras. Physical defense is often a matter of pure response, depending on the existence of formed paramilitary units capable of standing up to operational shock. Such standing up may require the formation of more HRT-level SWAT groups capable of rapidly mobilizing to swarm a certain point, as Bill Tallen argues in the *Homeland Security Affairs Journal*.[34] But if this attack can be stopped through municipal or regional-level processed intelligence and early warning it is clearly preferable to beating back a criminal or terrorist assault.

Emergency response integration with high civilian participation functioning at a local level also allows civilians to function in smooth integration with police and military forces. This allows the city to mobilize itself as an adaptive whole to construct a layered defense that can soak up the attack's operational shock. Furthermore, it also blunts the impact of the attack upon the bonds and relationship between the city, its government, and people. Sharing in the defense as a collective bond will make us more psychologically resilient as all share in the defense instead of being helpless and afraid.

Urban operations also demand a new type of policing—the full spectrum police officer. Full spectrum policing requires building specialized hybrid forces capable of operating in a range of environments and missions. They must be able to transition between community policing and investigations to public order and riot control missions to high-intensity operations ranging from gang control to counterterrorism and counterinsurgency. These gendarmerie or constabulary units combine the survivability of military forces with the investigative skills and policing skills of metropolitan police officers. Europeans have long relied on these versatile formed police units of this type for internal security and policing. Similarly, Israeli police have developed Joint Operations Forces (JOF) to bridge police and military urban operations requirements.

Crucial to urban policing and full spectrum police operations is the development of operational art doctrines for policing. Police forces across America do not have operational art, only a series of tactics. Without operational art there is no way of aligning ends with means and properly allocating resources. Only with functioning operational art can resources be properly allocated to identify threats, emerging groups, and criminal support networks. Police operational art allows each tactical echelon walking their beats to be integrated into a greater strategy, combining police efforts with greater civilian and government functions. Crucial to the construction of effective police operational art is interlocking concepts of operational swarming and "geosocial" intelligence. Each concept addresses the central idea of police as a mechanism that builds on and reinforces social control.

Operational swarming, first articulated by John Arquilla and David Ronfeldt, is a process of massing dispersed forces into a large amorphous mass of forces striking a decisive point. Attacks are constant and disorienting. This has been a method of military assault for many centuries.[35] Applied to policing, operational swarming is applied in both tactical and operational contexts. Tactical operational swarming involves the convergence of paramilitary forces and formed police units to quickly crush urban assailants before they do real damage. This is especially important in cases of a distributed assault like Mumbai, in which terrorists open multiple fronts. Utilizing interior lines, urban operations forces must quickly respond and smash each individual front.

The enemy will use deception and coordinate with Blackberries and other handheld communication devices. The goal of operational swarming in such a defensive context is to quickly restore public order by maximum concentration of public resources on the opponent. Paramilitary terrorists are likely to disperse their forces into small cells and disperse them throughout the city to cause maximum chaos. But if each cell can be isolated and fixed it can be destroyed in place. Stopping their kinetic motion will cause them to lose relative advantage and fall before superior weapons and numbers. This is nothing new—William McRaven records in his book *Case Studies in Special Operations Warfare Theory and Practice* many armed assaults that failed once the attackers lost their kinetic momentum and the relative advantage.[36]

The longer chaos continues the more difficult it becomes to crush entrenched enemy units, some of whom may have accumulated hostages. Public response also grows panicked and news media begin to substantially interfere with operations and the element of surprise. Formed police units capable of transitioning quickly to high-intensity conflict are important in such a scenario, as are "cloned" Tier-1 counter-terrorist units capable of being the main tactical effort. Many modern terrorist and criminal insurgent groups carrying out paramilitary groups will be heavily trained and heavily armed and destroying them with a minimum of harm to civilians requires professionals capable of rapid response, dealing with tactical deception, and fighting through Beslan-style entrenchments.

In the case of purely offensive swarming against an entrenched opponent in a feral city, purely operational shock swarming can be used in the Israeli context to establish tactical advantage. But operational shock is only one part of clearing feral cities and feral communities where criminal or terrorist non-state forces have a strong presence within a small urban hub. This kind of scenario also involves swarming, but a predominately non-kinetic sense as forces are concentrated to provide public order, protect the population, and prevent the enemy from freely maneuvering among the people.

Swarming as an operational art involves the deployment of stability police to specific neighborhoods as units in a larger strategy to carry out an inkblot counterinsurgency. Urban guerrillas' key disadvantage is the lack of strategic depth inherent in the small neighborhood points they occupy, and they overcome this by reinforcing and withdrawing units along both informal and formal lines of transportation. Resources devoted to building up citizen networks in order isolate guerrillas from popular sustenance in conjunction with expanding inkblots will allow the full force of the people and the state to be brought to bear.

In such a conflict there is no separation between kinetic operations and information operations. Kinetic operations *are* information operations, and vice versa. In a defensive scenario maintaining public morale is just as important as coordinating a defensive response. Likewise, utilizing interior lines to quickly and ruthlessly crush enemy emerging fronts in a defensive operation is a process of letting the population (and the news media) know that you have re-established social control over the battlespace. In an offensive swarming operation designed at re-establishing order over failed communities, the utmost care must be taken to stay within legal and moral norms.

Of course, such a policy must be the main effort of a strong political strategy designed to either organize the city in unified defense or resolve the conditions that give rise to failed communities. It goes without saying that networked, multi-ethnic diasporas are likely to be the primary battlegrounds. Building operational art for navigating these unique arenas requires a special kind of intelligence production for police and internal security forces. The cultural "human terrain team" must be replicated for full-spectrum policing, especially in local conflicts with global implications.

This task requires local-global-local analysis and synthesis, as well as the "co- production" of intelligence among distributed intelligence fusion efforts.[37] Such as process was foreseen in the terrorism early warning (TEW) model, where linked TEW groups co-operated to develop a broader understanding. Among the tools required are "geosocial" analysis (analysis of communities and places) and Intelligence Preparation for Operations (IPO), a civil analog of Intelligence Preparation of the Battlespace (IPB) adapted for civil public safety missions.[38] Red teaming is also a valuable tool for developing understanding of the interactions between threat actors and local conditions.[39]

Most important is the concept of the right to the city. The ultimate strategic goal of both urban siege defense and operations in feral cities and failed cities is the building and sustenance of free and public spaces for political and cultural expression. Every act of force should be evaluated against this goal and checked to see how it can contribute to the building of these spaces. This is not something that military or police forces can do on their own—it requires working with civilians and building the security necessary to help them realize their dreams. This is the ultimate form of resilient security infrastructure, as it draws its strength not from masses of barbed wire or bunkers but the energy and creativity of the people.

Much of recent writing about cities either is gloom and doom narratives of decaying slums or terror-infested "feral cities." This does describe a rather frightening reality of urban decay and disorder. But modern cities are also hives of innovative creative activity, cultural expression, and thriving political and commercial life. The modern *agora* is a zone of exchange worth defending with all our reason, endurance, and power.

Notes

[1] Saskia Sassen, "Cities and New Wars: After Mumbai," *OpenDemocracy*, November 29, 2008. http://www.opendemocracy. net/article/the-new-wars-and-cities-after-mumbai-0.

[2] Archer Jones, *The Art of War in the Western World*, Urbana: University of Illinois Press, 2001, p.11.

[3] Jones, p. 194.

[4] John Robb, "The Coming Urban Terror," *City Journal*, Summer 2007. http://www.city-<journal.org/html/17_3_urban_terrorism. html>.

[5] William M. Wadell, "Tai-erh chaung, 1938" in Col. John Antal and Maj. Bradley Gericke, *City Fights*: *Selected Histories of Urban Combat from World War II to Vietnam*, New York: Ballantine Books, 2003, p. 1.

[6] David P. Dilegge and Matthew Van Konynenburg, "A View from the Wolves' Den: The Chechens and Urban Operations" in Robert J. Bunker (ed), *Non-State Threats and Future Wars*, London: Frank Cass, 2003, p. 172.

[7] Anthony James Joes, *Urban Guerrilla Warfare*, Lexington: University of Kentucky Press, 2007, p. 1.

[8] Joes, p. 6.

[9] John Robb, "The Bazaar's Open Source Platform," *Global Guerrillas*, September 24, 2004. http://globalguerrillas.typepad. com/globalguerrillas/2004/09/bazaar_dynamics.html.

[10] See Adam Elkus, "Simulated Black Swans: National Security, Perception Operations, and the Expansion of the Infosphere," in Michael Tanji (Ed.), *Threats in the Age of Obama,* Ann Arbor: Nimble Books LLC, 2009.

[11] See John P. Sullivan and Adam Elkus, "State of Siege: Mexico's Criminal Insurgency," *Small Wars Journal*, August 19, 2008. http://smallwarsjournal.com/mag/2008/08/state-of-siege-mexicos-crimina.php.

[12] See Graham Hall Turbiville, Jr., "Outlaw Private Security Firms: Criminal and Terrorist Agendas Undermine Private Security

Alternatives," in Robert J. Bunker (ed), *Criminal-States and Criminal-Soldiers*, New York: Routledge, 2008.

[13]   Arthur Itassu, "Violence in Brazil: All Are Targets, All Are Guilty," *OpenDemocracy*, May 16, 2008. http://www.opendemocracy.net/node/3555.

[14]   Mike Davis, *Buda's Wagon: A Brief History of the Car Bomb*, Verso: New York, 2007, p. 117.

[15]   Davis, p. 111.

[16]   Bill Tallen, "Paramilitary Terrorism: A Neglected Threat," *Homeland Security Affairs Journal*, June 2008. http://www.hsaj.org/?article=4.2.6.

[17]   Tom Philips, "Blood on the streets as drug gang and police fight for control of Rio favelas," *The Guardian*, June 19, 2007. http://www.guardian.co.uk/world/2007/jun/29/brazil.international.

[18]   "Police Accused Over Rio Killings," BBC, Friday, June 29, 2007. http://news.bbc.co.uk/2/hi/americas/6254876.stm.

[19]   See "Brazil: Caveirão—Rio's real "bogeyman," Amnesty International, March 13, 2006. http://www.amnesty.org/en/library/asset/AMR19/009/2006/en/dom-AMR190092006en.html.

[20]   Joshua Partlow, "To Rid Slums of Drug Gangs, Police Try War Tactics," *Washington Post*, January 6, 2009. http://www.washingtonpost.com/wp-dyn/content/article/2009/01/05/AR2009010502741.html.

[21]   See Dr. Sergio Cantignani, "The Israeli Defense Forces and the Al-Aqsa Intifada," in Carter Malkasian and Daniel Marston (eds), *Counterinsurgency and Modern Warfare*, Oxford: Osprey Publishing, 2007, p. 241.

[22]   Eyal Weizmann, "The Art of War," *Frieze*, Issue 99, 2007. http://www.frieze.com/feature_single.asp?f=1165.

[23]   Steven Erlanger, "A Gaza War Full of Traps and Trickery," *New York Times*, January 10, 2009. http://www.nytimes.com/2009/01/11/world/middleeast/11hamas.html?_r=1&hp.

[24]   See Mark Bowden, *Killing Pablo: The Hunt for the World's Greatest Outlaw*, Washington: Atlantic Monthly Press, 2001.

[25] Richard Norton, "Feral Cities," *Naval War College Review,* Vol. 56, No. 4, Autumn 2003, pp. 97-106, available at *www.nwc.navy. mil/press/Review/2003/Autumn/pdfs/art6-a03.pdf.*

[26] See John Rapley, "The New Middle Ages." *Foreign Affairs* 85.3 (May/June 2006): 95-105.

[27] Martin van Creveld, *The Transformation of War*, New York: The Free Press, 1991, p. 198.

[28] Louise Shelley, "The Unholy Trinity: Transnational Crime, Corruption, and Terrorism," *Brown Journal of World Affairs*, 11 (2), 102.

[29] Ibid.

[30] See John P. Sullivan and Keith Weston, "Afterword: Law Enforcement Response Strategies for Criminal-States and Criminal-Soldiers," in Robert J. Bunker (Ed.), *Criminal-States and Criminal-Soldiers*, London: Routledge, 2008, pp. 287-300.

[31] See Michael Hardt and Antonio Negri, *Empire*, Cambridge: Harvard University Press, 2000.

[32] See Hakim Bey, *The Temporary Autonomous Zone*, New York: Automedia, 1991.

[33] Virilio is a prolific author. The best introduction to his thought is *Speed and Politics*, Cambridge: MIT Press, 2006.

[34] Bill Tallen, "Paramilitary Terrorism: A Neglected Threat," *Homeland Security Affairs Journal*, June 2008. http://www.hsaj. org/?article=4.2.6.

[35] John Arquilla and David Ronfeldt, *Swarming and the Future of Conflict*, Santa Monica: RAND, 2000, http://www.rand.org/ pubs/documented_briefings/DB311/.

[36] See William McRaven, *Spec Ops: Special Operations Warfare in Theory and Practice*, New York: Presidio Press, 1996.

[37] John P. Sullivan, "Terrorism Early Warning and Co-Production of Counterterrorism Intelligence," unpublished paper presented to Canadian Association for Security and Intelligence Studies, *CASIS 20th Anniversary Conference*, Montreal, Quebec, Canada, 21 October 2005, available at http://www.projectwhitehorse.com/ pdfs/6.%20CASIS_Sullivan_paper1.pdf.

[38] See John P. Sullivan and Alain Bauer (Eds,), *Terrorism Early Warning: 10 Years of Achievement in Fighting Terrorism and Crime*, Los Angeles: Los Angeles County Sheriff's Department, 2008, available at http://www.lasd.org/tew/TEW2009.pdf for a comprehensive history and doctrinal template of the LA TEW.

[39] See John P. Sullivan and Adam Elkus, "Red Teaming Criminal Insurgency," *Red Team Journal*, January 30, 2009.

Chapter 4

The Future of Terrorism: Mass Hostage Taking in Russia and Mumbai

Luke Allison

First Published 4 May 2010

Terrorism has a future; terrorism always has a future. The question is: can the application of terror morph into something inherently capable of distorting strategic countermeasures? The answer is probably yes, because a states' fundamental responsibility is to maintain sovereignty by protecting its population. The problem with this responsibility in relation to terrorism is that it is debilitating in terms of being predictable. Predictability is not a strategy; it is the absence of strategy.

The future of terrorism is to isolate instances where the state is compelled to act predictably. The best example of this type of terrorism is an approach that involves mass hostage taking in conjunction with the use of barricades. This is quite remarkable, because ". . . the idea of taking hostages and placing the responsibility for their fate into the hands of the opposing government was a highly effective tool. . ."[1] For the purposes of this article, a mass hostage taking incident occurs when between one hundred and two thousand people are held involuntarily under the threat of serious physical injury. Examples of mass hostage taking incidents will be restricted to those occurring in public buildings such as: schools, theaters, hospitals, and hotels. Similar incidents taking place on airplanes, busses, or other modes of transportation will be considered outside the scope of inquiry.

Ostensibly, the concern about mass hostage taking is the trepidation associated with possibly observing the next major adaptation in the application of terrorism. It is unclear how long mass hostage taking can or will remain in a nascent stage. There is a perverse irony when a new type of terrorism is proven effective: it becomes the new applicable standard of normalcy. Incidentally, the introduction of suicide bombing stimulated both terrorist groups and state security services to adapt organizationally. It is important to realize that situations like this are truly transformative. Something is transformative if it simultaneously introduces anomie and adds complexity. The time has come now that there is a considerable disaggregation between organization size and capabilities. The idea that large groups or states will continue to dictate to smaller groups is on the verge of being passé. There is a certain feeling that, "Over the last few years, small groups' ability to conduct terrorism has shown radical improvements in productivity—their capacity to inflict economic, physical, and moral damage. These groups, motivated by everything from gang membership to religious extremism, have taken advantage of easy access to our global super-infrastructure, revenues from growing illicit commercial flows, and ubiquitously available new technologies to cross the threshold necessary to become terrible threats."[2] New found power leads to an expanding horizon of possibilities. The current era is a time of unprecedented change. Many groups still view the application of terror as a useful approach. While political dissatisfaction seems largely endemic to the human condition: the thought that new sensational displays of violence might help reorder society is never entirely outmoded. The continued appeal is the notion (at least conceptually) that terrorism can become easier to apply, but harder to counter. Basically, the framework here is a type of schism that increasingly negates strategic prevention, but intentionally courts sanguinary pitched battles. In that respect, someone is always thinking about what comes next, and:

"There are several reasons behind this trend. One is the terrorists' natural tendency to 'out-do' their previous attacks, stimulated by the perception that if the present level of violence has thus far failed to succeed in forcing a radical change in the status quo, the campaign needs to be intensified. Another reason is the fact that no matter how horrific a terrorist campaign might be, the intended audiences become desensitized to the current level of violence over time, forcing the terrorists to escalate further in order to maintain or heighten the atmosphere of panic and fear among the general population, and to stay in the spotlight. An escalation in terrorist violence is also sometimes stimulated by the actions of other organizations with which the given group competes for power or popularity. Another reason for the gradual escalation of overall terrorist violence over time has been the formation of new groups. Upon emergence, new violent organizations usually do not undergo the full step-by-step process of radicalization, but rather pick up at the level of violence where other organizations active in the same struggle have left off. Alternatively, many existing organizations can give birth to new formations through the process of splintering, which usually results in the new entity being more radical and more violent than the core group."[3]

Mass Hostage Taking

The reason to reevaluate the phenomena of mass hostage taking is that the inherent lack of a strategic response makes similar situations inevitable in the future. Having the capability to take several hundred or several thousand people hostage makes a very loud statement about the seriousness of a terrorist organization. It is important to realize that mass hostage taking is a new type of terrorism, but it is still a type of armed political theater preformed for the explicit purpose of influencing an audience. Essentially, the problem with mass hostage taking situations that involve barricades is that the standard responses from security forces are simply too dangerous. However, this is not to say that large scale hostage rescue is impossible (both German and Israeli forces are known for thwarting attacks on large commercial planes). The difficulty is that most of the strategic responses do not scale up to handle the myriad of tactical problems caused by mass hostage taking situation that involve barricades.

Technology

In Mumbai, India, the importance of technology had never been so apparent until a series of coordinated assaults eventually turned into a mass hostage taking situation that lasted from November 26th until November 29th 2008. The crisis in Mumbai was exacerbated to a considerable degree by the terrorists' use of widely available technology. Additional details and implications about these attacks will be addressed in a later section. Unfortunately, the willingness to leverage seemingly banal technology signals a disturbing increase in capabilities and ingenuity. Counter-Terrorism expert John Robb explains how the Mumbai attackers leverage global infrastructure and technology to facilitate the attack:

- Boat navigation was by GPS for precision.
- Satellite phone, found onboard one of the vessels, for coordination en route.
- Constant use of cell phones for tactical communication.
- Blackberries for real-time tactical analysis of media coverage (which provided details on the status of forces arrayed against them). Also, an ability to check Web sites, including that of the police, for tactical data and global media coverage for strategic direction. This allowed them to route around attempts to sever their connectivity.
- E-mail and remailers for communication to the local media.[4]

It remains sufficiently challenging to project the influence for new application of technology in mass hostage taking situations. Objectively, the variety of technology available appears to only augment the terrorists' aspiration to develop capabilities that are archetypal situations where they can project power in a specific manor that must be dealt with in real-time. Almost every unique facet involved with mass hostage taking appears to be included in the process based on some potential for disrupting established strategic countermeasures. Without the advent of strategy, the state and its various security bureaucracies can be forced to respond to situations where they are at best on equal terms, or potentially, at a decided disadvantage against hostage takers. Clearly, the status quo is changing, but "In addition to shifting the traditional balance of power in the hostage takers' favor, the proliferation of communication technologies will probably also strongly influence the very process of negotiation itself. Firstly, the terrorists' immediate ability to consult with their leadership via mobile phone will deprive the negotiators of much of the influence they typically strive to gain by disrupting the hostage takers/ chain of authority, thus forcing the perpetrators to make their own decisions in isolation from their leadership."[5]

If you were to engage in a simple word association experiment by asking someone to say the first thing that comes to mind when they think of hostage taking chances are the response would be something approximating negotiation. Negotiation is a legitimate strategy to defuse a hostage situation. The availability of communication technologies makes it possible to not only subvert the negotiation process, but to gain information dominance across a vast array of media formats and platforms. The entire premise of negotiation is based on the prospect of mutually advantageous compromise. The likelihood that the state has some asset the hostage takers actually need or want is remote. The importance of controlling communication was much more influential when "…terrorist hostage takers of the past had often gone on operations with minimal instructions from their leaders, and thus frequently found themselves in a position of having to make decisions on their own, today's technological reality that gives the terrorists immediate access to their superiors has radically altered the situation."[6] The new design and implementation of mass hostage taking has largely invalidated the edifice of negotiation. Without negotiations there are very few scalable methods available to the state capable of exerting pressure for coercive purposes. Essentially, in a hostage situation the state functions relatively predictably somewhat like a hammer or any other single purpose tool. As long as all hostage problems look like nails that want to be fixed by a hammer then the state can cope just fine. Conversely, if the hostage takers want a solution the state is either unwilling or incapable of providing the situation can reach its nadir rapidly. Interestingly, "Since the leaders-unlike the hostage takers-will not be confined to the location under a constant threat of immediate forceful resolution, the processes that form the baseline foundation of the contemporary practice of crisis negotiation will not take place, making the task of lowering the terrorists' expectations much more difficult. Further, the availability of surveillance technology that can potentially aid the terrorists in eavesdropping on communication channels used by the security forces will also introduce new challenges."[7] As was the case in Mumbai, the value of email and the Internet became readily apparent. There is an obvious structural problem with not being able to anticipate where the Internet will be used, if it will be used to gather information prior to an attack, coordinate an attack, disseminate information after an attack, or some combination.

In the future, the Internet (and its various applications and functions) might be the definitive example of problems associated with dual use technology. Duel use technology can do everything from the pedantic to enabling terrorists. The implications are profound as ". . . the global reach of the Internet will present the terrorists with an independent communication channel to the media and the outside world, which will allow them to present their own version of events along with documentary evidence, making censorship and media manipulation a much less effective or even counterproductive incident management tool than in the past. Moreover, in such a situation, providing access to the media as a minor concession used to initiate trades will also become a decreasingly important instrument in the negotiators' toolbox."[8] A peripheral goal of mass hostage taking is to establish an ability to leverage technology and global infrastructure that the state cannot conceivably respond to effectively.

Often the only remaining viable option is to initiate a rescue attempt by force. State security services can be at a decided disadvantage if they are forced to storm a building to rescue hostages. Such an attack is not a favored approach because it lacks the element of surprise. Also, the absence of surprise makes the process of building entry highly predictable. It is almost certain that in a mass hostage situation the hostage takers will be well prepared for an impending assault. Curiously, "Such measures will likely take the form of employment of large teams of hostage takers armed well enough to repel a possible raid, strategic positioning of snipers, use of surveillance technology and booby traps to monitor and obstruct possible entry points, and the deployment of potent explosive devices among the hostages to make any attempt to rescue them by force as costly in terms of loss of human life as possible."[9] Essentially, these defensive positions are a series of fixed ambush points. Both sides in a hostage situation are aware that if conditions deteriorate quite a few people are going to die. If the theory behind these attacks is to create human carnage irrespective of the countermeasures used; then mass hostage taking is a frightening advancement in the application of terror. Mass hostage taking as a form of stylized terrorism clearly exhibits a number of disproportionate advantages for the hostage takers. Adam Dolnik and Keith M. Fitzgerald explain that, "In combination with the aforementioned greater readiness to die in the incident, and the overall decline in political sensitivity associated with killing innocents, this situation has essentially converted the barricade hostage scenario into a potential 'win-win' situation for the terrorists. If the hostage takers achieve their demands they win. If the government troops storm the location and the terrorists are killed in the shootout (along with many hostages) then the outcome of dying a martyr's death is also perceived as a victory."[10] The dynamic of almost certain death places a unique strain on the negotiating process to reach a resolution.

Chechen Mass Hostage Taking

Mass hostage taking is example of how the conflict between Russia and Chechnya was being pushed in new directions that no one ever expected. The following section will address three incidents involving Chechen separatists' as the hostage takers. The connected incidents comprise a trinity in terms of their discernable intensification and linear quality.

The formative incident occurred on "On June 14, 1995, Chechen warlord Shamil Basayev personally led a 162 strong commando unit for 'Operation *Jihad*' in Russian territory in order to 'strop the war [in Chechnya] or die."[11] To provide some context, between 1994 and 1996 the Russian Republic of Chechnya was at war with Russia. Reasons given for the war vary, but then Chechen President Dzhokhar Dudaev is often cited for his attempts to gain autonomy for Chechnya, and for his permissive stance on criminal behavior. A brutal and sloppy Russian invasion created the proper conditions to inspire reprisals in the form of terrorism. As the attack began:

> ". . . Basayev's original target was the Mineralniye Vody Airport, where the group allegedly planned to seize an aircraft and fly it into the Kremlin in a 9-11 style operation. For his part, Basayev claimed the convoy was heading to Moscow. In any case, the convoy made it through no less than twenty-two checkpoints all the way up to the village of Praskaeva near the Russian town of Budyonnovsk, but reportedly having run out of bribe money, the group was arrested and brought to the police station in town. Once there, previously undiscovered fighters emerged from the trucks and with swift action seized a number of key buildings in the city, eventually retreating with some 2,500 hostages into a hospital. During the initial takeover as many as 41 people were killed a number that would reach no less than 130 dead and 415 injured by the end of the crisis five days later."[12]

The initial observation is the unexpected deviation from the original target. Without going into unnecessary details, Basayev's unit was robust enough in terms of capabilities and capacity to facilitate a change of targets. Secondly, the availability of a series of secondary targets shows the range of different places that can be selected for mass hostage taking attacks. Third, even though Russian police ultimately prevented Basayev's unit from reaching the Mineralniye Vody Airport: this strategic success had little impact on the unit's ability to perform at the operational or tactical level in relation to taking and killing hostages. While the attack was off to an inauspicious start:

> "On the next day events took an ugly turn, as the terrorists executed another five captives after their morning deadline for staging a press conference had repeatedly been ignored. In order to avoid further killings, the Russian authorities finally allowed a group of journalists to enter the hospital and hold a press conference inside. During the event, Basayev proclaimed: 'Your pilots killed my family-eleven people, including women and children. But we do not fight women and children. They will be killed by your own soldiers. Your imperial army.' This statement would turn out to be prophetic, as on the next day at 4:55 A.M., the Ministry of Interior (MVD) and Federal Security Service (FSB) troops indeed launched an armed operation in an attempt to free the hostages by force. Russian forces led by the elite Alpha commando unit assaulted the Chechen positions but were forced to retreat, partially due to the terrorists' use of hostages as human shields. The four-hour assault was not completely without success however, as eighty-six people were rescued while the terrorists were forced to retreat from the wings into the main building. Still, more than thirty hostages were killed by the rescuing troops, and the lives of the ones remaining inside came

under a direct threat due to a fire that had erupted throughout the building."[13]

There are several curious factors about this incident that warrant further examination before moving on. The total of 2,500 hostages involved is truly astonishing. It is impossible to believe that Russian MVD or FSB troops came away with any meaningful lessons learned (worth synthesizing) that would help to significantly modify future response tactics, techniques, and procedures (TTP) for incidents of similar magnitude. However, "At the same time, it must be recognized that the terrorists apparently did not originally plan to take hostage in Budyonnovsk, which likely contributed to their eventual acceptance of a free passage offer."[14] We also know form this case that hostage rescue attempts done by force without the benefit of some strategic advantage seriously endanger the lives of hostages. Honestly, it is unclear what useful information can be extrapolated from this case in terms of forming guidelines or doctrine. There must be some amount of second guessing surrounding the decision to let Basayev leave considering the significant role he continued to play in the war with Russia until his death in 2006. Although, ". . . at this stage of the Chechen War, Basayev still tried to attract international support for his cause, which strongly influenced the strategy with which he approached the standoff. However, following the events of Kizlyar and the Moscow theatre hostage crisis, his approach to barricade incidents would assume an ominous escalatory trajectory leading directly to the tragic events of Beslan."[15] Finally, Basayev later entered politics, but his role in the Budyonnovsk attack was cited by Russia as a sign he could not be trusted.

The other two visceral examples of this type of attack perpetrated by Chechen fighters included: the October 2002 Moscow theater crisis and the September 2004 siege of Beslan School Number One. Initially, "On October 23, 2002, a group of 53 heavily armed Chechens seized the crowded Dubrovka theater in central Moscow during a performance of the Nord-Ost musical. The captors declared that unless Russia granted in-dependence to Chechnya and immediately withdrew its troops from the region, they would blow up the building with roughly 980 hostages inside. Although most of the hostages were saved when Russian spetsnaz forces stormed the theater on October 26, the rescue operation ended with the deaths of nearly 130 hostages, all but 2 of whom succumbed to the potent anesthetizing gas used by the rescuers."[16] Again, the new measures and countermeasures adopted during the ongoing conflict between Russia and Chechnya proved to have deadly consequences. The large scale tactical use of an anesthetic gas during a hostage rescue was unprecedented. The use of gas was an innovative attempt to maintain some semblance of a strategic advantage. Specific determinations about the exact nature of the anesthetic gas and its use bring up a lengthy series of concerns. Unfortunately, there seems to be considerable disagreement about what the gas actually was. Various sources concluded that the gas was likely an opiate derivative. Other sources were unable to make a determination because the gas did not fit the profile of any known opiate derivative anesthetic gas. Not being a chemist or anesthesiologist, this discrepancy is something that exists considerably beyond my understanding. Of course, the situation has proven to be nearly impossible to resolve and potentially irresolvable due to the unwillingness of Russia to provide details about the gas, and its origin. Serious questions linger about the application of gas in the Dubrovka theater. Specifically, was the gas itself and it use consistent with applicable norms regarding the use of chemical weapons?

Finally, looking carefully at the Beslan School siege, it is a continuation but also an improvement on the attack at the Dubrovka theater. In terms of specific changes during the 2004 Beslan school siege, "The hostage-takers laid mines around the perimeter of the building and strung up powerful explosives all over the gymnasium so that they could blow it up instantaneously. Having learned from the October 2002 crisis, the terrorists broke the windows in the gymnasium to disperse any gas that might be pumped in, and they took numerous other steps, such as monitoring the School grounds constantly on all sides and sealing off the plumbing and ventilation systems, to ensure that they could not be overpowered by Russian security forces before detonating the munitions."[17] The improvement made between the

2002 and 2004 attacks indicates a linear development that might be expected from any capable professionals. Mass hostage taking is the type of attack appropriate for small groups because they can be incredibly responsive to rapid tactical and technological amelioration. The ability for small organizations to adapt and restructure themselves is a considerable advantage in these instances. Conversely, state security services are slower to adapt because they are essentially extensions of a centralized bureaucratic system. In essence, ". . . the increased ability to learn from past experiences of groups in other countries, as well as the ability to conduct more detailed casing and analysis of possible targets, will probably lead to the terrorists' greater preparation aimed at eliminating any possibility of a successful rescue operation."[18] To say that the Chechens increased their proficiency for mass hostage taking is certainly true. However, it is also true that they became considerably more depraved in terms of target selection and methodology. The willingness to export terror well outside the boarders of Chechnya was likely a necessary step to validate the unpredictable nature of this new threat to a wider audience. There is also something disturbing about the need for terrorism to continually grow in complexity. It is unclear what drives this desire to continually grow and improve this particular type of political violence. Theoretically, it is possible that the conflict between Russia and Chechnya was a constant impetus for a more creative application of violence: a laboratory of death so to speak. Our last example of the phenomena of mass hostage taking occurred, "On September 1, 2004, a group of heavily armed fighters stormed a school in the town of Beslan, taking some 1,150 children, teachers, and parents hostage and demanding the withdrawal of Russian forces from Chechnya. Two days later, in a chaotic and violent battle, 330 hostages and nearly all the pro-Chechen fighters were killed by explosives set off by the hostage-takers and by gunfire from all sides. Radical Chechen field commander Shamil Basaev later claimed responsibility for the Beslan school assault."[19]

Mumbai

A series of coordinated terrorist attacks across the city of Mumbai in November 2008 demonstrated yet another dramatic increase in sophistication for attacks involving mass hostage taking. Bill Roggio notes, "Almost two days after terrorists attacked the Indian financial hub of Mumbai, the Indian military is still working to root out the remnants of the assault teams at two hotels and a Jewish center. More than 125 people, including six foreigners, have been killed and 327 more have been wounded. The number is expected to go up, as Indian commandos have recovered an additional 30 dead at the Taj Mahal hotel as fighting has resumed."[20] The list of adaptations and improvements used in the Mumbai attacks that require additional scrutiny is likely to include: an ability to disrupt infrastructure, a refined focus on soft targets, cultivation of terror and panic, effective use of various communication technologies, propaganda and media strategies, swarming, and buddy pairs. As noted previously, the use of various communication technologies to facilitate the attack is probably the most troubling development. The first time the world realizes that a terrorist organization has significantly greater or more refined capabilities is never a good day. During the assault, "Hundreds of people had been captive in the two hotels, many locking themselves in their rooms or trying to hide as the gunmen roamed the buildings . . . The gunmen were well-prepared, even carrying large bags of almonds to keep up their energy during the fight. Their main targets appeared to be Americans, Britons and Jews, though most of the dead seemed to be Indians and foreign tourists caught in the random gunfire."[21] The major difference between the Chechen cases and the case in Mumbai is that while they both involve mass hostage taking the attack in Mumbai was based much more on targets of opportunity rather than strict operational planning with the intent to take hostages.

The other noteworthy development during the Mumbai attack was the use of something called swarming:

"The basic concept is that hitting several targets at once, even with just a few fighters at each site, can cause fits for elite counterterrorist forces that are often manpower-heavy, far away and organized to deal with only one crisis at a time. This approach certainly worked in Mumbai, India, last November, where five two-man teams of Lashkar-e-Taiba operatives held the city hostage for two days, killing 179 people. The Indian security forces, many of which had to be flown in from New Delhi, simply had little ability to strike back at more than one site at a time."[22]

Swarming at its root is a type of biological intelligence. Very simple tasks can be controlled through simple interaction. Basically, swarming is what ants do; the problem with Mumbai was the process turned extraordinarily violent and proved difficult to stop. Incidentally, "That's how swarm intelligence works: simple creatures following simple rules, each one acting on local information. No ant sees the big picture. No ant tells any other ant what to do. Some ant species may go about this with more sophistication than others."[23]

This type of organization is an interesting departure from traditional hierarchical structure. The process of swarming allows for the just-in-time interjection of chaos at the local level: being incredibly responsive and opportunistic is clearly a desirable modus operandi. The potential damage this approach is capable of is obvious, but there should be additional related concern about further deterioration of viable strategic countermeasures. Shlok Vaidya of Naxalite Rage explains that:

"Instead of depending on local assets to expand the assault team, the terrorists made use of command and control hubs, located inside the two hotels, to out maneuver the Indian security apparatus. Each phase of the operation, every tactical movement, every step was coordinated via Blackberry, computer, and satellite phone in real time. This served as a force multiplier:

by acting in concert, they manipulated security force
and media estimates of their capabilities, allowing them
more time and space within to maneuver. When their
ability to travel around the city was cut off by police
forces, these rooms also provided a ready location to
fortify and sustain a siege."[24]

The Group Behind the Swarm

Pulitzer Prize-winning American journalist and writer Steve Coll
provided tremendous timely insight into the responsible terrorist group
Lashkar-e-Taiba. Having spent time with the group recently, Coll is
uniquely positioned to give an illuminating schematic of this mysterious
Hezbollah like group:

> "The tactics employed by the attackers will be instantly
> recognizable to Indian investigators because they bear
> the signature of the more sophisticated groups operating
> in and from Kashmir, particularly the banned terrorist
> group Lashkar-e-Taiba and its various splinters, allies,
> and ideological affiliates. In recent years, these Islamist
> networks have repeatedly engaged in what participants
> often refer to as 'fedayeen' attacks against Indian
> government targets. These attacks are suicidal, in
> the sense that the boys recruited to carry them out
> undertake reckless, gun-spraying penetrations of a type
> that make it very unlikely that they will emerge alive.
> Also, the assaults usually don't involve getaway plans
> or tactical exit strategies other than martyrdom. At the
> same time, these are not 'suicide attacks' in the sense
> that the attackers don't wire themselves up as human
> bombs. The guerrillas will penetrate a police station,
> government compound, or, as it seems in this case,
> softer targets such as hotels and a synagogue, fight for

as long as they can and finally accept their fates at the hands of opposing security forces."[25]

The Strategic Response

John Arquilla of the Naval Postgraduate School probably has the best potential response in terms of dealing with mass hostage taking situation. He explains that, "We've actually had a good test case in Iraq over the past two years. Instead of responding to insurgent attacks by sending out large numbers of troops from distant operating bases, the military strategy is now based on hundreds of smaller outposts in which 40 or 50 American troops are permanently stationed and prepared to act swiftly against attackers. Indeed, their very presence in Iraqi communities is a big deterrent. It's small surprise that overall violence across Iraq has dropped by about 80 percent in that period."[26] Consistent with typical military guidance, the ability to dramatically increase speed and decrease response times could alleviate some of the pressure associated with mitigating mass hostage taking incidents.

Conclusion

The essence of mass hostage-taking is that any large gathering is a potential target. More importantly, mass hostage-taking is strategically sound because these attacks strike essentially indefensible targets utilizing sophisticated planning to significantly reduce the availability of appropriate operational and tactical countermeasures for state security services.

Notes

[1]   Adam Dolnik & Keith M. Fitzgerald, *Negotiating Hostage Crisis with the New Terrorists,* 15.

[2]   John Robb, *The Coming Urban Terror: Systems disruption, networked gangs, and bioweapons.* http://www.city-journal.org/html/17_3_urban_terrorism.html (accessed March 8, 2009).

[3]   Adam Dolnik & Keith M. Fitzgerald, *Negotiating Hostage Crises with the New Terrorists,* 12.

[4]   John Robb, *Journal: Off the Shelf Leverage.* http://globalguerrillas.typepad.com/globalguerrillas/2008/12/journal-off-the.html (accessed March 8, 2009).

[5]   Adam Dolnik & Keith M. Fitzgerald, *Negotiating Hostage Crises with the New Terrorists,* Westport, CT: Praeger Security International, 2008. Page 17.

[6]   Ibid.

[7]   Ibid.

[8]   Ibid.

[9]   Ibid., 16.

[10]   Ibid., 24.

[11]   Ibid., 45.

[12]   Ibid.

[13]   Ibid., 46.

[14]   Ibid., 48.

[15]   Ibid.

[16]   Mark Kramer, *The Perils of Counterinsurgency: Russia's War in Chechnya,* 50-51. http://belfercenter.ksg.harvard.edu/files/kramer.pdf (accessed March 8, 2009).

[17]   Ibid., 54.

[18]   Adam Dolnik & Keith M. Fitzgerald, *Negotiating Hostage Crises with the New Terrorists,* 16.

[19]   Stuart D. Goldman, *Russian Political, Economic, and Security Issues and U.S. Interests,* 9. http://www.fas.org/sgp/crs/row/RL33407.pdf (accessed March 8, 2009)

[20]   Bill Roggio, *Analysis: Mumbai attack differs from past terror strikes.* http://www.longwarjournal.org/archives/2008/11/analysis_mumbai_atta.php (accessed March 8, 2009).

[21]   Ramola Talwar Badam, Indian commandos storm besieged Jewish center. http://www.huffingtonpost.com/2008/11/26/

indian-terror-shootings-i_n_146708.html (accessed March 8, 2009).

[22] John Arquilla, *The Coming Swarm.* http://www.nytimes. com/2009/02/15/opinion/15arquilla.html (accessed March 8, 2009).

[23] Peter Miller, *Swarm Theory.* http://ngm.nationalgeographic. com/2007/07/swarms/miller-text (accessed March 8, 2009).

[24] Shlok Vaidya, *Mumbai Overrun: The Evolving Threat.* http:// naxaliterage.com/?page_id=192 (accessed March 8, 2009).

[25] Steve Coll, *Decoding Mumbai.* http://www.newyorker.com/ online/blogs/stevecoll/2008/11/decoding-mumbai.html (accessed March 8, 2009).

[26] John Arquilla, *The Coming Swarm.*

Chapter 5

London Riots: Decentralized Intelligence Collection and Analysis

Alex Calvo

First Published 9 August 2011

Identifying Occasional Criminal Insurgents

The purpose of this paper is to comment on one of the developments arising from the current riots in the United Kingdom, where a website has been set up so that the public can identify those involved and report them to the Police. The use of modern technology to identify insurgents could be a response to the lack of working censuses in many areas where stability operations are conducted, seen by some observers as a major weakness.

The central idea is to tell friend from foe, or in classical Maoist terminology, fish from the water, using some of the widely available tools which, on the other hand, seem to be used to spread the violence in the UK.

The use of a website to spread pictures of violent incidents and have the perpetrators identified by the population would be a way to plug a gap in police capabilities, since the British authorities are unlikely to have the necessary manpower and knowledge to do so on their own.

This is why we can talk of "decentralized intelligence collection and analysis."

Looking Beyond the Protection of the Population

The current riots in London and other cities in the United Kingdom[1] have led to widespread calls for a wider police presence in the affected areas, and the social media have reflected some of these complaints, featuring stories about flashpoints where the population was left unprotected in the face of what could be described as a combination of urban guerrillas[2] and occasional criminal insurgents.[3][4]

With the riots still raging, it is obviously too early to draw any in-depth conclusions in terms of policing, and, furthermore, the complex nature of the incidents would make it inappropriate to concentrate on any single factor. It is obvious that the Police cannot be everywhere, and, furthermore, their duty to protect the population is a key organizational weakness of government forces[5] in the face of insurgents of any sort.[6]

This forces us to look beyond the protection of the population as a goal and ask ourselves how to identify those responsible for the violence so that they can be arrested[7] and, ideally, those who may join them in the future deterred.

The Challenge of Identifying Urban Guerrillas and Occasional Criminal Insurgents

In past post-conflict stability operations some observers have pointed out at the lack of a population census as a major weakness in attempting to identify the enemy, hidden among the population.[8] It is one of the capability gaps behind the calls for the deployment of military units with police training and skills.[9]

This is however where we can notice a key difference between London and other British cities currently under siege and the battlefields where our troops have been fighting in the last decade, since the former's population is already recorded on a number of databases.

We must however be careful before we jump to the conclusion that, given the ample available footage and pictures of the criminals, their identification will be a simple task, to be undertaken at leisure once order has been restored. For the time being, the software tools which may in the future allow the automated matching of pictures to identities are still not available, and the resulting volume of man-hours necessary to accomplish the task is probably beyond the capabilities of the London's Metropolitan Police Force and other British police forces and security agencies.

To make matters worse, even if such a feat could technically be accomplished, it is not clear whether the resulting intelligence would translate into legally admissible evidence, something that the rioters, or at least some of them, seem to be aware of, judging from the text of a pamphlet found in one of the scenes of devastation in Great Britain's capital, which among other pearls of wisdom reads "Don't assume that because you can identify yourself in a video, a judge will be able to as well. 'That isn't me' has got many a person off before now."[10]

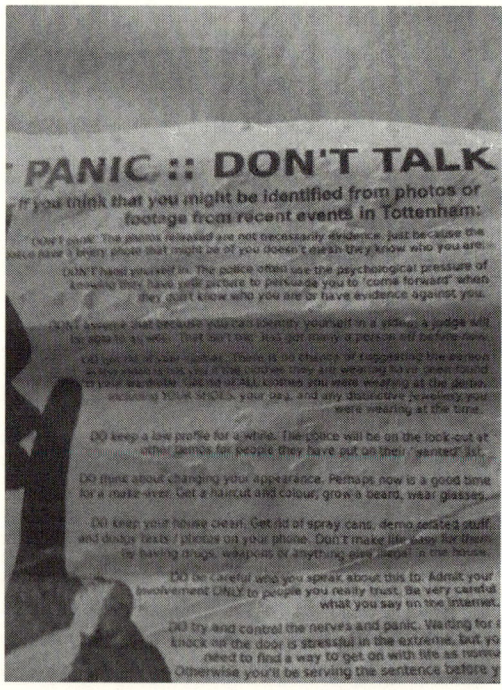

Figure Two. Don't Panic, Don't Talk Leaflet, available
at http://yfrog.com/z/h07mxcyzj.[11]

The leaflet also refers to the problems posed by the identification of photographed rioters, reminding its readers that "just because the police have a blurry photo that might be of you doesn't mean that they know who you are."[12]

A Decentralized Approach to Occasional Criminal Insurgent Identification

It is this problem, the inability of the Police to identify all the participants in the violence and mayhem, that seems to have prompted an interesting grassroots initiative, namely a website where the public can post pictures and look at them in order to identify the participants in the violence and call the authorities. Under the name "Catch a Looter," the website aims at "Collating all images of looters from the London riots." and invites readers to "contact Crimestoppers on 0800 555 111" if they "recognise anyone."[13]

The owner of the website is careful to make it clear that "This site does not support vigilante action; merely using social media to collate all images in one place," and, furthermore, warns that it is "Worth mentioning that some of these photos *may* be innocent bystanders who happen to have [been] shopping. It's not up to me to decide if they have committed a crime; I'm just helping to collate and perhaps provide a central place for these pics."[14]

These statements make it clear that there is no question of replacing the security forces, but rather of aiding them in a task for which they do not have the necessary manpower and expert knowledge:[15] the identification of criminals involved in the rioting and looting.

*Figure Three. One of the looters whose picture has been
posted at the Catch a Looter website*[16]

Unless this or similar efforts succeed, the proportion of rioters arrested will remain low, since the hundreds taken into Police custody to date are but a small fraction of the criminals involved. This will mean, as has been the case in similar instances in the UK and other countries, that crime will pay, given the low likelihood of being arrested and punished.

Effective deterrence requires the identification of as large a proportion as possible of those responsible for the wave of violence which has hit the United Kingdom, so that, using Mao's terminology, the fish cannot remain hidden in the water.

A Look at the Use of Modern Technology by Criminals and Security Forces

We can conclude by briefly referring to the widespread reports that the occasional criminal insurgents have made extensive use of modern technology to coordinate their actions. Reporting on this, Radio Free

Europe stressed the role of "Blackberry's instant message service (BBM) in the riots," which, as first pointed out by Blogger Jonathan Akwue,[17] "is an instant messenger system that has become popular for three main reasons: it's fast (naturally), it's virtually free, and unlike Twitter or Facebook, it's private." This privacy[18], together with "the ability to broadcast messages, which then go to all your contacts, and can quickly go viral," seems to be among the reasons for its popularity.[19]

This is yet another reminder that technology in itself is often neutral, potentially aiding both criminals and insurgents on the one hand, and government forces on the other.[20]

In addition to the possibility of fellow rioters gathering to strike at targets, another risk posed by modern communication technology may be disinformation. Reports of false incidents on social networks may have confused first responders and aggravated the lack of boots on the ground.[21]

However, despite all these instances of usage by occasional criminal insurgents and their moral sponsors of modern communication equipment and technologies, the birth of a website devoted to the collection of pictures of the incidents with a view to the identification by the population of those responsible and their reporting to the Police is clear evidence that these same technologies can be employed to deter violent crime. Websites like the one discussed above can plug a gap in the capabilities of security forces, using a decentralized approach to collect and process intelligence, turning the mere collection of thousands of pictures we all have seen in the media over the last few days into useful, actionable, intelligence leading to the arrest of those who thought they could maim, steal, and burn, with impunity.

In a way, this would be a replication of the variable-geometry networks currently destroying Britain's main cities. Just like all sorts of criminals have joined forces to concentrate, gaining local superiority at their chosen schwerpunkts, mainstream society, the population that the security forces must protect, would also join together, to repel them, providing the authorities with that most valuable of commodities in any struggle of this kind: intelligence. Just like the criminal insurgency networks at large often don't have overarching leaders, this would also be a horizontally coordinated, not vertically led, effort.

Finally, once these possibilities have been fully explored in largely stable and industrialized societies, it may be possible to adopt some of the lessons to the kind of scenarios where, as rightly pointed out by a number of observers[22], the inability to identify insurgents due to the lack of a census has hampered stabilization and reconstruction operations in the past.

Conclusions

When faced with widespread urban violence, which we can refer to using terms such as urban guerrilla or occasional criminal insurgency, security forces do not have the capacity to process the graphical information collected in order to identify and arrest the culprits. Since it is practically impossible to arrest them all on the spot, this means that unless an alternative way is found, deterrence will not work, because the chances of being caught will be statistically negligible, thus encouraging participation in future events of the same nature.

The security forces do not only lack the capacity to process all the information collected in the form of video footage and photographs, they are also unable to protect all the population and infrastructure and trying to do so may only result in being spread even thinner.

Therefore, only deterrence can diminish the likelihood and gravity of future riots, and as a result a way must be found to turn the large amounts of information on the identity of the culprits into actionable intelligence leading to their arrest. The existence of different government databases where the whole population is recorded means that part of the job is already done in advance, a welcome chance from many scenarios of recent counterinsurgency campaigns, but the key linkage of faces to names remains. It is here that the population at large can bridge the gap in police capabilities, by using the Internet.

Although the setting may seem very different, the key question in London and the rest of Britain right now is the same as in almost every insurgency: getting the population to provide intelligence to the government forces, so that they can isolate the insurgents, whatever their exact nature and motivations. Otherwise, hidden among the civilians, they will just wait for another opportunity to strike.

Notes

Editors' Note: To view *Figure One. One of the many disturbing sights published by the press* see Halliday Josh "London riots: BlackBerry to help police probe Messenger looting 'role'", *The Guardian*, 8 August 2011, available at http://www.guardian.co.uk/uk/2011/aug/08/london-riots-blackberry-messenger-looting.

[1] An interesting discussion of the likely wider causes of the violent wave which has engulfed the country can be found in Singh Sunny "London Riots: An Alternative 'Larger Context'", *Sunny Singh Online*, 9 August 2011, available at http://networkedblogs.com/lrDZy.

[2] As always, it is difficult to choose the right terminology to describe a diverse and mutating enemy. However, given the degree of violence and some of the tactics evident in the available footage of the incidents, urban guerrillas seems more appropriate than simply rioters.

[3] Occasional criminal insurgents refers to the members of organized (even if informal) criminal networks which usually refrain from openly confronting government forces and from seeking control of the territory, but which may change their posture and temporarily pursue both aims in circumstances such as the current ones. They are therefore different, despite sharing some traits, to the criminal insurgents described in the COIN literature, for a review of which one can see Sullivan John P. and Elkus Adam "Strategy and insurgency: an evolution in thinking?", *Open Democracy Net*, 16 August 2010, available at http://www.opendemocracy.net/john-p-sullivan-adam-elkus/strategy-and-insurgency-evolution-in-thinking.

[4] We should note the presence of third armed component, Islamist militias protecting the population of certain areas, in an open attempt to gain the legitimacy, prestige, and organizational skills, to achieve their aims of setting up self-policed enclaves ruled by Sharia, a goal repeatedly put forward in the last few months. "Bethnal Green—Gang of vandals broke the windows of an Islamic bank but were chased off by a rival gang Muslim youths who were standing guard outside the East London Mosque. Local shops attacked" Payne Sebastian and Quilty-Harper Conrad "London riots: all incidents mapped in London and around the UK", *The Daily Telegraph*, 9 August 2011, available at http://www. telegraph.co.uk/news/uknews/law-and-order/8689355/London-riots-all-incidents-mapped-in-London-and-around-the-UK.html.

[5] For the purposes of our discussion we shall not distinguish between the Police and the Military, since in non-conventional operations, such as post-conflict stabilization or counterinsurgency both can be employed and will have to resort to similar techniques. Actually, despite all the legal and constitutional problems this may imply, one of the key aspects of today's global security scenario is the confluence of police and military functions, as exemplified, in the US, by the setting up of a specialized USMC reserve battalion made up of civilian police officers. Sanborn James K., "Amos touts Reserve law enforcement unit"; *Marine Corps Times,* 15 April 2011, available at http://www.marinecorpstimes.com/news/2011/04/marine-amos-reserve-law-enforcement-battalion-041511w/; and Olesker Alex, "Cops in the Corps"; *Small Wars Journal,* 23 April 2011, available at http://smallwarsjournal.com/blog/2011/04/cops-in-the-corps/; the author would like to thank John P. Sullivan, Lieutenant at Los Angeles County Sheriff's Department, for having brought Alex Olesker's piece to his attention.

[6] Spreading them thin on the ground and preventing their concentration against groups of rioters and looters.

[7] It is beyond the scope of this paper to discuss the purposes of arrest and imprisonment, although this is an area where two

factors may force an in-depth rethink in the future. On the one hand, the overcrowding of prisons in many industrialized countries, and on the other the clear gap between the criminal law and the laws of war in terms of terrorism, with a dangerous and controversial gap obscuring the response to the phenomenon.

[8]   "The war would have been over in a month, had the insurgents worn uniforms. Throughout history, government forces have employed a census to sort out insurgents not wearing uniforms. It is a technique enshrined in all counterinsurgency manuals. I asked a four-star general in early 2005 why there was no census, complete with fingerprints. Why, he said, that could take a year to 18 months, implying the war would be over before then. On average, a military-aged male in the Sunni Triangle, which includes Baghdad, was stopped once or twice a year for a cursory identification check. But we never used the existing technology to take fingerprints on the spot and send a report back to a central data base for comparison with prints associated with unsolved crimes. This was the single greatest technical deficiency in the war. Most rifle companies tried to construct their own local census on laptops using digital photos, spreadsheets, and Google mapping. Millions of man-hours were wasted due to a failure at the top to understand how identification of the male population was equivalent to putting uniforms on the insurgents." West Bing, "Counterinsurgency Lessons From Iraq", *Military Review*, March-April 2009, pages 8-9.

[9]   Or, in the countries having them, constabulary-type police forces with military training and discipline.

[10]   *Don't Panic, Don't Talk* Leaflet, available at http://yfrog.com/z/h07mxcyzj.

[11]   http://yfrog.com/z/h07mxcyzj.

[12]   *Don't Panic, Don't Talk* Leaflet, available at http://yfrog.com/z/h07mxcyzj.

[13]   *Catch a Looter*, available at http://catchalooter.tumblr.com/.

[14]   Ibid.

Small Wars Journal

[15] "The lack of police officers living in some of the affected areas, with good local knowledge, has been identified by some observers as one of the failures to be addressed in the reaction to the riots. Another element of police practice contributed to their failure. The police do not have deep roots in most localities and especially areas such as Tottenham. Few, if any, officers live locally. In earlier times, policing was seen as primary prevention, based on a visible uniformed presence. Gradually, under pressure to appear more 'efficient', policing became more a matter of reaction and detection. Officers waited for calls and responded as fast as possible, while teams of investigators tried to solve past crimes. Only in the past couple of years has it begun to be accepted that primary prevention has its merits, and the Government is supposed to be moving towards neighbourhood policing with named officers covering particular areas and charged with getting to know everyone. An officer who knows the law-abiding locals as well as the miscreants is in a much stronger position when things go wrong than the officer whose 'response unit' has been called in to deal with some trouble every now and then" Green David, "London riots: why did the police lose control?", *The Daily Telegraph*, 8 August 2011, available at http://www.telegraph. co.uk/news/uknews/crime/8689004/London-riots-why-did-the-police-lose-control.html.

[16] *Catch a Looter*, available at http://catchalooter.tumblr.com/.

[17] Akwue Jonathan "The unlikely social network fueling the Tottenham riots", *The Urban Mashup Blog*, 7 August 2011, available at http://urbanmashup.wordpress.com/2011/08/07/ the-unlikely-social-network-fuelling-the-tottenham-riots/.

[18] "Chats on BlackBerry Messenger are encrypted and stored on Canadian servers; governments that want access to messages must go through Research In Motion, the Canadian company that owns Blackberry. In short, BBM is more secure than SMS for users living in restrictive communications environments." "Blackberry: The London Rioters' Tool of Choice." *Radio Free*

Europe, August 2011, available at http://www.rferl.org/content/blackberry_the_london_rioters_tool_of_choice/24290270.html.

[19] "Blackberry: The London Rioters' Tool of Choice." *Radio Free Europe*, 08 August 2011, available at http://www.rferl.org/content/blackberry_the_london_rioters_tool_of_choice/24290270.html.

[20] Something which should give pause for thought to those voices stressing the transforming effects of technologies such as drones, which we should not be surprised to soon see in the hands of non-state actors.

[21] "There is a bigger civic—and indeed—policing angle to this madness. Twitter, SMS, Facebook, have been hysterically reporting incidents where there aren't any, ensuring that anyone monitoring the situation would be constantly led astray. While leading police astray may seem like a laudable goal to some 'anarchist' sitting cosy at home, it merely added to the misinformation and most likely contributed to delayed responses by emergency services: if the cops were spread thin, were they following irresponsible leads to nonexistent incidents?" Singh Sunny "London Riots: An Alternative 'Larger Context'", *Sunny Singh Online*.

[22] Ibid. Page 8.

Chapter 6

Command of the Cities: Towards a Theory of Urban Strategy

John P. Sullivan and Adam Elkus

First Published 26 September 2011

Cities are likely to play major roles in the distribution of future global power. In 2008, over half of the world's 6.6 billion inhabitants lived in cities.[1] This development has led many observers to note that we now live in the "urban century." According to one view "Our future existence as a species is, inevitably, an urban one. By 2050, some projections have it that seven out of every 10 humans on earth will be living in a city."[2] With at least 200 cities of a million or more already in place or developing, urban warfare is now a strategic rather than operational or tactical question.

Urban warfare is remarkably diverse. Students of recent military history have observed and discussed urban sieges on the scale of Stalingrad, urban terrorist assaults like Mumbai, "Londonistan" type incubators of extremism, or feral feuds like those currently seen in the gang wars occurring in Ciudad Juárez and the world's "invisible cities" (global slums).[3] Here we attempt to stimulate the development of a theoretical framework for thinking about the command of the cities by states and other political communities.

Strategic Theories and the Commons

Beginning in the late 19th century, military theorists began to develop systemic theories about how military command of geography could lead to victory or defeat. Geography came to be seen—rightly or wrongly—as destiny. By the end of the 20st century, a set of different strategic schools oriented around different theories of strategic geography and their military applications emerged. These theories of geographic strategy culminated in Barry Posen's idea of the "command of the commons"—a unified idea about command of space and place.

One school of strategy—the Continental movement—encompasses theorists of strategy ranging from geopoliticians such as Halford Mackinger and Nicholas Spykman to more militarily focused landpower advocates. The Continental theorists concern themselves with political-military domination of crucial areas through either indirect political influence or manpower-intensive military strategies.[4] These theories have traditionally been the most influential. The Anglo-Afghan Wars, for example, were fought because British policymakers placed Afghanistan within the geopolitical framework of the Great Game and saw it as a strategic buffer for India that must be maintained in order to keep Britain's strategic position in Asia viable. A maritime school of theorists, with Mahan the most prominent, focuses on control of the high seas and more recently the littoral zones. With control of the seas, surface ships, submarines, and amphibious forces could dominate the mainland via blockades or naval 'descents' and strategic raids.

There are also aeronautical and astronautical theories of strategy focused on the domination of air and space for the purpose of deterrence and coercion. One might also say that information superiority is emerging (though perhaps explicitly non-geographic) as an equivalent school of strategy.[5] While airpower theory has been dissected, theories of information superiority as an element of geopolitics are still for the most part speculative.[6] Theories of cyber dominance are also, to some extent, still conceptually reliant on analogies on other models of power.[7]

Many of these theories were overly deterministic, but they served a useful function in identifying the strategic importance of geography and how military exploitation of different strategic commons can serve to shape strategic choices. The Cold War-era Maritime Strategy was a crucial aspect of the long-term strategic competition between the United States and the Soviet Union. Access to space gives the United States the ability to utilize sophisticated C4ISR (command, control, computers, communications, intelligence, surveillance, and reconnaissance) systems. American planners take command of the skies for granted during recent campaigns. And American strategy often places a high premium on preventing the emergence of a dominant hostile power in Eurasia.[8]

Command of the commons is the mega-theory of geographic strategy. In "Command of the Commons: The Military Foundation of US Hegemony," Barry Posen argued that the key to US hegemony was control of the commons:

> "The U.S. military currently possesses command of the global commons. Command of the commons is analogous to command of the sea, or in Paul Kennedy's words, it is analogous to 'naval mastery.' The 'commons,' in the case of the sea and space, are areas that belong to no one state and that provide access to much of the globe. ...Command does not mean that other states cannot use the commons in peacetime. Nor does it mean that others cannot acquire military assets that can move through or even exploit them when unhindered by the United States. Command means that the United States gets vastly more military use out of the sea, space, and air than do others; that it can credibly threaten to deny their use to others; and that others would lose a military contest for the commons if they attempted to deny them to the United States."[9]

Budget and strategy debates increasingly highlight the "command of the commons." In "The Contested Commons," Department of Defense officials Michele Flournoy and Shawn Brimley argued that a combination of irregular actors in the 'commons' and the ramping-up of anti-access capabilities by state and non-state actors poses a threat to the international system constructed around stable US-facilitated control of the commons.[10]

Urban Theories of the Commons: World Cities, Feral Cities, and A City-Based Geopolitics?

Might cities be considered a common akin to control of the cities and the air? According to Saskia Sassen, "Cities have long been sites for conflicts—wars, racism, religious hatred and expulsion of the poor— yet, where national states have historically responded by militarizing conflict, cities have tended to triage conflict through commerce and civil activity."[11] But although Sassen believes that cities are once again becoming a locus of conflict, her work has focused on the changing economic, political, and spatial role of the city.

There is a growing body of literature on so-called 'global cities' that act as pivot points of commerce. Sassen's pivotal book *The Global City: New York, London, Tokyo*, looks at the idea of 'world cities' as nodes in a global economic system. This idea is now so well known that it perhaps approaches some element of cliché, but is at the core of an emerging literature of popular urbanism trying to focus study of geopolitics away from nation-states back towards dynamic city-states.[12] We use the term "dynamic" because some writers, such as Jane Jacobs, write about cities as living entities. She stated in her famous final chapter in *The Death and Life of Great American Cities* that cities exhibited "organized complexity ... [which] present 'situations in which a half-dozen or even several dozen quantities are all varying simultaneously and in subtly interconnected ways'."[13] Cities are indeed complex adaptive systems whose evolution defies "high modernist" methods of explicit planning, and the research path that Jacobs outlined has been an inspiration to many urbanists.

Military and security theorists have also tried to keep pace with these developments. Martin Coward, for example, has explored the idea of 'urbicide'—the destruction of cities that provide a space for heterogeneous identities. Coward's monograph uses the destruction of cities in Bosnia as a paramount example.[14] Ralph Peters' seminal paper "The Human Terrain of Urban Operations" also added to the growing literature on cities and urban operations, with his taxonomy of different types of cities and different concepts of order. His idea of 'hierarchal cities' organized along command-and-control lines also parallels to some extent the writings of Paul Virilio about the military influence of urbanization in early modern Europe.[15] There is also the parallel idea of 'feral cities' expressed in military urbanist concepts with their visions of decaying metropolises as bases for enemies and criminals creating temporary urban autonomous zones.[16] This dystopian view is echoed in works that describe an emerging network of slum metropolises that are coming to span the globe.[17]

The common idea in all of these visions is an idea of an emerging network of mega-cities connected to each other through spatial flows, as elaborated by Manuel Castells in his works on the network city.[18] The notion of mega-cities parallels the concepts of sprawling slums laid out in dystopian urbanism and military urbanism, and for close to twenty years, military planners and theorists have anticipated the rise of mega-cities as micro theaters of operation for specially tasked urban forces.[19] The problem of mega-cities and slums have spawned a host of operational and tactical military concepts for pacifying unruly urban zones through a combination of older population control methods and newer networks of surveillance and control.[20]

The rise of the city also has political implications that have not gone unnoticed. Parag Khanna, an international relations scholar, asserts that the 21st Century "will not be dominated by America or China, Brazil or India, but by the city." In his view, "cities rather than states are becoming the islands of governance on which the future world order will be built…This new world is not—and will not be one global village, so much as a network of different ones."[21] Khanna's article has sparked a rather intense debate, but it is important to note that while the form of the future state and its role in the global order remains at best unclear, we can speculate that cities will comprise a 'space of flows' where the landscape's spatial transformation is a fundamental component of the social structure of the new global network society. This new spatial architecture demands an analysis of metropolitan regions and connectivity among (and within) these regions.

The Emerging Mega-City/Mega-Region: Terrain, Process and Conflict

Several scholars have attempted to characterize the spatial dynamics of this new global urban network. For example, urbanist John Friedmann conceptualizes cities as being arranged within a global hierarchy in which London, together with New York and Tokyo, are 'global financial articulations' while others such as Miami, Los Angeles, Amsterdam and Singapore are 'multinational articulations.'[22] Sassen envisions 'global cities' such as London and 'sub-global cities' with specialized roles such as Frankfurt (for banking), within this spatial dispersion. These hierarchical functions are the result of the internationalization of production and increasing centralization of the management and regulation of major multinational companies, financial and business services, and government.[23] Finally, world cities serve as control or command centers within the global networks of 'producer service' firms (financial and business services).

The 'space of flows' among and within these urban nodes—especially among the growing 'mega-cities' is determined by three factors: 1) material e-circuits (connectivity allowing the flow of information at anytime, anywhere); 2) nodes and hubs that are defined by strategic (or non-strategic) functions, with each 'place' having a specific hierarchical role, characteristics, and products to offer; and 3) spatial organization that foregrounds a social hierarchy where elites are increasingly cosmopolitan and people are increasingly local.

Communication technology is fostering multifunctional spatial decentralization. Some cities (and increasingly regions and especially nodes within regions) are able to specialize in form and function. As a consequence, parts of 'global cities' or 'mega-regions' are tightly coupled to the global grid—others are not. Elites are concentrated in key specialized neighborhoods of activity. Key global transport nodes (airports for example) create worldwide connectivity. Key neighborhoods attract core businesses (those that conform to the metro regional specialty), and then high-end hotels, restaurants, and cultural/entertainment venues will follow. Key decision-makers will concentrate in these neighborhoods and will link in real or chosen time with their colleagues globally. Networks of culture and people will connect these sectors of the metropolis (with like-situated persons globally and in other intra-metropolitan nodes). Intra-urban areas will continue to specialize locally and globally.

A potential consequence of this stratification is increased tension between those connected by new urbanism and those who are not. The contradiction between the 'space of flows' and the 'space of places' potentially promises to exacerbate the separation and isolation of those who are not well integrated into the global economy. Here, the concept of 'dual cities' is imperative.[24] Mega-cities (as nodes in the global hierarchy of mega-cities) are likely to be "spatially and polarized between high value-making groups and functions," vice "devalued social spaces and downgraded spaces." As a result, the urban process is likely to yield 'mega-slums' as well as 'mega-cities.'[25] Mega-cities and mega-slums are often discussed as opposites, but they are two sides of the same coin.

Urbanization and the desire to link to the global networked economy and reap its benefits are drawing people to mega-cities. Most of these persons are unable to reach the higher functioning positions within the megapolis and wind up in the world's growing slums. According to Davis by 2030 an estimated 5 billion of the world's population (which is estimated to be 8.1 billion at that time) will live in cities, about 2 billion of those (40%) will live in slums. The ratio of slum dwellers to elite (and middle class) will be variable throughout the world, and within mega-cities, but in some regions, it will be stark. For example, 80% of Nigeria's urban population currently resides in slums, while 4 million residents of Mexico City reside in the Neza/Chalco/Izta slum. An additional differential will be the distribution between inner city and peripheral slums. In each case, the position in the intra-metropolitan hierarchy will vary.[26]

Urbanization and favelazation[27] promise to be increasingly synonymous. As a result, slums/*desakotas*/*favelas* are likely to become important nodes in the embryonic megapolises of the future (Consider the emerging RSPER: Rio/São Paulo Extended Metropolitan Region as an extreme example of the polycentric mega-city). Parts of these slums will be 'lawless zones' or 'failed communities' where extreme violence will fester; others will be vibrant incubators of innovation. A good deal of slums are likely to be something in between. All will be complex local economies interacting in diverse ways within their own mega-city region. Global cities linking global economic circuits are also home to transnational criminals and global gangs. At times these illicit economy and illicit economic actors (gangsters) will link with gangsters in other mega-slums in a criminal parallel to the global network of mega-cities.[28] Mega-cities, or the polycentric megapolis emerging now and maturing in the future will as always be determined not by place, but by process.

The various nodes within each mega-conurbation will likely (as they do now) possess distinct social and architectural forms. Activities will continue to concentrate in specific districts (quarters or neighborhoods). The elite will continue to cluster to enjoy the benefit of shared company and fill the need for face-to-face decision-making. Advanced services and special functions will cluster within 'mega-politan' regions and continue to link with other nodes distributed globally (as well as within their region). Mega slums will surround and interact with the distributed cosmopolitan core.

Mega-slums will surround and interact with the distributed cosmopolitan core. Mega-regions will be dense with population and traffic congestion, and as a result, metro transit systems and high-speed rail to connect nodes intra- and extra region; as well as airports and rail terminals will become key terrain nodes. A range of associated services will cluster in the proximity of associated key terrain.

The dense traffic conditions will speed the process of urban elite cluster, which will continue to be surrounded by excluded zones (slums). As a result, security features will become increasingly proximate (as suggested by Davis). Walled and gated communities, video surveillance, and armed security will permeate the interface between mega-city and mega-slum. Operations in urban terrain will be common. The distinctions between urban and national strategy may increasingly blur, and significantly from an operational perspective, military and policing techniques and approaches will have greater mutual influence.

Bridging Operations and Strategy in Cities: Some Observations

Cities are not only hubs of commerce, political power, cultural difference, and geopolitical importance. They are fundamentally *contested* by police, military, criminal, and paramilitary forces. They are contested not because of a neoliberal design, as much contemporary urbanist literature suggests, but because they have become commons of political, economic, and thus strategic importance. The human experience of strategy over millennia suggests that which is valuable or gives a strategic advantage *will* become an object of contestation, despite whatever norms of cooperation have developed. And this is the case with the contemporary urban environment. The trends catalogued suggest possibilities beyond the current operations in places such as Grozny, Baghdad, or Rio de Janeiro—although a continuity of operations is also likely.

Tactics and operations inside urban zones, as everyone from Sun Tzu to RAND's Russell Glenn have noted, are fundamentally different than other military operations. The basics are familiar to everyone: command and control is fragmented, small-unit tactics assume even greater importance, and unorthodox uses of armor and airpower (particularly new intelligence, surveillance, and reconnaissance and unmanned platforms) are the key to military dominance. Indeed, the rise of operations in cities parallels other trends in military affairs in the 20th century in the greater demands on small-unit leaders and difficulties in command and control. Unorthodox maneuvers and concepts are key to mastering urban geography, as is more conventional isolation of the urban environment and grinding attrition. Both can be seen throughout military history.

Historically, cities derived military effectiveness from their ability to conserve manpower and sustainment by the substitution of fortifications for warm bodies on the front line. Cities could effectively dominate the surrounding countryside and serve as effective pivot points for armies to launch operations from. One could bypass a city but in doing so had to tolerate a hostile garrison in his rear. Moreover, cities were also full of resources, politically important, and sometimes capturing them could be the capstone to a war or campaign.[29] Although the advent of artillery solved one of the major problems of urban warfare—breaking through the siege walls and suppressing enemy firepower—it did not eliminate the numerous logistical, command-centric, and human challenges associated with capturing cities. In fact, these have in some ways increased. Many of these challenges are already familiar. One challenge, however, that has not been observed is one of *density*.

As Russell Glenn observed, many of the best-known urban battles occurred in environments that are considerably smaller than they are today:

> "Stalingrad, Manila, Seoul, and others are well known to those in the armed forces who see the world's ever-increasing urbanization as a harbinger of more such challenges to come. Yet these historical examples are perhaps less relevant than they might at first glance appear. The cities of Manila and Seoul boasted populations of only a million or so when Americans fought for their liberation in 1945 and 1950 respectively; today both measure residents and workers at well over ten times that number....Seoul was virtually an entity unto itself in the middle of the twentieth century, separated from neighboring small cities or towns by expanses of rice paddies and lightly occupied terrain. By the century's end, the city was awash in a much larger metropolitan area. Seoul and Inchon had seemingly merged. Tentacles of urbanization joined the heart of the capital with once remote and far northern Munsan, Uijongbu, and Tongduchon. That the numbers of

buildings, streets, vehicles, and people have increased is apparent in the comparison. The regional urban density has also increased. Whereas in 1953 built-up areas were the exception in the northwestern Republic of Korea, they are now predominant. Further, a city's components today are considerably more dense. More people now live and work in a square kilometer, a phenomenon made possible by ever-taller buildings and deeper subterranean structures. More vehicles pack the same downtown area; more offices, apartments, and commercial enterprises fill a unit of space than was the case in mid-century."[30]

The predominant strategic challenge of urban pacification and conventional urban operations in the 21st century is thus one that Sun Tzu and many ancients would have understood very well: one of cities swallowing armies. Today's professional armies are growing smaller and more expensive, while cities in turn are growing larger and more unruly. While, as Napoleon understood, a "whiff of grapeshot" in the face of a mob armed with inferior weaponry can have a force multiplication effect, pacification of urban megapolises will not be achievable by force alone—especially when political and logistical considerations limit the amount of force able to be brought to be bear. As Glenn notes, complexity and density should not be understood purely in terms of pure size. Rather, urban warfare also an issue of increasingly diverse and complex human intelligence issues, infrastructure, and urban networks.

For smaller forces such as police and paramilitary organizations, megacities comprise entire theaters of operation. While professional armies concern themselves principally with operations against other forces, internal security concerns the suppression of armed rebellion, protection of critical infrastructure, and counter-gang and high-intensity policing. The challenge of internal security, for many governments, will actually be front and central. Governments must control cities to maintain sovereignty internally. This has become a strategic challenge and will continue to be as mega-cities and slum cities continue their growth. It is entirely possible that cities will develop alternative identities hostile to that of the larger state, as already seen somewhat in the phenomenon of 'failed communities' within the Americas in which gangs have developed unique internal zones of difference and control.[31] This much is clear, and is generally accepted as a part of military planning and thought over what is now approaching two decades.

The response, however, has been entirely on tactical and operational levels. Concepts of 'swarming' or urban control have proliferated and have been implemented with some success in urban battles in Iraq. Of particular note are advances in network targeting and ISR integration. Tight and precise joint operations coordinated on the lowest levels have resulted in success in Iraq's urban warfare, although none of this has obviated the need to go 'house to house' in bloody battles that often unfold on the personal level. In the police realm, the revival of urban paramilitary shock attack in the Americas and South Asia has led to insights about focusing the full force of police and paramilitary elements throughout an urban theater of operation.

The importance of protecting and controlling key commercial nodes will be a military concern in conventional warfare. Urban density has the potential to swallow up armies attempting to contest control of cities and alternatively protect and destroy crucial commercial nodes. But the converse applies to internal threats. The power of relatively small groups to disrupt nodes and use interconnectedness to create widely dispersed operations across multiple urban "theaters" will challenge states' response capability. The temptation will be to either cordon off mega-slums and control them through periodic raids (as is the practice in some parts of Latin America) or demolish cities entirely to make a harsh political point (as did the Syrians in Hama in the 1980s and today). Neither response is more than a temporary expedient and depending on the nature of the response will only aggravate the situation.

On the other hand, strategists operating on the conventional end of the spectrum may grow so fixated on the purely economic aspects of the conflict that they may forget the importance of tying control of resources and nodes to political objectives. Contesting a fortress-city and losing many men and resources out of a false expectation that controlling the "pivot point" will lead to the other side either giving in or that certain nodes will deliver instant knockout blows to a nation's economy will repeat the worst excesses of the theories of economic war and industrial targeting that predominated during World War II and Vietnam. Armies that allow themselves to be trapped in cities, such as the Chinese Nationalists in the late stage of the Chinese Civil War, risk being swallowed up by their own fortresses and cut off.

Towards a Theory: Strategic and Political Context

The idea of the 'commons' is a starting point for a more strategic view, as many of the points elucidated about the importance of air, sea lines of communication, and cyberspace, can easily be extended into the urban realm. Alice Hills' look at post-conflict policing can also be a starting point, as her writing on the importance of political order and its production through the law enforcement profession can also help strategic theorists think about the unique challenges of urban strategy.[32] A theory of urban strategy would take a systematic look at the changing strategic environment, and determine the imperatives of police and military forces to successfully operate within and control urban spaces.

The model for such a theory would not be the theories of airpower that predominated in the early 20th century, nor the rather scattered landpower literature, but Julian Corbett's elegant and nuanced works on naval strategy. There are parallels between urban theory and seapower, to some extent, as urban operations present an environment of operations that poses special challenges requiring its own unique vocabulary. The terminology of sea control and contestation also has some analog in control of urban spaces.

The political context for a theory of urban strategy is the notion that internal and external security are roughly co-equal and in some cases flow seamlessly into each other, an problem that advanced Western states have not had to ponder for a while since the coercive power of the modern state has suppressed or indulged internal dissent to the point where external threats have been the only problems worth devoting extensive defensive resources. To some extent, the Cold War fears of internal Soviet subversion and present-day fears of Islamic radicalization have interfered with the external dimension of state security, but military-strategic thought and planning on the strategic level remains focused primarily on external threats.

It should also be noted that the "new" dialectic between interior and exterior security is a restatement of a very old problem. Old-school political realism, from the small-r republicanism of Machiavelli to Morgenthau and Kissinger, has concerned itself largely with the privileges of elite power and the restraint of the power of the popular mob and those who instigate them. Machiavelli was not only concerned with maximizing the power of his prince but also the politics of city-state dynamics. For Kissinger, the spread of destructive popular ideologies threatened the delicate balance of power internationally—as his work *A World Restored* focused on the attempts to put together antebellum Europe in the aftermath of the destructive Napoleonic wars.[33]

A key element of theory-building will be translating the nodal aspect of urban spaces into politics. One chief political issue will be the rift between the haves-and-have nots within cities and the challenge to order posed by those on the margins of that political order. In this light, Mike Davis's *Blade Runner*-like imagery of attack helicopters making incursions into slums and retaliatory car bombs is not an exaggeration of the future challenges. Elites will struggle to pacify unruly cities and "disconnect" them from other cities and spaces or close off cities as they exist in order to create expansive regimes of surveillance and control. The literature on "urbicide" also shows how cities are also spaces of political identity that make them targets for violence designed to totally destroy those spaces to quash certain identities.

Distinctions between national and domestic policing strategies, as mentioned before, will erode, which will require the ability to connect the urban element at the national level to military strategy, thus complicating issues of jurisdiction and shattering the fragile barrier between military and civil law operations in many democratic nations. Another corollary of this is that *urban policy* will also connect with grand strategic policy, as national prosperity (and the root of military capabilities) will increasingly become linked to the general health and prosperity of the global set of nodes that connect global cities and global slums.

What corporeal forms a theory of urban strategy will take is left up to the readers of this article. However, we wish to emphasize a point about the *human* dimension of cities often missing from discussions of urban operations. Command of the cities not only provides material gain and territorial integrity, preventing them from becoming so many holes of Swiss Cheese (the reverse inkblot) in a nation's territory but also should create an open space for urban residents to live, play, work, and grow to their full potential. Although the literature on cities and urban operations often casts connectedness—electronic, illicit, or commercial as dangerous, it also enhances human prosperity and happiness. Both of the authors grew up in major cities and have lived in the Greater Los Angeles mega-region and are often amazed by the fluid mix of cultures, nationalities, and trades. Cities should not be thought of merely as sources of danger or economic nodes but places of difference that add immense human and cultural value to a nation's fabric. This adds to the importance of protecting them without squelching their potential through security theater or collateral damage.

Such a balance will not be easy. The London riots demonstrate how flash mobs and swarms of people can lead to a lethal combination of government paralysis, popular fear, and ruinous destruction of property. Creating better security will take not only prudent political leadership but also knowledge of how to disperse and manage increasingly scarce manpower throughout larger and larger urban centers. At times, this will also hinge on involving citizens in their own security and prosperity rather than making them passive bystanders—a step that will be difficult for police forces and militaries wedded to the idea of monopolies of force to tolerate. Security in the mega-city is as much a matter of "population-centric" engagement in the local liquor store or taco truck as grand strategic calculations.

Notes

[1]   John Loring, *Cities, A Groundwork Guide*, Toronto: Groundwood Books, 2008, p. 7.

[2]   "The Big Question: The New Urbanism, In the future what will our cities look like?" *World Policy Journal*, Vol. XXVIII, No. 4, Winter 2010/2011, p. 3.

[3]   See for example, Antony Beevor, *Stalingrad: The Fateful Siege: 1942-1943*, New York, Penguin, 1999; John P. Sullivan and Adam Elkus, "Postcard from Mumbai: Modern Urban Siege," *Small Wars Journal*, 16 February 2009 at http://smallwarsjournal. com/blog/2009/02/postcard-from-mumbai/; Melanie Phillips, *Londanistan*, New York: Encounter Books, 2006; John P. Sullivan and Carlos Rosales, "Ciudad Juárez and Mexico's 'Narco-Culture' Threat," *Mexidata*, 28 February 2011 at http://www.mexidata. info/id2952.html ; and Mike Davis, *Planet of Slums*, Verso: London, 2006.

[4]   Joseph Collins, *Military Strategy: Principles, Practices, and Historical Perspectives*, Dulles: Potomac Books, 2002, p. 61.

[5]   Ibid.

[6]   See Will Goodman, "Cyber Deterrence: Tougher in Theory than in Practice?" *Strategic Studies Quarterly*, Fall 2010, Vol. 4., No. 3, pp. 102-135.

[7]   See Adam Elkus, "Legacy Futures in Cyberspace," *ThreatsWatch*, 03 March 2009 at http://threatswatch.org/commentary/2009/03/ legacy-futures-in-cyberspace/.

[8]   See Michael A. Lind, *The American Way of Strategy*, Oxford: Oxford University Press, 2006.

[9]   Barry R. Posen, "Command of the Commons: The Military Foundation of U.S. Hegemony," *International Security*, Summer 2003, Vol. 28, Issue 1, pp. 8-9.

[10]   Michele Flournoy and Shawn Brimely, *Proceedings*, July 2009, Vol. 135/7/1/, p. 277, http://www.usni.org/magazines/ proceedings/2009-07/contested-commons.

[11]   Saskia Sassen, "Saskia Sassen on War" in "The Big Question: The New Urbanism, In the future what will our cities look like?" *World Policy Journal*, Vol. XXVIII, No. 4, Winter 2010/2011, pp. 4-5.

[12]   See, for example, Saskia Sassen, *The Global City:* Princeton: Princeton University Press, 2001.

[13]   Jane Jacobs, *The Death and Life of Great American Cities*, New York: Random House, 1961, p. 433, quoted in Jeremiah S. Pam, "The Paradox of Complexity: Embracing Its Contribution to Situational Understanding, Resisting Its Temptation in Strategy and Operational Plans," in Christopher M. Schnaubelt (Ed), *Complex Operations: NATO at War and On the Margins of War*, Rome: NATO Defense College Forum, 2010, p. 3.

[14]   See Martin Coward, *Urbicide: The Politics of Urban Destruction*, New York: Routledge, 2009.

[15]   See Ralph Peters, "The Human Terrain of Urban Operations," *Parameters*, Spring 2010, pp. 4-12, http://www.carlisle.army. mil/USAWC/parameters/Articles/00spring/peters.htm and Paul Virilio, *Speed and Politics*, New York: Verso, 2006.

[16]   See Richard Norton, "Feral Cities: The New Strategic Environment," *Naval War College Review*, Autumn 2003, pp. 97-106.

[17]   See Mike Davis, *Planet of Slums*, New York: Verso, 2006.

[18]   See Manuel Castells, *The Information Age: Economy, Society and Culture. Vol. I, The Rise of the Network Society.* Oxford: Blackwell, 1996.

[19]   P.J. Taylor, "Worlds of Large Cities: Pondering Castells' Space of Flows," *Third World Planning Review*, 21 (3), (1999).

[20]   See Stephen Graham, *Cities Under Siege: The New Military Urbanism*, New York: Verso, 2010.

[21]   Parag Khanna, "Beyond City Limits," *Foreign Policy*, October/September, 2010. http://www.foreignpolicy.com/ articles/2010/08/16/beyond_city_limits.

[22]   J. Friedmann, "The World City Hypothesis," *Development and Change* 4, 1986, pp.12-50.

[23] Saskia Sassen, *The Global City* and *Cities in a World Economy*, London: Pine Forge Press, 1994.

[24] Manuel Castells, "The Informational City is a Dual City: can it be Reversed?" in Donald A Schön (*et al*) (Eds.), *High Technology and Low Income Communities*, Cambridge: MIT Press. 1998.

[25] Mike Davis, *Planet of Slums* and *City of Quartz: Excavating the Future of Los Angeles*, New York: Vintage, 1992.

[26] Ibid.

[27] Favelazation is the process of slum formation, it draws its name from Brazil's notorious slums of Rio de Janeiro and São Paulo.

[28] See John P. Sullivan and Adam Elkus, "Global cities–global gangs," *openDemocracy*, 02 December 2009 at http://www.opendemocracy.net/opensecurity/john-p-sullivan-adam-elkus/global-cities---global-gangs.

[29] See Lieutenant Colonel Lou DiMarco, "Attacking the Guts: Urban Operations Through the Ages," in William G. Robertson and Lawrence A. Yates (eds), *Block by Block: The Challenges of Urban Operations*, Ft. Leavenworth: US Army Command and General Staff College Press, 2003, pp. 1-29.

[30] Russell Glenn, *Heavy Matter: Urban Operations' Density of Challenges*, Santa Monica: RAND Corporation, 2000, pp. xi-xii.

[31] See for example John P. Sullivan, "Gangs, Hooligans, and Anarchists—The Vanguard of Netwar in the Streets," Chapter Four in John Arquilla and David Ronfeldt (Eds.), *Networks and Netwars: The Future of Terror, Crime, and Militancy*, Santa Monica: RAND, 2001, pp. 99-126.

[32] See Alice Hills, *Policing Post-Conflict Cities*, London: Zed, 2009.

[33] See Dan Trombly, "Old School Realism and the Problem of Society," *Fear, Honor, and Interest*, August 12, 2011, http://fearhonorinterest.wordpress.com/2011/08/12/old-school-realism-and-the-problem-of-society/.

Chapter 7

Urban Land Use by Illegal Armed Groups in Medellin

Geoffrey Demarest

First Published 17 October 2011

This article poses ideas about counterinsurgency, law enforcement and stability operations in the context of "land-use planning." Land-use planning carries many of today's dominant theoretical currents as to centralized direction of urban life.[1] Here, seven proposed categories of illegal slum land use are tested against a recent, complex Latin American case. Admittedly, this application of the term—land-use may be overly literal and is to be distinguished from "land-use planning." That latter term generally connotes a set of theoretical norms and objectives centered, in part, on the concept of 'sustainability' (often presented in planning literature as a balance or reconciliation of environmental stewardship, social equity and economic maximization).[2] Land-use planning also connotes a specialized set of opinions and plans coming from persons whom we can stereotype as technocratic and bureaucratic—as governmental.

Government land-use planning in Medellín, Colombia has sought to achieve the values supposed by 'sustainability,' but in the process has had to wrest land-use dominance from violent illegal armed groups, and to provide the population physical security and conflict resolution services. In such a violently conflictive urban geography, land-use planning has to account for illegal, violent land use. In the long run, attainment of basic sustainability goals facilitates peaceful social contracts, but, in the nearer term, some aspects of urban design must directly address ease in policing and perhaps even effectiveness of military operations. If experiences in Medellín foretell anything, it is that security planners' conversation will necessarily shift toward land use, and the conversation of land-use planners toward security.

Non-autochthonous (outsider) illegal armed groups (IAG) pursue and enjoy eight principal, overlapping uses of urban slum land in relation to their illicit pursuits. These eight land uses, in no particular order, are: 1. taxation; 2. free trade; 3. sanctuary; 4. clandestine manufacture or processing; 5. staging for violent operations outside the slum; 6. safe transit of contraband; 7. recruiting; and 8. as a prison or graveyard for their victims. The eight categories could be used as part of taxonomy for geographic profiling (predictive geographic forensics).[3] The IAG land-use categories are suitable as variables (field descriptions or attribute names—the titles of the columns at the top of an SQL spreadsheet perhaps) in a forensic police/military Geographic Information Systems (GIS) data table.[4]

While such use of GIS may be the most immediate or directly relevant application to government reduction of illegal armed groups, other uses, such as informing urban building and street design, may yield the more important longer–term security benefits. A correct GIS taxonomy, moreover, can speed the testing of broader insurgency and counterinsurgency theories and metrics, and hopefully fuel land-use planning strategies for building peaceful social contracts. It is probably safe to assert that the common sense possessed by experienced detectives remains the primary source of successful predictions regarding points and times where an IAG member or asset is likely to be found. It appears that such experiential common sense constitutes the backbone of police intelligence methods for anticipating criminal whereabouts in most foreign cities.[5] A more sophisticated epistemology, constructed as a GIS, can nevertheless improve, extend and accelerate common sense predictive victories. With that optimism in mind, we consider the case of Medellín, which has been one of the most complex and challenging urban battlefields on the planet.

Medellín, Colombia

Although some reference is made herein to other urban conflicts, the paper focuses on the case of *Comuna 13*, a borough in Medellín, Colombia, that suffered critical levels of internal violence in this first decade of the 21st century.[6] Although many IAGs were spawned within *Comuna 13*, outsider entities included drug cartels from greater Medellín and from other parts of Colombia, and revolutionary and paramilitary organizations born in other regions of Colombia. These latter groups were of greater concern to the formal Colombian governments at all levels, even if not to the *Comuna 13* neighbors. The individuals most able to control illicit land use within *Comuna 13* were often those most able to apply resources associated with the more powerful non-autochthonous IAGs.

Before considering each of the illegal land-use categories, some descriptive introduction to the Medellín area is warranted. Urbanized terrain inside and around the city of Medellín is home to a little over three million Colombians. It has at least since the early 19th century been a city of entrepreneurs and early adopters of technologies.[7] It felt all the various pulses of Latin America's accelerated 20th century migration to the cities, but in the late 1970s and early 1980s experienced a storm of urbanization.[8] That storm was formed by at least four identifiable contributors worthy of mention, as follows:

- Basic demographics—Medellín, in Colombia's northwest, is surrounded by one of Colombia's most densely populated rural areas, but itself sets at a disproportionately greater distance from other Colombian urban centers, thus being a more immediate magnet to a relatively greater surrounding population;[9]

- The countryside in counties of eastern Antioquia Department surrounding Medellín was a key battlespace in the accelerating insurgent war against the government of Colombia. People in those counties violently displaced were most likely to escape to Medellín;[10]
- Populist city leaders turned a blind eye to mass squatting in the cities peripheries, even encouraging it for electoral designs; and
- Medellín had always been (and is still) perceived as the Mecca of labor opportunity.

Those who migrated to the city, whether they compelled or not, did not necessarily find a peaceful alternative to their rural lives. Several other factors militated against a peaceful social environment, making Medellín not just one of hyper-accelerated growth, but one of the most violent cities in the world. Following are some of these factors:

a. In the context of the greater insurgent war, Medellín, due to its traditionally entrepreneurial ideological stamp and its seeming strategic vulnerability, became a territorial objective in an urban strategy of the principal insurgent guerrilla organizations, especially the Revolutionary Armed Forces of Colombia (FARC).[11] Late in 1998, the government of Colombia and the FARC began a peace process that included concession by the government of a large zone in eastern Colombia from which government authority and force were withdrawn. During most of the peace process period, Colombian President Andrés Pastrana constrained the military from taking any major offensive actions, including within Medellín. This nearly unilateral constraint lent a degree of freedom of action to various armed groups, including and especially the FARC.[12] On February 20, 2002, President Pastrana announced that the peace process was terminated, conceding to detractors of the process that the FARC had not been acting in good faith and that no progress toward peace had been achieved.[13] This event, and public realization regarding the *mens rea* of the FARC leadership, radically changed the parameters of engagement in Medellín, releasing the army and national police to act. During the middle months of 2002, after May elections, which brought the more militarily assertive administration of President Álvaro Uribe Vélez to power, *Comuna 13* became center stage of a series of government efforts at pacification and control in the city. These operations, dubbed in general, 'Mariscal,' appeared to be failures until October, when Operation Orion finally succeeded in changing the security condition within the borough.[14] (The relative success of Operation Orion stemmed from a decision on the part of the military and civilian authorities to maintain a permanent, physical presence of all parts of the government within the *Comuna*, often on the most conflictive pieces of terrain.)

b. Medellín was a geographic focus of leading anticommunist/anti-FARC armed self-defense consortiums, the dominant and prevailing among these becoming the Self Defense Forces of Colombia (AUC). The AUC gained widespread popular and political support in northwestern Colombia, including among wealthy business interests. Perceived inadequacy of the Colombian government under President Pastrana's administration to effectively challenge the FARC militarily, along with a legacy of official paramilitary institutional organization, led to vigilantism on a significant scale.[15] This vigilantism paralleled and melded with illicit drug operations, metastasizing to become as much of a menace to public security as was the FARC, at least in some of the country's departments.[16] While perhaps effective against the FARC in some battle zones, the AUC soon joined the ELN and FARC on the US State Department's official list of terrorist organizations due to its immane behavior.[17] It also joined in the fight for *Comuna 13*.

c. The international cocaine trade had begun to boom in the 1980s, and with it new and powerful criminal organizations, several of which were headquartered in Medellín. Pablo Escobar was killed in Medellín in late 1993, but his legacy was a city overfilled with dispersed, experienced and ruthless drug networks. Moreover, takedown of the Escobar organization, and along with it the reduction of other Aburrá Valley cartels, opened seams to competition from Cali-based drug lords.

d. Preferred transportation routes for the movement of everything (including drug processing precursor chemicals and weapons) between the northwestern coasts and central Colombia are constrained into the Aburrá Valley, which the city straddles. Especially while rural violence pushed, and illicit money pulled people to the city, smaller areas of terrain within the metropolitan area became objects of intense violent competition. These competition geographies seem to be defined by typical urban economic considerations. Needy and entrepreneurial individuals apparently chose proximity to urban services and jobs, informality of land ownership, and price.[18] Partly, the violence can be traced to spontaneous reaction to infrahuman conditions. Absence of basic services such as sewers and restrooms, for instance, would spark offenses to personal dignity, leading to the rapid formation of alliances for protection and revenge.[19] Other groups formed around electricity, cable or potable water piracy. Aside from these primordial needs (if the need for cable TV can be so designated), a more sophisticated violence arose, also encouraged by the absence of formal authority, but in response to the potential illicit uses of the peripheral slums as described in the first paragraph above. Some uses were influenced by larger war strategies, especially of the government and the FARC. Their 'peace process' allowed some additional freedom of presence and action on the part of some IAGs, including leftist guerrilla organizations, but, on the other hand, spurred antiguerrilla paramilitaries to organize, which in some locales had the effect of stymieing guerrilla advances, but via violent confrontation. These war-induced decision factors aligned with the existing currents of urbanization to assure deadly competition among more than a half-dozen ruthless identities. Listed briefly, these included Medellín Cartel remnants, the Cali Cartel, the FARC, the Ejército de Liberación Nacional (ELN), urban splinters of the FARC and ELN, the AUC, local militias/brigands, especially an ELN spin-off calling itself the Comandos Armados del Pueblo (The Peoples' Armed Commandos, CAP), as well as an assortment of free-lance local thugs.[20] These various IAGs took on a slang categorization with a musical referent as *bandas, combos* or *orquestas*. Add to the friction a not-always noble and incorruptible police force.

The developmental histories of autochthonous slum IAGs are significantly different than those of outside groups, and this is reflected in their land use.[21] Violent groups that form from within a slum do so in relation to relatively un-valuable or un-exportable services and commodities, and so are undercapitalized, often wanting of effective leadership and without strategic objectives or ideological emotive power as compared to outside groups.[22] This is, to a degree, self- evident, given that the more powerful external IAGs are able to venture into the slum from a distance precisely because of their relative power.[23]

The Illicit Land Uses Considered

1. **Taxation.** *Comuna 13* is for the most part a hilly borough comprised of 20 *barrios* or neighborhoods. Several of these are relatively more affluent than the rest. The owners and residents of lower-middle and middle-class apartments and condominiums suffered depredations from the near-by, up-hill and more lawless neighborhoods of the *Comuna*. Statistics compiled on market movement and rental values of properties over time show a clear pattern of value exhaustion as the more formal (usually downhill) properties suffered their proximity to the less formal areas.[24] Moreover, local real estate experts claim certain exceptions, such as property values in the immediate proximity of *moteles* (rent-by-the-hour trysting facilities especially popular in some Colombian cities). The exceptions can reflect the greater

disciplining capacity of outside IAGs, who are more likely to be financially or socially invested in moneymaking activities that attract monies from outside the *Comuna*. In the two or three years preceding Operation Orion, apartment vacancies rose in the *Comuna*, and many condo owners abandoned their real estate altogether or rented for almost nothing in order to have someone occupying them. Allegedly, many of the stay-behind individual renters in these fire-sale properties were agents of outside IAGs. In effect, residential and commercial real estate proximate to areas of organized criminal competition and territoriality is highly price-sensitive.[25]

For the autochthonous gangs, taxation will be a cruder form of protection racket than for the larger IAGs. The outsider gangs are likely to invite the local gangs either to participate directly with them or pay tribute. The squeeze is on when two competing outside gangs offer similar deals to the same local gang. The autochthonous gang is generally forced to decide for one outside IAG or another, and typically then becomes subject to proofs of loyalty that involve acting as the front-line troops for that IAG. An advantage that the local gang holds often comes in the form of personal relationships with local authorities, which offers the possibility of effectively informing on one of the outside gangs. The risk in this option often lies in the fact that the larger the outside gang, the greater the possibility that it has infiltrated the police apparatus to some degree.

2. **Illicit free trade**. As in many polities, legitimate government in Medellín looked at sinful behavior with an eye toward regulation, believing that a measured level of regulation could allow satisfaction of the basic demand and provide tax revenues while still limiting the exposure of protected classes (children) to the sin. For instance, rules were developed to regulate prostitution. Prostitution was legalized, while pimping (managing the commercial activities of a prostitute) remained illegal. All prostitutes had to have registered electronic accounts, and a great portion of the business went to a prepaid format in

which customers would buy pre-paid cards and all the money from the use of the cards would go to the registered accounts. As with most enterprises, regulation implies business costs, which are avoided by the business if possible. The measures tended mostly to separate economic classes of the prostitutes. Nevertheless, one clandestine activity leads to or attracts another. As the sale of drugs, drugs for guns, computer hacking etc., began finding space in or near *Comuna 13* (because formal law enforcement found it less and less possible to safely enter the borough), those activities also began to shadow, to some degree, the prostitution for reasons of money laundering, communications, etc. Still, gains by the police against the anonymity enjoyed by one form of criminal behavior were likely to break down the anonymity of other illicit activities. For the autochthonous groups the advantages of free trade are similar, but for goods and services of lesser value, if of greater immediate need, e.g., water, electricity. Some highly point-specific locations were identified as most coveted for predation, and so the real estate around these points became some of the most dangerous.

3. **Sanctuary**. Beyond free trade, outlaws need places to rest, recuperate, plan and heal. Distant rural areas present the same challenges of access and supply to the outlaw as they do to everyone else, so for some IAGs, having a closer-in urban harbor is a significant advantage. Yoni Rendón transmits the explanations of a reinserted *Comuna 13* youth who had belonged variously to a local gang, the Army, the ELN and later the ELN again. The young ELN guerrilla would typically transfer members wounded in combat, say, in the Catatumbo area near the Venezuelan border, to *Comuna 13* in Medellín for medical care and recovery. It is worth noting in regard to urban sanctuary that the seeming absence of some individuals in specific locations is as revealing for some intelligence purposes as is their presence. Because of the inconsistency between medical care and active defense, the ELN might feign absence from parts of the city.

Sanctuary for the autochthonous groups has a distinctly different calculus in that they are likely to enjoy the favor and protection of family, but this simultaneously makes many locations inapt as sanctuaries for the same obvious forensic reason.

4. **Clandestine manufacture or processing**. Counterfeiting CDs, money, tickets, ID cards, uniforms, keys, etc. is typical for some slum areas, including parts of *Comuna 13*. As the outside IAGs became customers, they all but invariably wanted to exclude other IAGs from a particularly lucrative, empowering, or protective activity, causing much of the cross-cutting and violence mentioned regarding free trade and taxation. As any process becomes more complex, such as counterfeiting IDs, which requires knowledge beyond the confines of the locality, outsiders are more likely to be seeking sanctuary inside the locale, rather than the local groups seeking larger markets.

5. **Staging for violent operations outside or on the fringes of the slum**. The FARC had long maintained a strategic vision that included an eventual urban offensive. In this context of the larger insurgent war, ideologically motivated and driven by large scale interpretations of national key terrain, some of the IAG activity in *Comuna 13* was prospective—in preparation to implement the call for sabotage, compartmentalization of streets, strangulation of official movement, and popular uprising that had long been made a staple of Latin American guerrilla design since outlined by Guevarra, Marighella and Debray.[26] Medellín, for its strategic location, economic significance, new-urban demographics, and its being a bastion of neoconservative and anticommunist thought, was always on the guerrillas' strategic short target list for eventual take over. Implantation of FARC cadres and solidarity-building within the peripheral slums seemed a necessary step, one the FARC attempted to accelerate in the 1990s. The FARCs advantage lay in its ability to maintain rural presence outside the city. The ELN also coveted urban space in Medellín, for compatible reasons, if with a more

regionalized emphasis: the strategic lines of communication for the ELN moved in part through Medellín northeast through what is known as the Medio Magdalena (middle reaches of the Magdalena Rive centering around Barrancabermeja) toward the border of Venezuela. Given the evident importance of Medellín to the guerrillas, the paramilitary AUC began to take a subsequent interest in control of the city's periphery. Major drug dealers became major land owners of mountain ranches and villas just uphill from the city.

Beneath the national strategic designs of the communist and anticommunist irregular armies, lesser IAGs found some neighborhoods in the *Comuna* to be ideal staging areas for out-of-borough predatory attacks in the more central parts of the city. Kidnappings, robberies, and even assassinations in service of the larger IAGs could best be conducted from the peripheries, often using motorcycle techniques, multiple taxi systems or other methods for efficient perpetration and then retreat to sanctuary.

6. **Safe transit of contraband**. An ancient rural trade route from Urabá Department and the border areas with Panama leads through Santa Fe de Antioquia (now a tourist center to Medellín's northwest), then passes through *Comuna 13* on the way into and through Medellín. There are several major routes in an out of Colombia, but this is one of the best for moving east to west. Because of the presence of many industrial and manufacturing enterprises in the Aburrá Valley, the movement of illicit drug precursors or war materiel enjoys natural concealment and ease of explanation. The local gangs only find this to be an advantage to the extent they can safely affect tolls for going through their territory. Depending on their ability and willingness to bring violent force to bear, they will share in the tolls, surrender an informal easement to the larger IAGs, join those IAGs, or be killed.

7. **Recruiting**. Recruiting assassins, hostage-takers, drug transporters, informants and messengers became widespread

in the *Comuna*. These jobs, however, were paid best and most quickly by the illicit drug dealing organizations. In the period of increasing violence during the two years before Operation Orion in October of 2002, the ELN and the FARC both conducted presence operations in *Comuna 13*. These followed a basic pattern of observation and identification of personality types suitable for a variety of missions, followed by selective threats and recruitments. The ELN, however, withdrew months before Operation Orion began. In part this was due to incipient armed confrontation between the FARC and the ELN, which the ELN felt it could ill afford to wage. It was more significantly due, according to evidence found in captured computer materials, to a determination by ELN leadership that the individual character of the recruitment-age males in the slums was unsuited to the revolutionary cause. The ELN had been spending resources in slum areas with the intention of recruiting revolutionaries, but seems to have found that, unlike many rural youths, the slum teen-agers were defiant, disrespectful, gratuitously violent, relatively lazy except to party hearty, and unimpressed by revolutionary arguments—especially when they did not include a distribution of booty. The male population at least had been infected by a drug and youth gang culture unsuited to the establishment revolutionaries.[27] Meanwhile, other agents found many young men perfectly suited to their business models. The FARC, for instance, had mastered outsourcing, especially for kidnapping and assassination. Moreover, the more vicious and entrepreneurial IAGs offered employment for very young males (eight or nine years-old to make deliveries and as outlooks) and for teen and preteen girls (mostly as informants, sexual servants or both).

8. **Storage and disposal of victims**. *Comuna 13* was used as a temporary holding location for kidnap victims and was ostensibly used as a disposal zone for corpses. The nature of this latter use is so controversial and emotionally and forensically sensitive that it cannot be described with any detail at this

point, and substantial use of the zone for this purpose has not yet be shown to a degree sufficient to move any prosecutions. However, it is clear that many bodies were dropped at the nearest hospital in San Lorenzo (one of the *comuna's barrios*), a few common graves were uncovered and anecdotal evidence suggests that more will eventually pop up.

Counter-IAG land-use response

A prevailing economic theory posits violence as a simple preference. Douglass North, in particular, outlined the idea of transaction costs as related to conflict.[28] People will resort to violence when the cost of so doing is perceived to be less than the cost of nonviolent transaction.[29] The land-use activities posited above each can be considered in light of the fact that nonviolent mechanisms for determining (especially among IAGs) who would enjoy unfettered and unsanctioned illicit land uses were often not available. Meanwhile, illicit land-use activities displayed specific architectural preferences, market evidence, legal quirks or deficiencies, or associated human habits signaling or canalizing the whereabouts of IAG perpetrators.[30]

The responses to illicit land use by the government in Medellín were, in great measure, land-use responses. The city administration decided to build a cable car (as an extension of the metropolitan public train system) that would open the neighborhood at depth. The administration created a planned neighborhood for new arrivals to the city that was separated from the older neighborhoods of the *Comuna*, thus taking pressure off small territorial conflicts. The city finished an auto tunnel that would shift and canalize licit traffic through the borough. It centralized and rationalized the registration of and payment for city services. It formalized all streets and addresses so that warrants could be legally served on the basis of an accurate census.[31] The payoff to government police and military comes in the form of forensic geography—profiling likely locations of IAG members at times when they can be apprehended or served process. Licit enterprises requiring legal land uses within the neighborhoods, especially those in formal tax compliance, are less likely to coexist in places subjected to IAG taxation. Correlations of real estate with active legal taxation and regulatory compliance, as well as the availability of land-use conflict resolution mechanisms, are themselves evidence geographically outlining the presence of internal and external IAGs.

While land-use categorization and mapping can reveal patterns and correlations useful to geographic profiling and other forensics, they can also form the basic information with which to build and maintain a peaceful social contract over the long-term. In *Comuna 13*, the government secured those points of land which had prompted the fiercest competition. The police built a fort in the most militarily dominant terrain within the *Comuna*, and the Colombian Army stationed detachments in various properties that had also been the most contended.

Government planners determined that certain acts of violence correlated to the absence of public utilities, as opposed to territorial fights over illicit trafficking routes. Partly on the basis of this analysis they were able to redirected or relocate some marginally licit activities, create and manage programs to keep children in school buildings, create safe places where residents could report evidence of strangers and criminal organizing, etc. Perhaps most intriguing, the government assured that streets were clearly named, addresses specific, residents registered by location and ownership rights formalized. Among other effects, this allowed legal searches and the presentation of valid arrest warrants. Today in 2011, *Comuna 13* has been suffering a moderate relapse into gang violence, although the leadership and membership has changed. That is to say, the land-use changes and analyses applied by Medellín do not address the whole challenge of urban peace. Medellín's government has proven that they help. The military and civilian decision in 2002 to take back, hold, and then build within *Comuna 13*, both in terms of physical infrastructure and governance, permanently changed the scale and nature of the security challenge.

Looking at IAG presence through the lens of land use can contribute positively to the construction of an urban counter-crime, counterinsurgency, and sustainable development method (probably in Geographic Information System (GIS) format). The government in Medellín had already been constructing its understanding of city management around land-use planning principles and the use of high-end GIS technologies. Success of the Colombian security forces in Medellin can be attributed, in part, to their acceptance and adoption of city planning language and method.

Notes

[1]   See generally, for instance, Philip Berke, et al, *Urban Land Use Planning, Fifth Edition* (Urbana: University of Illinois Press, 2006).

[2]   Ibid., p. 10.

[3]   A GIS-based urban field research effort was conducted in Medellín in 2008. Local researchers sought expanded methodological guidance, and, along with violent acts, land use became one conflict-related phenomenon the research attempted to map. Their research and mapping sought out other directions and phenomena as well, including, for instance, human fear. For a relevant bibliography on Medellín, see, David J. Keeling, *Bowman Expedition to Colombia*, The American Geographical Society, http://www.amergeog.org/bowman-colombia.htm.

[4]   Geographic Information Systems have become indispensable tools for accelerating geographic profiling, with the most important function of that profiling being prediction of the whereabouts of criminal perpetrators and their assets.

[5]   The search of control and speed human problem solving by aiding the processes of experience-based common sense is often called heuristics. We can say that geographic information science, with its relational databases and visual displays of spatial correlations, is a heuristic tool.

[6]   As a principal source of this hypothesis, see Ricardo Aricapa, *Comuna 13: crónica de una Guerra urbana* (Borough 13: chronicle of an urban war) (Medellín: University of Antioquia, 2005). Of

course, the assertion that autochthonous IAGs are less significant or dangerous than entities whose origins are from outside the slum may be overcome in a given case.

[7]   For instance, a group of Medellín entrepreneurs established a commercial airline in September, 1919. See Mauricio Savena B., "5 de diciembre de 1919': Se funda SCADTA" in Planeta, *50 días que cambiaron la historia de Colombia* (Bogotá: Planeta, 2004), pp. 163-166. Unfortunately for the Antioqueños, they had selected French Farmas made of wood and fabric, while their rivals, from what would become Avianca, chose the German metal Junkers. Avianca claims to be the second oldest surviving airline in the world after KLM.

[8]   "This advance led to the emergence of five new communities: La Independencia I, La Independencia II, La Independencia III, Nuevos Conquistadores, and a good part of El Salado, which in approximately five years accommodated more than five thousand families; at the time, the advance was worthy of being considered the most voracious invasion of Latin America, or rather the largest development in the least amount of time—more voracious than the slums of Mexico City and the favelas of Sao Paulo..." Aricapa, pp. 7-8.

[9]   Instituto Geográfico Agustín Codazzi, *Atlas de Colombia*, (Bogotá: Imprenta Nacional de Colombia, 2002) pp. 196-197.

[10]   For a thorough, if tendentious, statistical analysis in support of this assertion, see, Claudia López Hernández, ed., *Y refundaron la patria...De cómo mafiosos y politicos reconfiguraron el Estado colombiano* (And They Re-founded the Nation...How Mafiosos and Politicians Reconfigured the Colombian State) Most of this books' data comes from the Resource Center for the Analysis of Conflict, CERAC. See http://www.cerac.org.co/en/.

[11]   From author interviews with Colombian military personnel who wish to remain anonymous. To the author's knowledge, this is not a disputed assertion. See, Semana, "La primera batalla final," 10 November, 2003, *Semana*, http://www.semana.com/nacion/primera-batalla-final/74497-3.aspx.

118 *Small Wars Journal*

[12]   See, for instance, Ramiro Ceballos Melguizo, "The Evolution of Armed Conflict in Medellín: An Analysis of the Major Actors" Latin American Perspectives, Vol. 28, No. 1, *Colombia: The Forgotten War* (Jan., 2001), 110-131. "The Colombian State has neither the power nor the authority to settle social conflicts or enforce the law. It is obliged to negotiate its own sovereignty with the other, alternative powers." Ibid., p. 112.

[13]   See, Andres Pastrana, "Final Proceso de Paz-Alocución Presidencial-Febrero 20, 2002," *Vimeo*, http://vimeo.com/27208756.

[14]   Names of operations in order.

[15]   The argument or justification for Colombian vigilantism is encapsulated by the statements of Carlos Castaño, deceased leader of the AUC, in Mauricio Aranguren Molina, *Mi Confesión* (My Confession), (Bogotá: Oveja Negra: 2001). In synthesis, Castaño argues that the war has lasted 40 years because of corrupt governments who have been in a symbiotic relationship with the guerrillas to the benefit of a few and the expense of the majority. See p. 283, ibid.

[16]   See, for instance, Ramiro Ceballos Melguizo and Francine Cronshaw "The Evolution of Armed Conflict in Medellín: An Analysis of the Major Actors" *Latin American Perspectives*, Vol. 28, No. 1.

[17]   On the question of Colombian massacres see, Geoffrey Demarest, "Section 18: Massacres" in *Winning Insurgent War: Back to Basics* (Ft. Leavenworth: Foreign Military Studies Office, 2011), pp. 55-57.

[18]   That the decisions were 'natural' requires some additional argument, for which I depend generally on Robert Ardrey, *The Territorial Imperative: A Personal Inquiry into the Animal Origins of Property and Nations*. (New York: Antheneum, 1966).

[19]   See, Aricarpa, p. 10.

[20]   For a description of the evolution of Medellín IAGs, see generally Ceballos and Cronshaw, Ibid.

[21]   The term *ontogeny* is appropriate if the biological analogy is not overly pursued, but *suppuration* might be a better term yet.

[22]   These outside groups must be taken as collective *identities* rather than as stable organizational units (a given identity may or may not be stable as to membership) because service to, solidarity with or membership in an outside group may or may not include slum-originated individuals, and any individual associations may be part or full time.

[23]   Concomitantly, the degree of danger to the larger city and region outside the slum correlates to the out-sidedness of the IAG. That is to say, if the IAG identity is original to the greater metropolitan area, but not the slum, it will not be as dangerous to the surrounding city or to the nation as an outside-the-slum IAG original to another region, and less dangerous still than one with significant origins in another country.

[24]   See, La Lonja de propiedad raiz de Medellín y Antioquia, *Real Estate Consultancy Medellín Comuna 13*, (Medellín: La Lonja de propiedad raiz de Medellín y Antioquia, 2008).

[25]   While it is difficult to measure the illicit 'taxation' suffered by local residents in terms of its amount or frequency, criminal predation probably has a finely quantifiable effect on real property prices.

[26]   See, Brian Loveman and Thomas Davies, *Che Guevara Guerrilla Warfare*, (Lincoln: University of Nebraska Press, 1985), pp. 75-77 for a concise assertion regarding the urban insurgent sabotage mission, need to propagandize, and the normal vulnerability of the guerrilla in urban areas.

[27]   Perhaps the best Colombian book to deal directly with the nature of gang culture in Medellín is Alonso Salazar J., *No nacimos pa'semilla: La cultura de las bandas juveniles en Medellín* (We were not born to (sow) seeds: the culture of youth bands in Medellín) (Bogotá: Planeta, 2002); Also well-known and dealing directly with the violence in Medellín slums is Jose Alejandro Castaño, *Cuánto cuesta para matar a un hombre?: relatos reales de las comunas de Medellín* (How much does it cost to kill a man?: real stories from the slums of Medellín (Bogotá: Norma, 2006).

[28]   Douglass C. North & Robert Paul Thomas, *The Rise of the Western World, A New Economic History* (Cambridge: Cambridge

University Press, 1973); and *Structure and Change in Economic History*, New York: Norton, 1981. North asserts that peaceful transaction costs would be higher than violence if it were not for the invention of systems that encourage fulfillment of contractual obligations.

[29]　John R. Umbeck, *A Theory of Property Rights: With Application to the California Gold Rush* (Ames, Iowa: The Iowa State University Press, 1981). "No individual would be willing to accept a contract in which he was assigned property rights of less value than he could obtain by personal violence." Ibid, p. 9.; These theories are not incompatible with the body of political science theoretical writings on so-called war-economies. See, for instance Nazih Richani, "The Political Economy of Violence: The War-System in Colombia" *Journal of Interamerican Studies and World Affairs*," Vol. 39, No. 2 (Summer, 1997), pp. 37-81.

[30]　Recognition of the correlation between informal real property ownership and organized urban violence has been substantial in Colombian government and academe. See, for instance, Carlos Alberto Montoya C., "Ilegalidad de vivienda=limitación para el desarrollo urbana" (Illegality of residences equals limitation for urban development) in Presidencia de la República, *Medellín: Alternativas de Futuro* (Medellín: Consejería Presidencial para Medellín y su Area Metropolitana, 1992), pp. 287-290.

[31]　Ongoing *Comuna 13* research benefits from detailed daily logs of police and military activity during the pair of years before Operation Orion, as well as select information from interrogation and arrest reports. These and other data may expose physical, actuarial and psychological signatures of illicit slum land-uses.

Chapter 8

The Strategic Challenge of Riots: Riot Action and Crowd Power

John P. Sullivan and Adam Elkus

First Published 13 February 2012

Abstract: Are we entering an age of disorder? Recent events worldwide, and the continuing threat of global economic downturns, suggest the potential for large-scale civil disturbances. If so, public order maintenance and containing riots and disturbances will become key concerns as states and their security forces (the police and military) respond to an age of political and economic uncertainty. An operationally sound response to riots, mobs, and other forms of disorder has strategic implications for governments across the world. This essay looks at the dynamics of riots and order maintenance. We examine the politics of crowd power in a networked environment and suggest approaches to develop sound intelligence to understand the range of riot and crowd control issues that security services encounter in urban riot control. While the complex operations literature has understandably focused on overseas operations, domestic public order maintenance is an equally demanding undertaking with far-reaching political consequences. Operations must simultaneously prevent harm and disorder while avoiding provocation and respecting the right to voice dissent. Managing public order, in turn, requires an understanding of the nuances of crowds and mobs and the dynamics of domestic interagency coordination.

Economic turmoil, a lack of opportunity—perceived or actual—and the seeming emergence of a networked global protest movement suggest that police and military services need to prepare for a range of public order missions. As the London riots, growing "Occupy Wall Street" and "Indignados" movements suggest, disorder, protest, disturbances, and urban unrest are once again key security issues. During the Rome riots, cars were torched and banks and public buildings were attacked, demonstrating that economic populist movements connecting the "have-nots" or economically fragile can create a powerful backlash.

As the London and Rome riots so painfully demonstrate, mass social disturbances are not just a matter of policing or crowd control tactics. In his review of operational riot intelligence, Alex Calvo recently noted that the riots in London and other UK cities were punctuated with accounts of "flashpoints where the population was left unprotected in the face of what could be described as a combination of urban guerillas and occasional criminal insurgents."[1] Riots are a bridge between tactical disturbance and wider social unrest, with possible violent implications.

Government failure to correctly handle civil disturbances can have wide-ranging strategic consequences. The threat of violent crowds—whether mostly spontaneous or the result of deliberate provocation and instigation—is perhaps the oldest internal threat to organized governance. From the ancient world to the era of totalitarianism, intellectuals and politicians have feared the wrath of the crowd and placed a premium on restraining political and criminal mob violence. While the fundamentals of riot control—a firm hand that applies overwhelming yet proportional suppressive force at the outset of civil unrest—have not changed, the challenge of 21st century civil disturbances demand a more cohesive style of command. Key to riot suppression in future actions is the ability to organize tactical actions in time and space to accomplish strategic objectives.

Riots are neither purely "political" nor "criminal events." We are tempted to view them as either rebellions of the repressed or pure criminality. They arise from a complex array of motivations ranging from political grievance to pure boredom. Some mass social disturbances—like the perennial tendency of Los Angeles sports fans to riot after LA Lakers games—are completely criminal in nature and reflect the influence of strong drink rather than socioeconomic inequalities. Others, like the 1864 New York Draft Riots, are the violent outcome of larger political disturbances. Most riots are a combination of both "criminal" (profit and experience-seeking) and "political" (disputes over justice and power relations) causes.

Broadly "political" causes lie in the background of many riot situations. A recurring theme in mob violence is the struggle for political power. The Gracchi brothers, who tried to further the power of the Plebeians in ancient Rome, were murdered by armed mobs of aristocrats. The history of Italian city-states, particularly Machiavelli and Dante's home of Florence, is marked by internecine conflict and civil war. In Iraq, Muqtada al-Sadr and other local figures have been remarkably successful in instigating crowds of followers to engage in violent protests. Mobs—instigated by charismatic figures—are the oldest tool in organized politics for securing power and influence. Perhaps the most famous example of crowd power in literature is Shakespeare's rendition of Mark Anthony's funeral speech oration for Julius Caesar, which incites the mob to drive Gaius Brutus and his fellow conspirators from Rome.

United Nations peacekeeping and stabilization missions have also repeatedly dealt with crowds of militia and supporters of local warlords in many nations who aim to present them with the hard choice of using force—and hurting unarmed civilians—or ceding ground and possibly endangering their own lives. Such operations are made even more difficult by the intermixing of armed men with protesting civilians, and the presence of the mass media.

Deep political, ethnic, and economic divides have also historically sparked rioting. Ethnically inspired riots have been particularly pernicious, as communities have increasingly grown less ethnically homogenous. This is not to say, however, that they are always the product of "ancient hatreds." Many civil disturbances that are thought to be the product of spontaneous eruption of never-ending tribal hatreds are in fact the consequence of deliberate instigation by political elites seeking to manipulate existing prejudices for their own advantage or the actions of irregular groups fighting for larger political causes. This is not purely a modern issue, as the recurring horror of the blood libel in Europe over the centuries reflected deliberate instigation of mass violence against Jews. Conversely, not every riot has a clear point of origin. Academic research and practical experience has long shown that riots are a "tipping point" phenomenon. A small group of violent rioters is all that it takes to derail a peaceful protest and generate increasingly high-intensity property violence and motivate less politically motivated looters to take to the streets.[2]

The Range of Action: Typology of Disorder and Riots

Riots are complex events. Their complexity lies not only in the range of motivations, but the fact that riots—or violent outbursts of mass action—occur within a spectrum of crowd and mob activity resulting from a variety of underlying and proximate causes. This is further complicated by the fact that they are transient events that generally occur at low frequency making preparedness problematic for both political and security authorities. At the simplest level, riots can result from the spontaneous convergence of a number of contributory factors fueled by the acute interaction of precipitating events with a specific catalyst at a specific flashpoint. For example, protests (which are generally lawful and protected speech) can erupt into disorder when demonstrators are confronted by counterdemonstrations or unskilled police response (known as "police riot.) Another variation of spontaneous eruption is the case of "celebratory" sports riots. At the other end of the spectrum are organized, deliberate violent outbursts, such as football (soccer) hooliganism or orchestrated political violence. A variation that may fall into either spontaneous or orchestrated events is the "flash mob."

Crowds and Mobs

Different levels of mobs exist. At the highest end of the mob power spectrum are disorganized militia that cannot quite be called professional soldiers nor designated entirely civilians, who swarm with cheap weapons and even their bare hands. Perhaps the largest and most gruesome example of militia mobs is the 1994 Rwandan genocide, painstakingly organized by Hutu political elites. Historically, these riots require some level of organization or at least consistent political mobilization—especially if risk exists or the task is too large for spontaneous organization. Even so, political mobilization is no guarantee of effectiveness in the face of cold, hard, steel. Napoleon's famous "whiff of grapeshot" blew away political opponents that surely would have butchered him and the assembled Directory holding court at the Tuileries in 1795 if their fervor had not been met with overwhelming violence.

At the lowest end of the spectrum are rioters in major metropolitan cities, usually unarmed and mainly seeking to carry out opportunistic crimes to take advantage of the temporary lifting of domestic order. These riots are as much a product of rioters taking the path of least resistance—casually looting storefronts and avoiding police patrols as they scamper to bring their new high-def flat screens home—as strong and passionate rage.

A typology (or order of battle) describing the range of actors that may become involved in disorder and riots is useful. Crowds can be casual, cohesive, expressive or aggressive. Crowds can morph into mobs with the right catalyst(s). Mobs can be aggressive, expressive, acquisitive, or seek escape. All of these variations are possible in hybrid combinations.[3] A brief description of each crowd/mob variation follows:

Casual crowds are composed of individuals gathered in a common space with no common purpose; they have no emotional tie to the crowd. *Cohesive crowds* assemble for a common purpose such as a sports event or concert; members identify themselves as individuals but the collective can possess strong internal discipline and react with high levels of emotion. *Expressive crowds* gather for a unified purpose such as a demonstration or protest, they have common purpose and display of range of emotions. They can become frustrated and agitated and quickly erupt if frustrated or provoked. *Aggressive crowds* have a strong unity of purpose and a strong sense of group identity. They can be stimulated or provoked into destructive and lawless behavior. They are the most dangerous crowd form since they can transition into an aggressive mob.

Aggressive mobs engage in violent and lawless behavior. Violence is usually transient and can be directed against persons or property. These are primarily emotion-driven and can trigger sustained rioting. *Expressive mobs* view violence as a legitimate tool of rebellion, resistance, or protest. *Acquisitive mobs* seek to acquire something. They can be looters exploiting chaos or confusion. They have little emotional investment and can be controlled effectively be police intervention. The final mob type is the *escape mob*, or persons fleeing imminent danger. These are extremely difficult to control since they are sustained by fear.

Orchestrated Political Violence or the "Deadly Urban Riot"

Horowitz described a range of orchestrated political violence in his landmark work *The Deadly Urban Riot*.[4] These violent episodes are all characterized by selective targeting. They include: violent protests, pogroms, feuds, lynchings, genocides, terrorist attacks, gang assaults, and ethnic fights. They can be used individually or an in range of hybrids, such as the contemporary narco-blockades (or *narcobloqueos*) seen in Mexico's criminal insurgencies. The blogger Shlok Vaidya has also reported on *bandhs*, large-scale infrastructure disruption by crowds in India and their usage as a political tool.[5] The culmination of the orchestrated disorder is the deadly urban riot (or communal violence). These can be concentrated (occurring in a single location) or dispersed (occurring at multiple locations in a single neighborhood, city, or region, multiple cities or finally globally networked in multiple cities across multiple regions).

Networked Disorder

Contemporary disorder, protest, riots, and communal violence can be events can be focal, distributed, or networked. That is, they can occur in a range of settings due to advances in Internet Communications Technology (ICT). New media, such as social networking sites and tools allow mobs to coordinate and synchronized their actions.

ICT acts, in this context, as a force multiplier. As Jack McDonald notes, historically, one of the major advantages of the state was information dominance. The state and its bureaucracies used superior access to information as a tool to mass larger amounts of resources against its opponents. Politically "neutered" populations gradually ceded the ability to make violence to the state and its security services. Of course, this ability never really went away, but always lay dormant—contingent on perceptions of the state's power and legitimacy. The ability of individuals to organize themselves using person-to-person (P2P) technologies enhances the traditional small core of rioters always seen at the forefront of violent disturbances. The essence of flash-mobbing is the ability to create highly focused bursts of intense violence. This resulting "democratization" of violence allow a few people to turn a large city upside down.[6]

McDonald is also echoed by the netwar literature pioneered by John Arquilla and David Ronfeldt.[7] Perhaps the most important insight of the netwar literature is that riots and street revolutions are a product of diverse groups of actors—activists, opportunistic looters, anarchist "black bloc" members, and other networks—coalescing on a single spot. Indeed, in revolutionary "coup d'street" as the fabric of order and state dominance breaks down, direct action—whether for political purpose, criminal gain, or sheer boredom—becomes more viable. The implications of this convergence, as Bruce Crumley notes, is more violence spread around a larger geographic area and with actors not typically seen in the typical American and European riot experience, such as well-off students and professionals in addition to the stereotype of the typical aggrieved slum-dweller.[8]

Corresponding to the increasing diversity of actors and network mobilization is the rise of "global cities"—large, extended sprawl zones that serve as hubs of commerce and cultural relations, and their dark cousins, slum-cities, that expand large global sums to form large mega-cities of terrifying size and scale. As Sophie Body-Gendrot notes, these spaces and the economic and political mismatches they engender are flash rods for disruption.[9] The rise of "global cities" and "global slums" can result in networked diasporas of discontent that may fuel future riots and revolt.

However, the network form is not so much important in the case of mass social disturbances as the *tactical* dynamics of swarming and the stresses this places on police response. Police are good at responding tactically to individual threats, and if need be flooding an entire city with numbers if they can afford them. Yet high-impact violence geographically distributed across a large urban operational space—and in some cases several cities at once—imposes massive coordination costs on a threadbare command and control system optimized for dealing with one incident at a time. Police are spread thin, finding themselves unable to marshal enough force to deal with incidents that are concentrated in time rather than space. In the military, the art of using tactics to build a larger portrait that corresponds to the needs of strategy is the art of operations. Yet in the police sphere this understanding is sparse.

Operational Art for Public Order Management

The lack of appreciation and application of police operational art unfortunate, as riot response is one of the most important truly "operational" police situations. The defense of a large, complex capital city or urban center—such as London, the District of Columbia, or Los Angeles—bridges policy and strategy concerns with very minute and detailed tactical maneuvers and movements.

Police and emergency response to riots is truly a "whole of government" operation in miniature, requiring integration between political executives, the interagency community, and dispersed police commands struggling to concentrate their scattered sector-level concerns into a unified operational response. The function of operations are to make tactics achieve strategy, and serve as a kind of connective tissue binding purely spatial tactical actions into a coherent mass that serves an overall strategy of suppression. A large urban center and its peripheries (for large-scale, countrywide disorders), for police and paramilitary services, is essentially a theater of operation requiring the integration of theater strategy-like cognitive and planning devices.

The essence of containing a riot in progress is quick action to contain trouble spots before they metastasize, cancer-like, into greater dysfunction. As McDonald notes, in some ways the metaphor of putting out forest fires is very accurate. While this sounds simple enough in practice, there are a number of factors that can result in ruined cities and intense political blame games.

At the top level, strong political direction is needed to contain the situation. Policing—always a high-stress endeavor—is also an outgrowth of municipal (and the case of riots in capital cities, national) politics. In Los Angeles, the impact of the Rodney King beating induced excessive political caution that impeded the ability of the Los Angeles police department to train effectively for civil disturbances that might result afterwards and restrained police from deploying in strength during riot itself. Poor coordination and distrust between the mayor and the police chief also resulted in a confused and disaggregated planning and response.[10]

At the police executive level, systematic training and drills on both agency and multi-agency levels for civil disturbances and mass arrest situations are essential. Specific plans for civil unrest must be communicated, and the police executive must command in person. At the level of the emergency operations command, a breakdown in both the physical and human elements of command and control networks are often decisive as police commands find themselves isolated and overwhelmed by operational frictions. At the lowest level, proper personnel and equipment, logistical and technical support, and a willingness to engage emerging incidents are essential tactical elements of riot response.[11] During riot operations officers, without firm operational direction, revert to a reactive tactical mode. A lack of direction and coordination results in excessive force, poor discipline, tactical timidity in the face of danger, and poor force flow to trouble spots.

A key to operational response in riots is the civil equivalent all-arms capabilities. A major urban region hoping to quell a mass disturbance, like the Marine Air-Ground Task Force (MAGTF) must have all of the necessary assets necessary to carry out full-spectrum stabilization. Emergency response means far more than riot gear and mass arrests. Tactical medical response, fire control, aerial reconnaissance, and bomb squad and counter-explosive operations are only a sampling of the many functions that civil authorities must deal with in high-intensity riot situations. Obviously, the key to employing them is a resilient and effective organization and command and control organization.

In the United States, the Incident Command System (ICS) provides a standardized model of unity of command across organizations. Yet ICS alone is unlikely to provide the cohesion necessary to manage fluid incidents in time. One alternative—yet ICS-compatible—model of disaster response is the Emergent Multi-Organizational Networks (EMONs). Developed in the late 80s by Thomas Drabek, the concept calls for a temporary organization that can be scaled up and down as need be as disasters either expand or lessen. EMONs, while decentralized in execution, have a clear chain of command and delineated roles for multiple organizations. Former Los Angeles Sheriff's Department officer and police theorist Sid Heal would later use the EMON and the MAGTF concepts as the centerpiece for his police tactics book *Sound Doctrine*.[12] Organizations are also only as effective as their ability to manage situations in time, something that requires full-scale watch capabilities, particularly in collecting, analyzing, and disseminating tactical and operational intelligence in real-time.

Even more important than riot action is proactive policing. In a multicultural environment, a consistent effort to carry out effective community policing to develop a presence in communities regarded by police as "no-go" areas is necessary. The alternative model, a "raiding" concept in which police contact with locals consists mainly of sharp raids and gunfights followed by tactical withdrawal—does little and starves police of information and community knowledge necessary to quell riots. During tense incidents that have yet to erupt into force, overt show-of-force can actually be counterproductive compared to more dispersed patrolling and crowd control designed to quickly break up small disturbances and pre-empt large-scale disorder. Intelligence preparation for operations (IPO), a modified form of the military Intelligence Preparation of the Battlespace (IPB) concept also can help police pre-empt riots by making arrests, identifying likely causes of violence and instigators, and better positioning assets to make use of scarce resources before events.[13]

Intelligence Preparation (IPO) for Public Order

Intelligence to support counter-netwar activity (riots and networked swarming) requires active intelligence, as well as tactical and operational synchronization. Intelligence Preparation for Operations (IPO) can be a foundation of this needed situational understanding. Building from IPB's four steps: 1) Defining the Operational Environment, 2) Describing the Operational Environment, 3) Identifying and evaluating the threats, and 4) Developing Course of Action for Adversary, other threats, and non-aggressive groups, IPO seeks to identify the threat envelope in a dynamic fashion and craft corresponding courses of action to mitigate and resolve the disorder situation.

Specifically, active intelligence for addressing distributed riots requires an understanding of the geosocial construction of actors involved. This includes knowledge of the type of disturbance (focal, dispersed, networked), as well as insight into spatial dynamics (terrain)—both physical and in cyberspace—and crowd composition (crowd or mob typology). The density and complexity of urban terrain (physical and human) complicates this understanding making intelligence support critical to mission success. Specific intelligence requirements for public order events include:

- Spatial Dynamics
- Location(s)/Terrain
- Temporal Dimensions (Time/Duration; Day/Night)
- Crowd Size (number of persons)
- Crowd Composition (range of actors, violent/non-violent)
- Crowd Dynamics (type of crowd/mob; profiling key actors/ agitators; counterdemonstrations and factions)
- Media/Social Media Influences

Tactical and operational objectives include assessing the crowd/mob, containing and isolating disruptive activity, and dispersal of violent and unlawful actors. Tactically, this demands an assessment of alternative dispersal routes, knowledge of crowd composition and dynamics (including focal/convergence points and axis of crowd movement), and a description of closed areas. Crisis mapping, red teaming (alternative analysis), CyberInt (or cyber intelligence that gains understanding of social media), and an understanding of our own organizational capacities are needed to navigate the space of emerging disorder.

Conclusion: Avoiding Pathways to Failure

Civil disorder is fraught with complexity and misfortune. Dissecting failure also helps future operations by going beyond individual use of force to look at systemic failures. In this way, Eliot Cohen and Michael Gooch's concepts of military failure in *Military Misfortunes* can be usefully applied to the civil realm. Most studies of civil failure center around "simple failures"—individual failures to learn, adapt, or anticipate that are nevertheless survivable and in some cases are inherent to complex endeavors. Much more dangerous are aggregate failures— where a combination of two simple failures build up to something larger—or a catastrophic failure when three simple failures occur simultaneously or consecutively, leading to a complete organizational breakdown.[14]

Cohen and Gooch's critical failure methodology can be utilized to look at the 1992 Los Angeles riots. As seen in Los Angeles, a failure to learn, anticipate, and adapt coalesced to resulted in catastrophic failure. Crucial to understanding that breakdown was the dysfunction of command and control across all levels of command for the counter-riot response (*strategic*: political, police executive; *operational*: senior command, and *tactical*: field command). "[B]reakdowns at all levels, each compounded by lapses within each critical task [lead to the} ultimate outcome of catastrophic failure."[15]

Addressing complex civil disturbances, disorder, and riots is likely to be a staple of contemporary security operations (police, constabulary/gendarmerie, and military) operations globally for the foreseeable future. Negotiating this unstable civil environment will require an understanding of the dynamics of crowds and mobs in physical and cyber space to discern between constitutionally protected speech and dissent and unlawful mobs of many types. It can be anticipated that these dynamics will occur simultaneously demanding adept and adaptive operational responses and agile intelligence support over a broad area of (distributed) operations.

This portends many complicating factors. Most dangerous is complacency. Make no mistake—what occurred in London (and Rome) may happen in the US and elsewhere. What occurred in London is less the consequence of ethnic tension but a large-scale epidemic that struck even affluent districts.[16] The difference between local failure and catastrophic failure will be government response (including civil-military interoperations) and preparation by all echelons of political and civil order.

Notes

[1]   Alex Calvo, "London Riots: Decentralized Intelligence Collection and Analysis," *Small Wars Journal*, 09 August 2011 at http://smallwarsjournal.com/jrnl/art/london-riots -decentralized-intelligence-collection-and-analysis.

[2] Edward Glaeser, "How Riots Start, and How They Can Be Stopped," *Bloomberg News*, 12 August 2011, http://www.bloomberg.com/news/2011-08-12/how-riots-start-and-how-they-can-be-stopped-edward-glaeser.html.

[3] See Christopher Kozlow and John Sullivan, *Jane's Facility Security Handbook*, Alexandria: Jane's, 2000, 277-280.

[4] Donald L. Horowitz, *The Deadly Ethnic Riot*, Berkeley: University of California Press, 2003, *op cit.*

[5] Shlok Vaidya's reports can be found at the blog *India's Naxalite Rage*: http://naxaliterage.com/.

[6] Jack McDonald, "The Leviathan's New Clothes: Information and Power Relationships," *Kings of War*, 10 August 2011, http://kingsofwar.org.uk/2011/08/the-leviathans-new-clothes-information-and-power-relationships-by-jack-mcdonald/.

[7] John Arquilla and David Ronfeldt (eds), *Networks and Netwars: The Future of Terror, Crime, and Militancy*, Santa Monica: RAND, 2000.

[8] Bruce Crumley, "The Paris and London: A Tale of Two Cities," *Time*, 9 August 2011, http://globalspin.blogs.time.com/2011/08/09/the-riots-of-paris-and-london-a-tale-of-two-cities/.

[9] Sophie Body-Gendrot, "Disorder in World Cities: Comparing Britain and France," *OpenDemocracy*, 15 August 2011, http://www.opendemocracy.net/ourkingdom/sophie-body-gendrot/disorder-in-world-cities-comparing-britain-and-france.

[10] John P. Sullivan, "Critical Pathways: Responding to the 1992 Los Angeles Riot," *Journal of California Law Enforcement*, Vol. 30, No. 1, 1996, 14-18.

[11] Sullivan, ibid.

[12] Thomas E. Drabek, "Managing the Emergency Response." *Public Administration Review*, Vol. 45, 1985, 85-92 and Sid Heal, *Sound Doctrine: A Tactical Primer*, New York: Lantern Books, 2000, 41-51.

[13] John P. Sullivan, Hal Kempfer, and Jamison Jo Medby, "Understanding Consequences in Urban Operations," *On Point*, 2005. Available at http://www.riskintel.com/wpcontent/uploads/

downloads/2011/07/Understanding-Consequences-in-Urban-Operations.pdf.

[14]   Eliot A. Cohen and John Gooch, *Military Misfortunes: The Anatomy of Failure in War*, New York: Free Press, 1990.

[15]   Sullivan, "Critical Pathways: Responding to the 1992 Los Angeles Riot."

[16]   Crumley, ibid.

Chapter 9

Somalia 20 Years Later—Lessons Learned, Re-learned and Forgotten

Michael A. Marra and William G. Pierce

First Published 11 September 2013

Twenty years ago, on 3 October 1993, a desperate battle took place on the streets and in the air of the coastal city of Mogadishu, Somalia between American Soldiers and irregular militia from Clan of Mohamed Farrah Aideed from the Somali National Alliance (SNA). The battle, fought mostly within and above a single square mile of dense urban sprawl, would rage for nearly the entire day.

That fateful day would end with 17 Americans killed in action—two of which earned posthumous Medals of Honor, another 85 wounded some grievously, and an estimated 1,500 Somali casualties either killed, wounded captured or missing.[1] The battle epitomized the desperate struggle of modern urban warfare in tribal terrain— negating many of the advantages that technology usually offers the better equipped force, and drove small groups of fighters on both sides into desperate hand-to-hand combat that U.S. troops had not experienced in several decades. This was a tactical engagement to be sure, but the strategic implications of this comparatively minor battle reverberated around the world and are still evident in our psyche and policies today, 20 years later.

Like so many epic battles though history, this was a tactical event with strategic effects due to the advent of "instant access" via the new 24/7 news broadcasts. In 1993, at the leading edge of the Information Age, the era of the video camera on the battlefield had come to full-maturity and the means to capture moving battlefield images and project them worldwide through new, never-ending "24/7" news media had permanently arrived. The Persian Gulf War of 1991 had raised the standard of information-sharing, and now Mogadishu became the event de jure for audiences conditioned for constant stimulation from wartime venues. The entire world was captivated by horrific scenes of dead United States soldiers being dragged through the streets of Mogadishu by cheering, wild Somali mobs around them, seemingly celebrating the battle—as if killing any U.S. Soldier constituted victory.

In fact, the special operations mission that day had technically succeeded. The U.S. led force captured twenty-four key planners and operators in the Somali National Alliance (SNA) and inflicted significant damage on Aideed's forces. Unfortunately, the military success was a Pyrrhic Victory, and world opinion viewed this operation as a clear U.S. failure—not just in the battle, but ostensibly for the entire effort in Somalia.

Worldwide audiences did not concern themselves with the tactical military implications of the battle and who was captured or even to the damage suffered by the Somali irregulars. The prevailing narrative only focused on the Americans, fresh off of an overwhelming victory in the 1991 Persian Gulf War, being humiliated and overcome by mobs of lightly armed militia. This militia used human wave tactics and the knowledge of their city as an advantage to kill or capture as many as soldiers as possible, and then gleefully celebrated over their stripped and mutilated corpses of U.S. personnel. To say this was shocking to the world, the U.S. population, and the U.S. military would be a vast understatement. It was an event-horizon that ushered in a turning point for the way national security professionals viewed complex catastrophes where the worst of nature and mankind intersected to create a miasma of misery, destruction, and death.

So, what happened in Somalia 20 years ago and why does it matter today? How did a mission with such good, humanitarian intentions reflecting the very best of American values of helping a struggling nation and feeding a population about to starve to death devolve into a merciless bloody street fight that set new levels of ferocity, intensity and outright ruthlessness? What changed in the environment there and what produced the spark that lit the proverbial powder-keg of hostility in that city? Why does Somalia still serve as an example to represent the very best of our intentions but the very worst of our arrogance?

Somali Child, Mogadishu, 1993—Credit Defense Visual Information Center

The purpose of this paper is to reflect on the events surrounding the U.S. involvement in Somalia 20 years ago and learn from it as U.S. national security professionals ponder intervention in a myriad of similar locations today. It is a chance to review the paradoxical nature of this conflict that fundamentally changed the way the U.S. would view involvement in complex catastrophes, and how the same conflict, seen through the eyes of U.S. adversaries and rivals, provided different set of lessons. The paper will briefly describe the situation in Somalia, outline the history leading up to U.S. involvement in relief operations in the early 1990's, describe what went right, what went terribly wrong, what the U.S. military learned, and perhaps what it has already forgotten when pondering military intervention in contemporary complex catastrophes.

Prior to 3 October 1993, national security professionals would use the moniker of "Desert One" to describe a kind of military misfortune that degenerated into a major strategic political and diplomatic failure. This phrase originates from the ill-fated 1979 attempt by U.S. military forces to rescue U.S. hostages held in Iran.[2] The force sent to accomplish the mission experienced a major mishap in the desert outside Tehran resulting in multiple U.S. deaths, the destruction of aircraft, and the abandonment and cancellation of the mission.[3] The reverberations from this failure were enormous, with many believing this singular event cost President Jimmy Carter his Presidency. Upon investigation, the causes of the disaster were many, and the aftereffects of this disaster directly lead to many changes in the way the U.S. military trains, organizes, and fights. Some would go as far to say it made Goldwater Nichols Act (The Department of Defense Reorganization Act of 1986) possible.[4] The Act lead to the establishment of the Special Operations Command and many other changes in the way the U.S. employs forces worldwide.

After 3 October 1993, the new parlance for a military disaster of this magnitude with comparable strategic effects was called a "Black Hawk Down" event, describing the lexicon used during the battle for multiple UH-60 helicopters shot down by simple rocket propelled grenades fired from rooftops by Somali irregulars. The term "Black Hawk Down" was introduced to our lexicon through a major series of riveting newspaper articles written by Mark Bowden in the Philadelphia Enquirer which later became a book by that the name Black Hawk Down: A Story of Modern War, which was published in 1999 by the same author.[5] Later, in 2001, a major motion picture directed by Ridley Scott, "Black Hawk Down," won multiple awards.[6] More recently, during the U.S. raid on Osama Bin Laden, when an American assault helicopter experienced a mishap and crashed, the flashbacks of Mogadishu rapidly resurfaced and the term "Black Hawk Down" was euphemistically used by national security personnel to exclaim what was happening during the early stages of the raid.[7]

Somalia Today...

Somalia today is a failed state by nearly every measure. In fact, it is ranked number one on the Foreign Policy Failed States Index for 2012 and has held the top spot since 2008. The Index is the eighth annual collaboration between Foreign Policy and the Fund for Peace where Somalia has far outdistancing Iraq, Afghanistan, Sudan, and Chad.[8] Government is fractured, economy is in shambles, the infrastructure is in serious decay, and there is no rule of law. It is a hotbed of piracy and illegal trafficking, and even Al Qaeda finds it to be a rough neighborhood to establish a base.[9] The last best hope for Somali ended with the withdrawal of American forces after the Battle of Mogadishu. The next section will describe the events that precipitated this disaster.

Background—A Brief History of U.S. Involvement

Many books, monographs and articles have already been written about this effort, which will not be replicated here, but a brief overview to provide some background and context against the thesis of this piece is in order to understand what occurred and why. Like many military operations that start with one set of intentions and devolve or "creep" into others, the operations in Somalia went through three different and distinct phases over the years 1992 to 1995:

Airlift to Mogadishu, Somalia—Credit Mike Marra, 1993

- An airlift that provided food relief and medical supplies to a multitude of sick, starving people;
- An intervention force that combined continued humanitarian assistance activities with military operations meant to provide better security for relief efforts; and
- A military force that provided the bulk of the combat power for the first "peace enforcement" operation in the history of the United Nations.[10]

CJCS GEN John Shalikashvili with Army and
U.N. Peacekeepers, Somalia, 1992—
Credit Defense Visual Information Center

Along with these phases came different names of the Operation which tried to emphasize different lines of effort:

- United Nations Operation in Somalia I (UNOSOM I), April-December 1992, which tried to reconcile warring Somali factions but collapsed from bureaucratic infighting and an inability to provide safety and security for relief operations;
- United Nations Task Force (UNITAF) December 1992—April 1993, a multinational force approved by the United Nations and led by the United States, which quickly provided that safety, started a low-key political process, and maintained working relationships with all Somali factions and groups;

- United Nations Operation in Somalia II (UNOSOM II), May 1993—March 1995, the U.N.-led operation that comprised an overreaching, "nation-building" phase (May-October 1993) and a scaled-back, accommodative phase (November 1993—March 1995) triggered by the October 3, 1993, firefight in Mogadishu, the departure of the preponderance of U.S. forces in March of 1994, and total withdrawal of UN forces by 1995.

In addition to underlining the complexity of peace operations, these three distinct phases show that, as the level of conflict intensified, some things changed more than others. The specific mission elements examined here also provide a sobering glimpse of the challenges associated with efforts to stabilize a country in chaos, where the effects of by clan warfare and the absence of government were exacerbated by the harsh natural environment. Although drought conditions were partially responsible for this situation, civil war had devastated this already threatened country. Since 1988, this civil war had centered on more than fourteen clans and factions that made up Somali society, all of which fought for control of their own territory.[11]

The Somali culture, which the U.S. barely understood at the time, stressed the idea of "me and my clan against all outsiders," with alliances between clans being only temporary conveniences. Guns and aggressiveness, including the willingness to accept high casualties, were intrinsic parts of this culture, with women and children considered part of the clan's order of battle. (This later became painfully evident when Somali irregulars used women and children as "human shields" against Pakistani UN Peacekeepers, resulting in the death of 39 Pakistani Soldiers.)[12] This hostile environment was further fueled by a plentiful supply of individual and heavy weapons left over from Somalia's changing alignments during the Cold War. These weapons found their way from government control to clan armories and individuals.[13]

After the fall of the Siad Barre regime in 1991, the political situation deteriorated, with the clans in the northern part of the country trying to secede. With continuing drought conditions coupled with the already inadequate food situation, clan warfare and banditry gradually spread throughout Somalia. By early 1992, these conditions brought about a famine of Biblical proportions: more than 500,000 Somalis had perished of starvation and at least a million more were facing the same fate.[14] "Somalia" had become a pejorative expression for disaster rather than for a geographical location, nation or country. The technologies associated with the information age beamed scenes of starvation and death, orphans clinging to dead parents, and overall chaos around the world daily. The scale of the human suffering in Somalia had, by 1992, captured the attention of the international community and the President of the United States.[15]

U.N. Convoy, Somalia, 1994—Credit Mike Marra

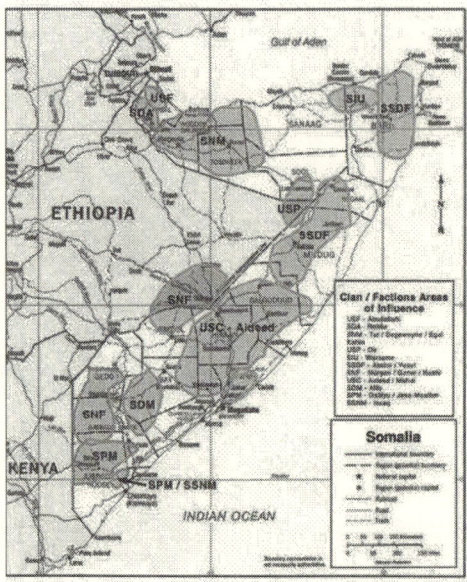

Somali Clan Territories, 1993—Credit U.S. Defense Mapping Agency

The initial U.N. intervention transformed Somalia from a famine-stricken disaster area where brutal warlords and khat-intoxicated gangs ruled over helpless innocents, into a test-bed for new theories of "world order," U.N. peacekeeping, and NGO cooperation. Perhaps, ironically, the impressive leadership, coherence, and dramatic success of the U.S.-led UNITAF phase made it look too easy, facilitating the "mission creep" that produced UNOSOM II's vast nation-building mandate. The sheer ease of intervention, combined with the mastery with which it was initially conducted in Washington and in the field, helped produce the slide toward a modern version of trusteeship over an ex-colonial territory, triggering a violent backlash mounted by a powerful Somali faction.[16]

But the goodness was not to last. Within months the situation deteriorated rapidly into ever escalating violence and disorder climaxing in the Battle of Mogadishu on 3 Oct 1993. Now, 20 years later, it is time to reflect on that painful experience, to learn from it and make better informed decisions to address contemporary situations where military intervention remains a strategic option. Each conflict through history is different, and it is very easy to misapply lessons learned from event to event. Still, there are valuable lessons to be learned which could illuminate some of the unintended consequences of future interventions.

What went right?

The intervention saved lives and helped avoid continuing famine. Tons of food and medical supplies arrived from around the globe, and human capital was infused into a dying nation not a moment too soon, resulting in perhaps hundreds of thousands of lives saved. The specter of mass starvation was checked through U.S. military logistics capability honed in the Gulf War. The combined logistical genius of the U.S. and coalition forces deftly used Air, Land and Seapower to synchronize and harmonize aid from all over the world. Although there were only a few viable air and sea ports and unimproved roads to set up key distribution points, the coalition was able to rapidly deliver aid to the people who needed it desperately. This was a marvel akin to the Berlin Airlift in 1947, where combined military forces saved Berlin through the air with enormous political implications. While the political stakes were not analogous to the situation in Somalia, the many lives saved by effective military capability were obvious. How large a tragedy the intervention prevented is impossible to know, but, judging by the Somali death toll of 1992, one could reasonably estimate that the intervention saved upwards of 500,000 Somali lives. The intervention in Somalia was not a failure as measured by the standards first set by President Bush in avoiding a lethal famine.

Food Arriving the Mogadishu Airport, 1993—
Credit Defense Visual Information Center

The United States effectively shaped a unified effort with a willing coalition. Fresh off the stunning coalition victory in the Gulf War, the United States parlayed that political capital into a true coalition of capable nations who delivered aid and provided security under the flag of the United Nations. Unlike the formation of most coalitions, this one was comparatively easy to form based on the positive relations developed during 1990-91 Operation Desert Storm. The U.S. had the prestige and gravitas as a world leader in a "New World Order" and Somalia would be one of the first test-cases. There have been approximately 60 officially sanctioned United Nations "peacekeeping" operations since 1948, illustrating how difficult this is to achieve.[17] Operation Restore Hope was an act of human solidarity without regard to race, religion, or region. That is why the Congress and the American people supported it—just as they supported the 1991 effort to protect Iraqi Kurds and many other such operations where there was no direct correlation to core national interests.

U.S. Army M1A1 Tank, Somalia, 1994—Credit Mike Marra

The United States military worked well with Non-Governmental Organizations vis-a-vis cooperation, information, security and the building of genuine trust. While not initially the case due to the strong emphasis on combat operations in Desert Storm, coalition forces rapidly learned to cooperate with many NGO's and learned where the humanitarian needs were the most compelling rather than simply taking the word of pseudo-officials from the failed Somali government. This resulted in more effective and efficient aid distribution. Similarly, by providing protection and security, the NGO's were able to do much more good than ever before when various rival groups would "use" their services as bargaining-chits for political power and influence in given regions.[18] These NGO's firmly believed local Somalis had to be part of the solution and be seen as "in the lead" in rebuilding their nation—a critical optic for a nation in need of a unifying belief that they could help themselves. The Somali people are proud, strong and generally self-reliant. They did not wish to become a "donor state" and by leveraging their local leadership as opposed to national leadership or clan leadership, they realized modest successes. This success in Somalia was to be replicated many times over following this operation.

While the Somalia intervention was not all bad news, national security professionals must examine the negative aspects of the operation if they are to critically think through what happened to avoid future pitfalls in responding to complex catastrophes in the future. While many other papers outline the operational and tactical details, the following strategic shortfalls are not so obvious.

Somali policeman, Mogadishu, Somalia, 1994—Credit Mike Marra

What went wrong?

Faulty Assumptions. The U.S. deployed believing this was a peacekeeping mission, but in fact, there really was no peace to keep. It has to be imposed on the warring factions. Dag Hammarskjöld, Former UN Secretary-General *once said, "Peacekeeping is not a job for soldiers, but only soldiers can do it."* While coalition presence had an immediate positive effect on the entire situation, this respect and admiration was not to last long. U.S. and other coalition forces continued to be challenged to the point of outright confrontation often ending in violence and bloodshed, thereby escalating hostility amongst the populace. The American belief was that if it is there to help, then surely the population would be happy to see the U.S. and cooperate. This was not an accurate or realistic assessment of the situation, as many warlords were already clashing. The famine was simply just another context to operate within, and for some factions, conflict offered opportunities for competitive advantages for political power. When the U.S. arrived and started re-distributing food, the new "coin of the realm," it changed many competitive advantages and resulted in anger, distrust, and acrimony within the society the coalition was trying to help.

Unrealistic Time Horizons. The U.S. and the UN had a very optimistic idea of what it would take to get Somalia back to a place where it could function without being on international life-support. The pace of such an operation must match that of the culture or it is hampered by constant friction and frustration—and this is where the time horizons diverged. Coalition forces wanted change and reformation in Somalia much more than did the Somali's, which created one of the core issues of conflict and tension. While the U.S. saw a hierarchical system of governance which drove subsequent distribution of aid assets, the existing system was actually tribal and worked on a completely different system of "...who got what—where, where and how." U.S. domestic timelines that revolved around elections and other political agendas should have been set aside, but the political aspects of any conflict nearly always rule, and Somalia in 1993 was no exception.

Strategy/Resources Mismatch. In reflecting on the mission to Somalia, General Freeman, who had been involved extensively in U.S. Central Command's planning for Operation Restore Hope, stressed "interests, ends, means, all three have to be in balance" in any future intervention of this type. The U.S. never balanced resources to execute the strategy in Somalia. Because no feasible end-state was ever articulated by the U.S., the efforts were not synchronized toward any clear goal, but rather a nebulous and ambiguous state where the situation was "normalized." In a nation where there is no "normal" but varying levels of chaos, the goal moved and shifted until the coalition could achieve a minimum acceptable level of stability. While the UN Security Council was interested in helping Somalia climb out of its abyss, it never gave commensurate resources to UNOSOM II to accomplish the mission. "This was the huge frustration we had out in the field," claimed one participant. "'Give us the tools,' we cried. And it wasn't that I wasn't asking for them constantly." With regard to military input at the national level, General Montgomery, the commander of U.S. forces added: "I think it is the responsibility of senior military people to tell the policy level what it is they need in terms of military means to do the job and not to try and pre-guess what will fly politically or not. You need to say, 'Here's what we need to do the job.' And let them say yes or no before you start deciding what might fly politically."[19]

Knowing what went right and wrong in the U.S. intervention in Somalia is important. The more difficult and subjective analysis must take place to enable the artful application of lessons learned for contemporary situations where a myriad of issues will be different, but the core issue of addressing a complex catastrophe at the strategic level will remain constant.

Egyptian Peacekeepers in Somalia, 1992—Credit
Defense Visual Information Center

Lessons Learned

Environmental framing can never stop. Whenever the U.S. or a coalition deploys forces into a third country, the environment changes, driving new assessments and iterative approaches to framing the environment, defining the problem, and devising various approaches or strategic options. This lesson is now being addressed by U.S. military doctrine and in professional military education at all levels.

Security works hand in hand with development and diplomacy but has to come first and foremost in contested and austere environments. This security, defined by a belief that one could exist in the society without fear of personal harm, or fear of being relived of all possessions is essential and imperative. Security was essential in order to control the mostly ungoverned area long enough to establish some order which in turn enables development of stable institutions of governance and infrastructure. At a minimum, the objective has to be the establishment of a responsible state entity that can ensure the well-being and safety of its people.

Military Interventions Change the Existing Balance of Power. This lesson of Somalia may be the most humbling to those countries capable of providing humanitarian assistance like the United States. Despite good intentions, the environment will change with the introduction of military power. Just as humanitarian relief may temporarily disrupt a local economy, changing the stakes of conflict and even, perversely, fueling it; military intervention may alter the regional and local balance of power. The effort in Somalia was a painful example of this axiom. The UN coalition's presence temporarily strengthened Somalia's vestigial civil society and challenged the warlords' political monopoly. By freezing in place the factional strife, it also checked the stronger factions and protected the weaker ones. Thus, the die was cast for a showdown on 3 October 1993 in the streets of Mogadishu. The strategist looking at the next intervention must have a viable follow-on to military intervention which will lead to a peaceful transition to civil authority, lest they be deployed there into perpetuity.

U.N. Convoy About to Depart Mogadishu Airport, 1994—Credit Mike Marra

The United States was not the only nation to learn from Somalia. Many adversaries and potential challengers saw the operation as exposing some vulnerabilities of the "…World's only superpower," as America was labeled in the 1990's. Several of these perceptions still exist as evident by U.S. enemies' strategies and tactics against throughout the conflicts in Iraq, Afghanistan and elsewhere.

What U.S. Adversaries Perceived

The world saw the U.S. rapidly withdraw from Somalia after the Battle of Mogadishu based on a high casualty count. While there was a "plus up" of forces in the region directly afterward, including more Air, Land, and Seapower assets, the die had been cast for a complete withdrawal by March of 1994 Statements made by President William J. Clinton after the battle tried to placate American dismay over the sordid and tragic images and narrative of the Somalia mission gone bad. Potential U.S. adversaries left with the perceptions that America would fight for many things, but would not die for seemingly peripheral causes, and that inflicting casualties and making those losses public was a strategy to erode U.S. will leading to U.S. disengagement.

Adversaries saw the U.N. as a viable place to dialog and joust diplomatically, but as a weak and ineffective organization for running military operations. The U.N. military effort was often fragmented on policies, rules of engagement, doctrine, equipment and overall capability. While this is not different from other U.N. actions, Somalia perhaps reached a new low in cooperation. After Somalia, opponents of the U.N. concepts of statehood and rule of law were emboldened to do as they pleased, as the U.S. saw in the Balkans in Srebrenica. There, U.N. forces were disarmed without a struggle, and genocidal atrocities continued unabated. These actions clearly underscored the lack of fear and respect for these peacekeeping forces.

There is no such thing as a purely humanitarian operation when the military is involved. The operation in Somalia calls attention to the question of how humanitarian intervention can evolve into a long-term stability as opposed to simply addressing symptoms of a problem. The Bush and Clinton administrations insisted on a quick handoff to the U.N. It is hard to escape the conclusion that an appeal for outside force must be accompanied by a political strategy for the nation and for the region before committing military forces. As Chester Crocker put it, "...unleashing the dogs of war while healing the wounds of war."[20]

USMC Cobra Attack Helicopter, Mogadishu Airport, 1994—Credit Mike Marra

After Somalia, the U.S. had another opportunity to act in Rwanda in 1994, but decided not to deploy forces, due in large part from the ghosts of Mogadishu. Those seeking power through force in countries around the world were embolden to act, knowing that the absence of the bi-polar balance left a security vacuum in many regions that would go unfilled with the lack of Cold-War competition for access and influence.

Today the U.S. is poised to act to similar crises around the globe. The clarion-call for intervention comes in many forms and in many places too numerous to list here, but there is continuous pressure on any U.S. President to act under a new concept called Responsibility to Protect, or "R2P" for short.[21] Secretary of State Madeline Albright championed this concept. But, before the U.S. heeds her advice and others like Senator John McCain, who has vociferously advocated "doing something" in Syria, the U.S. leadership should consider these seemingly forgotten lessons from Somalia.

Lessons Forgotten

Strategy formulation. As a nation, no operational or tactical events are powerful enough to overcome a lack of comprehensive strategy for a situation, nation, or region. As the U.S. deployed into Somalia in 1992, not enough strategists put thought into "...and then what?" There was little talk of the Horn of Africa as a whole, but only of ameliorating the famine in Somalia itself and making those images of starvation go away. This lack of a regional approach is sometimes seen today, as in Syria, Egypt, Afghanistan, and in other areas where "fixing" a singular nation is clearly not the total answer. An end-state with a realistic transition into the future must be designed from the start.

LtGen Anthony Zinni, USMC with Maj Michael McDaniel, USAF, Somalia, 1993— Credit Defense Visual Information Center

The value and utility of Landpower. If the U.S. really wants to affect what is happening on the ground in any nation during a complex catastrophe, it will take "boots on the ground." This is the one thing most politicians seek to avoid when edging near military action and seeking popular approval. There are times when ground forces are not appropriate, but immediately ruling them out far in advance of any intervention is generally ill-advised. While the U.S. has developed strong anti-bodies to this type commitment over the last decade, it simply can't be ruled out from the start as a strategic option lest we severely limit our military options and provide any adversary with one less set of challenges to confront.

Shaping vs. reacting. As the U.S. has learned, re-learned and forgotten many times, it is much more costly to do consequence management than it is to do prevention or pre-emption in these predictable catastrophe situations. Waiting until a nation utterly fails and falls into chaos before acting is far more difficult, dangerous, and costly. The geographic combatant commands and their functional components know and understand this, and work closely with Dept of State and U.S. AID experts to preclude these from becoming far worse than if left unattended.

The 3D approach. The "military-only solution" is not and should not be the first and only tool the U.S. leadership reaches for in a catastrophe. Any strategic option the U.S. considers should be a blend of "diplomacy, development and defense," as complex catastrophes are rarely solved by just one element of power.

Conclusion and a Warning for the Future of Intervention

President Kennedy once commented, "Success has a thousand fathers, but failure is the orphan child."[22] No military organization celebrates or enjoys recalling catastrophe or operational failure. For U.S. military forces, Somalia was both humiliating and costly. But, failures are often the situations where a nation or organization can learn the very most, as the cost in blood and treasure is both deep and impressionable.

President Clinton Awards Medals of Honor to the Wives of U.S. Army SFC Shughart and MSGT Gordon—Credit Defense Visual Information Center

Lieutenant General Thomas M. Montgomery, U.S. Army, who served concurrently as Commander of U.S. Forces in Somalia and Deputy Commander of United Nations Forces in Somalia (UNOSOM II) from March 9, 1993 to March 28, 1994, and then as Commander of the Joint Task Force in Somalia during his final four months there captured this best: In the United States, the aftermath of the operational failures in Somalia, has haunted U.S. foreign policy to this day. And if you're reading the press on Afghanistan and Iraq, the ghost of Mogadishu on 3 October 1993 looms very large even today. It certainly looms large in the minds of many of our soldiers in the field. The fact that potential lessons from Somalia have not been shared widely was an explicit concern for many who realized that complex contingencies and failed states have great salience today. Having lived through the dark and brutal night depicted in Black Hawk Down, the veterans of Somalia wanted their experiences disseminated to avoid the need for young Americans in the future to relearn them the hard way—on the battlefield.[23]

Notes

[1]   Richard W. Stewart, PhD, "The US Army in Somalia," The Army Center for Military History, December 2002, Printed by AUSA, p. 19.

[2]   Mark Bowden, "The Desert One Debacle," The Atlantic, May 2006, p. 1.

[3]   Ibid., p. 5.

[4]   Goldwater-Nichols Act of 1986, US Code, Cornell University Law School web page. http://www.law.cornell.edu/uscode/text.

[5]   Mark Bowden, *Black Hawk Down: A Story of Modern War.* Atlantic Monthly Press. Berkeley, California (USA). (March 1999).

[6]   Ridley Scott, *Black Hawk Down*, the film, Columbia Pictures, (18 Jan 2002), 144 minutes, based on *Black Hawk Down: A Story of Modern War,* by Mark Bowden (March 1999).

[7]   Mark Bowden, "The Finish: The Killing of Osama Bin Laden," 19 Oct 2012 *New York Times*, Sunday Book Review.

[8]   Failed State Index for 2012, *Foreign Policy*, Sunday, 1 Sep 2013, page 1. http://www.foreignpolicy.com/failed_states_index_2012_interactive.

[9]   Hassan M. Abukar, "The Letters, How Al Qaeda Failed in Mali and Somalia," April 18, 2013, Copyright http://www.wardheernews.com/the-letters-how-al-qaeda-failed-in-mali-and-somalia/© 2013 Wardheer News, all rights reserved.

[10]   Kenneth Allard, PhD, COL, USA *Somalia, Lessons Learned*, CCRP Publication Series Univ Pr of the Pacific (April 2002), Introduction, page xvii.

[11]   Chester A. Crocker, "Ambush in Mogadishu, Not Everything Went Wrong," *Foreign Affairs*, May-June 1995, Vol. 74, number 3, 1995, Copyright 1995 by the Council on Foreign Relations, 1995, page 1. http://www.pbs.org/wgbh/pages/frontline/shows/ambush/readings/lessons.html.

[12]   Pakistan Army Report, report of 39 fatalities during UNOSOM I and II, 1993 to 1995, Pakistan Army Web Portal, 2009-2013 http://www.pakistanarmy.gov.pk/AWPReview/TextContent.aspx?pId=57.

[13]   Clayton K.S. Chun, *Gothic Serpent*, 2012, Osprey Publishing, Long Island, NY, p. 4.

[14]   Col Dennis P. Mroczkowski, USMC, *Restoring Hope—in Somalia with the Unified Task Force,* History Division, USMC, Wash, DC, 2005, page 7-8.

[15]   Chun, *Gothic Serpent*, page 6-7.

[16]   Walter S. Poole, *The Effort to Save Somalia, Aug 1992 - March 1994*, Joint History Office, Office of the Joint Chiefs of Staff, Wash, DC Aug 2005, pages 23-26.

[17]   United Nations Official Web Site—list of Peacekeeping Operations since 1948; http://www.un.org/en/ and http://www.un.org/en/peacekeeping/documents/operationslist.pdf.

[18]   Allard, *Somalia, Lessons Learned*, pages 59-60.

[19]   Lieutenant Colonel Frank G. Hoffman, U.S. Marine Corps Reserve (Retired), "One Decade Later—Debacle in Somalia," *Proceedings*, January 2004, pages 1-3, http://www.military.com/Content/MoreContent1?file=NI_Somalia_0104.

[20]   Crocker, *Foreign Affairs*, page 3. http://www.pbs.org/wgbh/pages/frontline/shows/ambush/readings/lessons.html.

[21]   *The Responsibility to Protect*; Report of the International Commission on Intervention and State Sovereignty, Published by the International Development Research Centre, PO Box 8500, Ottawa, ON, Canada K1G 3H9, http://www.idrc.ca. © Her Majesty the Queen in Right of Canada 2001, as represented by the Minister of Foreign Affairs, National Library of Canada, International Commission on Intervention and State Sovereignty.

[22]   J. F. Kennedy, *There's an old saying that victory has 100 fathers and defeat is an orphan.*[1961 J. F. Kennedy *News Conference* 21 Apr. in *Public Papers of Presidents of U.S.* (1962) 312]; http://www.answers.com/topic/success-has-many-fathers-while-failure-is-an-orphan#ixzz2dm9bCofa.

[23]   Hoffman, "One Decade Later—Debacle in Somalia," pages 1-3.

Chapter 10

Into the Cities: Dark, Dense, and Dangerous

Frank G. Hoffman

First Published 10 October 2013

David Kilcullen, *Out of the Mountains: The Coming Age of the Urban Guerrilla*. New York: Oxford University Press, 2013, $27.95, 352 pages, photos.

Reviewed by F. G. Hoffman

Urban conflict has been a routine working context for the American military for some time (Beirut, Los Angeles, Panama City, Baghdad, Fallujah, Kabul, etc) although it is often ignored in defense planning scenarios. Numerous studies have recognized the simple reality that the world's population is increasingly migrating to cities. Both the Joint force development community and the Marine Corps used to have urban warfare centers focused on this potentially troublesome battlefield.

Now that Operation *Enduring Freedom* is winding down towards advisory and tailored counter-terrorism tasks, we need to step back and look forward to the future. That future looks increasingly urbanized. Not just more cities, but large, more populated, denser and more dangerous megacities. As the prophetic Ralph Peters wrote so dramatically in 1996:

> "Cities always have been centers of gravity, but they are now more magnetic than ever before. Once the gatherers of wealth, then the processors of wealth, cities and their satellite communities have become the ultimate creators of wealth. They concentrate people and power, communications and control, knowledge and capability, rendering all else peripheral. They are also the post-modern equivalent of jungles and mountains— citadels of the dispossessed and irreconcilable. A military unprepared for urban operations across a broad spectrum is unprepared for tomorrow."[1]

What was evident to forward thinkers like Peters so far back is much clearer today. We past a major tipping point in April 2008, when over half of humanity found itself living in cities. By 2030, nearly 60 percent of the humans on this planet will live in a city, and within 100 miles of a coast. Just about all the world's population growth, over 2.5 billion souls, will be concentrated in the developing world. We need to recognize both the potential for prosperity built into future trends like urbanization, and recognize the dark side in shortfalls in government, the rise of tech-savvy gangs, and fetid slums. This is what makes this new book so by the Australian soldier/scholar David Kilcullen so timely and relevant.

Out of the Mountains paints a vivid and compelling picture of a world rushing upon us. The author's argument is quite simple, we face a future security environment that could be more contested, congested, and conflicted than the last decade.

Kilcullen's central argument is not about the kinds of threats we may face in the future (the "who"). He acknowledges the limits of prediction and the near certainty that all forms of human conflict will continue to exist. However, the real threat will come from the environment and *context* itself, not any particular group or actor (the "where"). Our future security environment will be shaped by four megatrends that Kilcullen defines as having a significant impact on our collective future, including conflict. These include rapid population growth, extensive urbanization, littoralization (the congested clutters along coasts and waterways), and high levels of connectivity. This rapid urban growth in coastal, underdeveloped areas overloads economic, social and governance systems, strains city infrastructure and overburdens the carrying capacity of cities. In Kilcullen's words:

> "...the trends are clear: more people than ever before in history will be competing for scarcer and scarcer resources in poorly governed areas that lack adequate infrastructure, and these areas will be more and more closely connected to the global system, so that local conflict will have far wider effects."

Thinking through these effects and their impact on the character of potential contingencies that might involve U.S. forces is sorely needed. These far wider effects could influence policymakers into direct U.S. involvement, as it has in the past.

Overall, this is an engaging, well-structured book. It is part Thomas Friedman, part Tom Barnett, with a strong dose of Robert Kaplan all rolled into one tightly researched package. Like Friedman, Kilcullen understands the power of connectivity. From Barnett, the notion of the under-governed "gap" emerges, and from Kaplan one senses a new "coming anarchy." Kilcullen says little about the urban guerrillas themselves or what motivates them but he excels at describing their tactical prowess and ability to fuse various methods appropriate to their needs. He includes detailed vignettes of the attacks on Mumbai, U.S. combat operations in Mogadishu, (which just passed its 20th anniversary), Libya, Egypt, and Syria. All these conflicts underscore his conception of urban operations, the flows of urban megacities, and the tinderbox of violent potential they hold. Moreover, these case studies show how modern media tools can be a great accelerant of progress or networked chaos. The recent attack on Nairobi's Westgate Mall makes this book's argument even clearer.

Some may find this book dystopian, but I think you can extend its arguments on technology even further given how low the barriers to entry are becoming in so many fields including UAVs and biotechnology. There may be only a few urban guerrilla organizations out there, but they will be more dangerous. In fact, as noted by Eric Schmidt and Jared Cohen in their *The Digital Age*, "What gives terror groups in the future an edge may not be their members' willingness to die for the cause; it might be how good their command of technology is."

Military theorists have been searching for a unified field theory for complex operations for some time, despite the variegated contexts and forms this portion of the conflict spectrum can take. Kilcullen draws upon some early writings of the late Bernard Fall to postulate a theory of "Competitive Control" over populations. This theory implies that much of our traditional counterinsurgency notions (especially the social-economic underpinnings of "hearts and minds") may need to be rethought given the altered context in which insurgencies increasingly operate within. In Kilcullen's theory, "the local armed actor that a given population perceives as best able to establish a predictable, consistent, wide-spectrum normative system of control is most likely to dominate that population and its residential area." The author demonstrates how a range of current nonstate actors like Al Qaeda, Hezbollah, and the Taliban operate across a spectrum of persuasion, services and coercion to entrap or corral a local population. Once entrapped by the "fish trap" it is exponentially more difficult to lure the populace away from the armed nonstate group.

Kilcullen makes it clear that armed actors are increasingly able to generate coercive and disruptive power out of growing "feral" nature of urbanizing society in the developing world.

A special benefit of *Out of the Mountains* is his explanation of modern cities as a system. Kilcullen offers analytical tools for conceiving of urban centers as biological organisms with distinctive "metabolic" rates. He brings out a number of fascinating insights from the urbanist Mike Davis that should lead to further study in urban security challenges.

Kilcullen's notions about the importance of increased resilience over stability and the dynamic disequilibrium of urban complexes offers some ideas about prevention. Current Joint doctrine in the United States, JP 3-06 "Joint Urban Ops," is under review with an end of year revision due and should benefit from these insights.

The author has designed the book for general readers, but a detailed appendix proposes numerous and specific force development priorities for doctrine, mobility, sustainment and force structure for a military audience, particularly Army and Marines, and perhaps the Special Operations community. Marine thinking and investment in concepts like hybrid threats, Distributed Operations, unmanned systems, and the Marine Corps Warfighting Laboratory's work on Company Landing Team experiments are in line with the author's recommendations. This is a great chapter that confirms a decade of concepts and experiments, but more importantly identifies areas for detailed follow on work in light of the trends in connectivity and technology that Kilcullen has illuminated.

The most likely conflict scenarios for the future can be easily summed up: *Crowded, Complex, Connected,* and *Coastal.* The threats we face in this environment, when policy makers determine that U.S. interests warrant an intervention, will be on home ground. Furthermore, they will understand both the culture and urban "flows" better than we do and will tailor a unique *convergent* mode of fighting that makes our nice academic categories (Traditional, Terrorist, Irregular, Criminal) meaningless. *Out of the Mountains* is highly commended for its vivid portrait of tomorrow's operating environment and its proposed tactical solutions. This book should interest anyone who is concerned about an all too predictable and violent future. A military unprepared for security operations in urban settings is certainly unprepared for tomorrow.

Notes

[1]   Ralph Peters, "Our Soldiers, Their Cities." *Parameters*. Spring
       1996, pp. 43-50, http://strategicstudiesinstitute.army.mil/pubs/
       parameters/articles/96spring/peters.htm.

Chapter 11

The 'New' Playbook? Urban Siege in Nairobi

John P. Sullivan and Adam Elkus

First Published 24 November 2013

Multiple teams. Suicide commandos. Hostages. Automatic rifles. Grenades. Improvised fortifications. And indications that the attackers dug in for a long fight designed to maximize media attention. Once again terrorists used a page from the 'urban siege' playbook; this time at Nairobi, Kenya's up-market Westgate mall.

It's been about two months since al-Shabaab gunmen employed the new playbook. On Saturday, 21 September 2013 squads of gunmen affiliated with the Somalia terrorist group al-Shabaab armed with assault rifles and grenades attacked[1] the Westgate mall. They came to kill—and also came to die. With hostages and access to a large supermarket, they also prepared to dig in for the long haul. As of the writing of this piece, the siege is recent, and undoubtedly post-event analysis will reveal much more relevant information about the assault than we currently possess.

Al-Shabaab Strikes Westgate

At least 6 suspects, including a woman,[2] were involved in the armed, hostage-barricade assault on the Westgate mall. The attack began at about 12:30 pm on a Saturday afternoon. According to a *Guardian* report,[3] four men approached the entrance firing at cars. Then the first grenade detonated. About 150 meters away, a second attack squad drove through barriers, and then dismounted and engaged bystanders with gunfire and grenades. The attack led to a four-day standoff yielding at least 72 deaths and hundreds of persons injured. Five attackers were killed, and one has reportedly escaped. This was not al-Shabaab's first strike; it has been active in both Somalia and Kenya since it split from the Islamic Courts Union in 2007. Indeed, it has conducted nearly 550 attacks killing over 1,600 and wounding more than 2,100 prior to this attack. Almost a quarter of its attacks have occurred in Kenya, but this was its first 'urban siege.' To date, this was their first hostage-barricade raid, yet Al-Shabaab's attack preferences including bombings and armed assaults (72.6 of their historical attacks) prepared them for this innovation.

What is 'Urban Siege'?

Urban siege entails combined arms, 'swarming' attacks that bring multiple assault squads into play to attack a target or targets. The goal is to draw in defenders to prolong the attack and maximize casualties and disruption. By leveraging multiple, simultaneous assaults (known as swarming) response is complex. As a result, fog, friction, and the smog of terrorism is amplified. As the START Background Report[4] on the attack noted, extended hostage-barricade attacks with durations over 24 hours are nearly five times as lethal as those that end within a day.

The most notable antecedent to the Westgate siege was the Mumbai attack. In that 2008 action Lashkar-e-Taiba (LeT) conducted a series of assaults—including complex hostage barricade situations—on seven separate targets in Mumbai, killing 171 and wounding over 250 during their three-day siege. We viewed that as a seminal event in contemporary urban siege. Indeed in our paper[5] "Postcard from Mumbai: Modern Urban Siege" we called it a 'Back to the Future' incident where terrorists returned to urban guerilla tactics.

Though armed attacks and hostage situations are as old as terrorism itself, the urban siege is of a particularly recent vintage. Attackers do not aim to get out alive. Instead their goal is to kill as many as possible, taking hostages and building improvised fortifications to delay their own deaths and drag out the siege. Multiple teams are employed, often designed to overload the target's response capability and operational command and control. The attackers succeeded in complicating response in Nairobi. As recounted in the *Guardian* report,[6] disorganized response, punctuated by infighting and a clash of egos among authorities—including a friendly-fire incident that led to disrupting the counter-assault—allowed the terrorists to regroup and actively hunt victims. The security forces (police and military) violated the first goal of counter-assault for urban siege. They failed to 'stop the kinetic momentum!'

Response and Coordination Challenges

The latter point is not obvious to readers that visualize police tactical response as a simple matter of bringing overwhelming force to bear on a small number of attackers. In the aftermath of the Boston Marathon Attack,[7] the Boston Police Department, for example, was roundly criticized for locking down the city and deploying massive amounts of heavily armed officers to combat *two* young men.

Consider, however, the chaotic environment inside a police incident commander's headquarters in such a situation: conflicting reports are streaming in from every direction, the location and composition of the attack force is unclear, and it is still possible that there may be more attacks on the horizon. Response must be instantaneous, and an alphabet soup of agencies and departments must cooperate to ramp up from normal operations to emergency footing in the blink of an eye. Overnight, both regular and tactical law enforcement officers trained to de-escalate violent situations must embrace extreme violence to put down fanatical, heavily-armed murderers to prevent them from killing any more innocents. Bostonians were lucky that the attack force was minuscule, geographically confined, and acting alone. A larger, more distributed, better equipped, and better-trained force might have severely taxed police operational response.

Responding to urban siege is complex and outside the experience of most police departments. Traditional police practice calls for responding officers to contain the site of a hostage-barricade situation and then call for specialized responders—SWAT teams—to respond and neutralize the complex threat. Indeed, according to reports from the scene Nairobi's police flying squad followed this dated approach when they arrived at 1:10 pm. It wasn't until three and a half hours after the initial shots were fired that Kenya's 'recce group' a SWAT capability, responded at about 4:00 pm. Kenyan military forces (including infantry and rangers) arrived at about the same time, leading to conflict over command and a friendly-fire shooting with the commander of the 'recce group' killed and three police and one soldier injured. By the time the event ended on Tuesday, 24 September, blasts, mayhem, and killing had ensued. The political dynamics of the event also went viral.

It may be tempting to attribute the difficulty of police response in locales like Mumbai, India, Beslan, Russia and Nairobi to lack of government capacity and proper training. Such chauvinistic criticism overlooks the fact that police in such places—though perhaps under-resourced—have extensive experience dealing with heavily armed criminals and domestic terrorism that their Western counterparts generally lack.

The bitter truth is that a true armed assault by a dedicated, resourced, and fanatical opponent would tax the resources of any competent police department. Urban sieges are exceptional events that usually surpass the usual sequence of police roles and functions. They bridge the local/national/global levels, bringing to bear considerations, entities, risks, and responsibilities that go much higher up than the world of dragnets and squad cars. Indeed, this is a case of a local, tactical event having profound global, strategic consequences. From the onset of the Nairobi attack, Twitter became engaged. As one report notes,[8] "Twitter captured the confusion of the attack in real-time as users first reported what they thought was an explosion. Shortly after noon, news started trickling through the social network that something had gone horribly wrong at Westgate mall." By the time the siege was over, the public, Kenya's President Uhuru Kenyatta, al-Shabaab (#AlShabaab) and global civil society had weighed in. Indeed, as David Kilcullen has observed, the attackers' (in both Mumbai and Nairobi) focus on foreigners combined with the intimate nexus among attackers and victims demanded by gun battles, which are more protracted than bombings alone, lead to enhanced terror effects and seems to have been calculated to maximize international attention. Mobile phones and social media became tools of command and control, and amplified carnage for the terrorists. As a result, we posit that urban siege is intrinsically global in impact.

Counter-Swarming for Urban Siege

All is not lost. Police can train to fight and defeat armed assaults. The answer, however, does not necessarily lie in military-style police operators, tactical vehicles or Boston-style clampdowns. While these are all part of the solution, the most important aspects of defeating urban sieges lie in operational command, training, and synchronization among emergency response agencies. Incident command systems must be able to quickly scale up and direct a response force composed of many different government organizations and both process and red-team intelligence in real-time. Lines of authority, interagency relations and cooperation, and emergency response routines and subroutines must be clear and well-rehearsed, not improvised on the spot. Effective 'counter-swarming for urban siege must build from a baseline 'full-spectrum policing' capacity. Police must be able to quickly shift from community policing to formed units that are able to repel and contain threats. Addressing active shooters and combined arms swarms require immediate, adaptive, decisive counter-force action.

This must build from the concept that the first responding police must immediately engage the attackers and stop the kinetic momentum. This requires more than good tactics or MAC-TAC (Multi-Assault Counter-Terrorism Action Capabilities) training. Full Spectrum Policing must be grounded in operational art. Police operational art[9] must integrate operational swarming, maneuver, and real-time intelligence support across the urban operational (battle) space. This must be synchronized with community protection, political understanding, and media appreciation by both traditional and new media (social media) entities. Civil police, military, intelligence, private security and governance structures must also be synchronized to address attacks on soft infrastructure like malls, public transport, and downtown districts.

All of this is infinitely more important than technology and gear. After all, the first line of defense will not be a heavily armed tactical trooper but a regular police officer. The Mumbai, Beslan and Nairobi attackers all exploited the early chaos of the assault to kill wantonly and then entrench. The "golden hour" of an urban siege is far before the cavalry arrives to save the day. And the success of the entire effort depends on the command, control, and cooperation of the incident command units on various political scales of authority.

Conclusion: Adjusting Our "Playbook"

We are not helpless against urban siege. But first we must acknowledge it is a threat, and that worldwide terrorist attackers are eying malls, schools, sporting events, and urban centers as the next soft target to strike to further their political objectives. As David Kilcullen[10] aptly asserts, "urban environments, including complex pieces of urban terrain like shopping centres, hotels and industrial facilities, are the battlegrounds of the future. And the urban siege, with its commando-style tactics and guerrilla infiltration of a big city's ebb and flow, is increasingly the tactic of choice for a wide range of adversaries." The Westgate attack is a simplified variation of Mumbai's urban siege. The target set was more limited, but the principles the same. We have seen this set of tactics employed in South Asia,[11] and now Africa. It is as Daveed Gartenstein-Ross noted[12] "not a question of whether the Nairobi attack will be modeled, it will, and likely with a Western country as the target." Once we acknowledge the threat, we must next develop doctrine and training to counter it. We must build our counter swarming playbook for urban siege.

Notes

[1]   Mark Hosenball, "U.S. examines Kenya information about foreign link to mall attack." *Chicago Tribune*. 23 September 2013, http://articles.chicagotribune.com/2013-09-23/news/sns-rt-us-kenya-attack-usa-20130921_1_shabaab-kenyan-authorities-u-s-authorities.

[2]   Nima Elbagir and Lilian Leposo, "Source: 6 suspects behind Kenya's Westgate mall attack, including woman." *CNN*. 7 October 2013, https://edition.cnn.com/2013/10/07/world/africa/kenya-mall-attack.

[3]   Daniel Howden, "Terror in Nairobi: the full story behind al-Shabaab's mall attack." *The Guardian*. 4 October 2013, https://www.theguardian.com/world/2013/oct/04/westgate-mall-attacks-kenya.

[4]   *Al-Shabaab Attack on Westgate Mall in Kenya*. Background Report. National Consortium for the Study of Terrorism and Responses to Terrorism (START). September 2013, https://www.start.umd.edu/sites/default/files/publications/local_attachments/STARTBackgroundReport_alShabaabKenya_Sept2013.pdf.

[5]   John P. Sullivan and Adam Elkus, "Postcard from Mumbai: Modern Urban Siege." *Small Wars Journal*. 16 February 2009, http://smallwarsjournal.com/jrnl/art/postcard-from-mumbai.

[6]   Daniel Howden, "Terror in Nairobi: the full story behind al-Shabaab's mall attack." *The Guardian*. 4 October 2013, https://www.theguardian.com/world/2013/oct/04/westgate-mall-attacks-kenya.

[7]   "Boston Marathon Terror Attack Fast Facts." *CNN*. 3 June 2013, https://edition.cnn.com/2013/06/03/us/boston-marathon-terror-attack-fast-facts/index.html.

[8]   Omar Mohammed, "How the Nairobi Mall Attack Unfolded on Social Media." *Global Voices*. 23 September 2013, https://globalvoices.org/2013/09/23/how-the-nairobi-mall-attack-unfolded-on-social-media/.

[9]   John P. Sullivan and Adam Elkus, "Preventing Another Mumbai." *CTC Sentinel*. Vol. 2., Iss. 6., June 2009, https://ctc.usma.edu/app/uploads/2010/06/Vol2Iss6-Art2.pdf.

[10] David Kilcullen, "Westgate mall attacks: urban areas are the battleground of the 21ˢᵗ century." *The Guardian*. 27 September 2013, https://www.theguardian.com/world/2013/sep/27/westgate-mall-attacks-al-qaida.

[11] John P. Sullivan and Adam Elkus, "Urban siege in south Asia." *OpenDemocracy*. 9 November 2009, https://www.opendemocracy.net/opensecurity/john-p-sullivan-adam-elkus/urban-siege-in-south-asia.

[12] Daveed Gartenstein-Ross, "The Westgate Mall Attack and the Future of Terrorism." *Georgetown Journal of International Affairs*. 23 September 2013, https://www.georgetownjournalofinternationalaffairs.org/online-edition/the-westgate-mall-attack-and-the-future-of-terrorism-by-daveed-gartenstein-ross.

Chapter 12

Mega Cities, Ungoverned Areas, and the Challenge of Army Urban Combat Operations in 2030-2040

David Shunk

First Published 23 January 2014

The Worst Policy is to Attack Cities. Attack Cities Only When There is No Alternative.[1]

Sun Tzu, *Art of War*

Convinced that Hitler would employ whatever forces were necessary to seize the city [Stalingrad]...the sole function of the [Soviet 62ⁿᵈ & 64ᵗʰ Armies] was to lure combat ready German forces into the city..., sap their strength in the kind of street combat for which German soldiers were neither trained nor accustomed to fighting. By staying close to the German attackers and contesting every block, the Soviet soldiers deprived the Germans of the greatest advantages: firepower and maneuver.[2]

David Glantz, *Armageddon in Stalingrad*

Mega cities will complicate and greatly challenge Army urban combat missions in the 2030-2040 timeframe. By 2030 three out of five persons are forecast to reside in cities. This migration will bring competing interests into conflict and raise the chances for urban combat operations. Urban combat is the great leveler. Standoff technologies are negated and the city fight is still street-to-street, floor-to-floor, and often face-to-face. This paper will discuss mega city challenges and characteristics, the problems of ungoverned areas, offer historical examples of urban combat and the challenges of land combat in mega cities in 2030-2040. The Army should study urban combat in mega cities to develop the capabilities required for success in 2030-2040.

What is a Mega City?

So, what is a mega city? As defined by the United Nations, a mega city is defined as a city with more than 10 million inhabitants.[3] Today twenty four mega cities exist and by 2025 at least twenty seven cities will be classified as mega cities.[4] The current largest mega city, Tokyo, has a population of over 32 million and a city area that is 56 miles wide and 16 miles long. Any type of Army mission in a mega city will face daunting challenges.

Mega cities will further complicate the political, social, and military landscape in 2030-2040. Megacities and regional groupings are likely to assume increasing political and economic powers, whereas countries and global multilateral institutions will struggle to keep up with the rapid rise of their power.[5] With the rise of the mega city autonomy what are key mega city characteristics and problems?

Characteristics and Problems in Mega Cities:

- Potential for massive poverty and social unrest, especially in third world mega cities.

- Potential for massive infrastructure problems with communications services, basic infrastructure maintenance, transportation and congestion.
- Potential for environmental concerns, such as contaminated water, air pollution, and sewage.
- Potential for increased disease transmission due to over-crowding, drug-resistant strains of infection, and lethal environmental conditions.
- Potential for ungoverned spaces within the mega city.
- Potential for littoralization—the propensity for mega cities to cluster on coastlines.
- Population can be quickly mobilized with social media during times of social unrest.
- Demographics indicate higher birth rates, city migration and a young unemployed population.

Taken together these mega city characteristics demonstrate the possibility of instability over stability. Mega cities hold a high potential for unrest, disruption and disorder on a large scale:

> _Life in megacities will deteriorate as populations surge beyond their capacity_. The teeming populations of Lagos, Karachi, Cairo, and Dhaka have few options. In Lagos one could almost say that the rule of law does not exist.
>
> Moreover, some of what we term indigenous _"non-state actors"_ and nongovernment organizations (NGOs) _have the potential to become so powerful within megacities as to be virtually invulnerable to the power of the governments of their respective states_.[6]

P.H. Liotta and James F. Miskel,
Real Population Bomb

Potential for Disorder and Conflict in Mega Cities

David Kilcullen in his book, *Out of the Mountains: The Rise of the Urban Guerrilla, forecasts a world with conflict focused on megacities due to these factors:*

- Urbanization—tendency for migrations to larger and larger cities
- Littoralization—the propensity for people to cluster on coastal cities
- Connectedness—the increasing connectivity among people, wherever they live.[7]

He predicts conflict will occur in the sprawling coastal cities and in urban slum settlements of the Middle East, Africa, Latin America and Asia. Cities, rather than nations, may become the critical component for future conflict. Mega cities may permit the reemergence of the city state.

The greater danger for the future may not be failed states, but the possibility of failed mega cities. When states fail to provide protection and other basic services within a mega city an ungoverned region may rise within the mega city:

> *Increasing urbanization worldwide, combined with growing attention to illicit actors in remote areas, suggests that "hiding in plain sight" in urban and suburban areas or rural villages will be a strategy that illicit actors are likely to increasingly follow. Many cities, even in Western liberal democracies, have entire housing projects, neighborhoods, or slums that are known to be controlled by drug traffickers or other illicit actors and are "no go" areas for police; many favelas, urban slums, shanty towns, refugee camps, and squatters' villages outside of major cities lack police protection or government oversight.*[8]

> Office of the Deputy Assistant Secretary of Defensefor Policy Planning, *Ungoverned Areas and Threats from Safe Havens*

With no government, no courts, no law, and no university
there was no work … in Mogadishu. How could these
bloody Ranger raids alter things? [9]

Blackhawk Down

Mega City Disorder and Conflict May Result in Ungoverned Areas

Cairo, Mumbai, Dhaka, Karachi, Lahore, Lagos, Kinshasa, Nairobi, and Rio de Janeiro all have something in common—ungoverned spaces. All of these cities have ungoverned sectors in which the government is incapable of providing law enforcement, public health, education, and other basic services.

What is an ungoverned area in a mega city? It is a sector where the government has lost control and the capacity to manage the population. Security is challenged by non-state actors such as terrorists, insurgents, criminals, and extremist organizations.

Non-state armed groups may become a governing factor in mega cities. These groups may provide localized medical care, reconstruction, education and religious instruction aiming to win control of the people when the government fails to provide these services.

Within an ungoverned area the Army may be required to accomplish missions such as restoring order, seizing chemical or nuclear weapons. Any combat operation in a mega city will be a formidable challenge.

An urban area can constitute a major military obstacle. Its population poses major logistical, administrative and security problems for the invader:

Tactically, a city's closely packed buildings, basements,
alleyways and sewer systems offer cover, concealment,
and ready-made defensive positions to the defenders.[10a]

2d Battalion, 26th Infantry, at Aachen, October 1944

Generally, a modern city magnifies the power of the defender and robs the attacker of his advantages in firepower and mobility:

> A city can ingest an invading army, paralyze it for weeks on end, and grind it down to a state of ineffectiveness.[10b]

2d Battalion, 26th Infantry, at Aachen, October 1944

Combat Operations in a Mega City

With the potential for future combat operations in highly networked and densely populated mega cities, what can one expect? As demonstrated in Mogadishu, efforts that begin as humanitarian assistance or noncombatant evacuation may face an all-out urban conflict with little notice.

Army forces in mega city combat may face several types of adversaries as shown by history:

1. Grozny—state versus terrorist/guerrilla/irregular forces.
2. Stalingrad—state on state war within a city.
3. Mogadishu—city militia turns on U.S. forces.

The problems of urban combat in a mega city may be greatly magnified. Due to their size combat in mega cities will be complex, offer more dangers and larger entrapments. Additionally, in 2030-2040, prevalent technologies such as improved UAVs, 3D printing, and robotics will greatly empower the adversaries. So, what are some basic characteristics of urban combat?

> *Survival meant moving like your hair was on fire. As he moved he thought about making every one of his shots count. They were in a 360-degree battlefield.*[11]

Delta Force SFC Paul Howe, *Blackhawk Down*

*[In the streets of Mogadishu], <u>the Rangers</u> on the lost convoy
<u>took better than 50 percent casualties moving through the</u>
<u>streets in vehicles.</u>*[12]

Blackhawk Down

*In the Battle of Stalingrad, shock group and assault parties
spent days fighting for single buildings or blocks of buildings,
struggling for hours over separate rooms, single bunkers and
foxholes, cellars and twisted pieces of destroyed machinery.
The <u>sheer attrition took a terrible toll on both sides, quickly</u>
<u>depriving units of their combat effectiveness.</u>*[13]

David Glantz, *Armageddon in Stalingrad*

Basic Characteristics of Combat in Urban Terrain:

- Easy to enter, hard to extract forces in urban operations (think Mogadishu)
- Restricted movement
- Funneled approaches
- Constant threat of ambush
- Multi-level operations: subterranean, street level, and elevated terrain (buildings)
- Infantry intensive operations
- 360-degree battle
- High expenditure of ammunition and other expendables
- Potential for high causalities
- Terrain favors the defense
- Attacker firepower and mobility advantage is lost

To illustrate some of the challenges of urban combat, a look at the past will help view the future. Four examples from recent history illustrate three challenges and one possible solution.

Historical Examples Illustrating Three Urban Combat Challenges and a Solution

- Stalingrad 1942—Ultimate city conflict—state on state, tremendous casualties
- Mogadishu 1993—City wide militia rises up to attack U.S. forces
- Gronzy 1995—Russians rush to disaster, destroyed in detail
- IDF Nablus 2002—One solution, fighting through city walls

Stalingrad—Extreme Causalities

Stalingrad is the ultimate example of nation on nation warfare fighting for a city and the potential for extreme losses. The defensive phase of the battle for the city of Stalingrad battle lasted 126 days and the Russians lost 324,000 dead and 320,000 wounded/sick resulting in 644,000 total causalities producing an average of 5,100 casualties per day.[14] The battle created 600,000 Russian refugees.[15]

Mogadishu 1993—City Militia Rises Up

A planned ninety-minute mission to capture warlord Mohammed Farah Aidid turned into a seventeen-hour firefight when the city militia attacked the Ranger and Delta Force in the urban environment. An armored relief column rescued the trapped Rangers and Delta Force but the Americans suffered eighteen dead and eighty-four wounded. The geopolitical consequence saw U.S. national resolve defined by casualties resulting in disengagement from Somalia.

Grozny (Chechnya) 1995—Rush to Destruction

In the 1995 battle for Grozny the Russians initially used urban penetration tactics to move on multiple axes to seize an objective and then isolate and protect it from the enemy. The Russians moved on multiple axes to seize the presidential palace, railroad station and radio/television center.

The Russians moved unopposed until deep in the city, where the Chechens attacked and destroyed them. The Chechen opposition learned not to provide permanent strong points that would provide a focus for Russian air, artillery and maneuver forces. Rather, the Chechens employed temporary strong points and a great deal of internal mobility to deploy and redeploy strong points throughout the city.[16] Technology superiority did not guarantee victory for the Russians.

Nablus 2002—Walking Through Walls

At Nablus 2002, the Israeli Defense Forces (IDF) soldiers used none of the streets, roads, alleys or courtyards that constitute the city, and none of the external doors, internal stairwells and windows that constitute the order of buildings, but rather moved horizontally through walls, and vertically through holes blasted in ceilings and floors. This form of movement, described by the military as 'infestation', sought to redefine inside as outside, and domestic interiors as thoroughfares.

The three-dimensional progression through walls, ceilings and floors across the urban mass reinterpreted, short-circuited and recomposed both architectural and urban rules of combat. The IDF's strategy of 'walking through-walls' involved a conception of the city as not just the site, but the very medium of warfare—a flexible, almost liquid medium that is forever contingent and in flux.[17] Innovation provided new tactics and success in this urban fight:

> *There is excellent reason to believe that future enemies of the United States will look more like the Chechens than the Russians. Therefore, it behooves the United States to prepare for urban combat. As the Russians have learned, avoiding it, although preferable, is often impossible.*

U.S. planners should also recognize that <u>a resident</u> *<u>insurgency force enjoys significant advantages over even</u>* *<u>a technically superior foreign aggressor</u>. <u>It is better to</u>* *<u>learn from the</u> experiences of others than to repeat their* *mistakes.*[18]

RAND, *Russia's Chechen Wars 1994-2000*

Conclusion

Mega cities and the potential for the Army to engage in mega city combat operations in 2030-2040 fit the definition of 'wicked problem.' Leadership and intellect will be required to overcome the significant and complex challenges of mega cities.

It would be easy to dismiss urban combat in a mega city as a potential mission due to the dangers and limitations. However, by studying urban combat in mega cities the Army can best develop the capabilities required to face this challenge in 2030-2040.

Never under estimate the enemies in mega cities and never over estimate your own capabilities. Remember the warning of Sun Tzu.

Notes

[1]   Samuel Griffith translator, Sun Tzu, *The Art of War*, (London, England: Oxford University Press, 1963), 78.

[2]   David Glantz, *Armageddon in Stalingrad, September-November 1942*, (Lawrence, Kansas: University of Kansas Press, 2009), 705.

[3]   European Association of National Metrology Institutes, Mega Cities, 1. http://www.emrponline.eu/call2013/docs/MegaCities. pdf (Accessed 20 Nov 2013).

[4]   P.H. Liotta and James F. Miskel, *The Real Population Bomb: Megacities, Global Security and The Map of the Future*, (Dulles, Virginia: Potomac Books, 2012), 2.

[5]   National Intelligence Council, Global Trends 2030: Alternative Worlds, 57. http://www.dni.gov/index.php/about/organization/global-trends-2030 (Accessed 20 Nov 2013).

[6]   P.H. Liotta and James F. Miskel, 10.

[7]   David Kilcullen, *Out of the Mountains: The Coming of Age of the Urban Guerrilla*, (Oxford Publishing: Oxford, England, 2013), 22.

[8]   Robert D. Lamb, *Ungoverned Areas and Threats from Safe Havens*, Final Report of the Ungoverned Areas Project, Prepared for the Office of the Under Secretary of Defense for Policy, Office of the Deputy Assistant Secretary of Defense for Policy Planning, 2007, 25.http://www.cissm.umd.edu/papers/files/ugash_report_final.pdf (Accessed 20 Nov 2013).

[9]   Mark Bowden, *Black Hawk Down*, (New York, New York: Penguin, 1999), 75.

[10] [10a&b] Roger Spiller, *Combined Arms in Battle Since 1939*, (Fort Leavenworth, KS: Command & General Staff College Press, 1992), 163. http://usacac.army.mil/cac2/cgsc/carl/download/csipubs/spiller.pdf (Accessed 20 Nov 2013).

[11] Mark Bowden, 175.

[12] Ibid, 339.

[13] David Glantz, 709.

[14] Micheael Desch, *Soldiers in Cities: Military Operations On Urban Terrain*, Army War College, Strategic Studies Institute (SSI), October 2001, 24. http://www.strategicstudiesinstitute.army.mil/pdffiles/pub294.pdf (Accessed 20 Nov 2013).

[15] S.J. Lewis, *Battle of Stalingrad*, Web Source, 30, 35. http://www.strategique.org/3.cours/3.Documentations/3.2livres/Livres/Urban_Operations_XX-Century/chp2.pdf (Accessed 20 Nov 2013).

[16] Lester Grau, *Urban Combat: Confronting the Specter*, Military Review, July-August 1991. http://cgsc.contentdm.oclc.org/utils/getfile/collection/p124201coll1/id/314/filename/315.pdf (Accessed 20 Nov 2013).

[17]   Eyal Weizman, *Lethal Theory,* 2006, 81. http://www.skor.nl/_files/
       Files/OPEN18_P80-99%281%29.pdf (Accessed 20 Nov 2013).

[18]   Olga Oliker, RAND, *Russia's Chechen Wars 1994-2000*, Grozny
       Summary, 2001, xv. http://www.rand.org/content/dam/rand/
       pubs/monograph_reports/MR1289/MR1289.sum.pdf (Accessed
       20 Nov 2013).

Chapter 13

Narco-Cities: Mexico and Beyond

John P. Sullivan

First Published 31 March 2014

Transnational crime and its associated transnational illicit networks pose a challenge to sovereignty and governance by fostering corruption and impunity. These groups—gangs, cartels, and mafias—operate at the intersection of 'spaces and places.' That is, they dominate local territory (neighborhoods, cities, and states) in both urban and rural settings. These actors negotiate the global illicit markets (a space of flows) from tangible spatial entry points. As such, local and national gangs can become transnational criminal actors and as such are important targets for intelligence analysis.

This essay briefly assesses the role of urban criminal actors (violent non-state actors) in challenging security and state solvency (legitimacy and capacity) providing alternate governance in 'other-governed spaces' as part of their strategy to navigate global illicit markets.[1]

Violence, Gangs and Cities

Extreme gang and cartel violence grabs daily headlines and influences daily life in contested cities. As the Mexican Drug War has demonstrated, multi-year contests for criminal supremacy can yield high levels of violence in cities, towns, and states that challenge the ability to govern (Sullivan, 2013).

Violence is in itself an important component of understanding 'narco-cities' (*'narco-ciudades'*). Indeed, high levels of gang violence are one indicator that 'criminal insurgency' (Sullivan and Bunker, 2012 & Grillo, 2011) may be present. In Mexico, for example, the "10 most dangerous cities" are all contested within the drug war. These cities are: Reynosa, Acapulco, Tijuana, Torreón, Durango, Tepic, Culiacán, Mazatlán, Chihuahua, and Ciudad Juárez.[2] The world's deadliest cities are also linked to the *narcos*. These have been listed in descending order as: San Pedro Sula, Honduras; Ciudad Juárez; Maceio, Brazil; Acapulco (also known as 'Narcopulco'); Distrito Central, Honduras (Tegulcigalpa and Comayaguela); Caracas, Venezuela; Torreón; Chihuahua; Durango; and Belem, Brazil.[3]

For a while Ciudad Juárez was the murder capital of the world earning the nickname 'Murder City'[4] The battle for Juárez, left over 11,400 persons murdered.[5] The Sinaloa and Juárez Cartels, along with their gang proxies killed rivals, assassinated police, employed car bombs, intimidated journalists, and engaged in social cleansing to eliminate their rivals from operating.

The top ten cities for murders in Mexico in 2013 were: 1) Acapulco (883 homicides); 2) Distrito Federal (753); Tijuana (564); Culiacán (479); Ciudad Juárez (453); Ecatepec (312); Guadalajara (297); Monterrey (266); Zapopan (258); and Chihuahua (251).[6]

So intense is the violence in many of Mexico's small cities and towns that the residents flee the violence and become internally displaced persons.[7] In Guerrero state for example at least 20 'ghost pueblos' resulted when the residents abandoned them in the face of cartel violence.[8]

This use of extreme violence to control narco-turf is a hallmark of criminal warfare. In Mexico, *narcos* have utilized beheadings, at least one crucifixion, dismemberment and mass graves (*narcofosas*) to make statements and intimidate rivals (the use of both symbolic and instrumental violence).[9] In Buenaventura, Colombia the public is besieged by warfare between the BACRIM (*bandas criminales emergentes*), in this case the *Urabeños*, rival gangsters such as *La Empresa*, and the security forces.[10] Criminal gangs, including the Camorra in Naples (Saviano, 2006), the PCC, Red Command, and Pure Third Command in Brazil's *favelas* join the *narcos* (in Mexico and Central America) in dominating urban space.

Indeed, in Naples, the Camorra dominated a wide range of enterprises criminal and otherwise enforcing their will through violence and corrupting officials. Naples is a prototypical narco-city. The Camorra dominates the drug trade. Indeed, this criminal cartel dominates all criminal and much grey and legitimate commerce in Campania. The narco trade in Naples includes retail, open-air drug markets and wholesale trafficking: hashish, heroin, cocaine, meth, all move through the Camorra's supply chain. Building from traditional criminal enterprises, including drug trafficking and extortion, the *Camorristi* moved into legitimate businesses. Starting with textiles and garments the Camorra was able to undercut rivals producing goods at a lower cost and exporting them via their well-established narco-circuits.

Naples provides a template for understanding *narcos* in mega-cities. From inner city neighborhoods, through villages and suburbs throughout Campania the Camorra clans command both criminal enterprise and political processes. They suborn mayors and elected officials to shape their operating environment. In doing so, they built a 'system' (often called the '*Secondgliano* System' after the name of one of the enclaves controlled by the clans). The system entails an economic and financial structure backed by military power. From their nodes in Naples' mega-city region, the Naples narco-city became a key node in an international criminal empire.

In Brazil the PCC (*Primeiro Comando da Capital*), Red Command (*Comando Vermelho*), and Pure Third Command or TCP (*Terceiro*

Comando Puro) control street life and commerce in the *favelas*, colluding with corrupt police to dominate trade in drugs and extract street taxes. In the Brazilian context, we see clear evidence of gangs moving into political action as 'third generation gangs' (Sullivan, 2002). Brazil's gangs dominate the *favelas* which have become "other governed zones;" criminal enclaves ruled by gangs.

Brazil's gangs have been known to stimulate riots, attack police and public transit to assert command of their turf.[11] For example the PCC has conducted synchronized attacks in prisons and on the street. On Friday, 12 May 2006 the PCC's criminal rebellion against state authority led to attacks on symbols of authority (police, public buildings, and buses) as well as prison riots in 73 separate correctional facilities.[12] The PCC controls *favelas* where the gang has supplanted civil administration.

In the case of the PCC we also see a firm link between dominating prisons and controlling the street in the PCC, which has its base in Brazil's prisons, controls *favela* action and conducts urban attacks to maintain its hold. This prison-street overlap is also seen with *Barrio Azteca* in Texas/Chihuahua and the *Eme* (Mexican Mafia) in California. Police responses to gangs in Rio de Janeiro and São Paulo have focused on a counterinsurgency type response known as 'pacifying police units' (*Unidade de Polícia Pacificadora* or UPP).[13]

The intensity of violence in cities can be the result of many factors, but the most likely is that the terrain is contested. That is one or more cartels and associated gangs are fighting to dominate the turf and opportunity space for criminal enterprise. In the Mexican context, these spaces are known as *plazas*. The *plaza* is the lucrative transshipment space for drugs across frontiers. The gang or cartel that controls the space levies a tax (known as a *"piso"*) on the criminal enterprises that transverse the *plaza* (Sullivan and Elkus, 2009a).

In Mexico it is estimated that 40% of municipalities are under daily threat from organized crime—a threat that has resulted in over 1,200 municipal employees, including at least 43 mayors and hundreds of police.[14] Similar situations exist in Central America where *maras* (especially MS-13) have gained effective control of village level political processes and see themselves as community champions (essentially social bandits) (Sullivan, 2012a & 2012b).

'Narco-cities' take several different forms. As demonstrated in Mexico, they can be characterized by: 1) '**hyperviolence**' where a type of feral, failed city exists as seen in Ciudad Juárez during the height of the Sinaloa incursion; 2) '**contested zones**' when the cartels begin to challenge political mechanisms and civil society to assert their power as seen in the *narcobloqueos* in Monterrey; or they cab be 3) '**narco-controlled**' as in the case of Culiacán; or home to 4) '**hidden financial power**' as seen in Mexico City.[15]

While cartels and gangs operate across cities (and national frontiers) they usually have strong ties to specific cities. The Sinaloa Cartel, for example has strong ties to Culiacán, the Tijuana and Juárez Cartels to those cities respectively, *Barrio Azteca* to El Paso, and the *Mara Salvatrucha* (MS-13) to Los Angeles and San Salvador. These ties are natural. Neighborhoods or barrios are often the starting point for gangs. They build from local affinities and then link with larger more dispersed entities. In the case of MS-13 transnational linkages can emerge through emigration and deportation. These transborder links are often reinforced through diaspora communities, as seen in the Sinaloa Cartel's presence in Chicago.[16] Similar dynamics are seen in *La Familia Michoacana/Los Cabelleros Templarios* links in California. Just as global cities link global economic circuits, 'narco-cities' link transnational criminals and global gangs (Sullivan and Elkus, 2009c).

Fragile, Failed and Feral Cities

The growing political might of cities is increasingly recognized. Saskia Sassen's work on global cities (Sassen, 2001) and Parag Khanna's assertion that a new urban age is replacing the age of nations (Khanna, 2010) combine with Mike Davis's assessment of global slums (Davis, 2006) to fuel the discussion of fragile, failed, or feral cities. Robert Muggah describes cities challenged by *narcos*, crime, conflict, and poverty as 'fragile cities' (Muggah, 2013). Certainly, cities like all human endeavors are fragile and, in our context, can be challenged by *narcos* and violence indeed cities in conflict have been linked to state fragility and state transformation (Beall, Goodfellow, and Rodgers, 2011).

Richard J. Norton (2003, 2010) described the potential security challenge of feral cities. In his 2010 essay Norton defined a feral city as: "a metropolis in a nation-state where the government has lost the ability to maintain the rule of law within the city's boundaries. These cities nevertheless remain connected to the greater international system through such avenues as trade and communication." For Norton this would include the city losing the ability to sustain the rule of law.

Norton defined three levels of ferality (green, yellow, red) for cities at risk. Green connoted no risk, yellow marginal risk, and red denoted a city becoming feral. Bunker and Sullivan (2011) expanded this framework to include two additional levels (purple and black). The purple level denotes a 'fully feral' city and the black level denotes a 'beyond feral; criminal city.' The purple feral city is one where there is an absence or vacuum of state governance (what Sullivan refers to as a lack of 'solvency' (*i.e.,* state legitimacy and capacity; Sullivan 2012a & 2012b) that is filled by a non-state entity (gang, cartel or warlord).

A black feral city would be a city where the external trappings of vital urban life have returned but are 'hollow' shells of a functional city. The black city is one that would be ruled by the criminal enterprise and the gangsters provide security. The illicit economy is prime and the state is absent. Neither the purple nor black feral city exists yet. They are projections. However, there certainly are purple and black neighborhoods. No city is fully feral (at any level) yet 'narco-cities'/'*narco-ciudades*' raise that potential.

Narco-cities (Narco-ciudades)

Narcos rule entire regions of Mexico and certainly cities, slums, *favelas* and *barrios* elsewhere. These criminal enclaves are essentially 'criminal cities.' It is important to note that 'narco-cities' are not solely products of hyperviolence. As mentioned earlier, violence plays a role and is a sign of ferality and a lack of state solvency, but other factors corruption, co-option of government officials, dominance of commerce and trade also figure into *narco* dominance.

In Mexico it has been estimated that up to 71.5% of *municipios* (cities and towns) have been captured or are under control of *narcos*. This figure has been steadily rising during Mexico's drug war as seen here: in 2001 the number of *municipos* under *narco* control was assessed at 34%; in 2006 that rose to 53%; in 2010 it was estimated at 73%, then dropping to 71.5% in 2011.[17] The result is a neo-feudal situation where stratified governance exists: the gangs and cartels rule some functions while the state rules others. Complicating the situation is the rise of *autodefensas* (self-defense groups or vigilantes) sponsored by businessmen, farmers, or rival cartels. *Autodefensas* are estimated to operate in at least 68 *municipios* in 13 Mexican states.[18] Currently Michoacán, including an embattled Apatzingan, is site to multipronged conflict among *Los Cabelleros Templarios*, rival groups of *autodefensas*, the *Cártel de Jalisco Nueva Generación*, and the state.[19]

The rise of the narco-state ('*narco estado*') is feared by many observers of the drug cartel war and its violence. For example, in *Narco Estado*, photographer Teun Voeten looks at the violence and their state transforming potential (Voeten, 2012). For Voeten the narco-state entails "the erosion of civil society and its gradual takeover by organized crime, the nascency of a new class of excluded and disposable people that choose a criminal career that ends in certain death, the devaluation of human life. All these elements present a nightmarish scenario of how our future could look like. The worst we can do is to close our eyes and ignore these developments."[20] The *narco estado* is exemplified for Voeten by the images of Ciudad Juárez and Culiacán, narco-cities where drug barons, their serfs—the *sicarios*—and their victims exemplify a new life a *narcocultura* (Sullivan, 2012b) where violence and the illicit economy punctuated by fear and terror reign.

Assessing Narco-cities: Intelligence Analysis and Red Teaming

In *Cartels at War*, Paul Rexton Kan (2012, p. 242) advises that it is useful to "Think of Narco-Cities Rather than a Narco-State." Kan notes that the violence associated with the *narcos* is largely limited to specific geo-criminal areas. Hence policy (and implicitly intelligence analysis informing policy) should focus on not only on those cities experiencing violence but also those with little violence. This would contribute to understanding the differential impacts of *narcos* and organized crime on different cities. Those with little violence may be captured or feudalized by the *narcos* those with hyperviolence may be contested. Kan suggests that analysts focus on state and local governments when assessing "how patterns of drug trafficking and violence may shift" (p. 242).

The first step in analysis of the dynamics of a narco-city is defining what it is. A narco-city is an urban area (including small cities and neighborhoods within a mega-city) that is controlled or contested by criminal cartels or gangs engaged in drug trafficking. As such they are "other governed zones) criminal enclaves and include fragile, failed and feral cities and neighborhoods where *narcos* exert political influence or *de facto* control.

Intelligence analysis of narco-cities must include analysis of the 'geosocial' dynamics of that conurbation. That means both terrain analysis and social network analysis of the criminal actors and their political links with state and sub-state political organizations, as well as assessment of market (black, grey, and legitimate) conditions must be assessed. For assessing terrain, it is important to recall that urban terrain is difficult for security (police and military forces) to operate in. Restricted movement, funneled and channelized movement, high potential for ambush, population and structural density, three-dimensional operational space (including subterranean, surface, and elevated terrain) are all features. The criminal actors have the advantage in many cases (urban terrain favors the defense)[21] Non-combatants complicate engagements between the security forces and gangsters. The gangs utilize terrain, as well as look outs (*halcones*) to sense incursions by the police or military.

Urban IPB (Intelligence Preparation of the Battlefield or Battlespace) is an essential component of assessing the geo-social dynamics of a narco-city. Urban IPB[22] is essentially a four step process: 1) Define the Operating Environment; 2) Describe the Operating Environment's Effects; 3) Identify and Evaluate Threats and Relevant Influences; and 4) Develop Opposing Courses of Action.

There are four key factors in assessing the importance of a narco-city in the circuit of illicit global flows. These are: 1) presence of transport/lines of communication, 2) ethnic make-up and presence of diaspora communities that may be exploited by gangsters, 3) the size of the city and its illicit trade, and 4) the cities gangs culture. From this starting point, analysts need to look at the presence and degree of corrosive cartel/gang influence. The corrosive factors include:

- Co-option of state, community, and corporate functions; especially co-option/corruption of police, judicial, and elected officials (mayors, city council members)
- Growth of criminal subculture (*narcocultura*)
- Links and alliances with other criminal enterprises
- Resource Extraction (ranging from street taxes through extorting profit from mining, logging, agriculture).

Finally, analysts need to define the current and evolving operational status of the criminal cartels and gangs in the narco-city. What is the operational posture of the gangs/cartels? Are they avoiding state interference? Are they engaged in collusive corruption with state actors? Are they confronting the state and/or other cartels/gangs? Are they targeting critical infrastructure? What tactics, techniques, and procedures (TTPs) do they employ? What firebreaks are they likely to cross as gang warfare intensifies, etc.? When conducting these assessments ground truth from informants, active police investigators, and journalists are essential sources of raw information. These, along with open source (OSINT) reports and studies should be assessed to develop working hypotheses that can be tested by on-going investigations and trough analytic red teaming (Sullivan and Elkus, 2009b).

Assessing the status and evolution of narco-cities is an essential intelligence task for police and security services (military and intelligence). This analysis must include geosocial assessment of the individual narco-city as well as the position and linkages of the narco-city within the global illicit network of flows. Since these situations are fluid—alliances and factions shift over time as described by Saviano, "In the face of [gang] war, danger, and defeat, allies and enemies are interchangeable" (p. 80).

During the course of gang and cartel conflict the status of forces will change. Gangs and cartels are protean, adaptive actors. Often violence, not economics will dictate the evolution, as Saviano recounts, "Groups, alliances, and enemies, will take shape afterward. But first the shooting has to start" (p. 80). This demands 'co-production' of intelligence to accurately gauge the situation and place it into context (Wirtz and Sullivan, 2009). As gangs and criminal cartels (violent non-state actors) expand their reach and potentially challenge states such intelligence analysis and geosocial assessment of narco-cities will become increasingly important.

References

Jo Beall, Tom Goodfellow, and Dennis Rodgers (2011) "Cities, Conflict and State Failure," *Working Paper no, 85, Cities and Fragile States, Crisis States Working Paper Series No. 2*, London: Crisis States Research Center, London School of Economics and Political Science.

Robert J. Bunker and John P. Sullivan (2011) "Integrating feral cities and third phase cartels/third generation gangs research: the rise of criminal (narco) city networks and BlackFor," *Small Wars & Insurgencies*, 22:5, pp. 764-786.

Mike Davis (2006) *Planet of Slums*, Brooklyn: Verso.

Ioan Grillo (2011) El *Narco: Inside Mexico's Criminal Insurgency*, New York: Bloomsbury.

Paul Rexton Kan (2012) *Cartels at War: Mexico's Drug-Fueled Violence and the Threat to U.S.*Washington, DC: Potomac.

Parag Khanna (2010) "Beyond City Limits," *Foreign Policy*, 16 August at http://www.foreignpolicy.com/articles/2010/08/16/beyond_city_limits.

Robert Muggah (2013) "The Fragile City Arrives," *E-International Relations*, 23 November 2013 at http://www.e-ir.info/2013/11/23/the-fragile-city-arrives/.

Saskia Sassen (2001) *The Global City*, Princeton: Princeton University Press.

Roberto Saviano (2006) *Gomorrah*, New York: Picador.

John P. Sullivan (2002) "Terrorism, Crime and Private Armies," *Low Intensity Conflict & Law Enforcement*, Vol. 11, No. 2/3 (Winter), pp. 239-253.

John P. Sullivan (2013) "Chapter 10: How Illicit Networks Challenge Sovereignty," in Miklaucic, M., and Brewer, J. *Convergence: Illicit Networks and National Security in the Age of Globalization*. Washington, DC: National Defense University; pp. 171-187.

John P. Sullivan and Robert J. Bunker (2012) Mexico's *Criminal Insurgency: A Small Wars Journal Anthology*, Bloomington: iUniverse.

John P. Sullivan and Adam Elkus (2009a) "Plazas for Profit: Mexico's Criminal Insurgency," *Small Wars Journal*, April 2009 at http://smallwarsjournal.com/jrnl/art/plazas-for-profit-mexicos-criminal- insurgency.

John P. Sullivan and Adam Elkus (2009b) "Red Teaming Criminal Insurgency," *Red Team Journal*, 30 January 2009 at http://redteamjournal.com/2009/01/red-teaming-criminal-insurgency-1/.

John P. Sullivan and Adam Elkus (2009c) "Global cities-global gangs," *OpenDemocracy*, 02 December 2009 at http://www.opendemocracy.net/opensecurity/john-p-sullivan-adam-elkus/global-cities---global-gangs.

John P. Sullivan and James J. Wirtz (2009) "Global Metropolitan Policing: An Emerging Trend in Intelligence Sharing," *Homeland Security Affairs*, Vol. 5, Issue 2, May at http://www.hsaj.org/?article=5.2.4.

John P. Sullivan (2012a) "From Drug Wars to Criminal Insurgency: Mexican Cartels, Criminal Enclaves and Criminal Insurgency in Mexico and Central America. Implications for Global Security," Paris: Fondation Maison des sciences de l'homme, FMSH-WP-2012-09, April at http://halshs.archives-ouvertes.fr/FMSH-WP/halshs-00694083.

John P. Sullivan (2012b) "Criminal Insurgency: Narcocultura, Social Banditry, and Information Operations." *Small Wars Journal*, 03 November at http://smallwarsjournal.com/jrnl/art/criminal-insurgency-narcocultura-social-banditry-and-information-operations.

Teun Voeten (2012) Narco *Estado: Drug Violence in Mexico*. (Photographs by Teun Voeten with introduction by Howard Campbell and Javier Valdez Cardenas), Lannoo Publishers: Tielt, Belgium.

Notes

[1] This article was presented as a paper to the Panel on "Geosocial Intelligence for Deviant Globalization: Analyzing the Spaces and Places of Transnational Crime," International Studies Association, *55ᵗʰ Annual Convention* (ISA 2014), Toronto, Ontario, Canada, 26 March 2014.

[2] These ratings change over time as the conflict and crime ebbs and flows. This listing is found at "10 Most Dangerous Cities in Mexico," *Gadling* at http://www.gadling.com/photos/10-most-dangerous-cities-in mexico/#!slide=955568 (downloaded 10 March 2014).

[3] Alicia P.Q. Wittmeyer, "The world's 10 deadliest cities," *Sydney Morning Herald*, 10 October 2012 at http://www.smh.com.au/travel/the-worlds-10-deadliest-cities-20121010-27cnz.html.

[4] See Charles Bowdin, *Murder City: Ciudad Juarez and the Global Economy's New Killing Fields*, New York: Nation Books, 2011.

[5] Molly Molloy, "The Mexican Undead: Toward a New History of the "Drug War" Killing Fields," *Small Wars Journal*, 21 August 2013 at http://smallwarsjournal.com/jrnl/art/the-mexican-undead-toward-a-new-history-of-the-"drug-war"-killing-fields.

[6] "Ciudades más violentas en el sexenio de Enrique Peña Nieto en 2013" in "Los primeros 23 mil 640 muertos de Enrique Peña Nieto," *Zeta*, 17 March 2014 at http://www.zetatijuana.com/ZETA/reportajez/los-primeros-23-mil-640-muertos-de-enrique-pena-nieto/#sthash.A7FD5Hj8.dpuf.

[7] See Robert J. Bunker, "Mexican Cartel Strategic Note No. 8: 230,000 Internally Displaced Persons (IDPs) in Mexico and 'Narco-Refugee' Potentials for the United States," *Small Wars Journal*, 19 November 2011 at http://smallwarsjournal.com/blog/mexican-cartel-strategic-note-no-8 and Paul Rexton Kan, *Mexico's "Narco-Refugees": The Looming Challenge for U.S. National Security*, Carisle: Strategic Studies Institute, U.S. Army War College, October 2011 at http://www.strategicstudiesinstitute.army.mil/pdffiles/PUB1083.pdf.

[8] Richard Fausset, "Mexican towns, once frozen with fear, now frozen in time," *Los Angeles Times*, 26 February 2013 at http://articles.latimes.com/2013/feb/26/world/la-fg-mexico-ghost-pueblos-20130227.

[9] See John P. Sullivan and Adam Elkus, "Tactics and Operations in the Mexican Drug War, *Infantry*, September-October 2011, pp. 20-23.

[10] "Buenaventura, entre fuerza pública, bandas criminales y narcotráfico," *La F.M.*, 22 March 2014 at http://www.lafm.com.co/noticias/buenaventura-entre-fuerza-157552#ixzz2wkeHcFF4 and James Bargent, "War for Cocaine Corridors Consumes Colombia's Busiest Port," *InSight Crime*, 14 February 2014 at http://www.insightcrime.org/news-analysis/war-for-cocaine-corridors-consumes-colombias-busiest-port.

[11] Most recently uprisings in Rio's *favelas* have led to attacks on police stations and requests for federal assistance; See Paul Kiernan, "Rio Seeks Federal Help to Stem Attacks on Police Force," *Wall Street Journal*, 21 March 2014 at http://online.wsj.com/news/articles/SB10001424052702304756104579453382489507704?mg=reno64-wsj&url=http%3A%2F%2Fonline.wsj.com%2Farticle%2FSB1000142405270230475610457945338489507704.html.

[12] William Langewiesche, "City of Fear." *Vanity Fair*, April 2007, pp. 158, 165-177.

[13] See Victoria Baena, "Favelas in the Spotlight: Transforming the Slums of Rio de Janeiro," *Harvard International Review*, Vol. XXXIII, No. I, Spring 2011, pp. 34-37; and Flavie Halaia, "Pacifying Rio: what's behind Latin America's most talked about security operation," *openDemocracy*, 12 March 2013 at http://www.opendemocracy.net/opensecurity/flavie-halais/pacifying-rio-whats-behind-latin-americas-most-talked-about-security-oper.

[14] Dudley Althaus, "Death and Corruption: Organized Crime and Local Govt in Mexico," *InSight Crime*, 18 October 2013 at http://www.insightcrime.org/news-analysis/mexico-mayors.

[15] See Inma Gil and Julián Miglierini "México: 4 ciudades a la somra del narco," *BBC Mundo*, 30 July 2010 at http://www.bbc.co.uk/mundo/america_latina/2010/06/100621_mexico_ciudades_narcotrafico_introduccion.shtml for a journalistic account of the different forms of narco influence on cities and states.

[16] Jason McGahan, "Why Mexico's Sinaloa Cartel Loves Selling Drugs in Chicago," *Chicago Magazine*, 17 September 2013 at http://www.chicagomag.com/Chicago-Magazine/October-2013/Sinaloa-Cartel/ and "How Sinaloa Cartel Influences Chicago's Violence," *NPR*, 24 February 2014 at http://www.npr.org/2014/02/24/281916686/el-chaop-cartel-influences-chicagos-violence.

[17]   Doris Gomora, "Narco controla 71.5% de municipios del país,"
       El Universal, 02 January 2012 at http://www.eluniversal.com.mx/
       nacion/192540.html.

[18]   "Grupos de autodefensa operan en 68 municipios del país,"
       Animal Politico, 02 March 2014 at http://www.animalpolitico.
       com/2013/03/grupos-de-autodefensa-operan-en-68-municipios-
       del-pais/#ixzz2wklbvAnZ.

[19]   Eduardo Stanley, "Autodefensas of Michoacan, infights, a dark
       past and, a darker future? *VOXXI*, 21 March 2014 at http://voxxi.
       com/2014/03/21/mexico-vigilante-infighting-violence/.

[20]   Cited at Jean-Paul Marthoz, "Narco Estado by Teun Voeten: so
       close to us," *Media and Human Rights*, 04 March 2013 at http://
       www.humanrightsmediaproject.org/2013/03/narco-estado-by-
       teun-voeten-so-close-to.html.

[21]   See David Shunk, "Mega Cities, Ungoverned Areas, and the
       Challenge of Army Urban Combat Operations in 2030-2040,
       Small Wars Journal, 23 January 2014 at http://smallwarsjournal.
       com/jrnl/art/mega-cities-ungoverned-areas-and-the-challenge-of-
       army-urban-combat-operations-in-2030-2040.

[22]   See Jamison Jo Medby and Russell W. Glenn (2002) *Streetsmart:
       Intelligence Preparation of the Battlefield for Urban Operations*,
       Santa   Monica: RAND   at   http://www.rand.org/pubs/
       monograph_reports/MR1287.html.

Chapter 14

A Proposed Framework for Appreciating Megacities: A US Army Perspective

Michael Bailey, Robert Dixon, Marc Harris, Daniel Hendrex, Nicholas Melin and Richard Russo

First Published 24 April 2014

Abstract

Cities with populations of ten million or more are given a special designation: Megacity, a term coined by the UN in the 1970s [1]. There are currently over twenty megacities in the world, and by 2025 there will be close to forty [2]. This article presents a framework for assessing megacities to better appreciate the unique and unprecedented challenges and opportunities that may confront the U.S. Army in these rapidly evolving environments. The key components of this framework are context, scale, density, connectedness, and flow. These characteristics combine in varying ways, depending on the megacity. By assessing individual megacities through this framework, the U.S. Army can better understand how it might operate as part of a joint, interagency, intergovernmental, and multinational (JIIM) force within them. Making individual megacities (vice a generic megacity) the unit of analysis will lead to better DOTMLPF (doctrine, organization, training, materiel, leadership, personnel, and facilities) solutions, increase commander's appreciation, and provide better options for the conduct of successful operations.

Introduction

A global urbanization trend has pushed the number of megacities (a city or combination of cities with a total population over ten million) worldwide from two in 1970, to ten in 1990, to twenty-three in 2011. By 2025, the United Nations predicts there will be thirty-seven megacities [2], many of which will be in the developing world where drivers of instability will be numerous. The probability that the U.S. Army will be called upon to operate in a megacity will only increase. Although the Army has recent urban combat experience during Operation Iraqi Freedom in Fallujah (pre-war population estimate 350,000) and Baghdad (pre-war population 6 million), it has not yet conducted operations in megacities [i]. Recent writing and thinking about megacities attempt to characterize these large urban areas, explore their inherent risks and opportunities [3], and map their economic importance [4]. But little has been written about how the Army might prepare itself to operate in these environments. This article seeks to add to that discussion. Our hypothesis is that megacities are a unique category of operational environments that the Army does not fully appreciate or understand; by analyzing megacities through a strategic framework like the one described here, the Army can prepare itself to operate more effectively within them. This framework, applied to specific megacities, will begin to provide the foundational understanding the Army must have to operate successfully in megacity environments.

The Army has considerable recent experience in urban environments, particularly in Fallujah and Baghdad during Operation Iraqi Freedom. But even Baghdad, with a 2003 population of roughly 6 million, is not fully comparable to megacities that have two or three-times that population. While there are undoubtedly lessons to be learned from this and other urban operations of the past, those examples may not represent fully relevant historical models for future operations. While attempting to determine what, exactly, makes a megacity different from other urban environments, a framework emerged that has five central components: scale, density, connectedness, flow and context. These characteristics combine with each other in unique ways in several of the megacities that we examined. What emerged from our analysis is a typology ranging from cities that are highly integrated (e.g. New York City or Tokyo) with hierarchical governance and security systems, to cities that are loosely integrated (e.g. Lagos, Nigeria or Dhaka, Bangladesh) with alternatively governed spaces and security systems. Some cities exhibit a combination of the two (see Figure 1).

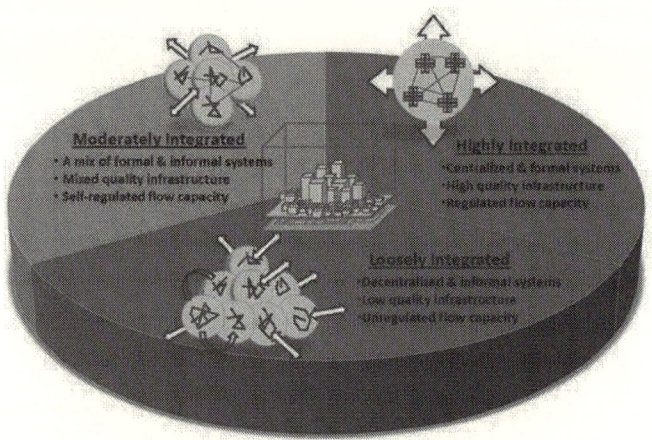

Highly integrated systems are characterized by strong formal and informal relationships among its component parts. These relationships manifest as highly ordered hierarchical structures with formalized procedures and norms, and open communication among its various parts. Highly integrated systems are inherently stable, show high degrees of resilience (ability to absorb change) and manage growth in a relatively controlled manner. Loosely integrated systems, on the other hand, lack many of the formal relationships that keep highly integrated systems stable. Weak control and communications systems, and lack of consistent rules for interaction amongst component parts lead to low resilience and unregulated growth. This growth, in turn, contributes more component parts that aren't formally integrated into the system, creating a downward spiral of instability.

Drivers of instability in megacities range from glaring wealth disparity to environmental risk factors. Some megacities, particularly highly integrated cities, are capable of coping relatively well when instability arises, while others will have their service and security capabilities quickly overwhelmed. Where vital US interests are at stake, the Army may be called on to conduct operations in and around megacities to achieve strategic goals that protect those interests. Lacking relevant historical examples to base training, education and planning, we believe the Army is not prepared for operations in these unique operational environments. Entirely new concepts are needed to prepare the Army to conduct operations in the megacity environment. A framework based on context, scale, density, connectedness, and flow is presented to encourage new thinking on the subject (see Figure 2). This framework can be used to uncover key nuances in operational environments that are incredibly complex. It is not meant to provide a model for understanding all megacities; such a thing is not possible. Nor is it meant to take the place of existing analytical tools (PMESII-PT[ii] or METT-TC[iii] for example) that help tactical planners focus their efforts, but instead can be used as a precursor to tactical planning to provide an urban-centric strategic appreciation of the megacity system.

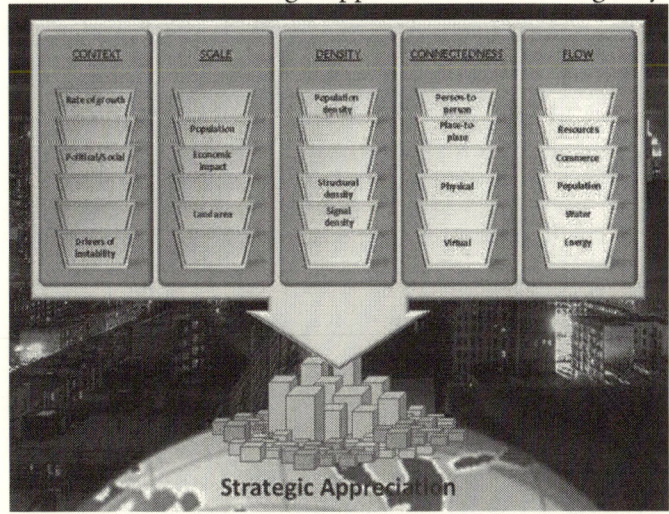

Context

Every megacity is unique and must be understood within its own historical, cultural, local, regional and international context. Politics and geography further complicate the human terrain and leave military planners with a potentially overwhelming problem set. Knowledge of the rate and characteristics of a megacities' growth may enrich our contextual understanding, as will knowledge about certain drivers of instability, including the geographic complexities which might increase the likelihood of environmental catastrophe.

In 1950 there were 2 megacities, New York and Tokyo. Today there are nearly 30. Some have grown very rapidly (Table 1), while others have grown slowly and methodically. The pace and nature of a city's growth are essential to understanding context. Economic and environmental forces drive migration from rural areas to cities resulting in either slow, gradual growth, or explosive growth depending on the nature of work being done there [5]. There is a difference between large, complex, economically essential megacities that came to be through well-understood economic processes and megacities that are just as large and economically essential but grew into what Jacobs terms 'economic grotesques' which are simpler economies based on dependency and exploitation [6]. Growth of this kind is rapid, largely unchecked, and relies on people and resources from surrounding rural areas to migrate to the city, which in some cases can create instability in both areas. New York City's growth, for example, happened because it was an engine of diverse economic growth. People migrated to New York City gradually, creating an economic base from which to develop infrastructure at a reasonable pace. Rural areas were able to keep pace with the gradually increasing demand to supply the urban center with food and other resources [7]. But less integrated cities, such as Dhaka, are growing at a pace that the formal system cannot cope with. Rapid growth of this kind can lead to a rise in informal economic activity which can destabilize the labor market [8]. In the case of Lagos, Nigeria, the urban center attracts rural migrants because of insufficient opportunities in the rural areas, not because of inherent, stable economic opportunities within the city itself [9]. The nature of the growth is therefore fundamentally different, which shapes the nature of the relationship between migrants and city itself.

	Population (M) 1950	Population (M) current	Fold Increase
Lagos, Nigeria	0.28	12.2	43.2
Dhaka, Bangladesh	0.42	13.6	32.4
Sao Paulo, Brazil	2.4	19.9	8.3
Mumbai, India	2.9	17.3	6.0
Tokyo, Japan	11.3	37.2	3.3
New York, USA	12.3	20.3	1.7
London, UK	8.7	9.5	1.1

Table 1: Population (in millions) increases in selected megacities from 1950 to Today. Note the relationship between typology and rate of population growth.

Additionally, places like Lagos and Dhaka will continue to grow despite the fact that the government provides neither services nor, in many cases, economic opportunity to migrants. Megacities in the developing world risk becoming gathering places for the dispossessed to a greater extent than they already are, and not magnets for opportunity as one might hope they would be. Another concept worth understanding is the primate city, one that "stands alone in a different order of magnitude and significance from those of all other cities…"[10]. A primate city is an order of magnitude larger than other cities in the country and its economy is essential to the entire nation. Primate cities are often the home of national governments and security forces, and central hubs for business. The security and stability of the city has a direct impact on the security and stability of the nation. London and Paris are examples of Western primate cities. Lagos and Dhaka are examples of primate cities in the developing world. They are not simply big cities. They are places of such significance that any military effect may be magnified many times over due to their regional and international importance.

New York City has a rich history dating back to the mid-16th century. It has been a focal point in American history from its founding and its cultural significance is perhaps unparalleled in history. New York City is a local, regional, national and international economic superpower. While it is not a capital city, one could reasonably make the case that it is one of the most important places on earth. By virtue of its great wealth and highly integrated structure, New York City reaps the benefits of layers upon layers of government entities and service providers that are effectively resourced to deal with whatever problems may arise there, whether infrastructure, governance or security related. This will not be true of many megacities because they did not all grow out of similar processes.

Rio de Janeiro is also a culturally significant global city. Rio grew by a largely separate process than New York City. Its *favelas*, or slums, make up a significant portion of the city, and grew somewhat unintentionally in the late 19th and early 20th century when disaffected veterans and freed slaves essentially squatted in areas around the city [11]. This context provides some understanding of how these places, kept at arm's length by the government while the rest of the city grew, evolved separately and were populated by people without strong ties to the local or national government. Knowing this, it is perhaps not surprising that during a recent *favela* clearance operation government forces planted a national flag in the center of the *favela*, as if they were claiming some foreign territory [12]. Understanding political and social nuances like this will be essential for Army leaders hoping to engage effectively with local partners in future operations.

Finally, contextualizing megacities according to geography is important. The global urbanization trend is being accompanied by a trend towards littoralization [13], or movement towards the coasts, where they are more vulnerable to severe weather events including flooding (Kilcullen, 2013). A recent study analyzed economic (coastal population growth), institutional (uncontrolled planning zones) and natural (severe weather event frequency, river discharge, soil subsidence, and others) factors in an effort to identify cities at increased risk of flooding. Shanghai (pop. 22M), Dhaka (pop. 14M), Calcutta (pop. 14M) and Manila (pop. 22M) were found to have the highest Flood Vulnerability Index ratings [14]. The populations of those cities are at high risk from severe weather events. Other natural disaster risk factors include earthquakes; numerous megacities (Tokyo (pop. 37M), Los Angeles (pop. 15M), Tehran (pop. 13M), and Mexico City (pop. 20M) to name a few) are located on active geological fault lines [15].

Economic, cultural, historical, and geographical context amplify drivers of instability. Understanding a megacity's context is essential for military planners and leaders tasked to operate in there. Appreciating context provides insight into the needs of the population, their receptiveness to foreign military assistance, and the Army's ability to affect real change. Context is an essential component of the commander's appreciation and must be central to considering operations in any megacity.

Scale

The scale, or relative size, of megacities differentiates them from other urban environments and presents a fundamental challenge to the Army's doctrine and force structure. Scale can be expressed in multiple ways; one is the scale of population. By 2025 cities with populations at or near 20 million will be more common; places like New York (23.6 million), São Paulo (23.2 million), Dhaka (22.9 million) and Lagos (18.9 million) (2). New places will be added to the list of megacities including Kinshasa (14.5 million), Bangalore (13.2 million), and Bogota (11.4 million). To put these numbers in context, the entire population of the country of Afghanistan, where U.S. forces have operated over the last decade, is 28.9 million [16]. Another way of understanding scale is in terms of land area. New York City's five boroughs cover 301 square miles [17]. This does not capture, however, the entire megacity area. When the area of shared infrastructure and industry that surrounds New York City's urban core is included the metropolitan area expands to 4,495 square miles, and crosses from New York State into New Jersey and Connecticut [18].

The scale of the economic impact of megacities also places them in a separate category from other cities. New York City's Gross Domestic Product (GDP) is on par with Canada and larger than South Korea[19]. Lagos' GDP is as large as that of the country of Kenya [20]. In many cases megacities have more in common with nations than with smaller urban environments. For military strategists, megacities may have more in common with operational theaters than with areas of operation.

Although all urban environments can be understood better by examining their density, connectedness, flows and context, within a megacity these characteristics manifest themselves on a far greater scale. Take, for example, the scale of density. While it might not be evident on the surface, the cities of Macau, China and Karachi, Pakistan share a common characteristic; they both have similar population densities: Macau 61,400/km², Karachi 59,100/km². Macau packs its 553,000 people into twenty-three square kilometers, while Karachi's has nearly twenty million people spread over 945 square kilometers [18]. Macau is dense, but within an area that could potentially be manageable to a military force using existing doctrine. Karachi's population, on average, is equally dense over an area far too large to manage with current doctrine and available force levels. This example illustrates how each of the characteristics detailed in this study is magnified and made unique by the sheer scale of these urban environments.

The scale of megacities challenges the underlying tenets of force sizing (methodology and doctrine) for urban operations. The Army's methodology for tailoring the size of the force for an operation is based on historically derived ratios. However, the Army lacks relevant historical examples that adequately apply to mega urban environments. Simply scaling historical ratios quickly exceeds capacity by orders of magnitude. Based on analysis of counterinsurgency campaigns such as British operations in Malaya and Northern Ireland, US Army Field Manual (FM) 3-24 *Counterinsurgency* advises that the counterinsurgent force possess a minimum strength of 20 to 25 soldiers per every 1,000 people in an area of operations [21]. Likewise, the foundational ratios utilized in major combat operations, as presented in the Army's premier doctrine for operations, *Unified Land Operations* [22] and shown below (Table 2) originate from analysis originally conducted by the German General Staff during the Franco-Prussian War of 1870 [23].

The usefulness of these ratios is called into question by the scale of megacities. Execution of counterinsurgency operations in a large urban environment with a population of 20 million would require 400,000

Soldiers according to the ratio defined in FM 3-24. That number is exclusive of support personnel and assumes the operating environment is isolated from its surroundings. This surpasses the largest commitment of U.S. and allied forces in Iraq and Afghanistan (195,100 Soldiers, Airmen and Marines in November 2007), and approaches the current end strength of the entire active component of the U.S. Army [25]. Thus, some current force planning factors are obsolete when considering megacity environments.

Density

A major characteristic of urban environments is density, or quantity per unit area. Density comes in several forms and will impact any operation in a megacity. The challenges associated with managing population density is one form, but there are others (e.g. vehicle density leads to traffic congestion, structural density limits growth and maneuverability, and electronic signal density presents myriad problems in terms of bandwidth congestion and confounds signal-based targeting). Joint doctrine describes density as an overriding aspect of the urban environment and Army doctrine recognizes the difficulty of maneuver in urban environments [26]. But even these descriptions fall short of describing the impact that urban density at scale has on an Army's ability to operate. Under the pressure of extreme density, effects begin to blur and coalesce between specific urban patterns as the scale of the urban environment increases [27]. This limits a formation's ability to mass its formations and causes a disaggregation of combat power.

Increased vehicle density in large urban areas can result in congestion on surface roads and reduces the potential approach speeds of maneuver elements [28]. Population density can, intentionally or unintentionally, disrupt flows on fixed capacity lines of communication in and around the urban environment. In highly integrated megacities increases and fluctuations in population can be forecasted and planned for. On the island of Manhattan, for example, workforce commuting causes the population to expand from 1.6 million on weeknights to 4 million during weekdays [29]. This is an example of a daily fluctuation, but similar changes occur on other timelines in other places. For example, the mass migration of people throughout east Asia during the Chinese Lunar New Year results in what has been called "Traffic Armageddon" as billions of commuters and migrant workers journey home for the holiday [30].

Population, structural, and signal density in the urban environment produce physical and virtual clutter which reduces the effectiveness of intelligence collection and complicates target acquisition. Market saturation of cell phones and other web-enabled devices produce a signal-dense environment which complicates target acquisition and Signals Intelligence (SIGINT) collection [31]. Further, the three-dimensional maneuver spaces in urban environments present a departure from the horizontal target engagement Army maneuver forces are accustomed to:

> "… the high density of urban areas affects every level of operations. At the tactical level mental and physical exhaustion is exacerbated by the high noise levels reflecting off hard surfaces. More infrastructure, people and activity means situations change rapidly so more decision are needed, but the time available for decision is contracted. Density's cumulative negative effects can also create a scenario of sensory and capability overload. Activities at the operational and strategic level are complicated because a single area can soak up manpower and other resources. Density, like the linked notions of tempo and fragmentation, thus represents a way of understanding the dynamics of operations. For the result of density, vibration and increased temp is magnification; everything becomes intense, expensive and noisy [32]."

Connectedness

Now more than ever it is obvious that cities don't exist in isolation: not only are they part of a region or state, but modern, highly integrated cities are players on the global stage. The relationship between the city and its environment (local or global) is a product of the connections between them. In systems terms, the connections describe the city's *external connectedness*, and it reflects the myriad interactions to various places around the world. These interactions take the form of trade (goods or services), information, economics and finance, entertainment, social, etc. and form the basis of the city's function and purpose.

The complex web that describes modern cities' connectedness is integrated in more and faster ways than ever before. Instantaneous information transfer, robust international shipping on the surface and in the air, and mass migration (legal and illegal) connect the cities around the world in ways undreamed of only decades ago. The ability of a shopkeeper in Brazil, for example, to instantly contact a supplier in Beijing and receive a package the next day is a commonplace expectation.

Robust and redundant external connectedness makes isolating a modern city nearly impossible. Indeed, recent attempts at shutting down social media in Turkey [33], Egypt and Libya [13] illustrate how resilient modern communications systems are becoming. This robust connectedness can be used to great advantage see and understand the system, even from remote locations. An example of a global network leveraged to understand and inform a tactical situation is the work of a group of disaster response experts know as Crisis Mappers:

> "Crisis Mappers leverage mobile & web-based applications, participatory maps & crowd sourced event data, aerial & satellite imagery, geospatial platforms, advanced visualization, live simulation, and computational & statistical models to power effective early warning for rapid response to complex humanitarian emergencies. As information scientists we

also attempt to extract meaning from mass volumes of real-time data exhaust [34]."

In the 2010 earthquake in Haiti, Crisis Mappers members based in Boston and supported by volunteers around the world used real time data enabled through social media and SMS messaging to dynamically map crisis response needs. This dynamic map was used by US Marine Corps and US Coast Guard personnel on the ground to locate and rescue hundreds of earthquake victims [35].

Real-time global news coverage of events is another form of connectedness that solidifies global connectedness. This dynamic serves to flatten the strategic-operational-tactical hierarchy and increase the impact of seemingly local events. Instantaneous worldwide communication of news appears to be reliably consistent, so much so that terrorists attacking Mumbai in 2008 used news feed from global media sources as their primary feedback mechanism to their control center in Pakistan [13].

Megacities also serve as physical conduits through which goods, services and traffic flow. Sea ports and international airports serve both the city itself and the surrounding region. New York City's port, for example, is the largest port on the East Coast of the United States, serving 35% of the country's population. Its three airports account for 25% of the nation's air imports and almost 20% of its exports. Regional and national road and rail networks also converge on these large urban environments acting as conduits for traffic to and through the city. For example, over 1.1 million vehicles pass through New York City each day, making it the most active traffic hub in the Northeast between Boston and Washington, D.C. The ramifications of interrupting this flow are so profound that cities across the region established an agency, *Transportation Operations Coordinating Committee* [36], to continually monitor the traffic conduits through New York City and issue alerts so that outlying areas can react to the effects of even one highway closing in the city within hours of its occurrence [37].

Interrupting the conduits of physical connectedness is likely to complicate military operations, as seen during the responses to urban areas in the 2010 Haiti Earthquake and Typhoon Haiyan in the Philippines in 2013. While neither affected a megacity, the cases illustrate the potential for widespread devastation. The Haiti earthquake, which demolished over 100,000 structures and damaged 200,000 more, devastated not only the internal physical connectedness of Port-au-Prince but also the national transportation grid. With a devastated port, marginally functional international airport and rubble-blocked roads, responders discovered that their ability to provide relief to the rural periphery could not proceed until these connective functions were restored [38].

Cities are also connected internally to their own structure. The relationships and flow systems that connect the various component parts of a city are the primary factors in defining the structure and behavior of the city. In viewing cities as complex systems, it is often easiest to notice the elements of the system because they are thought to be visible, tangible things [iv]. But a system cannot be understood absent an understanding of the connections between them. Some of the interconnections in the system are actual physical flows, such as roads, power lines or waterways. But non-physical flows of information are increasingly becoming the primary connective tissue that holds cities together. Information-based relationships are difficult to see in most systems but are essential to understanding the city [39]. But the increasing proliferation of mobile communications is making internal connectedness more robust at the personal level. The International Telecommunications Union (ITU) expects the number of cell phone accounts to rise from 6 billion now, to 7.3 billion in 2014, compared with a global population of 7 billion. Over 100 countries have more cell phone accounts than people [40]. However, non-digital information flows remain an important form of internal connectedness and are more difficult to see than digital systems. In many cities, information is still spread by word of mouth: in the market, on the street, or from the pulpit.

Military operations in the urban environment will continue to become more transparent with deeper mobile communication penetration. Cell phone capabilities (voice, text, and data (cameras)) may deny us the element of surprise during operations; the density of information and communication technologies (ICT) may slow the ability to identify actionable intelligence; and as developing countries gain parity in ICT, our ability to influence an adversary may be restricted.

Flow

Flow is the movement of people, resources or things into or out of a megacity. Just as a living organism relies on flows in (food, air and water), and flows out (waste) to stay alive, a city also requires flows. Vast amounts of energy and other vital goods must flow into the megacity, these goods must circulate throughout the urban space, and waste must flow out if the megacity is to remain healthy. The quality and efficiency of these flows are often referred to as the metabolism of the megacity, relating the importance of internal and external flow to its health. Some of these "lifeline" commodities are obvious: water, food, electricity and the removal of trash and sewage. Current Army doctrine outlines what technical infrastructure information should be collected, including the above areas plus others such as transportation networks, fuel distribution, and communications [41]. The economic impact of even temporary interruption of flow can be significant: the interruption of internet service in Egypt in 2011 for five days, for example, resulted in an estimated economic loss of $90 million (3-4% of GDP) [42].

Internal flow systems emerge naturally throughout the city to enable every moveable thing (goods, people, ideas, electricity, information, etc.) to flow in an increasingly efficient manner. While some flow systems (e.g., road networks, digital network architecture, and subways) are relatively static, the patterns of use of these systems are shaped by the nature of what travels along them. Absent constraint, flow systems continually evolve to increase efficiency, and new flows self-generate where necessary. This constant change in flows results in complexity that can be both challenging to understand and difficult to map [43]. This complexity makes it difficult to predict the consequences of even minor, temporary interruptions to flow, and gives rise to non-linear effects that confound analytic prediction.

Regardless of the type of operation, militaries operating in large urban areas are necessarily affected by their myriad flow systems, and this will be especially true in megacities. Among them are the flow of the population, friendly and enemy forces (maneuver, mobility, and logistics), information, and lifeline commodities (food, water, electricity, sewage, etc.). Many of these systems will compete for the same physical and electronic terrain. Commanders must, by necessity, seek to make sense of the various flow systems, and identify where flow systems are potentially in conflict. In fact, increasing flow system efficiency may be a central mission in a megacity environment.

Conclusions

Current Army doctrine acknowledges that "The dynamic relationships among friendly forces, enemy forces, and the other variables of an operational environment (PMESII-PT and METT-TC) make land operations exceedingly difficult to understand and visualize [22]." In a megacity it may not be possible to fully understand the complex and dynamic environment. Developing a robust strategic appreciation that considers the city as a holistic entity existing within a specific context is the most viable tool for military planners and commanders to begin making sense of the operation. Here we present a city-centric framework that acknowledges that any given megacity may not be fully understandable using a general analytical process and may not be responsive to traditional doctrinal methods. This framework, if used in advance of any operational or mission planning, updated as frequently as possible, and used to inform DOTMLPF [v] requirements, may help Army planners and commanders prepare for operations in highly complex megacity environments.

Current doctrinal approaches are underpinned by two fundamental assumptions: The Army will have the ability to isolate the urban environment, and ground forces will be able to utilize ground approaches from the periphery for maneuver into the city [27]. For megacities, both of these assumptions may be badly flawed. By virtue of their scale, density, connectedness, flows and context, isolation of a megacity (or even significant portions of it) either physically or virtually may not be possible or desirable. Attempting to physically control an urban population of tens of millions of people spread over hundreds of square miles either ignores the force ratios defined in doctrine or demands massive mobilization. In the future, optimal force ratios may have to be determined in real time based on dynamic circumstances in a megacity and must include innovative use of external (non-US) forces. The flexibility to man, train and equip a force rapidly enough to deal with such an environment will be essential. Virtual isolation of a megacity is even more improbable given that cell phone saturation in urban environments worldwide is already approaching or even exceeding 100% and global interconnectedness through the World Wide Web and satellite technology is ubiquitous. Ground maneuver from the periphery is also unrealistic. The congestion of ground avenues of approach combined with the massive size and density of the megacity environments make even getting to an objective from the periphery questionable, let alone achieving operational goals.

The very nature of megacities, coupled with the increasing likelihood of their being the key terrain of the future security environment, demands new thinking and new operational approaches. Megacities are a fundamentally new operating environment where traditional approaches are unlikely to work. It will not be possible to attack the problem one neighborhood at a time. The Army must endeavor to view the system as a whole, like a living organism, and understand its context, density, connectedness, and flow, all at an unprecedented scale. The Army must learn to shape itself to this environment. One size will not fit all in these places and developing a one-size-fits-all Army will lead to failure in megacities. Increasing our understanding based on the framework discussed here may enable the Army of the future to operate effectively in these highly complex environments.

Acknowledgements

Thank you to Dr. David Johnson and Dr. Christopher Rice, Director and Deputy Director of the Chief of Staff of the Army's Strategic Studies Group (SSG) for valuable guidance and review and to our colleagues in the other SSG Concept Teams for their input and ideas. This work was done as part of a one-year fellowship at the SSG during which Fellows seek to provide the Chief of Staff of the Army with Independent, Innovative and Unconstrained ideas about future Army challenges.

The views expressed in this article are those of the authors and do not necessarily reflect the official policy or position of the U.S. Army or the Department of Defense.

Bibliography

[1]   IRIN. In-Depth: Disaster Reduction and the Human Cost of Disaster. [Online] June 2005. [Cited: April 3, 2014.] http://www.irinnews.org/in-depth/62448/14/africa-the-special-case-of-mega-cities.

[2]   United Nations. *World Urbanization Prospects, 2011.* Department of Economic and Social Affairs. New York: s.n., 2012.

[3]   Hazel, G. & Miller, D. *Megacity Challenges, A Stakeholder Perspective.* Munich: Siemens AG, 2006.

[4]   Dobbs, Smit, Remes, Manyika, Roxburg, Restrepo. *Urban World: Mapping the Economic Power of Cities.* s.l.: McKinsey Global Institute, 2011.

[5]   Jacobs, Jane. *Cities and the Wealth of Nations.* New York: Vintage, 1984.

[6]   Taylor, P.J. *Mega-Cities in Theoretical Perspective.* Leicestershire, UK: s.n., Feb 28, 2011. GaWC Research Bulletin 373.

[7]   Hughes, Jonathan and Cain, Louis. *American Economic History.* New York: Harper Collins, 1994. pp. 169-171.

[8]   NRC. *Population Growth and Economic Development: Policy Questions.* Working Group on Population Growth and Economic Development, National Research Council. Washington, DC: National Academy Press, 1986. pp. 70-73.

[9]   Falola, Toyin. *Violence in Nigeria. The Crisis of Religious Politics and Secular Ideologies.* Rochester: University of Rochester Press, 1998. p. 148.

[10]   Jefferson, Mark. The Law of the Primate City. *Geographical Review.* April 1939, Vol. 29, 2.

[11]   Martin, Molly. *Mega-Cities & Mega-Events: Lessons from Favelas for the Future.* [Online] Spring 2012. [Cited: Feb 25, 2014.]

[12]   Domit, Myrna. Brazilian Forces Claim Victory in Gang Haven. *New York Times.* November 28, 2010.

[13]   Kilcullen, David. *Out of the Mountains: The Coming Age of the Urban Guerilla.* Oxford: Oxford University Press, 2013.

[14]   Balica, S.F. *A flood vulnerability index for coastal cities and its use in assessing climate change impacts.* October 2012, Natural Hazards, Vol. 64, pp. 73-105.

[15]   Achenback, Joel. Under the world's greatest cities, deadly plates. *Washington Post.* February 23, 2010.

[16]   Goode, Steven. *A Historical Basis for Force Requirements in Counterinsurgency.* Carlisle: US Army Strategic Studies Institute, 2009-2010.

[17]   nycgo.com. New York City Official Guide. [Online] 2014. [Cited: March 5, 2014.] http://www.nycgo.com/articles/nyc-statistics-page.

[18]   Demographia. World Urban Areas. [Online] 2013. [Cited: March 5, 2014.] http://www.demographia.com/db-worldua.pdf.

[19]   Florida, Richard. If U.S. Cities were Countries, how would They Rank? *The Atlantic.* [Online] July 21, 2011. [Cited: March 5, 2014.] http://www.theatlantic.com/business/archive/2011/07/if-us-cities-were-countries-how-would-they-rank/241977/.

[20]   Economist. *The Economist.* [Online] April 13, 2013. [Cited: March 5, 2014.] http://www.economist.com/news/

middle-east-and-africa/21576135-africas-giant-waking-up-it-still-looks-unsteady-its-feet-lurching-ahead.

[21] HQDA. Field Manual 3-24, Counterinsurgency. Dec 2006.

[22] —. *Army Doctrine Reference Publication 3-0.* Washington, DC: s.n., 2012 йил.

[23] Mearsheimer, John. *Assessing the Conventional Balance: The 3:1 Rule and Its Critics.* Spring 1989, International Security, Vol. 13, p. 59.

[24] Zanella, James. Combat Power Analysis is Combat Power Density. Fort Leavenworth, KS: School of Advanced Military Studies, 2012.

[25] Belasco, Amy. *The Cost of Iraq, Afghanistan, and Other Global War on Terror Operations Since 9/11.* Washington, DC: Congressional Research Service, 2011.

[26] HQDA. FM 2-91.4. [Online] Mar 2008. [Cited: Feb 25, 2014.] https://www.fas.org/irp/doddir/army/fm2-91-4.pdf.

[27] —. Field Manual 3-06. [Online] 2006. [Cited: Feb 25, 2014] https://www.fas.org/irp/doddir/army/fm3-06.pdf.

[28] *Does Accessibility Require Density or Speed?* Levine. Spring 2012, Journal of the American Planning Association, pp. 157-172.

[29] Moss, M.L. & Qing, C. *The Dynamic Population of Manhattan.* New York, NY: Rudin Center for Transportation Policy and Management, Wagner School of Public Service, NYU, 2012.

[30] Huang, G. [Online] Feb 5, 2014. [Cited: Feb 25, 2014.] http://www.cnn.com/2014/01/27/travel/11 things lny/.

[31] Moore, M.R. *Regional and Broadband Wireless Technologies.* Oak Ridge, TN : Oak Ridge National Laboratory, 2008.

[32] Hills, Alice. *Future War in Cities: Rethinking a Liberal Dilemma.* New York : Frank Cass, 2004.

[33] Rawlinson, Kevin. Turkey blocks use of Twitter after Prime Minister attacks social media site. *The Guardian.* March20, 2014.

[34] CrisisMappers. CrisisMappers: The Humanitarian Technology Network. [Online] 2014. [Cited: April 10, 2014.] http://crisismappers.net/.

[35]	Meier, Patrick. How Crisis Mapping Saved Lives in Haiti. *National Geographic.* July 12, 2012.

[36]	TRANSCOM. Transportation Operations Coordinating Committee. [Online] 2014 йил. [Cited: 2014 йил 24-March.] http://xcm.org/XCMWebSite/Index.aspx.

[37]	Ascher, Kate. *The Works: Anatomy of the City.* New York: Penguin Books, 2005.

[38]	Cecchine, Gary. *The U.S. Military Response to the 2010 Haiti Earthquake: Considerations for Army Leaders.* Washington, DC: The RAND Corporation, 2013.

[39]	Meadows, Donella H and Wright, Diana. *Thinking in Systems: A Primer.* White River Junction: Chelsea Green Publishing, 2008.

[40]	SiliconIndia. World to have more cell phone accounts than people by 2014. [Online] January 2, 2013. [Cited: March 4, 2014.] http://www.siliconindia.com/magazine_articles/World_to_have_more_cell_phone_accounts_than_people_by_2014-DASD767476836.html.

[41]	HQDA. FM 3-3 4.170, Appendix C, Engineering Reconnaissance. Washington, DC: s.n., 2008.

[42]	Young, Mirae. *The Collision of Social Media and Social Unrest: Why Shutting Down Social Media is the Wrong Response.* Fall 2013, Northwestern Journal of Technology and Intellectual Property.

[43]	Bejan, Adrian. *Design in Nature: How the Constructal Law Governs Evolution in Biology, Physics, Technology, and Social Organization.* New York: Doubleday, 2012.

Figure Legends

Figure 1: Proposed Megacity Typology ranging from Highly to Loosely integrated. Highly integrated megacities have centralized, formal systems of governance and security systems, high quality physical and technical infrastructure, and an ability to regulate the flows of people, resources and economic activities. Loosely integrated megacities have decentralized and informal governance and security systems, low quality physical and technical infrastructure and have considerable difficulty regulating the flow of people, resources and economic activity. Moderately integrates megacities exhibit combinations of these two. It is also worth noting that this is a general typology and does not fully describe the environment. Even the most loosely integrated megacities will have pockets of highly integrated systems, and conversely highly integrated megacities will have pockets of loosely integrated systems.

Figure 2: Proposed analytical framework of Context, Scale, Density, Connectedness and Flow. Based on initial analysis these elements, and sub elements are important factors to achieve a strategic appreciation of a megacity environment, but this list is not all-inclusive. Each analysis will likely result in other elements and sub-elements that will add to understanding and appreciation.

Notes

[i]   Population estimates vary widely depending on source data. Whenever possible we used population data from United Nations Statistical Division available at http://unstats.un.org.

[ii]   PMESII-PT analysis can be used to examine the following operational variables: political, military, economic, social, information, infrastructure, physical environment and time.

[iii]   METT-TC analysis is done upon receipt of a warning order or mission. It is used to explore the following mission variables: mission, enemy, terrain and weather, troops, time available and civil considerations.

[iv]   Elements of complex systems do not have to be physical things: intangible elements in social systems such as solidarity, factionalism, and belief systems can be very important elements to the system. *See* Meadows, pp. 11-15.

[v]   DOTMLPF: Doctrine, Organization, Training, Materiel, Leadership, Personnel, Facilities.

Chapter 15

On Megacities

Geoffrey Demarest

First Published 11 June 2014

This comment responds to the the *SWJ* publication of "A Proposed Framework for Appreciating Megacities: A US Army Perspective."[1] I applaud the Strategic Studies Group for choosing the topic, and found the paper refreshing and significant. I noted some years ago a tendency in our war-gaming to simply pretend that these huge conurbations did not exist, so troubling were the geographic challenges they presented. That the Chief of Staff has thrown that strategic method out in favor of the Myamoto Musashi approach is great progress. We are going to have to fight in urban areas, so let's figure it out. I found the concluding sentence of the abstract especially encouraging: "Making individual megacities (vice a generic megacity) the unit of analysis will lead to better DOTMLPF…and provide better options for the conduct of successful operations. With that in mind, I notice that Dhaka and Lagos seem to get pinged for special attention. The *SWJ* article appeared in my inbox only days after Dr. Charles Ehlschlaeger's anthology from the Strategic Multi-Layer Assessment (SMA) and U.S. Army Engineer Research Development Center (ERDC), "Understanding Megacities with the Reconnaissance, Surveillance, and Intelligence Paradigm."

The two (The Strategic Studies Group article and the ERDC White Paper) don't seem aware of each other, or at least do cite each other or share references. They share 'mega' and, interestingly, the ERDC also pings Dhaka and Lagos. It seems like somebody somewhere has it in for those two places.

There are a few points I would like to bring to the attention of the group of authors for their consideration. One comes from a word search of the Strategic Studies Group document. The terms 'built-environment' and 'land-use planning' cannot be found in it. This is probably no big thing, but it might bespeak a gap in references or a failure to engage, and it might present an opportunity. The conversation in academe and the vocation of urban management has had these two terms near their core for some decades. The group's paper seems unimpressed by that conversation. It just seems odd to me that in the group's consideration of sources, something wouldn't tend to compel use of (or at least a nod to, since the paper is about an analytical framework) the common urban studies terms. Another thing, and this is perhaps even more picayune, is an appearance that maybe the "megacities" notion is some sort of current think-tank shiny object. I see that the subject is megacities not cities, and the paper clearly expresses the idea that a megacity is something apart and different than the mere huge city or, say, a peripheral non-primate burb of just three million. OK, but (keeping in mind that most megacities are places where the United States military is just not going to go, and that the number of megacities where we might in fact go is maybe not enough to occupy all the digits on one hand) the current fascination with 'mega' might be detouring intellectual resources from the geographies that count—these latter probably being a number of cities that are mid to large in size—like the Fallujah-size to Bagdad-size that the group mentions in passing.

Which brings us to a central offering of the article, the analytical framework the group summarizes as 'context, scale, density, connectedness, and flow.' That is thought-provoking and perhaps a valuable tool for understanding, but I doubt it is sustainable as a guide for organizing and operating. I think, for instance, that prompts like 'distances,' 'ownership,' 'energy,' 'convocation,' 'collective identity,' and 'waste management,' and a few others might be better categories of analysis, but that's just me. Regardless— good read, congratulations Strategic Study Group.

P.S. From the BBC we get, "The population of Stalingrad—now Volgograd—fell from 850,000 to just 1,500 at the end of the war." So, I guess what armies do in a city can have an effect.[2]

Notes

[1]   Michael Bailey, Robert Dixon, Marc Harris, Daniel Hendrex Nicholas Melin, and Richard Russo, "A Proposed Framework for Appreciating Megacities: A US Army Perspective." *Small Wars Journal*. 24 April 2014, http://smallwarsjournal.com/jrnl/art/a-proposed-framework-for-appreciating-megacities-a-us-army-perspective-0.

[2]   "On this Day: 1943: Germans surrender at Stalingrad." *BBC*, 2 February, http://news.bbc.co.uk/onthisday/hi/dates/stories/february/2/newsid_3573000/3573003.stm.

Chapter 16

Intelligence Challenges in Urban Operations

James Howcroft

First Published 20 July 2014

Military operations in an urban area are not normally thought of as a "Small Wars" concern, yet they are an important capability that will remain relevant as we address the issue of security in the 21st century. From my experience, we avoid them like the plague, for good reasons, until we have no option but to commit resources and go in. Our foes see great value in operating in urban areas. Urban operations are a form of asymmetric warfare, which degrades a number of advantages possessed by well-equipped and well-trained militaries. (David Kilcullen's recent book *Out of the Mountains: The Coming Age of the Urban Guerrilla* addresses these aspects in great depth). The population of our world is increasingly urbanized. Both the World Bank and CIA agree that more than half the world's population now lives in urban areas. There are the mega cities of Africa and Asia to consider, but the issue is equally important in the hundreds of thousands of smaller cities and towns throughout the world. The Ukrainian military is dealing with this issue in the summer of 2014 in Donetsk and Luhansk in eastern Ukraine. The Nigerian military will have tough decisions to make to in its fight against Boko Haram. Eventually, the Iraqi military will need to retake the towns and cities of central and northern Iraq lost to ISIS and its allies in June 2014.

As a Defense Attaché assigned to Moscow in the 1990s, I observed and reported on Russian combat operations in Grozny during the two Chechen Wars (1995-2000). I served in the Second Marine Division during Desert Storm in 1991 as part of the operation to liberate Kuwait City. I was the G2 of First Marine Division for the capture of Baghdad in 2003 and G2 of First Marine Expeditionary Force (MEF) during the unsuccessful assault on Fallujah in 2004. I observed firsthand a number of **important conditions for success** throughout these urban operations that remain relevant for any fighting force. There are many doctrinal publications, lessons-learned handbooks, and first-person accounts that are certainly worth reading. My modest list is not meant to replace these resources nor is my list exhaustive. These seven are merely challenges in urban operations I personally encountered over the past 20 years that have constrained the ability to provide intelligence to those organizations and commanders I supported.

1. Plan Ahead for the Challenges and Opportunities of the Cordon

One of the initial tasks will be to establish a cordon to isolate the urban area of concern. This is an extremely resource-intensive job that will immediately draw upon the troops and tools you are assembling to use once you move into the city. One of the most important initial intel tasks will be to determine how the local population moves in and out of the city, to help the commander focus his limited forces on disrupting the flow. You will never have enough assets to be able to completely stop the traffic. The intelligence officer, based on his assessment of the environment and foe's capability and intent, has to help the commander decide not only *where* to focus, but also *how much* movement to try to block and *who* in particular you will use your finite resources to screen and search. You need to keep hostile forces out of the city obviously; but who do you let out? Everyone, so there are fewer noncombatants in the line of fire? Families only? Do you want to leave a way out for your foe so you can then engage them outside the cover and concealment of the city? In April 2003, after fighting 600 kilometers from Kuwait to the Diyala River outside Baghdad, orders to my Division from higher headquarters were merely to "put a cordon around Baghdad," … a city of 5 million people. Our request for clarification and guidance regarding rules of engagement, end-state, etc. was met by silence. Fortunately for us, by mid-April there was little movement by the population out of the city and little regime capability remained to reinforce Baghdad, so the cordon didn't turn out to be quite the problem I had feared.

Unfortunately, my fears were realized a year later when establishing an effective cordon around Fallujah, prior to our assault in April 2004, proved to be a much bigger problem. Large numbers of the population were anxious to leave. Foreign fighters and extremists were trying to get into the city to fight from within the urban confines. We had to uproot Marine battalions from their ongoing security mission throughout Al Anbar Province in an attempt to impose a cordon and isolate the city. We did not have adequate resources or experience to effectively screen those coming out of the city to identify and segregate the bad guys. We quickly learned of the need for trained and trusted personnel, including hundreds of linguists, to question the population regarding the situation in the city. This exiting population was mainly families with their possessions, anxious to move out of the danger area. They were not interested in stopping their flight to talk to us. The fleeing population had the best, most up to date information about what was going on in Fallujah, but we didn't have a system in place or enough resources allocated to tap into this knowledge. The campaign didn't end well for either side.

2. Knowing Where Things are Located Isn't Enough

Once the cordon is functioning, it's time to move into the city. The information demands of your force will be staggering. There are certain areas you will always need to understand when entering an urban area—with the purpose of then controlling it and the population. These are the building layout and composition, transportation, electrical, sewage and water, and natural gas systems and the locations/status of key subcomponents—bridges, gas stations, power stations, high tensions power lines, neighborhood substations/transformers, underground sewage canals, water purification plants, gas lines and their depth under roads (so they aren't crushed by your tanks). Other considerations are the locations of all police stations—either to get them on your side or to disarm them as they are the easiest sources of weapons at the beginning of an occupation—other civic buildings necessary for the running of the city trash department, finance department, banks, city hall, fire departments, key cultural areas, and political party headquarters amongst a few as well as the locations of the tallest buildings not only for fields of fire and observation but to locate the radio relays necessary for VHF communications systems. The USMC *Urban Generic Information Requirements Handbook (UGIRH)* was a useful tool to identify and organize the vast range of information our force required.

As the intelligence officer, you will need to know not only about the physical characteristics of the town and the capabilities and intentions of your foe, you must know the ***current*** composition and power of whatever group or groups is running the city. Knowing how the city was run or organized under the former regime is probably irrelevant. You need to know the tools and levers of power and personalities of the current group or groups **now** calling the shots. Where are they successful in the city? What can't they do and why not? Whatever groups may be running the city's neighborhoods day by day may not necessarily be the foe you are going into the city to defeat. Can those running various sections of the city be our ally or are they aligned and supportive of the armed foe inside the city? If they support them, is it out of ethnic loyalty or fear? Is the looming destruction of their city sufficient motivation for local powerbrokers to force foreign fighters out?

Tools and assets that allow you to tap into the timely, detailed knowledge of the population are essential; but they can rapidly become overwhelmed by the size and scale of the task. The ability to exploit the language and cultural expertise of trusted local individuals, organizations and units will be crucial to your success. During the Russian assault on Grozny in 2000, the Russians exploited the experience, knowledge and connections of warlord Bislan Gantamirov's militia to guide operations in the city and obtain timely intelligence from the local population. Conversely, we lacked Iraqi units that could play such a role when we attacked Fallujah in April 2004. All but one of Iraqi military units that were to assist the Marines deserted, except for a single Kurdish battalion. They were well-led and brave, competent fighters, but they were Kurds in a Sunni city and thus little help in engaging local power brokers and learning from the population. If you don't have local allies that you and the population trust to assist your efforts you will fail; if not in the initial assault then certainly in your longer- term efforts to secure the city.

3. Impose a Single, Common Tool to Visualize the Urban Area

There is a requirement for a single, common visualization tool or product that depicts the city or town that **EVERYONE** involved in the operation has access to. "Everyone" includes the infantry, resupply, medevac, supporting arms, air support, UAV operators, interrogators, de-briefers, engineers, local police, the UN and NGOs. This has to be **unclassified,** easy to reproduce and available as paper copies that can be handed out like candy to everyone at every coordination meeting as well as disseminate electronically on smart electronic devices. You need a product with various scales that a user can turn/toggle the page from the detailed zoomed view of individual buildings on a particular block up to the overview of the city showing routes, power supplies and important buildings. This document will be a common planning and coordination tool and provide a single, common naming convention and symbols. This can help eliminate the maddening tendency for every unit or organization to give the same feature a different name, and for newly arrived units to rename a feature to reflect their unit's history and heritage. Is it Leatherneck Highway, Route Tampa, Highway 7 or what the population calls the road? Keep in mind you need to identify a simple way to update it as you receive corrections and changes and you need to decide who will be empowered to add these updates; everyone or a centralized authority?

4. Building a Useful Collection Capability Takes Time, Imagination and Flexibility

The nature of the urban environment will negate or degrade much of your intelligence and reconnaissance (ISR) capability. It is nearly impossible for reconnaissance or HUMINT teams to infiltrate covertly and remain undetected. Because of the risk associated with their employment, these assets were of little value in <u>this</u> role in either Baghdad or Fallujah. The urban structure and nature of the communications environment limit the ability to collect signals intelligence. Low power, commercial devices designed for short distances will largely be outside your capability to collect. If local features and your resources do allow collection, you will be overwhelmed by the vast amount of signals traffic from the large, urban population to translate, analyze, pass for action, and store for later use. Having only recently decided to address the urban area, you won't necessarily have the baseline template of the communications environment that is so important to signals intelligence. It takes time to develop this template. Time was a luxury the commanders I supported never had. Find a way to get your SIGINT guys in place working the signals environment as soon as possible.

Scalable UAVs have proven extremely useful in many urban efforts, but the limitations of imagery, whether UAV or a satellite, to see between densely packed buildings or within structures are obvious. Furthermore, the overhead imagery perspective will not match the ground eye orientation of the force on the ground. The individual on the ground, being shot at, awash in a sea of gray concrete or dust will orient and navigate by items of color, i.e. the building with the red roof or the house with the blue door, while the imagery analysts or UAV operator is usually looking from a perspective above at a black and white video screen or black and white infrared or radar imagery. The common visualization tool previously discussed can aid in this regard by providing a common block and building reference capability.

The local population will be the best source of intelligence. Locals that don't notice subtle changes in their environment don't survive. The large numbers to be screened and questioned will quickly overwhelm your resources. If they can be trusted (both by you and by the population), the local police and military are well suited for this task. Don't forget about identifying a culturally appropriate way to engage the female half of the city's population. It took years for the US Army and Marine Corps to field female engagement teams to talk with the mothers, wives and sisters of Baghdad, Fallujah and Kandahar. That's a lesson we can't let fade from our corporate mentality. Just like SIGINT, it takes time to set up HUMINT networks in a new city. HUMINT professionals need time to understand the ethnic/tribal makeup and power dynamics of the city, which will have an effect on who reports on whom and how reliable that reporting will be. It will be tough to ascertain the reliability and truthfulness of local population reporting—after all, it is your actions that are bringing death and destruction to their neighborhoods, putting their families at risk and causing them to flee. They don't know yet if you are going to win or how long you will be around. Talking to you compromises their families.

Media reporting can also be of great value to your intelligence collections operation. Reporters will be able to access places and people you may not be able to reach. What they have to say and what the people they are interviewing are expressing is of tremendous value to your assessment. Observation of the view over the shoulder of the correspondent can also be a valuable tool in assessing the status of buildings, key infrastructure or enemy equipment. Air Force analysts assessed that strikes in 2001 on the Taliban's Ministry of Vice and Virtue in Kabul were successful based on looking over the shoulder of a journalist reporting in front of the building. In April 2003 after seizing the northern half of Baghdad, my Division was tasked with short notice to send a Task Force another 200 kilometers north to seize Tikrit, Saddam's home town. Our objective had only ever been Baghdad, but the Turkish government's refusal to allow their territory to be used to invade Iraq from the north left Tikrit unsecured. It took time to reorient collection assets further north. My initial assessment to Task Force Tripoli that the city had been abandoned by the military and was undefended was based on watching a *CNN* report. The widespread growth in social media, especially in young, urban populations, opens up another lucrative source of real-time, street level reporting, as recently seen in Damascus, Tripoli, and Mosul.

5. Have a Method to Separate the Bad from the Good that Doesn't Alienate the Population

There is a requirement to separate the bad guys from the innocent. Not every 25-year-old male is the enemy. Not only is interning every male of fighting age a huge resource drain, it also alienates the population. Your understandable "better safe than sorry" approach results in actions that push the population away from you. A local populace that feels the occupying military has its interests in mind, can meet their needs and hasn't indiscriminately interned their husbands and fathers is more likely to provide reliable and useful information. An ignored, alienated population is less likely to carry out your directions and directives, or to identify concealed combatants, cached weapons and booby traps. At best, an alienated population is neutral. Worst case, they provide intelligence to the enemy and join their side.

There must be a fast and easy initial screening process that can be employed, as your forces clear buildings and neighborhoods. People with gunshot wounds and military related equipment on them will be easy, but how about the rest? The Russians in Grozny in the 1990s checked shoulders for bruises, sleeves and forearms for powder burns and sniffed for the smell of gunpowder. Initially, our biometrics won't be of use, we are unlikely to have had the time or opportunity to have built a database. One solution to identify combatants could be the use of gunpowder residue tests which police and forensics teams' use in civilian police departments. Once you do identify the bad guys, you need a plan to figure out where they go and how to interrogate them. Most likely the town's jail was set up and run for a small number of criminals, not hundreds or thousands of detainees with uncertain legal status. Even if there are vacant prisons conveniently now empty and available as a result of your actions, you will need trained and well-led professionals to administer whatever system of interrogation, evidence and justice your mandate and circumstances dictate. We did this poorly in Iraq in 2003-2004; the resulting Abu Ghraib scandal was a huge setback in our efforts to develop trust and cooperation with the Iraqi population.

6. Do Not Underestimate the Power and Importance of the Media

The media will have a huge impact on the perceived success or failure of your mission. Combat in a city is ready-made for a huge impact on TV and social media. The media can get close to the action and capture a real-time stream of powerful images and video of damaged buildings, craters, burning vehicles and destroyed lives. They will have access to hundreds of poignant frightened and injured civilians and children to photograph or interview that will be appear in homes and capitols around the world. Innocents will get killed in this type of fight. Your force will be the one bringing the destruction, you will get the blame, not those who chose to occupy buildings and build bunkers in neighborhoods. As the Ukrainian military had retaken Slavyansk in July 2014, the media was focused on images of the destruction caused by the Ukrainian military, not on the guilt of those who initially chose Slavyansk as the battleground. My commanders' prescient warnings prior to the assault on Fallujah in April 2004 to senior US leadership of the likely media impact of sending a Marine infantry division into a city were ignored. These civilians were aghast when those warnings became reality. The Marines had to cease operations and withdraw from the city because of the impact on world opinion of the destructive images being shown on international media.

Chechen mistreatment of journalists coupled with the deliberate Russian effort to keep the international media out of the second battle of Grozny in 2000 meant that the Russian destruction of a city of half a million of their own citizens was not shown on domestic or international media outlets; giving the Russians freedom to use supporting arms to level the city block by block and eliminate the Chechen force in Grozny. International media coverage of the carnage and destruction of the cities of Syria in 2014 has dwindled after the targeting of journalists has made Syria the most deadly country in the world for journalists to work. This is a trend likely to continue as regimes recognize the power of media driven information operations and take action to shape the message. While the Russian and Syrian regimes were able to intimidate journalists so that independent reporting of the fighting was impossible, America and NATO operate under public and transparent rules and laws that prohibit this type of action. Our operations <u>will</u> be seen by the world. We have to anticipate the powerful impact of our operations and be willing and prepared to engage with the media to help them present an accurate and balanced message. General Mattis, when serving as the First Marine Division Commander, often challenged us by saying; "*There will be a story about our actions on the evening news tomorrow, what are we doing to make it the right story?*" If you chose to ignore the media, you cede this powerful tool to our foes.

7. Realize Your limitations and Decentralize Your Effort

Intelligence for urban operations must be centrally planned and coordinated at the senior headquarters level in order to incorporate the insatiable needs of the multiple actors addressing a difficult mission in a complex environment. But when it comes time to move into the city and begin the clearing operation the fight becomes decentralized down to the small unit level, squads, platoons and companies. Decentralized operations of this type require decentralized intelligence. Platoons and companies need intelligence of immediate value and precision. Knowing that *"Al Jawan neighborhood has a high concentration of former regime fighters"* is useful and adequate at your headquarters level. The platoon needs intelligence that tells them "T*he three-story building on the north side of the next block in Al Jawan has a newly dug tunnel connecting it with adjacent buildings allowing the defenders unobserved lateral movement and resupply.*" It is extremely unlikely that a higher headquarters would be able to collect that information and be able to disseminate it down to the supported small unit in time to be useful. The headquarters who own intelligence assets need to acknowledge this fact and be willing to strip personnel and capabilities from their level to push down in direct support of the small level units in the fight. I learned that the time to do this is sufficiently prior to the launch of the assault to give the supported commander the chance to understand how to use the capability he now owns and enough time for the attached intel professionals to have the opportunity to understand the needs of those they now support. Intelligence attachments can be useful; last minute attachments are a distraction.

Final Thoughts

Urban operations are difficult, resource-intensive missions for every war fighting function within a unit. This is equally true for intelligence, both during the planning and execution phases of the mission. More collection platforms, more systems and more technology won't necessarily make you successful. The common thread needs to be the issue of dealing with the population. They are the reason we go into the city; it isn't about the structures or statues. The people have the best information to fill your gaps. Dealing with the huge amount of data at your disposal and turning in it usable, relevant, actionable intelligence for the wide range of consumers counting on you for answers is a daunting task and it has to be done. Because it is tough doesn't mean it can be ignored, wished away or pushed off to some other distant headquarters. I cannot honestly say that I did a great job supporting initial urban operations in Baghdad in 2003 and Fallujah in 2004, but my Marines and I did what we could, we learned hard lessons as we went along and these lessons paid dividends for those who followed us in Iraq. It is those lessons that I offer for future use among my peers and comrades in arms.

Chapter 17

Employing Armor Against the Islamic State: The Inevitable Urban Combined Arms Fight

Dennis A. Lowe

First Published 26 September 2014

> A: Where is the shooting?
>
> B: Everywhere! In every area.
>
> A: What is it, artillery?
>
> B: Artillery, mortars, tanks—everywhere.
>
> A: Where are you?
>
> B: By the flour mill.
>
> A: Are they attacking the flour mill?
>
> B: Yes, and they are attacking us too. The artillery is destroying us. All of Fallujah is in ruins. Not a house left standing. What can stand? The tanks come down every street with artillery falling ahead of them.
>
> —Intercepted jihadist cell phone conversation, November 12th, 2004.[1]

ISIL cannot be destroyed relying solely on airstrikes, guided missiles and special operations. The Russians made a critical mistake thinking artillery and airstrikes could bend the Chechen's to their will in 1994 and 1999. Military options confined to these capabilities will hinder ISIL in the short term. Ultimately, they will adapt to survive the circumstances imposed by external actors operating without a significant and stable ground presence. As long as ISIL controls territory and shelters among civilian populations in easily fortified urban environments, a combined arms ground force will be required to root them out and establish alternative governance. Essential to a major combined arms effort is the enlightened employment of armor and the mobile, protected firepower it provides.

Lacking the capability to engage a well-trained combined arms force in conventional maneuver warfare, ISIL will seek to level the playing field asymmetrically by choosing to fight in urban environments. Cities mitigate many of the technological and numerical advantages of Western-style conventional forces. Their topographic and human complexity impedes analysis and therefore effective planning. Such constraints make cities difficult to seize without significant collateral damage. Although ISIL will harass forces outside cities through IED's, ambushes and raids, they will seek victory in the concrete jungle. Unless the world is prepared to adopt an indefinite containment policy against an ISIL pseudo-state in the heart of the Middle East, we will find ourselves waging war in cities against a well-prepared foe.

Past urban conflicts provide valuable lessons for a possible fight in ISIL controlled cities. Had U.S. forces used armor in Mogadishu, Somalia in 1993, some of the ground force losses may have been avoided. A crucial component missing in Task Force Ranger were vehicles that could sustain multiple hits from an array of enemy weapon systems and keep moving. This is a recurring need in urban warfare that was neglected to the detriment of the forces involved.

In Chechnya, the failures of Russian armor commanders to effectively employ their forces in Grozny led to disastrous consequences. The hard-won lessons of the Russians serve as an important guide for any force contemplating action in the urban landscape.

The second battle of Fallujah in 2004, however, is an excellent case study in the successful combined arms employment of armor to take and hold urban terrain. Here a range of armored vehicles, centered on the Marine M1A1 Abrams, provided indispensable protection and firepower for the infantry who cleared the city room by room. Moreover, the shock effect that this armor brought to bear had both a physically and psychologically crushing impact against the insurgent defenders.

Few sources discuss the role of armor in Syria's civil war and the renewed conflict in Iraq. Both Syrian and Iraqi forces have employed armor but not to decisive effect. The full potential of armor in these contexts has not yet been realized. This paper aims to alleviate the deficit in material covering the usage of armor in these conflicts. I explore how a conventional combined armed force could most effectively employ armor assets against ISIL given what we know about the organization's current and projected practices. Although the recommendations contained herein are intended primarily for U.S. planners, the general principles may be applied to regional allies who employ armor against ISIL in the near future. Finally, this paper is not a call for a major U.S. intervention in the Middle East. Such an opinion is well beyond the scope of my qualifications and professional mandate. This paper is an exploration of possible improvements on armor practices given the real possibility of a renewed ground force commitment in the Middle East. Should the U.S. or regional powers choose this course, armored forces will be vital.

Understanding the Enemy

At a minimum, our point of departure must orient towards an understanding of ISIL and how it fights. Much of the contemporary material discussed in this paper comes from open sources such as news articles, journal publications, and social media outlets. The synthesis of sources provides insight into how this enemy fights and will likely fight, especially against an armored threat.

The primary limitations of this article stem from the lack of publicly available intelligence regarding the current Syria and Iraq conflicts. Nevertheless, the introduction of a Western combined-arms formation would present an unprecedented challenge for ISIL. It is a threat they have not yet faced. ISIL, like us, would initially rely on past experiences to inform their course of action and subsequent innovations would arise from circumstances we cannot yet predict. All recommendations are based on likely courses of action developed from lessons learned in similar conflicts.

LTC Aaron Bazin understands ISIL as a complex adaptive system; an organization that has no centralized hierarchy but rather functions as an aggregate of actors unified by a common cause. In this case Abu Bakr al-Baghdadi's Caliphate and its brand of Jihadist dogma are ISIL's ideological foundations.[2] Although al-Baghdadi functions as the self-proclaimed Caliph his command of ISIL is decentralized. He disseminates strategic and operational intent while subordinate commanders act on their own initiative in accordance with this higher guidance.[3] This is similar to the network-centric model described by Kilcullen.[4] These networks are an interwoven mesh of militants, supporters (both local and transnational), and leadership cadres that operate without a rigid or linear hierarchy. The leadership in such networks is best understood as actors who serve as nodes of influence within overlapping networks. The elimination of one such node simply gives rise to or augments the power of another without seriously degrading the capability of the whole.

At the tactical level, ISIL employs a "rule-based swarm maneuver system" similar to that of the Somali militants that Kilcullen describes.[5] Adapted from General Mohamed Farrah Aidid's tactics in 1993 this system operates according to a simple set of rules: "Maintain an extended line abreast, keep your neighbors just in sight, but no closer, move to the sound of the guns, dismount when you see the enemy, when you come under fire, stop and fire back."[6] It is a self-synchronizing system that requires minimal command and control and is adaptable to almost any situation. ISIL's maneuver warfare, if not deliberately developed from Somali practice, draws upon congruent methodology.

Once ISIL takes control of a population center it seizes local essential resources thus creating a dependency that yields compliance whether or not residents agree with ISIL's political-religious agenda.[7] Ultimately,

ISIL's power is dependent on its control of populations and the flow of resources. Therefore, control of cities is its primary objective. Retired Colonel Gary Anderson rightly acknowledges that a large, competent combined arms force is the only way to completely defeat ISIL and drive it from its urban strongholds.[8] This means we must look at the potential vulnerabilities that such a force will face in urban terrain.

Likely the primary ISIL anti-armor threats will not be other armored vehicles but small ATGM/AT[9] teams and IED's. They will seek to avoid our conventional maneuver strengths by avoiding direct conflict outside urban areas. Any large-scale engagements will occur in cities where ISIL can maximize its strengths as a decentralized fighting force, reducing the gap between their capabilities and ours. Additionally cities provide ISIL with a readily available, technically skilled population capable of leveraging workshops and industrial facilities to craft a number of homemade armaments, communications equipment and explosives.[10] Insurgents did exactly this in Fallujah, 2004.[11] Bashar al-Assad's forces have encountered similar "Do it Yourself" warfare techniques in Syria as well. As new innovations in DIY warfare arise on the battlefield testing grounds in Syria and Iraq, they will be disseminated and readily available online for future combatants.

Since ISIL began its conquest of Iraq earlier this year, it has proved adept at employing a number of anti-tank systems such as 9K11 Kornet ATGM's, RPG[12] variants, and the Yugoslavian M70 Osa rocket launcher.[13] During these engagements militants damaged at least twenty-eight Iraqi M1A1 Abrams tanks, five of which suffered full armor penetration.[14] Clearly, ISIL understands how to target our tanks' weak spots and accurately employ AT fires against them. Furthermore, ISIL has demonstrated its technical savvy in leveraging cyberspace to disseminate its message abroad in numerous languages, recruit fighters and collect intelligence. If it is capable of producing multi-language content and distributing it to a wide audience then it is capable of scouring open-source repositories for crucial technical and doctrinal data about how we and our allies operate. They will understand how to attack our vulnerabilities better than we may realize.

ISIL AT tactics and weapons systems are similar if not identical to those used by other militant groups fighting in the region. For example, Hezbollah fields a variety of ATGM systems against Israeli Merkava tanks to include: Milan, Metis-M, Sagger AT-3, Spigot AT-4 and Kornet AT-14 systems.[15] Many of these have seen action in Syria's civil war where ISIL first gained prominence. Additionally, Chinese manufactured Norinco HJ-8 Red Arrows have been widely used against Syrian armor formations.[16] Numerous militant and rebel groups use these systems and we must assume that ISIL is familiar with their operation. Should the U.S. and allies use armor against ISIL they will likely encounter such weapons.

Although many of the aforementioned AT assets have maximum ranges up to 3-4 kilometers, many militants choose to engage targets at much closer ranges in order to increase the likelihood of a catastrophic kill.[17] Videos posted online show Syrian rebel groups operating in small teams from high ground such as rooftops and hills in urban and peri-urban environments. In one example an Islamic Front ATGM team is set up on either a rooftop or an upper story. A hole knocked in the wall serves as the ATGM firing port, concealing the system in shadows while the wall provides small-arms cover for the team. Throughout the engagement, the team communicates via radio to what is likely an OP[18] or another ambush element.[19] This is one instance of the type of urban fighting that will likely occur should ground forces move against ISIL controlled cities. In this kind of fighting, small teams move through "rat holes" knocked between rooms and buildings, enabling movement through the urban battlefield without crossing open streets and intersections. The U.S. encountered similar tactics in Iraq's urban battlefields.[20] It is essential that the lessons from those fights are remembered.

Another example of AT employment shows a Syrian Army T-72[21] engaging an RPG team that fires from the darkness of a partially destroyed school building. Potentially lower level training is indicated here because the team engages the tank's frontal armor and main weapon systems instead of targeting weaker spots from safer positions. In this engagement the Syrians employ infantry dismounts on adjacent rooftops to likely spot targets for the tanks and provide close-in security.[22] Similar tank-infantry coordination met with success in Chechnya and Iraq.

The Syrian rebels also have employed recoilless rifles, IED's, and dismount grenade attacks against regime armor.[23] ISIL can be expected to operate in a similar manner against an armored threat. In Iraq, ISIL used dismount teams to place explosive charges directly on Iraqi Abrams that lacked infantry support in close terrain.[24] Additionally, ISIL's predecessor ISI used RKG-3 anti-tank grenades against coalition forces in Iraq.[25] RKG-3's are useful in densely populated areas due to their compact size. They are easily concealed on one's person and may be thrown from a crowd, making retaliation difficult if not impossible without serious civilian casualties.

Overall, we can be sure that armor, whether U.S. or allied, will be a prime target for ISIL should a combined-arms force be sent against them. Tanks are the quintessential embodiment of military might. The destruction of tanks, especially American tanks hold immense propaganda value for ISIL.[26] Although ISIL does not have the capabilities to defeat a Western-style combined arms force that employs heavy formations, it does have the capability to wage an effective war of attrition, especially in the urban environment, using small, semi-autonomous AT teams in conjunction with remote observers, C2[27] nodes and highly mobile infantry squads. The rest of this article will discuss recommendations on the employment of armor against ISIL given lessons learned from both previous conflicts and the current fight.

Preparation

"If the fundamental principles of combat are identical for all arms of service, their application is strongly conditioned by the technical means that are available."[28]

—General der Panzertruppen Lutz

Whoever understands the city best and how to array capabilities within it will hold a significant advantage. Often this advantage goes to the defender. In Chechnya, the Russians did not conduct thorough IPB[29] and this led to needless casualties.[30] The Chechens on the other hand meticulously prepared an urban defense, utilizing the city's planners to develop their defensive scheme.[31] Without adequate urban IPB, the commitment of a large ground force in a city will be extremely risky. Fallujah, 2004 provides an excellent case study in which good IPB led to the successful employment of armor in urban terrain. IPB, however, is beyond the scope of this article.[32] It suffices to note that the success of armor in any terrain is as much the result of good planning as the intrinsic capabilities of the platform.

Training is the second prerequisite for successful armor employment in cities. The Russians suffered heavily in both Chechen wars because they sent hastily cobbled together crews to the front lines in order to augment under strength armor units.[33] In the early days of armor, Heinz Guderian noted a truth that still holds today:

> "Tank service builds small unit cohesion in a quite remarkable way; there can be no distinctions— officers, NCOs and men alike share the same testing conditions of combat, and everyone must play his part to the full. Armored equipment is expensive and rather complicated, which calls for a fairly large establishment of long-service soldiers."[34]

The cohesion and training required of a successful armor unit takes time and good leadership to achieve. The risk posed to under strength U.S. armor units is similar to that of the Russians in Chechnya. In order to mitigate this, it would be beneficial to combine already proficient but under-strength units into fewer full-strength formations, keeping individual crews together as much as possible.

Additionally, armor units should focus on both joint and combined arms training to adequately prepare for the requirements of an urban fight. The following discussion explores areas that armor units preparing to fight in cities should consider incorporating into their training and planning.

Nomad Method

In 1999 a Russian company in 136th Brigade developed an effective tactical innovation for the employment of their small fleet of T-72BM's against Chechen rebels operating in the countryside. An individual T-72BM worked independently from the rest of its company as a raiding tank. Nicknamed the "Nomad Tank," it drove "covertly, but at high speed into the area indicated. The tank would move independently, without accompanying infantry. Moving off-road along mountain ravines, the tank remained unnoticeable to observers until it reached a suitable firing position, where the crew would fire four to five rounds at the target indicated and then disappear back into the ravines."[35] A similar method would work well in Iraq and Syria when combined with SOF[36] coordination or aerial observation. A further innovation would be to utilize tank-APC teams for the same purpose. The addition of an APC[37] such as a Stryker, LAV[38] or Bradley would enable greater tactical flexibility for diverse mission sets. Infantry dismounts open the possibility of raiding compounds, taking prisoners and gathering intelligence. Operating at night (something Russian conventional forces in Chechnya rarely did due poor training and broken optics) the Nomad method would further enhance shock effect. Designed for use outside cities, the Nomad method would target ISIL's logistics, communications and resource domination, weakening its power over local populations. Moving unpredictably at night, away from major roads and trails, the Nomad method would avoid IED ambushes and be difficult to counter given the enemy's current capabilities.

This method has applications in the built environment as well. Kilcullen states that "the ability to quickly aggregate and disaggregate (mass and disperse) forces and fires is the critical aspect of organizing for urban combat."[39] Nomad is the modular embodiment of this concept. U.S. Marines used a version of the Nomad method in April, 2004 leading up to their autumn assault on Fallujah. An M1A1 tank section was called to reinforce a Marine infantry patrol in heavy contact.[40] At nightfall, after relieving pressure on the embattled Marines, the tank section penetrated deep into the city, destroying targets of opportunity while an AC-130 gunship provided over-watch and aerial fires. The tank-gunship team wreaked havoc on Fallujah's streets until the tanks had to return to their assembly area to refuel and upload ammunition. Had there been an effective (protected) means to re-arm and refuel forward, the only limiting factor would have been the endurance of the crews. Moreover, prior combat air control training for individual tank commanders would have further enhanced the team's communication and effectiveness.

The Urban Fight

The underlying principles for the successful employment of armor have not changed since the inception of the arm in WWI. Guderian notes: "We may summarize the requirements for a decisive tank attack by the concepts of: suitable terrain, surprise and mass attack in the necessary breadth and depth."[41] Urban terrain is suitable insofar as it is properly analyzed through IPB and allows for adequate support. Some types of urban terrain may be unsuitable for armor. For example, canal cities or those built in precarious locations such as some Brazilian favelas and Afghan towns. The key point here is that urban characteristics do not make terrain inherently unsuitable for armor. It is the interaction of natural and human factors that coalesce in any given city which determines armored viability. Guderian's remaining principles are similar to the American doctrinal concept of SCAT (surprise, concentration, audacity and tempo); the fundamentals of the offense. The specific application of SCAT will vary depending on analysis of the urban environment.

Urban terrain often favors the well-prepared defender. The multi-dimensionality of urban warfare makes it the most complex type of terrain, offering increased tactical opportunities for those prepared to exploit them. Often these opportunities present themselves to light infantry while mounted forces struggle with a diversity of limitations.

After the defense of the Flesquières salient in WWI, Guderian noted that "infantry are perfectly capable of holding a great variety of locations against armored attack, provided that those places are properly evaluated and exploited; conversely unsupported armor cannot always be guaranteed to wipe out defending infantry."[42] Insurgents exploited Fallujah's terrain, attempting to limit vehicle mobility by blocking streets with Jersey barriers, HESCOs, and earthen berms. They covered these obstacles with direct and indirect fires as well as complex webs of IEDs, including entire explosively laden buildings.

The defenders turned private dwellings into bunkers and fortified seemingly ordinary structures, creating kill zones hidden inside buildings that would have to be cleared by infantry.[43] Compounding challenges for U.S. forces, the insurgents returned to infest previously cleared buildings and neighborhoods if these locations were not permanently occupied or monitored.[44] Similar Chechen tactics required lightly armed, semi-autonomous teams, each bearing a man-portable AT system and crew served weapon, to negotiate the urban battlefield with greater agility than their foes.[45] In both Fallujah and Grozny control of space often went to whoever happened to occupy it at the moment.

The Chechen defenders of Grozny ambushed Russian armor columns in the streets, shooting from upper stories and basements where main guns could not engage.[46] A dilemma in urban combat is overcoming the advantage conferred to the defender against light skinned vehicles and infantry given the difficulty of employing purely armored and mechanized forces which have the requisite protection to withstand the enemy fires. Kilcullen differentiates between two types of protection on the battlefield: indirect and direct. "Direct protection is the ability to survive a hit; indirect protection is the ability to avoid being hit in the first place… what's mostly needed in a populated urban environment is direct protection.[47] He points to the battle of Mogadishu mentioned earlier as an instructive case. The planners of Fallujah also recognized the importance of an armored spearhead. As

Lowry points out, "The lead vehicles needed to be able to take a hit because they were going to draw intense fire."[48]

There are several ways a heavy force may overcome the defender's advantage on its own terms. One is taking a proactive approach to altering urban terrain. Cities provide some of the most malleable terrain in warfare, enabling a wide latitude of possibility that spans the limits of a given commander's creativity. Urban defenders are not the only ones able to modify to urban environment to their advantage. Armored forces have the protection and capabilities required to convert the urban fabric to the advantage the attacker. Marines in Fallujah used armored D9 bulldozers to clear obstacles, collapse building and make new passageways.

Combined with robust engineer capabilities, infantry-armor teams seized and kept the initiative by changing the urban landscape to their advantage, severely disrupting the enemy defensive plan in the process. In the second Chechen War (1999-2000) the Russians employed infantry-tank teams using armor to support the forward advance of infantry "storm" detachments.[49] Russian fratricide rates, however, were high in both Chechen wars. In order to mitigate this, the Marines in Fallujah kept armor in the lead with infantry covering rooftops and building interiors on the tanks' flanks and rear.[50] The Marines found success using tanks and infantry in wide streets, AAVs[51] and LAVs in narrower streets and gun trucks in the smallest alleys. All moved using the Same-Axis-Same-Speed technique developed in WWII.[52] In this way they achieved SCAT and contributed to low fratricide rates.

An additional consideration for armored urban warfare is the integration of armored platforms beyond the Tank-APC duality. While tanks and APC's provide critical capabilities in the urban environment, their level of armor protection and mobility has creative applications across every war fighting function.[53] Examples that have already been tried with success are armored engineer assets such as the D9 used in Fallujah. In Chechnya the Russians used armored anti-aircraft platforms to engage targets that tanks and APCs could not. U.S. forces already have the CROWS[54] on many vehicles which enables similar urban targeting.

A further innovation was the Buratino, a multiple rocket launcher system mounted on a T-72 tank chassis.[55] This weapon system utilized thermobaric (fuel-air) munitions to eradicate targets inside buildings and other enclosed spaces. The Buratino essentially combined the armored protection of a tank, the fires of rocket artillery and the thermobaric munitions concept of the smaller, man-portable RPO-A Schmel system. Such combinations of capabilities suited to urban warfare are extensive. While a Buratino type platform would likely run counter to a U.S. strategy seeking to minimize collateral damage, thermobaric warheads could be integrated in existing weapon systems to great effect. Examples might include the Mk 19 grenade launcher, M320 grenade launcher[56] and 120mm tank main gun.

Several expedient innovations for the U.S. army exist in the sustainment realm. The Field Artillery Ammunition Support Vehicle (FAASV) is an armored 155mm ammunition carrier utilized by Paladin platoons. This vehicle could be augmented with explosive reactive armor, a CROWS and modified to carry Abrams and Bradley ammunition. This would be an effective step towards overcoming the problem of protected resupply on the front lines. Similar armament modifications are conceivable for existing fuel vehicles. Alternatively, the dismount compartments of surplus APCs and up-armored trucks could be converted to carry fuel, albeit less than current light-skinned fuelers. Nevertheless, fuel capacity is a worthwhile trade-off for increased protection and mobility in urban terrain.

Additionally, the M88 recovery vehicle already possesses substantial armor. The addition of reactive armor and a CROWS would further enhance its survivability in urban terrain. The Russians commented on the need for such protected sustainment capabilities during their operations in Chechnya.[57] Furthermore, the historical precedence for armored sustainment dates to WWI when modified supply tanks brought munitions, equipment and other supplies to the front lines.[58] Given the immense sustainment requirements of urban combat, especially in ammunition and fuel classes, these recommendations are worth serious consideration.

Finally, any urban operation will likely have to contend with non-combatants on the battlefield. Unless a successful non-combatant evacuation and subsequent cordon is achieved as in Fallujah, 2004, unintended civilian casualties will become propaganda fodder for insurgents. Ultimately, domestic and international support for any major war effort hinge on perceptions of the justice of the cause. Media coverage of civilian deaths is a surefire way to erode this support.

Armored vehicles play a unique role in this aspect of the urban fight. Their protection enables crews to take additional time to positively identify targets or decide not to engage at all. Vehicle optics further increase the crew's ability to distinguish between friends, foes and non-combatants. The integration of remotely operated weapons enables crews to employ lethal and precise small arms fires against threats where volume of fire was once used for the same purpose.

A variety of non-lethal systems are available and widely used in cities by police forces. Some of these could be integrated with existing combat vehicles to provide commanders with a broader array of engagement options. One example would be the use of crowd-control agents to disperse civilians caught in dangerous situations. Many other non-lethal combinations, whether chemical, sonic, optical or electronic, could be used towards the same end. Of course, armor and infantry teams would have to develop tactics for the employment of non-lethal agents when mitigate effects on nearby friendly dismounts. The flexibility offered by non-lethal systems, however, outweighs the burdens of additional training. Additional research is necessary for this and the other recommendations offered. If the topics mentioned are compelling enough to spark further investigation then this paper will have achieved its primary objective.

Conclusion

The record of past urban fights provides an informed guideline for future operations in cities. In the short to medium term, the Army will have to adapt using its existing organizational structures and equipment.

In the long term the Army needs a unit dedicated specifically to urban warfare much like the 10th Mountain and 82nd Airborne Divisions were originally formed to master unique military competencies. This will preserve lessons learned in a living organization, preparing the Army for future urban conflicts better than books and papers ever will.

Warfare is a crucible of adaptability that culls those who fail to innovate. We must recognize that any enemy will adapt to the limitations imposed on it by airstrikes and raids. Although the West and its allies can destroy ISIL's conventional capabilities using such means, it cannot loosen their grip on the populations that inhabit occupied territories without the significant commitment of ground forces. In light of this quandary, the recommendations in this article are intended to provoke further reflection and discussion. Their application is contingent upon a thoughtful approach to ground conditions and the given mission's political objectives.

The views expressed are the author's own and do not reflect those of the Department of Defense or United States Army. Please reference footnotes for clarification of acronyms and doctrinal terms.

References

Anderson, Gary. "The Coming War with the Caliphate." *Small Wars Journal.* http://smallwarsjournal.com/blog/the-coming-war-with-the-caliphate (accessed September 16, 2014).

Anderson, Gary. "Abu Bakr al-Baghdadi and the Theory and Practice of Jihad." *Small Wars Journal.* http://smallwarsjournal.com/jrnl/art/abu-bakr-al-baghdadi-and-the-theory-and-practice-of-jihad (accessed September 16, 2014).

Bazin, Aaron. "Defeating ISIS and Their Complex Way of War." *Small Wars Journal.* http://smallwarsjournal.com/jrnl/art/defeating-isis-and-their-complex-way-of-war (accessed September 16, 2014).

Binnie, Jeremy. "Iraqi Abrams losses revealed." *IHS Jane's 360*. http://www.janes.com/article/39550/iraqi-abrams-losses-revealed (accessed September 16, 2014).

"Deadly Duel: Syrian Tank vs RPG Jihadists." *LiveLeak.com*. http://www.liveleak.com/view?i=77a_1381931775 (accessed September 16, 2014).

Geibel, Adam. "Some Russian Tankers' Experiences In the Second Chechen War." *ciar.org*. http://www.ciar.org/ttk/mbt/armor/armor-magazine/armor-mag.2001.ja/4chechen01.pdf (accessed September 16, 2014).

Grau, Lester W. and Timothy Smith. "A 'Crushing' Victory: Fuel-Air Explosives and Grozny 2000." Foreign Military Studies Office Publications. http://fmso.leavenworth.army.mil/documents/fuelair/fuelair.htm (accessed September 22, 2014).

Guderian, Heinz. *Achtung-Panzer!: the development of tank warfare*. London: Cassell, 1999.

Holliday, Joseph. "The Syrian Army Doctrinal Order of Battle." *understandingwar.org*. http://www.understandingwar.org/sites/default/files/SyrianArmy-DocOOB.pdf (accessed September 16, 2014).

"Islamic Front destroy regime tank with ATGM." *LiveLeak.com*. http://www.liveleak.com/view?i=efe_1392139117 (accessed September 16, 2014).

Kilcullen, David. *Out of the Mountains: The Coming Age of the Urban Guerrilla*. New York: Oxford University Press, 2013.

Lowry, Richard S. *New dawn: the battles for Fallujah*. New York: Savas Beatie, 2010.

McGregor, Andrew. "Hezbollah's Creative Tactical Use of Anti-Tank Weaponry." The Jamestown Foundation. http://www.jamestown.org/single/?tx_ttnews[tt_news]=876&no_cache=1#.VBjOIxZ6Q_g (accessed September 16, 2014).

Oliker, Olga. *Russia's Chechen wars 1994-2000: Lessons from Urban Combat*. Santa Monica, CA: Rand, 2001.

"RKG-3 Anti-tank Grenade thrown at Humvee." *LiveLeak.com*. http://www.liveleak.com/view?i=379_1331224886&comments=1 (accessed September 21, 2014).

Stevens, Michael. "Islamic State: Where does jihadist group get its support?" *The BBC*. http://www.bbc.com/news/world-middle-east-29004253 (accessed September 1, 2014).

"Syrian Arab Army Tank Losses Since March: 534 tanks, 77 BMPs, /r/syriancivilwar." *Reddit*. http://www.reddit.com/r/syriancivilwar/comments/1m0b29/syrian_arab_army_tank_losses_since_march_534/ (accessed September 16, 2014).

"Syrian rebels use HJ-8 'Red Arrow' ATGM to destroy SAA T-62." *YouTube*. https://www.youtube.com/watch?v=Oh83gB2VXJg (accessed September 16, 2014).

Notes

[1] Richard S. Lowry. *New dawn: the battles for Fallujah*, 172.

[2] Aaron Bazin. "Defeating ISIS and Their Complex Way of War."

[3] Gary Anderson. "Abu Bakr al-Baghdadi and the Theory and Practice of Jihad."

[4] David Kilcullen. *Out of the Mountains: The Coming Age of the Urban Guerrilla*, 226.

[5] Ibid., 84.

[6] Ibid.

[7] Michael Stevens. "Islamic State: Where does jihadist group get its support?"

[8] Gary Anderson. "The Coming War with the Caliphate."

[9] Anti-tank Guided Missile/Anti-Tank.

[10] David Kilcullen. *Out of the Mountains: The Coming Age of the Urban Guerrilla*, 226.

[11] Richard S. Lowry. *New dawn: the battles for Fallujah*, 6.

[12] Rocket Propelled Grenade. Often a man-portable, shoulder-fired weapon.

[13] Jeremy Binnie. "Iraqi Abrams losses revealed."

[14] Ibid.

[15] Andrew McGregor. "Hezbollah's Creative Tactical Use of Anti-Tank Weaponry."

[16] "Syrian rebels use HJ-8 'Red Arrow' ATGM to destroy SAA T-62." *YouTube.*

[17] Andrew McGregor. "Hezbollah's Creative Tactical Use of Anti-Tank Weaponry."

[18] Observation Post.

[19] "Islamic Front destroy regime tank with ATGM." *LiveLeak.com.*

[20] Richard S. Lowry. *New dawn: the battles for Fallujah*, 20.

[21] A Soviet era main battle tank that still serves in militaries around the world.

[22] "Deadly Duel: Syrian Tank vs RPG Jihadists." *LiveLeak.com.*

[23] "Syrian Arab Army Tank Losses Since March: 534 tanks, 77 BMPs, /r/syriancivilwar." *Reddit.*

[24] Jeremy Binnie. "Iraqi Abrams losses revealed."

[25] "RKG-3 Anti-tank Grenade thrown at Humvee." *LiveLeak.com.*

[26] Andrew McGregor. "Hezbollah's Creative Tactical Use of Anti-Tank Weaponry."

[27] Command and Control.

[28] Heinz Guderian. *Achtung-Panzer!: the development of tank warfare*, 19.

[29] Intelligence Preparation of the Battlefield. The processes of analyzing pertinent data about the battlefield and turning that data into actionable planning considerations.

[30] Olga Oliker. *Russia's Chechen wars 1994-2000: Lessons from Urban Combat*, xi, 9.

[31] Olga Oliker. *Russia's Chechen wars 1994-2000: Lessons from Urban Combat*, 19.

[32] *Street Smart: Intelligence Preparation of the Battlefield for Urban Operations* by Jamison Jo Medby and Russell W. Glenn is an excellent resource for planners seeking a greater appreciation for the nuances of the built environment.

[33] Adam Geibel. "Some Russian Tankers' Experiences In the Second Chechen War," 27.

[34] Heinz Guderian. *Achtung-Panzer!: the development of tank warfare*, 176.

[35] Adam Geibel. "Some Russian Tankers' Experiences In the Second Chechen War," 25.

[36] Special Operations Forces.

[37] Armored Personnel Carrier.

[38] Light Armored Vehicle. A personnel carrier used predominantly by the United States Marine Corps.

[39] David Kilcullen. *Out of the Mountains: The Coming Age of the Urban Guerrilla*, 283.

[40] Richard S. Lowry. *New dawn: the battles for Fallujah*, 10-14.

[41] Heinz Guderian. *Achtung-Panzer!: the development of tank warfare*, 181.

[42] Ibid., 83.

[43] Richard S. Lowry. *New dawn: the battles for Fallujah*, 61.

[44] Ibid., 218.

[45] Olga Oliker. *Russia's Chechen wars 1994-2000: Lessons from Urban Combat*, 17.

[46] Ibid.,13.

[47] David Kilcullen. *Out of the Mountains: The Coming Age of the Urban Guerrilla*, 289.

[48] Richard S. Lowry. *New dawn: the battles for Fallujah*, 45.

[49] Olga Oliker. *Russia's Chechen wars 1994-2000: Lessons from Urban Combat*, 45.

[50] Richard S. Lowry. *New dawn: the battles for Fallujah*, 11.

[51] Amphibious Assault Vehicle.

[52] Ibid., 73-74.

[53] Army Warfighting Functions: Intelligence, Command and Control, Movement and Maneuver, Sustainment, Protection, and Fire Support.

[54] Common Remotely Operated Weapon Station. Allows vehicle crews to fire a variety of weapons remotely utilizing both thermal and daylight optics.

[55] Lester W. Grau and Timothy Smith. "A 'Crushing' Victory: Fuel-Air Explosives and Grozny 2000." Foreign Military Studies Office Publications.

[56] The experimental 40mm XM1060 round already exists for this weapon and has seen service in Afghanistan.

[57] Adam Geibel. "Some Russian Tankers' Experiences in the Second Chechen War," 26.

[58] Heinz Guderian. *Achtung-Panzer!: the development of tank warfare*, 111.

Chapter 18

A Case for Reflection: On the Ground in Iraq, Afghanistan, and Detroit

Kirby Dennis, Kris Karafa and Rebecca Patterson

First Published 18 November 2014

Abstract

The military's lessons from a decade of war can be particularly useful for a domestic audience facing similar challenges. For example, Detroit faces urban blight, high unemployment, low literacy rates, social and economic inequality, and pervasive insecurity—issues confronted by those who served in Iraq and Afghanistan. The authors use the framework of counterinsurgency to examine how lessons from Iraq and Afghanistan apply to Detroit. The importance of security as a precursor to economic development, government legitimacy, and the impact of economic growth on stability are highlighted with suggestions of how such lessons apply domestically. Harnessing the experience of veterans could be particularly impactful for municipal leaders as they address challenges similar to those faced by military officers in Iraq and Afghanistan.

Introduction

During a recent trip to Detroit, we were struck by the glaring similarities that a once proud and thriving American city shares with two increasingly well-known countries—Iraq and Afghanistan. In our interactions with Detroit municipal leaders during our visit these connections became increasingly apparent, and indeed, reflect many of the issues faced by American military leaders over the past thirteen years of conflict. The U.S. military fought counterinsurgency campaigns in Iraq and Afghanistan, and thus engaged in activities that affected the political, economic, and social systems of these countries. Many argue that the U.S. went far beyond a military campaign in these two particular cases, and instead sought to implement wholesale societal transformation or nation-building.[1] Like municipal leaders at home, the U.S. military dealt with issues that included urban blight, high unemployment, low literacy rates, social and economic inequality, and high rates of violence. These problems represented fundamental impediments to America's ability to foster sustainable peace in the war-torn areas of Iraq and Afghanistan, and in many ways are commensurate with the current issues facing Detroit.

More similarities exist between Iraq, Afghanistan, and Detroit than the casual observer might expect. One should consider the following: Detroit has been listed by *Forbes* as America's most dangerous city for the past five years; the city possesses $18 billion in debt obligations; the unemployment rate is roughly 16% which tripled from 2000-2012; the city experienced a 77% decrease in property value over the past 50 years; and, the city witnessed a population decline from its peak of 1.8 million in 1950 to 700,000 today, including a 50% decline in employed residents from 1970 to 2000.[2] Given these bleak statistics, it is important to consider how recent lessons learned from the last decade of war could inform Detroit's policymakers in their efforts at home. The following analysis seeks to capture several key lessons from the U.S. military's experience in Iraq and Afghanistan, and ultimately draw similarities to the current situation in Detroit. We believe these lessons can be useful for Detroit's leaders as they chart a way towards a better future for the Motor City.

Counterinsurgency Tenets—A Framework

Through the lens of the Iraq and Afghanistan experience, several broad categories exist for analyzing similarities and lessons learned. Economic, security, political, and leadership categories—which mirror several core tenets of counterinsurgency doctrine—are particularly useful for this analysis in that they provide a clear framework for assessing the case of Detroit. We acknowledge that counterinsurgency theory does not provide a basis by which all of Detroit's ills can be assessed. Nonetheless, broadly speaking, we believe that there is utility in assessing the similarities and lessons presented within this framework, as they may provide useful insight, perspective, and even possible solutions to domestic audiences seeking to address challenges at home. The lessons are not intended to provide ready-made answers for Detroit's complex problems. However, as a result of our interactions with government, non-profit, and civilian leaders during our visit to the city, we believe enough parallels between Detroit, Iraq and Afghanistan exist to warrant further exploration. What follows is an examination of lessons learned from our own experiences with counterinsurgency, as well as suggestions as to how they may apply in future efforts to revitalize Detroit.

Similarities & Lessons Learned

Security is a necessary precursor to economic development. In the case of Iraq and Afghanistan, providing security to local populations was of paramount importance—namely to instill confidence and provide the necessary space for economic growth to occur. Although there is not a well-defined metric by which levels of security trigger economic activity, it is clear that local populations will engage economically once they assess security to be at an acceptable level—an idea buttressed by personal vignettes of counterinsurgents across the military.[3] In the case of Iraq and Afghanistan, security investment was manifest in the growth of both national security forces as well as the surge of U.S.

military forces in 2007 and 2010. Take for example the national police force in Iraq, which grew from a force of 27 battalions in 2007 to 44 battalions by the end of 2008.[4] In the case of Afghanistan, President Karzai sought and exceeded an incredibly ambitious goal to field over 350,000 Afghan National Security Forces in a little over 10 years, requiring a major capital investment by Afghanistan, the U.S., and the international donor community.[5] In the end, this exponential growth in host nation forces coupled with a large influx of U.S. troops set the necessary conditions to tamp down violence in key areas so that political and economic initiatives could take hold.

The importance of police forces in both conflicts warrants specific mention, as their performance was often linked to the legitimacy of the central government. Although in both Iraq and Afghanistan the number of police battalions grew exponentially over the course of the war, the quality of the police force itself was every bit as important as quantity. Whereas the Iraq and Afghan Armies enjoyed high levels of public support, the police were generally viewed as corrupt and incompetent—this despite public recognition of their importance to improving security. In the early stages of the Iraq war, 62% of residents in Baghdad stated that growing an adequate police force in terms of size and capability was their number one priority.[6] Unfortunately, Iraq and Afghanistan struggled to field impartial and capable police forces early in the war. Consequently, local police functions were often assumed or influenced by militias that operated at the behest of local strongmen—a dynamic that often stymied the efforts of U.S. military commanders to improve security.

Like Iraq and Afghanistan, Detroit has struggled with escalating violence and an underdeveloped police force. Not only has Detroit ranked first on the *Forbes* "Most Dangerous City" list for the last five-years, but it also has a crime rate that far exceeds both domestic and international norms, to include Baghdad and Kabul.[7] This dubious distinction has not only damaged the psyche of Detroit residents, but has also prevented potential economic investment from taking hold. Detroit citizens have expressed their outrage, evident in a 2012 *Detroit News* poll that indicated that 40% of the population would leave the city within a 5-year span primarily because of the crime problem.[8] Perhaps more alarming, the same poll found that 58% of Detroit residents believe that crime is their foremost problem—an issue that eclipsed unemployment during a period in which some estimates placed the real jobless rate at close to 50%.[9] To compound matters, investment in the Detroit police force is not commensurate with the security problems that currently exist. Specifically, members of the Detroit police force are paid less than their suburban counterparts, and recruitment efforts for new police hires were virtually non-existent up until late 2013.[10] From 2012-2013, police rolls decreased by 300 personnel and the police budget was cut by 18% from the previous year—two trends that cannot continue if Detroit hopes to economically rebound.[11]

While the current leadership in Detroit has acknowledged the need for increasing investment in the police force, the security situation has already resulted in far-reaching consequences—chief among them is Detroit's stagnant economy. In a December 2013 *Forbes* statistical analysis of major metropolitan areas that gauged economic vitality, Detroit ranked last.[12] Not surprisingly, the study highlights population influx as a key indicator of a strong economy. Given the *Detroit News* poll that underscores crime as the impetus for population flight, the resulting economic ramifications come as no surprise. The security situation in Detroit is no doubt complex, as its roots run deep in economic, political, and social sectors. However, there is broad agreement that investment in security forces is a necessary step in reversing trends—a concept proven by the large growth of Iraqi and Afghan security forces from 2007-2011. As Detroit faces difficult prioritization choices in the coming months, investment in its police force should be near the top.

Government legitimacy is paramount. In addition to the aforementioned reasons for security force investment, it is critical to point out that performance and professionalism of security forces are directly tied to government legitimacy—which is vital to achieving long-term stability. Populations today expect their government to provide essential services such as education, health care, rule of law, and infrastructure maintenance as a means of sustaining and promoting economic activity. When governments in a conflict zone cannot fulfill these responsibilities, malign actors often exploit the existing vacuum and undermine its authority.

A key component of legitimacy is government leadership. As history has shown time and again, effective leaders garner popular support for government efforts while corrupt leaders denigrate the institutions they are meant to represent and alienate the populace. The U.S. military campaigns in Iraq and Afghanistan are rife with examples of good and bad leadership across military, civilian, and host-nation organizations. Although certain environments proved to be indifferent to leadership no matter how strong, in many cases leadership was a decisive variable in advancing counterinsurgency efforts for the U.S. military. Broadly speaking, leadership proved essential to progress. If nothing else, the campaigns in Iraq and Afghanistan prove that leaders who understand security, economics, society, government, and culture are better equipped to build consensus and achieve goals in complex environments. The most successful leaders in both campaigns were able to effectively communicate a vision and unite stakeholders and were thus successful in guiding disparate organizations toward a common purpose.

While economic, social, and political factors led to the downfall of Detroit, a persistent failure of leadership is equally to blame.[13] The city has demonstrated the steep cost of poor government leadership perhaps better than any other municipality in America. Sadly, it has suffered from a rash of corrupt or ineffective leaders for the past several years, and no better example of this exists than the tenure of Mayor Kwame Kilpatrick. Mayor Kilpatrick led Detroit from 2002-2008, and was convicted on counts that included extortion, racketeering, and obstruction of justice. The government's lack of legitimacy resulted in severe consequences for the city and its residents.

The problem of an illegitimate and corrupt government system in Detroit is much more pervasive than merely the example of Mayor Kilpatrick though. In addition, five Detroit police chiefs have been replaced in the past five years, and two of the past four city council presidents have been embroiled in scandal.[14] These examples, along with many others, are a key reason for emergency manager Kevyn Orr's description of Detroit's government as "dysfunctional and wasteful" and plagued by "years of budgetary restrictions, mismanagement, crippling operational practices, and, in some cases, indifference or corruption."[15] The dearth of government legitimacy in Detroit has led to a disillusioned public with little confidence in government leaders and institutions—verified by a 2012 poll in which 63% of Detroit residents expressed no faith in the mayor or the city council.[16]

The rapid promotion of competent leaders and their placement in the right positions is perhaps more important than any other aspect of Detroit's recovery. Local opinion in Detroit indicates that the election of Mayor Mike Duggan was a good start in achieving this goal. However, the campaigns in Iraq and Afghanistan illustrate that effective leadership must be sustained over the long run. Moreover, the military's experience proved that effective leadership is not only required at the top of an organization but must also be present throughout its lowest levels. Detroit must bear this in mind as it builds its next generation of leaders to assume critical positions across government, business, charitable and education sectors.

Economic growth is fundamental to stability and must be carefully facilitated. Economist Paul Collier has argued convincingly that poor nations with little economic growth have a greater tendency to experience conflict and violence.[17] No doubt, Collier's premise applies to troubled municipalities as well. Targeting the most impactful sectors for economic growth will be as vital in Detroit as they were in Iraq and Afghanistan. For example, a vital part of economic recovery is private sector development—the private sector creates jobs and provides a sustainable source of tax revenue. While it took the U.S. military longer than expected to address economic problems in Iraq, the ultimate response was impressive. By 2007, each brigade combat team was assigned a Provincial Reconstruction Team to oversee economic initiatives, and commanders were authorized to spend significant sums of money to jumpstart the economy through the Commander's Emergency Response Program—two initiatives that not only helped enable economic growth vis-à-vis small business expansion, but also contributed to reducing levels of violence.[18] While the decline in violence was the result of a wide scope of efforts, it is clear that an improving economy was a key component to a more secure environment. As Iraq's economy grew approximately 5% a year between the years 2008 to 2012, violence declined significantly.[19] Detroit's leaders would do well to consider the positive impact that private sector development can have on security and stability—a notion highlighted by the American military experience in Iraq.

Moreover, a critical lesson learned in the Iraq and Afghanistan conflicts was the importance of a coherent, unified spending strategy among stakeholders—an issue strongly tied to economic recovery. An early impediment to economic recovery in Iraq was linked to the lack of financial coordination between the U.S. and multilateral institutions.[20] Synchronizing financial efforts between multinational institutions in war-torn regions is difficult business, but its importance to forging unity of effort among stakeholders has become increasingly central to success in modern warfare. That said, there can be unintended consequences when external monies flood conflict zones. Indeed, such financial assistance proved to be a double-edged sword in Iraq and Afghanistan. On the one hand, external support was vital to jumpstarting economic recovery. On the other hand, as the number of stakeholders proliferated so too did the likelihood for duplication of effort in terms of programs and projects.

Similarly, the number of organizations involved in the recovery of Detroit has drastically increased. Since the public announcement of Detroit's bankruptcy in July 2013, funding from a variety of sources has flooded the city. Whether in seed money from JP Morgan's recent $100 million investment, or the recent $25 million non-profit injection to boost community initiatives, the current landscape in Detroit is rife with well-intentioned ideas backed by cash.[21] Though high levels of funding have the potential to transform Detroit into a place where people want to live and work, oversight is required to ensure that funds are channeled into the most impactful sectors. Without oversight and unified objectives between government, businesses and non-profit sectors, the potential for an artificial economic spike is likely—rather than the stable economic platform that Detroit so desperately needs.

Indeed, if stakeholders are too eager for quick results, they can spoil the overall intention of sustainable economic development—a lesson learned by many military units in Iraq and Afghanistan. As Detroit moves forward, it must ensure that initiatives are synchronized and coordinated to advance a coherent economic agenda.

Conclusion

One of our most common refrains in America is to learn from the past. Over the last 13 years of conflict, the U.S military has displayed its ability to learn and adapt to changing environments. While arriving at change is not easy and often met with bureaucratic obstacles, the ability to adapt is imperative to success—a notion underscored in Iraq and Afghanistan, two campaigns in which the U.S. military had to meet changing circumstances with creativity and fresh thinking to succeed. Moving forward, the challenge facing the military was best summarized by Secretary of Defense Robert Gates, who asked "How can the Army break-up the institutional concrete, its bureaucratic rigidity…in order to retain, challenge, and inspire its best, brightest, and most-battled tested young [leaders] to lead the service in the future?"[22] The answer to this question will be critical to future military success. Detroit, like other municipalities across America, should be asking themselves the same question.

Given the aforementioned similarities faced in Detroit with those in Iraq and Afghanistan we believe that the hard lessons learned from war should not just be data to fill the history books but should be applied to problems faced at home. The experiences of Iraq and Afghanistan veterans across the country should be harnessed and brought to bear on the nation's toughest problems, whether at the municipal level or the national level. This terse analysis has hopefully illustrated the critical lessons learned from Iraq and Afghanistan that are most applicable to domestic problems. Importantly, these lessons were forged through the hard work and sacrifice of military veterans who possess incredible insight, perspective and leadership—skills that can help municipalities tackle some of their most vexing problems. As local government leaders seek creative ways to address economic, political, security, and leadership challenges, they would do well to tap a readily available pool of talent, resident in our military veterans.

The views expressed herein are those of the authors are not are representative of the U.S. Army, the Department of Defense or National Defense University.

Notes

[1] For example, see Francis Fukuyama, ed. *Nation-Building: Beyond Afghanistan and Iraq,* (Baltimore: Johns Hopkins University Press, 2006).

[2] In list order: Matthew Dolan, "Detroit Debt Proposal Favors Pension Funds," *Detroit Free Press,* January 30, 2014, accessed September 21, 2014, http://online.wsj.com/news/articles/SB10001424052702304428004579353451973478 672; "Unemployment Rate," U.S. Bureau of Labor Statistics, accessed September 21, 2014, http://www.google.com/publicdata/explore?ds=z1ebjpgk2654c1_&met_y=unemployment_rate&idim=city:CT2622000000000:CT1714000000000&fdim_y=seasonality:U&hl=en&dl=en; Nancy Kaffer, Stephen Henderson and Matt Helms, "Detroit: How the Motor City went bust," *Detroit Free Press,* July 19, 2013, accessed August 23, 2014. http://www.usatoday.com/story/news/nation/2013/07/18/detroit-files-for-bankruptcy/2567159; City of Detroit, *Proposal for Creditors* (Detroit, June 14, 2013), http://www.detroitmi.gov/Portals/0/docs/EM/Reports/City%20of%20Detroit%20Proposal%20for%20Creditors1.pdf.

[3] Crane, Keith, et. als. *Guidebook for Supporting Economic Development in Stability Operations.* (Santa Monica: RAND, 2009).

[4] GEN David H. Petraeus, "Multi-National Force-Iraq, Charts to accompany the testimony of GEN David H. Petraeus," (Testimony to Senate Armed Services Committee, Washington, D.C., April 8-9, 2008), accessed September 7, 2014. http://www.defense.gov/pdf/Testimony_Handout_Packet.pdf.

[5] North Atlantic Treaty Organization, "Afghan National Security Forces: Training and Development," *Media Backgrounder*, accessed on July 14, 2014. http://www.nato.int/nato_static/assets/pdf/pdf_2012_12/20121205_121205-ansf-backgrounder-en.pdf.

[6] Richard Burkholder, "Gallup Poll of Baghdad: Iraq's Police-Now Targets Themselves-Are Key to Security," *Gallup,* November 4, 2003, accessed on August 27, 2014. http://www.gallup.com/poll/9637/gallup-poll-baghdad-iraqs-police-now-targets-themselves.aspx.

[7] Daniel Fisher, "Detroit Again Tops List of Dangerous Cities as Crime Rates Dips," *Forbes*, October 22, 2013. UNODC (2013), "UNODC Homicide Statistics 2013", in UNODC, *Global Study on Homicide: Trends, Contexts, Data*, United Nations. http://www.unodc.org/unodc/en/data-and-analysis/homicide.html.

[8] Christine MacDonald, "Poll: Crime drives Detroiters out; 40% expect to leave within 5 years," *Detroit News,* October 9, 2012, accessed on September 23, 2014. http://www.detroitnews.com/article/20121009/METRO01/210090369.

[9] Ibid.

[10] "Salaries driving Detroit police officers to the suburbs," *myFOXdetroit.com*, March 18, 2014, accessed on August 14, 2014. http://www.myfoxdetroit.com/story/25010627/salaries-driving-detroit-police-officers-to-the-suburbs.

[11] "Detroit Fire, "Police Departments Suffer Deep Cuts," *CBS Detroit,* last modified July 3, 2012, accessed on August 28, 2014. http://detroit.cbslocal.com/2012/07/03/detroit-fire-police-departments-suffer-deep-cuts/.

[12] "The Metro Areas with the Most Economic Momentum Going Into 2014," *Forbes*, December 26, 2013, accessed September 23, 2014. http://www.forbes.com/sites/joelkotkin/2013/12/26/

Small Wars Journal

the-metro-areas-with-the-most-economic-momentum-going-into-2014/.

[13] Jena McGregor, "What killed Detroit? Let's not forget the 'who.'" *The Washington Post,* July 19, 2013, accessed August 30, 2014. http://www.washingtonpost.com/blogs/on-leadership/wp/2013/07/19/what-killed-detroit-lets-not-forget-the-who/.

[14] Ed White and Corey Williams, "Detroit police chief steps down amid sex probe," *The Seattle Times*, October 2, 2012. http://seattletimes.com/html/nationworld/2019375732_apusdetroitpolicechief.html?_ga=1.79760402.444395523.1412253620.

[15] City of Detroit, Office of Emergency Manager, *Financial and Operating Plan,* (Detroit, May 12, 2013), http://www.detroitmi.gov/Portals/0/docs/EM/Reports/City%20of%20Detroit%20-%20Final%20Financial%20&%20Operational%20Plan%20_45%20Day%20Pl.pdf.

[16] Darren A. Nichols and Leonard N. Fleming, "Poll: Detroit Residents Have Little Confidence in Leaders," *The Detroit News,* October 10, 2012, accessed August 29, 2014, http://www.detroitnews.com/article/20121010/METRO01/210100361.

[17] Paul Collier, *The Bottom Billion*, (Oxford: Oxford University Press, 2007).

[18] Eli Berman, Jacob N. Shapiro, and Joseph H. Felter, "Can Hearts and Minds Be Bought? The Economics of Counterinsurgency in Iraq," *Chicago: Journal of Political Economy*, Vol. 119, No. 4 (August 2011): 766-819.

[19] The World Bank, "Iraq Annual GDP Growth," 2013. http://data.worldbank.org/indicator/NY.GDP.MKTP.KD.ZG/countries/IQ?display=graph.

[20] Stephen Lewarne and David Snelbecker, *Economic Governance in War Torn Economies: Lessons Learned from the Marshal Plan to the Reconstruction of Iraq*, U.S. Agency for International Development, Office of Development Evaluation and Information Bureau for Policy and Program Coordination, Contract No. 2941-1729-0-P-01 (Washington, DC: United States

Government Printing Office, 2004), 133. http://www.oecd.org/derec/unitedstates/36144028.pdf.

[21] Jim Tankersley, "JP Morgan is betting $100 million on Detroit. Can it leverage a lot more?" *The Washington Post,* August 15, 2014, accessed on October 3, 2014. http://www.washingtonpost.com/news/storyline/wp/2014/08/15/jpmorgan-is-betting-100-million-on-detroit-can-it-leverage-a-lot-more/.

[22] Robert M. Gates, "United States Military Academy (West Point, NY)," speech delivered at West Point, NY, February 25, 2011. http://www.defense.gov/speeches/speech.aspx?speechid=1539.

Chapter 19

Urban Siege in Paris: A Spectrum of Armed Assault

John P. Sullivan and Adam Elkus

First Published 2 February 2015

In 2009, we laid out a conceptual model of terrorist "urban siege" based on the Mumbai attacks.[1] As noted by several observers, the recent terrorist attack in Paris on the *Charlie Hebdo* offices may have succeeded due to the unfortunate fact that security officials expected other attack modes (such as airline bombs), not a run and gun in the heart of an urban center.[2]

While it would be tempting to posit Paris as another bloody data point explained by our conceptual schema, Paris is in fact cause for broadening and expanding it. Unfortunately, the world faces urban security threats that span a spectrum of organization and lethality. Future threats may look like Mumbai (as has been seen in the Mumbai-like operation against the Westgate shopping mall in Nairobi) or they may resemble Paris.[3] And there is a large spectrum of threats that occupy the threat envelope in between.

Here we review the timeline of the attacks, analyze continuities and complications with urban siege schemas and relevant incidents, review relevant analysis that could inform a more robust analysis of urban siege, and close with a set of our own questions for researchers and practitioners about what assumptions we need to make in planning for, training to stop, and red-teaming urban siege scenarios.

Urban Siege in Paris

In France, the new year opened with a horrific urban siege. This latest installment of urban guerilla action involved armed assault and massacre, execution of police, a massive manhunt and two hostage-barricade situations. Three days of terror saw the deployment of 88,000 personnel from the French Interior Ministry—ranging from community police to specialized gendarmerie, augmented by a large military contingent.[4]

On Wednesday 7 January, a car pulled up in front of the offices of *Charlie Hebdo*, a satirist magazine in Paris' 11th Arrondissement. Two men—the Kouachi brothers, Cherif and Said—got out of the car; they were dressed in black and carried automatic weapons. After making inquiries the made way to the office and opened fire, killing one. When they arrived at the office they again opened fire killing the editor and 9 others including a police officer guarding the editor, as well as a police officer Ahmed Merabat, the first responding officer to the scene.[5]

After the attack the self-styled Mujahideen fled the scene. The next day (8 January) they robbed a gas station near Villers-Cotterets. The same day a female police officer, Clarissa Jean-Phillpe was killed in Montrouge, a Paris suburb by Amedy Coulibaly (who has been linked to the Kouachi brothers). On 9 January, the Kouachi brothers robbed a car in northeast Paris. A few minutes later the Kouachi brothers took a hostage and the suspects were chased by helicopters in a massive manhunt. Area schools and businesses were put under lockdown and large numbers of officers from the National Police and Gendarmerie (including GIGN and RAID respectively) were deployed with support from the Army.[6] The suspects settled in for a hostage-barricade situation (the second siege) at a printer's suite in Dammartin-en-Goele. The suspects boasted they would become martyrs.

A third incident at the Hyper Cacher, a kosher grocery, was conducted by Amedy Couliby to support the Kouachi brothers.[7] This siege, which resulted in the death of Couliby and four hostages, was terminated by a police counter assault. The counter assaults were coordinated, simultaneous actions with the takedown of the Kouachi brothers to limit risk to the hostages at the grocery since Couliby said he would execute them if police assaulted the Kouachis' location.

The aftermath of the assaults includes questions about intelligence failure, fear of follow-on attacks conducted by activated sleeper cells, threats to police, and the threat of attacks in The United Kingdom and United States.[8] Finally, the conflict has both physical and virtual dimensions as seen by a wave of attacks against French websites. Hackers, responding to the French public's defiance in the face of terror, hit 19,000 French websites with denial-of-service attacks.[9] A group of pro-Syrian regime hackers briefly commandeered the French newspaper *Le Monde*'s Twitter account, tweeting a message mocking the post-attack hashtag #JeSuisCharlie.[10]

Analyzing the Paris Urban Siege: Continuity and Complication

On one end of a spectrum of urban assault lethality and sophistication is the Mumbai attacks. The attackers belonged to a cohesive and organized terrorist organization and received guidance, direction, and real-time information support from an offsite handler. On the lowest end is a garden variety "active shooter" more akin to the Columbine school shooters—no training, no guidance, no resources, no contacts but nonetheless possessing a willingness to kill and die. The organized terrorist group type of attacker is obviously capable of waging urban siege. Operating in small squads, they can challenge police command and control and on-site response through dispersion, firepower, and entrenchment.

As David Kilcullen observed in an application of our work to the Westgate mall attack, the Mumbai attack also was terror by "remote control"—the attackers utilized Skype, cellphones, and satellite phones to connect to an offsite operations team in Pakistan monitoring social media and news reporting concerning the ongoing attack. The Nairobi attack exhibited similar characteristics.[11] Six suspects affiliated with al-Shabaab executed a hostage-barricade assault against the mall complex.[12] Multiple squads executed a coordinated attack and successfully entrenched within the mall complex for four days. 72 people died before Kenyan security forces could retake the mall.

As with Mumbai, the Kenya attackers prepared for an entrenchment scenario, fused various weapons and teams, and thwarted a disorganized and bureaucratically disjointed security force response long enough to exact a gruesome toll. The attack, though novel in its ferocity, sophistication, and toll, was preceded by a drumbeat of urban terrorist attacks in which al-Shabaab demonstrated urban assault capabilities. The catastrophic impact of poor command and control cannot be overstated. An extensive *Guardian* report suggested that disputes over police and military command and control delayed response. Not only were attackers able to entrench and kill more victims, but a friendly fire incident also occurred and militants were able to foil a first joint police-army counterattack with sniper fire.[13]

Nor has Kenya been the sole instance of a suicide commando assault since Mumbai. In December of last year, the Pakistani Taliban launched a gruesome attack on a school for children of Pakistan army officers.[14] In a repeat of previous urban siege patterns, attackers provisioned for a long attack quickly pushed into the school. However, unlike in Beslan there would be no entrenchment and hostage situation. Pakistani forces responded within 15 minutes and killed all of the attackers. However, the security forces were too late to save the 132 children and 10 school staff slaughtered by the terrorists during the initial attack. Pakistani Taliban, Afghan Taliban, and al-Qaeda urban operations continue within urban centers in South Asia, a site C. Christine Fair has noted is one large "urban battlefield."[15]

While we do not suggest that older hostage and armed attack scenarios were simple, the operational challenges associated with these types of attacks dwarf the typical single-site, hostage-barricade assumptions seen in terrorist operations such as the 1970s Munich Olympics incident or the spate of aircraft hijackings seen during the wave of terror that preceded the current wave of radical Islamist terror. As J. Paul D. Taillon noted in his study of hijacking and hostages, successful counterterrorist operations involved forward base access, cooperation, and specialized units capable of dislodging attackers.[16] In contrast, modern urban sieges will require first responders to meet attackers head-on, regardless of sophistication and armament. Such direct police action is necessary to stop the 'kinetic momentum' and minimize casualties.[17]

For example, in June 2014 a team of heavily armed Pakistani Taliban militants assaulted the Jinnah International Airport in Karachi.[18] Attackers disguised themselves as airport personnel and were successfully held off by security personnel and finished off by military reinforcements. They were provisioned for a long siege but failed to survive long enough to inflict major damage.[19] Whatever damage (material, human, and symbolic) they inflicted, it could have been far worse had airport security officers not immediately responded to the incident.

For police, responding to simple, single site attacks requires a high degree of tactical proficiency. Larger, more complex, area-wide simultaneous assaults require a high degree of coordination and the employment of operational art. Urban operational art for the police demands integration of patrol, special operations (tactical response including SWAT, bomb squad, riot/crowd control, media/public information, detectives and investigation, and intelligence, as well as synchronization with the fire service, emergency medical services (EMS), emergency management, civil authorities, and potentially the military. Such coordination may be needed at multiple locations in a single jurisdiction or among authorities spread across multiple jurisdictions.

Our ability to comment on the Paris attacks is limited and based on details currently known in the open source. However, we can observe several important similarities and distinctions to the urban siege model we have outlined in prior work.

Some aspects of the Paris attacks had at least superficially to other observed urban terrorist attacks. While the main actual attack itself was relatively brief, the attackers themselves hid out in the Paris metropolitan area, lengthening the period of terror and fear. The incident reached a bloody climax when the assailants—seeking martyrdom and desiring a fight to the death—holed up in a small warehouse with a hostage and subsequently died at the hands of French law tactical responders.[20] Both gunmen received tactical training related to basic weapons usage, and one gunman may have visited Yemen to receive further instruction and financing.[21]

The distribution of the siege is also relevant. The *Charlie Hebdo* incident must be understood as an integrated whole, with the opening assault against the newspaper offices just one (high-profile) component. For three days, attackers went on a killing spree, distributing their attacks in time and space around Paris and its environs. During this time, the French security authorities were forced to deploy an enormous force to find, fix in place, and neutralize the suspects before they could accumulate a larger kill count. The attacks were synchronized to achieve maximum impact, and police faced enormous difficulties handling both situations simultaneously.

The Hyper Cacher hostage taker, for example, demanded that authorities cease their pursuit of the Kouachi brothers. While the police raid that broke the siege at the Hyper Cacher may seem improvised and amateurish to some observers, it was also conducted under extremely unfavorable conditions.[22] Both police raids had to be synchronized for hostages to survive. Moreover, coordinating a massive interagency response is complex and should be considered an operational success for the French security authorities given that difficulties in interagency coordination are an impediment to many operational responses and notably operational response to the Nairobi mall attack in 2013.[23]

While these elements may be familiar to those that respond to, and/or analyze urban siege, other elements of the attack were more novel. Analyzing the Paris attacks, Clint Watts argued that the future of jihad was "inspired, networked, and directed:"

The jihadi movement may have finally become what its original luminaries always wanted it to be—and in Paris of all places. The amorphous connections between the Charlie Hebdo attackers, the Kouachi brothers— who attributed their actions to "al Qaeda in Yemen"— and kosher market attacker Amedy Coulibali—who pledged allegiance to the Islamic State in a recently released online video—may reflect exactly what some early jihadi strategists intended: broad based jihad via a loose social movement. …. Years ago, Bruce Hoffman rightly proposed a spectrum approach to understanding al Qaeda comprising of a core, affiliates, and locals. His framework was appropriate but now needs some updates with the rise of the Islamic State. With two competing poles and a spectrum of adherents littered throughout at least five continents, jihadi plots and their perpetrators might best be examined through the blending of three overlapping categories: 'directed', 'networked' and 'inspired'. These three labels should not be seen as discrete categories but instead as phases across a spectrum—some plots and their perpetrators will bleed over these boundaries.[24]

Counterterrorism analysts have often argued over whether the future of jihad lies with centralized, hierarchal (if not completely top-down) groups capable of organized and lethal attacks or small groupings of alienated, mostly self-directed local attackers.[25] Watts suggests that this dichotomous understanding is ultimately misleading—it may be possible for an attack to feature such strange incongruities as terrorists belonging to two rival organizations (the Islamic State in Iraq and al-Qaeda) cooperating together.

Indeed, Islamic State supporter Coulibaly (with logistical support from other men that French authorities have detained) operated alongside al-Qaeda-identifying gunmen.[26] All three were part of a known network of French domestic extremists that orbited around a charismatic yet amateur and unofficial religious figure.[27] We leave discussion of what this means for the global terrorist threat landscape to counterterrorism specialists who will be informed by additional data. However, these debates, typologies, and considerations have practical meaning for operational authorities tasked with preparing for and countering urban attacks.

The three-day Paris siege complicates the assumptions of the conceptual schemas we and others have laid out regarding urban siege and urban terrorism.[28] Attackers did not belong to a single group—they were part of a common network that somehow received inspiration and possible direction from two ideologically opposed terrorist organizations. Investigators are still hunting for possible leads, but it is safe to say that the attacks were a "tangled" mess that involve uncertain connections between the attackers, local terrorist connections in Europe and external organizations in the Middle East.[29]

The threat of simultaneous attacks, follow-on attacks, and the tangled web of influence this situation involves complicates operational response. Police must assume from now on that attackers might derive logistical support, inspiration, funding, and/or direction from a diverse combination of local, regional, and extra-regional sources. Moreover, they cannot also assume that one large attack by an attacker group is all they must contend with—synchronized attacks may occur designed to augment the execution and impact of one attack mission. Campaigns containing multiple simultaneous (or near-simultaneous) and/or sequential attacks (including attacks or engagements during exfiltration and escape) must be accounted for and demand the development and employment of operational art for urban battle.[30]

While much of the urban sieges since Mumbai demonstrate continuity, complications and change suggest the need for new thinking, including full-spectrum policing, operational art, including operations-intelligence integration to support command.

Diagnosing Urban Siege: Towards A Spectrum of Armed Assault

Deriving problem classes of urban siege requires a look at both the organizational dimension of the attack and the actual means of operational preparation, planning, and execution.

As per Watts' typology of terrorist organization and influence, we believe that the organizational dimension of the attack matters a great deal in creating reasonable assumptions for training, response planning, and wargames/red-teaming efforts. We summarize his typology below. While we make no claims that Watts' typology is the only or necessarily the most accurate template for analyzing jihadist organization, we believe it at least illustrates many of the analytical challenges involved.

First, there are obviously the most traditional kind of attack organization. "Directed" attacks, Watts notes, assume a large degree of central organization by an external group and high lethality and capability. These attacks have become seemingly less likely as improved Western law enforcement, intelligence, and military efforts have made it difficult for attacks to be organized from the top-down. However, as Gartenstein-Ross and Leah Farall have noted, one should not count these attacks out.[31] Moreover, hierarchal organization does not necessarily assume a rigid, military-style command and control structure, and Gartenstein-Ross has noted that our understanding of the global jihad remains too fragmented and incomplete to make sweeping judgements about the likelihood of directed attacks.

"Networked" attacks will assume fighters with some degree of training (perhaps derived from overseas conflicts) and some degree of connection to overseas terrorist organizations or communities of terrorist practice. But, in contrast to elaborately planned directed attacks, Watts notes, networked attackers will constitute a "swarm" that brings together operatives, resources, and perpetrators as needed. Key variables in networked attacks include the local strength of foreign fighter networks, availability of weaponry, and the Western security environment that jihadists must contend with. Watts has suggested elsewhere that the chain of foreign fighters and radicals that being funneled to and from Western states to foreign battlefields may be modeled with the collective intelligence optimization technique known as ant colony optimization.[32]

Finally, "inspired" attacks feature "bungled plots and random violence" by "jihadi wannabees." While directed attacks and networked attacks demand a complex interagency operational response, "inspired" attacks may not typically not fit the urban siege conceptual schema. Competent law enforcement should be able to handle it, as "inspired" but often incompetent jihadists are frequently just as much of a danger to *themselves* as they are to their targets. However, one cannot rule out that directed or network attacks may spawn copycat inspired attacks, complicating security response, intelligence, and investigation before, during, or after an urban siege scenario. It is possible that future "inspired" cells may develop sophisticated capacity on their own or through interaction with other cells over time (although it is expected that this is difficult to achieve).

Next, we summarize Gartenstein-Ross and Daniel Trombly's October 2012 report on the use of small arms by terrorists.[33] Gartenstein-Ross and Trombly note that the use of small arms figures highly in terrorist strategic thought and must be analyzed as a function of a larger jihadist war of attrition. Al-Qaeda documents outline a strategy for a war of attrition rooted in a combination of complex, multi-member operations and smaller attacks. Complex and large-scale missions force the target to expend significant resources to prevent future attacks of that type, while smaller operations create a constant threat stream and foster an atmosphere of fear and paranoia while driving up costs gradually.[34] A vehicle for this is the use of firearms and armed assault:

> For both large-scale and small-scale attacks, firearms figure prominently in al Qaeda's strategy. A considerable corpus of written works underlies the significant role given to small arms. For years, al Qaeda and other jihadi organizations have published documents on the

value of these weapons. In Abd al Aziz al Muqrin's *A Practical Course for Guerrilla War*, a book based on writings that first appeared in al Qaeda's online journal Mu'askar al Battar, multiple chapters describe tactical and operational planning for urban warfare. Techniques covered include assassination, hostage taking, attacking motorcades, assaulting and clearing fixed targets, and setting up ambush positions. Additional volumes cover the acquisition and maintenance of small arms.[35]

Having outlined the strategic aim behind al-Qaeda contemplation of armed assault, Gartenstein-Ross and Trombly create a typology of urban assault types. Assasination attacks involve terrorist targeting of a high-profile individual. Single-shooter attacks aim for a symbolic target or location of importance to the enemy. Two-shooter teams allow terrorists to conduct more sophisticated attacks over extended periods of time. Mass attacks and frontal assaults denote terrorist operations against fixed targets. Finally, complex urban warfare attacks include multi-man teams and hybrids of the aforementioned attacks. Terrorists may also mix hostage taking, robberies, and defensive siege combat with any one of these attack types.[36]

Both the Watts and Gartenstein-Ross and Trombly typologies address essential aspects of an urban siege scenario. The organizational capacity and style in one of the categories Watts outlines may dictate the nature of the small arms attack drawn from Gartenstein-Ross and Trombly's study. Moreover, as we have previously suggested, an attack of one Watts type may lead to follow-on and/or concurrent attacks featuring another Watts organizational attack type and multiple possible Gartenstein-Ross and Trombly small arms attack types.

Murky and ill-structured incidents like the Paris incident suggest the need for greater integration between the levels of analysis in both surveys. Both cover core elements of the problem—operational direction and mechanism of attack respectively—but understanding organizational capacity and the causation of attacks may help explain the overlaps between attack execution types that Gartenstein-Ross and Trombly note at the conclusion of their report. "With firearms attackers have great flexibility," Gartenstein-Ross and Trombly rightly note. Once an attack has begun, they can select new targets and counter law enforcement."[37]

This, when coupled with the potential for a more unpredictable attacker set composition, suggests that conceptual integration is of more than just academic or high-level policy relevance. It matters very much for operational preparation for countering armed assaults. In order to train, prepare, red-team, plan, and allocate resources properly *before* the attack, police and other security agencies need to have scripts, scenarios, and models of how an attack is organized, rehearsed, and executed.

Questions about Future Urban Siege

While we do not propose our own typology, the Paris attack and newer research and analysis by Watts, Garteinstein-Ross and Trombly, and others suggest some pressing questions for both researchers and operational responders to consider when pondering urban siege post-Hebdo. In pondering these questions, we hope that researchers and operational responders can grope towards some conceptual synthesis between the levels of analysis that Watts and Gartenstein-Ross and Trombly cover in their analyses. We list them below:

1. *What kind of organizational assumptions should we utilize when building urban terrorism scenarios?* Both the Mumbai and Paris urban sieges had similar results—prolonged mayhem by multiple groups of attackers. However, in one operation (Mumbai) the terrorists belonged to one group distributed into multiple teams. During the Paris attack the terrorists belonged to a loose common network but only loosely coordinated their synchronized operations. This created two different kinds of command problems for the first responders. Of course, the police may not and likely won't know which type of adversary they are facing during the initial course of an actual attack sequence and must

rely upon real-time intelligence and operational reports to develop situational assessments.

During the Mumbai operation first responders struggled to handle the command and control problem of countering a distributed operation. But in the Paris attack state capacity was high and this was not as grave of a challenge. Rather, the primary challenge was locating the perpetrators, connecting disparate incidents, and later during the hostage situations dealing with the new problem of an attacker that synchronized an attack to coincide with a main operation. This demanded synchronized police response, which was achieved.

The command implications most relevant for an urban siege problem will depend greatly on what kind of organizational assumptions we make about the connection between attacks in the urban terror scenario. But this question also pertains very much to the prevention of attacks before they happen.

A Mumbai-like scenario requires extensive preparation, planning, a forward base, and attack vector that might expose planners and operatives to vulnerability. The terrorist "kill chain" in this case may be amenable to detection and penetration. In contrast, a Paris-like scenario does not have to be analyzed by the familiar recourse to "intelligence failure" explanations—it is perfectly possible that an attack like Paris might occur absent the systemic intelligence-sharing and indications and warnings flaws observed after Mumbai.[38] Here the terrorist "kill chain" may be more obscure and difficult to penetrate.

2. *How should we weight maximum casualties and maximum disruption in the assumptions we make about terrorist mission planning?* One issue that Gartenstein-Ross and Trombly implicitly raise is the dichotomy between disruption and casualties as objectives in an urban siege scenario. Certainly, killing a lot of people can induce disruption and disrupting a key site or system can lead to a substantial amount of casualties. But they ought not to be regarded as interchangeable. One can induce a substantial amount of disruption and fear without Mumbai or Peshawar kill counts—the toll of the Paris attack sequence was small compared to those incidents yet it also induced a massive

mobilization of French security forces and led to fear, suspicion, and a backlash that may complicate future counter-terrorism efforts.[39]

This raises some core questions about urban siege scenarios from the point of view of the attacker. Is there a tradeoff between casualties and disruption? How many casualties are necessary for disruption? Is one kind of objective easier to achieve than the other in an urban siege? Do attacker objectives change dynamically during the middle of an incident in response to new information? It should be noted that attackers themselves also may not see a distinction between casualties and disruption or heavily consider it in their planning. Enough casualties automatically suggest disruption, and disruption may be a primary objective with casualty count as a side effect.

All of these questions bear heavily on organizational assumptions and choice of attack tactics and weapons. As Gartenstein-Ross and Trombly note, firearms allow tremendous flexibility both prior to and during the prosecution of an urban siege. Police will be better able to model, red-team, and train for urban siege scenarios if they have a greater idea of how terrorists themselves view success and failure conditions for urban sieges.

3. *How should we think about social media information and operational security during urban sieges?* We devote the most space to this issue due to the fact that operational security (OPSEC) in response has become more acute due to changes in the social media landscape since we last wrote on urban siege.

The issue of social media and OPSEC is by no means new. The Mumbai attacks were one of Twitter's first real-time crises, with both locals and foreigners giving contradictory and confused play-by-play as the event unfolded. However, the increasing saturation of social media platforms and the ubiquity of Twitter and other social media platforms are increasingly bringing uncertainties about social media and OPSEC to the fore.

In this attack sequence, social media played a significant role for police, the media, the community, and terrorist organizations alike. Jihadists and their supporters used social media to praise the attacks, and the #JeSuisCharlie meme went viral extremely quickly.[40] Additionally, Twitter became a tool for tracking terrorists and developing situational awareness (for all actors), and social media became a key operational security concern as the tactics, techniques, and procedures of security forces are now broadcast in real time by both new and conventional media and terrorist can track that presence as seen in the warning for police to keep a low profile on social media minimize the potential for terrorist ambush.[41]

Both everyday citizens and major news media organizations maintain social media presences. Social media increasingly drives news during crises and fusing social media information has grown easier over time due to the increasing maturation of third party client applications. It has become easier for perpetrators of incidents to monitor feeds, as long as they have manpower to spare or are suitably entrenched in a manner that allows them to monitor feeds unimpeded.

While it is important to remember that attackers (if they successfully infiltrate) begin with the advantage of surprise and responders face an uphill challenge in sorting through contradictory information, so do attackers as well. More research and assessment needs to be done about cognitive and organizational limitations on how attackers receive, process, and utilize social media information during crisis scenarios.

The human factors and emergency response literature is replete with analysis about how the incident commander's situational awareness challenges, but we know comparatively little about that of the attacker group.[42] It is plausible that information fusion and processing difficulties may be negated by external support and planning (like the Mumbai attack's handlers), but it also may just add yet another information channel to process as an extra burden. It is only by modeling the information processing challenges attackers face (and how technology may help or worsen them) that law enforcement organizations can gain a realistic idea of OPSEC considerations in future crisis scenarios and justify them to external audiences.

Conclusion: Are We Charlie?

The first question routinely asked after every major terrorist attack is "can it happen here?" Until more information is available about the *Charlie Hebdo* attacks, it is hard if not impossible to even offer informed speculation about the answer. Our own work is based on news reports and others' analyses and we will eagerly monitor how well they hold up as more detailed information continues to emerge about the attacks.

Our purpose in writing this piece, however, is not to argue about the potentials for urban siege. We know that armed assault and urban siege is likely to remain a dangerous threat in both the developed West and the developing world.[43] However, noting that the possibility for urban siege exists is no longer sufficient or useful. What increasingly matters is *how* the attack will occur, and we hope that our analysis and questions will spur others to move forward in intensely studying and wargaming the variations and permutations of urban siege.

We titled our first piece on urban siege: "Postcard from Mumbai: Modern Urban Siege." It is our sincere hope that, whatever the tangled aftermath of Paris, we do not see too many more lethal "postcards" of urban siege from any more cities.[44]

Notes

[1] John P. Sullivan and Adam Elkus, "Postcard from Mumbai: Modern Urban Siege," *Small Wars Journal*, 16 February 2009, smallwarsjournal.com/blog/journal/docs-temp/181-sullivan. pdf and "Preventing Another Mumbai: Building a Police Operational Art," *CTC Sentinel*, West Point: Countering Terrorism Center, 15 June 2009, https://www.ctc.usma.edu/posts/ preventing-another-mumbai-building-a-police-operational-art.

[2] Shane Harris, "US Spies Expected Airline Bombs—And Got The Paris Attacks Instead," *The Daily Beast*, 17 January 2015, http:// www.thedailybeast.com/articles/2015/01/17/u-s-spies-expected-airline-bombs-and-got-the-paris-attacks-instead.html.

[3]   David Kilcullen, "Westgate Mall Attacks: Urban Areas Are the Battleground Of the 21ˢᵗ Century," *The Guardian*, 27 September 2013.

[4]   *BBC*, "Charlie Hebdo Attack: Three Days of Terror," *BBC*, 14 January 2015, http://www.bbc.com/news/world-europe-30708237 and Pierre Bienaime, "France Has Mobilized 88,000 Personnel After the Paris Shootings," *Business Insider,* 8 Jan 2015. http://www.businessinsider.com/france-has-mobilized-88000-personnel-after-the-paris-shootings-2015-1.

[5]   Emma Graham-Harrison, "Paris Policeman's Brother: Islam Is A Religion of Love. My Brother Was Killed by Terrorists, By False Muslims," *The Guardian*, 10 January 2015, http://www.theguardian.com/world/2015/jan/10/charlie-hebdo-policeman-murder-ahmed-merabet.

[6]   *CBS News*, "The Special Forces Behind France's Rescue Operations," 9 January 2015, http://www.cbsnews.com/news/the-special-forces-behind-frances-rescue-operations/.

[7]   Griff Whitte, "In A Kosher Grocery Store In Paris, Terror Takes A Deadly Toll," *The Washington Post*, 9 January 2015, http://www.washingtonpost.com/world/europe/paris-kosher-market-seized-in-second-hostage-drama-in-nervous-france/2015/01/09/f171b97e-97ff-11e4-8005-1924ede3e54a_story.html.

[8]   Ray Sanchez, Laura Smith-Spark, and Hakim Almasmari, "Source: Terror Cells Activated in France," *CNN,* 11 January 2015, http://edition.cnn.com/2015/01/10/europe/charlie-hebdo-paris-shooting/, and Shashank Joshi, "Charlie Hebdo attack: A French Intelligence Failure?" *BBC*, 10 January 2015, http://www.bbc.com/news/world-europe-30760656.

[9]   Christian de Looper, "Post-Charlie Hebdo Attack, "Islamist Cyberattacks' Cripple French Media: About 19,000 Websites KO'd," *Tech Times*, 19 January 2015, http://www.techtimes.com/articles/27228/20150119/post-charlie-hebdo-attack-islamist-cyber-attacks-cripple-french-media.htm.

[10] *AFP*, "Hackers Took Control of a French Newspaper's Twitter Account and Tweeted 'I'm Not Charlie'", *Business Insider*, 20

January 2015, http://www.businessinsider.com/afp-syrian-group-hacks-french-newspapers-twitter-account-2015-1.

[11] Kilcullen, ibid.

[12] For an overview of that operation, see John P. Sullivan and Adam Elkus, "The New Playbook? Urban Siege in Nairobi," *Small Wars Journal*, 24 November 2013, http://www.isn.ethz.ch/Digital-Library/Publications/Detail/?lng=en&id=175657.

[13] Howden, ibid.

[14] Sophia Saifi and Greg Botelho, "In Pakistan, Terrorists Kill 145, Mostly Children," *CNN*, 17 December 2014, http://www.cnn.com/2014/12/16/world/asia/pakistan-peshawar-school-attack/.

[15] C. Christine Fair, *Urban Battle Fields of South Asia: Lessons Learned from Sri Lanka, India, and Pakistan*, Santa Monica: RAND Corporation, 2004.

[16] J. Paul D. Taillon, *Hijacking and Hostages: Government Response to Terror*, Westport: Praeger, 2002.

[17] John P. Sullivan and Adam Elkus, "Preventing Another Mumbai: Building a Police Operational Art," *CTC Sentinel*, West Point: Countering Terrorism Center, 15 June 2009, https://www.ctc.usma.edu/posts/preventing-another-mumbai-building-a-police-operational-art.

[18] *BBC,* "Gunmen kill 13 at Karachi's Jinnah International Airport," 8 June 2014, http://www.bbc.com/news/world-asia-27757264.

[19] Taimur Khan, "Karachi Attack Shows Pakistani Taliban Fighting to Re-Assert Itself," *The National,* June 2014, http://www.thenational.ae/world/pakistan/karachi-attack-shows-pakistani-taliban-fighting-to-reassert-itself.

[20] "Cornered French Suspects Vow to Die as Martyrs," *USA Today*, 9 January 2015, http://www.wusa9.com/story/news/nation/2015/01/09/report-hostages-taken-northeast-of-paris/21487097/.

[21] Scott Bronstein, "Cherif and Said Kouachi: Their Path to Terror," *CNN*, 14 January 2015, http://www.cnn.com/2015/01/13/world/kouachi-brothers-radicalization/Erich Schmitt, Mark Mazzetti, and Rukmini Callimachi, "Disputed Claims Over Qaeda Role in Paris Attacks," *The New York Times*, 14 January 2015, http://

www.nytimes.com/2015/01/15/world/europe/al-qaeda-in-the-arabian-peninsula-charlie-hebdo.html.

[22] Some have snarkily compared the operation to the infamous "Leeroy Jenkins" raid in the computer game *World of Warcraft*, mixing the audio dialogue from the failed multiplayer mission with the video of the Hyper Cacher police assault. See, for example, https://www.youtube.com/watch?v=cKw65EN_JtE.

[23] Daniel Howden, "Terror in Westgate Mall: The Full Story Of The Attacks That Devastated Kenya," *The Guardian*, 4 October 2013, http://www.theguardian.com/world/interactive/2013/oct/04/westgate-mall-attacks-kenya-terror#undefined.

[24] Clint Watts, "Inspired, Networked, and Directed: The Muddled Jihad of ISIS and Al-Qaeda Post-Hebo," *War on the Rocks,* 12 January 2015, http://warontherocks.com/2015/01/inspired-networked-directed-the-muddled-jihad-of-isis-al-qaeda-post-hebdo/?singlepage=1.

[25] For an overview of the debate, see Daveed Gartenstein-Ross, "Is Al Qaeda A Global Terror Threat Or A Local Military Menace?", *The Globe and Mail*, 28 May 2014, http://www.defenddemocracy.org/media-hit/gartenstein-ross-daveed-debate-is-al-qaeda-a-global-terror-threat-or-a-local-military-menace/.

[26] Maia de la Baume and Dan Bilefksy, "France Vows Forceful Measures Against Terrorism," *The New York Times*, 21 January 2015, http://www.nytimes.com/2015/01/22/world/europe/amedy-coulibaly-paris-gunman-france.html.

[27] Griff Witte and Anthony Faiola, "Suspect in Paris Attack Had 'Long-Term Obsession' Carrying Out Terrorist Attack," *The Washington Post*, 8 January 2015, http://www.washingtonpost.com/world/europe/suspect-in-paris-attack-had-long-term-obsession-carrying-out-terror-attack/2015/01/08/b36f6c90-974e-11e4-aabd-d0b93ff613d5_story.html.

[28] See David Kilcullen, *Out of the Mountains: The Coming Age of the Urban Guerrilla*, Oxford: Oxford University Press, 2013, Anthony James Joes, *Urban Guerrilla Warfare*, Lexington: The University of Kentucky, 2007, and John Robb, *Brave New War: The Next*

Stage of Terrorism and the End of Globalization, Hoboken: Wiley, 2007 for a sampling of academic and practitioner writings on urban guerrilla operations.

[29]   Mariano Castillo, "Following the Tangled and Treacherous Trail After France Terror Attack," *CNN*, 15 January 2014, http://www.cnn.com/2015/01/13/europe/france-charlie-hebdo-attack-trail/.

[30]   The Boston Marathon Bombing Attack (2013) was followed by the shooting of an MIT police officer, carjacking, a manhunt, and firefight. See J.M. Hirsh, "Boston Bombing Overview: The Unfolding of A 5-Day Manhunt For Suspects," *Huffington Post*, 21 April 2013, http://www.huffingtonpost.com/2013/04/21/boston-bombing-timeline_n_3127079.html.

[31]   Gartenstein-Ross and Farall's analysis is reviewed in Adam Elkus, "Leader of the Pack," *War on the Rocks*, 31 October 2013, http://warontherocks.com/2013/10/leader-of-the-pack/.

[32]   Watts, "Foreign Fighters and Ants: How They Form Their Colonies," *Geopoliticus: The FPRI Blog*, June 2013, http://www.fpri.org/geopoliticus/2013/07/foreign-fighters-and-ants-how-they-form-their-colonies.

[33]   Daveed Gartenstein-Ross and Daniel Trombly, *The Tactical and Strategic Use of Small Arms by Terrorists*, Washington, DC: The Foundation for Defense of Democracies, 2012.

[34]   Gartenstein-Ross and Trombly, 6.

[35]   Ibid., 7.

[36]   Ibid.,7 8.

[37]   Ibid., 21.

[38]   Sebastian Rotella, James Glaz, and David E. Sanger, "In 2008 Mumbai Attacks, Piles of Spy Data, But an Uncompleted Puzzle," *ProPublica*, 21 December 2014, http://www.propublica.org/article/mumbai-attack-data-an-uncompleted-puzzle

[39]   Steven Metz, "The Paris Attacks and the Logic of Insurgency," *World Politics Review,* 16 January 2015, http://www.worldpoliticsreview.com/articles/14873/the-paris-attacks-and-the-logic-of-insurgency.

[40]   Ben Hubbard, "Islamic Extremists Take To Social Media To Praise Charlie Hebdo Attacks," *The New York Times*, 10 January

2015, http://www.nytimes.com/2015/01/11/world/europe/islamic
-extremists-take-to-social-media-to-praise-charliehebdo-
attack.html?_r=0&gwh=DEF452EB18676C551C641B70
B2D85FFF&gwt=pay.

[41]   Noah Ryman, "How Twitter Tracked the French Terror Suspects,"
Time, 8 January 2015, http://time.com/3659307/twitter-tracked-
terror-suspects/ and Sanchez et al., ibid.

[42]   See, for example, Alexander Kott(ed), *Battle of Cognition: The
Future Information-Rich Warfare and the Mind of the Commander*,
Westport: Praeger, 2007, and Christine Owen (ed), *Human Factors
Challenges in Emergency Management: Enhancing Individual and
Team Performance in Fire and Emergency Services*, Farnham:
Ashgate, 2014.

[43]   David Kilcullen "New terror paradigm after Charlie Hebdo raids,"
The Australian, 17 January 2015, http://www.theaustralian.com.au/
in-depth/terror/new-terror-paradigm-after-charlie-hebdo-raids/
story-fnpdbcmu-1227187609376.

[44]   Postscript: As we completed this piece another urban siege attack
transpired in Tripoli. Libya. This attack on 27 January 2015
involved a combined assault (car bomb and gun attack) against
the Corinthia Hotel killing at least three and injuring a half
dozen more. See UN News, "Terrorist attack on hotel in Libyan
capital," *Scoop*, 30 January 2015, http://www.scoop.co.nz/stories/
WO1501/S00251/terrorist-attack-on-hotel-in-libyan-capital.htm.

Chapter 20

Book Review: The Robin Hood Guerrillas

Michael L. Burgoyne

First Published 1 July 2015

The Robin Hood Guerrillas
The Epic Journey of Uruguay's Tupamaros
By Pablo Brum
402 pp. $15.00

> *Until men learn that of all human symbols, Robin Hood*
> *is the most immoral and the most contemptible, there will*
> *be no justice on earth and no way for mankind to survive.*
>
> —*Ayn Rand, Atlas Shrugged*

In *The Robin Hood Guerrillas; The Epic Journey of Uruguay's Tupamaros*, author Pablo Brum provides us with a fascinating look into the history of a little known and little understood 20th century insurgency. *The Robin Hood Guerrillas* is the first complete English language history of the Tupamaros, a group that launched an innovative insurgent campaign against the Uruguayan government in the 1960s and 1970s. Through his comprehensive study, Brum illustrates the tragedy of a violent quest to achieve utopia which destroyed the very democratic system that would, in the end, lead to the elected victory of former insurgent Jose Mujica. Brum delivers an extremely valuable case study that belongs on the shelf of every latin-americanist and student of unconventional warfare. The case of the Tupamaros is especially relevant today as increasing worldwide urbanization continues to make urban insurgency a more important strategy in internal struggles for power.

Perhaps one of the most striking themes of Brum's history is the avoidable nature of the conflict. In the 1960s, Uruguay's government was already left leaning. It was difficult to promote radical revolution when much of the socialist platform was already being pursued within the democratic system. Fidel Castro said that Uruguay's broad plains did not provide the proper conditions for an insurgency and none less than Che Guevara cautioned that Uruguay's revolutionaries should pursue democratic channels rather than armed struggle. Brum captures the sentiment of the Uruguayan revolutionaries brilliantly. "Why should they be condemned *not* to have a revolution only because they happened to have been born in cities?"

Despite the unfortunate lack of proper conditions, the Uruguayan revolutionaries moved forward with a unique insurgency strategy. They decided on an offensive, Cuban *foco* styled, uprising that would be necessarily based out of the cities due to the lack of complex terrain. The National Liberation Movement (MLN) or Tupamaros were born, taking their name from the Incan leader Tupac Amaru II who fought the colonial Spanish.

A key early aspect of the MLN strategy was armed propaganda. Every act was designed to send a message more than it was designed to inflict military harm on the government. Brum provides the reader with several riveting accounts of Tupamaro bank robberies, prison breaks, and radio station seizures. Despite the criminal nature of the acts, the reader cannot help but root for the Tupamaros as Brum narrates their daring feats. These largely non-violent antics helped build the group's reputation with the population and attacked government legitimacy. It could be argued that the Sandinistas in Nicaragua would become the next stage of evolution in the armed propaganda techniques used by the MLN. Insurgency expert TX Hammes believes that the Sandinistas were able to eliminate the need for a final military offensive by successful political messaging which eventually led to government collapse.[1]

The early success of the MLN's creative and almost playful escapades gradually descends into a darker more violent insurgency. Brum narrates the MLN's spiral into more aggressive methods. MLN kidnappings began in 1968, targeted at first and then later cast with a wider net. In 1969, the seizure of the town of Pando resulted in the death of an innocent civilian. Later the kidnapping and murder of US diplomat Dan Mitrone seemed to be an end of innocence for the group. Finally, the MLN "Plan Cacao" unleashed bombings and attacks that impacted the general public.

The government response was initially as limited as the MLN insurgency. Largely police led, the interrogations were light and torture was limited if at all. Like the insurgents, the government seemed interested in conducting a war, but not to the extreme. However, as Brum explains, the government response would ramp up with the more violent MLN tactics. In the end, the military is placed in charge of the counterinsurgency mission. Drawing largely from the lessons of French counterinsurgents like Roger Trinquier, the Uruguayan military attacked the MLN with a vengeance. Torture became more common, more effective, and more brutal. The military systematically dismantled the MLN, arresting members and seizing safe-houses. However, in the end, the military realized that military action alone could not solve instability. The democracy that even Che Guevara praised fell into military dictatorship for 12 years.

Those desperate to have "their revolution", damn the conditions, caused the destruction of democratic institutions in Uruguay. Brum notes "their remarkable pursuit of high ideals and principles became a tragic story as they progressively violated all of them." 37 years later, in a remarkable turn of events, Jose "Pepe" Mujica, the MLN guerrilla, would find himself elected president of Uruguay. The very democratic institutions that Mujica had undermined eventually allowed him to take power. Moderated by the years, Mujica would say "I believe we have to favor capitalism, so that its wheels keep turning and then take our quota of resources to give to the weakest. But we should not paralyze it."[2]

Brum's excellent case study of the Tupamaros offers lasting lessons applicable to current security challenges. One key point from the conflict is the often-noted need for a "whole of government" approach. In the case of the MLN, the Uruguayan government eventually turned to the military to take on the problem. However, the military, versed in the French experiences in Algeria, identified the social and economic factors that were driving the insurgency. Like the French military's move to take power in 1961 in the middle of the Algerian War, the Uruguayan Army sought out the necessary powers to address their own problem. Uruguay's cautionary tale, once again highlights the need for civilian agencies to be a critical part of any government response to an insurgency.

The Tupamaro case study provides historical data points for those studying the increasingly common phenomenon of urban insurgency or urban conflict. The Tupamaros developed a unique and largely effective urban campaign based on the works of Abraham Guillen and Carlos Marighella. Guillen stated that "the Tupamaros have served as the best revolutionary academy in the world on the subject of urban guerrilla warfare; they have taught more through actions than all the revolutionary theories abstracted from concrete situations."[3] One need only look at the conflict in Iraq, where the insurgency was largely urban based, to see that urban insurgency is a valid course of action for a devoted force. Security scholars like David Kilcullen, John Sullivan, and Robert Bunker among others are sounding alarms about evolving unconventional threats and the growing importance of urban terrain in warfare. Students of warfare and security can mine extensive lessons from Brum's study including the Tupamaro use of subterranean networks, safe-houses, communication techniques, and the utility of varied government responses. The lessons in *The Robin Hood Guerrillas* will be ever more valid as warfare continues to move into the cities.

Few experts in security studies have taken the time to review the story of the Tupamaros. There has been significant study of rural guerrilla movements in Central America, Colombia, and Peru; however, future insurgencies may look more like the urban battles fought in the Southern Cone. The urban nature of the Tupamaro's campaign and the evolution of the government response are highly relevant today. Pablo Brum has written an objective and detailed look at one of the finest case studies in urban conflict. Students and practitioners of warfare and public security should read this book to better understand current and future conflicts that are increasingly urban. The reader comes away from the book feeling Brum's sense of tragedy and the futility of the entire enterprise. The MLN's transformation from idealists to murderous insurgents and the destruction along the way of a functioning democratic system is heartrending. One can only ask "why?" This becomes especially ironic given that all of this conflict and pain ends with a more moderate Mujica gaining power, not by assassination or bombings, but through the ballot box. Perhaps if those who still cling to the idea of violent revolution read Brum's cautionary tale they will seek to achieve their aims democratically in the market of ideas rather than through intimidation and subversion. When they do not, this book provides valuable insights on how to stop them.

The views expressed in this study are those of the author and do not reflect the official policy or position of the Department of the Army, Department of Defense, or the U.S. Government.

Notes

[1]   TX Hammes, *The Sling and the Stone*, (Minneapolis, MBI Publishing and Zenith Press, Minneapolis, 2006), 76-88.

[2]   Jonathan Gilbert, "Uruguay's Most Unexpected Champion of Capitalism," *Fortune*, January 23, 2015.

[3]   Abraham Guillen, *Philosophy of the Urban Guerrilla*, ed. Ad trans. Donald C. Hodges, (New York, William and Morrow, 1973), 276.

Chapter 21

City As a System Analytical Framework: A Structured Analytical Approach to Understanding and Acting in Urban Environments

Mark Lomedico and Elizabeth M. Bartels

First Published 4 August 2015

Introduction

On-going research on "mega-cities" highlights aspects of large, unplanned cities that make them an operational challenge. This work has a clear perspective on the potential threats posed by cities and makes the case that current doctrine is ill prepared to manage these problems. However, these research efforts have focused on the conceptual challenges of cities rather than practical approaches to analyzing and operating in urban environments. In response, Caerus Associates has created an analytical framework to enable military analysts and planners to develop a systems perspective of the urban operational environment. The framework is designed to enable the continuous updating of analysis and premised on the idea of iteration in the face of a changing environment. This article discusses the characteristics of urban environments, suggests opportunities, as well as challenges, resulting from urban complexity, and describes the framework's approach to understanding and acting in urban settings.

Background

Caerus Associates developed an analytical framework for assessing urban environments to support current military planning and analysis processes. The purpose of the project was to develop a nuanced way of understanding hyper-connected cities, highlighting interactions between the physical and social domains. Building on ideas developed by Caerus founder David Kilcullen in his book *Out of the Mountains*, the team's work drew on current social science research, best practices curated through interviews with military and intelligence organizations, and team members' own operational experience. Caerus rigorously tested the framework using workshops, case studies, and wargames over the course of 15 months. These engagements with general purpose and special operations forces, the intelligence community, and academia ensured that the framework was useful to, and usable by operational staffs during analysis and planning.

The Urban Environment's Challenges

Rapid and unplanned urbanization continues to concentrate the global population in cities. A growing consensus of military thinkers argue that as cities struggle to plan for and manage this growth, threats to US interests will require US military engagement.[1] In some cases, these threats will take the form of non-state actors empowered by gaps in host-nation capacity. In others, normal urban functions will be overcome by natural disasters or popular unrest. As a result, the US military will be called to conduct decisive action (offense, defense, stability, or defense support of civil authorities[2]) in cities.[3] Many of these missions will not be adversary-centric, requiring analysis of the environment be given the same level of emphasis traditionally given to the adversary.

In order to be successful in cities, military analysts and planners will require tools to understand urban environments. The City As a System Analytical Framework describes the urban environment and recommends a systems approach to analysis. Cities are complex, adaptive systems due to their connectedness; their unique terrain; and the diversity of territorial controllers (each explained in more detail below). These qualities lead to a high density of interaction between the population, infrastructure, and the physical terrain, which overwhelms traditional reductive analysis. Systems approaches to analysis seek to understand these interactions and how they contribute to broad patterns of behavior over space and time.

The framework is not unique in advocating a systems approach to understanding the connected, complex nature of urban environments. Many academic and military thinkers have argued that adopting a systems approach is crucial to understanding urban environments. For example, urban operations subject matter expert Russell Glenn wrote: "Urban areas are by nature systems, which are themselves parts of even larger systems."[4] More recent writings within the military have also taken this approach. The Chief of Staff of the Army's Strategic Studies Group stated: "...Simply understanding the behavior of individual parts of a complex system is insufficient. One must develop an appreciation for the whole of the system to comprehend the behavior of its sub-components."[5] Other Army thinkers have agreed, arguing: "Megacities can be best described as systems of systems, comparable to a living organism. They are dynamic environments that change not only block by block, but day to day. While this is not a new idea, the magnitude of the challenge to gain situational understanding is significantly greater due to the complexity, density, and scale of the physical and human terrain."[6]

Connected and Data Rich

Cities are saturated with information due to their internal and external connectedness. The constant interaction between people and between people and physical terrain creates a large amount of information, which is collected by ubiquitous sensors throughout the urban environment. This rich data offers big data analytical opportunities, but it can also be overwhelming for analysts, risking the loss of critical signals in the noise of the city. For example, those seeking concealment in urban environments must work carefully to remain unobserved, but for those who are able to blend into the daily patterns of urban life, detection can be extremely difficult. Data is also difficult to interpret, and changes rapidly over time. Residents cope with size, density, and complexity by developing personalized understandings of the city, which can cause conflicting interpretations and observations of how elements of the urban environment work and their importance. Cities also change due to both outside stimuli and due to interactions between elements of the city over time.

As a result of urban connectedness, methods for gathering necessary information about cities differ from methods used in traditional environments. Analysts need to be prepared to leverage open source information and local perspectives. However, they must also be prepared to synthesize multiple, conflicting perspectives and dynamic information. Better intelligence collection requirements, and structured but flexible approaches to store and share date will be critical to sense making in these environments. Additionally, traditional analytical methods that silo information do not enable analysts to observe relationships that exist in the environment. This presents a problem— one that the framework seeks to remedy—as the urban environment is hyper-connected and thus yields many cross-cutting relationships.

Unique Terrain

As a result of the growing size of cities and connectivity, cities no longer terminate at their administrative edges. Expanding populations settle in outlying neighborhoods, slowly connecting cities to neighboring urban centers to form uninterrupted areas of settlement. Resulting urban agglomerations—such as the northeast corridor of the US with its string of urban settlements from Washington DC to Boston—function as an integrated whole, even when outdated political divisions remain. Infrastructure, such as utility systems and transit networks, also extend past administrative boundaries. Social networks connect the city to people outside of the city, whether 5 miles outside or 5,000. These networks can influence certain sectors of a city's population through information sharing, messaging, and an influx of money. As a result, areas of operation determined by political boundaries fail to encompass the true extent of the cities' social and physical reach, removing potential threats and vectors of influence from the analysis.

Edgelessness requires a fundamental change in approach to urban operations. Existing joint concepts stress the importance of isolating cities before undertaking urban operations.[7] Caerus' findings, however, conclude that it is very difficult to cordon and lay siege to a medium or large city. Urban agglomerations do not terminate in permissible areas, making it difficult to emplace walls and checkpoints needed to isolate the city. Systematic clearing of city blocks requires battalions of forces that are rarely available, leaving openings for enemies to re-infiltrate cleared areas. Even when resources are available, cordoning a city and cutting off the flow of goods and people can cause long-term damage to the health of the city, risking strategic defeat despite tactical victories. Instead, US forces can achieve micro-isolation by denying the problem system of certain critical flows and nodes that may be accessible to friendly forces. Alternatively, friendly forces may be able to work within the existing system, by strengthening some aspects of the problem system allowing cities to continue to function while removing potential threats. In some cases, these approaches can be achieved from outside of the city as urban connectedness enables US forces to influence systems from afar.

Diversity of Controllers

Cities are rarely controlled by a single coherent actor. Most cities have social, political, economic, and infrastructure hubs located in multiple places throughout the city. These hubs are often controlled by different actors who influence the population by permitting or denying access to areas, people, goods, and services. While the state attempts to create rules to make these centers legible and accessible to state rule,[8] often cities are too overwhelming to be completely managed by one actor. To compensate, the state will devolve control to sub-state actors or non-governmental entities. In some cases, this is done in a very controlled, official way, by granting authority over specific aspects of the city to approved entities, like religious organizations and businesses. For example, states sometimes grant authority to churches to manage behavior of their congregations. However, in other cases devolution occurs because the state lacks the capacity, allowing unauthorized actors to gain control over an area.

As a result, analysts of, and operators in cities must be prepared to navigate interactions with a range of powerful actors. Understanding the relationships between different actors, and how friendly and adversary forces are connected as part of systems, is critical to effective operations. Furthermore, it is critical to understand how territorial logics of the physical environment empower and constrain actors' behavior. The natural and man made physical terrain shapes the behavior of adversary forces, friendly agencies, and the population. Territorial logic refers to the strategies and behaviors of systems and actors resulting from the limits of terrain.

City Size

Caerus' findings indicate that population size is not a proxy for connectivity, unique terrain, or the diversity of actors in the city. The difficulty of managing urban problems is not meaningfully reduced by operating in a smaller city, if that city is still hyper-connected, edgeless, and exhibiting fractured control. Size also rarely predicts whether a city is relevant to US national security interests, or permissible to US actors on the ground.

Many stakeholders in the urban operations community of interest place an emphasis on megacities—cities of 10 million or more people—and their size, rapid growth, and scale. However, Caerus research shows that megacities are not growing as quickly as are medium sized cities. In fact, the fastest growing cities are cities with 500,000 to 1 million people in Asia and Africa.[9] Furthermore, there are many more medium sized cities than there are megacities. In 2014, there were 952 cities with populations between 500,000 and 5 million, 43 cities with populations between 5 and 10 million, and only 28 megacities, with populations 10 million or more.[10] Caerus is not alone in reaching this finding.[11] The complex, adaptive nature of cities is present in small and large cities as well as megacities. The quantity of middleweight cities might mean that the US military is more likely to operate in these medium sized cities than in megacities. A similar argument is made in "The Case Against Megacities" by Michael Evans in *Parameters*.[12]

City as a System Analytical Framework

In light of these urban challenges, Caerus built a framework to enhance existing doctrinal planning and analysis techniques. The framework is a method for developing a holistic perspective of the urban environment and its problem systems in order to better aid US military course of action development and course of action analysis. The framework also motivates data collection and organization practices to address critical gaps, as well as long term collection to support baselining.

Design Principles

The framework encourages analysts to take a broad view of the urban operational environment by combining adversary-, population-, and terrain-centric approaches that are common to various military planning processes. The complexity of the urban environment makes it impossible to isolate these aspects of the environment from one another. Terrain and infrastructure shape the behavior of not only friendly and adversary forces, but also contribute to the behavior of the population. Adversary action affects both the behavior of the population and the physical terrain of the city. In order to account for these relationships, the framework encourages the consideration of friendly and adversary actors as part of the environment, rather than as an isolated element of analysis.

Relatedly, the framework elevates the importance of the environment (to include physical and man-made terrain, infrastructure, and the population) to the same level of emphasis given to the adversary. Traditional intelligence preparation of the operational environment (IPOE) focuses heavily on the adversary, their tactics, techniques, and procedures, and their most likely courses of action (COAs). The framework posits that other aspects of the environment—like infrastructure and the population—contribute to urban problems as much as, and perhaps more than, the adversary. Giving the environment this level of emphasis and importance ensures analysts and planners are considering how the system of systems across the physical and social domains impact the operational environment, a key component of IPOE step 2.

Process

The framework is a three step process: define the urban operational environment, frame and map urban problem systems, and develop and analyze urban COAs.

Step I: Define the Urban Operational Environment guides analysts to develop an understanding of the current and historical operational environment. The framework's techniques offer lines of questions for staffs to work though in order to gain an initial understanding of the urban environment. The framework provides an ontology for urban environments that highlights 13 Significant Characteristics (illustrated in Figure 1 below), and commonly occurring "types" for each.

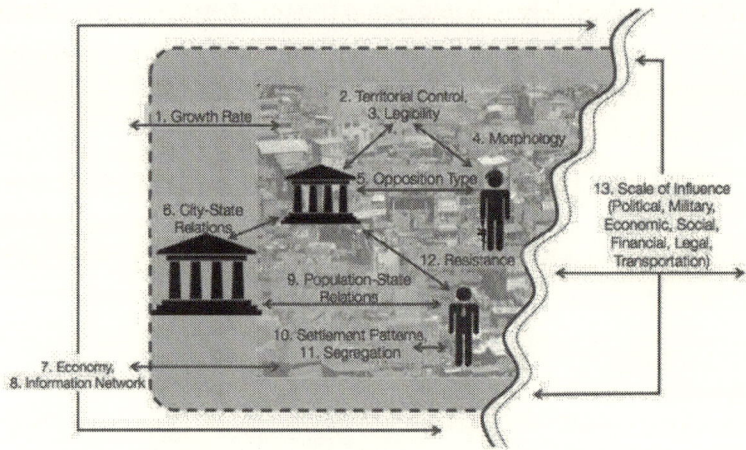

Figure 1 Significant Characteristics of the
Urban Operational Environment.

These characteristics and the research that goes into defining them helps analysts and planners understand the connections between elements of the Urban Triad[13]—the population, infrastructure, and physical environment of the city. In contrast to traditional approaches like the operational variables (PMESII[14]), the framework does not encourage a reductive method but helps tease out the important systems that exist within an urban environment. The Urban Triad also supports cataloging and storing data to encourage collection over time and coordination between units. Figure 2 illustrates this approach with some notional (though frequently relevant) elements of the environment. It is important to note that the framework does not use the Urban Triad as a mandatory matrix to populate as part of a deep dive. It is merely a method to catalog research.

Taken together, the techniques provided in Step 1 of the framework generate a picture of the current and historical state of the environment. It improves on current practice by guiding analysts to collect and analyze information that highlights the relationships between elements of the environment. This approach integrates adversary-, terrain-, and population centric perspective to create a more holistic picture.

Population					Infrastructure									Physical Environment		
Political	Military	Economic	Social	Information	Sewage	Water	Energy	Academics	Trash	Medical	Safety	Food	Other	Natural	Man-made	Time

Figure 2 Example of the Urban Triad.

Step II: Frame and Map Urban Problem Systems directs analysts and planners to develop problem statements and understand the elements and interactions of the environment that contribute to the problem. The framework's structured process for defining the urban operational environment in Step I enables comparison of the current state of the environment to the desired future state defined by commander's guidance in order to identify problems. The framework then guides the analyst to identify elements of problem systems in systems terms. The framework identifies flows and nodes as the elements of problem systems. Flows are the tangibles and intangibles, whether in constant or periodic motion, that serve as a system's inputs and outputs and enable system capability. Nodes are the shipping, storage, and receiving locations of various flows. The framework offers a structured approach, called FASCOPE,[15] to identify and document elements of the system and their key considerations.

After determining the problem system and identifying its elements, the framework directs analysts and planners to analyze the problem system as a whole by conceptually diagramming and geospatially mapping it. Depicting how these elements of the environment interact can help provide an explanation why and how systems behave and reveal the associated territorial logics. Conceptual and geospatial mapping is crucial to developing a sense of systematic behavior and territorial logics as they can be used for process and flow pathway tracing. Simply inputting information about a system into an Excel spreadsheet or a PowerPoint deck will not reveal these logics. It is important to reiterate that problem systems can include the adversary, friendly forces, the population, infrastructure networks, and elements of the physical terrain.

Step III: Develop and Analyze Urban Courses of Action provides the analysis needed to determine how best to affect the environment through the identification of Environmental Centers of Gravity (E-COGs). Based on the maps of the problem system developed in Step II, analysts and planners can begin to identify E-COGs. E-COGs are the nodes and/or flows—of which there can be one or many—that are most critical to a problem system. As a result, affecting these components can have a sizeable impact on the broader system.

E-COGs expand traditional adversary-centric center of gravity analysis to be used for examining urban problem systems in order to identify the elements on which the system critically depends. The concept also picks up on themes from newer applications of systems thinking to military analysis and planning such as the 2003 Institute for Defense Analyses ideas of nodal capture and nodal isolation, as mentioned in the Kevin M. Felix and Frederick D. Wong article, "The Case For Megacities," in *Parameters*.[16] However, the E-COG concept introduces the possibility of isolating important nodes (and flows) outside the scope of the adversary. Furthermore, the E-COG concept seeks to stress that not all E-COGs must be destroyed, degraded, neutralized, or isolated. Some E-COGs—for example a potable water infrastructure network—must be buttressed, protected, or improved.

After identifying the E-COGs of problem systems, analysts and planners can begin developing tentative COAs to degrade or buttress E-COGs and understanding how the COAs might impact the broader environment. Analysts and planners can assess COAs for their acceptability and feasibility, by returning to their conceptual diagram and thinking through how the proposed COAs might affect the elements of the problem system. This visualization and accompanying narrative can serve as a way to promote discussion amongst the staff and also as a briefing tool to the commander. Planners should also brainstorm how the COAs can affect systems that are related to the problem system. Because consequences of military action do not unfold neatly and linearly, the staff and commander must return to their definition of the urban operational environment (Step

I) and re-assess how the COAs will impact the significant characteristics of the urban operational environment. The commander and staff must identify whether the COAs' actions on the E-COGs will contribute to achieving the desired future state.

Conclusion

The community of interest concerned with future urban operations generally agrees on the types of challenges the urban environment poses. While there are slight disagreements with regard to city size as a driver for force and concept development, there is a growing effort to devote time and resources to study the problem. With this in mind, Caerus sought to ground and operationalize these concepts in the creation of the framework. By developing a process for establishing a systems perspective of the city and its problem systems, Caerus believes it addressed a gap in urban operations doctrine guiding analysis and planning.

For more information about the framework, its components, and its development process, contact Caerus Associates regarding the City as a System Analytical Framework at info@caerusassociates.com or (703) 649-5300.

Notes

[1] David Kilcullen, *Out of the Mountains: The Coming Age of the Urban Guerrilla*, 2013.

[2] "The term *decisive action* replaces the term *full spectrum operations* as the concept of continuous, simultaneous offense, defense, stability, or defense support of civil authorities. *Defense support of civil authorities* replaces *civil support* as a task under decisive action." Army Doctrine Reference Publication 3-0 "Unified Land Operations," 2012, v.

[3] US Army Training and Doctrine Command Pamphlet 525-3-1 "The U.S. Army Operating Concept," 2014, 12.

[4]   Russell W. Glenn, "Managing Complexity During Military Urban Operations: Visualizing the Elephant," RAND, 2004, x.

[5]   "Megacities and the United States Army: Preparing for a Complex and Uncertain Future," Chief of Staff of the Army, Strategic Studies Group, 2014, 10.

[6]   Kevin M. Felix and Frederick D. Wong, "The Case for Megacities," *Parameters*, Spring 2015, Vol. 45 No. 1, 24.

[7]   William G. Adamson, "Megacities and the US Army," *Parameters*, Spring 2015, Vol. 45 No. 1, 51-52.

[8]   For more on this, see James C. Scott, *Seeing Like a State: How Certain Schemes to Improve the Human Condition Have Failed*, Yale University Press, 1998.

[9]   "World Urbanization Prospects: The 2014 Revision," United Nations, 2014, 2.

[10]   "World Urbanization Prospects: The 2014 Revision," United Nations, 2014, 13.

[11]   See Diane E. Davis, "Insecure and Secure Cities: Towards a Reclassification of World Cities in a Global Era," *MIT International Review*, Spring 2008, p 30-41.; Christopher Paul et. al "Identifying Urban Flashpoints: A Delphi-Derived Model for Scoring Cities' Vulnerability to Large-Scale Unrest," *Studies in Conflict & Terrorism*, 31:981-1000, 2008.; and Brett G. Sylvia, "Megacities: Geopolitical Dominator or Distractor?" *USAWC Strategy Paper*, 2014.

[12]   Michael Evans, "The Case Against Megacities," *Parameters*, Spring 2015, Vol. 45 No. 1, 36.

[13]   Joint Publication 3-06 "Joint Urban Operations," 2013, I-2.

[14]   Political, Military, Economic, Social, Information, Infrastructure. Joint Publication 2-01.3 "Joint Intelligence Preparation of the Operational Environment," 2009, I-1.

[15]   Flows, Areas, Structures, Capabilities, Organizations, People, and Events.

[16]   Kevin M. Felix and Frederick D. Wong, "The Case For Megacities," *Parameters*, Spring 2015, Vol. 45 No. 1, 29.

Chapter 22

The Role of CCTV in Terrorist TTPs: Camera System Avoidance and Targeting

Christopher Flaherty

First Published 9 November 2015

The object of this article is to develop a conceptual framework, to critically evaluate the role of closed circuit television (CCTV) in terrorist TTPs (Tactics, Techniques, and Procedures), focusing on camera system avoidance and targeting. This will be examined in terms of the interplay of tactics and technology, between surveillance (provided by CCTV) and its avoidance, or destruction, as these serve as a precondition to successfully committing an act of terrorism, from an operational and tactical perspective.

The pervasive presence of CCTV in cities underpins much of contemporary security, policing and defence, against anti-social behaviour, crime and terrorism. The dominate debate as to its effectiveness is not the object of this article; instead the question addressed here—is does the presence of CCTV factor in terrorism TTPs? The argument made here is that CCTV coverage is regularly used in post-incident analysis of acts of terrorism. This has been a factor previously in terrorism planning, either avoiding it for greater operational security, or using it to document jihad resolve.

The question remains, do trends in crime and activism to actively destroy CCTV suggest any alternative terrorist TTPs? This article will examine this shift in terrorist TTPs specifically addressing the perception (admittedly an assumption), that a terrorist actor in the future will see CCTV systems as a potential operational and tactical threat; and that predicatively given current trends to destroy CCTV assets in cities, as a means to aid criminal or activist activity. Therefore, one future indicator of a pending major terrorism attack is likely to be the 'downing' of local CCTV.

TTPs Overview

The role of TTPs in terrorism analysis is that this concept is used to identify individual patterns of behaviour of a particular terrorist activity, or a particular terrorist organisation (Sullivan, Bauer, 2008). The concept of TTPs helps examine and categorize more general tactics, and weapons used by a particular terrorist activity, or a particular terrorist organisation. The current approach to terrorism analysis involves an examination of the behaviour of an individual terrorist, or that of a terrorist organisations, in particular their use of specific weapons, used in specific ways; and which may include different tactics and strategies being exhibited. Normally, the 'technology' aspects of tactics, techniques and procedures are treated as indiscreet elements within TTPs. However, a specific focus on CCTV as an 'opponent', so to speak, raises an interesting focus on the specifics of a technology that encourages a counter-tactic/operation to be created. In this case the specific need to destroy, or render useless the capacity of police, security or defence to surveil an area, collect information, and digital images of people's activities. As stated, the dominate debate to do with CCTV is its effectiveness in crime prevention; however, viewed alternatively, that a terrorist actor likely sees CCTV systems as a potential operational and tactical threat, an analogy can be made with known criminal and activist perceptions (which will be explored further in this article), who do target CCTV specifically. It is argued that a likely outcome based on the need to achieve operational security, is the 'downing of CCTV' as a precondition for a successful attack. This latter point will be examined next, in two sections: actual instances of attacks on CCTV equipment; and, a recent example of CCTV avoidance strategy in a case of terrorism.

Attacks on CCTV Equipment

Actual instances of attacks on CCTV equipment are regularly reported, and these cover a spectrum from drunken attacks on a single unit, such as the 2015 Australian case of a terrorist sympathiser (who had posted a series of tweets that supported the Sydney siege gunman Man Haron Monis), who was fined for a CCTV attack (Flower, 2015). In that case, the defendant, "who defended himself, had no explanation for his violent outburst... allegedly told police he was drunk when he attacked the camera in broad daylight." (Flower, 2015) Another instance, involving actual criminal intent, was a recent UK case, where two criminals smashed a camera during an armed-raid (Wheatstone, 2015). The 'Camover 2013' campaign, is an instance of actual systematic attacks on CCTV. This particular campaign was started by German dissidents who turned their attacks into a game, and their deliberate vandalism of CCTV equipment was to protest the rise of surveillance technology in the country (Blagdon, 2013). This was reported as "a competition unfolding across the country, in which teams attempt to destroy as many CCTV cameras as possible." (Blagdon, 2013) According to a *Guardian* report the activist's objective, was to: "see all surveillance cameras removed from public spaces,... taking matters into their own hands, by taking down as many cameras as possible ahead of February's European Police Congress" (Stallwood, 2013). In the Camover 2013 campaign:

> "bonus scores are given to the teams that display the most creativity in destruction. In... video invitation... you can see ski-masked 'players' (self-described shoplifters,

graffiti sprayers, homeless, and squatters) tearing the
cameras down with ropes, smashing them out with
hammers, and blacking them out with billowing clouds
of spray paint. Teams are encouraged to upload their
conquests to the Camover website." (Blagdon, 2013)

According to one activist online magazine, the Camover 2013
campaign: "game ended in February 2013, at least 60 cameras had
been smashed in Germany, Finland, Greece and the USA." (Disabling
Surveillance, 2014) In the U.S., a Camover group in Washington State
released a statement... saying that they destroyed 17 surveillance cameras
(Kane, 2013).

A 2014 online magazine article on the Camover 2013 campaign (still
available online at the time of writing this article—as the Camover 2013
website was itself removed from several servers, during policing action
against the group in 2013-2014) shows several diagrams illustrating how
activists can destroy cameras in various locations, and ways (effectively
providing an online TTPs manual on CCTV destruction). The methods
listed: "1. Beat It; 2. Snare It; 3. Tape it Over; 4. Bag It, Blind It; 5.
Cut the Power; 6. Spray the Lens; 7. Laser Dazzling; and, 8. Block
Drop" (Disabling Surveillance, 2014). As well, this magazine edition
encourages its readers: "Take a quasi-revolutionary name like Berlin's
Black Rabbit of Death Commando, or the Sternburg Export Fraktion
(named after a German beer), then mask up, wreck cameras, video the
vandalism and post the footage online." (Disabling Surveillance, 2014)
It is interesting to note, that in relation to item '4. Bag It, Blind It'. The
actual origin of this method was an observation made by activists, how:
"Camover recommends gluing a plastic bag over a camera. In 2010,
police in Birmingham, UK, were forced to do the same (without the
glue) to 218 of their own cameras, after local activists revealed police
cameras were disproportionately concentrated in relatively low-crime,
predominantly Muslim areas." (Disabling Surveillance, 2014) This last
example, illustrates that TTPs are an evolving mythology, where in this
case the actions of Birmingham police are observed, copied and then
extended.

The examples illustrated in this article, from 2013 and 2015, demonstrate that actual attacks on CCTV equipment commonly occurs. The reasons range from acts of lone rage, part of a criminal plan to deny policing CCTV evidence of a crime, to systematic campaigns by activists. In the next part of this article the focus will be to look at CCTV avoidance altogether as a strategy.

CCTV Avoidance Strategy

In recent news reporting on the case involving a Sydney teenager Raban Alou, charged with several offences under Australian anti-terrorism law in 2015, in relation to procuring a weapon said to have been used in the shooting murder of police accountant Curtis Cheng at the Parramatta police headquarters, earlier in 2015. Part of the reporting referred to police alleged incident, where the accused "handed a revolver to Parramatta gunman Farhad Jabar in the female section of the Parramatta Mosque where there was no CCTV coverage" (Rubinsztein-Dunlop, 2015).

This set of circumstances emphasises how the presence of CCTV can be a factor in terrorist TTPs. In particular, the choice of a specific location for the arming of an assailant, where there is no CCTV. While, it may seem an obvious choice, to find a location where an illicit transaction can take place, looked at from a tactical and operational perspective, two fundamental operational objectives are in fact achieved:

The initial avoidance of detection and intervention by security, which has the potential to disrupt the terrorist operation from going ahead, to start with.

The latent-advantage that without CCTV coverage a key element in policing is denied, with the lack of real-time physical evidence being available post-the-terrorism event, during investigations, leading to prosecutions—which again, which has the potential to disrupt future terrorist operation from going ahead.

In the UK context, for example, these two elements disrupt the 1999 strategy, usually called the 'four 'P's of security/policing counterterrorism strategies: Prevent, Pursue, Protect, and Prepare' (UK Home Office, 2011). In the first case, the adoption of an avoidance strategy using CCTV blind-spots denies the 'Prevent' portion of the basic security strategy. The lack of evidence also denies the 'Pursue' portion of the basic security strategy. This later point, namely, the longstanding function of CCTV has been to permit post-incident analysis in the investigation of crime and facilitate the prosecution and detection of crime. In the case of terrorism, this is a significant operational problem. Namely, it is a significant factor that major, even minor attacks have all led to the subsequent rolling-up of the terrorist group involved, and its network of supporters, leading to a significant degrading in any future capacity to wage further attacks.

CCTV Evidence Used in Previous Post-Terrorism Investigations

According to research on al Qaeda: "Allegedly, a number of minor operatives have been arrested after being spotted on CCTV uploading al Qaeda communications at Internet cafes." (Atwan, 2006) The instance of CCTV evidence being used in previous post-terrorism investigations, for the purposes of this article, are best demonstrated by the 2005 attacks in London on the Underground. Famously, in that case CCTV was available showing the bombers entering the London Underground, and having identified the individuals involved, their prior movements were back-tracked, allowing police to find not only their car parked in Luton, but their flat in Leeds, where the bombs had been made. Two weeks later, the same set of circumstances was replayed, when police used CCTV footage to start a manhunt for Yassin Omar and his co-conspirators (in the failed second attempted terrorist attack on the London Underground).

From an operational perspective, one of the core concepts is 'operational security', where the object is to deny an opponent any capacity to view or know of an impending attack. Instances, when this general adage of warfighting is subverted, can be where the attacker wants an opponent to know what he or she is doing. In the case of the London Underground attacks in 2005, it was clearly the case that the terrorists involved wanted everyone to see their actions—in this case they appear to consciously want themselves to be captured on CCTV. In fact, the historical footage seems to show them 'playing to the camera' especially in the case of the now famous footage of Mohammad Sidique Khan, and this group, in the lead-up to the attack, where they appeared unconcerned that their actions were being filmed. The rational for this, is that the attackers wanted their actions filmed in order to prove their jihad; as much as it was irrelevant that they were being filmed in the first place, as their actions were innocuous—enough not to draw any attention to them (this can be compared to the case of Sydney teenager Raban Alou discussed above, where he needed a CCTV blind-spot to exchange a gun).

The argument that can be made, is that the 'desire to be filmed' is purely an expression of the operational concept viz to be 'proved to be the jihadist who make the attack'. This can be argued to be a vital part of the whole attack methodology: which was to demonstrate 'jihadist resolve'. If however, there was a fundamental shift in the operational paradigm, namely an embedded strategy—such as the PIRA (Provisional Irish Republican Army) campaigns in the 1970s and 80s where the perpetrators deliberately sought anonymity in order to preserve the terrorist structure. This was cleanly the case, when the 1977 PIRA's 'restructuring strategy' memo, known as the Staff Report was found, and this instructed:

> "This old system with which the Brits and the [Special] Branch are familiar has to be changed. We recommend reorganization and remotivation...We emphasize a return to secrecy and strict discipline. Army men must be in total command of all sections of the movement... Anti-interrogation lectures must be given in conjunction with indoctrination lectures...Cells of four volunteers with be controlled militarily by the Brigade's/Command Operations Officer...Cells should operate as often as

possible outside of their own areas: both the confuse
Brit intelligence (which would increase our security)
and to expand out operational areas." (Coogan, 1996)

The interplay with CCTV, between PIRA tactics evolved much later, with the development of the City of London's ring of steel in the 1990s. In this particular example, CCTV cameras were deployed in deliberated narrowed street lanes, forcing traffic to slow to allow drivers, vehicles and number plates to be more easily recorded. It has been argued, that the presence of this system, compelled the republicans to shift focus onto targets outside central London, such as the 1996 Docklands attack.

The 1996 Docklands attack illustrates that CCTV has been factored into terrorist operational concepts, to the extent that its presence arguably led the PIRA to avoid central London and attack a target where there was less-likelihood of interdiction by security authorities. It is also the case of later London attacks that terrorist groups like al Qaeda, the attack mythology changed to be less depended on vehicle-borne attacks (which central London security is designed to interdict), to smaller people-borne attacks, which in the 2005 cases of the Underground attacks, were somewhat depended on CCTV being present to document their jihad. This suggests two competing sets of terrorist TTPs, as to potential the use of CCTV:

- Rely on its presence as form of historical recording. In which case, the CCTV system has become a defacto-tool of terrorists to promote their actions after the attack.
- Avoid CCTV as part of the operational security methodology.

The adoption of an avoidance strategy in regards to CCTV may also signal a much broader operational shift by terrorist groups towards conservation of assets, than have been seen in the past. Where the rolling-up-arrests of people involved in terrorism following an attack has been the norm, to a posture based on maintaining secrecy and anonymity where the same group (operating more like a conventional insurgency) can continue with their attacks on an ongoing basis.

Extrapolated into a future-paradigm, it can be argued that in order to allow future attacks to take place then a completely different strategy must come into play, namely the downing of local CCTV as a prelude to attack. This operational concept will be discussed next. This analysis will then be recast as an example of an interposing tactics problem.

Downing of Local CCTV as a Prelude to Attack

The argument, is that CCTV coverage is regularly used in post-incident analysis of terrorism acts, and this factor leads to the suggestion, that predicatively given current criminal and activist trends to destroy CCTV assets in cities as a means to aid their activities, one likely indicator of a major terrorism attack is likely to be 'downing' of local CCTV. This may even extend to the systematic targeting of the CCTV system, its power as well as data storage centres. The argument is that 'destruction of the CCTV system' across a city will by necessity form an important part of the overall operational concept in a future act of terrorism. The question arises how will this be accomplished, without tipping local security or policing that a major act of terrorism is about to be launched?

One potential set of events, could be the employment (as a mode of operation) utilising radicalised street-people, or people acting as street people, operating as the irregular force to disrupt and degrade on a substantial scale the very means that conventional security for city centres is dependent (much the same as Camover 2013). This sort of attack can be viewed as an example of "skid row terrorist TTPs" (Flaherty, 2013), where the attackers—such as in Camover 2013—are camouflaged into the urban landscape as homeless and vagrants. For instance, people talking on these roles, may in fact only be a few, who rapidly move along the street and building landscape, at all hours ripping down cameras and cutting cabling; even deploying small easy to construct IEDs (Improvised Explosive Devices), such as gunpowder pipe-bombs to attack offices where CCTV watching and recording takes place, and well as destroy digital assets; "the use of the homeless beggar on the streets sitting on the ground covered by dirty blankets and bedding outside transport hubs and alongside roads presents the perfect mechanism for smuggling in and deploying IEDs" (Flaherty, 2014). This inconspicuous element could also just as easily occupy pedestrian, shopping, and entertainment thoroughfares. Such a mechanism (the beggar) can move silently into the city infrastructure of underground tunnel systems, simply vandalising cabling, etc.

The significance of attacks such as these is that damage to the civil infrastructure equally affects security. For instance, in the U.S., domestic access to civil power grids by U.S. military bases can be severely affected by simple blackouts:

> "In the first six months of 2011, the U.S. civilian power grid suffered 155 blackouts affecting an average of 83,000 people with 36 blackouts affecting over 100,000 people. Despite these staggering numbers, U.S. military bases rely solely on the civilian grid to power 99% of their war fighting capabilities, homeland security missions, and rescue and relief operations." (Sater, 2011)

While the above example is given in relation to the effect of power blackouts on the operation of U.S. domestic bases, much the same impact is largely seen in civil security systems as well.

Interposing Tactics

The role of CCTV in terrorist TTPs, cast in terms of interposing tactics argument (Flaherty, 2009) has relevance to constructing how future major terrorist operations may develop. Typically, in an interposing tactics problem, both the enemy and friendly elements move through the same space and time, each operating on the same road network, etc., and usually in the same direction. This situation illustrates two opposing force elements that are both using interposing tactics and shows that thinking about the 'theater of operation', traditionally set within the Jomini-defined square field (Jomini, Baron de. 1862), had become defunct in the sense that forces are not coming from a base of operations and moving to supply a force (which the insurgents attack), rather, there is space over which both enemy and friendly continue to move through and around each other. This model combined with the basic premise: the sharing of the logistic base, by friend and foe alike; leads to a situation of the embedding of the terrorism element organising the attack into to the local power, and information infrastructure—the same system(s) that the defending security are themselves dependent. In short, both friend and foe alike actually share the same logistics infrastructure, a direct consequence of the regional and global connectivity of information and power systems.

Conceptually, this merging of the friend-and-foe's logistic base, into one-and-the-same, has fundamental implications for the use of CCTV systems. For instance, if we see the modern urban battlespace as a completely saturated 5D-operational space where competing force elements exist in a state of operations, and tactically speaking more akin to a fluid suspension medium; then within this fluid suspension medium of operations competing force elements constantly interpose or interject each other. The basic idea(s), underpinning interposing tactics:

- Drawing a parallel with the game of chess, an interposing move would be one in which a player moves a piece between his or her king and the opponent's piece which has placed the king in check.
- A tactical situation describing the action or activity that interrupts a particular process.
- In basic terms, interposing tactics is the deployment of forces to block and cover friendly from hostile.

An extension of this idea involves opposing forces dispelling or scattering much more freely within an operational area to achieve the effect of blocking and covering all friendlies from hostiles. These moves and counter-moves in the urban landscape directly bring onto play the relationship with CCTV, this network of surveillance assets need to be controlled or denied in order for one force to achieve dominance over the other.

The interposing tactics model was developed to illustrate a phase in security operations where the combatants are reduced to individuals, and individual pieces of technology, and are completely mixed together operating within the same space and time, particularly in an urban environment, where there is also present a population, who are divided in support for the combatants, or neutral and are equally intermixed. Combined with factors such as the merging of the logistics base for friend and foe, and in the case of CCTV the 'battle' would be to both to destroy and/or utilise. For instance, the destruction of individual CCTV units to deny security, policing and defence 'eyes on the ground', and/or the co-opting/reconfiguring of these systems. Any of these methods would give a terrorist element embedded in the urban landscape far greater situational awareness.

Illicit Use of CCTV

The question of illicit use is a significant likely extension of terrorist usage of CCTV. Based on copying the actions of criminals as well as the cartels, either hacking into existing CCTV, which is technically possible (Zetter, 2012), or setting up illicit CCTV cameras in order to give greater intelligence coverage of potential targets. This is part of a strategy to remotely surveil potential targets, rather than take more risky surveillance operations in-person, which have become a well-known part of terrorist planning, and which are watched-for by local security. In regards to this later point, a scenario involving terrorists or activists potentially co-opting/reconfiguring of CCTV systems, there is a parallel case of the cartel use of CCTV for its own intelligence benefit. In 2015, there was a report of the 'Tamaulipas state authorities in northeastern Mexico, who recently dismantled an internet-operated video surveillance network used by a criminal group to monitor both government security forces and civilian life' (Anderson, 2015). This reported illicit CCTV network comprised 39 cameras, with each camera capable of being controlled wirelessly via modem, video card and data encoder, and power feeder. These cameras were scattered across Reynosa, a border town and coveted entry point into the U.S. for crime syndicates trafficking in narcotics and humans. Using an example of the 'merging of the logistics base for friend and foe' (discussed in this article), the "bulk of the cameras had been installed on telephone poles serviced by the Federal Electricity Commission, a public utility, and Telmex, the largest privately-held telco in Mexico.... the camera network drew power from electric lines strung above Reynosa's streets, and connected to the internet via phone cables tethered to those same poles" (Anderson, 2015).

Concluding Remarks

The problem illustrated by interposing tactics is how does one or the other combatants effectively control or direct forces when they are fragmented throughout each other, in order to achieve a tactical/operational outcome? The original literature on interposing tactics argues that this scenario illustrates how each combatant's organisational character has progressed to the point of a complete devolution, only operating in single entities, and in new forms of autonomous actions. Cohesion is achieved through each element possessing superior situational awareness, and thereby knowing when, and where to interdict an opponent, or reach a friendly and assist in the task. Viewed from this perspective, the control of CCTV system(s) locally and city-wide has fundamental implications.

Instances of vandalism of the CCTV system(s) as a criminal enterprise are a common occurrence in cities, and the extension of this into a formal campaign, as a prelude to a major terrorist attack, represents a natural extension of these actions into the realm of terrorist TTPs. The new modes of operation, is likely to be radicalised street-people, or terrorists acting in this role as the irregular force seeking to disrupt and degrade on a substantial scale the very means that conventional security for city centres is dependent. Systematic targeting of the CCTV system, its power as well as data storage centres will by necessity form an important part of the overall operational concept in a future act of terrorism. In closing, given that TTPs are universally applicable, the techniques for destroying CCTV have been established, documented and promulgated in how-to-do-it manuals, as well as tried and tested during the Camover 2013 campaign, it is anticipated that any operational concept in a future act of terrorism, will used the exact same approach. As a final note, it is also a likely extension of terrorist usage of CCTV, to copy the actions of criminals as well as the cartels, and either hack into existing CCTV, or set up illicit CCTV cameras in order to give greater intelligence coverage of potential targets, remotely surveilling these rather than the more risky in-person surveillance operations that have become a well-known part of terrorist planning, and which are watched-for by local security.

References

Anderson, B. 2015 Big Brother Narco: Cartels Are Building Their Own CCTV Networks. *Motherboard (Vice)*, 27 May 2015. Viewed 23 October 2015, http://motherboard.vice.com/read/cartel-cctv.

Atwan, A.B. 2006 *The Secret History of al Qaida*, Saqi Books: London.

Blagdon, J. 2013 Anti-Surveillance Activists Turn Smashing CCTV Cameras into a Competitive Game. *The Verge.com* (January 27, 2013), viewed 23 October 2015, http://www.theverge.com/2013/1/27/3922840/anti-surveillance-activists-turn-smashing-cctv-cameras-into-sport.

Coogan, T.P. 1996 *The Troubles: Ireland's Ordeal 1966-1996 and the Search for Peace*, Roberts Rinehart Publishers, USA.

Disabling Surveillance, Germany. 2014 Smashing Surveillance Cameras is Now a Game Called Camover, *COLORS#88* (March 17, 2014), viewed 23 October 2015, http://www.colorsmagazine.

com/stories/magazine/88/story/smashing-surveillance-cameras-is-now-a-game-called-camover.

Flaherty, C. 2009 Interposing Tactics, *Red Team Journal,* viewed 23 October 2015, http://redteamjournal.com/2009/12/interposing-tactics/.

— 2013 Skid Row Terrorist, *OODA LOOP,* viewed 23 October 2015, www.oodaloop.com/security/2013/07/26/skid-row-terrorist/.

— 2014 3D Vulnerability Analysis Solution to the Problem of Military Energy Security and Interposing Tactics. *Journal of Information Warfare.* (13)1: 33-41.

Flower, W. 2015 Terrorist Sympathiser Khodr Moustafa Taha Fined Over CCTV Damage *News Limited* (September 4, 2015). Viewed 23 October 2015, http://m.heraldsun.com.au/news/law-order/terrorist-sympathiser-khodr-moustafa-taha-fined-over-cctv-damage/story-fni0fee2-1227513349587.

Jomini, Baron de. 1862 *The Art of War.* New York: G.P. Putnam (trans. Capt. G.H. Mendell and Lieut). W.P. Craighill, USA.

Kane, A. 2013 Smashing State Surveillance: Group Breaks CCTV Cameras on the Street, *AlterNet* (August 19, 2013), viewed 23 October 2015, http://www.alternet.org/german-group-smashes-surveillance-cameras.

Rubinsztein-Dunlop, S. 2015 Unemployed Sydney teenager handed revolver to gunman in Parramatta Mosque, police allege, *ABC News,* 15 October 2015, viewed 23 October 2015, http://www.msn.com/en-au/news/australia/unemployed-sydney-teenager-handed-revolver-to-gunman-in-parramatta-mosque-police-allege/ar-AAftbaq?li=AA4RE4&ocid=mailsignout.

Sater, D. 2011 *Military Energy Security: Current Efforts and Future Solutions,* report, Global Green, Washington, D.C., USA.

Stallwood, O. 2013 Activists Destroy CCTV Cameras in Germany, *The Guardian* (26 January 2013), viewed 23 October 2015, http://www.theguardian.com/theguardian/shortcuts/2013/jan/25/game-destroy-cctv-cameras-berlin#start-of-comments.

Sullivan, J.P. Bauer, A. 2008 *Terrorism Early Warning: 10 Years of Achievement in Fighting Terrorism and Crime.* Los Angeles Sheriff's Department (December, 2008). Viewed 23 October 2015, http://file.lacounty.gov/lasd/cms1_144939.pdf.

UK Home Office (UK Government). 2011 *The Prevent Strategy.* Viewed 23 October 2015, http://www.homeoffice.gov.uk/ counter-terrorism/review-of-prevent-strategy/.

Wheatstone, R. 2015 Dramatic CCTV Footage Shows Armed Robbers Pulling up in Porsche for Terrifying Gun Raid, *Mirror* (31 July 2015). Viewed 23 October 2015, http://www.mirror.co.uk/ news/uk-news/dramatic-cctv-footage-shows-armed-6170033.

Zetter, K. 2012 Popular Surveillance Cameras Open to Hackers, Researcher Says. *Wired* (15 May 2012). Viewed 23 October 2015, http://www.wired.com/2012/05/cctv-hack/.

Chapter 23

Operational Environment Implications of the Megacity to the US Army

Darryl Ward

First Published 9 February 2016

Megacity Defined

The United Nations (UN) and the United States National Intelligence Council (NIC) define the megacity as a metropolitan area whose population exceeds 10 million people. While other definitions exist, this is the definition used as the basis for understanding future impacts of megacities to US Army operations. Depending on the statistical reference, there are between 23 and 30 megacities in the world. Statistical numbers vary primarily due to different interpretations of metropolitan limits and surrounding areas. However, regardless of how megacities are quantified, trends within the global operational environment (herein referred as the "OE") indicate that the number of urban areas will continue to rise.[1]

Global Drivers and Trends

In order to predict future impacts of megacities to the US Army, the global drivers and trends leading to megacity development must be identified. Drivers (as defined for this paper) are forces that always exist, such as demographics (people), natural resources (water, oil, land), and globalization (interconnectivity). Drivers constantly impact the OE.

Drivers are impacted by trends, which have life cycles with associated impacts on drivers. Trends are constantly analyzed in terms of their impacts to drivers. This article is not all inclusive but highlights some trend-driven impacts on drivers and resulting potential for involvement of the US Army across the range of military operations.

Demographics

Progressive ideologies; war; youth population bulges; unemployment; climate change; and scarcity of food, water, and medicine are among the reasons that human migration to urban areas is a trend expected to continue for several decades. The UN estimates that approximately 180,000 people move into urban areas every day and the Defense Intelligence Agency (DIA) estimates that 60 percent of the world's population will live in cities by 2030.[2] This constant influx of population is certain to stress megacity infrastructures, resulting in the potential for certain population groups to perceive disenfranchisement and leading to US Army military urban engagement in cooperation with host nation forces.

Demographic trends can greatly affect political decisions in countries striving to continue economic growth, maintain a military, generate tax revenue, and maintain alliances. Among demographic trends, the NIC estimates that by 2030 the world will have contracted from 80 to 50 countries whose populations will have a medium age of 25 years or less. Most countries maintaining a youth bulge are located in Sub-Saharan Africa, the Middle East, and in South and Central Asia.[3] Those countries without a youth bulge in 2039 are located in Eastern

Asia, North America, and Europe. In fact, the DIA estimates that by 2050 the most prevalent age group in Europe will be in the 55-69 year old category.[4]

Natural Resources

Megacities are susceptible to natural and manmade disasters due to their physical proximity to large bodies of water. All of the top ten megacities fall into this category and eight of the ten are on a coast. Furthermore, the UN estimates that over 50 percent of the world's population lives within 120 miles of a coast.[5] Indeed, water near population centers has always been necessary for commerce, food, sanitation, etc. However, extreme water events caused by floods, hurricanes, typhoons, and tsunamis exacerbate life threatening situations in areas of increased urbanization. The US Army is likely to experience an increase in crisis response operations requiring foreign humanitarian assistance in large-scale urban environments.

Another complication megacities present is vertical growth. This is especially true in cities along coastlines, where expansion is naturally inhibited. Design and development of high-rise cities could lead to greatly compromised military operations in urban settings where the effectiveness of precision guided munitions; elevation of weapon systems; and intelligence, surveillance, and reconnaissance (ISR) collection platforms are limited.

Globalization

Globalization as a driver creates OE interconnectivity. As societies become more connected, events unfolding in one area of the world are communicated and affect other areas. Some examples of potential manifestations of globalization and demographic interaction include: an increasing influx of Middle Eastern and African youth into Europe. Many of these migrants arrive without a formal education and are unemployed. Countries such as China wanting to attract migrants from low income countries to supplement its declining youthful workforce in order to sustain its economy.

The NIC forecasts that the need to support economic growth combined with the lack of opportunities in areas of the world that maintain a youth bulge will create even faster demographic shifts than those that occurred in the last quarter of the 20th century.[6] A huge migrant influx into megacities and urban areas in general has the potential for increased xenophobic feelings and conversely, perceived inequities may lead to violence and acts of terrorism as the world has already witnessed in megacities such as London and Paris. A question to consider is, at what point do states begin to enculturate the character/culture of rapidly increasing ethnic minorities?

A PMESII-PT Megacity Analysis

The following is an analysis of some of the trends affecting drivers from the perspective of the US Army doctrinal taxonomy of PMESII-PT. It is intended to articulate how these trends might affect or involve the US Army but is not a detailed PMESII-PT megacity analysis.

Political: Futurist Thomas Frey notes that democracy could be viewed as an inferior form of government by 2030.[7] In fact, a number of megacities or large urban areas are located in democracies with a high risk of failure due to religious extremism or other trends. Even in states where democracy is not threatened, it is important to consider that disenfranchised populations often harbor feelings of deprived rights and may tend to incite violence as a means to force political change. For instance, megacity gangs taking this approach could stress already taxed law enforcement to the point where the US military would be requested to provide foreign security assistance.

Military: An ever-narrowing gap between military capabilities, organization, and influence (due in part to globalization) is increasingly blurring distinctions between regular and conventional forces, irregular forces, and insurgents. When criminal elements are considered, a "hybrid threat" as defined in Army Doctrinal Reference Publication 1-02 emerges. While the term "hybrid threat" is relatively new, the concept behind it is not. There are many examples in military history of groups with military capabilities that unite either formally or informally to achieve a mutually desired outcome.

Hybrid threats (threats) seek ways to counter perceived strengths of their adversary. US Army military strengths such as situational awareness through mission command systems and ISR platforms, precision guided munitions (PGM), and protection/lethality provided by armored fighting vehicles (AFVs) afford the advantage to see, know, and act decisively. Threats study these advantages and deduct their own lessons learned. For instance, drawing US forces into urban areas compromises our technological advantages. Megacity congestion limits movement and predictable movement corridors will make the US Army susceptible to improvised explosive devices (IED), explosive formed projectiles, and an array of dual-warhead antitank (AT) missiles and rocket propelled grenades (RPGs). A recent RAND Corporation study "Comparing US Army Systems with Foreign Counterparts" noted the increasing weight in AFVs to protect against IEDs and other urban combat threats. Added weight, due to reactive armor, urban survival kits, and other protective enhancements affects vehicle dimensions and power train transfer. In an urban setting, conditions such as bridge classifications or road widths may prohibit where AFVs can travel as well as reduce AFV performance (vehicle power requirements vs. weight). The US Army must balance protection requirements while maintaining mobility.

Weight issues also apply to urban conflicts involving light infantry. The RAND report also noted the increasing loads that infantrymen are required to carry. One hundred pounds or more was cited as common practice.[8]

Threats are subject to some of the same challenges. However, the OE will affect the threat much differently than it does the US Army. It is highly possible that initial US Army entry into a megacity and/or urban area will be expeditionary in nature and opposed by the threat. Operations will be primarily offensive and lines of communication (LOCs) will be under development. In addition, LOCs will be under the same scrutiny of predictability by the threat and hence subject to interdiction. Therefore, US Soldiers will be required to carry additional supplies (ammo, batteries, night vision, water, etc.) that at least initially threats will not face the same burden. When superior US military forces enter, threats will adapt to defensive operations while maintaining limited offensive actions such as raids and ambushes. Therefore, while threats still have logistical requirements, they have advantages in that they can cache supplies, do not need to carry loads similar to US infantrymen, and enjoy (at least initially) more mature LOCs.

Economics: The lure to megacities and urban areas because of employment opportunities is a trend that is likely to continue through 2030, especially for economies that are developing or want to sustain growth. The NIC cites not only current economic leaders (e.g., China, Europe, or Japan) but also developing economies such as Columbia, Indonesia, Nigeria, and others are becoming increasingly important to the global economy. As previously mentioned, a number of established economies are challenged because an aging workforce may look to migrants from low income countries to replace labor needs. This could lead to megaslums if local economies and infrastructures cannot react in concert with the rapid influx of migrants. Slums tend to exacerbate disenfranchisement and lead to conflict. Strategist and counterinsurgency expert David Kilcullen writes in *Out of The Mountains: The Coming Age of the Urban Guerrilla* that it is time to take what we have learned from the war in Afghanistan and think how it applies to future conflicts consisting of "…urban, networked, guerrilla warfare occurring in megaslums and megacities."[9]

Social: The UN estimates that 180,000 people migrate to urban areas daily. The cities and megacities of Brazil, China, Democratic Republic of Congo, India, Indonesia, Mexico, Nigeria, Pakistan, Philippines, and the US are forecasted to make up approximately 60 percent of the global urban growth through 2030.[10] Diaspora from youth bulging countries bring their cultures, ideologies, and most important, expectations. However, increasing migration to urban areas could at least, initially result in the expansion of slums and the materialization of acute poverty. A rapid increase in minorities could erode social fabric and lead to violent friction and the potential for overwhelming state security force capabilities. This could lead to generating domestic and international requests for the US Army to provide military engagement, security cooperation, and deterrence.

Infrastructure: In addition to employment opportunities, another major contributor to urban growth is the need for food, fresh water, housing, and energy. Megacities and large urban areas in general have infrastructures to provide these life supporting necessities. However, the NIC estimates that the demand for food, water, and energy will increase by 35, 40 and 50 percent respectively over the next 40 years and that housing demand will equal the entire volume of construction worldwide to date.[11] These figures are staggering and will surely stress infrastructure capacities. The effort to meet demands could result in poor construction quality, gridlocked transportation networks, and utility service failures. In addition, the fact that most megacities are located along coasts restricts horizontal development. Vertical development is more vulnerable to natural (earthquakes, tsunamis, typhoons, etc.) and man-made disasters. US Army assistance for civil support and civil-military operations may be in greater demand than ever before.

Information: Urban areas tend to have the most mature radio, television, and cellular networks. Information can be passed by the adversary using a variety of means with almost instantaneous results. High rise buildings afford nearly unobstructed signals for jamming of US PGM and unmanned ISR platforms therefore reducing US military technological advantages.

Physical terrain: Urban settings are dominated by buildings and roads that develop predictable man-made mobility corridors. Buildings can both impede and improve observation. High rise buildings provide both commanding observation and concealment for individually operated anti-tank launchers. They also create elevation issues for AFV weapon systems targeting such threats while serving as obstacles to acquiring aerial ISR platforms. Urban settings also have mature sub-surface structures such as sewer, drainage, and subway transit systems. Underground mobility is an important aspect of urban warfare. The use of existing subterranean features and tunneling can create elaborate defensive networks. Hence, megacity physical terrains present three-dimensional threat challenges to the US Army in that threats may occur simultaneously above, at, and below surface levels.

Time: It is assumed that potential US adversaries have developed operational plans that involve adaptive operations within urban settings. The use of urban terrain by militarily inferior opponents against superior opponents has been exercised throughout military history. Chechen tactics against the Russian military[12] and Hezbollah's defense[13] against the Israeli Defense Force are recent examples of how urban terrain is used to engage and prolong conflict while using information operations to generate world opinion. Potential adversaries understand that the US has transitioned to primarily an expeditionary force, which could at least initially favor the adversary. Future adversaries do not need to win; they just need to avoid losing to force a stalemate.

Replicating Future Complexities at US Army Training Centers

What emerging technologies and capabilities should the US Army consider replicating in live, constructive, and virtual (LVC) training environments in order to realistically represent OE complexities?

Physical destruction in urban areas will further degrade the infrastructure and alter perception of non-combatants once supportive of US forces. Therefore, we must place more emphasis on employment of non-lethal weapons for more affective riot control and against military targets. Various types of stun guns, mood-altering gasses, and other temporarily incapacitating capabilities are needed to train for military engagement, security cooperation, and deterrence.

In addition, constructive and virtual gaming simulations must accurately reflect munitions effects ranging from small arms to artillery on different types of buildings and also reflect physical properties of how these buildings are constructed. The current multi-integrated laser equipment system (MILES) is ill-suited for registering effects in urban terrain. We need MILES to reflect partial and catastrophic destruction inflicted on buildings by both US and threat weapon systems. We also need improved personnel and equipment MILES that factor material used for cover in the probability of hit/probability of kill codes.

We must be able to see-through urban environments. We need ultrasound and x-ray technology that permits squad level US Soldiers to penetrate walls and below the surface in order to acquire adversarial information. Dual warhead AT missiles and RPGs also pose a real threat to US Army AFVs. AFVs need the ability to automatically acquire, track, and launch countermeasures to neutralize and/or defeat these weapons.

Urban settings (physical structures, subterranean, population, etc.), reduce US stand-off weapon and ISR superiority, requiring close in combat to identify friendly vs. foe. Robotic platforms that serve a multitude of functions such as the ability to acquire, assimilate, and transmit biometric data and serve as weapon platforms are needed to offset the challenges presented by urban environments.

Conclusion

History shows it is difficult to predict with clarity what future conflict will look like. However, drivers and their trends analyzed through the lens of PMESII-PT lend some form of credence as to what future challenges megacities pose to the US Army. As such, the US Army must continue to prepare its training centers for replicating urban settings by establishing LVC training conditions that include the aforementioned emerging technologies and capabilities.

Notes

[1]   *Global Trends 2030: Alternative Worlds*, (National Intelligence Council, December 2012).

[2]   *DIA: Long Range Futures Brief,* Mr. Jesse Fairall (Defense Intelligence Agency, 29 July 2015).

[3]   *Global Trends 2030: Alternative Worlds*, (National Intelligence Council, December 2012).

[4]   *DIA: Long Range Futures Brief,* Mr. Jesse Fairall (Defense Intelligence Agency, 29 July 2015).

[5]   *UN Atlas of the Oceans, Human Settlements on the Coast*: http://www.oceansatlas.org.

[6]   *Global Trends 2030: Alternative Worlds*, (National Intelligence Council, December 2012).

[7]   *Dramatic Predictions,* Mr. Thomas Frey: http://www.wfs.org/blogs/thomas-frey/33-dramatic-predictions-for-2030.

[8]   *RAND Research Report: Comparing US Army Systems with Foreign Counterparts*, John Gordon IV, John Matsumura, Anthony Atler, Scott Boston, Matthew Boyer, Natasha Lander, Todd Nichols (RAND Corporation, 2015).

[9]   *Out of The Mountains: The Coming Age of the Urban Guerrilla,* Dr. David Kilcullen. (Oxford University Press, 2013).

[10]   *Global Trends 2030: Alternative Worlds*, (National Intelligence Council, December 2012).

[11]   Ibid.

[12]   *Fangs of the Lone Wolf: Chechen Tactics in the Russian-Chechen Wars 1994-2009*, Mr. Dodge Billingsley and Mr. Lester Grau. (Combat Films and Research, 2012).

[13]   *CALL Newsletter 11-34 Preparing for Hybrid Threats: Improving Force Preparation for Irregular Warfare,* Mr. William Fleser (Center for Army Lessons Learned, June 2011).

Chapter 24

Technical Challenges for Simulation and Training in Megacities

Jon Watkins and Chuck Campbell

First Published 12 February 2012

Introduction

Megacities, urban areas with populations over 10 million people, are of growing importance to the military, and thus are of growing importance to training. Training needs vary widely based upon maneuver or fighting in open desert, urban environments on the streets, and building interiors (room clearing). Training applications span aggregate commander and staff constructive trainers to individual combatant virtual simulation. It is critical for Modeling and Simulation (M&S) applications to represent those environments and situations which are inherently unusual or difficult to train live. An example of this is urban areas, which are difficult to recreate realistically for training. It is impractical to impossible to fully recreate megacities (like we do with MOUT sites) or to get access to real-world cities for live training. As a result, simulation becomes critical for both training and analysis use cases (i.e. analysis to assess if a particular weapons system or offensive plan might work better than another).

Figure 1: (L) Metro entrance in Canada, showing an example of the layers of features and activity at a single location; (R) Underground Mall in Taipei, showing the importance of advanced underground modeling.

As the threats to the U.S. change, megacities become increasingly relevant and important for preparing for the future. Violent extremist groups regularly innovate in their approaches to terrorism, creating new threats to U.S. troops. They operate out of a wide variety of locales around the world, to include large urban areas and megacities. In addition, a conventional war with a major power like China, North Korea, or Russia would inevitably involve urban environments. Modeling and simulation must be able to represent these megacities so that U.S. forces can more efficiently prepare to combat threats arising within the megacities of our world. Accurately representing megacities and dense urban environments provide particular challenges to the simulation and training community. This paper discusses those challenges from a Synthetic Natural Environment (SNE) standpoint.

Within modeling and simulation systems, higher level models operate on, around, and within the synthetic natural environment. The SNE is the foundation of M&S capabilities and must be designed and developed to meet new and far-reaching requirements. If the SNE representation lacks a critical data element required for a model to function, then training may be impeded. For example, if the material characteristics of walls are critical for calculating damage, building collapse, mouseholes, or weapon penetration, then the SNE must contain that data or a reasonable approximation of it. Current SNE capabilities can be applied to the challenges with representing megacities in limited ways but must advance exponentially to meet 2025+ challenges.

The two major challenge focus areas presented here are data representation and the environment model. While data collection and processing are a major concern for simulation of megacities, we do not focus on these issues here, since collection and processing is also an issue for operational situations as well, and thus is not unique to simulation and training. We do, however, reference collection and processing where we see M&S-specific issues.

Background

The authors have practical, real-world experience with SNE as it is designed, produced, and used in M&S today, and we are familiar with both strengths and weaknesses of the current state of the art. We have a long-standing history of pushing SNE technology towards the future, having contributed to the design and development of the SNEs on many of the Army's simulation and training systems over the past 20 years, including WARSIM, CCTT, OneSAF, SE Core, and others. The authors are currently leading research efforts for the M&S community looking at complex urban environments, including megacities in general and underground representations in particular. This work is being conducted primarily for the U.S. Army Research, Development and Engineering Command (RDECOM) Army Research Lab (ARL) Human Research and Engineering Directorate (HRED) Advanced Training & Simulation Division (ATSD).

While the overarching scope of our work is to investigate the future direction of SNE for simulation in general, we are looking at megacities as a key area requiring improvement. This paper summarizes the high-level concerns with megacity representation as we see it (relative to today's state of the art in fielded M&S systems).

Challenges

Inevitably, SNE requirements for the future must be driven by functional needs, since ultimately any SNE implementation exists to provide the context and surrounding environment for a larger system. For example, one training use case may consider it critical to represent power outages if power lines are damaged while others may consider this irrelevant. However, we can still extract several larger themes of concern with accurate portrayal of megacities, given the inevitable desire for increased fidelity and realism.

Data Representation

A new approach is needed for data representation. Current data representation approaches do not scale to the extent needed for the ultra-dense urban environment, as is seen with a megacity. Megacities will naturally require a wider breadth and higher density of data than is currently used in M&S applications. In addition, to keep up with the increasing availability of new data and notifications of changes to existing data, mechanisms are needed to quickly update and modify data. Technology advancements enable rapid, continuous bursts of new information from the field, which should be integrated into the data to improve the representation of the environment within simulation. Several challenges arise when considering megacities:

Increased density. In terms of the environment, this means an increase in non-specific environment features such as clutter; items like benches, trash, signs, etc. Buildings will be large, close together, and will often require both interior and sub-subterranean representation. Transportation networks will be increasingly complex, requiring representation of roadways, railways, water ways, and subways, many of these transitioning frequently from above ground to below ground.

Figure 2: (L) A simple roadway interchange; basic traffic laws are obeyed by simulated vehicles; (R) A complex highway interchange in Boston, MA; will require advanced representation and models.

Increased flexibility. Megacities have many characteristics in common, but training in one city is not directly applicable to training in another city. Simulations must be able to represent the key characteristics of various megacities so that training can occur in geo-specific locations around the globe. This diversity requires increased flexibility in how SNE data is represented. Every mission brings new and unfamiliar challenges. Just as the military must adapt quickly to overcome adversity, training simulation must respond accordingly to remain effective. Megacity representation requires a fluid SNE specification able to rapidly change to provide training for future, often unpredictable threats.

Vast relational challenge. Increases in urban density compound the complexity of relationships between infrastructure components. Critical infrastructure such as transportation networks become progressively complex as the interactions between environment features (roads, tunnels, railways, traffic signals, etc.) and moving actors (vehicles, pedestrians, etc.) become more frequent, with a greater number of variables and possible outcomes. Other infrastructure representations are in their infancy, such as computer and cellular networks, and challenges must be overcome to accurately represent these as well.

Streaming information at appropriate levels. Given the ubiquity of sensors and sensing platforms, live, up to the minute data is often available, and should be leveraged to maintain the environment representation accurately. This challenge has not yet been tackled in the modeling and simulation community to a level that is applicable for megacities. Data filtering becomes increasingly important with the rise of augmented reality systems.

Multiresolution representation. Megacity training objectives will be wide and varied. Some applications will need very detailed information while others will only need an abstract representation. For example, one trainer may need to simulate disabled power to a section of the city, whereas another may need to disable the power to a particular building. The effects of urban modeling should correlate at every level. In the power disruption example, the power grid is represented by power being distributed from power plants, across lines, through substations, transformers and other equipment. While this example focuses on electricity, the concepts apply to many SNE representational areas, including transportation/supply lines (including shipping and air), potable water, structural materials, communication, medical facilities, shelters, weather, and more. The SNE must be equipped to be able to manage the timely provision of high-resolution data in specific areas when it is required.

Environment Model

Megacities are inherently intricate in terms of how people interact with them, including complex effects on entities, secondary effects (such as damage to power lines causing lights to go off), implied or expected behaviors (such as traffic lanes or areas where civilians are likely to congregate), and multi-dimensional context (such as airport versus hospital/school versus police station). At least some of these complex effects must be captured in simulation in order for training to be effective and realistic:

Improved fidelity. In order to accurately portray the increasing complexity discussed above in relation to infrastructure, flexibility, and increasingly available data, environment models need to be more advanced, more capable, and of a higher fidelity. For example, models must take into account the difference between types of clutter. Clutter may create obstacles and change line of sight, but higher fidelity models should distinguish between a movable, non-blocking obstacle (trash bag) and a stationary, blocking obstacle (dumpster). As another example, advanced vehicle models will be able to use road lane and traffic signal data and obey basic traffic laws of the city in which they are operating.

Cascading effects. Many environment models in M&S today effectively simulate the single function for which they are designed. As interactions between various models within the simulation increase, so do possible outcomes, issues, effects, etc. Infrastructure failure such as a water main break is one example of a cascading effect in an urban environment. Often what follows are flooded streets and subways, localized loss of electricity, increased vehicle traffic, etc. In addition, political, economic, and social models will need to be incorporated in order to support training for combating terrorist activities.

Weather realism. While weather is not specific to megacities, Army simulations currently have minimal representation and modeling of weather. Weather affects real world operations, and similarly should affect training, but it has not yet been a focus of Army simulations. Two critical components are required to achieve weather realism in modeling and simulation: accurate and complete weather models, and usage of the resulting weather data by other models in the simulation. Accurate weather models and weather data are available, although not often leveraged in M&S, and other models rarely consider weather conditions. Weather affects much of what happens in the real world (fog, haze, smog, precipitation, etc. all effect movement, visibility, etc.), and weather realism in simulation is a complex challenge. Localized weather effects can induce the need for immediate deployment of first responders to help those in need and quarantine unsafe areas. Considerations for weather in megacities are often unique and may require additional data and models (e.g. the uncharacteristically high amount of snow in Boston, MA in 2015 presented new challenges with snow removal—there was nowhere to dispose of the excess snow from plowed roadways).

Figure 3: Rain is accumulating in the dug hole and changing the composition of the soil. Dignitas added weather modeling and effects to a Construction Equipment Virtual Trainer (CEVT).

Current State of the Art

While the simulation and training community has made great strides in some areas related to dense urban environments, the community lacks the current capability to represent megacities at a sufficient level.

Current SNE capabilities exist in some key areas, which can be applied and leveraged to represent dense urban environments. For instance, high fidelity representation of building interiors has been achieved and applied in simulation training for tasks such as room clearing or attacks within a building. In addition, advances have been seen in visualization technologies, where visualizing urban and high-density environments is no longer a struggle, and specialized, expensive hardware is no longer a necessity. Computers have gotten faster, smaller, and more capable over the years, while visualization algorithms have improved, making it possible to visualize complex 3D scenes on inexpensive hardware. Representation of high density features has been achieved in support of computer generated forces as well. Simulation systems such as OneSAF, Close Combat Tactical Trainer (CCTT), and JCATS offer support for limited urban areas and building interiors. Although some strides have been made, many key elements of urban environments are notably missing from modern simulation systems.

The authors see the modeling and simulation community as largely unprepared to accurately represent the physical environment in a simulation context. Innovation to address this challenge must come through targeted research to provide a foundation on which programs of record can base future requirements. Visual systems required for virtual simulation are generally in a better position to represent complex urban environments, although much work remains in the detailed geometry, topology, and physical modeling of the environment required to provide supporting services.

Figure 4: The Dignitas Veritas 2D/3D Viewer is used by LVC-IA and SE Core and runs on inexpensive laptops or desktop computers, with no specialized hardware requirements.

Below we discuss a selection of the issues that exist with the current state of the art:

Specialized Attribution Requirements. The modern battlefield is characterized by unparalleled access to data from a wide range of sensors. Open environments, such as those seen from air or space or easily observed from the ground, can be visualized and sensed in real-time. However, obtaining realistic and geospecific data for megacities is more complicated. Techniques that scan environments can be hindered by physical blockages (such as visibility into buildings or underground), as well as lack the ability to capture the intricacies of the man-made environment (such as such as material characteristics, access points, mobility information, etc.). Accurate simulation of a megacity synthetic environment will require access to these types of information or the ability to realistically infer or derive such data. These content requirements, of course, will be driven by training and functional requirements. If a training use case requires accurate representation of underground fire or smoke propagation, then issues like airflow, venting, etc., become important. If structural collapse or simulation of mouseholes is important, then structural attribution becomes more important.

Leveraging Commercial Data and Technology. In times of limited budgets, it is critical that the Army adapt to development of systems and technology that can more readily leverage commercial solutions. Current Army M&S solutions are stove-piped, built through specialized development with only limited reuse of open and commercial solutions. While specialized development may remain necessary in many areas, reuse can be increased.

Traffic and Crowd Modeling. The density and variety of human activity is a critical component in urban operations. Even in wartime situations, there may be civilians hiding out in cities, fleeing the hot zones, or congregating in the city's outskirts. When there is little warning of impending conflict, civilians may be *the* critical factor in operations. Military operations may need to be carried out with regular civilian activities occurring, as in Baghdad. Simulation of civilians requires specialized data in SNE, including things like traffic information (lanes, stop lights), designation of areas of heavy traffic (e.g. transportation hubs or malls would have more civilian traffic than a warehouse), etc. Public gathering locations such as stadiums, parks, hospitals, and churches can serve as terrorist targets or opportunities for civil unrest.

Underground and Interiors. While the Army has extensive recent experience in urban environments and building clearing, regional differences can make a tremendous difference. Clearing a high-rise building requires different approaches than clearing a small building in a walled compound. Similarly, underground environments represent special risks due to factors such as collapse, access, and even air flow (for fires or smoke propagation).

Civilian Infrastructure. Megacities will have complex and widely varying types of civilian infrastructure including power networks, lights, water lines, specialized buildings (hospital, power plant), etc. This infrastructure can matter in physical ways (damage to gas pipes could be physically dangerous, knocking out power will disable lights) as well as in conceptual ways (approaches will vary for a hospital versus school versus police station). Large, open areas such as stadiums, playgrounds, and parking lots can have military significance in providing locations for displaced civilians, holding areas for detainees, or logistics support.

Physics Effects and Interactions. Complex physical interactions will be critical in representing urban environments, including structural collapse, weapon penetration of walls, cratering of roads, collapse of tunnels, etc. In more open, rural environments, these effects could often be minimized or avoided except at key chokepoints. Megacities are large aggregations of critical chokepoints.

Urban Clutter. In most Army simulations, the training environment is largely sterile and lacks dense clutter like dumpsters, parked cars, street side market stalls, utility poles, etc. Urban clutter is especially important for high-fidelity training where objects can reduce visibility, provide cover and concealment, and hamper movement.

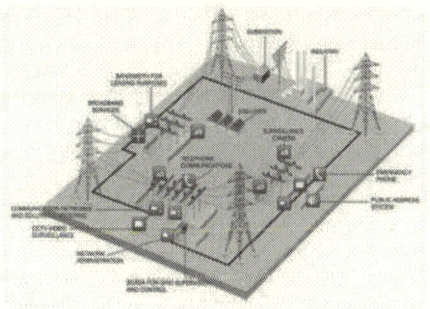

Figure 5: Complex civilian infrastructure must be modeled and considered in megacity operations.

Emerging Technology

Keeping an eye on emerging technologies across the industry ensures re-use candidates can be identified and used as appropriate.

There is an emerging trend of crowd-sourced data and increased timeliness of geospatial and infrastructure data available from multiple sources. For example, navigational data on smart phones and GPS systems is updated frequently with up to date traffic data to indicate whether traffic is flowing smoothly or is backed up. Some navigational apps also include crowd sourced data, allowing users to input accidents, road hazards, and detours. However, such data sources must be carefully considered since they could easily provide a pathway for misinformation to enter into military systems. Critical areas and categories of data will remain difficult to obtain trust-worthy sources for, especially in foreign countries or network denied areas.

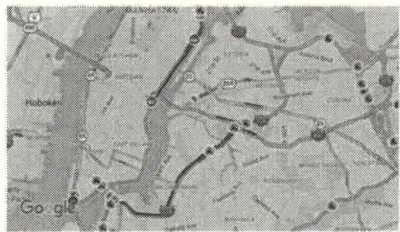

Figure 6: Google maps and GPS systems show live traffic status via colored lines (red for heavy traffic, green for clear) and icons for construction zones and accidents.

Game engines continue to evolve, but their focus is often in areas that are not important in military applications. Game engines often excel at providing highly realistic visual environments and compelling physical interactions, but the focus is generally on visual effect and gameplay rather than realism. Realistic effects are of utmost importance to military simulations to avoid negative training. Similarly, realistic-looking effects in game engines are often achieved through extensive manual effort from artists and scenario developers. This approach is cost-prohibitive if representing large areas or when rapid turnaround is needed from source to training.

*Figure 7: Realistic video game visuals require
extensive manual designs and illustrations.*

Cloud-based, thin-client solutions are a growing trend that could help facilitate training at point of need. As a download repository, cloud technology has no impact on SNE representation. But the notion of streaming SNE database information adds an additional layer of complexity to the solutions needed for megacity representation. To help combat delays caused by network latency, a number of techniques are available, including optimized data structures, compression, composition (configure what data is needed per application), predictive caching, and procedural generation of SNE features. Investigation and experimentation is needed to determine which technique or combination of techniques deliver best "bang for the buck" results.

Future Focus of Science and Technology Investments

We believe concentrated investment in government development is needed to meet military needs. Crowd-source and commercial technology is widely available but doesn't fully meet military needs and is susceptible to injection of misinformation. We also need pathways to connect simulation and training applications over to classified data or networks, and operational data to enhance training and realism.

The authors' current research efforts are investigating methods to represent geometry and topology in separate ways yet providing some assurance of correlation between them. Megacities will require complex geometries which will make it extremely difficult to automatically derive key behavioral aspects needed for automated opponents, such as logical firing and over watch positions. Current Army simulation systems have structured yet comparatively simplistic SNE data to reason on, often making broad assumptions (such as not worrying about overhead clearances). In megacities, these assumptions will not hold up. Our research will also consider how to use a mixture of automation, machine learning, and very targeted human in the loop attribution (for heavily used training areas) to support behavioral aspects.

Defining what types of data are needed for megacity simulation is critical for success. This will include not just obvious information… such as locations of buildings, bridges, and roads…but potentially far more complex data such as material characteristics, support structures (load bearing walls for collapse), topological information (turn lanes, stop lights, paths where civilians often travel on foot), and more. Since elements of this data will be difficult to collect from standard sources (e.g. interiors and below ground geometry), it will be important for such information to be derivable in geotypical, realistic ways. Our research will focus on what is needed for runtime functional needs rather than considering methods for collection.

Megacity simulation will require different data and services for various training use cases. For example, an immersive simulation for individual soldiers will require a different type of detail and information than a strategic bombing simulation. However, to ensure communications and interoperability between simulations, these varying representations would ideally be derived from and relate back to a common overarching representation which can handle multiple resolutions or levels of detail. Our research will investigate techniques for how to represent varying levels of detail in a correlated and realistic fashion, while also supporting highly selective data use wherein a given simulation system only loads data that is relevant and useful to its use case.

The authors believe it important that future simulations support just in time data delivery and flexible paradigms for computing platforms and environments. A simulation run one day in the cloud, might be run on network denied devices the next. In addition, we expect frequent updates to geospatial, topological, and human behavioral data from a wide range of sources in the future. This concept requires the ability to distribute the latest data rapidly, consistently, and selectively so as to get maximum benefit out of limited bandwidth for edge devices. Just in time data processing and delivery will enable different data use cases, such as cloud-based simulation using data centers or highly select data sets for resource- and bandwidth-limited devices.

As data sources, content, and updates increase in complexity, the mechanisms and processes for verifying consistency, relationships, and interdependencies must grow. Seemingly simple changes in basic geometry for feature data can have complex secondary effects on other data. For example, if data becomes available for changing the function of a building (from office building to embassy, for example), it can impact secondary data, including crowd modeling flows, behavioral cues, and more. As we build up content requirements and update mechanisms in early years, the later years of our research will look at ways to reconcile all of this data and maintain consistency where it matters.

Work is needed even in areas where the Army simulation community has extensive previous experience, such as calculation of cover, conceal, or hide locations, basic movement planning, and line of sight. These algorithms will require a different level of complexity with different tradeoffs when working in complex megacity environments.

Conclusion

As the U.S. military adapts to operating in megacities, it will be critical to enable realistic training through simulation so that warfighters are able to refine and practice their procedures. This is necessary not just for training and experience, but also to assess effectiveness of new weapons systems and platforms. The simulation and training community faces a wide range of challenges to enabling this training, especially with regards to realistic representation of dense urban environments. The authors believe focused investment is needed to ensure the simulation and training community can meet the technical challenges required to enable analysis and training in megacities. We welcome feedback from and collaboration with other Army agencies and contractors working in this domain.

Chapter 25

Megacities: The Good, the Bad, and the Ugly

Russell W. Glenn

First Published 17 February 2016

Introduction

> "When [U.S. military] officers objected that Kahn was ill-equipped to speak on military affairs…he'd shoot back, 'How many thermonuclear wars have you fought recently?'… They admitted they had no actual experiences with these weapons. 'O.K., Kahn would grin, 'Then we start out even.'"[1]

> —Ghamari-Tabrizi, *The Worlds of Herman Kahn*

Today's armed forces and those accompanying their security efforts worldwide have no more conducted major operations in a megacity—those urban areas in excess of ten million population—than have they participated in a nuclear war. Fortunately, however—and unlike the case with the officers above—recent experience and history's lessons from undertakings in cities short of the ten million mark have much to offer. Much, but those offerings will fall short of the comprehensive. The same is true for those in civilian clothes—government and otherwise. Megacities are sure to challenge every member of a coalition.[2] How these urban areas might do so in the intelligence realm in the near future is the primary focus of this offering, one that can but provide but a brief taste of the sweet, savory, and bitter implications involved.[3]

The facts are well known, some so often repeated as to be all but common knowledge. Among them:

- Over half the world now lives in urban areas; nearly a quarter resides in those with over one million population.[4]
- Eighty percent of the world's population lives within one hundred miles (160 kilometers) of a shore, most in cities.[5]
- There were 132 cities of population one million or more in 1965. Such urban areas numbered 494 in 2015, thirty-four of which were megacities (urban areas with populations of ten million or more).[6]

Though the waters are muddied by varied definitions of "city," "urban area," "metropolitan area," and others, it is inescapable that the world increasingly urbanizes and its largest cities/urban areas/metropolitan areas tend to swell at an even greater rate.[7] Implications for coalitions are numerous and far-reaching. Non-state actors in particular have turned to urban terrain's density of hides, firing positions, and civilians providing sustainment willingly or otherwise to avoid confronting superior Western military technology and training, both of which tend to be designed for more open environments. Fortunate indeed will be the future military leader finding his enemy willing to evacuate a city as did the Iraqi Army Basra in 2003.[8]

Were these not challenges enough, the varying definitions conceal social, political, and economic implications no less problematic. The *city* of Los Angeles proper—the political entity—is home to a population of but 3.8 million within the greater Los Angeles *urban area* of 15.1 million beings.[9] (Thus Los Angeles qualifies as a megacity.) A coalition operating in such a region would find itself coordinating with hundreds of administrative jurisdictions: political, fire, law enforcement, transportation, and health to touch on a few, this regardless of whether the mission at hand involves armed force or not. Nor would opposing force's evacuation of an urban area guarantee relief. Removal of what might well have been coercive authorities too typical of the Third World removes the lid from a simmering pot; looting, surging criminality, and latent sectarianism could be only three of the newly arrived rewards for assuming responsibility.

Yet all is not darkness. Though man has no more conducted major operations in a megacity than had those in Herman Kahn's audiences fought a thermonuclear war, we need to remind ourselves that similarities between undertakings in smaller urban areas have much to offer coalitions confronting others when a population exceeds ten million mark. The remainder of this essay will only sparingly touch on these commonalities. Analysis instead seeks to focus on issues particular to megacities. As the title suggests, operations and campaigns in these environments will provide the good (opportunities), the bad (challenges), and the ugly (especially difficult issues).

The Good

A recent chief of the US Army Capabilities Integration Center's Future Warfare Division stated, "Dense urban terrain favors the defender," a daunting prospect when one considers the expanses of tightly packed man-made structures characteristic of the world's largest urban conglomerations.[10] Reality fortunately confounds this common belief. Defense of cities, especially the vast expanses that are megacities, presents a situation akin to that described by Clausewitz in his contemplations of mountain complex defense:

> Defensive mountain warfare…. Is it meant to last only a certain time or to the end in definite victory? Mountains are eminently suited to defense of the first type…. For the second type, on the other hand, they are, except for a few special cases, generally not suited at all…. A small

post can acquire extraordinary strength in mountainous terrain. [However,] in a decisive battle, mountainous terrain is of no help to the defender; on the contrary… it favors the attacker.[11]

As in extensive mountainous terrain, the megacity defender will tend to lack the manpower, weaponry, and knowledge to prevent circumvention of its defensive positions. Further, unlike the Persians at Thermopylae, there will be no need for reliance on the good fortune of finding the singular individual knowledgeable in this regard. Residents familiar with their city and willing to guide a force to surface, subterranean, or super-terranean bypasses should not be hard to locate.

A first lesson is therefore to recognize that megacities' substantial populations, geographies, infrastructures, and other features offer benefits in addition to difficulties. Existing doctrine, past experience, and theory will all offer points from which to adapt. Factors more likely found only in these largest urban areas will enhance these opportunities. Larger built-up areas tend to offer a breadth and depth of information lacking in less populated environments. The navigation application Waze, for example, can be of limited value in infrequently traveled rural regions. Relying on user-submitted data, it is of notable value in densely populated areas, however. Waze tells users not only how to get from point A to point B but also provides real-time status regarding ongoing construction, accidents, roadway debris, and (yes) police speed trap and fixed camera locations amongst other information. The app employs this input to redirect users from their normal home-to-work and other routes to less congested alternatives. Military units could conceivably adapt such applications, allowing for inclusion of secure inputs regarding threat locations, raw material stockpiles of potential operational value, and suspicious road conditions (e.g., possible spots where an improvised explosive device might have been emplaced), perhaps linking drivers' observations targeting assets. Integrating secure with Waze (or a similar application's) open-source information would at once increase routing efficiency and force protection while reducing opportunities for theft of supplies. (Armed robbers in Lagos, Nigeria, for example, routinely rob occupants of vehicles trapped in the city's notorious traffic jams.)[12]

Urban areas are also hives of official and commercial demographic information. Robert Dixon's "Bringing Big Data to War in Mega-Cities" discussion regarding the types and value of urban databases applies equally to humanitarian response and other contingencies not involving combat.[13] Census information, marketing survey results, and property records are but a sampling of what military and broader coalition authorities would find beneficial for addressing tasks inherent in urban undertakings. Cell phone data has especially notable potential to assist a coalition during crises. Call data records providing the number, time, and cell tower location of use have already been used to track malaria outbreaks in Africa.[14] Captured in a timely fashion, they could similarly help trace the flow of commuters later found to have been contaminated in a biological agent attack. As with an interactive traffic application, larger urban populations enhance the potential value of analyzing cell phone record data; those in cities are more likely to possess cellphones than others in remote rural areas. The sophistication of databases and their potential value may surprise. Geo-profiling shows promise for finding terrorists via analysis of where incidents occur. Most attacks are within a short distance of perpetrators' residences or materials storage locations, reducing chances of confronting checkpoints when moving to targets. Further, extremists may avoid certain neighborhoods due to discomfort with activities there, e.g., those in which the sex trade is commonplace.[15] Police records and accompanying analysis software in some US cities provide timely color coding regarding risk levels associated with individuals and addresses. Dispatched officers receive in-route evaluations after database searches regarding information such as whether a resident has a record of weapons possession or past violent crimes.[16] These capabilities could be used in conjunction with local knowledge as possessed by members of Terrorism Early Warning Groups (TEWG) such as that found in Los Angeles. TEWGs offer arriving coalition members valuable local and broader regional knowledge memberships that include representatives from police, fire, coast guard, federal law enforcement, and other organizations familiar with both the immediate urban area and more far-flung reaches. (Links between various city's TEWGs or similar organizations can likewise be invaluable when an event in one megacity threatens distant locations, e.g., when the aforementioned bio-contaminated individual departs for another destination.) Knowing how to access, organize, and make good use of these various troves of information will take practice. Training with megacity authorities such as those in TEWGs would provide insights regarding both the specific urban area represented and others more generally applicable to such megalopolises.

Nor should one assume capabilities of this type are restricted to the First World. When Liberian Patrick Sawyer collapsed on arrival in the Lagos, Nigeria airport, local authorities soon recognized he— and potentially passengers on his plane—posed a potential medical disaster. Sawyer had brought the Ebola virus to Africa's and one of the world's largest megacities, estimated population 30.6 million. Despite the city's doctors being on strike, refusal of the Nigerian Medical Association's chairman to terminate the strike in the face of the threat, and exposure of hundreds to those confirmed or possibly infected, actions by working medical personnel, aggressive and successful efforts to trace and get in touch with the 891 individuals possibly or actually exposed, and coordination of operations by a Gates Foundation-funded clinic converted into an emergency command center precluded wider infection.[17] The quick reaction included nongovernmental, inter-governmental, commercial, and governmental organizations in addition to mobilized volunteers and the United States Centers for Disease Control.[18] That Lagos was so large an urban area increased the likelihood that appropriate medical facilities were on hand. (Two laboratories in the megacity were able to test for the Ebola virus.) That Nigeria's capital was also an epicenter of the country's educated and the expert and vying a "wired city" was fundamental to the disease being interdicted with only twenty infected and a total of eight deaths. A doctor in the hospital to which Sawyer was taken not only recognized the symptoms; she prevented the uncooperative patient from forcibly leaving the medical facility and resisted pressures that included those from the Liberian embassy.[19] World megacities are more likely to have similar in-place emergency response procedures and other resources key to effective crisis response. Even preparations for dislike events have potential to assist a coalition's urban operations. Provisions for action in the aftermath of a major earthquake, for example, will have value during responses to other disasters, e.g., a major terrorist attack.

Access to megacity information, authorities, and other key resources will assist not only during general planning and conduct of urban area operations. They will likewise be invaluable in determining what specific communities within a built-up area (or country or region more broadly) offer greatest promise for supporting (or impeding) coalition objectives. No force will be large enough to control an entire megalopolis. Knowing likely hotspots, identifying centers or gravity and decisive points, and locating acceptable base areas from which to conduct operations will do much toward making the apparently overwhelming a manageable undertaking.

The Bad

A megacity is the un-consumable elephant; the number of bites needed to address all of its requirements would far exceed any coalition's capabilities. Progress and ultimate success is further made difficult in that the armed forces likely to lead such ventures have doctrines that go little beyond generalities when it comes to dealing with the largest of urban agglomerations. A United States Marine Corps comment from over a decade ago holds true both for its specific topic and other functional areas during urban operations:

> Formal, written urban combat reconnaissance doctrine—the foundation (at least in theory) for the planning and execution of operations and training, the development of organizational structure, and the basis for equipment procurement—is essentially nonexistent.[20]

The need for more urban (and megacity)-specific doctrine is evident to any who since 2002 found themselves in Baghdad, Kandahar, Fallujah, or any other of the many urban environments in which the men and women of the US and its closest partners have served. There will be "other-governed" communities, those ruled by less-than-official (but not necessarily less effective) authorities, often with criminal or other nefarious intentions, Sadr City in Baghdad being an exemplar. Misnomers, misunderstandings, and mistakes left unaddressed in recent guidance pose threats to urban operations success; they portend outright disaster when the numbers involved grow to double-digit millions. The assumption that provision of aid and quality of life improvements is fundamental to gaining and maintaining public support is one perhaps resting on dubious foundations. Eric Hoffer's classic *The True Believer* warns of a conundrum rarely recognized: the destitute are too worried about the source of their next meal to have interest in rebellion or resistance. Lifting them from this hand-to-mouth existence, however, threatens creating tinder ready to flare given expectations of yet further improvement, expectations that may be beyond the abilities or intentions of a coalition to meet, particularly one confronting the scope of issues inherent in megacity operations.[21]

Intelligence implications are clear. Far more than estimates of conventional enemy capabilities and intentions will be called for. Those of the many insurgent, criminal, militia, and other armed threats will be no less important. Identifying key formal and informal power brokers in neighborhoods and political jurisdictions and determining the most effective means of communicating with both these social nodes and the population at large will be fundamental to maintaining even minimal control. The larger the urban area, the greater the number of threat groups and the wider the regional dependencies linked to the city. Collection of the information needed to feed what is sure to be a voracious intelligence beast will demand manpower and equipment resources in excess of any currently available to even the most ambitiously conceived deployed force. The sheer extent of megacity operations-related information from human, visual technology, acoustic and vibratory sensor, signals collection, and other sources will overwhelm today's analytic capabilities. Add to this quantity the vast expanses of line-of-sight terrain and additional influences such as having to separate relevant information from the mundane inherent in the habitual "noise," "hum," or vibration of megacity daily activities and the challenge is further exacerbated.

The Ugly

> *Munitions are now delivered reliably from distant launch systems and brought onto target by units that can remain hidden....It means the demise of infantry battalions, tank regiments and armoured brigades as they are currently structured for major combat operations.*[22]

> —*Christopher L. Elliott*, High Command: British Military Leadership in the Iraq and Afghanistan Wars

Not so fast, general. Let us not fall victim to believing that past activities will accurately reflect the nature of those yet to come. The same marines decrying doctrine's lethargy in meeting 21st-century urban reconnaissance demands found "controlling fires is difficult for us" urban area's ubiquitous buildings, the smoke and smog degrading both vision and laser designation, and polished surfaces reflection of those beams. Hamas and other foes confronted by the Israel Defense Forces (IDF) during recent operations increasingly make use of urban subterranean hides, headquarters, and passageways to deny observation and targeting. Below ground facilities are already inherent physical features of today's cities, their number and dispersion increasing as does population growth and accompanying structural spread. Detecting entrances and exits to facilities can be extremely difficult; determining their underground route nearly impossible given the depth of some such infrastructure and clever concealment of air shafts.[23] Even when detected, valuable targets may be left unhindered due to their being positioned under proscribed civilian infrastructure. A Hamas command center remained unscathed beneath Gaza's largest hospital during 2014 Operation Protective Edge despite IDF leaders knowing its location.[24] Determination of favorable laser designation and launch system locations; analysis of rotary-wing flight routes minimizing exposure to likely enemy air defense weapons sites; development of algorithms to support such analyses in operationally relevant timeframes; and commitment of resources to detecting, tracing, and targeting subterranean facilities all pose worthy challenges for the intelligence community.

Nor is it only those in uniform who will find megacity challenges overwhelming. Demands for capabilities essential to aiding so large an urban area's recovery may exceed what international and coalition governments can bring to bear even for a short period. The problem will be more difficult yet should years of assistance be necessary, a problem magnified if that assistance be needed beyond the bounds of the megacity alone. Difficulties are made worse yet when inappropriately manned advance parties and early information collection efforts fail to identify and thereafter focus on priority challenges.

No less ugly are cases in which shortfalls during previous urban campaigns are repeated. The commander drawing militarily-typical unit boundaries along physical features such as roads, rivers, and the like will find those boundaries become self-inflicted wounds should they not be realigned once combat operations recede. Savvy leaders can instead minimize liaison, communications equipment, and other demands by realigning boundaries with existing administrative jurisdictions. It is a lesson unfortunately repeatedly learned and forgotten, two of the most recent instances being during the Los Angeles 1992 riots and in 2003 Baghdad. Intelligence personnel's recognizing the importance of identifying administrative delineations, then providing them to operational planners could preclude yet another recurrence.

Toward Solutions

To describe megacities as "information rich" environments is an understatement. No less than their towering buildings and teaming masses, the information oceans can seem an overwhelming flood. Some simple—and logical—first steps can provide a means of lending form to the seeming deluge. Regarding these environments in terms of underlying terrain, buildings, infrastructures (physical, social, and informational), and people creates "bins" to assist in managing collection and analysis…given that the bins do not become stovepipes hindering system-wide analysis. Likewise, recognizing that megacities' physical, human, and other characteristics can differ from smaller urban areas in terms of familiar concepts such as density assists in making the seemingly ungraspable graspable.[25]

Innovation will prove an indispensable commodity. Recognizing how lessons from previous operations in sub-megacities and during counterinsurgency operations can be molded in the service of new challenges would be a significant step forward. Modifying proven and well understood concepts will likewise provide payoff. Bringing maneuver into the 21st century would be one such re-forging. Previous operations—both urban and counterinsurgency—demonstrate the value of a comprehensive approach during which military, government civilian, and other relevant participants cooperate. All the more reason to embed the essence of maneuver's traditional definition:

> Employment of forces in the operational area through movement in combination with fires to achieve a position of advantage in respect to the enemy[26]

And in a more encompassing conceptualization:

> The employment of relevant resources to gain advantage with respect to select individuals or groups in the service of achieving specified objectives.[27]

Similarly, the long-held understanding of a coalition as "an ad hoc arrangement between two or more nations for common action"[28] would benefit from recognition that the scope of efforts requires synchronization of more than national assets alone. A better definition would account for nongovernmental, inter-governmental, private, and other organizations able to offer needed capabilities, making a coalition "an ad hoc arrangement between two or more organizations in the interest of common action."[29] Conceiving of "intelligence coalitions" along similar lines could significantly increase the number of information providers in support of megacity events. Much of the information needed to support intelligence requirements implied both explicitly and implicitly above is available in open sources. Pre-deployment and reach-back employment of interns and others to mine databases could dramatically increase the number of assets providing data. Much of the information would require revalidation, particularly in cases where physical destruction due to natural or man-made disasters is extensive or the numbers of displaced persons high, making large numbers of those capable of datamining an even greater asset. Manning would have to include sufficient personnel to confirm and reconfirm findings. Information sources inevitably conflict; some official sources are notoriously little more than fabrications designed to keep in-place authorities in power. It is obvious that training data miners should be undertaken before future operations the better to identify likely information requirements and minimize response times.

On the urban ground itself, the infantryman, pilot, NGO aid provider, truck driver, and every other participant becomes a potential source of information and recipient of resulting intelligence products (understanding all such participants are not equal when it comes to intelligence provision given differences in security clearances). Embedded personnel assisting with various government organizations should wear multiple hats. Those assisting in building governing capacity should at the same time be incorporated into information collection efforts, thereby enhancing understanding of megacity key relationships, fault lines, vulnerabilities, emerging requirements, and sources of opportunity in the service of coalition objectives. These same individuals will ideally be monitors confirming or alerting responsible parties when activities put short and longer-term objectives in tension as did one command in Iraq when members proposed providing small business startup grants at the same time other coalition authorities hoped to establish a program of bank micro-loans.

The far-reaching consequences of getting it right (or wrong) during operations in megacities demands not only innovative thinking, fresh doctrine, and multi-disciplinary assessments. Extreme war-gaming must become the norm. The Arizona Market outside Brcko, Bosnia-Herzegovina was a brilliant initiative, reestablishing as it did regional ties with that small city after years of violence had shattered previously longstanding economic links. Yet the immediate benefits gave way to the market's becoming a center of black marketing, fencing high-value products from Western Europe, and trafficking of women.[30] Rigorous and frequent war-gaming of possible alternative outcomes linked to intelligence collection regarding market activities should have been required the better to identify factors likely to promote slippage of the facility into illegitimacy. Such failing to actively monitor and analyze events during operations in a megacity could have adverse consequences extending well beyond the immediate region. The implications are once again complex. War games would require robust computer support given the rapid spiraling of second, third, and higher-order effects inherent in any action taken in megacities' innumerable and compacted interrelationships. Those interrelationships (and therefore those effects) will undoubtedly have regional, probably nationwide, and quite possibly worldwide effects. (Consider the global impact of the 9/11 attacks on New York City.) Change may be hard to detect given the constant and varied levels of activity in these megalopolises alluded to earlier. This need to war-game the status quo—what could happen from the situation as it is now—suggests the analysis will have to be nearly continuous. To assume otherwise is to overlook the very real possibility that today's brilliant successes are potentially seeds for tomorrow's disasters. The implications reach into pre-operation preparations: backward planning should begin at an end condition well beyond the re-assumption of governing responsibility by local authorities.

This monitoring and war-gaming assumes an understanding of a megacity's routines and patterns. Determining these patterns and variations therefrom will necessitate data compilation and analysis beyond anything available to coalition leaders today. Sophisticated use of the aforementioned big data, overhead monitoring by long on-station systems, and establishment of and reporting by contacts in local governments (e.g., police, fire personal, building inspectors, and tax collectors to mention only a few) and communities (taxi drivers, delivery personnel, neighborhood watch volunteers, and those manning hospitals) will have to be constant. Those in coalition militaries will be crucial components of this pattern definition. Logistics providers and foot patrols are among those from whom reporting should be frequent and for whom debriefings must be thorough, both of which will be enhanced by assigning these individuals "beats" similar to those of neighborhood policemen to the extent feasible. Those interviewing members of the population will have to be schooled in intelligence tradecraft. Anti-gang squads in Los Angeles, for example, canvas entire neighborhoods or city blocks in order to conceal the identity of the one individual from whom they know information is forthcoming. Robots, security cameras, and other means could provide additional monitoring. Shortages of interpreters can to an extent be overcome via reach-back sessions employing Skype- or Facetime-like connections with language speakers remote from the city itself. Simpler translation needs might be met one or more of the smartphone applications or other software currently available.

The challenges inherent in undertaking operations in a megacity will extend well beyond the sampling of intelligence-related concerns touched on above, instead permeating every military function and many civilian as well. New challenges will be commonplace, adapting lessons from those confronted before a routine necessity. New yes, but little will qualify as revolutionary. The urban-experienced soldier, sailor, marine, and airman will be a valuable asset, as will any who are well-read in the ways of urban operations, megacities, and fields with obviously applicable insights such as the previously mentioned counterinsurgency. Demanding as future megacity contingencies will be, however, innovations and initiative in drawing upon professional education and experiences are sure to provide far more of value than overzealous claims of having discovered a heretofore never seen form of conflict. The observations of both Eran Zohar and General James Mattis provide pertinent closing thoughts in this regard:

> *Wars became hybrid wars.... Being an old tactic practised by armies and guerrilla rebels, the "new" idea of an enemy that "disappears" from the battlefield and wages urban warfare is a fraud.... That rhetoric characterizes an organization that fails to conserve its memory and learn lessons from the past."*[31]

—Eran Zohar

> *"Israeli military intelligence's understanding of the security environment in light of the Arab Awakening"*
> *For all the "4ᵗʰ Generation of War" intellectuals running around today saying that the nature of war has fundamentally changed, the tactics are wholly new, etc., I must respectfully say... "Not really": Alex the Great would not be in the least bit perplexed by the enemy that we face right now in [2013] Iraq, and our leaders going into this fight do their troops a disservice by not studying (studying, vice just reading) the men who have gone before us.*[32]

—General James Mattis

Notes

[1]   Sharon Ghamari-Tabrizi, *The Worlds of Herman Kahn: The Intuitive Science of Thermonuclear War*, Cambridge, MA: Harvard University Press, 2005, 48-49.

[2]   21ˢᵗ-century operations and campaigns—those in larger urban areas in particular— demand more than a "coalition" as currently defined in US joint doctrine: "an arrangement between two

or more nations for common action." [Joint Chiefs of Staff, Department of Defense Dictionary of Military and Associated Terms, Joint Publication 1-02, Washington, D.C.: Joint Chiefs of Staff, November 8, 2010 as amended through January 15, 2016, 34, http://www.dtic.mil/doctrine/new_pubs/jp1_02.pdf (accessed February 3, 2016)] A broader conceptualization is called for: "an ad hoc cooperative arrangement between two or more organizations in the interest of supporting a common action." [Russell W. Glenn, *Band of Brothers or Dysfunctional Family: A Military Perspective on Coalition Challenges During Stability Operations*, Santa Monica, CA: RAND, 2011, 41, http://www.rand.org/pubs/monographs/MG903.html (accessed February 3, 2016).].

[3] That many if not all observations made regarding megacities herein apply to the larger of world's cities with somewhat smaller populations is a given. Westerners' liking for multiples of five and ten should not cause us to limit insights to the serendipitous choice of the ten million mark.

[4] *Demographia World Urban Areas*, 11th edition, 2015, 2, http://www.demographia.com/db-worldua.pdf(accessed January 28, 2016).

[5] Jonathan W. Greenert (Chief of Naval Operations, US Navy), "The World is Dependent Upon the Oceans...," presentation hosted by the Strategic and Defence Studies Centre, The Australian National University, Canberra, Australia, January 8, 2015.

[6] Statistic for 1965 from Ronan Paddison, ed., *Handbook of Urban Studies*, Thousand Oaks, CA: Sage, 2001, 24. 2015 statistics from *Demographia World Urban Areas*, 11th edition, 2015, 2, http://www.demographia.com/db-worldua.pdf (accessed January 28, 2016).

[7] Statistics such as those just cited suffer from these sometimes-considerable differences in definition. I will use the following descriptions for urban-related terms in this essay: "An urban area is best thought of as the 'urban footprint'—the lighted area that

can be observed from an airplane (or satellite) on a clear night. National census authorities in Australia, Canada, Denmark, Finland, France, the Netherlands, Norway, Sweden, the United Kingdom and the United States designate urban areas. Except in Australia, the authorities use a minimum urban density definition of 400 persons per square kilometer (or the nearly identical 1,000 per square mile in the United States) …. Urban Areas Contrasted with Metropolitan Areas: An urban area (built-up urban area or urban agglomeration) is fundamentally different from a metropolitan area…. A metropolitan area is a labor market and includes substantial rural (non-urban) territory or area of discontinuous urban development (beyond the developed urban fringe)." *Demographia World Urban Areas*, 11th edition, 2015, 3-4.

[8]   Christopher L. Elliott, *High Command: British Military Leadership in the Iraq and Afghanistan Wars*, Oxford: Oxford University Press, 2015, 151-152.

[9]   2015 city of Los Angeles population estimate from "Suburban Stats: Current Los Angeles, California Population, Demographics and stats in 2014 and 2015," https://suburbanstats.org/population/ california/how-many-people-live-in-los-angeles (accessed February 2, 2016); Los Angeles urban area population estimate from *Demographia World Urban Areas*, 11th edition, 2015, 35, http://www.demographia.com/db-worldua.pdf (accessed January 28, 2016).

[10]   William Matthews, "Megacity Warfare: Taking Urban Combat to a Whole New Level," *Army* (February 12, 2015) http://www. armymagazine.org/2015/02/12/megacity-warfare-taking-urban- combat-to-a-whole-new-level (accessed January 3, 2016).

[11]   Carl von Clausewitz, *On War*, ed. Michael Howard and Peter Paret, Princeton, NJ: Princeton University Press, 1976, 419, 420, and 423. (emphasis in original).

[12]   "Paralysed: Urban traffic," *The Economist* (November 7, 2015), http://www.economist.com/news/middle-east-and-africa /21677665-why-nigerias-largest-city-even-less-navigable-usual- paralysed (accessed February 2, 2016).

[13]   Robert Dixon, "Bringing Big Data to War in Mega-Cities," *War on the Rocks*, January 19, 2016, http://warontherocks.com/2016/01/ bringing-big-data-to-operations-in-mega-cities/ (accessed January 19, 2016).

[14]   "Call for help; Ebola and big data," *The Economist* 413 (October 25, 2014), http://www.economist.com/news/leaders/21627623-mobile-phone-records-are-invaluable-tool-combat-ebola-they-should-be-made-available (accessed February 2, 2016).

[15]   "Shrinking the haystack: Counter-terrorism," *The Economist* 418 (January 16, 2016): 78-79, http://www.economist.com/news/ science-and-technology/21688368-software-helping-search-guerrillas-and-terrorists-safe-houses-and (accessed January 24, 2016).

[16]   Justin Jouvenal, "The new way police are surveilling you: Calculating your threat 'score'," *The Washington Post* (January 10, 2016), https://www.washingtonpost.com/local/public-safety/ the-new-way-police-are-surveilling-you-calculating-your-threat-score/2016/01/10/e42bccac-8e15-11e5-baf4-bdf37355da0c_story. html (accessed January 14, 2016).

[17]   Michael Bailey and John Via, "Military Medical Implications of Future Megacity Operations," *Small Wars Journal* (February 13, 2015), http://www.smallwarsjournal.com/printpdf/21402 (accessed January 3, 2016); Geoffrey York, "Ebola: How Nigeria and Senegal stopped the disease 'dead in its tracks'," *The Globe and Mail* (October 19, 2014, updated October 20, 2014), http://www.theglobeandmail.com/news/world/ebola-how-to-stop-the-disease-dead-in-its-tracks/article21159394/ (accessed February 2, 2016); and Akintunde Akinleye, "Nigeria isolated Lagos hospital where Ebola victim died," *Reuters*, July 25, 2014, http://www.reuters.com/article/us-health-ebola-nigeria-idUSKBN0FX15420140728 (accessed February 2, 2016).

[18]   International Federation of the Red Cross and Red Crescent Societies, "Emergency Plan of Action Final Report-Nigeria: Ebola Virus Disease," August 31, 2014, http://reliefweb.int/

sites/reliefweb.int/files/resources/MDRNG017FR.pdf (accessed February 2, 2016).

[19]   John Tozzi, "How to Avert an Ebola Nightmare: Lessons From Nigeria's Victory, *Business Week* (October 20, 2014), http://www.bloomberg.com/bw/articles/2014-10-20/ebola-how-nigeria-averted-a-nightmare-in-densely-populated-lagos   (accessed February 2, 2016); and Will Ross, "Ebola crisis: How Nigeria's Dr Adadevoh fought the virus," *BBC*, (October 20, 2014), http://www.bbc.com/news/world-africa-29696011 (accessed February 2, 2016).

[20]   Russell W. Glenn, et al., *Honing the Keys to the City: Refining the United States Marine Corps Reconnaissance Force for Urban Ground Combat Operations*, Santa Monica, CA: RAND, 2003, 11-12.

[21]   Eric Hoffer, *The True Believer*, NY: Time, 1963, 29-30.

[22]   Christopher L. Elliott, *High Command: British Military Leadership in the Iraq and Afghanistan Wars*, Oxford: Oxford University Press, 2015, 238-39.

[23]   During the 2014 Operation Protective Edge in Gaza, for example, IDF soldiers could not find tunnel exits in buildings despite being aware of the general location of the egress points and searching for them extensively, later suffering surprise attacks after Gazans emerged behind Israeli positions. Russell W. Glenn, *Short War in a Perpetual Conflict: Implications of Israel's 2014 Operation Protective Edge for the Australian Army* (draft), 2015, to be published in 2016, 123.

[24]   Russell W. Glenn, *Short War in a Perpetual Conflict: Implications of Israel's 2014 Operation Protective Edge for the Australian Army* (draft), 2015, to be published in 2016, 26.

[25]   For a further discussion of urban densities and their influence on military operations, see Russell W. Glenn, *Heavy Matter: Urban Operations Density of Challenges*, Santa Monica, CA: RAND, 2000.

[26]   Joint Chiefs of Staff, *Department of Defense Dictionary of Military and Associated Terms*, Joint Publication 1-02, Washington, D.C.: Joint Chiefs of Staff, November 8, 2010 as amended through

January 15, 2016, 145, http://www.dtic.mil/doctrine/new_pubs/jp1_02.pdf (accessed February 3, 2016).

[27] Definition from Russell W. Glenn, *Rethinking Western Approaches to Counterinsurgency: Lessons from Post-colonial Conflict*, Abingdon, UK: Routledge, 2015, 270.

[28] Joint Publication 1-02, *Department of Defense Dictionary of Military and Associated Terms*, Washington, D.C.: Joint Chiefs of Staff, November 8, 2010 as amended through January 15, 2016, 34.

[29] Russell W. Glenn, *Band of Brothers or Dysfunctional Family? A Military Perspective on Coalition Challenges During Stability Operations*, Santa Monica, CA: RAND, 2011, xiv.

[30] Dina Francesca Haynes, "Lessons from Bosnia's Arizona Market: Harm to Women in a Neo-liberalized Post-conflict Reconstruction Process," *University of Pennsylvania Law Review* 158: 1779, 1781 and 1794-98, http://scholarship.law.upenn.edu/cgi/viewcontent.cgi?article=1163&context=penn_law_review (accessed February 3, 2016).

[31] Eran Zohar, "Israeli military intelligence's understanding of the security environment in light of the Arab Awakening," *Defence Studies* 15:3, 216-17 [complete article 203-234].

[32] Geoffrey Ingersoll, "General James 'Mad Dog' Mattis Email About Being 'Too Busy To Read' Is A Must-Read," *Business Insider* (May 9, 2013), http://www.businessinsider.com.au/viral-james-mattis-email-reading-marines-2013-5 (accessed January 19, 2016).

Chapter 26

How to Hold or Take a Big City— Seven Lines of Effort

Geoff Demarest

First Published 18 February 2016

This essay proposes adoption of a specific planning framework for urban operations.[1] An American armed force smaller than, say, that used in Sadr City, Baghdad might well achieve victory in a future urban environment.[2] The imagined geographical context for the presentation of this planning framework is that of a large city, and the situation one that features active opposition by at least one well-armed organization of significant organizational and communications capacity. How large a city and how powerful an opposing force are of course consequential questions. Cities considerably smaller than what are generally taken as megacities still present significant, unique military challenges.[3] The armed opposition imagined here does not include the committed military of a large country that might assign significant national resources to either taking or holding the city with regular formations. The imagined opposing force might nevertheless be able to move several thousand-armed fighters and employ a range of sophisticated weapons and surveillance systems to include those mounted on aerial drones. Regardless of the size and sophistication of the opposing force, the lines of effort for success in taking or holding a city can be placed in basically the same seven proposed categories. The reader is invited to assume that opposition entities (there likely being more than one) will not share with us the same scruples or social and political delimitations regarding how they will apply coercive violence. That is to say, as to any dissimilarity in the mixes of resources available to the contenders, moral asymmetry may be the most pronounced and consequential.

We can measure victory (our own or that of any of the competing entities) cartographically. The physical geographic space within which a contender can effectively punish its opponents, plus the geographic space in which a contender can remain impugn from that punishment (sanctuary) will constitute the definitive map.[4] If throughout the city one of the parties to the contest were able to apply concepts and processes of justice as it sees fit, and can simultaneously protect individuals it chooses to protect from punishment by others, that party is *eo ipso* the complete victor. Perhaps total control of the whole urban place never becomes a practicable goal for any contender. Nevertheless, if the cartographic extent (within which whole or partial impunity is achieved) exceeds an entity's goals, one can fairly argue that it succeeds exactly to that extent. As to an American force overseas, at least a partial victory reasonably could be claimed if the US force could be withdrawn without the balances of impunity changing unfavorably, that is, without there being a change in the boundaries of sanctuaries.

Not contemplated here as part of the definition of victory is the attainment of any particular conditions of material life such as electoral suffrage, infant mortality, showers taken, calories consumed or political legitimacy. While perhaps rightfully interested in the improvement of material wellbeing, or justified in pursuit of such progress for its own sake, material improvement may have insignificant if any measurable, timely influence on the outcome of an armed competition as to who dominates whom.[5] In some areas and to some degree, the conditions of human suffering and injustice (or, perhaps, how a populace sees how the parties addresses such conditions) can have a recognizable effect on relative competitive prospects. Sociocultural conditions are not to be ignored, but they are best understood as potential influences on, and not conflated with measures of military success. Impunity can be gained or lost almost irrespective of socioeconomic conditions.

We can assume that a conflict may end in some sort of settlement, the result perhaps of a formal negotiation. Such a settlement would be the price of real or perceived relative weakness, however. In other words, ignorant of the situational details, we cannot claim that any contending party would necessarily have enough strength to dominate totally. It probably will not. The degree to which party A might have to settle is a fair measure of the extent to which it did not win, since negotiated settlement would mean that its opponents enjoy some degree of impunity from A's coercion, or perhaps that they retain some capacity to impose punishment on A. Experiences indicate that some areas of a city may be hotly contested while other areas are fully controlled by one party or another, and these variously controlled locales may or may not be contiguous. Contestants may have to either take or hold according to a patchwork of urban sectors. There are likely to be more than two major contestant organizations, not simply a government versus an anti-government resistance or defiance. In addition, urban areas are intertwined with surrounding geographies we might prefer to categorize as suburban or rural or sea or hinterland.[6] With all the caveats in mind, however, seven lines of effort provide a reasonable starting template for planning.

They are as follows:

1. Maintain and improve advantage in anonymity
2. Maintain and improve advantage in competitive distances
3. Control the disruption of service flows
4. Control convocation spaces
5. Progressively reduce enemy sanctuary space
6. Pursue the *mens rea*
7. Punish the enemy
Measure the physical geography of all of the above
Ultimate goal: Dominate the granting of impunity

1. **Maintain and improve advantage in anonymity.**[7] Implement specific actions and programs whose immediate goal is to tip the balance of anonymity, that is, encourage and enable the reporting of information, especially regarding the whereabouts of elements of the enemy's armed members and leadership. These actions can include construction of reporting websites and phone numbers or designing offices wherein a citizen can report without being seen doing so by an agent of an opposing force. The side currently able to openly occupy space can more easily flood public places with closed circuit cameras, for instance, but some use of cameras will be available to the other side as well. Include here also a number of considerations for the preservation of secrets, such as polygraphing, background investigations, oaths and the like. Those implementing siege of urban territory or the take-over of buildings have less opportunity for actual, physical presence by which to instill a 'rule of silence.' For them, the creation of psychological presence is made more difficult, but hardly impossible.

2. **Maintain and improve advantage in competitive distances.**[8] One of the most significant lines of effort is the building of walls, doors and bridges.[9] This is best done in an overall urban plan that considers travel distances among police stations, public convocation sites, likely sites of opponent perpetrations and government enforcement initiatives. Conversely, for the siege, approach distances to service nodes, convocation areas, and other valuable terrain need to be prepared.[10] Especially this initiative needs to anticipate withdrawals or escapes. Tunnels are a classic siege preparation, but way-stations made from the offices of front organizations, or the coopting of transportation networks are now typical. In Bogota, the FARC had briefly converted the immense garbage disposal network into a back-alley taxi service.

3. **Control the disruption of service flows.**[11] As cities grow they tend to change in step fashion. That is, urban phenomena may appear fairly rapidly to bring the city to a new stage or status that has direct bearing on prospects in armed competition. For instance, a small city might overnight be home to a radio-controlled taxi network while a megalopolis might finally gain a third major airport, bringing a closer coordination of airspace control and all but sealing out some classes

of aircraft. Also, among the effects of scale may be a tendency toward single contract or single network consolidation of some services, for instance, sewage removal. As a service provision becomes monopolized or centrally regulated, it also acquires a vulnerability in that the geography of the reins of control may become centralized or present very specific nodes or constrictions. These need to be physically protected, as do the executives or key technicians who wield control. Because large cities often find economic advantage in consolidated service systems, the nodes and constrictions in these systems present geographically specific targets, targets that can not only be physically occupied, but the occupation of which can be defended for sufficient time to make power concessions appear economically and politically attractive.

4. **Control convocation spaces**.[12] Convocation (causing crowds to form) is hardly a new tactic, but social media has augmented their practicability. Rules of operational art still apply, however, to actions based on the massing of people, including protests, demonstrations, or marches. Regardless of the speed of instruction, coordination, and movement of such aggrupation, the characteristics of the spaces to which people can go to accumulate count for a great deal when it comes to how consequential or dangerous a crowd might be to the survival of an established governmental or economic structure. Some cities, because of ancient land use planning, have open areas that straddle important lines of communication or threaten significant economic nodes. If, on the other hand, a formation of large crowds can be diverted to open spaces that present little threat to principle transportation links or other pieces of economic terrain, the ability of resistance leadership to extort concessions from government is greatly reduced. For the government planner, in other words, it is smart to orchestrate the architectural, spatial relationship of constrictions and access points to open spaces such that, whatever the speed of social media, there is a lessoned potential for economic threat resulting from the fact of a crowd itself.

5. **Progressively reduce enemy sanctuary space**.[13] A sanctuary is that space within which a contestant cannot be punished by their opponent. Sanctuary may be attained through anonymity, legalities, moral and electoral risk, and physical distance. Sanctuary is in any case

a physical material place. One either enjoys a place wherein they are safe from the punishments that their foes can be impose upon them, or they are not. As such, the sanctuary space can be mapped, and while the cartographic delineations of sanctuary space will be hypothetical, it is that hypothesis exactly that can guide the application of competitive resources in order to shrink the sanctuary space of one's competitors and to increase one's own. In addition, every attempt should be made to map the likely routes to and from sanctuary spaces.

6. **Physically pursue of the *mens rea*.**[14] The challenge posed here is more than just a 'small fries' versus 'big fish' distinction. The locus of dangerous intent is the human mind, and while it may profit us to work intellectually against those ideas and messages that we find in some way dangerous, sending our opponents a stark physical message can be ultimately influential. To the extent it is apparent to our opponents that we can and will bring dire physical consequences upon those who lead others to act in ways we cannot abide, our goal of holding or taking the city will be more economically achieved. A competitor is most likely to be effective who can mount constant, physical pursuit of the human initiative of what aggravates him. It is leaders' corporeal impunity from punishments (and in turn the impunity they can grant to others) that must be challenged and dismantled. If there exists a single imperative for any durable victory, it is that we definitively disprove any suggestion that our opponent can bestow physical impunity to his followers. If the good guys are not capable of physically pursuing the bad guys within whom resides the *mens rea*, it is unlikely that the good guys are making progress in the direction of durable victory.

7. **Punish the enemy.**[15] This to an extent is a repetition of line of effort 6 above. Pursuit of the *mens rea* is valuable in itself in that a vigorous pursuit keeps the opponent off balance, makes it difficult for him to take initiative, and whittles at his moral. However, the act of pursuit is not a goal. Punishment alone is proof of the absence of impunity. The punishments might include no more than the stripping of wealth or of public authority, but to be absolutely effective the punishment of the *mens rea* probably has to be corporeal, that is, confinement or death. The operant psychology is one of visibly extending punishments to the

enemies' *mens rea*. This may mean capturing or sniping leaders. To the extent it becomes clear that 'we' have a monopoly of punishment over 'them', that is, we can punish them, but they cannot punish us, we win and can negotiate from strength in view to the future. If on the other hand, they can close our sanctuary space, that is, they can occupy and use the mayor's office, the court building or the police station, etc., or they can kidnap our daughters at the school or theatre, then we are well along the way toward losing. Ultimately, for winning (that is, controlling territory, that is, effective/efficient/sufficient influence, that is, controlling impunity, that is, 'we dominate them'), we must be capable of punishing them and they not capable of punishing us.

How to Organize the Study of a Big City to Support the Seven Lines of Effort

This section proffers a separate list, suitable for research or intelligence, of phenomena on which to focus in order to make an explanatory description of a large urban area. I propose twelve research categories. All are relevant to resourcing and implementing the seven lines of effort, although some of the twelve more clearly allude to a specific line of effort:

1. Constriction points in the lines of supply into the city (water, power, food, and telecommunications)

    a. Practical distance to and from ('practical' meaning cost or friction distances from a party's start points or bases, i.e., time, fuel, money etc.)

    b. What organizations control
        — Headquarters locations
        — Practical distance to and from

2. Constriction points in the lines of waste in and going out of the city (garbage, sewage, hazmat, death and medical)

   a. Practical distances to and from
   b. What organizations control
      — Headquarters locations
      — Practical distance to and from

3. Key control points for city services within city (vulnerable nodes) (transportation, convocation, comfort)

   a. Practical distances to and from
   b. What organizations control
      — Headquarters locations
      — Practical distance to and from

4. Most commercially valuable terrain (banks, by the way, are valuable. That's where the money is)

   a. Practical distances to and from
   b. What organizations control
      — Headquarters locations
      — Practical distance to and from

5. Key events times, locations, movement and normal participations (both recurring and special events)

   a. Practical distances to and from
   b. What organizations control
      — Headquarters locations
      — Practical distance to and from

6. Key recreation (especially sinful recreation) locations, times, normal participations (for a party's own members as well as for opponents', but especially for opponent parties' leadership)

   a. Practical distances to and from
   b. What organizations control
      — Headquarters locations

— Practical distance to and from

7. Collective identities of note (political, ethnic, gang affiliation, etc.)

a. Physical locus, scale and range
b. Representation (agents, especially exclusive agents)
 — Physical locus, extent, density and movements
 — Means of wielding influence
 — Capacities for physical coercion

8. Exclusive agents (those who set themselves up as representatives of others and are jealous of that representation—like lawyers, politicians, union bosses, priests, etc.)[16]

a. Physical locus and movements
 — Practical distance to and from
b. Means of influence
c. Instruments of physical coercion
d. Available resources
e. Known vulnerabilities and locations in time
 — What they love
 — Practical distance to and from
f. Level of will (ruthlessness, courage, etc.)
g. What nodes, constrictions, and key locations they control or occupy; which they do not control but are attempting to control, and which should they logically want to control.

9. Grievances of note

a. Associations of grievances with namable collective identities
b. Representation, especially exclusive representation of the grievance Resolution possibilities and physical locus and range of resolution mechanism (i.e. jurisdictions)

10. Symbols of note (flags, songs, historical and literary figures, etc.)

    a. Physical locations where found, density or duration of occurrence
    b. Depth and extension of awareness and affectation regarding symbols
    c. Psychological, affective and political correlations

11. Known relevant attitudes (regarding us, allies, enemies, etc.)

    a. Location, density, intensity, range, durability
    b. Reflections in symbols, events, communications

All of the categories are inter-related and if for some reason facts asserted within a category do not reconcile with those of others, then something is amiss which requires a disclaimer, reconsideration of the assertions and probably more field research. A competitive objective, for instance, would be to control nodes physically—the other factors (like knowing who exactly controls those nodes, the sources of their power to do so, and especially their physical vulnerabilities, feeds into possibilities of physically changing control the node, or alternatively, to protect the status quo.

Once nodes, etc. are identified along with their respective 'ownership', we can begin to measure how much strength it would take for other competitors to hold or to take, and to remain. If we correctly identify the nodes, constrictions and most valuable terrain, then the next step would be to understand the cost and risk distances in getting to those places and staying there. How far is each in practical terms, what resistance could be generated against getting to and staying in each place, as well as the likely useable routes of escape and withdrawal from attempts to take or hold the key locations—all this is subject to geographic study.

What may seem as an emphasis on physical locations and their control is not a dismissal of the psychological or sociological elements (perhaps the 'subjective' dimensions and options), but it is intended to seek relative efficiency and appropriateness in the short-term use of coercive force.[17]

The views expressed in this article are those of the author and do not necessarily represent the official policy or position of the Department of the Army, Department of Defense, or the U.S. government.

Notes

[1]　Meaning the range of armed coercive force available to a city's government along with the forces in play from any of the higher administrative levels to which a city might belong (department, nation, region, coalition, etc.). Units might include police military paramilitary militia, intelligence etc.

[2]　See, regarding urban operations in Iraq see, Chris Bowers, "Future Megacity Operations—Lessons from Sadr City." *Military Review*, May-June, 2015.

[3]　See, on this point, Michael Evans, "The Case against Megacities: The Megacity Myth," *The United States Army War College Quarterly, Parameters*, Vol 45 No 1 Spring 2015, pp. 33-43.

[4]　The idea of the use of the control of impunity as a proxy for victory is adapted from Geoffrey Demarest. *Winning Irregular War: Conflict Geography*. Ft. Leavenworth, Kansas: Foreign Military Studies Office (FMSO), 2015, http://fmso.leavenworth.army.mil/documents/Winning-Insurgent-War/WIrW_2015.pdf.

[5]　For expansion on this point see, "Section 39, Socioeconomic Causation," ibid. pp. 155-158.

[6]　To expand on this theme see, "Section 34, Urban or Rural," ibid. pp. 133-136.

[7]　To expand on this theme see, "Section 2, Anonymity," ibid. pp. 4-5.

[8]　To expand on this theme see, "Section 64, Measuring Distance and Comparing Power," ibid. pp. 262-66; "Section 32, Land-use Planning," ibid. pp. 126-129.

[9]   See, on this point, "Section 32, Heavy Machines," ibid. pp. 119-120.

[10] To expand on this theme see, "Section 33, Engineers and the Built Environment," ibid. pp. 130-132.

[11] To expand on this theme see, "Section 91, Forts and Walls," ibid. pp. 366-370; "Section 94, Poop," pp. 379-380; "Section 63, Roadblocks and Checkpoints," pp. 258-261.

[12] To expand on this theme see, "Section 27, 'Nonviolent' Action," ibid. pp. 110-115.

[13] To expand on this theme see, "Section 7, Sanctuary," ibid. pp. 22-27; "Section 23, Mens Rea," pp. 96-98.

[14] To expand on this theme see, "Section 23, Mens Rea," ibid. pp. 96-98; "Section 10, Decisive Battle," ibid. pp. 36-39.

[15] For more on this theme see, "Section 1, Impunity," ibid. pp. 1-3.

[16] For more on the theme of exclusive agency see the index entry of that term in *Winning Irregular War*, ibid.

[17] Pardon a bit of atmospherics, but the terms 'long-term effect' and 'short-term effect' are themselves relative, and it might be vanity to claim long-term goals are fundamentally better than short-term goals, or that 'long-term' is, without specific context, a more strategic notion than 'short term'.

Chapter 27

U.S. Army Mega City Operations: Enduring Principles and Innovative Technologies

Frank Prautzsch

First Published 22 February 2016

"…and the worst policy of all is to besiege walled cities. The rule is, not to besiege walled cities if it can possibly be avoided. The preparation of mantlets, movable shelters, and various implements of war, will take up three whole months; and the piling up of mounds over against the walls will take three months more.

The general, unable to control his irritation, will launch his men to the assault like swarming ants, with the result that one-third of his men are slain, while the town still remains untaken. Such are the disastrous effects of a siege. Therefore, the skillful leader subdues the enemy's troops without any fighting; he captures their cities without laying siege to them; he overthrows their kingdom without lengthy operations in the field."

—Sun Tsu, *The Art of War*, 500 B.C.

Introduction

By 2050, urbanization will arguably be the most consequential event in the history of mankind. Out of every 100 children born at that time, 57 will be Asian, and 22 will be African. The majority of those new babies will live in cities. Over the last two decades, developing nations have added 3 million new people per week. This is the equivalent of adding the city of Seattle to the planet *daily*. Starting in 2018 the world's global rural population will peak at 3.5 billion and then proceed to fall by almost a billion new migratory city citizens.[1]

In conjunction with a massive demographic shift to urbanization, there are also shifts in wealth and in aging. The developed world is losing its edge over developing nations in wealth, while Central and South America bear the brunt of a radically aging population.[2]

For the U.S. Army to conduct future missions, Sun Tsu's principles may be more fitting than ever. While U.S. Army may not always lay siege to a city, the preparation for any military urban operation is not a short-term event, nor is the planning ad hoc. The spectrum of operations spanning non-combat and combat missions in the face of natural or adversarial threats, makes this preparation a multi-dimensional problem requiring significant attention and forethought. As we proceed to investigate and plan for Mega City operations there are a few key points that must be made:

> Mission success is contingent upon the will of the population, as well as the coalitions, governments, religions and tribes in occupancy not purely the strategy, tactics and planning of the U.S. Army.

The U.S. Army cannot "fight its last war". Lessons learned from battles such as Fallujah, Aleppo, or throughout densely populated Palestine don't scale well, and are miniscule in size and scope compared to a Mega City battle.

Mega City warfare is a highly 3-dimensional event. Unlike rural warfare with focus upon capturing mountaintops, resources, and roads, urban key terrain belongs to the defender and suggests skyscrapers, bridges, tunnels, subway systems, energy and water distribution, telecommunications, airports and rail stations are the discriminators.

Mega Cities with a subterranean network, capable of threat transit (subway, water drainage, sewage) will offer a compounded advantage to a defender or asymmetric threat. Most subterranean geospatial data is a non-integrated stack of reference materials, maps, and overlays. Often these references don't exist or are completely unreferenced or surveyed resulting in C2 and situational awareness failures.

The U.S. Army must understand that technologies that would be used for missions in 2040 Mega Cities don't exist yet. However, those technologies that do exist, may point towards needed future technical capabilities in some form or function.

The U.S. Army must assume that if specific technologies exist for supporting future operations, that an adversary may also have access to a derivative of such technology.

The value of C4ISR, mobile networks and unmanned/autonomous systems are exponentially more significant than today. With this comes an implied task to have spectrum supremacy or the above capabilities are useless.

The resources of the U.S. Army may be called upon in more non-combat missions to protect or sustain life. (Power generation, water purification, water pumping, health care, engineer support, air drops, evacuations, psychological operations, sanitation, graves operations)

A determined adversary or a disgruntled population has time and mass on their side.

Logistics and energy rule. The "Achilles Heel" for a Mega City involves the lines of communication for power, water and food supplies.

Emerging, Enduring, and Endearing Technologies

The U.S. Army should carefully evaluate, mature and mutate selected commercial technologies that aid Mega City operations. Each of these technologies exists or is emerging today and has some value in further research:

Broadband over power lines (BPL): Simply stated one key asset that most Mega Cities have is a reasonably well-defined power grid. Today BPL technologies allow for networked and point-to-point transmission of 200-500 Mbps over simple modems and integrated network control capabilities. This is significant to spectrum supremacy, covert operations, remote sensing, and C2. Most wireless phone antennas are horizontally polarized and start to lose service at altitude above about 600 feet. Thus, communications in the highest floors of a skyscraper can be complicated by a lack of wireless quality of service which can be somewhat offset by BPL. Many BPL and Network Control capabilities can also interface on ad hoc with fiber, terrestrial and satcom systems at some designated nodes.

Tethered and Untethered C4ISR Sensors: In a Mega City environment the need for persistent surveillance is paramount. While UAVs are vogue in 2016, the need for small positive buoyant gas envelops with sensors and visualization for hours-days is of necessity. Numerous systems exist today that are controlled or on tether. Additionally, controlled small airships afford the ability to conduct sustained observation of a target or area of interest, and also perform such functions as bottom side bridge inspection or bomb sniffing.

Manned, Unmanned and Autonomous Systems: Such capabilities are not limited to urban airspace, but also littoral and harbor areas with USVs, streets, tunnels and high-risk areas with UGVs, and undersea operations along coastal and harbor areas with UUVs. New systems such as VTOL jetpacks, manned quad copters and air mules need to be considered for rapid equipment and team displacement, remote sensor placement, security and vantage of urban high ground, sniper and counter sniper operations, incident response, combat evacuation, and search and rescue.

Subterranean Vehicles: More research is in order at developing capabilities that can allow the US Army to more effectively use rail and subway systems within a Mega City. This could include a rail gauge-scalable light armor assault and recovery vehicle that is both road and rail capable for supporting a squad infiltration or an evacuation/ recovery of critical area when/if mass transit fails. (e.g. towing a metro rail train without power during a mass casualty evacuation)

Internet of Things: If there was ever a consideration that plays heavily into remote sensing, security, and situational awareness in a future Megacity, it will be the Internet of Things. Retail wireless companies already have the option of purchasing 15 thousand edge sensor devices smaller than a credit card, and an integrated router system that can aggregate all the devices, (one and 2-way), and wireless connectivity at up to 2.5 miles in unlicensed spectrum. Such COTS capabilities are both an enabler and a threat as they are not ITAR and can be implemented across a Mega City in hours.

Tunnel and Bridge Emergency Management: By far the biggest choke points and symbolic targets for a Mega City relates to bridges, tunnels and ferryboat operations. Inflatable plugs and barriers exist for sealing tunnels both to fire and to catastrophic breaches in their outer walls. While the Army has a longstanding history and portfolio of expeditionary bridging capabilities, the expertise and experience for tunnel operations, advanced bridge security, and the security of ferryboat operations is perhaps an important future competency needed. In addition, most bridges and tunnels are conduits to Mega Cities for power, telecommunications, and in some cases, gas and water lines. Robotic and sensor integrity and inspection systems are essential. Failure to control and secure bridges and tunnels make any Mega City operation impossible.

Non-Lethal Weapons: Many missions in Mega Cities will likely have the potential of migrating from a peaceful and organized event, to a limited engagement and disorganized chaotic event. Intermediate capabilities to control crowds and incapacitate via non-lethal means can retain the will of the people with the U.S. Army whereas casualties, however justified, could instigate disastrous consequences. While the Marine Corps continues to research future joint non-lethal weapons, much more must be done in non-lethal weapons research, breaching and riot systems, IT and PNT denial, micro-area cyber operations, localized

Marx generation to incapacitate electronics, and non-lethal weapons for incapacitating insurgents or riotous masses.

Disease, WMD and CBRNE Detection: Mega Cities are both an incubator and a target for the worst of all scenarios. Greater sensor and detection systems and field response systems are now emerging in the scientific and consumer market. Such systems allow for field optical stereoscopy and spectroscopy for characterization of substances, DNA sequence analysis and Chemical-Biological Pathogen detection and field vitals and triage in handheld or small portable devices.

Augmented Reality, Night Vision and Situational Understanding: Electronics now exist that introduce affordable augmented reality in high resolution for the war fighter. These systems will mature dramatically in form factor, and content over the next two decades. It is safe to say that some form of augmented reality eyewear or headwear will be normal attire for the war fighter in Mega City operations. Current technologies in EO/IR have taken away the "ownership of the night" from the U.S. Army. Night vision modules that attach to intelligent phones cost less than most of the phones. Innovation in graphene points to phase shift single molecular layer carbons that will ultimately introduce a night contact lens. Of greater importance than the greatness of gadgetry, is the need for integrated understanding of intelligence and sensor feeds. It will not be adequate to have situational awareness but understanding. The motives, patterns, behaviors, and predicted next steps of a threat will be the "new normal" for missions. In a Mega City, future commanders won't decide courses of action without understanding the motives and intent of the adversary.

Illumination: Technology now exists to provide high lumen lighting in an area the size of a football field in a hand-carry device. LEDs give us a distinct advantage in crisis lighting for subterranean, catastrophic point-of-event, and emergency services operations. Such systems are now DC powered and operate with up to 400w/45000 lumens in hand carry form factor. Such a capability would also be practical for integration on selected autonomous or unmanned systems and selected urban terrain vantage points.

Through-obstacle Detection and Characterization: Current systems exist that can detect life under up to 27 feet of rubble by measuring the displacement of the lungs and processing respiratory level and pulse rates. While such ultra-wideband systems are a mercy tool for earthquakes, explosions, and bombings it can also be an important tool in determining threats behind closed doors or walls. Additionally, such a system can identify elevated heart and respiratory rates in a crowd, acting as a physiological marker to a potential threat. In 2016, mobile technology to monitor though-walls is smaller than a breadbox. For free space monitoring of heart and respiratory rates the entire module is the size of a small paperback book.

3D/4D Geospatial Referencing: By 2050, most all image sciences will be 3D and also include a fourth dimension of time. Current systems in LIDAR, light field camera techniques, 2/3D ortho-recification against point clouds, and structure internal GIS mapping and referencing will be the norm for navigation and negotiation of Mega City movements and coordination. This will also include 3D synthetic geospatial night vision mosaics. 3 and 4D systems will not only aid the war fighter in understanding context, but also vertical, subterranean, and hidden threats. In addition, the geospatial data will be essential to autonomous systems operation.

Weather and Micro-weather: Weather is not limited to trafficability and complications to operations in rural areas. Mega City operations in adverse weather introduce unexpected threats, opportunities and consequences. Systems exist now to introduce micro-weather prediction by analyzing weather formations and road conditions from traffic cameras. One system today has an aggregate capacity of over 165K cameras that provide integrated hyper local weather and environmental intelligence.

Specialty Vehicles: Consideration should be given to vehicles that can operate in more than one domain. Platforms exist today that can cover transitions between land and water, air and sea, surface and subsurface and air and land. These systems are essential in Mega City operations for mission agility, selected concepts of operation, surprise, and range extension.

Communications: By 2050, the world will have embraced 5 and 6 G wireless services and ad-hoc networks between mobile platforms and users will involve transmissions from 5 Gbps-1 Terabyte/second. 5G starts fielding in 2020 and should move to consumer acceptance by 2025. Laser high fidelity communications are currently under demonstration and testing. LI-FI will soon supplement or replace selected WI-FI applications in urban areas. Since LI-FI does not consume RF spectrum and operates at significantly higher data rates, it will gain acceptance for selected network applications. Basic 5G speeds will exceed 4G LTE service by a factor of 65000. 4D Virtual reality, instantaneous downloads, mission rehearsals, and multi-intelligence, multi-language machine learning systems will be commonplace. With communications and networks our ability to rationalize the future is most difficult and we have successfully written requirements for capabilities that have been surpassed by technology time and time again. Additionally, old technologies in acoustics and older spectrum such as HF may have a calling for mission specific support, operations during RF spectrum denial, or surprise.

Gunshot and Explosive Detection and Characterization: Force protection will always be an issue with Mega Cities. While the need for new and protective forms of armor and TALOS-like exoskeletal capabilities are needed, the ability to deal with snipers and improvised explosives, and trigger systems can only expand exponentially in a gigantic population center. The ability to disguise and surprise with asymmetry, calls for improved acoustic geolocation, predictive crime models, and new sensors such as graphene trough sensors or piezo-electric cantilever sensors that can detect explosive particle residue at range.

Armor and Blast: While the metallurgical and ceramic armor communities continue to develop plating solutions, new inventions in flexible body armor from spider silk, tight woven hemp, advanced plastics, Kevlar, and graphene are redefining ballistic protection that is flexible and agile, while still maintaining the performance of plating techniques. The use of syntactic foams with tailored density resins and tailored size micro-balloon glass particles introduces unique blast protection features as the foam distributes energy radially and radically from the highest point of an acoustic wave impact and distributes that blast energy in effective nullification. Such a capability offers progressive and aggressive force blast protection by introducing such capabilities in the platforms, building processes, and troop protection. Advanced electro spray techniques allow for the development of active armor that has different molecular composition at different levels in the armor. Such armor changes the Vickers Index properties of the materials from which it is made (e.g. aluminum armor) and allows for boutique armor capabilities against different threats using heat or shaped charges, higher grade explosives, or high velocity projectiles from the blast effect.

A New "MacGuyver" Squad [3]: For each prevailing Mega City, a subject matter expert cadre should be passively maintained, that are versed *in that Mega City*, have lived in that Mega City, or have insight on capabilities involving its government and its infrastructure. Such a Squad must be able to facilitate host nation and Mega City support, telecommunications, emergency shelter, fuel, energy, water, and how to operate critical infrastructure, such as transportation, with or without city employees. This should include HUMINT and several insights on technical, religious, and political intelligence about that Mega City. This squad should be "doers" that can improvise anything, and not be totally contract/transactional support.

Conclusion

Mission support within Mega Cities, across the continuum, on an objective timeline, 24-years away, requires vision, invention, innovation, technical ingenuity, commercial off-the-shelf solutions, host nation support, and legacy systems integration. The technology vectors professed in this paper are critical future Mega City missions. They will emerge with or without U.S. Army involvement, since in various forms, each of these technologies *already exists in 2016*. It is our charge to challenge the "Art of the Possible", not await or monitor it. The U.S. Army cannot simply study or analyze Mega City warfare.

Failure to prepare for statistically inevitable Mega City peaceful or violent missions is beyond foolhardy. Unlike Sun Tsu's warnings about impatient generals that will not tolerate 6 months of preparation to besiege a city, the U.S. Army may not have such luxury of time.

Notes

[1]   Laurence C. Smith, *New North: The World in 2050*, (London: Dutton Publishing/Penguin Group, 2010.

[2]   Ibid.

[3]   Richard Dean Anderson, MacGuyver. TV Series, ABC TV, Hollywood, CA and Vancouver Canada, 1985-1992.

Chapter 28

Megacities and Dense Urban Environments: Obstacle or Opportunity?

Dawn A. Morrison and Colin D. Wood

First Published 23 February 2016

Introduction

The United Nations (UN) projects that by 2030 there will be more than 41 megacities, with the majority of them located in Africa and Asia. These 41 cities alone will house approximately 9% of the world's population, as rural life declines.[1] Approximately 54% of the world's people are now urban residents, with 66% expected to be urban by 2050.[2] More alarming, the number of people worldwide living in urban slums has increased by 33% since 1990.[3] As rural to urban migration continues to increase, experts expect more frequent requirements for the U.S. military to be involved in responding to conflicts and disasters in densely populated urban environments. As more of the world population resides in littoral cities, natural disasters such as hurricanes, floods, health epidemics, and resource scarcity could pose significant challenges for military intervention. "While the U.S. military continues to protect U.S. national security interests across the globe, it must focus on protecting those interests where they are in most jeopardy. The greatest potential threats to those interests lie in Asia and the Middle East, and the U.S. Army's role extends to both."[4] Of the 41 projected megacities, 25 are located in the Asia-Pacific and Middle East regions. Doctrine further recognizes the potential for urban areas to become redoubts for enemy forces and acknowledges that "joint operations will require land forces capable of operating in congested and restricted urban terrain,"[5] thus indicating U.S. doctrinal intent to operate within megacities and dense urban environments. In short, megacities and dense urban environments are firmly on the horizon as likely and potential environments for future warfare and humanitarian engagements. Are we prepared?

Current military thinking tends to present the megacity and dense urban environment as challenging, intimidating, and as a source of anxiety for military commanders who contemplate its operational environment. While megacities and dense urban environments *are* challenging and complex, we argue that the unique characteristics of these environments offer many opportunities and leveraging points that future U.S. military forces can use to their advantage to conduct successful military operations. The first step toward this new paradigm requires a solid method for understanding the operational environment of megacities and dense urban areas. We believe this can be done by operationalizing the megacity framework proposed by the Chief of Staff of the Army's Strategic Studies Group.[6] Not only does this framework allow megacities and dense urban environments to be understood as a system of systems akin to a living organism, it also categorizes the level of integration between the systems. Operationalizing this framework was accomplished in Morrison et.al. (2016).[7] Here we discuss how the resulting composite index (Table 1) that was generated may be helpful in understanding the operational environment of different megacities, including the challenges of operating in these environments. By examining these challenges, however, we discovered that the framework allowed us to re-conceptualize the megacity *not* solely as an impossible military challenge, but rather as a place of potential opportunity offering several leverage points advantageous to future forces if new technology, tactics, techniques, and procedures can be adopted. This paper presents a brief overview of the operationalized megacity framework and demonstrates how it may be used to better understand the future operational environment. We consider the challenges presented to the military by the megacity and dense urban environment under current military thinking. Lastly, we explore several ways in which the military might meet and overcome these challenges by leveraging the megacity environment to its advantage and capitalizing on the opportunities afforded by the complex environment.

Defining the Area of Regard (Megacity and Dense Urban Environments)

The megacity concept has a common operating definition: an urban or metropolitan area with a population of 10 million people or more.[8] Less well-defined is the concept of dense urban environments. There is currently no standardized, metric-based definition for what constitutes a dense urban environment or for determining the point at which an area switches from urban to dense urban. The U.S. Census Bureau defines the minimum threshold to be considered urban as an area with 50,000 or more people with a minimum threshold of 1000 people per square mile, but does not define anything beyond the dichotomy of urban/rural.[9] The fields of urban planning and urban design often factor in floor area ratio (FAR) and dwelling units per area (DU/Area) along with population density, and then examine the persistence of these metrics over scale, ranging from block or developmental parcel upwards to neighborhood, then district to city or region.[10] Using these metrics, we can begin to understand dense urban environments as places where either all three metrics—FAR, DU/Area and Population—are high (e.g., high rise districts of Tokyo, London or New York), or where DU/Area and Population remain high while FAR decreases (e.g., favelas of Rio de Janeiro or the slums of Dhaka). Employing a combination of these metrics may help provide a more accurate determination of urban density as they normalize population by infrastructure capacity, thereby allowing us to better identify and measure dense urban environments for the purposes of planning and execution of military operations. These metrics enable planners to understand the spatial distribution of the density and whether it is stacked vertically (high FAR, DU/AREA and Population) or concentrated at ground level (low FAR, high DU/ Area and Population).

SSG Megacity Framework

To better understand megacities and dense urban environments, we implemented the megacity framework presented by the SSG.[11] The SSG megacity framework is based on five characteristics—Context, Scale, Density, Connectedness and Flow—which are used to determine the level of integrated systems—Highly Integrated, Moderately Integrated and Loosely Integrated—found in each megacity. Integration, in turn, is based on the level of formal versus informal systems, the quality of infrastructure, and how regulated is the flow capacity of goods, resources, people, and information. Morrison et. al. (2016) operationalized the SSG megacity framework by compiling a composite index for each of the U.N.'s projected 41 megacities (Table 1) based on an extensive data matrix assembled from open sources. Metrics collected in the data matrix were selected to cover the five characteristics above, and then cross-walked to address the integration areas of system types, infrastructure quality and regulated flow capacity. For example, data was collected on such topics as governance, rule of law, stability, quality of life, politics, airports, seaports, railroads, roads, economic growth and performance, communication, demographics and other associated human geography variables.[12] Much of the data used to compile the index is drawn from regularly updated metrics so that the operationalized framework has the ability to remain current over time. We believe this index adequately represents the level of integrated systems for each megacity and allows opportunity to better understand both the positives and negatives of the megacity and dense urban environment in terms of military operations and how they will vary depending on the level of integration; for example, responding to a natural or man-made disaster in a highly versus loosely integrated megacity.

Morrison et al (2016) further connected the operationalized megacity framework to data compiled from the Global Conflict Risk Index (GCRI) and NASA's Socioeconomic Data and Applications Center (SEDAC) to assess the level of risk associated with conflict and environmental hazards for each projected megacity.[13] They found that according to the GCRI, more than 70% of the projected megacities are situated in countries with a high probability for conflict in the near future. Similarly, over half of the projected megacities are at risk for environmental hazards (e.g., drought, flood, cyclone, landslide, and earthquake), including both highly integrated cities such as Tokyo and Los Angeles, as well as moderately and loosely integrated cities such as Kolkata, Bogotá, Lahore and Manila. These findings support the June 2014 SSG report which posited that instability and environmental stressors are likely to be what leads to U.S. military intervention in a megacity. Since 1980, the U.S. military has responded to a wide variety of threats and operations impacting national security, but the majority of these operations have consisted of humanitarian assistance/disaster relief (HADR) operations, both CONUS and OCONUS, rather than major combat operations.[14] With climate change and sea-level rise, we should expect to see drastic change in many of the world's littoral areas in the coming decades, and a U.S. response to follow.

Given this, the U.S. military needs to consider and be prepared for how the type of megacity (i.e., loosely, moderately or highly integrated) presents varying orders of magnitude to the complexity of operations. Conducting any type of operation in a highly integrated city such as Tokyo, London or Paris, even with host nation cooperation, will still be challenging, but those challenges may differ significantly from conducting similar operations in a loosely integrated megacity such as Dhaka, Lahore or Lagos. The operationalized megacity framework, by looking at and evaluating the level of interconnected systems within, throughout and between megacities, characterizes the dense urban environment in the narrative of a living organism. As with all living organisms, megacities and dense urban environments have strengths, weakness, and leverage points that can be identified by understanding the level of formal versus informal systems, the quality of infrastructure, and the regulation of the flow capacity of goods, resources, people and information.[15] These circumstances, while perhaps challenging to conventional military wisdom, may actually present spaces of opportunity for military advantage from a different perspective.

Framework Applied: Regulated Flow Capacity

The operationalized framework is useful for understanding the military operational environment of megacities and dense urban environments; knowing whether a place is highly or loosely integrated will significantly impact how the U.S. approaches a mission, as well as the expected consequences of various military activities. If military action affects the flow of a city (e.g., cordoning off the city or parts thereof, blocking access points, etc.), the effects could be tremendous. Depending on the market importance of the city, world economies could quickly experience adverse effects. Looking at various global indices[16] that assess urban areas based on their business activity, economic status, culture, politics, information exchange, human capital, productivity, infrastructure, environment and quality of life metrics, we find that the highly integrated megacities (e.g., Tokyo, New York, Paris, London) tend to be ranked near the top of each list, as expected. However, we also see cities such as Istanbul, Turkey; Chengdu and Shanghai, China; Delhi, Mumbai and Kolkata, India; Jakarta, Indonesia; Buenos Aires, Argentina; and Sao Paolo, Brazil ranking relatively high on these lists due to their economic importance, even though their systems are moderately or loosely integrated.[17] These indices also reflect the level of difficulty that would be involved with attempting to isolate any of these cities, or subparts therein, and the potential cascading impact on the world's economy that could result. Indeed, even the most loosely integrated megacities (e.g., Lahore, Karachi, Dhaka, Ahmadabad, Dar es Salaam), play significant roles in the world economy such that isolating them will have ramifications in places far flung. For example, Dhaka has a $19 billion/year garment industry which makes up 77% of its total merchandise export economy, and is second only to China in the world ready-made garment economy; cordoning off any part of Dhaka, and disrupting the garment industry would have rippling effects far beyond Bangladesh's borders.[18]

Framework Applied: Infrastructure Quality

Quality of infrastructure within a megacity and dense urban environment is also critical to understanding the operational environment and the effects and consequences of military action therein. For example, mobility in a megacity and dense urban environment will be greatly affected by the integration level of the city. Troop movement is dependent upon both built and human environments—the densities of people and structures in a megacity can be such that movement is slowed, sometimes to a standstill, as roads become impassable. This, in turn, impacts security: soldiers attempting to reach their objective may be forced to dismount from vehicles to cordon and search an area while they wait for a clearing, or sit in their stationary vehicles which quickly become targets for small arms, rocket, and IED attacks. Intratheater airborne operations may also be hindered due to the lack of appropriate ground-based landing zones (LZs), with skyscrapers and shanty structures providing additional obstacles that further complicate maneuverability.[19] Likewise, Medical evacuations (MEDVAC) may be significantly challenged in a megacity due to time and distance constraints imposed by quality and/or density of infrastructure and traffic congestion. There are certain time-frames within which casualties need to make it to a higher echelon of care (such as the "Golden Hour" and the "Platinum Ten")[20] to have a greater chance of surviving their injuries. While not hard and fast rules, such time-frames are essential to improving mortality rates in battle. A more highly integrated megacity may have better infrastructure than a more loosely integrated city to accommodate mounted movement, but population density often causes extensive travel delays and choking traffic. According to the TomTom Worldwide Traffic Index,[21] Istanbul, Mexico City, Rio de Janeiro and Moscow are the top 4 cities with the worst traffic, and 11 of the top 20 most congested cities in the world are on our list of megacities.

Intertheater maneuverability—with its reliance on commercial and military air and seaports—may also be challenged by the megacity and dense urban environment.[22] While all of the projected megacities have major commercial airports, accessing those airports will not always be straightforward, whether due to disrepair, or the inability to accommodate the weight and size of U.S. military aircraft. The placement of the airport within the urban environment and security issues related to landing within a dense urban environment immediately surrounded by potential enemy forces are cause for additional concern. For example, in September 2014, India's federal government asked Mumbai officials to clear the slums surrounding the Chhatrapati Shivaji International Airport due to increased concerns over terrorist attacks against airports in the region. The effort will involve removing 90,000 people—the population of a mid-sized American city—from roughly 309 acres of land.[23] Even in highly integrated megacities, the use of airports may be restricted to U.S. military forces due to congestion by commercial and industrial ventures that, if disrupted, could have consequences far flung beyond the area of operations. Port access is even further restricted than airports: 10 of the countries containing the projected megacities have port facilities with infrastructure quality rated at average or above, and only 16 of the cities have a major port, the rest either being landlocked or without access to a major body of water to support port facilities.[24]

Framework Applied: Systems

Human settlements, regardless of density or size, exist as a system of systems. How integrated and functional these systems are largely determining the success and livability of the settlement. As such, the operationalized megacity framework is useful in assessing the integrated system quality of each megacity and dense urban environment for purposes of projecting the effects of military operations in that environment. The need for positioning U.S. forces in such an environment is one clear example of the importance of understanding the impact of military operations on urban systems. Positioning U.S. forces often requires enough land to house personnel, materiel, and necessary facilities. General base camp land use planning factors for a Heavy Brigade Combat Team-sized element, for example, call for between 1,780 and 2,185 total acres in order to meet requirements.[25] In practice, contingency bases are often larger than this, such as Camp Diamondback in Mosul, Iraq, which was roughly 2,200 to 2,300 acres.[26] Finding that amount of space in a megacity or dense urban environment may be difficult, though, with the availability of airports and other urban industrial areas, not impossible. Still, population displacement will always be an issue under current military convention. Dhaka provides an excellent example of the tradeoffs that will need to be made if following doctrine for positioning U.S. troops. Areas that provide the requisite space may come at a cost to security, access to adequate utilities or expose deployed soldiers to environmental hazards and will likely require significant displacement of the local population, in some cases upwards of a quarter million people just to make room for a contingency base equivalent to the size of Camp Diamond Back in Iraq. It is important to note, however, that loosely integrated cities may have poorly designed and inadequate infrastructure to support contingency basing in these environments. Moreover, U.S. use of host nation space and infrastructure will tax already limited resources, potentially destabilizing both social and physical infrastructure beyond the scope of operations.

Megacity and Dense Urban Environments: Moving on Up!

Are megacity and dense urban environments challenging, complex operating spaces? Absolutely! As the above demonstrates, current military operating procedures and perspective may not be adequate to overcome these challenges. However, these environments also offer significant opportunity for military advantage and overmatch if we are willing to think outside of the box and look at the area of regard from a different angle. While the problems and obstacles associated with the megacity and dense urban environment are numerous and myriad, they create opportunities for the military to engage through adaptive technologies and methodologies. We believe the most fertile areas for creating military overmatch in these environments will be in exploiting the vertical space, leveraging the natural flows and patterns of life of the population and through technological advancement tailored to the specific challenges of a dense urban environment.

Rather than focus on the density of buildings, infrastructure, and people that may choke out traditional military tactics at the ground level, megacity and dense urban environments offer a manmade high ground—replete with over watch, standoff distance, free from urban canyon bandwidth affects and, with advancing technological support, potential for rapid ingress/egress with minimal local population engagement. We argue that the greatest advantage and opportunity afforded by these environments resides in exploiting the vertical space inherent in all urban centers. One of the larger issues of infrastructure often pointed to in a megacity is that of the vertical space. Tactically, the military has long known that taking and owning the high ground is advantageous. In an urban environment, however, "owning" the high ground   skyscrapers—is not only fraught with difficulty but can bring about other issues from a structural/physical security standpoint. New technological approaches to securing the space, providing greater stand-off from explosives, and options for areal refit (creating add-on LZ's for vertical lift capability) would greatly improve the outlook for a military operating in this environment. Current technological advances in net zero basing systems could also be developed to ensure a fully contained and controlled environment within the skyscraper for U.S. forces that is not reliant on the existing building systems. Further, distributed high ground basing throughout the megacity would also allow for greater command and control of the environment through extended visual over watch. Exploiting the vertical space would also entail greater use of unmanned systems in lieu of ground-based patrols.

The population of the megacity and dense urban environment—rather than being an obstacle to military operations—may be the next greatest leverage point of opportunity for future military operations if we are willing and able to change our perspective on how to conduct military operations. The local population is an organic landscape feature that unlike buildings, ebb and flow through the physical environment on dynamic temporal schedules that have daily, weekly, monthly, seasonally and yearly variance. In the megacity, and particularly in dense urban environments, we argue that the population creates incredible complexity and results in novel challenges for military operations. But, better understanding the spatial and temporal patterns of daily life will enable high-fidelity modeling and forecasting of population movement, behavior and reaction within the dense urban and megacity environment. Can we use this understanding to better blend in with the local context so as to also hide among the people? Likewise, if we can learn and adapt to the social and cultural systems and their associated patterns of life, could we train our soldiers to become adept at local "street smarts"? In the same way that Google Glasses now offer on the spot place-based information for way finding, could technology be developed that provided on-the-spot translation and interpretation of language, behavior, dress, and other social and cultural signs, symbols and cues? In this way, could we enable our future soldier to use the crowd as camouflage—ergo, get lost in the crowd, and not in translation? At the same time, new technological advances in analytical capabilities, such as those of IBM's i2 EIA, [27] will enable the future force to quickly identify key players in the crowd, as well as to better understand the connectivity among actors and persons of interest.

Understanding the patterns of daily life of the local population would also facilitate the ability to go "with the flow" of the dense urban environment rather than against it when trying to move large equipment and/or troops? In a megacity, there will always be a "flow", it is just a matter of being able to identify the one most suited to the mission set. Moreover, understanding the recurring temporal patterns inherent to how the local population moves through and makes use of their urban environment would also provide the future force with a built-in barometer for identifying adverse activities, sentiment and change that taps into the local knowledge base. For example, in Iraq, the noticeable absence of women and children and/or deserted areas that are normally busy potentially signaled an impending IED attack, or other adversarial action.[28] In the megacity and dense urban environment, particularly if we leverage vertical space which would allow the future force to more clearly see the ebb and flow of the local population, identifying aberrations in generally recurring patterns of life may provide a significant tactical edge.

Leveraging technology is another way that the U.S. can achieve overmatch in the megacity and dense urban environment. Future research and development, if tailored to the specific context of the megacity operating environment, could result in new technologies and techniques that take advantage of the opportunities presented by this unique environment. Are there technological solutions, perhaps in the field of robotics that can assist U.S. forces in bridging the gap between (current) required force strength ratios given the immense population size of the operating environment? Are there ways to leverage and use specific integrated systems or certain "flows" to cordon off and control sections of a city without disrupting global economic processes? Traditional fortification methods that create significant standoff distances between troop positions and the local population may be impractical in a megacity or dense urban environment, thus requiring technological solutions to compensate. Conversely, are there low-tech options ripe for advancement that would bypass the ever-growing reliance on energy and networks that may provide future forces with military overmatch in dense urban environments? What will be the future equivalent in matching the simplistic elegance of the Navajo Code Talkers?

Summary

It behooves the U.S. military to not only understand the megacity and dense urban environment in the context of a living organism wherein all elements are connected in an integrated system, but to be able to identify the strong and weak areas of the systems that can be used as leverage points to achieve success (ergo, where does the U.S. need to focus efforts to strengthen/buttress the system as well as where are the pressure points in the system that may trigger a desired end-state tipping point). Switching the emphasis from kinetic, human in the loop military tasks that focus on person-on-person interaction between our forces and the population of the megacity (inclusive of adversaries, neutrals and supporters), to strategically supporting, manipulating and/ or undermining the flows, infrastructure and systems of the megacity and dense urban environment as a whole itself may transform what was previously viewed as intimidating complexity with too many moving parts (all those millions and millions of people!) into a sophisticated, integrated, and manageable system of systems. By focusing on the integrated system of systems inherent to the megacity and dense urban environment, by leveraging and taking control of the vertical space, by fully understanding the population and—most importantly, by bringing to bear our capability for technological overmatch that will enable all of the above, we believe future U.S. military forces will have the ability to successfully operate in megacity and dense urban environments as they do now in open terrain.

City (Urban Agglomeration)	Country	Typology Score
Tokyo	Japan	3.0
London	United Kingdom	3.0
New York-Newark	United States of America	3.0
Paris	France	2.9
Los Angeles-Long Beach-Santa Ana	United States of America	2.8
Kinki M.M.A. (Osaka)	Japan	2.7
Johannesburg	South Africa	2.2
Istanbul	Turkey	2.2
Buenos Aires	Argentina	2.0
Ciudad de México (Mexico City)	Mexico	2.0
Krung Thep (Bangkok)	Thailand	2.0
Shenzhen	China	1.9
Shanghai	China	1.9
Kolkata (Calcutta)	India	1.9
Mumbai (Bombay)	India	1.9
Lima	Peru	1.9
Beijing	China	1.9
Chennai (Madras)	India	1.9
Hyderabad	India	1.9
Delhi	India	1.9
Chengdu	China	1.9
Rio de Janeiro	Brazil	1.8
Ahmadabad	India	1.8
Moskva (Moscow)	Russian Federation	1.8
Jakarta	Indonesia	1.8
Chongqing	China	1.8
São Paulo	Brazil	1.8
Bangalore	India	1.8
Guangzhou, Guangdong	China	1.8
Al-Qahirah (Cairo)	Egypt	1.8
Tianjin	China	1.8
Manila	Philippines	1.7
Bogotá	Colombia	1.7
Thanh Pho Ho Chi Minh (Ho Chi Minh City)	Viet Nam	1.6
Lahore	Pakistan	1.5
Karachi	Pakistan	1.5
Dar es Salaam	United Republic of Tanzania	1.4
Lagos	Nigeria	1.4
Dhaka	Bangladesh	1.3
Luanda	Angola	1.3
Kinshasa	Democratic Republic of the Congo	1.0

*Table 1: Projected megacities typology scores (sorted by score);
3 represents highly integrated, 1—loosely integrated*

Notes

[1]   United Nations, Department of Economic and Social Affairs, Population Division (2014). *World Urbanization Prospects: The 2014 Revision, Highlights (ST/ESA/SER.A/352).*

[2]   Ibid.

[3]   UN Habitat, *State of the World's Cities 2012/2013* (2013).

[4]   TRADOC Pam 525-3-0, 2-1c.

[5]   TRADOC Pam 525-3-1, 2-3.b(5).

[6]   Chief of Staff of the Army, Strategic Studies Group (April 21, 2013). "A Proposed Framework for Appreciating Megacities: A US Army Perspective," *Small Wars Journal.* See also, Chief of Staff of

the Army, Strategic Studies Group (June 2014). *Megacities and the United States Army: Preparing for a Complex and Uncertain Future.*

[7]   Dawn A. Morrison, Colin D. Wood, Timothy K. Perkins, Carey A. Baxter. 2016. "Extreme Environment Basing: Contingency Basing in Megacity and Dense Urban Environments," Center for the Advancement of Sustainability Innovations (CASI), ERDC/CERL SR-15-DRAFT (Forthcoming March 2016).

[8]   United Nations, Department of Economic and Social Affairs, Population Division (2014). *World Urbanization Prospects: The 2014 Revision, Highlights (ST/ESA/SER.A/352).*

[9]   U.S. Census Bureau Online. Geography Reference Section. http://www.census.gov/geo/reference/urban-rural.html.

[10]   For a good explanation of these metrics, see MIT's Density Atlas project: http://www.densityatlas.org/.

[11]   See Chief of Staff of the Army, Strategic Studies Group (April 21, 2013; June 2014).

[12]   Data is available upon request.

[13]   GCRI. http://conflictrisk.jrc.ec.europa.eu/. Website hosted by the Joint Research Center of the European Commission; Center for Hazards and Risk Research—CHRR— Columbia University, Center for International Earth Science Information Network—CIESIN—Columbia University, and International Bank for Reconstruction and Development—The World Bank. 2005. Global Multihazard Frequency and Distribution. Palisades, NY: NASA Socioeconomic Data and Applications Center (SEDAC). http://dx.doi.org/10.7927/H45718Z5. Website hosted by CIESIN at Columbia University.

[14]   Sukman, Daniel. "The Past as a Prologue: The Future of the U.S. Military in One Graphic." *The Strategy Bridge.* December 18, 2015. Retrieved from http://www.thestrategybridge.com/the-bridge/2015/12/20/the-past-as-a-prologue-the-future-of-the-us-military-in-one-graphic, February 02, 2016.

[15]   See Chief of Staff of the Army, Strategic Studies Group (April 21, 2013; June 2014).

[16]   E.g., City Prosperity Index (CPI), 2012, United Nations Human Settlements Programme, Global Urban Indicators Database; Global Power Index (GCPI) 2009, http://www.citymayors. com/economics/power-cities.html; http://www.citymayors.com/ economics/power-cities.html Global Cities Index (GCI), 2014, by AT Kearney; Global Metromonitor, 2014, Brookings Institution, Metropolitan Policy Program; Mercer's 2015 Quality of Living City Rankings, https://www.imercer.com/uploads/GM/qol2015/ h5478qol2015/index.html.

[17]   See Morrison et.al. (2016) for a detailed discussion and breakdown of how these, and other open source indices, were used to operationalize the megacity framework.

[18]   "Textiles on the WTO Website" http://www.wto.org/english/ tratop_e/texti_e/texti_e.htm. WTO Secretariat. See also, Hildegunn Kyvik Nordas (2004), "The Global Textile and Clothing Industry post the Agreement on Textiles and Clothing." Geneva, Switzerland: World Trade Organization.

[19]   TRADOC Pam 525-3-6, 3-4b.

[20]   The "Golden Hour" is the first hour following a trauma injury, which is considered the most critical for successful emergency treatment. Likewise, the "Platinum Ten" refers to the period in which medical personnel arrive on and assess the scene, initiate treatment, and transport for injured personnel.[xx]

[21]   TomTom Worldwide Traffic Index, 2015, http://www.tomtom. com/en_gb/trafficindex/#/list.

[22]   TRADOC Pam 525-3-6, 3-4a.

[23]   Anurag Kotoky (September 11, 2014). "Mumbai Airport Slum Removal Sought by India Over Terror," *Bloomberg Business*.

[24]   See Morrison et.al. (2016).

[25]   EP 1105-3-1, E-4.

[26]   Area calculations for Camp Diamondback were determined using ESRI GIS ArcMap 10.1 and images from Google Earth.

[27]   Tucker, Patrick. "Refugee or Terrorist? IBM Thinks Its Software Has the Answer." *Defense One*, January 27, 2016. Retrieved from: http://www.defenseone.com/technology/2016/01/refugee-

or-terrorist-ibm-thinks-its-software-has-answer/125484/?oref=d -channelriver, Feb. 02, 2016.

[28] U.S. Marine Corps, "Improvised Explosive Devices (IED) B3L4118 Student Handout," Pg. 8.

Chapter 29

Anticipating Megacity Responses to Shocks: Using Urban Integration and Connectedness to Assess Resilience

Shade T. Shutters, Wes Herche and Erin King

First Published 26 February 2016

Introduction

Over half of humanity now lives in cities, a proportion rising to 80% by 2100 [1]. With this rapid demographic shift has come a new type of geographical entity—the megacity [2]. Typically defined as an urbanized area with at least 10 million residents, 28 megacities exist in the world today—almost 10 times as many as the three that existed in 1970. And nearly 40 of these massive human agglomerations will exist just 10 years from now. In parallel with this trend is a diffusion of world power from traditional hegemonic states to networks of diverse types of actors, including non-state entities such as megacities [3].

The rapid emergence of these dense urban areas has led to their prominent role in recent U.S. operations, with urban warfare being an integral part of allied efforts in both Iraq and Afghanistan. Operations in Fallujah, Iraq in 2005 were described as, "the heaviest urban combat

Marines have been involved in since Hue City in Vietnam in 1968," [4]. In Afghanistan, a resurgent Taliban has concentrated its attacks on dense urban areas, forcing Afghan security forces into an urban warfare front for which they are ill-prepared [5]. Indeed, Iraq's recent announcement that it will construct a reinforced wall to surround Baghdad illustrates the ever-increasing emphasis of megacities and their security.

Given these recent experiences and prevailing trends there is clearly a need for a deeper understanding of dense urban environments at this unprecedented scale [6, 7]. What, if anything, fundamentally differentiates megacities from other cities? How does a contemporary military force confront an urban system of such immensity? While current military doctrine extends to urban operations, the sheer size of current megacities is beyond the scope of that doctrine. A recent report by the Chief of Staff of the Army's Strategic Studies Group [8] summarizes the gaps in our understanding of megacities and the potential implications for national security.

The report states that megacities "create a complex security environment which will challenge policy makers and military planners" and that megacities will be the strategic key in future U.S. military interventions. This presents a paradox for strategic planning and operations, framing urban warfare as a "wicked problem" [9-11]. By their nature, complex systems such as megacities cannot be controlled in a traditional military sense, but they can be influenced [12]. It is critical then to understand exactly how to influence the trajectory of these cities and how to anticipate their responses to that influence.

Urban Resilience

A primary objective of better understanding of megacities is to enable a proper evaluation of alternative tactical and strategic options. It is virtually impossible to evaluate a scenario for intervening in a megacity without the ability to anticipate the megacity's response.

And the magnitude and nature of a city's response to intervention is intimately related to the city's resilience.

Thus, we focus in this paper on a critical and fundamental attribute of megacities, and indeed of all complex systems—their resilience to shocks [13]. How well can a megacity respond to a shock? How long will that response take? What are its vulnerabilities and weaknesses? What policy interventions can affect its resilience? Quantifying that resilience is a crucial prerequisite for comparative analyses, for assessing the impact of policies, and for planning both strategic and tactical options. It is also central to anticipating whether a disrupted urban environment will eventually recover from a shock or transition into a haven for violent extremists.

Connectedness, integration, and interdependence

Ideally, our understanding of megacities, or any dense urban environment would include a theoretically-grounded, quantification of resilience, which many experts claim is virtually impossible to create [14, 15]. Analysts are thus forced to derive simplistic qualitative notions of resilience. This has led to a prevailing view asserting that tightly connected, highly integrated cities are the most resilient to shocks [16, 8, 17]. Cities such as London and New York, this view claims, will recover from shocks much more readily than the likes of Lagos or Dhaka.

This concept of integration or connectedness and its relation to resilience is sufficiently accepted so that it was used as the basis for the CSA's proposed megacity typology (Figure 1). As Harris et al [8] conclude:

> *Highly integrated systems are characterized by strong formal and informal relationships among its component parts. These relationships manifest as highly ordered hierarchical structures with formalized procedures and norms, and open communication among its various parts. Highly integrated systems are inherently stable, show high*

degrees of resilience (ability to absorb change) and manage growth in a relatively controlled manner.

Loosely integrated systems, on the other hand, lack many of the formal relationships that keep highly integrated systems stable. Weak control and communications systems, and lack of consistent rules for interaction amongst component parts lead to low resilience and unregulated growth. This growth, in turn, contributes more component parts that aren't formally integrated into the system, creating a downward spiral of instability.

The assertion that higher connectedness of a system increases that system's resilience comes largely from the engineering concepts of robustness and redundancy [18-20], where designed networks and engineered systems must be crafted to withstandshocks [17]. The rationale is that if one part of a system fails, higher connectivity enables the rapid replacement of resources and the uninterrupted flow of information through the system.

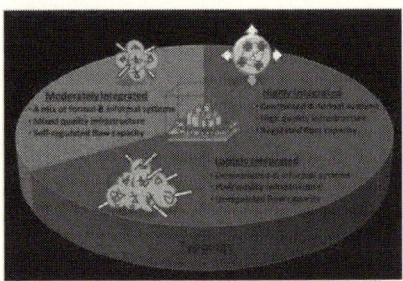

Figure 1: A typology of megacities defined by the level of a city's integration (from [8] p. 14).

Yet this prevailing view is not the only one. A contrary view, outlined in the seminal tome *Panarchy* [21] and originating in ecology-related fields, asserts that highly connected and integrated systems become brittle and susceptible to cascading failures [22, 23]. To better illustrate this counter view, we present a simple organismic analogy to cities.

An analogy from biology

Let us consider an illuminating analogy from the animal kingdom. Though this vantage point will be new to most readers, it is important to understand that an animal is a collection of numerous individual cells: individuals that communicate with each other, coordinate activities, carry out diverse functional tasks, change their behavior in response to their environment, regulate themselves, and depend on one another for survival. In other words, just like a city, an animal is nothing less than a complex adaptive social system [24].

Biologists typically place animals along a continuum of internal complexity with humans at one end (most complex) and sponges at the other (least complex). The human body is made of nearly 200 different types of cells, which form a highly integrated hierarchy of interconnected tissues, organs, and dynamic systems. These systems and their components show an incredible degree of self-regulation, feedback controls, interdependency, redundancy, and defense capabilities. On the other hand, sponges have no tissues, no organs, no systems at all, and are composed of only four types of cells. Thus under virtually any conceived scale of integration, connectedness, or interdependency, humans are far above sponges.

But which is more resilient? Consider the shock of discharging a firearm into both a human and a sponge. In humans a small area of localized damage can trigger a series of cascading system failures culminating in the collapse of the entire system and the death of the individual. And the sponge? Some of its cells would die but the system overall would be largely unaffected. With minimal integration between damaged areas and the rest of the animal, unaffected parts continue to function as if nothing had happened. In fact, a sponge can be subjected to chemical or mechanical stresses that virtually disintegrate the animal into a mass of unconnected cells and those cells will soon reconstitute into a single animal. Given this example it is difficult to argue that the highly integrated and hierarchical society of cells forming a human body is more resilient than a lowly sponge. Can the analogous social systems of cities be so different?

Recent empirical evidence

Partly to reconcile this apparent contradiction over the role of connectedness, a recent study attempted to craft a quantitative and anticipatory metric of urban resilience. Using massive government datasets on the economies of U.S. cities, Shutters et al [25] developed a quantitative measure of a city's "tightness" or level of economic integration. Using this metric, the authors found that, following the shock of the 2007-2009 "Great Recession," U.S. cities with tightly integrated economies actually had the largest percentage drops in several measures of economic performance. In addition, the highly integrated cities took longer to return to their pre-shock performance levels. In other words, the most integrated cities were the *least* resilient to this global economic shock.

Yet the authors of this study caution that resilience is likely very nuanced and contextual. Factors such as the type of shock, its geographical extent, its duration, etc., will ultimately determine what is and is not a resilient megacity. For instance, a disaster befalling a specific U.S. port city may have cascading impacts on the U.S. economy, but the nature of this geo-specific shock is likely quite different than the global economic shock described above. In any regard, clarifying the impact of increasing connectedness is paramount in today's world of increasing globalization and interdependency [26].

The Key to Urban Resilience

Thus far we have established that understanding the resilience of megacities is critical to planning interventions, evaluating options, and anticipating responses, but that typical thinking about urban resilience is both naïve and conflicted. So what is the way forward?

We believe the key to understanding urban resilience can be summarized in one word—networks. To appreciate this assertion, we must first accept that cities are complex adaptive systems. They exhibit emergent properties, evolutionary dynamics, and non-linear responses.

But more importantly, cities, like all complex systems, are composed of a network of interacting parts and subsystems. Complex urban systems are virtually defined as a multiplex of interacting complex networks [27-29].

Indeed, modern urban centers, and particularly megacities, are no longer isolated fortresses, but large, highly complex interconnected networks of networks. Those networks include transportation, financial, resource distribution, sewer and water infrastructure, electricity, communication and data, economic trade, social networks, and others. These networks can best be conceptualized as "Level 2" socio-techno systems under the Allenby and Sarewitz [30] framework of technologies and emergent technological systems that have co-evolved as integral parts of human beings and societies. Networks like traffic conduits and electrical delivery can be mapped through physical inspection, including remote sensing. On the other hand, financial and social networks, for example, require tools such as social media analytics and data mining. Still others, such as economic interdependence networks, require careful analysis with tools from information theory and other advanced techniques [31].

Quantifying the dynamics and topological features of these networks is key to understanding both their resilience and that of the complex systems they govern [31-33, 25]. This includes analyzing the diversity of networks embedded in dense urban systems. Thus, the tasks at hand include at least two major agendas: (1) determining how the different networks comprising a city are affected by various shocks, and (2) generating the high-quality data needed to inform models of urban resilience for developing nation megacities, where current data availability is limited.

Conclusion

Given current global trends in population growth, urbanization, and power dynamics, megacities and other dense urban environments will continue to grow in strategic importance. Thus, it is critical that we enhance our understanding these complex systems. This understanding will require embracing a complex adaptive systems framework focused on the networks that comprise urban systems.

In particular, assessing multiple policy and tactical options requires the ability to anticipate how a megacity will respond to intervention or shocks; and those responses are a function of the resilience of an urban system. Thus, the imperative is to better understand urban resilience, theoretically ground its assertions, and rigorously quantify it for enhanced decision making. We assert that the best way to accomplish these goals is through sophisticated analysis of the multitude of networks embedded within (and existing between) urban systems.

Notes

[1] United Nations Population Fund (2007). *State of the world population 2007: Unleashing the Potential of Urban Growth.* United Nations, New York.

[2] Dobbs, R. (2010). *Prime Numbers: Megacities.* Foreign Policy Magazine 181: 132-135.

[3] National Intelligence Council (2012). *Global Trends 2030: Alternative Worlds.* Office of the Director of National Intelligence, Washington, DC.

[4] Garamone, J. (2005). *ScanEagle Proves Worth in Fallujah Fight.* DoD News 11-Jan-2005, available at http://archive.defense.gov/news/newsarticle.aspx?id=24397.

[5] Smith, J. (2015). *Battle for Kunduz Draws Afghans into Urban Warfare. Stars and Stripes* Oct. 13, 2015, available at http://www.stripes.com/news/battle-for-kunduz-draws-afghans-into-urban-warfare-1.373072.

[6] Adamson, W. G. (2015). *Megacities and the US Army.* Parameters: The US Army War College Quarterly 45(1): 45-54.

[7] Felix, K. M. and F. D. Wong (2015). *The Case for Megacities.* Parameters: The US Army War College Quarterly 45(1): 19-32.

[8] Harris, M., R. Dixon, N. Melin, D. Hendrex, R. Russo, and M. Baily (2014). *Megacities and the United States Army: Preparing for a complex and uncertain future.* Office of the Chief of Staff of the Army, Strategic Studies Group, Arlington, Virginia, USA.

[9] Rittel, H. W. J. and M. M. Webber (1973). *Dilemmas in a general theory of planning.* Policy Sciences 4(2): 155-169.

[10] Camillus, J. C. (2008). *Strategy as a wicked problem.* Harvard Business Review 86(5): 98.

[11] Bebber, R. (2015). *The Wicked Problem of War.* MOC Warfighter, U.S. Naval War College 5, available at https://www.usnwc.edu/mocwarfighter/Article_M.aspx?ArticleID=40.

[12] Clark, A. (1999). *Leadership and Influence: The Manager as Coach, Nanny and Artificial DNA.* Pages 47-66 in J. Clippinger, editor. The biology of business: De-coding the natural laws of Enterprise. Jossey-Bass, San Francisco.

[13] Kilcullen, D. (2012). *The City as a System: Future Conflict and Urban Resilience.* The Fletcher Forum of World Affairs 36(2 Summer 2012): 19-39.

[14] Walker, B. and D. Salt (2012). *Resilience Practice: Building Capacity to Absorb Disturbance and Maintain Function.* Island Press, Washington, DC.

[15] USAID (2013). *The Resilience Agenda: Measureing Resilience in USAID, Technical Note 1866.* United States Agency for International Development, Washington, DC.

[16] Norton, R. J. (2003). *Feral Cities.* Naval War College Review 56(4): 97-106.

[17] Sterbenz, J. P. G., D. Hutchison, E. K. Çetinkaya, A. Jabbar, J. P. Rohrer, M. Schöller, and P. Smith (2014). *Redundancy, diversity, and connectivity to achieve multilevel network resilience, survivability, and disruption tolerance.* Telecommunication Systems 56(1): 17-31.

[18] Pavard, B., J. Dugdale, N. B. B. Saoud, S. Darcy, and P. Salembier (2008). *Underlying concepts in robustness and resilience and their use in designing socio-technical systems.* Pages 127-142 in E. Hollnagel, C. P. Nemeth, and S. Dekker, editors. Resilience engineering

perspectives: Remaining sensitive to the possibility of failure. Ashgate Publishing, Burlington, Vermont, USA.

[19] Smith, P., D. Hutchison, J. P. G. Sterbenz, M. Scholler, A. Fessi, M. Karaliopoulos, C. Lac, and B. Plattner (2011). *Network Resilience: A Systematic Approach*. Ieee Communications Magazine 49(7): 88-97.

[20] Krupa, M. B., F. S. C. III, and A. L. Lovecraft (2014). *Robustness or resilience? Managing the intersection of ecology and engineering in an urban Alaskan fishery*. Ecology and Society 19(2): 17.

[21] Gunderson, L. H. and C. S. Holling, editors. (2002). *Panarchy: understanding transformations in human and natural systems*. Island Press, Washington, DC.

[22] Kauffman, S. A. (1993). *The Origins of Order: Self-Organization and Selection in Evolution*. Oxford University Press, New York.

[23] Dorner, D. (1996). *The logic of failure: recognizing and avoiding error in complex situations*. Metropolitan Books, New York.

[24] Maynard Smith, J. and E. Szathmáry (1997). *The major transitions in evolution*. Oxford University Press, New York.

[25] Shutters, S. T., R. Muneepeerakul, and J. Lobo (2015). *Quantifying urban economic resilience through labour force interdependence*. Palgrave Communications 1(201510): 1-7.

[26] Ward, D. (2016). *Operational Environment Implications of the Megacity to the US Army*. Small Wars Journal 12(2): 02-Feb-2016.

[27] Craven, P. and B. Wellman (1973). *The Network City*. Sociological Inquiry 43(3-4): 57-88.

[28] Batty, M. (2013). *The New Science of Cities*. MIT Press, Cambridge, Massachusetts.

[29] Neal, Z. P. (2013). *The connected city: How networks are shaping the modern metropolis*. Routledge, New York, NY.

[30] Allenby, B. and D. Sarewitz (2011). *The techno-human condition*. MIT Press, Cambridge, Massachusetts, USA.

[31] Ulanowicz, R. E., S. J. Goerner, B. Lietaer, and R. Gomez (2009). *Quantifying sustainability: Resilience, efficiency and the return of information theory*. Ecological Complexity 6(1): 27-36.

[32] Buldyrev, S. V., R. Parshani, G. Paul, H. E. Stanley, and S. Havlin (2010). *Catastrophic cascade of failures in interdependent networks.* Nature 464(7291): 1025-1028.

[33] Parshani, R., S. V. Buldyrev, and S. Havlin (2010). *Interdependent Networks: Reducing the Coupling Strength Leads to a Change from a First to Second Order Percolation Transition.* Physical Review Letters 105(4): 048701.

Chapter 30

Using the Internet of Things to Gain and Maintain Situational Awareness in Dense Urban Environments and Mega Cities

Alfred C. Crane and Richard Peeke

First Published 26 February 2016

It may prove beneficial to leverage the internet of things (IOT) in order to provide our Soldiers, Sailors, Airmen and Marines the decisive advantage needed to fight and win future armed conflicts. It can be anticipated that connected devices such as game consoles, "baby monitors"[1] and "that smart meter (that) knows when you're home and what electronics you use when you're there"[2], for example, will be prolific in the future operating environment. With this in mind, the joint force will have opportunities to use these devices to gain and maintain situational awareness in a mega city or dense urban environment. Before Soldiers enter a building or deploy an unmanned system, they may have opportunities to access these existing "sensors" to build a picture of the building's interior. Also, being able to access personal electronic devices of the buildings occupants could, coupled with the deployment of unmanned systems, give the Warfighter a better picture of what awaits behind the next door, wall, room or floor.

Not only knowing about the location and patterns of life of enemy combatants in the building and the ability to find out where non-combatants are would increase protection of the Warfighter, as well as, reduce the risk of civilian casualties. The data obtained from these connected devices, personal electronic devices and deployed unmanned systems would be rapidly stitched together to render a real-time 3D model of the building, as well as, show locations of the structure's occupants. An example of this can be seen in the films "Prometheus,"[3] and "The Dark Knight".[4] This would give the Warfighter the needed edge to fight and win in complex urban terrain.

In addition to finding out how many occupants there are as well as their location, the Soldier will also need to gain and maintain situational awareness outside of buildings by being able to access traffic cameras, security cameras and so forth. Building a comprehensive, living model of a city or even a city block would enhance situational awareness and provide the necessary data for leaders to make rapid decisions and increase the protection of the combat element in an operational environment. This composited data could also be shared so that the operational commander would have a real-time view of the area of operations. Big Data Analytics and knowledge management / decision-making tools will be needed in order to filter and make sense of all of the data being obtained.

Of course, these connected devices can be used for defensive as well as offensive operations. By knowing where allies and noncombatants are as well as movement of suspect personnel in an area of operations by target acquisition and tracking of personnel using biometric sensors and software will give the Warfighter the needed information to be lethal, informed, and protected.

A draw back to this is that without power, access to these connected devices may not be possible. Also, if we have the ability to access and use these connected devices then it can be anticipated that the enemy will have this ability, as well. Counter-measures and technologies to spoof, trick or deny enemy access to these devices will also need to be developed.

One of many the challenges in the operational environment is to distinguish between enemy combatants, non-combatants and friendly forces. In order to mitigate fratricide and collateral damage, transponders would need to be developed, that are either worn by the Warfighter or are subcutaneous, which can be picked up by friendly forces. These would need to be visible in different spectra and frequencies.

Vignette

In support of ongoing operations, United States forces have been assigned to rescue hostages held in a high-rise building of a dense metropolitan area.

This is part of ongoing operations to remove hostile forces who are attempting to gain control of the capitol building and power grid.

Several hostages have been taken in order to pressure US forces to leave.

Multispectral, visual, as well as audio signals are used to locate the building where the hostages are being held.

As the US forces advance to the building they contact their Cyber Support Center (CSC) utilizing the cyber support officer (CSO) attached to their unit. As the CSC is contacted, unmanned aerial and ground systems that are organic to the unit are deployed.

A call for cyber effects is initiated in order to gain access to the city's security and traffic cameras. This coupled together with the sensors onboard the unmanned systems informs the small unit leader of the best avenue for advance.

Advanced recon to determine patterns of life and develop a target folder are initiated prior to advancement/execution of mission.

Simultaneously, an information campaign to provide a plausible cover story or shape public opinion against the hostage takers and delegitimize their insurgent movement is launched.

Once the safest route has been determined, the US element advances using visual and digital obscurants to cover their movement. A second cyber effect is requested to locate and gain access to connected devices and personal electronic devices in and around the building.

Swarming nano and small unmanned systems are deployed to map out the buildings floor plan and identify location of the occupants. After a few minutes, some cameras are accessed that are built in to game systems, security cameras, mobile phones, smart TV's and baby monitors. Access to these help develop a picture of where the building occupants are located. Two potential locations where the hostages are held are identified based on signals intelligence, cyber effects and the information gathered from the connected devices, mobile phones and unmanned systems.

The US forces enter the building and proceed with caution using the appropriate tactics, techniques and procedures to the two possible locations. After entering the building, US forces talk to a few civilians who have evaded capture and they are able to point out the target location.

A further cyber effect is requested and the location of the hostile forces within the room are identified through their mobile phones, a smart TV and a camera on an office computer. A diversion is created to distract the hostiles and using room clearing procedures, the US forces enter the room, eliminate the threat and rescue the hostages. Less than lethal/area-denial technologies to incapacitate the hostage takers and temporarily neutralize the threat to friendly forces are utilized.

Concluding Thoughts

Gaining and maintaining situational awareness in this age of technology can be challenging. If the Warfighter is left to fight and clear buildings in the same manner, same methods and same technology as seen in the battles of Stalingrad, Arnhem, Nuremburg or Fallujah we have failed.

In conclusion, investments in basic and applied research to develop the necessary technologies and software needed to gain and maintain access to personal as well as connected devices (to include denying access of these same devices to our adversaries) and utilizing elements such as Defense Innovation Unit X in Silicon Valley will be needed to make these concepts a reality.

This paper addresses Army Warfighting Challenge number 1, Develop Situational Understanding [5].

The authors would like to extend a special thanks to COL Bryan Denny and Mr. Curtis Austin for taking the time to review and provide valuable comments and suggestions that enhanced this paper. We are truly grateful for their input.

Notes

[1] DiGangi, C. (2016, January 28) *6 Things in Your Home That Could Get You Hacked*. Retrieved from http://www.foxbusiness.com.

[2] Kobie, N. (2015, May 6) *What Is the Internet of Things*. Retrieved from http://www.theguardian.com.

[3] Costigan, M. (Executive Producer), & Scott, R. (Director). (2012). *Prometheus*. United States: Twentieth Century Fox.

[4] De La Noy, K. (Executive Producer), & Nolan C. (Director). (2008). *The Dark Knight*. United States: Warner Brothers.

[5] ARCIC Future Warfare Division. (2015, October 7) Army Warfighting Challenges Army Operating Concept; Burrus, D. (2014, November) *The Internet of Things Is Far Bigger Than Anyone Realizes*. Retrieved from http://www.wired.com; Meek, A. (2015, October 16) *Body cams, smart guns and tracking darts: policing and the internet of things*. Retrieved from http://www. theguardian.com.

Chapter 31

It's in There: Rethinking(?) Intelligence Preparation of the Battlefield in Megacities/Dense Urban Areas

Richard L. Wolfel, Amy Krakowka Richmond,
Mark Read and Colin Tansey

First Published 2 March 2016

The complexity of the modern city has been a key conclusion in most Army research surrounding military operations in megacities/dense urban areas. This complexity is based on three fundamental concepts of the modern city. First, modern cities are multidimensional (subterranean, surface and vertical). Second, cities are interconnected through globalization, social media and modern methods of communication/ information dissemination. Third, cities are uncontrollable due to increased connectivity, rise of black market/informal economy, ineffective government control of slums and the rise of vulnerability in significant portions of the city. As the US Army considers the challenges of operating in dense urban areas, leadership requires a basic understanding of the operating environment. In such a complex environment, understanding the multidimensional, interconnected and uncontrollable elements in complex environments using traditional approaches of situational awareness, which emphasize discrete problem sets and well-defined regions, is problematic at best.

Intelligence sections provide a basic understanding of the operating environment. Military intelligence (MI) Concepts, such as Intelligence Preparation of the Battlefield (IPB), Areas, Structures, Capabilities, Organizations, People and Events (ASCOPE), Sewage, Water, Electricity, Academics, Trash, Medical, Safety, and Other Considerations (SWEAT-MSO), and Political, Military, Economic, Social, Information, Infrastructure, Physical Environment, and Time (PMESII-PT), have been used extensively within the MI community for decades in order to provide a snapshot of the operating environment. Before we go off and try to develop, or find the next new "it" concept, or gadget, we need to step back and critically evaluate what currently exists. How do traditional intelligence methods help inform situational awareness in dense urban environments? Where do these methods fall short? These gaps then become areas where new ideas and Science and Technology (S&T) developments can fill the void to fill in the picture. We need to avoid the urge to throw out what we have. As researchers have contemplated the next new idea, the aforementioned intelligence tools have stood the test of time and with a little modification, offer a solid approach to understanding and explaining the complexities of Megacities/Dense Urban Areas. Military intelligence doctrine provides a solid foundation on which to launch an expedition into identifying and explaining the complexity of the megacity that will increase situational awareness.

What is IPB and How is it Evolving in the Dense Urban Environment?

Intelligence Preparation of the Battlefield (IPB) is the systematic process of analyzing the four mission variables (enemy, terrain, weather and civil considerations) in an area of interest to determine their effect on operations (HQDA, 2014, ix). This is the foundation of all intelligence gathering exercises, to identify and explain these key variables that work to help the commander gain a clear situational awareness of the area of operations (AO).

One of the largest issues with this basic definition of IPB is that it often does not take into account how the variables explaining dense urban areas are increasingly interconnected. Change in urban areas is not a unidirectional process in which the individual agent influences change in the area of interest. As a result of interacting with the area of interest (AI), the agent is also influenced as a result of social and environmental change. Anthony Giddens refers to this process as the *Duality of Structure* (Giddens, 1979: 5). This duality is important in understanding dense urban areas. Often we look very directly at the influence of the mission variables, take them as given variables, well defined and unchanging, and do not address the recursive nature of society in which the enemy, the terrain and civil considerations often change rapidly based on the actions of agents in the area. For example, the enemy can shift dimensions and move from the surface to subterranean, introduce barriers to the terrain and develop a disinformation campaign that will fundamentally shift the societal characteristics of the area of operations.

Along with the recursive nature of mission variables, the interaction of variables has become almost more important than the variables themselves. For example, we are no longer able to extract terrain from the societal milieu and analyze it separate of civil considerations. Kilcullen (2013: 54), emphasizes the interaction of mission variables in his analysis of the attacks on Mumbai in 2008. The terrorists used the interaction of terrain (littoral situation of Mumbai) and civil considerations (the unregulated nature of the fishing fleet) to explain how the terrorists were able to gain access to the region virtually undetected. Neither the terrain, nor the civil considerations alone are adequate to explain the situation in Mumbai. The complex connection between the two gives one a clearer situational awareness of the battlefield.

What is the Operational Environment?

Joint Publication (JP) 3-0 (2011) identifies the area of operations as an area defined by the commander that is large enough to accomplish the mission and protect the force. There is a tendency to treat it as a discrete region that can be circled on a map and discussed in a vacuum. It also identifies the operational environment as a composite of the conditions, circumstances, and influences that affect the employment of capabilities and bear on the decisions of the commander. The problem in the modern dense urban environment is that the OE, including the area of operations, often extends much further than in the past. The impact of connections and linkages, facilitated by globalization, advances in communication technology, and media access challenge the traditional idea of a unique OE that can be isolated for analysis by an intelligence team. These connections must be addressed as part of the analysis. At an even more fundamental level, is the AO the appropriate scale of analysis in a dense urban area/megacity? Should intelligence analyses be conducted at the Area of Influence or Area of Interest level? How do we define these spheres? How do we isolate regions that cannot be isolated from outside influences? These are the challenging questions that face intelligence analysts as they conduct IPB and commanders trying to gain an awareness of an urban region.

One of the major challenges in defining a discrete Area of Operations, is the connectivity and complexity that defines the modern age of globalization. Wielhouwer (2005) addresses this complexity through the *urban triad*. The triad includes: "complex manmade terrain superimposed on natural terrain, a large and densely distributed population, and physical and service infrastructures. These characteristics interact to make each urban area a complex and dynamic system of systems, with a unique physical, political, economic, social, and cultural identity." (Weilhouwer, 2005: 2). Taken a step further, these systems are not static and, based on the recursive nature of societal change, always in flux as agents are influenced by the system and the system is influenced by the agents. The dynamic nature of the modern urban environment demands an expansion of traditional IPB thinking where terrain is fixed and generally unchanging. The *urban triad* helps portray a more complex terrain, both in terms of the amount of components that make up the terrain and also the continual nature of change on the terrain.

The IPB Manual, ATP 2-01.3 emphasizes the multidimensional nature of the operating environment but offers little instruction on how to address the complex, multidimensional environment. Multidimensionality is defined by the IPB Manual (HQDA, 2014: 9-1) as "a blend of horizontal, vertical, interior, exterior, and subterranean forms superimposed on the natural relief, drainage, and vegetation." *Blend* is the key word here. Groups utilize various dimensions in an effort to increase mobility through the urban region. Historically, our thinking about battlespace has been two dimensional. While the IPB Manual does mention and define multidimensionality, it provides little in operational advice or examples. Technologically, this is a huge gap to fill. Technology developments, including, but not limited to, the ability to track people in three-dimensional space and systems to promote greater situational awareness, are needed to increase situational awareness in three-dimensional space, from the subterranean through the vertical high-rise tower. The need for greater situational awareness is magnified as individuals will not stay on one level for an extended period, but rather will change dimensions to avoid detection, gain a tactical advantage, increase security or facilitate movement.

The traditional concept of the AO and the AI are also challenged by the connectivity of the modern urban center. The city is connected globally by many different means, including: economics, culture and social media. While the IPB Manual does address cross border threats (HQDA, 2014: 7-9), the role of information is different than military or paramilitary forces coming across a boarder and influencing an AO. The Arab Spring and the Occupy movements have demonstrated that the ability to control information in the modern age is limited, at best and how virtual communities and shared ideology are created using social media and modern communication/information dissemination techniques. These movements also demonstrated that as governments attempted to control access to social media, that attempt to seize control acted as a unifying force to bring together various, disparate, social movements under a common goal. (Castells, 2015: 62).

The other major area of concern highlighted by the IPB manual is the discussion of approach and mobility corridors. Table 4-2 (HQDA, 2014: 4-6) identifies the minimum distance between terrain features required for avenues of approach. In urban settings, the two-kilometer requirement for the battalion is not possible. This requires a rethinking of our mobility plans and how to control and maneuver through significantly narrower avenues of approach and to consider the possibility of nonstandard mobility corridors, those subsurface and overhead.

In addition, line of sight analysis will be substantially limited and visibility will be influenced by obstructions. For example, Begin Morning Nautical Twilight (HQDA, 2014: 4-18) will most likely not occur at 12 degrees below twilight as suggested by the IPB Field Manual. Buildings will obstruct view, shortening daylight hours in an urban environment as opposed to an open field. These small considerations could substantially impact operations in dense urban areas. Both mobility corridors and line of sight concerns show how the unique environment of dense urban areas challenge many standard conventions of intelligence preparation and situational awareness.

How do the Analytical Tools of Intelligence Inform IPB in Urban Settings?

ASCOPE, PMESII-PT, and SWEAT-MSO are used extensively as the foundational analytical tools for intelligence operators to provide information to promote situational awareness. While the foundational concepts are very useful in urban environments, it is essential to view these as not discrete elements, but as interconnected elements that interact with each other, change the environment and are changed as a result of interactions with each other and the social environment. For example, how do medical conditions interact with political and capabilities? No longer are these elements in a vacuum. It is necessary to view the connectivity in a complex and changing matrix.

Dense Urban Areas and Insurgency Theory

Along with interconnectivity, another key question is what happens when civil capabilities decline, or were never developed in a region? Who steps in to fill the void? This is the foundation of the 2006 version of the Army's counterinsurgency doctrine (HQDA, 2006: 1-3). As mentioned in the Counterinsurgency Field Manual (HQDA, 2006: 1-2), irregular threats strongly influence insurgencies. Also, due to the rise of asymmetrical warfare and increasing number of insurgencies, the nature of combat effectiveness has changed in the modern era. External support is critical in modern AOs. Often this is requested/provided through social media interactions, video uploads, onsite media, elements that are difficult to control. The IPB Manual (HQDA, 2014: 5-15) emphasizes that the "effectiveness of unconventional warfare depended heavily on support and relationships." The question is how do we measure support and how do we determine the strength of relationships? Social media analysis provides a starting point to see how people form social media networks, social media clout scores provide examples of an individual's influence on a specific movement/idea.

What causes the decline in civil capabilities? That becomes another key question in understanding the uncontrollable nature of dense urban settings. Vulnerability, declining environmental security and declining (or non-existent) political capabilities are key drivers in the decline of civil control in regions. One example of the decline of civil capabilities and the rise of vulnerability is in Kampala, Uganda. Kampala is Uganda's capital city with a population of 1.5 million in 2014. Uganda as a whole has one of the world's highest population growth rates and, like many African countries, half of its population under 15. During the last two decades, the city has expanded in all directions. Growth is primarily concentrated along main roads. Between 1989 and 2010 the total built-up area increased exponentially. Sprawling, unplanned urban growth often results in slum development. Slums are the primary destination for migrants and are generally informal settlements. Much of this migration is rural-urban, however there is also considerable movement between cities. Slums make up at least a quarter of the total city area in Kampala, housing roughly 40% of the total city population. The demand for municipal infrastructure is far out pacing supply. This creates countless human security challenges in the realms of sanitation, clean water availability, and environmental degradation.

Davis (2006: 87) also points to an example of loss of civil control in terms of land ownership. Often, public land is illegally controlled by various agents who extract significant rent from local poor who are forced to live on the periphery of the city. Often this land is marginal, vulnerable and is one of the breeding grounds for insurgent actions within the city. Thus, making them areas of prime interest for potential military operations in dense urban environments. The major problem here from the perspective of situational awareness is to understand who controls/ "owns" the land?

How to Model Overlapping Threats?

Weilhouwer (2005: 6), using the Army's primary lessons learned document about the war in Iraq, *On Point*, identified two deficiencies from joint urban operations in Iraq. First, the primary training facilities for U.S. forces are small towns or villages, rather than major metropolitan areas. Second, legacy computer simulations are insufficiently realistic to prepare joint force commanders and warfighters for urban operations. The first deficiency endures—urban training facilities will always be limited in size, and military units are limited in what kinds of training can be conducted in real built up areas. The second deficiency may be easier to overcome than the first, but simulations that are able to replicate the complexity of dense urban areas have yet to be created and will be very resource intensive. So, what might be done to better understand and plan for the complexities of operations in dense urban areas? Scenario planning offers some solutions.

Scenario planning was developed by military strategists following World War II and has been refined and adopted by others in the intelligence community, business, and academia. Most scenario planning exercises seek to satisfy one or more of the following objectives: to make sense of a confusing situation, to develop a strategy, to anticipate future events, or to facilitate organizational learning. Scenarios are especially appropriate for very complex problems that exhibit high uncertainty and involve numerous, uncontrollable variables (van der Heijden 2005). Unlike forecasts or models, which usually attempt to predict specific outcomes, scenarios seek to identify a limited number of *plausible* outcomes.

In the context of IPB and planning for operations in dense urban areas, scenario planning offers several constructive alternatives to more traditional methods. First, scenario planning can be done with limited resources. A scenario planning exercise can be conducted with a small group of people (as few as three or four, but scalable for much larger groups or staffs), and can last from a few hours to several days, depending on time available. Unlike modeling or forecasting, a simple scenario exercise requires minimal information-technology support. Second, scenario planning facilitates 'out of the box' thinking about complex problems. Instead of trying to understand and map the interaction of dozens or more variables, scenario planning constrains the number of variables considered, and forces participants to think about unique ways a few variables may interact over space and time. During the scenario planning process, groups develop plausible storylines that describe alternative futures. Often, during the development of such storylines, participants identify gaps in their understanding of the problem, or find new ways of thinking about a situation. Third, scenario planning can be done with groups who have no previous scenario planning experience— all that is required is a trained facilitator to explain the process, guide dialog, and capture the scenarios as they are developed. Finally, scenario planning exercises provide excellent forums for networking, team building, and learning among participants.

Scenario planning provides a method to come to terms with the complexity of dense urban areas. Scenario planning offers a tool to enhance IPB. Since scenarios are not predictive in nature, they allow for a number of plausible solutions and provide an opportunity to look at the process of working through the scenario to determine gaps in our knowledge. The basic concepts used by intelligence sections provide a point of departure as we begin to tackle the wicked complex problems of dense urban areas. The complexity does not lie in the basic concepts, but in the interconnectivity between discrete defining variables in the AO. Understanding the interconnectivity of ideas and spaces will be a major step forward in starting to grasp the complexity of dense urban environments.

Bibliography

Castells, Manuel. (2015). *Networks of Outrage and Hope: Social Movements in the Internet Age.* 2nd ed. Cambridge, UK: Polity.

Davis, Mike. (2006). *Planet of Slums.* London: Verso.

Giddens, Anthony. (1979). *Central Problems in Social Theory: Action, Structure and Contradiction in Social Analysis.* Berkley: University of California Press.

Headquarters, Department of the Army. (2006). FM 3-24: *Counterinsurgency.* Washington, DC: Department of the Army.

Headquarters, Department of the Army. (2014). ATP 2-01.3: *Intelligence Preparation of the Battlefield.* Washington, DC: Department of the Army.

Joint Chiefs of Staff. (2011). *JP 3-0: Joint Operations.* http://www.dtic.mil/doctrine/new_pubs/jp3_0.pdf. Last accessed: 10 February, 2016.

Kilcullen, David. (2013). *Out of the Mountains: The Coming Age of the Urban Guerrilla.* New York: Oxford University Press.

Van der Heijden, Kees. (2005). *Scenarios: The Art of Strategic Conversation,* 2nd Ed. Hoboken, NJ: Wiley.

Wielhouwer, Peter W. (2005). "Preparing for Future Joint Urban Operations: The Role of Simulations and the Urban Resolve Experiment." *Small Wars Journal* (2 July 2005). www.smallwarsjournal.com/documents/urbanresolve.pdf. Last accessed: 10 February, 2016.

Chapter 32

An Analytical Framework for Operations in Dense Urban Areas

William Hedges

First Published 11 March 2016

Introduction

The U.S. Army Operating Concept, (AOC) *Win in a Complex World*, "provides the intellectual foundation and framework for learning and for applying what we learn to future force development under Force 2025 and Beyond.[1] The AOC focuses on important questions; this paper provides a relevant framework supporting how we go about attempting to answer two of the questions presented within the AOC: "what is the environment we think Army forces will operate in, and what is the problem we are trying to solve?"[2] Both of these questions and potential resolution thereof are key to how we continue to tackle Army Warfighting Challenge #1, developing and sustaining a high degree of situational understanding against determined, adaptive threats. The AOC provides due consideration to anticipated threats and the future operating environment (OE) by outlining five characteristics of the future operating environment with likely significant impact on land force operations:

(1) *Increased velocity and momentum of human interaction and events;*
(2) *Potential for overmatch;*
(3) *Proliferation of weapons of mass destruction;*
(4) *Spread of advanced cyberspace and counter-space capabilities;*
(5) *Demographics and operations among populations, in cities, and in complex terrain.*[3]

Though the latter characteristic is the most compelling, it is important to note that the other future OE characteristics would indeed be exacerbated by the conditions found in dense urban areas (DUA). This paper provides a relevant analytic framework in support of framing, mapping, and developing courses of action (COA) for operations occurring in DUA today and in the future.

Background I—Dense Urban Areas

Discussion regarding DUA-oriented environments usually center on the roughly 28 megacities on the planet today. However, the increasing global pace of urbanization is not confined to just a megacities issue or perspective; recent United Nations studies portend a 60% population surge in urban areas by 2030.[4] Despite the scale and complexity of the world's megacities, there are almost 850 cities with populations between 500k and 9.9m—in essence, "middleweight" cities[5] that also represent interactively complex operating environments. Environments which may feature a dense and diverse population mix; further complicated by the potential for loose integration[6], a multitude of networks, and potentially volumes of big data[7] that present noteworthy challenges for information collection, much less its parsing, characterization, and understanding.

According to the National Intelligence Council's *Global Trends 2030: Alternative Worlds*, precipitous changes in world demographics are expected to perpetuate significant changes, or megatrends, in the world's diplomatic, economic, and military power.[8] Such change may undoubtedly lead to a potentially volatile and uncertain security environment where US interests and related national security concerns are increasingly vulnerable to a variety of actors and a range of threats.[9] In accepting that cities/dense urban areas represent the nexus of the megatrends alluded to above, the potential for US forces to operate in DUA is significant today and increasingly probable in both the near and far terms. Which presents the following questions, how do US forces develop critical situational understanding of such environments, and what would constitute a viable analytic framework for developing and placing that understanding into relevant and applicable context?

Background II—IPB: A Dated Methodological Approach

For the better part of four decades, Army intelligence has tackled operational challenges via an approach known as Intelligence Preparation of the Battlefield (IPB), which was embedded within the Military Decision-making Process (MDMP). Even though the Army has revised a great deal of its doctrine and associated tactics, techniques, and procedures in an effort to adapt to an evolving OE landscape, our situational understanding largely remains anchored to IPB's role as a MDMP catalyst for all environments. IPB's orientation is towards linear engagement areas and a specific threat methodology and model. It is essentially reductionist and quantitative in nature, still supportive of a structurally complex OE; but, often fails to gain sight of the dynamics between the components of problems within an interactively complex system. The dense urban area problem approach must be qualitatively focused and employ diverse heuristics[10] lines of effort rather than the rigidity invoked by the IPB analytic framework.[11]

The products for each step of IPB are not conducive to an interactively complex OE. These products fail to adequately unify the different elements found within the OE while seeking alignment to a threat or system of opposition[12] picture. One pointed example associated with the IPB construct, lies with the challenge of incorporating religion as an operational data layer specific to an OE. Presently, an analytic team focusing on a religious-themed impact – central to operational planning, would focus on the operational variables captured within a given city's OE assessment (note though that doctrinally, religion at present is not represented as a "stand-alone" variable). Such a religious-themed search (within PMESII-PT[13], F-ASCOPE[14], SWEAT-MSO[15], DIMEFIL[16], and even METT-TC[17] analysis) would potentially yield multiple and disparate religious informational elements, which is to be expected. However, the IPB construct does not afford a clear step for tying together several "like" elements into a single operational data layer and illustrating or modeling the relationship of that system upon other systems (IPB does not accommodate "modelling" until step 3 and that step/model is threat-centric).

The relevance of the example above highlights a significant gap within the IPB framework/process and the inability to truly support comprehensive mission analysis and problem framing, especially for the multitude of data layers found in DUA. Though religion is often cited within an OE assessment, there is little conduit via IPB to truly discern analytic value. In IPB, there exists the potential for such data to be "not considered" since it may be interpreted as having little to no value in either describing the threat or the threat COA. This example highlights another IPB-related challenge. How the Army doctrinally captures relevant operational variables is potentially problematic given that a very relevant operational variable like religion (or perhaps even tribal/familia factors) is buried within our PMESII-PT or F-ASCOPE snapshots despite the data point that religion continues to emerge as a dominant theme for a multitude of current and perhaps future operating environments.[18] IPB's role and suitability as a MDMP catalyst, directed towards an interactively complex environment focused on a city-system environmental challenge or a hybrid warfare[19]—oriented system of opposition—remains questionable.

An Urban Analytic Framework: City as a System

Dense urban areas represent the higher nexus of interactively complex operating environments. The IPB process' end-state provides an inadequate degree of situational understanding for such complex environs given its inherent threat-oriented slant versus a city as a system or all-encompassing environmental perspective. Adoption of this city as a system perspective will require adaptation of a significant portion of our Army doctrine and thus, lead to an urban analytic framework tailored to address the operational data layers found within urban centers, their environmental dynamism, and their state of connectedness.[20]

One such urban analytic structure has been developed by CAERUS Associates, championed by the Combatting Terrorism Technical Support Office (CTTSO),[21] and has been applied by elements within the special operations community. The overarching concept behind this framework is alignment with systems thinking, focusing attention on the relationships between different parts of the environment and working to understand the cumulative effects of these interactions.[22]

The CTTSO analytic framework certainly offers dividends as well as potential shortcomings. "Shoehorning" another analytic framework into IPB should not be the first objective. Instead, the Army should be focused on: the capture of the DUA's operational data layers; the display or modeling of those data layers; determination and analysis of city system Environmental Centers of Gravity (E-COG); the potential impact on friendly or threat/ systems of opposition COA; and the impact or urban consequences of friendly/threat COAs upon the city systems. All of these objectives should be contained within an analytic framework dedicated to understanding interactively complex and adaptive operating environments (i.e. DUA).

Creating a Tailored Urban Analytic Framework

The creation of a tailored urban analytic framework would build upon the merits of the CTTSO/CAERUS construct and incorporate additional elements essential to both development of a pertinent intelligence-oriented model and relevant support to Army staff action planners during the course of MDMP. Such a framework would stand-alone; and be the primary analytic process that develops situational understanding for DUA.

Such a framework could potentially look much like the following:

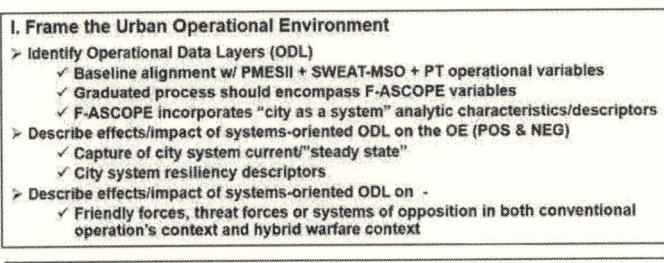

Figure 1. Proposed Urban Analytic Framework

Framing the Urban Operational Environment

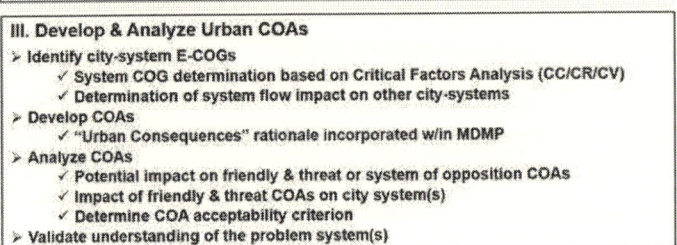

Figure 2. Framing the Urban Operational Environment

This first step is an initial assessment construct of a city's operational environment. It represents an assessment of existing OE conditions developed from both operational and mission variable analysis within the commander's area of operations, the area of influence, and the area of interest. This assessment is integral to planning and facilitating friendly force operations. The data visualization capture should provide for an initial city/system modeling construct, illustrating individual components within each city system, leading to the ability to display a layered (system upon system) operational view.

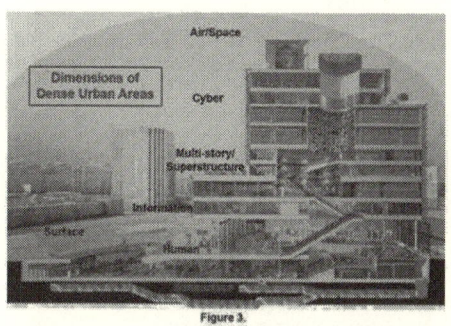

Figure 3.

Before we can begin to frame the problem, we must first understand the components of the potential problem system, therefore it begins with identifying the operational data layers associated with a specific urban environment. Note that historical application of IPB towards DUA usually resulted in a limited operational data layer perspective (i.e. three layers: terrain, weather, and the threat); yet, urban OEs (e.g. megacities and "middleweight" cities) will likely involve a multitude of diverse data layers.

Characterization or context of how the data applies assists the process of identifying relevant urban area data layers. Figure 3 captures the common themes related to the dimensions often associated with DUA,[23] and in effect, guides the "fit" of a data layer within the urban OE.

Using Figure 3 as a general guide, an initial analysis of population, infrastructure, and physical environment variables (described within the CAERUS framework as the Urban Triad[24]) would yield critical insight to the operational data layers relevant to a given DUA (See Appendix: "Select examples of operational data layers within Dense Urban Areas." The cited examples are reflective of an initial PMESII + SWEAT-MSO + PT analysis.)[25]

Further maturation of these initially identified data layers will be required in which F-ASCOPE context, particularly the "flow" or relationship aspect, is geared towards a "city as a system" perspective, and thus lay the groundwork for both individual system and system-on-system interaction analysis.[26] Each systems' perspective should continue to evolve, leading to a description of the positive and negative effects/impacts of the systems- oriented operational data layers on the OE from a holistic standpoint.[27] The overarching objective is to capture the city systems' status currently or from a "steady state" standpoint.[28] The resultant capture should include additional descriptors of each systems' resident capabilities which enable achieving or maintaining a degree of resiliency against internal or external forces/factors/variables.

This urban OE framing concludes with a transition from our examination of the city systems as federated entities, to one in which an analytic team then describes the effects/impact of systems-oriented data layers on friendly and threat forces, the latter of which may be addressed as systems of opposition[29] in order to achieve both a conventional and a hybrid warfare context.

Mapping Urban Problem Systems

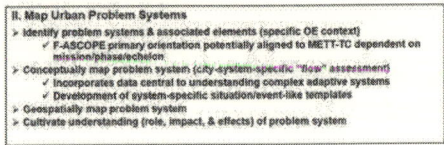

Figure 4. Mapping Urban Problem Systems

Mapping the urban problem system elaborates on the problem through system map visualization. Transferring this knowledge to a map/picture supports the identification of key accumulators/nodes and flows integral to the problem system itself and our understanding of the system in general. This mapping process assists key input to:

- Friendly forces concept of operation;
- Running intelligence estimate;
- Development, evaluation, and refinement of priority intelligence requirements;
- Facilitating the initial scoping of a unit's intelligence collection plan.

Whereas the initial urban OE framing is largely a strategic and operational undertaking (e.g. geographic combatant command aligned to corps and divisions), the mapping of the urban problem system step may largely fall to BCTs and below. In tactical echelons, F-ASCOPE evaluation and subsequent analysis[30] would be aligned with the applicable METT-TC variables, dependent upon specific mission, operational phase context, and the respective operationally engaged echelon. This mapping step should incorporate data central to understanding complex adaptive systems, essentially alluding to global graph[31] utilization; human domain mapping; human social culture behavior modeling; and emergent state phenomena.[32]

A definitive by-product of framing the urban OE, specifically the analysis of the relevant operational data layers and their systems' orientation, yields select identification of those problem systems along with their associated sub-elements (see Figure 5[33]).

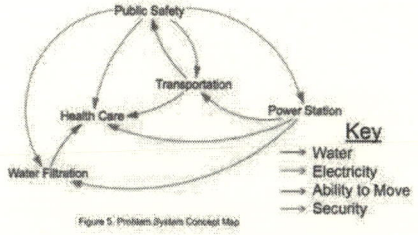

Figure 5. Problem System Concept Map

Concept Mapping is a key component of problem framing and is linked to TRADOC PAM 525-5-500, "Commander's Appreciation and Campaign Design," 200).

As the concept and geospatial mapping functions come together (See Figure 6 on following page) the data therein is critical towards enabling an analytic team the means to convert system patterns of operations (to include systems of opposition) to graphics. This visualization may take on a form similar to elements within the present IPB process in which situation and event-like templates are generated; thereby illustrating system and city key "terrain," potential/necessary objectives, named areas of interest, target areas of interest, and associated decision points.

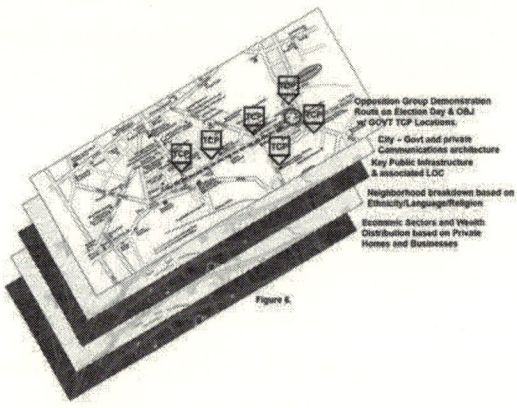

Figure 6 (above) is an example of the Urban OE visualization discussed on the previous page. In this figure's example, significant operational data layer examples (culled from the examples presented in the Appendix) were combined and framed in a visual array for a select portion of a city in support of a specific event.

In sum, mapping the urban problem system embodies a visual representation of the elements of the problem and their relationships. This step is an integral element towards truly facilitating and cultivating a deeper understanding of each system's role, impact, and effects. This step illustrates and affords:

- General understanding (and simplification) for how disparate parts of the system interconnect and interact to produce emergent phenomena and provides a visual means supporting systematic study of system parts.[34]
- Structural diagramming showing directional flows of resources and the connections between accumulators/nodes (based on the initial F-ASCOPE analysis). This diagramming technique results in a visual track of resource flow(s) through the problem system while building a holistic picture of the system(s) within the OE.[35]
- Understanding how the population, infrastructure, and key actors relate to the physical terrain. This in turn aids in revealing the territorial logic shaping the spectrums of behavior[36] of the key actors within the urban OE and potentially puts a face to each of the city's operational data layers.[37]

Fruition of the latter comment above is intrinsic to a maneuver commander's vision and intent as well as the unit's urban battlespace (or engagement) management. Analysis and subsequent data mapping should answer several significant questions relevant to friendly force operations, strategies, and objectives—contributing to the commander's understanding of system/city (urban) metabolism.

Developing & Analyzing Urban COAs

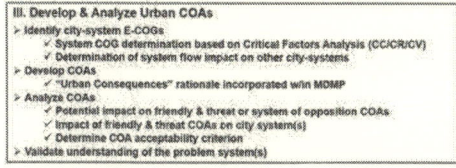

Figure 7. Develop & Analyze Urban COAs

This framework then moves from describing the problem to how to influence it[38] via identification of Environment Centers of Gravity (E-COGS). E-COGS are those accumulators/nodes and flows that appear to play a more central role in the viability and functionality of the system. E-COGs are the critical elements that truly enable the system to function to the degree required in order to fulfill its inherent system and city objective(s). E-COG identification may be aided by the location of potential E-COG within a city's overall systems diagram, the potential E-COG's centrality (degree of accumulators/nodes and flows interaction) and its loop positioning (where a closed sequence of causes and effects occurs).[39]

E-COG application extends traditional COG analysis from one that is adversary centric to one that embraces a systems-supportive environmental perspective. E-COG analysis resides within the premise that population, infrastructure, and the physical environment all provide resources to both friendly forces and systems of opposition as well as all those who rely on the city's systems for well-being, sustainment, and progress. There may be multiple E-COGs "in play" at the same time within the same DUA, with each or a combination thereof, extremely susceptible to change over time.

The key to E-COG application is giving each system found within the population, infrastructure, or environment (e.g. water, energy, communications systems, etc.) greater context or depth by stating the objective(s) of each of those entities (as opposed to a "threat intent" in traditional COG analysis). Alignment of an objective to a system enables tailored application of current COG or critical factors analysis using critical capabilities, critical requirements, and critical vulnerabilities descriptions, rendering a more refined intelligence portrait of system interaction and the impact on the DUA. E-COG identification, partnered with relevant critical factors analysis provides an important conceptual link between framing the environment, identifying and characterizing the problem systems,[40] and creating a model[41] that incorporates the elements/systems therein.

E-COG identification within the problem(s) system(s) remains key towards developing tentative courses of action (COA) designed to affect the E-COG and thus achieve a friendly force desired end-state.[42] Select examples of related system/E-COG-related friendly COAs may center around degradation of the E-COG to deny resources to a system of opposition or a clearly defined threat entity;[43] and reinforcement of an E-COG in order to ensure that that E-COG functions and contributes positively to the system users.[44]

This framework enhances the operations planning staff's ability to determine COA acceptability criterion specific to DUA through an urban consequences rationale developed within MDMP.[45] Urban consequences COA considerations may also be assisted by using imaginative advanced structure analytic techniques (e.g. outside-in thinking and morphological analysis[46]) to forecast how the COA may affect other not-yet-analyzed systems.[47] This process may also serve as a check against baseline system-on-system effects analysis, in which a relationship outcome may not be sufficiently captured or the relationship effects are now unfavorable to friendly force operations.

Preparing for the AOC's Future Operating Environment

DUA require an analytic framework specifically tailored to accommodate a city's system diversity. The analytic framework presented provides a structure that incorporates urban operational data layers and city as a system context and perspectives. It is a catalyst towards addressing AOC questions like, "what is the environment we think Army forces will operate in, and what is the problem we are trying to solve?" The potential for US forces to operate in DUA remains significant today and in the far term given the global pace of urbanization and the world's megatrends involving more complex diplomatic, economic, and military power. These trends are largely population-centric, and thus urban centric. As the Army's potential OE landscape continues to evolve, so must the Army's doctrinal framework, processes, and applications evolve as well. This framework is representative of our human domain[48] efforts (e.g. data collection and analysis) in understanding the human interface resident within DUA; it is an education enabler that prepares the Army for the "unknown."[49] It complements the Army's human dimension[50] educational effort as well, guiding both situational understanding and the knowledge acquisition necessary for managing and influencing an Army team (and those within the human domain) through a potentially challenging and relatively unknown problem set. Gaining further insight to the dynamics between the components of problems within a decidedly complex urban system and the potential for hybrid warfare therein will not be easy; but, it must be a requirement. Development of situational understanding for dense urban areas remains a critical component of Army planning; such understanding demands relevant context and a framework appropriate for content application.

Appendix

Select Operational Data Layers Examples Found Within Dense Urban Areas

The following examples are grouped or nested within an overarching concept (e.g. human geography) and shaped initially by the appropriate dense urban area dimensional perspective (see Figure 3 on page 9):

1. Human geography of the "cityscape" (Human/Cyber/Information/Surface)
2. Ethnicity/Language/Religion
3. Social groups and organizations
4. Select demographic group patterns of life capture
5. Attitudes; social networking near-term sentiment analysis
6. Health & medical
7. Significant events
8. Relative degree of urbanization & associated demographics (Human/Cyber/Information/Surface)
9. Geospatial visualization of dense urban core and peri-urban
10. Distributions of wealth (wealthy core vs. poor core & poor periphery (geospatial graphic representation))
11. Familia/tribal pockets; relationships, ideology influencers

12. Demographic dependencies on government or armed groups

13. Grievances; Identified coping mechanisms; opportunities to create resiliency

14. Identification of what one knows of the "social state," group or population movement (human condition mapping)

15. Analysis of urban inflow & outflows (Human/Cyber/Information/Surface/sub-surface)

16. Sewage, Water, Electricity, Academia, Trash, Medical, Safety, Food

17. Demographic/social movement (Dense urban core to peri-urban areas & peri-urban areas to dense urban core)

18. Traffic and commuter patterns (Road/rail/pedestrian/maritime/air)

19. Wealth and economic distribution patterns, means of economic control and infrastructure controls (Define "elite, middle-class, and poor" based on present conditions)

20. International trade flows into/from city (incl. Air and sea ports/other (rail/ground))

21. Economics (Human/Cyber/Information)

22. Basis and state of financial capital

23. Type/flow of commodities and remittance

24. Potential for stabilizing effects of illicit economies

25. Unemployment; rates, socio-economic aspects of affected divisions w/in general population

26. Systems of opposition (Human/Cyber/Information)

27. Identification, description, and their core interests

28. Opposition methods, span, and degree of control

29. System rivals/allies (active/potential)

30. Level of demonstrated or potential access to advanced lethal/military technologies available to the system of opposition

31. Population's reliance/dependence on the system (security, aid, conflict resolution, social rule, financial assistance) and impact on terms of support/acceptance of the system's authority or influence

32. Security controls/overwatch mechanisms (Human/Cyber/Information)
33. Government security forces; degree of presence, influence, and control
34. Internet and social media penetration; government internet policy
35. Identification of political/military influencers
36. Population's reliance/dependency on the city government (admin services, property rights, conflict resolution, social welfare/aid, education, and health) and impact on terms of support/acceptance of the government's authority or influence
37. Other "Actors" (not identified/discovered above) (Human/Cyber/Information)
38. Local administration (governance, military, law enforcement)
39. Religious/Business/labor
40. Illicit network "leads" or commodities providers
41. Hostile actors (not otherwise captured w/in system of opposition; e.g. gangs)

Notes

[1]   "The US Army Operating Concept," TRADOC Pamphlet 525-3-1 (Oct 14), i (Foreword).

[2]   Ibid. iii (Preface).

[3]   Ibid. 11-12.

[4]   "The US Army Operating Concept," TRADOC Pamphlet 525-3-1 (Oct 14), 12.

[5]   "Readiness in an Urban Era: Implications for the US Army," Strategic Initiatives Group—Lyceum, School of Advanced Military Studies (SAMS), Ft. Leavenworth, KS (May 15), i.

[6]   US Army Chief of Staff' Strategic Studies Group (Megacities), *A Proposed Framework for Appreciating Megacities: A US Army Perspective,* Small Wars Journal (Apr 2014), 2. System typology

often featuring decentralized and informal systems, low quality infrastructure, and unregulated flow capacity.

[7] Luciano Florida, *"The Fourth Technological Revolution,"* Oxford, UK, Oxford University Press (May 2014), 14-15.

[8] National Intelligence Council, *Global Trends 2030: Alternative Worlds* (Washington DC: Office of the Director of National Intelligence (2012), ii.

[9] SAMS, "Readiness in an Urban Era: Implications for the US Army," 1.

[10] Heuristics are strategies using readily accessible, though loosely applicable, information to control (or steer) problem solving.

[11] "Commander's Appreciation and Campaign Design," TRADOC Pamphlet 525-5-500 (Jan 2008), 6.

[12] Understanding the Threat as a System of Opposition," David Pendall, COL, USA, White Paper (Jan 2014), 4.

[13] Political, Military, Economic, Sociological, Infrastructure, Information—Physical Environment & Time. "Brigade Combat Team Intelligence Techniques," ATP-2-19.4 (FM 2-19.4) (Feb 2015), 1-3.

[14] Flow—Area, Structures, Capabilities, Organizations, People & Events. ATP 2-19.4, B-21.

[15] Sewage, Water, Energy, Academics, Trash—Medical, Safety, & Other Considerations. "Engineer Reconnaissance," FM 3-34.170 (Mar 2008), 6-14.

[16] Diplomatic, Information, Military, Economic, Financial, Intelligence, and Law Enforcement. Vulnerability Analysis Workbook, Understanding the Threat, Vol 1, US Army Asymmetric Warfare Group, Ft. Meade MD (Jun 2008), v.

[17] Mission, Enemy, Terrain & Weather, Troops & Support Available—Time Available & Civil Considerations. ATP 2-19.4, 1-3.

[18] Re-scoping how the Army views and applies applicable operational variables to a problem set like dense urban areas, could significantly add data dimensions not presently considered for urban-related mission analysis.

[19] Frank Hoffman, LtCol, USMCR (Ret.), "The Janus choice: Defining today's multifaceted conflict," Armed Forces Journal (Oct 2009). Combat operations characterized by the simultaneous and adaptive employment of a complex combination of conventional weapons, irregular warfare, terrorism and criminal behavior to achieve political objectives.

[20] "City as a System, Analytic Framework," Version 1.0, CAERUS Associates and the Combatting Terrorism Technical Support Office, Alexandria, VA (Jun 2015), 1.

[21] CTTSO was established in 1999 by the Assistant Secretary of Defense for Special Operations/Low-Intensity Conflict. It is charged with providing a forum for interagency and international users to discuss mission requirements to combat terrorism, prioritize requirements, fund and manage solutions, and deliver capabilities.

[22] "City as a System, Analytic Framework," 1.

[23] There exists minute differences for representing the dimensions of the urban landscape between various DoD entities as part of the dense urban area community of interest.

[24] "City as a System, Analytic Framework," 25-26. The CAERUS/ CTTSO Urban Triad Paradigm conceptually borrows from Joint Publication 3-06, "Joint Urban Operations," and contributes significantly towards defining the unique features of urban environments. This paradigm is represented by population (PMESII), infrastructure (SWEAT-MSO), and physical environment and time (as a latter sub-set of PMESII-PT application.

[25] "Dense Urban Areas & Megacities Challenge," Brief to US Army Intelligence Center of Excellence representatives, Dr. Rolf Halden, Arizona State University Research Enterprise (ASURE), Phoenix, AZ (24 Sep 15), slide 19. Multi-variable consideration creates multiple lines of information ingest, protects against data gaps, and thus better informs follow-on mapping and modeling efforts.

[26] David J. Kilcullen, *"The City as a System: Future Conflict and Urban Resilience,"* The Fletcher Forum of World Affairs, VOL 36:2 (Summer 2012), 36.

[27] Capture and analysis of negative effects/impacts regarding urban operational data layers is key to informing friendly COA development. There may be circumstances in which the effects of a city-related system are so adverse that an environmentally imposed condition like area anti-access/area denial is present.

[28] Comparing/contrasting current city steady-state with a desired future state, based on the urban OE's operational data layers analysis and a Commander's guidance/mission analysis will also require a structured analytic outline (see DIA & CIA structured analytics regarding diagnostic techniques, argument mapping, and contrarian techniques).

[29] Pendall, (Jan 2014), 4.

[30] Identification of critical city system flows may not be readily apparent to a planning staff via F-ASCOPE regarding a dense urban OE's effects on operations and the implications therein. This contention is reinforced by the CAERUS framework's apt descriptors of accumulators and nodes as related, yet hardly interchangeable concepts. These terms may require doctrinal re-visit in light of the critical application of F-ASCOPE in support of dense urban terrain analysis.

[31] A global graph is a scalable, operational environment-specific database that identifies, stores, and updates the relationships between hundreds of thousands to millions of entities. The relationships between entities are stored as fusion triples, i.e., as object-predicate-object. Future analytic teams would employ algorithms and artificial intelligence means to discover and explore not only those entities and relationships that are obviously relevant to their unit's mission; but more important, to discover and track those entities which were not previously known to the unit. Global graphs are foundational and fundamental to all future analytics, to understanding threat and non-threat networks of people, places, procedures, and underlying motivations, and

perhaps most importantly, to understanding complex operational environments as complex adaptive systems.

[32] Tom Pike and Eddie J. Brown, *"Populations as Complex Adaptive Systems: A Case Study of Corruption in Afghanistan,"* Small Wars Journal (Aug 2011), 3.

[33] "City as a System, Analytic Framework," Brief to US Army Intelligence Center of Excellence, CAERUS Associates and the Combatting Terrorism Technical Support Office, Alexandria, VA (14 Jul 2015), slide 16.

[34] "City as a System, Analytic Framework," 30.

[35] Ibid. 30-31.

[36] "Dense Urban Areas & Megacities Challenge," Brief, Dr. Rolf Halden, ASURE, terminology discussion.

[37] "City as a System, Analytic Framework," 35.

[38] Ibid. 37.

[39] Ibid. 39.

[40] Ibid. 38.

[41] Comparison between two or more dense urban OEs will likely yield contrasting elements or system-specific-interaction differences; therefore, model-linked experimentation efforts may require a very specific dense urban OE test subject and scenario in order to adequately convey and capture the resultant impact of a critical variable upon the other resident systems within the OE.

[42] "City as a System, Analytic Framework," 41.

[43] Ibid.

[44] Ibid.

[45] Ibid. 42. Urban operational consequences are not presently captured within MDMP as part of step 4 (COA Analysis—War Game) and step 5 (COA Comparison). A planning staff may need to return to the urban OE framing and mapping steps in order to re-assess how the friendly/threat COAs will impact the system-specific operational data layers.

[46] Richards J. Heur Jr., and Randolph H. Pherson, *"Structured Analytic Techniques for Intelligence Analysis,"* Washington, DC, CQ Press—Division of SAGE (2011), 108.

[47]   City as a System, Analytic Framework," 42.

[48]   Totality of the physical, cultural, psychological, and social environments that influence human behavior to the extent that the success of any military operation or campaign depends on the application of unique capabilities that are designed to influence, fight, and win in population-centric conflicts.

[49]   Thomas E. Ricks, *"The Generals,"* New York, NY, Penguin Press (2012), 346. The author's context was in relation to *"FM 100-5: Operations,"* in which that document was categorized as ". . . emphasized training, which prepares soldiers for the known, far more than education, which prepares them to deal with the unknown."

[50]   Cognitive, physical, and social (CPS) components of Soldier, civilian, leader, and organizational development and performance essential to raise, prepare, and employ the Army in unified land operations.

Chapter 33

Assessing Physiological Response to Toxic Industrial Chemical Exposure in Megacities

Danielle L. Ippolito

First Published 14 March 2016

Introduction

Megacities—urban areas with populations of ten million or greater—and other dense urban environments are emerging and growing globally, posing new challenges for U.S. military operations. The United States (U.S.) military can be better positioned for potential future operations within megacities as part of a joint, interagency, intergovernmental, and multinational team by increasing its understanding of megacity environments (Harris et al., 2014). Chemical exposures pose risk to the health and readiness of Service Members operating in these environments. The Naval Research Laboratory (NRL) prioritized a list of the top 30 chemicals of concern for global military operations based on physical characteristics and available toxicology data (Sutto, 2015). Occupational exposure to these chemicals increases risk of developing adverse health effects during mission operations or post-deployment. Policy guidelines specifying the use of the appropriate personal protective gear constitute the first line of defense to protect personnel by limiting exposure in the field. After a confirmed or suspected exposure event, far-forward diagnostic tools are needed to quickly and effectively determine and manage the risk of adverse health effects post-exposure in order to make informed command decisions about return-to-duty and treatment options. Identifying and quantifying biomolecular indicators in accessible biofluids such as blood, saliva, or urine is critically important for evaluating chemically-induced disease prognosis (Tawa et al., 2014; Ippolito et al., 2015). Biomarkers of end-organ toxicity can be integrated into a fieldable detection system to rapidly diagnose chemical exposure-induced adverse health effects in theater. Noninvasive or minimally invasive screening methods could enable early intervention, treatment, and informed decision making to optimize force readiness. Mapping biomolecular patterns of adverse health effects represents a promising solution to the complex problem of assessing health effects after exposure to mixtures of different chemicals and /or pollutants and aggregated exposure effects over time (Silins & Högberg, 2011).

This systematic literature review identifies and assesses the level of evidence for candidate far forward diagnostic technologies and biomarkers that may be used to detect emerging health effects from exposure to militarily-relevant chemicals. The review emphasizes a subacute exposure window (i.e., days to weeks) best suited to the short-term exposure scenarios anticipated in military operations and mission scenarios. Biomarker development demands meeting rigorous regulatory and clinical standards before adoption in the field, but military investment in this research and development process has the potential for significant returns in military healthcare during the deployment life cycle. Biomarker-based screening technologies can benefit routine health care screening, return-to-duty decision-making, triage during mass casualty exposure events, and/or guiding the development of diagnostics to inform treatment options. Biomarker-based far-forward diagnostic strategies and technologies have the potential to transform military healthcare in the changing face of warfare in megacities and dense urban operating environments

Methods

The peer-reviewed literature was surveyed to evaluate the weight-of-evidence regarding biomarkers for emerging health effects resulting from exposure to militarily-relevant chemicals (Table 1). The target list of militarily relevant chemicals was based on 30 prioritized megacity chemical hazards outlined in the *NRL Industrial Chemical Assessment for Hazard, Probability, and Biomarker Prioritization* (Sutto, 2015). A biomarker was defined as a molecular, cellular, or biophysical event linked to an emerging health effect.

Table 1. High Priority Megacity Military relevant Toxic Industrial Chemical Hazards. Adapted from NRL Industrial Chemical Assessment for Hazard, Probability and Biomarker Prioritization (Sutto, 2015)

Global Rank	Toxic Industrial Chemical	Global Rank	Toxic Industrial Chemical
1	Chlorine	16	Phosphoryl trichloride
2	Ammonia	17	Chlorine dioxide
3	Hydrogen chloride	18	Bromine
4	Sulfuric acid	19	Nitrogen dioxide
5	Hydrogen fluoride	20	Phosphorus trichloride
6	Formaldehyde	21	Fluorotrichloromethane
7	Mercury	22	Hydrogen sulfide
8	Nitric acid	23	Molybdophosphoric acid
9	Sulfur dioxide	24	Toluene-2,4-diisocyanate
10	Phosgene	25	Fluorine
11	Hydrogen bromide	26	Malathion
12	Nitric Oxide	27	Parathion
13	Octamethyl pyrophosphoramine	28	Acetylene tetrabromide
14	Boron trifluoride	29	o-Anisidine
15	Methyl bromide	30	Phosphine

Databases searched included PubMed, Web of Knowledge, Google Scholar, ClinicalTrials.gov, publicly available Department of Defense (DoD) technical reports (e.g., Defense Technical Information Center), non-DoD sources, and the Center for Disease Control Agency for Toxic Substance & Disease Registry and from the U.S. Library of Medicine Hazardous Substances Data Bank ("Agency for Toxic Substance & Disease Registry—Medical Management Guidelines Home Page," n.d., "U.S. National Library of Medicine—Hazardous Substances Data Bank," n.d.). Search terms were selected to identify studies that examined health effects associated with exposure to the high priority chemicals. The search was limited to articles published in English from January 2005 to May 2015.

Peer-reviewed articles were excluded if they (1) reported acute responses requiring immediate palliative care, (2) reviewed *in vitro* or computational toxicology sites that did not use publicly available data sets, and (30 discussed mechanistic biomarkers without clear implications for candidate prognostic markers suitable for fieldable detection devices.

An objective two-step grading approach based on the U.S. Preventive Services Task Force Grade Definitions was used to assess the internal validity of individual studies published in peer-reviewed journal articles that met the inclusion criteria. The first step in evidence grading methodology identified and ranked the study design within a hierarchy of evidence, and the second step assessed the study quality (good, fair, poor). Study designs included the following categories: preclinical research (e.g., animal models), clinical research (e.g., clinical trials, diagnostic studies), epidemiological research (e.g., cohort studies, intervention studies), and secondary research (e.g., meta-analysis, systematic reviews). If a publication contained both a preclinical study and a clinical study, a separate grade was assigned for each study.

Results and Discussion

A review of 57 current papers in the diagnostic device literature identified five classes of biomarker detection devices (Figure 1). Most of the devices in development are lab-on-a-chip designs and paper-based lab-on-a-chip (LOC paper) prototypes. Frequently portable and disposable, these designs may be amenable to military field settings (Shafiee et al., 2015). Unique technological challenges limit the utility of many prototype diagnostics for use in a far-forward operational setting. Further research, clinical trials, and validation are needed to advance the devices beyond the prototype stage (Hoenigl et al., 2014). Ruggedization and miniaturization of laboratory prototypes are significant challenges in fielding these devices (Greenwood et al., 2007).

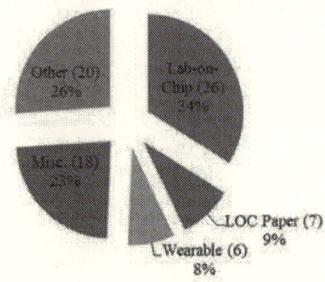

Figure 1. Biomarker detection devices under development identified by environmental literature scan. Modifications are necessary before many of these detection devices are available in far-forward diagnostic settings. (LOC, lab-on-a-chip)

Table 2 lists the target organs of adverse health effects following exposure to each of the chemicals. Table 3 reports the key acute, subacute, and chronic health effects for each target organ. Most of the data summarized in Tables 2 and 3 are derived from a scan of public toxicology data repositories (e.g., the Hazardous Substances Data Bank and related ToxNet resources). These repositories identify relevant studies outside the time frame of the systematic review (i.e., before 2005-2015).

Table 3. Top 30 prioritized militarily relevant toxic industrial chemicals by target organ adverse health effects.

Table 3. Key acute, subacute, chronic health effects by target organ associated with exposure to the top 30 prioritized megacity chemicals

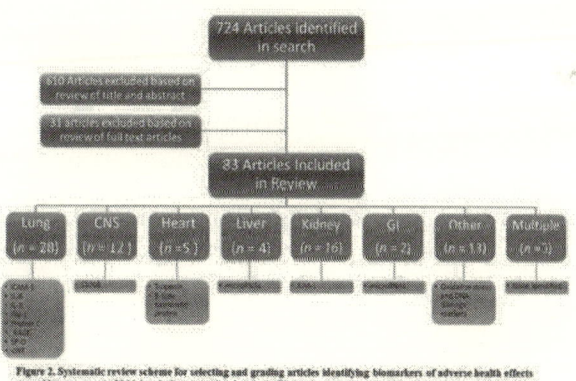

Articles meeting the inclusion criteria for adverse health effects were organized into eight specific target organ categories: lung, central nervous system (CNS), peripheral nervous system (PNS), heart, liver, kidney, gastrointestinal, other, and multiple (Figure 2). A summary of the literature review by target organ for five key target organs (lung, CNS/PNS, heart, liver, and kidney) follows.

Figure 2. Systematic review scheme for selecting and grading articles identifying biomarkers of adverse health effects caused by exposure to 30 high priority megacity chemicals. Biomarkers associated with each target organ are listed.

Lung. Several of the 28 lung-related articles identified biomarkers correlating with acute lung injury/acute respiratory distress syndrome (ALI/ARDS): RAGE, ICAM-1, KL-6, SP-D, vWF, IL-6, IL-8, protein C, PAI-1, TNFR1 and 2, and thrombomodulin (Agrawal et al., 2012; Calfee et al., 2008; Calfee et al., 2009; Collard et al., 2010;

McClintock et al., 2008; Parsons et al., 2005; Uchida et al., 2006). Many of these biomarkers were associated with clinical outcomes (e.g., ventilator-free days, organ-failure-free days, and mortality). Mean levels the proteins PBEF or MIF were significantly greater in serum of ALI patients than healthy controls although the specificity for ALI remains uncertain (Gao et al., 2007; Ye et al., 2005). Combining predictive markers improved predictive power. Low levels of protein C and high levels of PAI-1 were independent predictors of mortality, and the two markers had a synergistic interaction for the risk of death (Ware et al., 2007). Levels of RAGE, PCP III, BNP, ANG-2, IL-8, TNF-α, and IL-10 show potential as a diagnostic biomarker panel (Fremont et al., 2010). In two studies, combinations of clinical predictors and multiple plasma biomarkers measured in individuals with ALI/ARDS improved predictive power for mortality over either approach alone, with some evidence that trauma differentially affects odds of mortality (Calfee et al., 2011; Ware et al., 2010). Exposure to isocyanates (e.g., TDI and MDI) was linked to occupational asthma. Biomarkers associated with this clinical outcome included VDBP, MMP-9, VEGF, LSP-1, COR1A, HPX, and autoantibodies to tTG, CK18, and CK19 (Kim et al., 2011; Hur et al., 2008; Ye et al., 2006; Haenen et al., 2012). F_2-IsoP in plasma and lung tissue and SOD1 and COX2 in lung tissue may be associated with respiratory exposure to cadmium or silica nanoparticles (Coccini et al., 2012). Pulmonary fluid proteins and/or bronchial lavage proteins are biomarker candidates for lung injury, including ferritin, transferrin, CC16, ICAM-1, and PBEF (Hur et al, 2008; Kropski et al., 2009; Ye et al., 2005). Biomarkers in exhaled breath present an attractive alternative for accessibility in field settings (eNO and eCO_2 after exposure to chlorine and phosgene) or cytokines such as IL-4 after exposure to NO_2; Luo et al., 2014; Nath and Januszkiewicz, 2008).

Central and peripheral nervous system (CNS/PNS). The 18 articles associated with CNS/PNS injury included serum biomarkers associated with neurological sequelae, mostly associated with organophosphate pesticide (OP) exposure. These biomarkers of OP exposure and effect included a panel of autoantibodies (e.g., antibodies to NFP, TAU, MAP-2, MBP, GFAP, S100B), blood ChE/AChE, creatinine kinase,

AST, LysoPC hydrolase in erythrocytes, SOD activity and/or LPO concentration after exposure to organophosphate pesticides (Abou-Donia et al., 2013; Rohlman et al., 2011; Bayrami et al., 2012; Vose et al., 2007; Colak et al., 2014; Aygun et al., 2007). Biomarkers to non-OP-related chemical exposures included GRIA 1 and glial S100B after exposure to mercury (Park et al., 2012) and serum S100B after acute CO poisoning (Abou-Donia, 2013).

Heart. A combination of biophysical and serum biomarkers were identified for the heart. Isoforms of troponin and cardiac natriuretic proteins released into the serum were associated with myocardial injury. Hydrogen sulfide poisoning resulted in cardiac proteins TNI and CPK-MB increased over time in conjunction with ECG data (Hirakawa et al., 2013). OP poisonings were associated with elevated TNI detecting acute early phase of cardiac injury (e.g., within the first 48 hours) (Cha, Cha et al., 2014). There is strong evidence for the emerging utility of cardiac troponins in stratifying toxicity risk (Dolci et al., 2008). Biophysical biomarkers included ECG measurements to determine risk of myocardial injury and arrhythmias (e.g., transmyocardial repolarization parameters to myocardial injury, left ventricle ejection fraction), especially after CO poisoning and OP exposure (Akilli et al., 2013). An emerging literature identifies micro-ribonucleic acids (miRNAs) in the prediction, detection, assessment, or treatment of myocardial damage and cardiac dysfunction (Sandhu & Maddock, 2014).

Liver. Four articles identified liver biomarkers in serum, including miRNAs (serum miR-125a-5p, miR-192 and miRNA-122; Zheng et al., 2015; Zhang et al., 2010). Changes in miRNA levels assessed in liver tissue implicate miRNAs such as miR-34a as promising new candidates in serum or urine (Koufaris et al., 2012). Liver injury diagnosis is routinely made in conjunction with clinical chemistry data, including alanine amino transferase (ALT). A panel of plasma or serum biomarkers diagnosed liver fibrosis in animal models (fibrinogen precursor, ceruloplasmin isoform 1, insulin like growth factor binding protein, alpha-2-macroglobulin, and vitronectin) (Ippolito et al., 2015).

Kidney. The 17 kidney-related articles identified biomarkers in serum and urine. Acute kidney injury markers in serum included LG3, cathepsin L, NGAL, IL-6, soluble TNFR1 and 2, and PAI-1 as potential candidates (Haase et al, 2014; Liu et al., 2007). Clinical studies have identified promising urinary biomarkers of acute kidney injury and/or nephrotoxicity, including KIM-1 protein after TCE exposure (Vermeulen et al., 2012). Urinary panels include Alb, NAG and α1-MG as indicators of fluoride and arsenic-induced glomerular and tubular injury (Zeng et al., 2014). KIM-1 predicted kidney injury earlier than the traditional biomarkers, such as creatinine, BUN, and/or NGAL (Rached et al., 2008; Vaidya et al., 2010; Wunnapuk, Gobe, et al., 2014; Zhou et al., 2008). Many of the preclinical studies examined urinary biomarkers of kidney injury other than KIM-1 (e.g., Cal, Clu, KIM-1, Lcn2, the three-branched chain amino acids [leucine, isoleucine, and valine], OPN, TTF3) and provide important foundational information (Boudonck et al., 2009; Fuchs et al., 2014; Hoffmann et al., 2010; Wunnapuk, Liu, et al., 2014; Yu et al., 2010).

Other health effects. Other health effects with biomarker candidates included gastrointestinal, reproductive, cancer progression, blood, bone, and lymphatics (see Tables 2 and 3 and Figure 2).

Conclusions

As megacities and dense urban environments continue to grow in number and population size, there is an unmet need to understand the health threats of service members exposed to toxic chemicals and environmental hazards unique to the megacity operational environment. Properly validated biomarkers of exposure and effect can integrate with current biomonitoring systems throughout the soldier deployment life cycle to inform medical decisions during and after exposure events, especially in polluted megacity operational environments with increased risk of non-agent chemical exposure. Further research is needed to ensure the field-ability of ruggedized detection systems in the megacity environment.

Acknowledgements: This manuscript is based on a DTIC report submitted by Booz Allen Hamilton entitled "Biomarkers for Health Effects of Industrial Chemical Exposure Literature Review", submitted to USACEHR on behalf of USAMRMC-MOMRP on 26 June 2015. We gratefully acknowledge COL Thomas C. Timmes, USA, Commander of USACEHR, for programmatic support.

The views, opinions, and/or findings contained in this report are those of the author and should not be construed as official Department of the Army position, policy, or decision, unless so designated by other official documentation.

References

Abou-Donia, M. B., Abou-Donia, M. M., El-Masry, E. M., Monro, J. A., & Mulder, M. F. A. (2013). Autoantibodies to Nervous System-Specific Proteins Are Elevated in Sera of Flight Crew Members: Biomarkers for Nervous System Injury. *Journal of Toxicology and Environmental Health, Part A, 76*(6), 363–380. http://doi.org/10.1080/15287394.2013.765369.

Agrawal, A., Zhuo, H., Brady, S., Levitt, J., Steingrub, J., Siegel, M. D., ... Liu, K. D. (2012). Pathogenetic and predictive value of biomarkers in patients with ALI and lower severity of illness: results from two clinical trials. *American Journal of Physiology—Lung Cellular and Molecular Physiology, 303*(8), L634–L639. http://doi.org/10.1152/ajplung.00195.2012.

Akilli, N. B., Akinci, E., Akilli, H., Dundar, Z. D., Koylu, R., Polat, M., & Cander, B. (2013). A new marker for myocardial injury in carbon monoxide poisoning: T peak-T end. *The American Journal of Emergency Medicine, 31*(12), 1651–1655. http://doi.org/10.1016/j.ajem.2013.08.049.

Aygun, D., Erenler, A. K., Karatas, A. D., & Baydin, A. (2007). Intermediate Syndrome Following Acute Organophosphate Poisoning: Correlation with Initial Serum Levels of Muscle

Enzymes. *Basic & Clinical Pharmacology & Toxicology, 100*(3), 201–204. http://doi.org/10.1111/j.1742-7843.2007.00042.x.

Bayrami, M., Hashemi, T., Malekirad, A. A., Ashayeri, H., Faraji, F., & Abdollahi, M. (2012). Electroencephalogram, cognitive state, psychological disorders, clinical symptom, and oxidative stress in horticulture farmers exposed to organophosphate pesticides. *Toxicology and Industrial Health, 28*(1), 90–96. http://doi.org/10.1177/0748233711407243.

Boudonck, K. J., Rose, D. J., Karoly, E. D., Lee, D. P., Lawton, K. A., & Lapinskas, P. J. (2009). Metabolomics for early detection of drug-induced kidney injury: review of the current status. *Bioanalysis, 1*(9), 1645–1663. http://doi.org/10.4155/bio.09.142.

Calfee, C. S., Eisner, M. D., Ware, L. B., Thompson, B. T., Parsons, P. E., Wheeler, A. P., … Matthay, M. A. (2007). Trauma-associated lung injury differs clinically and biologically from acute lung injury due to other clinical disorders. *Critical Care Medicine, 35*(10), 2243–2250.

Calfee, C. S., Ware, L. B., Eisner, M. D., Parsons, P. E., Thompson, B. T., Wickersham, N., … NHLBI ARDS Network. (2008). Plasma receptor for advanced glycation end products and clinical outcomes in acute lung injury. *Thorax, 63*(12), 1083–1089. http://doi.org/10.1136/thx.2008.095588.

Calfee, C. S., Ware, L. B., Glidden, D. V., Eisner, M. D., Parsons, P. E., Thompson, B. T., & Matthay, M. A. (2011). Use of risk reclassification with multiple biomarkers improves mortality prediction in acute lung injury. *Critical Care Medicine, 39*(4), 711–717. http://doi.org/10.1097/CCM.0b013e318207ec3c.

Cha, Y. S., Cha, K. C., Kim, O. H., Lee, K. H., Hwang, S. O., & Kim, H. (2014). Features and predictors of myocardial injury in carbon monoxide poisoned patients. *Emergency Medicine Journal: EMJ, 31*(3), 210–215. http://doi.org/10.1136/emermed-2012-202152.

Cha, Y. S., Kim, H., Go, J., Kim, T. H., Kim, O. H., Cha, K. C., … Hwang, S. O. (2014). Features of myocardial injury in severe organophosphate poisoning. *Clinical Toxicology (Philadelphia,*

Pa.), *52*(8), 873–879. http://doi.org/10.3109/15563650.2014. 944976.

Coccini, T., Roda, E., Manzo, L., Barni, S., & Signorini, C. (2012). Isoprostanes as Biomarkers for In Vivo Evaluation of Nanoparticle-induced Oxidative Stress: a Study with Silica Nanoparticles Doped with Cadmium. *International Journal of Theoretical and Applied Nanotechnology*. http://doi. org/10.11159/ijtan.2012.001.

Çolak, Ş., Erdogan, M. Ö., Baydin, A., Afacan, M. A., Kati, C., & Duran, L. (2014). Epidemiology of organophosphate intoxication and predictors of intermediate syndrome. Retrieved from http://dergipark.ulakbim.gov.tr/tbtkmedical/ article/viewFile/5000022935/5000023173.

Collard, H. R., Calfee, C. S., Wolters, P. J., Song, J. W., Hong, S.-B., Brady, S., ... others. (2010). Plasma biomarker profiles in acute exacerbation of idiopathic pulmonary fibrosis. *American Journal of Physiology-Lung Cellular and Molecular Physiology*, *299*(1), L3–L7.

Dolci, A., Dominici, R., Cardinale, D., Sandri, M. T., & Panteghini, M. (2008). Biochemical markers for prediction of chemotherapy-induced cardiotoxicity: systematic review of the literature and recommendations for use. *American Journal of Clinical Pathology*, *130*(5), 688–695. http://doi.org/10.1309/ AJCPB66LRIIVMQDR.

Fuchs, T. C., Mally, A., Wool, A., Beiman, M., & Hewitt, P. (2014). An Exploratory Evaluation of the Utility of Transcriptional and Urinary Kidney Injury Biomarkers for the Prediction of Aristolochic Acid–Induced Renal Injury in Male Rats. *Veterinary Pathology Online*, *51*(3), 680–694. http://doi. org/10.1177/0300985813498779.

Gao, L., Flores, C., Fan-Ma, S., Miller, E. J., Moitra, J., Moreno, L., ... Garcia, J. G. N. (2007). Macrophage migration inhibitory factor in acute lung injury: expression, biomarker, and associations. *Translational Research*, *150*(1), 18–29. http://doi. org/10.1016/j.trsl.2007.02.007.

Greenwood, D. Q. (2007). *Reconstructing operational theory: A framework for emerging threats in a complex environment.* Marine Corps University, School of Advanced Warfighting. Quantico, VA.

Haase, M., Bellomo, R., Albert, C., Vanpoucke, G., Thomas, G., Laroy, W., ... Haase-Fielitz, A. (2014). The identification of three novel biomarkers of major adverse kidney events. *Biomarkers in Medicine*, *8*(10), 1207–1217. http://doi.org/10.2217/bmm.14.90.

Haenen, S., Clynen, E., De Vooght, V., Schoofs, L., Nemery, B., Hoet, P. H. M., & Vanoirbeek, J. A. J. (2012). Proteome changes in auricular lymph nodes and serum after dermal sensitization to toluene diisocyanate in mice. *Proteomics*, *12*(23-24), 3548–3558. http://doi.org/10.1002/pmic.201200264.

Harris, M., Dixon, R., Melin, N., Hendrex, D., Russo, R., & Bailey, M. (2014). *Megacities and the United States Army: Preparing for a Complex and Uncertain Future.*

Hirakawa, A., Takeyama, N., Iwatsuki, S., Iwata, T., & Kano, H. (2013). Delayed myocardial injury following acute hydrogen sulfide intoxication. *Chūdoku Kenkyū: Chūdoku Kenkyūkai Jun Kikanshi = The Japanese Journal of Toxicology*, *26*(1), 44–48.

Hoenigl, M., Prattes, J., Spiess, B., Wagner, J., Prueller, F., Raggam, R. B., ... Buchheidt, D. (2014). Performance of galactomannan, Beta-d-Glucan, aspergillus lateral-flow device, conventional culture, and PCR tests with bronchoalveolar lavage fluid for diagnosis of invasive pulmonary aspergillosis. *Journal of Clinical Microbiology*, *52*(6), 2039–2045. http://doi.org/10.1128/JCM.00467-14.

Hoffmann, D., Adler, M., Vaidya, V., Rached, E., Mulrane, I., Gallagher, W. M., ... Mally, A. (2010). Performance of novel kidney biomarkers in preclinical toxicity studies. *Toxicological Sciences*, kfq029. http://doi.org/10.1093/toxsci/kfq029.

Hur, G.-Y., Choi, G.-S., Sheen, S.-S., Lee, H.-Y., Park, H.-J., Choi, S.-J., ... Park, H.-S. (2008). Serum ferritin and transferrin levels as serologic markers of methylene diphenyl diisocyanate–induced occupational asthma. *Journal of Allergy and Clinical Immunology, 122*(4), 774–780.

Ippolito DL, AbdulHameed MDM, Tawa GJ, Baer CE, Boyle MH, Hobbs CA, Streicker MA, Snowden BS, Lewis JA, Wallqvist A, Stallings JD. Gene expression patterns associated with histopathology in toxic liver injury. *Toxicological Sciences.* 2016 149(1):67-88. doi: 10.1093/toxsci/kfv214.

Kim, J.-H., Kim, J.-E., Choi, G.-S., Kim, H.-Y., Ye, Y.-M., & Park, H.-S. (2011). Serum cytokines markers in toluene diisocyanate-induced asthma. *Respiratory Medicine, 105*(7), 1091–1094. http://doi.org/10.1016/j.rmed.2011.03.005.

Koufaris, C., Wright, J., Currie, R. A., & Gooderham, N. J. (2012). Hepatic microRNA profiles offer predictive and mechanistic insights after exposure to genotoxic and epigenetic hepatocarcinogens. *Toxicological Sciences*, kfs170. http://doi.org/10.1093/toxsci/kfs170.

Kropski, J. A., Fremont, R. D., Calfee, C. S., & Ware, L. B. (2009). Clara cell protein (cc16), a marker of lung epithelial injury, is decreased in plasma and pulmonary edema fluid from patients with acute lung injury. *Chest, 135*(6), 1440–1447. http://doi.org/10.1378/chest.08-2465.

Liu, K. D., Glidden, D. V., Eisner, M. D., Parsons, P. E., Ware, L. B., Wheeler, A., … Matthay, M. A. (2007). Predictive and pathogenetic value of plasma biomarkers for acute kidney injury in patients with acute lung injury. *Critical Care Medicine, 35*(12), 2755–2761.

Luo, S., Trübel, H., Wang, C., & Pauluhn, J. (2014). Phosgene- and chlorine-induced acute lung injury in rats: comparison of cardiopulmonary function and biomarkers in exhaled breath. *Toxicology, 326*, 109–118. http://doi.org/10.1016/j.tox.2014.10.010.

McClintock, D., Zhuo, H., Wickersham, N., Matthay, M. A., & Ware, L. B. (2008). Biomarkers of inflammation, coagulation and fibrinolysis predict mortality in acute lung injury. *Critical Care, 12*(2), R41. http://doi.org/10.1186/cc6846.

Nath, J., & Januszkiewicz, A. (2008). *Early Systemic Biomarkers of Acute Lung Injury: Application of Multiplex Proteomic Array Technology*. Walter Reed Army Institute of Research Silver Spring MD. Retrieved from http://www.dtic.mil/docs/citations/ADA505713.

Park, E., Ahn, J., Min, Y.-G., Jung, Y.-S., Kim, K., Lee, J., & Choi, S.-C. (2012). The usefulness of the serum s100b protein for predicting delayed neurological sequelae in acute carbon monoxide poisoning. *Clinical Toxicology, 50*(3), 183–188. http://doi.org/10.3109/15563650.2012.658918.

Parsons, P. E., Matthay, M. A., Ware, L. B., Eisner, M. D., & National Heart, Lung, Blood Institute Acute Respiratory Distress Syndrome Clinical Trials Network. (2005). Elevated plasma levels of soluble TNF receptors are associated with morbidity and mortality in patients with acute lung injury. *American Journal of Physiology. Lung Cellular and Molecular Physiology, 288*(3), L426–431. http://doi.org/10.1152/ajplung.00302.2004.

Rached, E., Hoffmann, D., Blumbach, K., Weber, K., Dekant, W., & Mally, A. (2008). Evaluation of Putative Biomarkers of Nephrotoxicity after Exposure to Ochratoxin A In Vivo and In Vitro. *Toxicological Sciences, 103*(2), 371–381. http://doi.org/10.1093/toxsci/kfn040.

Rohlman, D. S., Anger, W. K., & Lein, P. J. (2011). Correlating neurobehavioral performance with biomarkers of organophosphorous pesticide exposure. *Neurotoxicology, 32*(2), 268–276. http://doi.org/10.1016/j.neuro.2010.12.008.

Sandhu, H., & Maddock, H. (2014). Molecular basis of cancer-therapy-induced cardiotoxicity: introducing microRNA biomarkers for early assessment of subclinical myocardial injury. *Clinical Science (London, England: 1979), 126*(6), 377–400. http://doi.org/10.1042/CS20120620.

Shafiee, H., Asghar, W., Inci, F., Yuksekkaya, M., Jahangir, M., Zhang, M. H., Demirci, U. (2015). Paper and flexible substrates as materials for biosensing platforms to detect multiple biotargets. *Scientific Reports, 5*. http://doi.org/10.1038/srep08719.

Silins, I., & Högberg, J. (2011). Combined Toxic Exposures and Human Health: Biomarkers of Exposure and Effect. *International Journal of Environmental Research and Public Health, 8*(3), 629–647. http://doi.org/10.3390/ijerph8030629.

Singh, S., Kumar, V., Thakur, S., Banerjee, B. D., Chandna, S., Rautela, R. S., … Rai, A. (2011). DNA damage and cholinesterase activity in occupational workers exposed to pesticides. *Environmental Toxicology and Pharmacology, 31*(2), 278–285. http://doi.org/10.1016/j.etap.2010.11.005.

Sutto, T. (2015). *NRL Industrial Chemical Assessment for Hazard, Probability and Biomarker Prioritization* (No. NRL FR 6364-14-14, XXX) (pp. 1–35). Washington, DC: Naval Research Laboratory.

Tawa, G. J., AbdulHameed, M. D. M., Yu, X., Kumar, K., Ippolito, D. L., Lewis, J. A., … Wallqvist, A. (2014). Characterization of Chemically Induced Liver Injuries Using Gene Co-Expression Modules. *PLoS ONE, 9*(9), e107230. http://doi.org/10.1371/journal.pone.0107230.

Uchida, T., Shirasawa, M., Ware, L. B., Kojima, K., Hata, Y., Makita, K., … Matthay, M. A. (2006). Receptor for Advanced Glycation End-Products Is a Marker of Type I Cell Injury in Acute Lung Injury. *American Journal of Respiratory and Critical Care Medicine, 173*(9), 1008–1015. http://doi.org/10.1164/rccm.200509-1477OC.

U.S. National Library of Medicine—Hazardous Substances Data Bank. (n.d.). Retrieved June 9, 2015, from http://toxnet.nlm.nih.gov/cgi-bin/sis/htmlgen?HSDB.

Vaidya, V. S., Ozer, J. S., Dieterle, F., Collings, F. B., Ramirez, V., Troth, S., … Bonventre, J. V. (2010). Kidney injury molecule-1 outperforms traditional biomarkers of kidney injury in preclinical biomarker qualification studies. *Nature Biotechnology, 28*(5), 478–485. http://doi.org/10.1038/nbt.1623.

Vermeulen, R., Zhang, L., Spierenburg, A., Tang, X., Bonventre, J. V., Reiss, B., … Lan, Q. (2012). Kidney toxicity in Chinese factory workers exposed to Trichloroethylene. *Carcinogenesis*, bgs191. http://doi.org/10.1093/carcin/bgs191.

Vose, S. C., Holland, N. T., Eskenazi, B., & Casida, J. E. (2007). Lysophosphatidylcholine hydrolases of human erythrocytes, lymphocytes, and brain: Sensitive targets of conserved specificity for organophosphorus delayed neurotoxicants. *Toxicology and Applied Pharmacology*, *224*(1), 98–104. http://doi.org/10.1016/j.taap.2007.06.008.

Ware, L. B., Koyama, T., Billheimer, D. D., Wu, W., Bernard, G. R., Thompson, B. T., ... Matthay, M. A. (2010). Prognostic and pathogenetic value of combining clinical and biochemical indices in patients with acute lung injury. *Chest*, *137*(2), 288–296. http://doi.org/10.1378/chest.09-1484.

Ware, L. B., Matthay, M. A., Parsons, P. E., Thompson, B. T., Januzzi, J. L., Eisner, M. D., & National Heart, Lung, and Blood Institute Acute Respiratory Distress Syndrome Clinical Trials Network. (2007). Pathogenetic and prognostic significance of altered coagulation and fibrinolysis in acute lung injury/acute respiratory distress syndrome. *Critical Care Medicine*, *35*(8), 1821–1828. http://doi.org/10.1097/01. CCM.0000221922.08878.49.

Wunnapuk, K., Gobe, G., Endre, Z., Peake, P., Grice, J. E., Roberts, M. S., ... Liu, X. (2014). Use of a glyphosate-based herbicide-induced nephrotoxicity model to investigate a panel of kidney injury biomarkers. *Toxicology Letters*, *225*, 192–200.

Wunnapuk, K., Liu, X., Gobe, G. C., Endre, Z. H., Peake, P. W., Grice, J. E., ... Buckley, N. A. (2014). Kidney biomarkers in MCPA-induced acute kidney injury in rats: Reduced clearance enhances early biomarker performance. *Toxicology Letters*, *225*, 467–478.

Ye, S. Q., Simon, B. A., Maloney, J. P., Zambelli-Weiner, A., Gao, L., Grant, A., ... Garcia, J. G. N. (2005). Pre–B-Cell Colony-enhancing Factor as a Potential Novel Biomarker in Acute Lung Injury. *American Journal of Respiratory and Critical*

Care Medicine, *171*(4), 361–370. http://doi.org/10.1164/rccm.200404-563OC.

Ye, Y.-M., Nahm, D.-H., Kim, C.-W., Kim, H.-R., Hong, C.-S., Park, C.-S., … Park, H.-S. (2006). Cytokeratin autoantibodies: useful serologic markers for toluene diisocyanate-induced asthma. *Yonsei Medical Journal*, *47*(6), 773–781.

Yu, Y., Jin, H., Holder, D., Ozer, J. S., Villarreal, S., Shughrue, P., … Gerhold, D. L. (2010). Urinary biomarkers trefoil factor 3 and albumin enable early detection of kidney tubular injury. *Nature Biotechnology*, *28*(5), 470–477. http://doi.org/10.1038/nbt.1624.

Zeng, Q., Xu, Y., Yu, X., Yang, J., Hong, F., & Zhang, A. (2014). The combined effects of fluorine and arsenic on renal function in a Chinese population. *Toxicology Research*, *3*(5), 359–366. http://doi.org/10.1039/C4TX00038B.

Zhang, Y., Liu, X., McHale, C., Li, R., Zhang, L., Wu, Y., … Ding, S. (2013). Bone marrow injury induced via oxidative stress in mice by inhalation exposure to formaldehyde. *PloS One*, *8*(9), e74974. http://doi.org/10.1371/journal.pone.0074974.

Zheng, J., Zhou, Z., Xu, Z., Li, G., Dong, P., Chen, Z., … Yu, F. (2015). Serum microRNA-125a-5p, a useful biomarker in liver diseases, correlates with disease progression. *Molecular Medicine Reports*. http://doi.org/10.3892/mmr.2015.3546.

Zhou, Y., Vaidya, V. S., Brown, R. P., Zhang, J., Rosenzweig, B. A., Thompson, K. L., … Goering, P. L. (2008). Comparison of Kidney Injury Molecule-1 and Other Nephrotoxicity Biomarkers in Urine and Kidney Following Acute Exposure to Gentamicin, Mercury, and Chromium. *Toxicological Sciences*, *101*(1), 159–170. http://doi.org/10.1093/toxsci/kfm260.

Chapter 34

Atmospheric Impacts and Effects Predictions and Applications for Future Megacity and Dense Urban Area Operations

David Knapp, Robb Randall and Jim Staley

First Published 22 March 2016

Introduction

By 2030 it is expected that more than 60% of the world's population will live in dense urban centers and the majority of these Megacity/ Dense Urban Areas are/will be in complex terrain environments. Consequently, weather conditions within these dense urban and complex terrain (DUCT) environments will influence a greater populace and can negatively influence military operations, community services, and overall situational understanding needed for Intelligence Preparation of the Battlefield (IPB) and Intelligence, Surveillance, and Reconnaissance (ISR). Extreme weather conditions will impact DUCT areas often already overstressed by uncontrolled growth and a degraded public infrastructure. Unique weather conditions experienced within the DUCT will highlight, and even magnify, weather sensitivities affecting threat, civilian populations, and DoD weapons systems and operations.

Current state-of-the-science atmospheric sensing, characterization, and forecasting capabilities cannot accurately represent the rapidly changing and complex atmospheric processes in a DUCT environment. Therefore, innovative and disruptive solutions are required to revolutionize locally fine-tuned weather support for DUCT operations, information critical to IPB and ISR needs. If localized urban and complex terrain domain weather conditions can be accurately sensed, characterized, and predicted, such information will be a force multiplier for local commanders tasked with leading operations in these multifaceted and intricate domains.

Local DUCT Weather Concerns Impacting Operations

There are a variety of atmospheric environment concerns that must be addressed to improve the potential for success in a Megacity/DUCT battlefield. A few examples of topics that must be addressed by current and future atmospheric scientists are below:

- *DUCT Winds*: The local complex terrain (natural and man-made urban sprawl, etc.), can significantly influence near-surface wind patterns across just a few city blocks. Unpredicted wind funneling between, around, and over buildings can lead to small unmanned aerial system failure, inaccurate dispersion plume predictions (chemical, biological, smoke, etc., coupled with consequence management), and many other related environmental impacts and effects issues for warfighters in such domains. Significant research and development efforts are needed to determine such microscale wind effects within unique DUCT environments.

- *Severe Weather Concerns*: Flooding, drought, excess heat/cold, precipitation, and wind influences in each particular Megacity can be drastically different from day to day, hour to hour, and from one section of the Megacity to another. Questions regarding what the populace does during expected severe weather events and how best to militarily influence or control civilians during such events must be addressed. Equally important are questions regarding how best to address the need for new decision support applications to aid military planners through mission execution in such extreme weather conditions. Decision tools addressing how the severe weather effects food, communications, fuel, and service distribution, for both military and civilian operations, can enhance leadership's decision toolset for planning and execution.

- *Battlefield Sensor Performance*: The often complex and varied local weather conditions within a DUCT domain can wreak havoc on battlefield sensor performance. Since sensors are influenced by not only target, but also background signatures, the complex and oftentimes densely packed structures of the urban environment together with heating and cooling changes, precipitation, and atmospheric aerosol concentrations impact infrared and acoustic sensors and performance.

- *Scientific Work Needed*: The spatial resolution of fine-scale atmospheric prediction models must be continuously improved and validated for accurate predictions in difficult DUCT domains. What weather spatial resolution is required to effectively address DUCT weather effects? How often should fine-scale DUCT atmospheric prediction models be run to adequately depict the environment? This information and answers to the questions noted are critical for accurate microscale weather prediction model performance. Additionally, specific weather sensing requirements within the DUCT need to be addressed, insofar as determining ideal numbers, types, placement, etc., to insure weather prediction models are initialized using the most recent and accurate local conditions possible. These sensing advances will provide data to enhance the understanding of Megacity atmospheric processes critical to improving the underlying physics and dynamics of microscale atmospheric models tailored to such domains.

Specific Operational Challenges Within Megacity Domains

1. Military units deploying within a DUCT domain are likely to operate in small teams conducting short duration missions. These teams will often execute different types of missions within city blocks of each other. The DUCT environment can be heavily influenced by microscale weather conditions which are often significantly different from one block to the next.

2. Most DUCT environments are located near significant bodies of water (lakes, rivers, littoral), which further influence microclimates associated with these high humidity and valley terrain areas.

3. Aviation operations will likely be a preferred method of mission execution. Wind, cloud ceiling, visibility, precipitation, buildings, wires, communication towers, and urban terrain objects such as large signs and billboards within the DUCT domain will significantly influence all aviation operations.

4. Weather conditions within the DUCT domain effect threat operations just as they do friendly force operations. Determining the weather impact differences between friendly and threat forces can significantly contribute to the DUCT battlefield commander's IPB knowledge base. Other related challenges relate to weather's impact on concealment of operations for both friendly and threat forces.

5. Weather sensing and atmospheric characterization capabilities are lacking within DUCT environments. Reliable weather forecasting capabilities (weather forecast models) require local weather observations as input to accurately characterize current/initial atmospheric conditions. Sufficient numbers of weather observations enable meaningful mission watch. Mission watch provides operational commanders a real-time weather picture of the Area of Operations (AO) during mission execution. Effective weather "mission watch" provides atmospheric monitoring of

choke points, avenues of approach and even military objectives within the AO.

6. Lastly, addressing environmental intelligence for autonomous systems in Megacities, swarms of unmanned ground/air micro-vehicles could be equipped with weather sensors to dramatically improve currently inadequate local weather condition sensing and thus improve the accuracy of local DUCT atmospheric prediction models.

Needed Solutions: Weather Technologies to Change Warfare for Decision Makers at All Echelons

Looking ahead at the Megacity/DUCT battlefields of 2030 and beyond, there is an overwhelming need to revolutionize the science of atmospheric sensing, characterizing, and predicting local conditions in DUCT environments. The Battlefield Environment Division at Army Research Laboratory (ARL), in conjunction with research partners across the DoD, academia, and civilian public and private arenas, will be using a combination of existing very fine-scale resolution (microscale) meteorological tower arrays, unmanned system-hosted existing/emerging sensor technologies, and optimized sensor placement strategies to include crowdsourcing techniques to sense and characterize DUCT atmospheric domains. Applying sensor data and characterization improvements (separately and combined) to novel, forward-deployed microscale Nowcasting ("pocket modeling") technology hosted on computationally complex but extremely efficient General Purpose Graphics Processing Units (GPGPU) and smaller portable devices such as warfighter-hosted communications platforms is the way of the future for DUCT operational weather forecasting.

Observed data must be used to verify/validate the atmospheric modeling weather forecast improvements as related to value-added to the DUCT warfighter, showing how improved localized weather forecasts significantly enhance warfighter operations. Applying all such fine-scale technology improvement lessons learned to advanced automated state-of-the-science decision tools focused on predicting attrition rates from operations in adverse DUCT weather conditions will be one critical result this long-term effort. Thus, Megacity battlefield commanders will be provided with a full picture of predicted atmospheric effects and impacts on local operations, including expected losses due to hazardous weather. Pocket modeling (focused local atmospheric prediction technology hosted on personal communications devices), crowdsourcing sensed data, and GPGPU advances for atmospheric prediction computing are just a few of the disruptive technologies to be used as the capability to run a complex terrain atmospheric model is pushed to the lowest echelons in the battlefield which will positively affect current DoD processes. Development of deployable hardware and software system prototypes for weather effects intelligence and decision tools for DUCT environments is the planned culmination of ARL's work on meteorological sensor arrays, microscale atmospheric prediction systems, and unmanned system and atmospheric sensing platform resources to reach these technological goals.

There are a number of critical steps being addressed to move the science forward as the needed technological advances are developed:

- *Perform research to understand atmospheric processes in DUCT environments.* Effective weather sensing and atmospheric characterization of the AO will optimize mission execution by providing essential input to weather forecast models. This improves forecast accuracy and therefore confidence in planning and execution of all military operations; forecast accuracy improvements mean a safer operating environment for military and civilian personnel, with few, if any, weather surprises. Weather sensing in DUCT domains also provides critical, real-time situational awareness supporting current operations. A comprehensive understanding of current atmospheric conditions enables the commander's full utilization of the AO, in both time and space, allowing for the selection of tactics, weapons, and targets based, at least in part, on atmospheric conditions. Accurate and timely weather observations are a true force multiplier, protecting military and civilian operations from the uncertainty of mission-limiting weather conditions.

- *Advanced development of microscale models.* Develop DUCT fine-scale operational local atmospheric modeling capabilities suitable for forecast center and forward-deployed implementation on the smallest computational platforms possible. Such capabilities will support both operational theater forecast centers as well as the lowest battlefield echelons with on-scene local atmospheric predictions. These forecasts will have the capability to ingest the most current, locally-sensed atmospheric data. Local forward-deployed atmospheric modeling capabilities will ensure timely weather forecast updates to Megacity commanders and decision-makers down to actionable Soldier levels. Today, precise prediction of local weather events is limited by the resolution of currently fielded weather forecast modeling capabilities and the availability of weather observations. Improving the resolution of weather predictions, especially in the complex terrain of a Megacity, requires a significant increase in the number of weather observations and optimized placement of weather sensors in the domain to initialize the weather predictions. Research will consider the value of remotely-sensed observations (e.g. satellite, radar, etc.) as input to these improved forecast model capabilities. Weather sensing capabilities, combined with better model physics, will significantly improve the weather forecast accuracies within an urban environment. Additionally, developing forward-deployed and frequently updated small "pocket" computer platform atmospheric modeling capabilities, providing data to on-board weather decision tools will significantly enhance the local timeliness and accuracy of microscale DUCT weather predictions.

- *New weather-related decision aids include sensor performance tools for multiple modalities, including acoustic, infrared, radar, and seismic.* Urban routing tools must account for manned and unmanned ground and aerial vehicles. Decision aid development must include applications supporting a prediction of human domain conditions based on weather and climate combined with and including populace reactions to military operations. DUCT-focused ensemble probabilistic predictions will produce forecast confidence output for decision support tools of high interest and use by military commanders and decision makers within the Megacity.

Summary

Weather conditions significantly influence military operations within Megacity DUCT operational domains. Confident execution of military operations demands comprehensive weather support at spatial and temporal resolutions that accurately depict microclimates found in every DUCT environment. These weather conditions effect all aspects of the geospatial environment within the Megacity.

Increased resolution and accuracy of deployed weather support products is crucial, especially so in the DUCT environment. Effective weather sensing, atmospheric characterization and prediction will optimize mission execution by providing critical, real-time situational awareness supporting future operations as well as providing essential input to weather forecast models and decision support tools. This improves forecast accuracy and confidence in planning and execution of all military operations. Forecast accuracy improvements mean a safer operating environment for military and civilian personnel.

This disruptive based approach ensures DoD DUCT battlefield Commanders will have a full picture of predicted atmospheric effects and impacts on DUCT operations, including expected losses due to hazardous weather. The work highlighted in this paper will optimize our understanding and application of crucial weather conditions within the Megacity operations as future urban operating environments become the norm.

Chapter 35

Complex IPB

Tom Pike and Eddie Brown

First Published 24 March 2016

The right perspective makes hard problems easy while the wrong perspective makes easy problems hard.

—Scott Page

The last 15 years of conflict have shown the difficulty in understanding the internal dynamics of a foreign population. Understanding these internal dynamics, however, is essential to implementing policies and taking action to influence the foreign population's behavior in pursuit of U.S. goals. The U.S. Government must improve its capability to rapidly analyze foreign populations and the need for this capability will only increase as megacities, with their incredibly complex population systems become more numerous. Unfortunately, the challenge is not only finding effective approaches to understand foreign populations but also finding approaches that can integrate assessments from a Battalion Intelligence Officer all the way to a strategic level agency. This integration is necessary to synchronize the efforts of the large and likewise complex U.S. Government. Acknowledging these daunting challenges demands the U.S., and in particular Army intelligence, work to find and apply improved analytic frameworks for foreign population analysis.

Intelligence Preparation of the Battlefield (IPB) provides a strong nucleus to develop new frameworks but must evolve past its force on force focus to an approach that analyzes multiple groups competing within a population. The integration of new concepts from complex adaptive system theory provides rigorously tested concepts many of which have already been incorporated into common analytic software—such as Analyst Notebook, Palantir, and others—to cope with the problems of Yemen, Somalia, Iraq, Syria, and elsewhere. Complexity based approaches have also been the core of strategic assessments which have influenced the highest levels of government. The challenge is to operationalize these approaches so intelligence analysts, at all levels, can gain an understanding that leads to synergistic policy and action. A critical capability to support this evolution of IPB is the development and integration of Agent Based Models. Agent based Models, a proven tool of complex adaptive systems, can provide staffs and decision makers an option exploration tool to help them visualize possible effects of their policies and actions. Using IPB as the nucleus and integrating concepts from complex adaptive systems theory generates Complex IPB. Complex IPB is the next generation of IPB and has the potential to dramatically improve foreign population analysis as well as improve U.S. ability to influence foreign populations.

IPB

Define the Area of Operations
Describe environmental effects
Evaluate the threat
Evaluate threat courses of action

Complex IPB

Define the Area of Operations

Describe fitness landscape effects
Evaluate the major groups
Evaluate major groups' courses of action
Asses the groups interaction
Evaluate population behavior

The strength of IPB is its underlying logic. A reasonable prediction of threat behavior can be made by analyzing the situation combined with an assessment of the threat's capability. This logic is evident by reviewing the four steps of IPB. Step one is to define the operational environment. This is a description of the area of operations' significant characteristics that can influence friendly or threat courses of action. Step two is to describe the environmental effects on operations, for example a densely forested swamp would be severely restricted or no-go terrain. Together, these two steps are the constants, which the threat has little ability to change. Step three is evaluate the threat.[1] This is the threat's capability, through the context of the terrain and weather effect. What is the range of the threat's weapons and what is the threat's vehicles ability to negotiate the terrain accounting for the weather? What knowledge does the threat have in constructing IEDs? How easily is the threat able to move through the population without interdiction by local authorities? The conventional threat must choose different courses of action in a desert than in a jungle, while the insurgent threat must alter how it plants IEDs based on how freely it can move and its capacity to construct them. This is the simple elegance of IPB. The given situation and the threat's capability limits what they can and cannot do. This situation leads to the fourth step, evaluate threat courses of action, a reasonable prediction of what actions the threat can take reduced by the environmental and capability constraints.[2] These courses of action or hypotheses are then confirmed or denied through the implementation of a collection plan. The predictions of threat behavior allows friendly forces to maximize the limited capability of their limited collection assets to determine what course of action the threat adopted and how they are adapting. This logic can be applied not only to threat forces but also to groups in foreign populations. To understand how to do this it is useful to first examine the decision making of an individual.

The choices of an individual sitting within a population socio-cultural-political-ecosystem (fitness landscape for short) are constrained by the same general logic which IPB uses to analyze a threat force. When a person wakes up they will make decisions to generally maximize their situation. This individual confronts a fitness landscape which has an impact on what action the individual may take. This is similar to the terrain analysis and effects in IPB but with the added layers—politics, economics, social, information, infrastructure, environment and possibly more. The individual also has a capability (or fitness function) such as a profession, education, ethnic group, savings or family connections. A person survives or thrives based on their fitness function and its ability to extract resources from the fitness landscape. This simple dynamic is prevalent across time and space. In the 1980s, while the country faced a horrific insurgency from the Shining Path, a group from the Institute of Liberty and Democracy wanted to see how long it would take a person to set up a two-person sewing machine shop in a shanty town of Lima, Peru. It took more than 1800 hours, which when accounting for access to the government offices was more than 300 days and cost 32 times the monthly minimum wage.[3] When similar studies where done in Peru on everything from marriage licenses to property transfers the results were the same staggering obstacles.[4] The implications were clear, Peruvians in Lima's shanty towns were not joining the legal economy because the bureaucracy was such a daunting obstacle, severe no-go terrain, that it was impossible for them to do so. The government began to reform this situation and these reforms were seen as a crucial in defeating the Shining Path insurgency. In a lecture at the National Defense University, Dr. David Kilcullen described the choice for many Afghans working to find resolution to a dispute. If they went to the local Afghan Government official they would be beaten up and no action would be taken. If they went to the Taliban they could expect at least some sort of predictable, albeit harsh justice.[5] Many individuals therefore choose to ask the Taliban for justice, since at least there was a chance of resolution of their issue. The dynamic is the same as a threat commander making decisions in IPB, an individual has a capability to face the situation and from this develops courses of action.

The challenge then becomes analyzing hundreds to millions of people and their decisions instead of one threat unit. At first glance, this challenge seems overwhelming. Fortunately, complex adaptive systems have a property called emergence. Just as a threat unit is made up of a number of individuals but can be viewed as a single entity due to the military structure, emergence has a similar effect without the requirement of a centralized command structure.[6] Large groups of people will make the same decision without a centralized decision making process. This phenomenon is evident in the recent conflicts, where different tribes, ethnic groups and individuals decided to support either the insurgency or the government. Although each group or individual may have had different motives for their decision when these micro-decisions aggregated together the result was either the strengthening or weakening of the insurgency. Thanks to the property of emergence analysts, can look at groups of people and view them as a cohesive whole. Analysts do not need to understand each person, instead they can identify the key groups within a population and use the same IPB logic to try and predict these groups' courses of action by analyzing their situation and capability. Unlike IPB where the terrain is a constant, however, groups can actively shape the fitness landscape they are negotiating.

Arguably, the reason a fitness landscape of cultural, economic, social and other dynamics even exists is because it is the result of the interaction of lots of individuals and groups, who are negotiating it each day. The idea that each group contributes to the shape of the fitness landscape means different groups may be able to radically alter it. This is a significant difference from IPB as the threat, cannot turn a desert into a jungle, turn a machine gun into a tank, or make a secure radio suddenly compatible with a newly arrived foreign partner. Coalition actions in Iraq clearly demonstrate how a group can significantly change the fitness landscape of a population. Prior to the Iraqi invasion of 2003, being a Ba'athist in the Iraqi fitness landscape provided an avenue of approach to jobs and security. After the invasion the coalition made contentious decisions to bar Ba'athist members[7] which immediately and dramatically altered this terrain. Instead of having an avenue of approach, Ba'athist's now faced no-go terrain when trying to get government jobs or security. Unfortunately, these same individuals, were the people in the country who had many critical capabilities from technical knowledge of the infrastructure to organizational understanding of the government. This decision had cascading effects throughout the rest of the coalition's time in theater, with many arguing this decision drove key Iraqi leaders to the insurgency.[8] The Coalition dramatically reshaped the fitness landscape, but at the same time they had to negotiate the new landscape they created. Groups within a population have the ability to influence the fitness landscape which shapes the situation of the population every day and subsequently influences decisions. Evaluating group courses of action uses the same reasoning underlying IPB, however, the groups being analyzed have greater ability to shape the situation.

Evaluating group courses of action then leads to the next step of Complex IPB, assessing the groups' interaction. This step is effectively wargaming from the Military Decision Making Process (MDMP). Each group will be making decisions to maximize their situation and outcompete any perceived rivals. They will adjust their courses of action based on what their rivals are doing. Having multiple groups increases the complexity of what one is analyzing. For example, if there is an insurgency, with a government group, an insurgent group, and three more major groups (a total of five groups) in the population each with the three possible courses of action, there are 125 possible combinations. This challenge can be simplified as the possible behavior of concern will likely only have a few categories. Despite this large number of different combinations the effect of these combinations will still fall into four broad categories. The insurgency may be (1) expanding and gaining legitimacy (groups supporting the insurgents), (2) contracting and losing legitimacy (groups supporting the government), (3) is in a stalemate with neither the government nor insurgency gaining ground, or (4) an alternate group is rising up to take power from the government and insurgency. In addition, most of the combinations may fall into only one or two categories. This allows analysts to generalize the combinations and focus on those combinations leading to or away from US objectives.

The interaction of the groups and the courses of action they pursue leads to the population's behavior. This statement is significant because it fundamentally defies the Westphalian tradition, and the default view, of viewing foreign states as a single entity. Instead, foreign populations are more like ecosystems, where the various groups are in a delicate equilibrium and the government is only one part, albeit an important part, of the functioning of that ecosystem. Evaluating the population behavior is an assessment of the interaction of major groups within that population as they pursue courses of action. These interactions may result in an unstable state, a dictatorial regime, or an emerging democracy. Critically, this dynamic is scalable, whether the population is a village, a province, a nation, or a region of the world. Allowing analysts at all levels to use a common approach to understand the population of concern. The behavior of the population is a result of the interactions of the groups within it at all levels. This assessment of the population's behavior is also the culmination of Complex IPB. Applying the Complex IPB framework will provide decisions makers a better understanding of the internal dynamics which are driving the populations' behavior; this understanding should allow leaders to take more effective action and better synergize the instruments of power to achieve U.S. Objectives.

Applying the Complex IPB framework to population analysis will improve the situational understanding of any population in any environment, this understanding can be further enhanced through the development and integration of Agent Based Modeling tools into the analytic and decision-making processes. The primary tool to model complex adaptive systems is Agent Based Models (ABM). As Agent Based Models are unfamiliar to many readers please see the embedded graphic or if you would prefer a video please follow this link. The model the graphic below portrays is very relevant to Dense Urban Areas as it is a model of slum formation. On the left of the picture are the input parameters, which allows users to manipulate variables and see the impact of adjusting these variables. The output parameters are different ways of measuring the model's behavior to provide insight into what is happening.

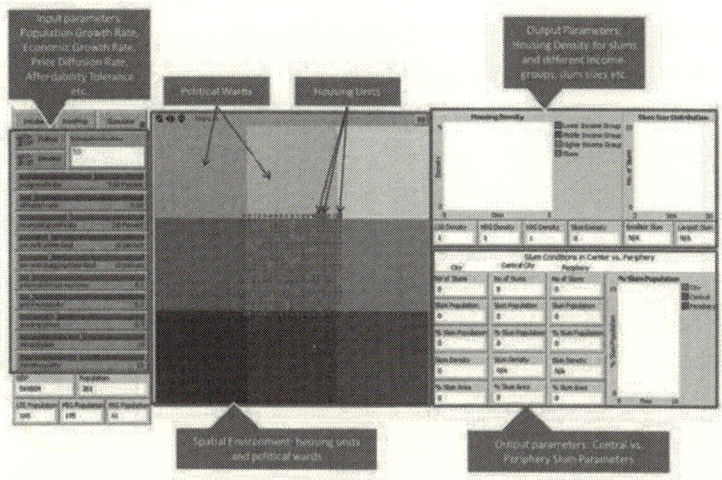

Graphic One: "Slums provide shelter for nearly one third of the world's urban population, most of them in the developing world. Slumulation represents an agent-based model which explores questions such as i) how slums come into existence, expand or disappear ii) where and when they emerge in a city and iii) which processes may improve housing conditions for urban poor.[9]

ABMs have already proven effective in analyzing and informing policy on everything from foreign population behavior to the US electric grid to leadership in organizations.[10] ABMs are proven tools which takes the perspective of the agents. An agent is a discrete entity with its own behavior and own goals. In the context of the Complex IPB framework, agents would represent the major groups and their internal variations. These agents then interact with each other. The fitness landscape is the terrain in which they interact. These interactions then produce a possible emergent behavior of the population. This emergent behavior is the U.S. objective. Are the groups supporting the insurgency or the government? Does the fitness function of one group allow it to gain dominance over the system undermining the democratic institutions? ABMs allow for the adjustment of variables within a group's fitness function or a manipulation of the fitness landscape. In the application, the action of the analyst may be to adjust the size of the money variable for a group's fitness function or adjust a variable of the fitness landscape to represent a change in the government process which may result in restrictive terrain becoming an avenue of approach for a previously excluded group. As the adjustments are made the analysts, staffs and decision makers would be able to see how multiple changes at different points in the system may affect the interaction of the groups and the subsequent behavior of the population. From this course of action development, they then may adjust how money is dispersed to influence the power of competing fitness functions, help pass new laws to provide access to previously excluded groups, and/or focus on attacking a different part of the insurgent network. A Complex IPB agent-based model application will provide analysts, staffs and decision makers an option exploration tools that gives them insights into how the different groups may react to U.S. policy and actions.

ABM and its integration into decision making processes does face hurdles for implementation. The first hurdle is "can a generic model be created that any analyst can set specifically enough to analyze the local problem set or will an Army element need to be created to build models specific to a Brigade Combat Team (BCT) and their particular problem?" In other words, can a universal application be created that is both effective and user-friendly enough that analysts can apply it to their local situation whether in humanitarian missions in Africa or active insurgencies in South Asia. Or, will a group of experts need to do the coding and formulas necessary for a realistic model to be created that analysts can further adjust to the specific situation of the local area. If a group of experts is needed to support ABM model, it cannot be experts working in isolation instead it must be a symbiotic relationship with the BCT forward, where the entities are working as a team to further refine and update the model so staffs can employ it to achieve their objectives. The second hurdle is these models will only ever give a probabilistic outcome and will have to be run multiple times to see what behavior has the highest probability. This is a reflection of reality and it often creates some computing challenges. The nature of the model, its complexity and the austerity of the environment will determine what is feasible. Even if Complex IPB must be completed in analog, it will still provide an improved understanding of the situation. ABMs enhance the approach they do not replace it. The third hurdle is the need to federate production when conducting a campaign. The analysis of a village will have an impact on the analysis of a region, which will have an impact on the analysis of the country. From step one, any plan to integrate ABM into decision making must look at how to link these ABMs together. National action has a local impact and local events can have a national impact. ABM can and must serve as a catalyst to help synchronize whole of government efforts when influencing the behavior of a foreign population. ABM is a powerful tool which must accompany Complex IPB and be integrated into decision making processes whether MDMP for a BCT or discussions by the National Security Council.

The foundation of IPB is a strong and powerful logic. Understanding a threat's situation and its capability within the given situation allows for a reasonable prediction of that threat's behavior. This same logic can be applied to most people who are fighting each day to maximize their situation. The property of emergence allows analysts to focus on the main groups of the population instead of trying to understand the millions of people who may be in the area of operations. Complex IPB then follows the same initial steps as IPB, but with a focus on groups and an incorporation of the more dynamic fitness landscape (the cultural, social, economic, information, government terrain): (1) Define the Area of Operations, (2) Describe the Fitness Landscape effects, (3) Evaluate the major groups (4) Evaluate major group courses of actions. Complex IPB must then add an additional two steps. (5) Assess the groups interaction and (6) Evaluate population behavior. These two steps follow logically from the base of IPB. Complex IPB can then be enhanced through development and application of a Complex IPB Agent Based Model application. Although its development and implementation faces some hurdles, ABMs are a proven tool, which can provide analysts, staffs and decision makers the ability to explore numerous options and combinations of options and visually see the possible effects. Complex IPB is the natural evolution of IPB and has the potential to improve analysis and influence of foreign populations.

Notes

[1]   Headquarters, Department of the Army, Army Techniques Publication 2-01.3, *Intelligence Preparation of the Battlefield*, (November 2014), 1-1-1-4.

[2]   Ibid, 1-1-1-4.

[3]   Hernando De Soto, *The Other Path: The Economic Answer to Terrorism*, (New York: Basic Books, 1989), xxi-xxxiv.

[4]   Ibid.

[5]   David Kilcullen, "Counterinsurgency," (lecture, Afghanistan-Pakistan Foundation Course, National Defense University, October 6, 2009).

[6]   *Understanding Complexity*, taught by Scott E. Page, Lecture 6.

[7]   *FRONTLINE: The Lost Year in Iraq*, (October 17, 2006) http://www.pbs.org/wgbh/pages/frontline/yeariniraq/ (accessed May 26th, 2014).

[8]   Ibid.

[9]   Patel, A., Crooks, A.T. and Koizumi, N,. "Slumulation: an Agent-based Modeling Approach to Slum Formation", (2012), http://www.css.gmu.edu/Slums/PatelCrooksKoizumi_Slumulation.pdf, (accessed 27 February 2016).

[10]   Joshua Epstein, *Generative Social Science: Studies in Agent-Based Computational Modeling*, (Princeton University Press, 2007).

Chapter 36

Megacity Madness

Gustav Otto and A.J. Besik

First Published 9 June 2016

Are you in an urban area? Can you look around without seeing anyone? Try talking without being in earshot of someone who can easily overhear your conversation. Try walking side to side, front or back without having to watch out for someone or something. Now imagine the size and frequency of these events, so vast it takes hours to get to a place where you don't have these experiences at every turn. If these all exist you're probably in a megacity. So, what is one? No one really knows, and that's a problem. Trying to define a megacity is hard enough, trying to win a decisive action, engage in governance and rule of law, or trying to provide relief? It could be maddening. So, what is a megacity? US Supreme Court Justice Potter Stewart is famous for a remark in 1964 about pornography that he knows it if he sees it.[1] That mental approach doesn't suffice when thinking of a megacity. More importantly we can't interact with it based on such a shallow understanding. The United Nations arbitrarily defines a megacity as something larger than 10 million people. John Wilmoth, Director of the UN's Department of Economic and Social Affairs (DESA) Population Division rightly states, "Managing urban areas has become one of the most important development challenges of the 21st century. Our success or failure in building sustainable cities will be a major factor in the success of the post-2015 UN development agenda."[2] The problem is bigger even than a megacity. It is how to consider one. How does the international community analyze megacities? Reviewing over 400 documents, website and blogs suggests there's no single analytic, comprehensive tool for analyzing this new phenomenon.[3] Arguably this is a classic interdisciplinary topic requiring a complex framework for analysis and evaluation, and ripe for innovation and creativity (design thinking).

The paper outlines a few ways to think about and analyze a megacity and make recommendations to prepare for operations in such an environment. The recommendations herein could not all encompassing, and likely never will be. It is an introduction by which a person or organization may consider the myriad of issues regarding a megacity, that when combined become vexing if not a wicked problem. But these problems are not insurmountable, nor impossible to operate in successfully.

Cities are often thought of as systems of systems. Utilizing this framework to conceptualize the issues in a megacity then allows the application of previous ideas that have been proven.

Problems may arise when the sheer scale of a megacity's issues come into play. This is where design thinking and generating multiple options rapidly allow for these issues of scale to be addressed, and thus be useful in the context of a megacity. We have lived and worked in some of these megacities and watch with great interest the growing number of megacities around the world. There are a number of trends driving and driven by their growth. Among the two greatest are the draw of urbanization and the increase in globalization. They are complimentary, not exclusive. They are not the only reasons for their growth either. The growth of urbanization is recognized by authors as wide ranging as Thomas P. M. Barnett, author of *The Pentagon's New Map*, to *The Christian Science Monitor* or *Forbes*, to global consultants such as Accenture, Deloitte and Frost & Sullivan and McKinsey & Company. Each of these has a different vantage point, and each is moving towards a more comprehensive consideration of this challenging discussion on megacities.

The term megacities itself is problematic. While an accepted benchmark, it fails to account for other factors including the sophistication of infrastructure or transient populations. Some cities are categorized as a megacity by outside organizations but not by their own municipal governments. Some are megacities, no matter what we call them, or if there's disagreement.

They present a rich, urban and dense location filled with endless challenges and opportunities for engagement, partnership, and profit. Therefore, accepting definitions of a city and a megacity differ is of little import. This paper seeks to look at a megacity as one might a computer—the combination of software, hardware and what the outcomes are. In the case of a megacity, the hardware may be the physical, the plants and facilities, the roads, electric and plumbing, the buildings, trains and tunnels. The software is what travels over, to and through the physical, and may include information or data, energy, even people. Finally, the outcomes, the humanistic realities others will have to recognize, deal with, and live by.

The hardware/software/outcomes framework of analysis for these urban areas is intentionally oversimplified because it lends itself to a set of parallel measurements allowing for improved analysis and evaluation with every iteration. Over the last two decades it seems the international community, scholarly and otherwise, settled on the number of 10 million. There's little good argument for this number. Rather it appears arbitrary with little rationale tied to it. It is important to recognize 10 million offers no additional value other than a fictitious threshold.

Does a city with 9.5 million behave in much the way one with 14 million? Yes. Size matters, but so do issues like population density and scale.

A recent example might be the impact the Zika virus is playing in and around the megacity of São Paulo. As we saw the reeling of the community to the sharp incline of microcephaly there were questions about its origin, its spread, its containment and the human impacts around the region and the globe. Some indicators suggest it was visitors to São Paulo for the 2014 World Cup games who brought the virus to the region, and fears by the International Community it will not be contained in time for the 2016 Olympics. Treatment of the virus, treatment of the mosquito and its vectors, and treatment of its victims vary, and there remains no cure.

Quarantine of São Paulo is next to impossible. Full scale assault by the International Community, along with armies of aid and health workers wouldn't solve the problem. How can we think of dealing with calamities such as this in a megacity?

Any operations normally conducted in a city will obviously occur in a megacity. Indeed, many such cities already have effective, established measures to continue with the day to day actions that those governments conduct. The likelihood of US forces of any type operating in such an environment is very high, including cities inside our own borders. According to the National Intelligence Council (NIC), by 2030 individuals will see a substantial increase in autonomy and prosperity. There's a growing notion that megacities are becoming their own little sovereign nations. The growth of the global population, especially in urban areas, will lead to a majority of the world's population residing in cities where more economic and education opportunities exist. This urbanization will lead to a middle-class that is the "most important social and economic sector in the vast majority of countries around the world." With better access to education, affordable health care, and sources of information, the individual will be the driving force behind global change. This change may take on the form of renewed economic growth in historically poor regions of the world or allow super-empowered people to challenge the security apparatus and governmental legitimacy. These areas are then fraught with the potential for emergencies, man-made or natural. Situations such as this can be seen emerging in some areas of the world.

Situations that appear similar to those the US has previously operated in successfully. Urban Combat, Humanitarian Assistance, Stability Operations, all have been conducted by US Government agencies within the last decade. Scale however rudely interrupts the best-laid plans. These aren't necessarily new problems, just ones that planners may have believed solved previously. Need to bring water and food into a city that has suffered a naturally disaster? This has happened on countless occasions around the globe, both with US and international involvement. However, what if the standard methods of bringing in supplies aren't feasible due to problems of sheer physics? If the normal seaport is closed and supplies must be trucked in but there are so many people to accommodate there is not enough physical space to park said trucks without clogging the supply routes. Issues that will compound when alternative remedies aren't available or don't meet the need in aggregate. So what kinds of analysis might prove useful in such an area? The list is long, and for the purposes of demonstration we offer only a few in the following paragraphs.

We're well served to think about communications and data and their growing importance to governance, awareness and human interaction. Consider well-developed megacities first. From London, to Seoul to Los Angeles, the physical infrastructure is governed by information. On the hardware front, information flows over copper wires, the airwaves and fiber-optics to keep things running smoothly. On the software front, data drives trains, planes and automobiles. On the outcomes front it cools towering high-rises so employees are more productive and computers don't break down and warms delivery rooms for babies. The importance of the human in the loop is greater in developing megacities but is *the primary factor* in all these systems. The presence of a functional technocracy keeps poor systems working. When these fragile systems are compromised the role of the technocrat becomes more apparent. Data isn't just important to the hard systems, they play a role in governance, especially during crises. How this data is developed, transmitted, consumed, etc., is more critical in a megacity than normal urban settings.

Another critical aspect to consider when analyzing any city is the population—as mentioned the primary human factor. This seems obvious, yet an in-depth understanding of populations is not always part of preparation. It is this fact that continues to vex US National Security Strategists in places like Iraq, Afghanistan, Syria and beyond. Cities exist to house, employ, and even contain human beings. The movement of people; their backgrounds, sociologies, education, ethnicity, gender and race; the culture(s) of the people living there; how these people choose to associate governance and politics; the work and social patterns of these people; the resultant rules and laws that are applied; how those rules and laws are upheld (or not); the services required for the people;

and finally, the tensions that exist, naturally, are all to be considered. Each of these could be layered in our conceptualization across four dimensions (three physical plus time = 4D = 3D + t). Unfortunately, there is little, perhaps no homogeneity or uniformity in these layers. To suggest we could just label each like a sheet of paper and lay them atop each other is naïve and misleading. It is important to stress the way these layers interact across and with each other, though not in a linear fashion.

The alluded to human factor plays out on various stages, from the electromagnetic to the physical. In some cases, those two above ideas of information and human landscape fuse as observed in the proliferation of social media. Decades ago, the Marine Corps had the foresight to describe the strategic corporal.[4] While not a perfect analog, the idea is well founded, that individual actions can reverberate and cause problems far beyond the scope of the original intent. When thought of in the nineties the concept brought attention to the idea that the action of an individual operating at a low level can be perceived various ways when transmitted through modern media and lead to unintended strategic consequences. More simply, when attempting to engage one person the effects can be felt by millions. Often times this can be negative, as perceptions can be manipulated or capitalized on by various factions. This idea takes on a new significance when the millions of people that may have acquired a negative view of your operations are not found around the globe, but within ten miles of your operating space. These kinds of effects were observed during the Arab Spring in 2011, when social media enabled mobilization on a scale that superseded the capabilities of the government to react.[5] Conversely, this could prove to be positive if leveraged properly. Imagine that when responding to a crisis that the local population actually becomes some of the best publicity as images of first responders handing out food or the removal of a particularly unsavory local character goes viral. This was present in nascent form on September 11, 2001 when the first responders of New York's emergency services became instant celebrities and people from Europe to Asia bought NYPD or FDNY tee shirts. This reality must be taken into account as technology only makes the capability easier. As observed by several police departments, anytime an officer stops for any reason, a camera is present, or should be assumed to be.[6] This must also be present in the preparation military or other groups' conduct prior to operating in such urban sprawls.

So, what can the US Government, the US Intelligence Community, and the Department of Defense, among others do to enhance the understanding of megacities? It must seek to resolve situations before they become problems. To accomplish that goal, members of those organizations need to be able to assess situations through frameworks that have not been the historical norm for the defense or intelligence communities. As with most problems, training and education are critical; a different mindset about solution development and employment, and less emphasis on fighting wars and more on avoiding them.

Training must instill an understanding of the challenges that will be encountered. Soldiers, intelligence operatives, a new breed of first responders, all should have an understanding of the megacity characteristics that may affect their operations. All must become comfortable operating in an area where they are likely to interact with the local population in any number of ways. Participating in multiple iterations of training is the underlying principle. Three broad areas, combining emergent technology and principles, come to mind that will enhance proper understanding through training:

• *Virtual Reality (VR).* The benefits of this technology are often improperly communicated. It is not a substitute for live training. It is a platform that can be leveraged to conduct iterative training. The US doesn't have a range or live-practice area where it can employ new concepts for engagement in a megacity. Therefore, well-crafted VR offers a way to work at an individual to group size level across the four dimensions of a megacity, with an appreciation of the hardware/software/outcome framework. Virtual Reality doesn't have to be cost prohibitive, it includes more than the idea of someone wearing goggles projecting images directly to their optical sensors. It can also involve systems younger operators are intimately familiar with, gaming platforms or computers. The base from which ideas for training are culled from must be expanded. Utilizing scenarios presented in media formats that would normally be viewed as skeptical (e.g. fiction) need to be considered. It is only through thinking in broad scope and considering possibilities however unpalatable that personnel will push their frameworks for understanding forward, even if the problems remain mundane in reality.

• *Specialization*. New specialties that deal with the realities of urban infrastructure and populations are essential. Perhaps a pilot group of professionals from Special Operations Forces (SOF) could work with members of the State Department's Conflict and Stabilization Operations (CSO) and select member of the Intelligence Community to develop or cross-functional tactics, techniques and practices to deal with uncertain scenarios before they become problems. These aren't normally areas that operators are trained in, certainly not military forces. Using new frameworks will allow the military to work better across a whole-of-government construct, and in this likely absence be more effective at advancing non-escalating solutions in a megacity environment. Further, an education component should be developed where select members of the USG are trained specifically on these types of situations. These personnel would then be tracked while in government service and on stand-by to advise various organizations who are confronted or confounded by a particular megacity. The education would include living and working in a megacity, deep exploration and evaluation of the hardware/software/outcomes framework and the thinking therein. These are often called broadening assignments by the military and have not yet fully matured. Indeed, it can be argued that despite the emphasis placed on them by some senior leaders, they are still not considered advantageous for personnel to participate in. This needs to change if there is going to be an expectation that defense professionals understand the various systems that may be encountered in megacities. It could lead to urban planning education tracks as the solutions are tested and approved over the next several decades.

• *Practice*. As with any endeavor, practice gives confidence to those that will conduct operations. Whether in small teams and coordinated live exercises in the future, in VR scenarios, or on tabletop exercises designed for failure, not success, practice is essential. The idea is to reinforce the necessity to conduct multiple iterations. This could be possible with physical training, either in Department of Defense owned bases that are nearly abandoned or in economically depressed cities. These costs may prove prohibitive, which is where Virtual Reality may prove a better avenue. However, it is enabled, multiple iterations will force trainees to think of different ways to overcome situations. This can be said of most any endeavor. The key to training for megacity operations will be to emphasize how to think of the various systems present. Easy to understand, easy to access templates can be established, *not* standards, for megacity challenges. Templates that convey understanding, not just lists, that explain why industrial or residential areas developed in a certain way in a geographic region. While no two cities have identical circumstances, there are well researched means of understanding the geographic layout based on history and resources. Why not more lists and standards? Standards are too static and fail to allow for the flexibility required in a dynamic setting like a megacity. Part of the practice, building from the previous paragraph, would find a select group of US Government employees, and possibly service personnel "stationed" in megacities, working with the Nation State, the city governance councils, industry and the USG to learn more lessons, map out functions and add to the depth of understanding available on this complex topic.

Next steps? Do you buy these arguments? Along the way you were thinking, "I've never been to a megacity, and these guys are crazy". Maybe you grew up in Delhi, Tokyo or New York, and you think "these guys are mad". You're right. The thing is, megacities are hard, issues and problems compound over things that were solvable in other environments. They as difficult a challenge to plan for than anything the US Government has tackled previously. Of course, if you believe, as we do, that megacities may quickly resemble mini-countries, that you just need to change your thinking, you're also right. What we want to demonstrate is the importance of talking about them. The importance of understanding a megacity, and that they are more than a scale issue is critical. Our culture and our minds are designed to limit choices, and when we're overwhelmed with data we tend to freeze. The time for this analysis paralysis is over, the time for movement and flexibility is here.

A hardware/software/outcome framework is part of the solution, but it is only a small part. A paper ten times this size will start to introduce the many factors each of these three criteria could consider. Even then, much work is left to do. As Andre Guide said "There are very few monsters who warrant the fear we have of them." We needn't fear megacities, we must start working hard to sort them though.

The views expressed in this article are of the authors, and do not necessarily reflect the view of the Department of Defense, the Defense Intelligence Agency, the U.S. Army, or any other agency of the Federal Government.

Notes

[1] Justice Potter Stewart's concurring opinion in *Jacobellis v. Ohio* 378 U.S. 184 (1964).

[2] UN Economic and Social Affairs Press release July 10, 2014. Accessed February 8, 2016 at esa.un.org/unpd/wup/Publications/Files/WUP2014-PressRelease.pdf.

[3] Collating the research materials and sources of the US Army Chief of Staff Strategic Studies Group white papers "Megacities and the United States Army", June, 2014 and "Readiness in an Urban Era," May 2015.

[4] General Charles C. Krulak, "The Strategic Corporal: Leadership in the Three Block War," *Marines Magazine*, January 1999.

[5] Taylor Dewey, et al. "The Impact of Social Media on Social Unrest in the Arab Spring" (Paper presented at Stanford University, March 20, 2012) 17-91.

[6] Author's Notes from "Readiness in an Urban Era," US Army School of Advanced Military Studies Lyceum White Paper, May 2015.

Chapter 37

People, Infrastructure, and Conflict: Analyzing the Dynamics of Infrastructure Disruption and Community Response

Natalie Myers, Jeanne Roningen, Ellen Hartman, Tina Hart, Scott Tweddale and Patrick Edwards

First Published 10 August 2016

Introduction

Human well-being is heavily reliant on infrastructure systems to provide food, water, power, communication, shelter, and transportation. In 2050, the world will have welcomed a net 2.5 billion additional people in areas characterized as urban, with most of this increase concentrated in Asia and Africa. In this urbanized future, societal dependencies on built infrastructure will remain, but it is highly likely that the organization, construction, maintenance, and governance of those infrastructures will have changed in response to increasing environmental, economic, and political pressures. Therefore, the ability to characterize the changing connections, additions, and disruptions between physical infrastructures and the people who depend on them is essential to fully understand future operational environments.

Military operations inevitably encounter and interact with complex infrastructure systems associated with an equally complex array of users. Infrastructure systems that distribute centrally-generated resources often coexist with infrastructure that is installed at the household or community level, but whose functioning in many cases has dynamic impacts on both supply of and demand for resources; infrastructure interdependencies therefore can occur across scales and are subject to dynamic changes and constitute complex adaptive systems (Rinaldi et al. 2001). The reaction of a population to a disruption to the infrastructure system due to conflict, terrorism, or natural disaster can transfer and aggravate the burden on surviving infrastructures, which may cause cascading secondary impacts. A fuller understanding of the function of infrastructure in the operational environment will enable mission planners to anticipate the effects of operations across all phases of conflict and potentially mitigate some of the effects of military interventions in urban areas where a heterogeneous mix of friendly, hostile, and neutral actors are in close proximity and share infrastructure networks.

Currently, resources for addressing doctrinal requirements in the area of infrastructure are insufficient. U.S. Army doctrine requires that commanders understand, visualize, and describe the infrastructure component of the Joint Operating Environment to accomplish the Army's missions of protecting, restoring, and developing infrastructure (Hart et al. 2014). The Army's current doctrinal tool (FM 3-34.170) for in-theater assessment of the operating status of infrastructure presents a collection of smartcards (i.e., checklists) on the following topics: (S)ewage, (W)ater, (E)lectricity, (A)cademics, (T)rash, (M)edical, (S)afety, and (O)ther Considerations, which include transportation networks, fuel distribution, housing, explosive hazards, environmental hazards, communications, places of worship, and attitude. SWEAT-MSO assessment is concerned with evaluating the operational status of essential services and the staffing level of critical positions; with securing infrastructure and the populace; and with ensuring civil order. However, tools are not available to help assess the dynamic interactions between these infrastructure services or between a population and the infrastructure network; or to integrate infrastructure into planning throughout all phases of conflict. Some people and groups are impacted differentially by disruptive events, react differently in the aftermath, adjust to circumstances in dissimilar ways, and recover in a different manner. Such differences are rooted in the societal characteristics of communities. The ultimate impact of disruptive events is the product of dynamic interactions between the built-environment (e.g., civil infrastructures) and the societal characteristics of the community, and these interactions are not adequately addressed in current methods of analysis (Myers et al. 2016). The consequences of disruptive events often extend beyond the geographic boundaries of the physically impacted region with the impacts spreading through multiple social systems and scales affecting governments, institutions, economic sectors, livelihoods, and people. Past experience in both conflict and natural disaster situations highlights the importance of accounting for the far-reaching societal impacts that are crucial for effective pre-event mitigation planning and optimal post-event resource allocation.

Desired outcomes of this research are improved abilities to 1) map, conceptualize, and model interconnected infrastructure networks, 2) quantify the effects of cascading disruptions across networked systems, 3) quantify and visualize the projected reactions of a population to a disruption, including switching resource providers and changing patterns of use of the infrastructure network, 4) define acceptable and tolerable levels of actual and perceived consequences to heterogeneous communities, 5) visualize the effects of disruptions on a population at a neighborhood level, and 6) assess social impacts of decisions to protect, destroy, or restore infrastructure assets across multiple operational phases.

Methods

Human-Infrastructure Systems Analysis (HISA) is an analysis method that accounts for both the physical/functional and social effects of infrastructure changes on society and local populations. A holistic analysis framework was developed that integrates infrastructure interdependencies and human community behaviors to evaluate a city's vulnerability to disruptions and to assess the impact of potential disruptions. To accomplish this, a game-theoretical equilibrium model was developed in a multilayer infrastructure network, to systematically investigate the mutual influence between infrastructures and communities. In this model, two types of infrastructure failure patterns were formulated to capture general network interdependencies; network equilibrium was extended into infrastructure and community systems to address redistribution of demand for life-supporting resources; and the societal impact of disasters was estimated based on resource demand loss, cost increase, and total infrastructure failure.

To further quantify the societal impacts of infrastructural disruptions, the HISA framework adopted the Capability Approach (CA) (Sen 1985). In CA, the impact of disruptions on individuals' well-being is evaluated in terms of genuine opportunities open to individuals to do or be things of value, like being sheltered, nourished, or mobile. The opportunity to achieve different functioning's collectively gives rise to a certain capability state that could be classified as acceptable, tolerable, or intolerable. To operationalize the CA, we identified 10 capabilities that capture various aspects of individuals' well-being and developed indicators for those capabilities based on census data and resource access cost values derived from the physical infrastructure model. For illustration purposes, the HISA framework is used to visualize the changes in access costs and capabilities of communities within the city of Maiduguri, Nigeria in the aftermath of disruptive event scenarios. The final product of the analysis is a series of maps that represent the spatial distribution of both access cost changes and capability states (from acceptable to intolerable) as a function of changes to an infrastructure network.

The Network Model

As disruption takes place in an infrastructure system, cascading failure begins to develop following certain failure propagation patterns that are inherent in the network, and people start to change the way they access resources. Eventually, the disrupted system arrives at a state where the remaining infrastructures and the impacted population behaviors fall into new equilibria. Modeling and querying the structure of these new equilibria aims to understand and visualize how local populations might be affected by particular infrastructure changes.

The framework therefore (a) generalizes various types of interdependencies among infrastructures with a layered network model, (b) estimates entangled system failure and equilibrium community behavior as part of a game-theoretical model, and (c) evaluates the cascading propagation of disruptions (due to interdependencies) and the consequential societal impacts (such as demand loss, cost increase, and capability state). We developed a heuristic algorithm to calculate the system equilibrium (Buldyrev et al. 2010; Lu et al. 2016). We performed numerical comparisons based on real-world data to examine the impact of cascading infrastructure failures on the population and explored model sensitivities.

Typically, especially after disasters, people access life-supporting resources by utilizing the transportation layer. The trivial case that people get resources within the community, e.g., tap water at each household, can be incorporated as traveling a distance of zero. Under disruption, fewer resource nodes remain functioning, which can lead to overwhelming demand concentration and associated long queuing, longer travel detours, and associated traffic congestion. This situation significantly increases people's resource access costs and may further lead to demand loss (i.e., people giving up service) if the costs exceed affordability for a given community. A variant of the traffic equilibrium model was implemented to capture this issue.

Two modes of failure propagation were represented in the network model. To maintain working status, some infrastructure nodes need resource supply, which are also transported via the transportation layer (e.g., a diesel generator accesses fuel from diesel tanks filled by tanker trucks). Therefore, the traffic congestion under the community behavior may significantly delay or block resource procurement as well, or even cause failure to the infrastructure. This type of failure is referred to as a *resource failure*. Secondly, infrastructure disruption could also be due to direct and obvious dependencies based on physical connections. For example, a water tank with an electrical pump must be supported by a nearby power source (e.g., a power grid). Such a dependency is normally established for the long run, at a large setup cost, and hence difficult to modify. This type of failure, caused by supporting infrastructure disruption, is referred to as *support failure*. Comparing the two types of failure, support failure is found to be one major cause of cascading disruptions. In particular, a network with a very dense presence of links (e.g., a tree) can be very vulnerable—the failure of the root node will propagate (cascade) and disrupt the entire system. In contrast, resource failure normally poses a potential risk, but one that is less obvious to foresee in advance. However, resource failure can also bring devastating damage to the entire system, especially when it happens at some critical node that can cause consequential cascading support failures.

Quantifying Social Effects

To develop the Capability Approach, we derived 16 indicators obtainable from census and survey data to quantify 10 capabilities, some of whose inputs are proposed to be analogous to infrastructure model outputs of access time to various resources (Table 1). A probabilistic predictive model was developed to determine the sets of indicators available from census data that were most correlated with capability scores derived from household surveys. Then, a fault-tree was developed that schematically illustrates how the combinations of different indicators collectively give rise to the capability states. The methods of system reliability analysis were used to obtain the corresponding probability of each capability state. (Gardoni and Murphy 2010). For illustration purposes, the proposed framework was used to visualize the capabilities of the communities in the city of Maiduguri in the aftermath of a disruptive event. The final product of the analyses is a series of maps that represent the spatial distribution of the well-being of the communities in terms of each capability as well as an overall capability score. While the physical network model output and associated resource access cost calculations are explicitly spatial in nature and limited by the fidelity of the infrastructure network, the spatial representation of the CA approach is limited by the smallest geographic area for which indicators derived from census data can be disaggregated.

Capability	Indicator
Meeting Physiological Needs	Main Source of Drinking Water
	Frequency of Problems with Supply of Drinking Water
	Frequency of Problems Satisfying Food Needs
Being Physically Safe	Do Members Feel Safe Walking on the Street at Night?
Being Sheltered	Frequency of Problems Paying House Rent
Having Access to Energy	Source of Electricity
	Number of Hours without Electricity in Previous 24 Hours
Earning Income	Household Financial Situation
Owning Property	Number of Household Durables
	Dwelling Ownership
Being Mobile	Time to Nearest Food Market
Being Educated	Time to Nearest Primary School
	Frequency of Problems Paying School Fees
Having Access to Medical Services	Time to Nearest Hospital
	Frequency of Problems Paying for Healthcare
Being Socially Connected	Can Household Depend on Religious Association during Difficult Period?

Figure 1: Selected Capabilities and Indicators for the Maiduguri Case Study End-User Applications

An end-user might want to know how to represent a case where there is incomplete information about the true fragility of infrastructure under the given failure propagation mechanisms. We therefore explored model formulations where, rather than presuming that infrastructure failure occurs completely and consistently when certain predefined failure conditions are met, instead a Monte-Carlo probabilistic failure analysis is used, whereby each failure propagation occurs based on a certain predefined probability of failure. This technique can help model results under incomplete information because the mean, range, and distribution of the results of multiple model runs can be analyzed to understand the implications of uncertainties in input failure probabilities.

In another "Restore-Recover-Rebuild" case study, the team was given an already-disrupted system and a set of nodes that could be restored or rebuilt in new locations. The infrastructure network model was viewed as a function that maps each subset of possible combinations of nodes to be restored to a set of social welfare indicators, such as the cumulative time for all communities to access water, markets, healthcare, etc. A method can then be set up to explore the best possible combination of nodes to restore, given that the aim is to maximize social benefits while only restoring/rebuilding a certain fixed number of nodes at any point in time. This method translates mathematically to a nonlinear non-convex optimization problem, which can be solved approximately but efficiently by using a genetic algorithm.

Additional modifications allowed the model to represent partial rather than complete failure; to represent resource limits or service capacities of a given infrastructure node; and to represent demand elasticity whereby demand decreases as a function of increasing cost to account for a community's tendency to make do with less as costs rise rather than using arbitrary cost ceilings at which demand collapses.

Case Study: Maiduguri, Nigeria

Maiduguri is the capital city of Borno State in northeastern Nigeria and has an estimated population of 1.2 million. Concurrent with rapid urban growth, the local government has been facing additional severe challenges. Maiduguri is located in the heart of the rebel activity of Boko Haram, experiencing frequent attacks on its infrastructure.

Boko Haram has, in the past three years, vandalized public infrastructure like telecommunication masts that had hitherto cut off various parts of Borno State from the rest of the world. The group had also used bombs and fire to destroy schools, hospitals, police offices, barracks and even cratering of roads. Their most recent attack on public infrastructure was the bombing of an ultra-modern drilling rig procured by Borno State at the cost of over N300 million at the site where it was mobilized to drill water for rural dwellers of the northern part of Borno State. (All Africa 2014)

Both active military events and terrorist attacks threaten people's daily life and the security of urban infrastructure (Ibeh 2015). Because of the ongoing conflict, large numbers of internally displaced persons (IDPs) flee from the surrounding countryside into Maiduguri after terrorist attacks. That influx in population further stresses the city's resources, resulting in increased demands on infrastructural systems (Haruna 2015).

A geospatially-referenced network model of the critical infrastructures in the city was developed using a combination of existing data and an understanding of how different infrastructure components are used in this location. In the network model of Maiduguri's infrastructure, the following utility, institutional, and community sectors were represented: Fresh Water, Fuel, Electricity, Transportation, Food, Schools, Medical Facilities, and Community. Subsequently, cascading infrastructure failures were propagated under different scenarios throughout the network, creating geospatially-referenced output representing before-and-after costs to access those different resources. The results of different failure scenarios were then assessed and several types of sensitivity analysis were performed to better understand both system and model behavior. Finally, this information was included in the CA method to derive spatially-distributed maps that relate infrastructure changes to changes in social well-being.

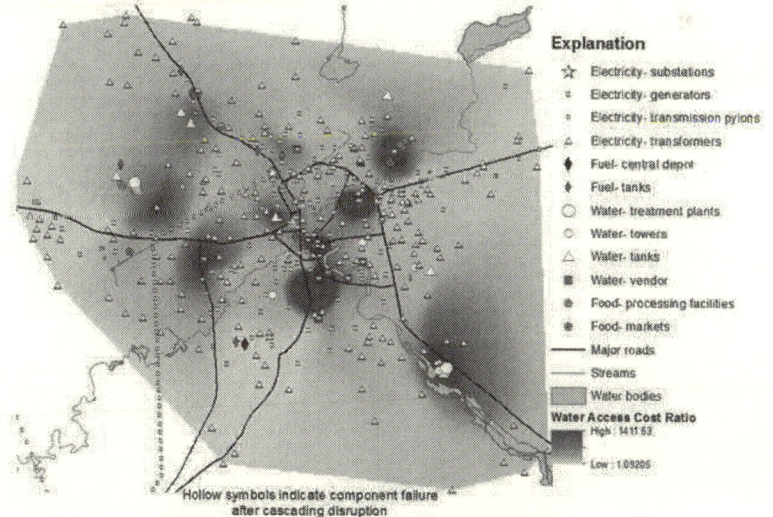

Figure 2: Change in Water Accessibility After
Disrupting the Main Power Substation

An example scenario was considered where disruption initiates at the main power substation in the center of the city, and the failure propagation and social impacts were then investigated. After propagating the network disruption, the system converges to equilibrium. As expected, all electricity transformers are shut down, the electricity network is disabled, while only local electricity generators can work based on fuel, providing limited power supply to nearby communities. Furthermore, the water network is also disrupted, while only local commercial water vendors that can pump water from wells using generators still function. As a result, educational institutions and healthcare facilities are disrupted due to the shortage of power and water. In Figure 1, the spatial distribution of changes in communities' water access costs shows that costs increased significantly around several of the commercial water providers as competition increases for those limited resources.

A set of simulations for this case study provided the means to explore potential system behavior. Predictably, resilience to disruptions increased with increased resource capacity. However, disruption that occurred at some apparently critical infrastructures (such as a water treatment plant) did not always produce catastrophic capacity reductions because the network of independent suppliers (e.g., commercially-run water wells) was able to replace that supply, although the spatial distribution of the attendant increased access costs varied. Under some scenarios, we observed that taking some infrastructure components offline actually produced overall benefits by supplying necessary resources or reduced congestion to other underserved parts of the system. Under other scenarios, dynamic interactions among infrastructures and communities led to new equilibria showing high-vulnerability risks to the system, with implications for operational planning. Our findings emphasize the importance of using a holistic model with dynamic community response rather than a one-way failure propagation model to correctly capture the interdependent relationships between the physical infrastructure systems and the population when evaluating system reliability and societal impacts.

Ongoing Research

Ongoing research aims to modify the model toward specific end-user objectives, for example, identifying the most critical infrastructure components in a given system. Based on this, geospatially-informed reinforcement or interdiction strategies can be sought that will best protect an urban system as a whole or certain vulnerable community within it. Currently, the model's framework only uses modeled values of access time to measure a community's generalized resource cost; this can be naturally expanded by considering additional cost components (e.g., volumes and/or prices of resources). Additional applications include optimization of an infrastructure system in order to produce maximum social benefit with a limited budget as well as derivation of the set of configurations that would restore system function to some threshold capability distribution. Finally, for effective use of this type of model for planning purposes, it will be critical to better understand the sensitivity of model outputs to the level of detail and structural differences in the input data that define the joint human-infrastructure network.

Conclusion

Accurately anticipating the sociocultural impacts of military interventions on infrastructure is particularly important to security and stability operations, in which appropriate engagement with the local population is essential for mission success. However, any human-infrastructure system is comprised of both centrally-planned utilities and community-level installations and infrastructure use patterns that are generated by efforts of the local population to provide for their own resource needs. As the number of expanding urban populations that outpace planned infrastructure is expected to grow dramatically in coming decades, models of the dynamics of infrastructure development, use, and failure propagation need to account for these realities. HISA enriches the understanding of the future battlespace through better visualizations of cascading failures of physical infrastructures and the resulting effects on populations, accounting for dynamic human responses to those failures. Military planners and strategists will benefit from human-infrastructure analysis when the results are integrated across tactical, operational, and strategic military planning processes.

References

Note—Only the Natalie Myers biography is provided in the original article.

All Africa. (2014). "Nigeria: Boko Haram Attacks Power Station, Plunges Maiduguri into Darkness." http://allafrica.com/stories/201407210823.html.

Sen, Amartya. (1985). Commodities and Capabilities. Amsterdam: North-Holland.

Buldyrev, S. V., R. Parshani, G. Paul, H. E. Stanley, and S. Havlin. (2010). Catastrophic Cascade of Failures in Interdependent Networks. *Nature* 464 (7291): 1025-1028.

FM 3-34.170. (2008). Appendix C, Infrastructure Reconnaissance, to FM 3-34.170, *Engineer Reconnaissance.*

Gardoni, Paolo and Colleen Murphy. (2010). Gauging the Societal Impacts of Natural Disasters Using a Capability Approach. *Disasters: The Journal of Disaster Studies, Policy and Management,* 34(3), 619–636.

Hart, Steven D., J. Ledie Klosky, Scott Katalenich, Berndt Spittka, and Erik Wright. (2014). *Infrastructure and the Operational Art: A Handbook for Understanding, Visualizing, and Describing Infrastructure Systems.* ERDC/CERL TR-14-14.

Haruna, K. (January 2015). "Maiduguri: A Troubled Capital City Overtaken by IDPs." http://leadership.ng/features/401050/maiduguri-troubled-capital-city-overtaken-idps.

Ibeh, N. (18 February 2015). "Nigerian Military Kills Over 300 Terrorists, Captures Many Others." http://www.premiumtimesng.com/news/top-news/177064-nigerian-military-kills-over-300-terrorists-captures-many-others.html.

Lu, Liqun, Xin, Wang, Zhaodong Wang, Yanfeng Ouyang, Jeanne Roningen, Scott Tweddale, Patrick Edwards, and Natalie Myers. (2016). *Assessing Socioeconomic Impacts of Cascading Infrastructure Disruptions in a Dynamic Human-Infrastructure Network*. ERDC/CERL TR-16-XX.

Myers, N., A. Rhodes, L. Whalley, G. Al-Chaar, J. Roningen, G. Calfas, T. Bozada, T. Hurt, D. Krooks, and D. Morrison. (2016). *Understanding the Effects of Infrastructure Changes on Sub-Populations*. ERDC/CERL TR-16-3.

Rinaldi, S. M., J. P. Peerenboom and T. K. Kelly. (2001). "Identifying, Understanding, and Analyzing Critical Infrastructure Interdependencies." *Control Systems*, IEEE 21 (6): 11–25.

Chapter 38

The Role of Network Science in Analyzing Slums in Rapidly Growing Urban Areas

Amy Krakowka Richmond, Chris Arney, Kathryn
Coronges and Matthew Simonson

First Published 13 August 2016

Introduction

In the coming decades the United States military will find itself operating in increasingly complex environments. New concepts of operations and new language in military doctrine are needed to address the complexities of these tactical, operational, and strategic environments. In particular, the complexities of urban and peri-urban—areas located in the "urban-fringe"—regions require new tools and concepts to develop more effective operations and supporting doctrine. Rapidly evolving social, economic, and physical structures throughout the world suggest that future operations will involve complex systems, unexpected scenarios, and nonlinear processes. As a basis for military decision-making, these systems have been described as having four components: volatility, uncertainty, complexity, and ambiguity (VUCA) (Kail 2010). VUCA features help explain political, social, informational, organizational, and physical infrastructure networks within complex environments.

The recent focus on the four VUCA features highlight the complex nature of modern military operational environments. This perspective calls on particular strategic approaches to deal with VUCA characteristics: *Volatility* refers to rapid, drastic changes in the environment—strategic plans that assume static environments become ineffective; *Uncertainty* refers to the unexpected and unclear environments faced by soldiers—military units cannot create useful situational awareness because past experiences do not necessarily help predict the future situation; *Complexity* refers to systems that are interactive, interdependent, and often multi-layered. Not accounting for the interdependencies and multiple dimensions of these systems will produce inaccurate assessments, which can be disastrous, setting off a cascade of unanticipated events. *Ambiguity* refers to the difficulty in determining, delineating, defining, and classifying the true problem—uncertainty must be quantified and accounted for in analysis. Supporting nation-building and humanitarian activities necessitates a deeper understanding of how these societal systems function.

Methods used to analyze VUCA environments are growing beyond traditional descriptive statistics, which inherently assume independence among components. During the past decade some of the most important advances towards understanding VUCA have been provided in context of network theory. Network science models capture a dynamic understanding of the interdependence among components, and the evolution of these relationships over time. Developing network models and theoretical approaches is critical to understanding, navigating and leveraging unfamiliar and complex social and physical terrains, particularly in large urban and peri-urban areas.

The megacity has quickly become a symbol of the 21st century human environment, with over 24 megacities in existence across the world in 2013. The rise of the megacity has brought forth significant issues in planning, authority, and stability as these rapidly expanding urban centers outpace the capacities of their municipalities. With populations in excess of 10 million, there are often extreme limitations in the abilities of formal municipal governments to plan space, infrastructure, and resources. This leads to issues of large-scale unplanned habitations, extreme stress on environmental resources, uncontrolled sprawl, pollution, informal governance structures, and dangerous power conflicts.

As this demographic shift to an urban society continues to cascade, it becomes increasingly important to understand this new terrain. As General Odierno, former Chief of Staff of the Army, and Michael O'Hanlon, a prominent Brookings Institute researcher, discuss in their recent article: "Scale is a major contributor to the complexity of urbanization. As cities grow, their vulnerabilities grow—often in nonlinear ways." (Odierno and O'Hanlon 2016) Massive growth creates new weakly governed spaces where criminals and extremists can flourish unabated. The challenge, as suggested by Pike and Brown (2016) is to operationalize existing military intelligence concepts so that intelligence analysts at all levels can gain understanding. For example, the Intelligence Preparation of the Battlefield (IPB) which is the systematic process of analyzing the four mission variables (enemy, terrain, weather, and civilian considerations), should consider the interconnectedness of the variables (Wolfel et al. 2016).

This paper stresses the importance of using network theory in analyzing the interconnectedness of different components of the operational and strategic environments. This type of analysis is particularly important in weakly governed spaces, such as slums and gang-controlled neighborhoods, where interactions between variables are mostly outside government control.

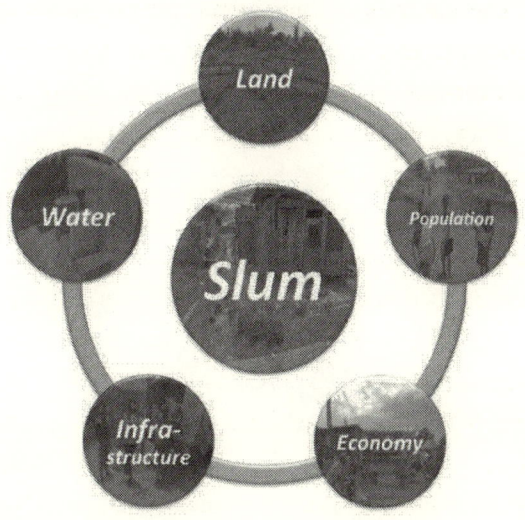

Weakly Governed Spaces in Urban Areas: Slums

Urbanization increasingly means that the poorest, most vulnerable people move into large, highly distressed slums. As a consequence, urban areas exhibit high levels of poverty and inequality. The risk is that these informal urban areas will detach themselves even further from effective government service and control, and instead build local political and military power structures that may come to constitute a threat to the city and ultimately, the state itself. The UN defines a slum household as a group of individuals living under the same roof lacking one or more of the following conditions (UN Habitat 2003):

- Access to improved water
- Access to improved sanitation
- Sufficient-living area
- Durability of housing
- Security of tenure

Often, all five of these factors are present. Slums are a clear manifestation of a poorly planned and managed urban sector. In rapidly growing cities, such as many sub-Saharan African cities, the majority of the population live in slums. Fifty-five million new slum dwellers have been added to the global population since 2000. ("UN HABITAT State of the World Cities" 2012)

There are five major components that perpetuate slum conditions and consequently contribute to household vulnerability. First, these settlements lack basic infrastructure such as waste management systems, sanitation, improved water sources, they have unpaved and poorly maintained roads and lack access to emergency services. Lack of adequate emergency services, such as functioning fire trucks, place these populations at a great risk in the event of a disaster. Even if emergency services were able to support the population, access to many of these slum neighborhoods is significantly restricted, if not impossible because of poor and non-existent transportation infrastructure. In many slum areas there are dwellings that do not have access to a single road because landlords have sold off adjacent plots with no room in between for vehicle traffic. To compound this, squatters set up their homes haphazardly leaving barely any room to walk effectively restricting vehicle access and reducing roads to footpaths. Municipalities cannot keep pace with the settlement process resulting in unorganized, densely populated, poverty ridden urban areas.

Second, land rights are exceedingly complicated in slum areas, resulting in differential access to land, water, and sanitation. In some cases, entire slums can be owned by just a handful of people who charge rent costs that the urban poor struggle to afford. In other cases, a convoluted legal system can make it almost impossible to legally determine who has rights to the land. Land is not only critical for providing residence but is also a means for growing food. One example of a functional informal economic system is urban agriculture, which is a key component of the urban mosaic and provides a significant source of nourishment, as food prices at local markets are often too high for the low-income population.

Third, rapid population growth, propelled by migration and high birthrates, results in both overcrowding and even more urban sprawl. The problem is exacerbated by the government's inability to implement or enforce zoning restrictions and building. Overcrowding therefore results in the inability of the municipality to provide crucial services such as garbage collection, which results in the accumulation of solid waste, and increases the risk of rapid spread of contagious diseases. Furthering the problem, sprawl encroaches on marginal lands, to include wetlands, steep hillsides, and low-lying areas, making inhabitants more vulnerable to natural disasters.

Fourth, the majority of slum dwellers operate in the informal economy—the part of the economy that is not regulated or taxed by the government. Many of the economic and infrastructural agreements are carried out with limited oversight of the government, therefore equity and safety of services cannot be ensured. Informality is an inevitable occurrence in developing countries simply because the formal sector cannot manage the sheer magnitude of the population. Informal sectors have become a critical component for the formal sector by providing essential distribution mechanisms. For instance, an unregistered kiosk owner might sell mobile money and cell phone airtime from a multinational telecom company. These entities have become so intertwined that they are often difficult to disentangle from one another. Informal sectors can also be sufficiently organized to affect political outcomes of the formal sector.

Finally, lack of reliable, clean water and sanitation is another crucial component in slums. Without established critical infrastructure, physical proximity and pollution frequently limit access to clean water. For example, in Kampala, Uganda, a city that is growing rapidly, and where 70 percent of the population lives in a slum, pollution from pit latrines, inadequate sanitation facilities, low ground water supply during the dry season, and the high cost for piped water from public taps all contribute to increasing household level vulnerability.

Using network concepts of governance, we propose that the underlying relationships that drive informal governance—a hierarchical system of power existing outside of state structure—to a large degree, drive the other factors of poor infrastructure, incongruent land rights, and overcrowding. We use network analytic perspectives to map what these informal power structures look like and suggest a quantitative framework for how to determine the impact of informal power networks on water sustainability. Quantitative network-based approaches may provide invaluable information for improving situational awareness and providing strategies for developing effective solutions. For example, if a natural disaster or a civil conflict were to occur, who would the US military or NGOs talk and coordinate with at the community level? Who in the city has the real influence and power in these situations? The complex and intertwined relationships between the informal to formal sectors lead to tactical and operational challenges. Tactical elements in these environments are likely to find they are mostly working within the informal network. At the operational level, host nation counterparts are more likely part of the formal structure of the city. The potential for alignment of mission elements and coordination of the US military's tactical/operational elements and cities' informal/formal networks may represent the most significant opportunity for mission effectiveness in urban operations.

Using Water Resources to Explain Informal Governance Structure

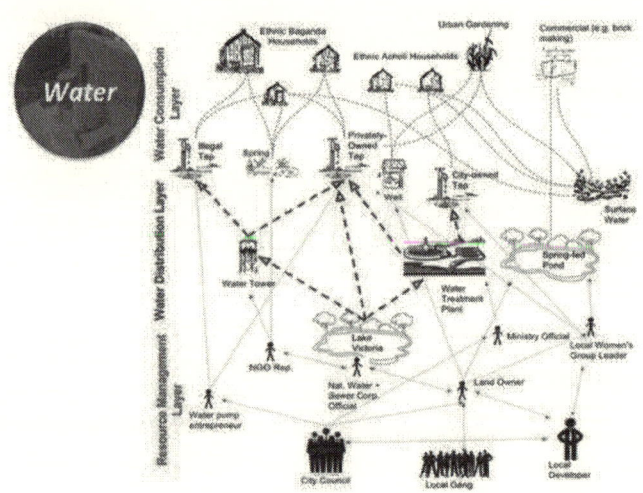

As water is critical for health and wellness of any community, its distribution is absolutely central for maintaining peace and coordination of a region. Urban and peri-urban communities of developing societies offer insights about how both formal government and informal power hierarchy can determine access and control of limited resources. We illustrate the utility of network models by exploring network maps of water availability in urban and peri-urban regions in the developing world. Historically, tension has been fueled when disparate social classes with numerous ethnic affiliations from distinct regions of a state are brought into close proximity and forced to rely on restricted resources. In many cases, political and other influential entities can act as informal gatekeepers, whose role can either aggravate or alleviate such tensions. The complexity of the problem is only made worse by the lack of centralized oversight of the various natural resources, such as water, food, and energy, as well as the physical land upon which these resources are drawn. We suggest that this problem be examined from a systems perspective, by mapping, quantifying and evaluating how well various interdependent systems related to water supply are maintained and balanced. In the figure above, we show the various networks that are likely involved in the access and consumption of water.

The water access and consumption network isolates where and how the resources directly impact the population. This network is bi-modal as it is made up two types of nodes: water consumers and water sources. The links indicate which households get water from which source(s). Water is consumed primarily by three sectors: agriculture, households and commercial operations. This network directly reflects constraints to water access—how far and how many sources can households access. Households can obtain water from multiple sources. In sub-Saharan Africa for example, a significant portion of the population lacks access to piped water and therefore households rely primarily on springs, communal taps, and open water sources such as lakes and rivers. Analysis of this network can show how water consumption relies on particular types of sources and which suppliers in turn wield the most economic and possibly social and political influence.

The water distribution infrastructure network traces how communal taps and other point-of-service water sources obtain their water. In most cities this supply network consists of multiple connected components of varying sizes and capacities. Successfully mapping the city's water distribution network could have important implications for residents' vulnerability in the event of conflict or the outbreak of a waterborne illness such as cholera. Understanding this layer of the network could be significant for the tactical forces in a military operation of any nature.

The resource management network shows which actors control and govern the use of communal resources, including food, water, sanitation, and land. For water, these actors include the city's official piped water supplier, city-wide agencies, local municipal councils, community organizations, local "strongmen" and their associates, as well as individuals who own or control particular taps, toilets, plots of land, and so forth. Understanding these connections can explain what barriers exist and which actors are needed to be included before operational changes can be implemented. In addition, network analysis can identify potential flashpoints for conflict over these resources, be they "turf wars" over the right to sell services, land-ownership disputes, resistance against the expansion of city services into new areas, or a conflict over resource control.

Importance of System Planning

Successful planning relies on good governance, yet city and national authorities are often unorganized, ineffective, and not trusted by local residents. Planning should not just focus on physical infrastructure but also on social sustainability. Mapping water consumption and management networks and their interdependencies would enable us to identify vulnerabilities to better understand the role of social factors in the governance of natural resources. For example, we can integrate these data to develop a multi-dimensional model that captures the interdependencies across resources and social structures. Multi-layer networks have been successful in modeling transportation infrastructure, optimizing traffic flow in a congested urban area, and forecasting water demand in a European city (Adamowski and Karapataki 2010). As Lily Kong at Singapore Management University states: when millions of people with different backgrounds and cultures come into contact with each other, managing social tensions becomes as important as providing essential infrastructure (such as housing and plumbing) and resources (such as food and water) (Yap 2016).

We can use these network approaches to quantify distribution strategies and evaluate specific approaches for how aid is provided in these regions. For example, there is debate over whether top-down state-led programs or privatization is better for improving water access in peri-urban settlements. A top-down approach of simply bulldozing unofficial squatter districts fell out of favor in the international community in the 1970s, giving rise to smaller, cheaper incremental improvements, such as "slum upgrading" projects such as building new wells, sanitation systems or footpaths. Though this approach achieved widespread popularity throughout the developing world from 1970s-90s, according to a recent continent-wide study, "the long-term sustainability of these projects is now seen as doubtful because of poor maintenance, lack of community capacity, difficulties of cost-recovery and deep-rooted social divisions" (Dagdeviren and Robertson 2011). By understanding how distribution strategies change the configurations of the various networks, we can estimate the effectiveness of the two approaches—top-down state-led versus locally driven—in terms of the second and third order effects.

Conclusion

Whether operating as small teams of specialized enablers or as a larger formation responding to crisis, US military forces engaging in a dynamic urban terrain must be able to find and interpret informal centers of gravity and spheres of influence. Moreover, the situational challenges may be *how* and *where* and at *what level* informal and formal powers mesh. Through network analysis of the connectivity of these systems, can we be more effective in this challenging operational environment, lowering the risk to our forces and the population, and increasing the likelihood of mission success.

Applications of network theory have the potential to generate new tools for the military in its efforts to facilitate stability in volatile urban environments, perhaps avoiding the need for costly military intervention. Mapping the networks of power, control, and resource-dependence in developing world slums, may soon be relevant to the U.S.'s efforts to keep terrorist groups from capitalizing on urban tensions, especially in African cities. From the perspective of international development, network theory has the potential to help researchers, decision-makers and warfighters understand how social networks control access to resources, so that they are better prepared to address the challenges facing the rapidly-growing cities within the developing world.

References

Adamowski, Jan, and Christina Karapataki. 2010. "Comparison of Multivariate Regression and Artificial Neural Networks for Peak Urban Water-Demand Forecasting: Evaluation of Different ANN Learning Algorithms." *Journal of Hydrologic Engineering* 15 (10): 729–43.

Dagdeviren, Hulya, and Simon A. Robertson. 2011. "Access to Water in the Slums of Sub-Saharan Africa." *Development Policy Review* 29 (4): 485–505. doi:10.1111/j.1467-7679.2011.00543.x.

Kail, Col Eric G. 2010. "Leading in a VUCA Environment: U Is for Uncertainty." *Harvard Business Review*. November 10. https://hbr.org/2010/11/leading-in-a-vuca-environment-1.

Pike, Tom, and Eddie Brown. 2016. "Complex IPB." *Small Wars Journal*, March. http://smallwarsjournal.com/jrnl/art/complex-ipb.

Raymond Odierno, Michael O'Hanlon. 2016. "The Future of Securing Global Cities." *The National Interest*. Accessed June 23. http://nationalinterest.org/feature/securing-global-cities-15563.

UN Habitat. 2003. "The Challenge with Slums."

"UN HABITAT State of the World Cities." 2016. Accessed June 23. http://mirror.unhabitat.org/documents/media_centre/sowcr2006/SOWCR%205.pdf.

Wolfel, Richard, Amy Krakowka Richmond, Mark Read, and Tansey. 2016. "It's in There: Rethinking(?) Intelligence Preparation of the Battlefield in Megacities/Dense Urban Areas." *Small Wars Journal*. Accessed June 23. http://smallwarsjournal.com/jrnl/art/it%E2%80%99s-in-there-rethinking-intelligence-preparation-of-the-battlefield-in-megacitiesdense-urb.

Yap, Samantha. 2016. "Give Citizens a Sense of Ownership in City Planning: SMU Provost—Channel NewsAsia." Accessed June 23. http://www.channelnewsasia.com/news/singapore/give-citizens-a-sense-of/2692304.html.

Chapter 39

Game Review: Operation Whirlwind— The Soviet Assault on Budapest, 1956

Michael Peck

First Published 21 December 2016

As the world watches Aleppo burn, the scenes of carnage and ruin bring to mind another rebellion in another city 60 years ago. In November 1956, it was Budapest [http://nationalinterest.org/blog/the-buzz/budapest-burning-the-hungarian-revolt-shook-the-soviet-18295] that burned as Soviet troops quashed a revolt against Communist rule. The photographs [http://time.com/3878232/the-hungarian-revolution-of-1956-photos-from-the-streets-of-budapest/] then are as haunting as the pictures of wounded Syrian children now: huge Red Army tanks clanking through the streets, smiling teenage boys and girls armed with Molotov cocktails, burning armored vehicles strewn across boulevards like junkyard trash.

Compared to the carnage of Aleppo, Budapest was tame: no barrel bombs, airstrikes or artillery barrages on civilian neighborhoods. The warriors of Stalingrad would hardly have called it a battle at all. Nonetheless, this was no mere riot or police action. It was urban warfare waged by conventional troops fighting house-to-house against armed insurgents. The Soviet intervention, code-named "Operation

Whirlwind," became a week-long struggle that cost the lives of 2,500 Hungarians and 700 Soviet soldiers.

That's the setting for *Operation Whirlwind*, a paper simulation of the Soviet assault on Budapest. Designed by prolific wargame designer Brian Train, who has tackled such obscure conflicts as the Shining Path insurgency in Peru and the Algerian Civil War, *Operation Whirlwind* puts two players in command of the Soviet and Hungarian insurgent forces.

This is no easy topic to capture in a board game. How do you simulate such an asymmetrical struggle between regular and irregular forces? This was a battle that the Soviets could not lose unless the West intervened (which would probably have triggered a nuclear war that everyone would have lost).

But *Operation Whirlwind* captures the essentials of the battle through some simple but clever game mechanics. The field of battle itself is a 17-inch by 22-inch paper map overlaid by thick red lines dividing the board into 34 areas, classed as either urban, suburban, industrial or recreational park terrain. In addition, 10 areas are marked with stars to indicate victory objectives, including Parliament, City Hall and Radio Budapest. Terrain offers defensive benefits during combat, but only to Hungarian units in rebel-controlled areas under attack by Soviet troops. Rebels attacking Soviet-controlled areas don't get any advantages, which make the insurgents better at holding ground then taking it.

The combatants are represented by 140 half-inch cardboard counters, red for the Soviets and green for the Hungarians. Soviet forces consist of the 2nd and 33rd Guards Mechanized Divisions plus attached corps-level formations, a mixture of motorized infantry, tanks and reconnaissance detachments. The Hungarians are a motley assortment of lightly armed Insurgent units, more heavily armed Militia and Sappers, plus 15 Civilian markers. There are also optional U.S. Special Forces A-teams and the 101st Airborne (more on them later). Each unit's effectiveness is marked with a Combat Rating, from 1 for Hungarian insurgents, to 3 for Soviet tank battalions, to a devastating 15 for Soviet motorized rifle regiments, underscoring the disparity in firepower between regulars and rebels. However, the Soviets begin with only six of those infantry regiments, reflecting a Soviet tendency to operate in big, clumsy formations. In fact, the Soviet only have about 25 pieces they can maneuver on the map, while the Hungarians have about 60. Soviets units are stronger, but with 34 areas on the map, the Red Army can't be everywhere.

Before the game starts, the Hungarian player rolls four dice, and randomly draws 4 to 24 Insurgent and Civilian counters that are deployed on the map. He also rolls to see how many Arms Points he receives, simulating looted and captured arms from Hungarian army depots, which he spends to upgrade Insurgents into Militia and Sappers (he also gets two anti-tank gun counters, representing captured artillery and partially dismantled tanks). He also places a marker for Hungarian military commander Pal Maleter, who gives a combat bonus to Hungarian fighters.

Soviet troops then enter the map from any edge. Every turn, representing 8 hours of game time (including a night turn every third turn), consists of Soviet movement and combat, followed by the Hungarians doing the same. Units can move an unlimited number of areas during a turn but must stop when entering an enemy-occupied area. However, the Hungarians can employ Infiltration Movement by rolling dice, with a small chance of the unit being eliminated and a greater chance that it will use alleyways and sewers to jump over Soviet blocking positions. With the limited number of Soviet pieces to cover the city, this becomes a problem—one that Syrian-Iranian troops in Aleppo, or American troops in Baghdad and Fallujah—could relate to.

A player can choose to initiate combat during his turn if friendly and enemy troops occupy the same area. Fighting is resolved by totaling the Combat Factors of each side's pieces, with each player rolling dice to see how many hits they inflict on the other. In theory, this should heavily favor the Soviets with their massive infantry regiments and powerful tank battalions, which get a combined arms bonus when attacking together.

But like an elephant battling a swarm of ants, it's a combination of little things that blunt the Soviet advantage. Besides defensive bonuses from terrain, the rebels can mount Surprise Attacks with their Sappers that inflict extra losses on the Soviets. It doesn't help that different Red Army divisions can't attack together because of rigid command and control.

The Hungarians enjoy three more advantages. First, the Hungarian rolls two dice every turn, which gives them 2 to 12 reinforcement units. Rebel troops die like flies but they resurrect like zombies, moving from the map to the dead pile, and then back again. In addition, every time a Soviet unit takes losses, the rebels get an Arms Point (captured equipment) to beef up their own troops. The Soviets take fewer losses, but when they do, there is a lesser chance they will be replaced.

Second, all Hungarian pieces are face-down, hiding their type and combat strength, unless they fire. The Soviets never know whether or not the area they are assaulting contains lightly armed Insurgents, or Militia or Sappers.

Which brings up the final rebel advantage, which is one that has plagued every counterinsurgency operation in history. The Hungarians have Civilian markers. If these markers are attacked by a Soviet infantry regiment and eliminated, a massacre has occurred and the Soviets lose 3 Victory Points each time. Because Hungarian pieces are face down, the Red Army doesn't know if the area it's attacking contains civilians.

Ah, but the Soviets have an alternative. Their infantry regiments normally operate in Assault mode, which allows them to attack at full strength. However, they can also choose to operate in Probe mode, which doesn't wipe out civilians. The problem is that Probe mode restricts them to attacking at half-strength, a dilemma that has hampered modern urban warfare from Budapest to Hue to Gaza. No one has yet to come up with a satisfactory answer, and neither will the Soviet player in this game, who must balance the risks versus rewards of unleashing his full firepower.

The game continues until the Soviets wipe out all the rebels, or they occupy all 10 victory objective areas. The winner is determined by Victory Points. The Soviets start with 50, and then lose them through killing civilians and suffering Red Army losses. If the Soviets end with 40 or more Victory Points, they achieve a "triumph for progressive

Socialist forces over the forces of reaction and fascism," according to the rules. If they have 24 or less points, "the operation was a success, but the patient died. Hungarian Moral Victory."

Operation Whirlwind features an intriguing what-if: U.S. intervention to support the rebels. Despite longstanding myths that the U.S. encouraged the Hungarian Revolt and supplied it with arms, it turns out that the CIA was caught by surprise. In fact, it only had only one case officer in Budapest, and he was stuck doing administrative chores [http://nsarchive.gwu.edu/NSAEBB/NSAEBB206/]. However, for those who want to experiment with history, the 101st Airborne and Special Forces teams can drop on Budapest (the paratroopers provide muscle, and the Special Forces provide Arms Points to equip Hungarian units). The downside is a huge Victory Point penalty, plus the Soviets get two extra divisions.

To say *Operation Whirlwind* is an ultra-realistic simulation of urban warfare would be a stretch. For example, the game continues indefinitely until the Red Army wipes out the rebels or seizes all the victory objective areas, which removes time pressure on the Soviet player. Nonetheless, while the game is fairly simple and abstract, this is also what makes it playable in a couple of hours. As a simulation, *Operation Whirlwind* broadly captures the challenges of a regular army attempting seize control of a city in armed rebellion.

The game's designer does have a recommendation for the outgunned Hungarians: play Beethoven's "Egmont Overture" over and over as long as the Soviets don't control Radio Budapest (apparently that was the only music the rebels could find when they took over the station).

Gallows humor, perhaps. But then, Hungary did become free 33 years later. The Soviet empire proved to be a sick joke that couldn't last.

Chapter 40

On the Likelihood of Large Urban Conflict in the 21st Century

Sean M. Castilla

First Published 25 March 2017

The Chief of Staff of the Army, General Milley, recently said "future war will be largely fought in urban terrain," and that the Army is currently "suboptimized for urban capabilities."[1] In recent years several articles have explored how to go about 'optimizing' for future combat scenarios in megacities—urban centers with populations of 10 million persons or more.[2] Despite this growing emphasis on megacity contingencies, many question the premise of U.S. participation in megacity conflict.

As Major John Spencer (Modern War Institute at West Point) recently noted, the counterargument is that megacity terrain is too challenging in terms of scale and complexity, and consequently it should be considered an "impossible mission and, therefore, not one we will undertake."[3] Like Major Spencer, I reject this notion.

This logic is flawed for four reasons. First, humans, and by extension sources of human conflict, are concentrating in urban areas. Second, our potential adversaries will continue to leverage complex terrain, such as large urban areas, to negate U.S. advantages.

Third, dismissing megacity conflict as extreme ignores the fact that conflict in large and complex urban terrain is a prominent feature of 21st century warfare. Lastly, as the sources of conflict grow increasingly consolidated in urban terrain it is the duty of military professionals to consider the character of such conflict and what types of military options we can provide our political leadership in a crisis. In this essay I will consider each of the four factors outlined above in further detail.

Global Urbanization Trends

By now, even the most casual reader on this topic knows that global urbanization trends are making conflict in megacity environments increasingly likely. Urbanization of the global population over the last five decades has been momentous; two centuries ago only three percent of humanity lived in cities, whereas today for the first time in history half of the world population lives in urban areas.[4] If current urbanization trends continue, over 70 percent of the global population will reside in cities by the year 2050.[5] Much of this urban growth will be absorbed in Sub-Saharan Africa and Asia, geopolitical areas that are challenged by rampant poverty and violence.[6]

The rising socioeconomic influence of megacities (14 percent of global economic output today comes from the world's megacities), compounded by multiple drivers of instability (i.e. unregulated growth, urban slums, ungoverned areas, income disparity, substandard infrastructure, corrupt governance, sectarianism, climate change, etc.), has significantly bolstered their strategic importance.[7] Cities are increasingly rivaling nation states in importance as the driving force in shaping global stability and development.[8] As General Milley recently noted, war is about politics and it will be fought where people live; in an urbanized world, large urban areas are the battlefields of the future.[9]

Unforeseen Drivers of Urban Conflict

Another potentially unforeseen, and less obvious, driver of conflict in megacities may prove to be the current modernization efforts of the U.S. and our potential adversaries. Having observed U.S. military operations in Iraq and Afghanistan, revisionist powers (i.e. states that seek to challenge the status quo of the international system, such as Russia) have adapted their military strategies and modernized their forces to counter U.S. strengths and exploit U.S. weaknesses.

These adversarial efforts seek to "fracture" the AirLand Battle paradigm by denying U.S. Joint forces supremacy and interoperability across all domains.[10] Focused on the current fight, the U.S. simultaneously allowed its modernization efforts to atrophy. Consequently, revisionist states have achieved technological parity, and in some instances superiority, with the U.S. by implementing robust anti-access/area-denial (A2/AD) networks comprised of a sophisticated array of sensors and cross-domain capabilities (e.g. precision-guided munitions, cyber/electronic warfare capabilities, etc.) designed to challenge U.S. domain supremacy.[11]

Recognizing these challenges, the U.S. Army is taking action to modernize its force, pacing its efforts on the technological advancements of near-peer competitors.[12] The Army seeks to enhance its air and missile defense, fires, communications, aviation, and cyber/EW capabilities as well as providing lethality and survivability upgrades for the Abrams, Bradley, and Stryker. Other emerging technologies, such as autonomous drones and artificial intelligence, are being developed to offset the advantages of potential adversaries.[13]

Ultimately, the goal of these modernization efforts, known broadly as the DoD's Third Offset Strategy, is to shore up the eroded credibility of U.S. conventional deterrence in order to ensure stability in an increasingly competitive multipolar international system.

If we assume that these modernization efforts prove successful in (a) negating competitor capability advantages in the near-term; and (b) regaining domain superiority in the long run; then it is logical to assume our modernization efforts may inadvertently compel revisionist state adversaries (or their proxies) to challenge U.S. supremacy in the very places we seek to avoid—areas of severely restricted terrain that deny U.S. land forces the ability to maneuver and mass its forces.

As the world grows increasingly urban, this includes the severely restricted terrain of megacities. Operating from within such crowded and complex terrain, revisionist states can challenge the international status quo indirectly using deception, misinformation, surprise and speed to engage us below the threshold of military escalation.[14] In a 2013 document outlining his view of 21ˢᵗ century warfare, the Russian Chief of the General Staff outlined exactly this kind of indirect approach:

> *Frontal engagements of large formations of forces at the strategic and operational level are gradually becoming a thing of the past. Long-distance, contactless actions against the enemy are becoming the main means of achieving combat and operational goals.*[15]

It may be that as the U.S. reestablishes the credibility of its deterrence capabilities, revisionist forces will choose to launch such non-frontal attacks from the cover and concealment that complex urban terrain provides.

Additionally, while U.S. defense spending continues to vastly exceed that of our competitors, it may be logical for potential adversaries to use complex urban terrain as a base from which to strike the U.S. rather than to continue their modernization efforts for linear force-on-force conflict.[16] Policy advisor and columnist Rosa Brooks recently wrote that U.S. military conventional capability dominance makes it "suicidal" for competitors to directly challenge us. Revisionist powers are forced to pursue asymmetric strategies (e.g. striking U.S. forces from complex, non-linear battlefields) to counter U.S. strengths and exploit U.S. weakness. Brooks notes:

> *We assume that military technological innovation is a one-way ratchet. High-tech measures taken by one side*

will be followed by high-tech countermeasures taken by the other, which will be met with still more advanced counter-measures, and so on, ad infinitum...for all our technological sophistication, warfare has never truly moved past sticks and stones—and even today, their bone-breaking power remains surprisingly potent...[sometimes] the most successful countermeasures are low-tech—and historically, this has been demonstrated just as often as has the opposite.[17]

Accordingly, it is unnecessary for potential adversaries to match current U.S. modernization efforts tit-for-tat. Urban terrain offers tactical advantages to the defender that is otherwise inferior at the operational and strategic level.[18]

By operating within a megacity environment, U.S. maneuver formations will be unable to maneuver with ease and unable to mass its forces at decisive points. It is not hard to envision scenarios in which U.S. technological advantages can be negated by technologically unsophisticated means in such environments.

Commercially bought quadcopters configured as low-tech bombers and vehicle-borne improvised explosive devices become just as effective as technologically sophisticated aircraft and tanks in such terrain. Drone swarms can be disrupted or rerouted by the combination of low-tech obstacles, small arms, obscurants and traps emplaced at urban canyon choke points (imagine our adversaries trawling for drones!). Robots using artificial intelligence to identify targets will find that, unlike the air and sea domains, the land domain is crowded and complex; they will find themselves drowning in the sea of humanity residing in megacities. Such scenarios evoke LTG McMaster's "vampire fallacy" which warns that faith in technology "neglects war's uncertainty based mainly on interactions with determined and elusive enemies."[19]

Before proceeding, let us then assume that it is plausible that future U.S. adversaries are just as likely to be near-peer, hybrid or asymmetric forces operating in megacities or large urban areas, as they are to be peer competitors conducting force-on-force warfare in open terrain.

Let us also assume that such conflict will be conducted amidst dense human populations that are burdened by poverty, sectarianism, and other social challenges.

Conflict in Large and Complex Urban Terrain is a Prominent Feature of 21st Century Warfare

Into just its 17th year, warfare in the 21st century has been notably urban in character. Consider the abundance of urban battles and campaigns that have occurred in just under two decades: Grozny; Nablus; Baghdad; Fallujah; Bint Jbeil; Nahr al-Bared; Tskhinvali; Rio de Janeiro, Gaza; Donetsk; Aleppo; etc. These conflicts are only the continuation of a trend towards the urbanization of conflict that intensified in the 20th century (reference Stalingrad, Manila, Hue City, etc.). Recent conflicts such as the Third Battle of Fallujah, operations in Yemen, and the ongoing Mosul campaign suggest that this trend towards urban conflict is not going away.

Despite evidence that war is growing increasingly urban, there are many that continue to dismiss the notion that we should prepare for megacity conflict because it is an unlikely scenario. Perhaps this reluctance is rooted in our cultural aversion toward conflict in urban areas. Whatever the cause, the notion that we shouldn't be preparing for megacity conflict because it is unlikely is akin to saying that we shouldn't have a React to Nuclear Hazard/Attack battle drill because that scenario is also unlikely. Training and preparing for the worst-case scenario is what we are paid to do. Choosing not to prepare for such scenarios neglects our duty to be prepared for conflict in whatever form it may arise. As Roger Spiller noted in *Sharp Corners: Urban Operations at Century's End*, "No fighting force is ever permitted to indulge its operational preferences with impunity. War and lesser forms of conflict do not organize themselves for anyone's benefit."[20]

Furthermore, as military professionals we must not lose sight of the forest for the trees. In discussing potential conflict in megacities, it is easy to get wrapped around the categorical distinction that they are comprised of 10 million persons or more. Megacity populations are daunting and it is hard to wrap one's mind around how to successfully operate in such an environment. Yet even if conflicts don't occur in the extreme megacity populations, the overarching argument in this paper is that conflict is likely to become increasingly urban. Conflict in cities below the megacity threshold will still feature the key characteristics of urban conflict: creating massive casualty rates; requiring considerable resources and time; causing civilian hardship, etc. The city of Aleppo, with a prewar population of approximately 2.3 million, has been no less ghastly than conflict in a megacity may be.[21]

It is Our Duty as Military Professionals to Consider the Character of Megacity Conflict

Urban conflict will likely continue to be a prominent characteristic of 21st century warfare. As large cities grow increasingly influential, it is reasonable to assume that we may find ourselves operating in severely restricted urban terrain. Urban fighting will be extreme. It will be complex, intense and offer our adversaries many advantages. It will not be ground of our choosing. But we must prepare ourselves for such contingencies. Spiller wrote:

> *Human behavior has always been equal to the savagery of war, no matter how extreme. And in the beginning, no other form of early combat posed the test of intense, prolonged, unremitting violence as did combat in and against cities.*[22]

Going forward I recommend research into the following areas: (1) the character of megacity conflict; (2) the types of operations required in megacity conflict; (3) the types of units required to conduct megacity operations; (4) how to conduct multi-domain Joint combined arms operations in a megacity area of operations.

Notes

[1]   Lee, Connie, (2017, March 21). "Milley: Army Will Have to 'Optimize' for Future War in Urban Environments," *Inside Defense*. Retrieved from https://insidedefense.com/daily-news/milley-army-will-have-optimize-future-war-urban-environments.

[2]   Army Capabilities Integration Center, *The Megacity: Operational Challenges for Force 2025 and Beyond*, 2014, http://www.arcic.army.mil/app_Documents/ARCIC_Report_Unified_Quest-14_The-Megacity-Operational-Challenges-for-Force-2025-and-Beyond_08MAY2014.pdf; U.S. Army, *ATTP 3-06.11: Combined Arms Operations in Urban Terrain*, June 2011, A-1.

[3]   Spencer, John, "What an Army Megacities Unit Would Look Like," *Modern War Institute at West Point*, March 8, 2017, http://mwi.usma.edu/army-megacities-unit-look-like/.

[4]   Jonathan Kalan, "Think Again: Megacities," *Foreign Policy* 206, May-June, 2014, 69; Halvard Buhaug and Henrik Urdal, "An Urbanization Bomb? Population Growth and Social Disorder in Cities," *Global Environment*, 23(1), 2013, 1, http://www.urbangateway.org/es/system/files/documents/urbangateway/an_urbanization_bomb_0.pdf.

[5]   Kalan, 69.

[6]   Buhaug, H., & Urdal, H. (2013). An Urbanization Bomb? Population Growth and Social Disorder in Cities. *Global Environment Change*, 23(1), 1-10.

[7]   Kalan, J. (2014). Think Again: Megacities. *Foreign* Policy, 206, 69-73; Harris, Marc; Dixon, Robert; Melin, Nicholad; Hendrex, Daniel; Russo, Richard; Bailey, Michael, *Megacities and the United States Army: Preparing for a Complex and Uncertain Future*, June 2014, 21, http://usarmy.vo.llnwd.net/e2/c/downloads/351235.pdf; Shunk, D. (2014, January 23). Mega Cities, Ungoverned Areas, and the Challenge of Army Urban Combat Operations in 2030-2040. *Small Wars Journal*, retrieved from http://smallwarsjournal.com/jrnl/art/

mega-cities-ungoverned-areas-and-the-challenge-of-army-urban-combat-operations-in-2030-2040.

[8] Robert Muggah, "Fixing Fragile Cities: Solutions for Urban Violence and Poverty," *Foreign Affairs*, January 15, 2015, http://www.foreignaffairs.com/articles/142760/robert-muggah/fixing-fragile-cities.

[9] Lee.

[10] Perkins, D. G., "Multi-Domain Battle: Joint Combined Arms Concept for the 21st Century," *Association of the United States Army,* retrieved from https://www.ausa.org/articles/multi-domain-battle-joint-combined-arms-concept-21st-century.

[11] West Point Society of Washington and Puget Sound. (2016). *General Mark A. Milley, AUSA Eisenhower Luncheon, October 4, 2016* [transcript]. Retrieved from http://wpswps.org/wp-content/uploads/2016/11/20161004_CSA_AUSA_Eisenhower_Transcripts.pdf; GEN David G. Perkins, "Multi-Domain Battle: Joint Combined Arms Concept for the 21st Century," *Association of the United States Army,* November 14, 2016, https://www.ausa.org/articles/multi-domain-battle-joint-combined-arms-concept-21st-century; Dr. Albert Palazzo & LTC David P. McLain III, "Multi-Domain Battle: A New Concept for Land Forces," *War on the Rocks,* September 15, 2016, https://warontherocks.com/2016/09/multi-domain-battle-a-new-concept-for-land-forces/.

[12] Pellerin, Cheryl, "Deputy Secretary: Third Offset Strategy Bolsters America's Military Deterrence," *U.S. Department of Defense*, https://www.defense.gov/News/Article/Article/991434/deputy-secretary-third-offset-strategy-bolsters-americas-military-deterrence.

[13] Judson, Jen, "Army Details Draft Robotics and Autonomous Systems Strategy at AUSA," *Defense News*, October 4, 2016, http://www.defensenews.com/articles/army-details-draft-robotics-and-autonomous-systems-strategy-at-ausa; Martin, David (Correspondent), & Walsh, Mary (Producer). (2017). The Coming Swarm [Television series episode]. In J. Fager (Executive producer), *60 Minutes*, New York, NY: CBS Television Network,

retrieved from http://www.cbsnews.com/news/60-minutes-autonomous-drones-set-to-revolutionize-military-technology/.

[14] Perkins.

[15] Galeotti, M. (2014, July 4). The 'Gerasimov Doctrine' and Russian Non-Linear War [Web log post]. Retrieved from https://inmoscowsshadows.wordpress.com/2014/07/06/the-gerasimov-doctrine-and-russian-non-linear-war/.

[16] Abadi, Mark, "The Only Chart You Need to See to Know That the US Spends More on Its Military Than the Next 11 Countries Combined, *Business Insider*, http://www.businessinsider.com/us-military-spending-dwarfs-rest-of-world-2016-5.

[17] Brooks, Rosa (2016). *How Everything Became War and the Military Became Everything: Tales from the Pentagon*. New York, NY: Simon & Schuster, pp. 329-331.

[18] Spiller, Roger J. *Sharp Corners: Urban Operations at Century's End*. Command and General Staff College, Fort Leavenworth, Kansas. Retrieved from http://usacac.army.mil/cac2/cgsc/carl/download/csipubs/SharpCorners.pdf.

[19] McMaster, H.R., "Discussing the Continuities of War: The Defense Entrepreneurs Forum," *Small Wars Journal*, http://smallwarsjournal.com/jrnl/art/icymi-discussing-the-continuities-of-war-and-the-future-of-warfare-the-defense-entrepreneur.

[20] Spiller, vii-viii.

[21] *Profile: Aleppo, Syria's Second City*. (2016, November 28). Retrieved from http://www.bbc.com/news/world-middle-east-18957096.

[22] Spiller, 38.

Chapter 41

Fighting in Megacities—The Army's Next Challenge

Gary Anderson

First Published 5 April 2017

When General Charles Krulak directed the Marine Corps to study the problems of urban warfare in the late 90s of the last century, he had considerable support in the Corps because many Marines were veterans of urban combat in Somalia. In addition, many Marines were aware of a brief done by a highly respected retired Marin General Officer, Mike Myatt. *CHAOS IN THE LITTORALS* showed how rural populations in the Third World are gravitating to cities, most of which lay on the seacoasts or close to them. When they get to the cities, many of these former farmers find their expectations dashed by the conditions they find in the urban areas; this will increasingly lead to conflict as it already has. The events of 9/11 and the wars it spawned overshadowed the Marine Corps' urban studies and experiments as the Army and Marine Corps turned to fighting the wars they were given. Recently, the current Army Chief of Staff (General Mark Milley) has pushed the Army to study the future of combat in the world's fast-growing megacities.

Unlike General Krulak, General Milley is getting some pushback from within his own organization. Some senior Army officers have concluded that megacities are "too hard to do" and they should be bypassed. The problem here is obvious. If the enemy knows that we don't want to fight someplace, which is where he will go. Consequently, I am squarely in General Milley's corner on this subject.

As the Director of the Marine Corps Center for Emerging Threats and Opportunities before 9/11, I directed Project Lincolnia which looked at urban warfare in megacities in the 2025-2030 timeframe (earlier Marine Corps experiments had concentrated on the problems of urban combat in the near to mid-term in conventional large urban areas). The scenario for Lincolnia was set in a megacity that was a kluge of Lagos, Rio de Janeiro, and Shanghai. The results of these games largely went into Marine Corps vaults as we turned to the wars at hand in Afghanistan and Iraq. However, I have some observations that might help General Milley and his people in their urban studies.

Most megacities consist of a modern and generally well planned urban core ringed by relatively affluent suburbs. As rural denizens flock to the cities, they tend to build shanty towns. As with immigrants to America, these people tend to nest together in familiar ethnic and religious groupings that mirror the places they came from. Most megacities are in essence, cities of villages. That is not necessarily a bad thing for western military planners as it allows them to look at the megacity in bite sized bits.

We know how to fight in the urban core from our experience in places like Fallujah, Ramadi, and Baghdad. The Iraqi experience in Mosul is also instructive, although most of it consists of negative examples. If each unit assigned to a certain area of the outlying shanty towns, it can concentrate on gathering intelligence on the location of regular enemy units and the attitude of individual urban villages in their assigned area of operations. This type of specialized cultural knowledge and situational awareness will make it easier to determine the attitude of populations toward American presence. If one such enclave is friendly toward us and does not hold enemy fighters, it can probably be bypassed allowing us to concentrate on hard spots giving us a map of the human terrain where we will be fighting.

The Army would be well advised to hire contract expatiates from these urban villages in the buildup to crisis (which the military calls phase Zero) and keep them on retainer. They can be activated and sent home on temporary duty to take the temperature of their respective urban enclaves prior to the conflict if one appears to be brewing. Once fighting starts, they can be activated and act as advisors to the commanders assigned to work in individual urban villages as well as to help with interpretation.

The army should also consider the development of advanced directed energy weapons that can immediately incapacitate everyone in a building, fighters and non-combatants alike, while minimizing the kind of fatalities we recently saw in Mosul where scores on non-combatants were recently killed in an airstrike on a building where civilians were used as human shields. There are objections to such weapons by human rights groups, but they may be more muted post-Mosul due to the horrific civilian death toll in the fighting in that unfortunate city.

Robotics is another area where fighting in the urban canyons and sewers of megacities could be helpful. These include human sized remotely controlled armed unmanned ground vehicles (UGVs) and micro robotic scouts. Fighting in high rises and sewers is intensely exhausting and dangerous work. Robots are tireless and harder to kill than flesh and blood humans. They are also relatively inexpensive. If each American urban assault platoon had an armed UGV to kick down doors, it would allow one squad in the platoon to clear a floor in a building while two others rest the are fresh to leapfrog to the next floor with the robot in the lead on every floor. We know that our potential adversaries are working on ground combat vehicles and that is another reason for us to invest in them. It would be a very bad thing to have to pit flesh and blood American against enemy armored systems in an urban brawl.

The United States has made use of miniature Unmanned Aerial Systems (commonly called drones) in reconnaissance. But these are less useful in urban environments where much of the action takes place in covered building and tunnels that airborne drones can't see. Very small and micro semi-autonomous ground systems can infiltrate building to send images of what is going on inside and even listen to conversations.

General Milley is right. We need to take on the megacity combat challenge. If the enemy know we can fight there and win, he is much less likely to fight there at all.

Chapter 42

Enabling Smart City Resilience Through Center of Gravity Analysis

Victor R. Morris

First Published 6 July 2017

Introduction

The "Joint Operating Environment 2035" assesses the center of gravity (COG) for the world's population is shifting from the developed world to the developing world. The security challenges present in dense urban areas include adversary convergence and unassimilated communities. Humanity is developing into an urban species, therefore the Smart City (SC) system of systems becomes the primary center of gravity for relevant populations. A SC is one that utilizes information and communication technology (ICT) to enable citizens and meet their demands. Moreover, a SC involves the community by incentivizing participation, encouraging ownership, and improving the lives of residents. Interdependent populations cope with environmental stressors and nonlinear escalation through a resilient city system. A high fitness landscape is the objective of a resilient SC system.

Urban and global trends present a variety of critical factors contributing to center of gravity analysis and resilience assessments. The increase of urbanization makes instability and conflict within dense population centers a real and emerging possibility.[1] Major wars of attrition between 2001 and 2017 turned millions of civilians into refugees and stateless populations.[2] Enduring resilience is critical to minimizing the effects of system perturbations or "butterfly effects" and developing effective coping strategies.

The proposed SC Resilience Framework employs 19th century Prussian General Carl von Clausewitz's Center of Gravity concept elucidated through SC critical factors analysis. The current definition of COG uses systems theory and refers to the primary entity that inherently possesses the critical capabilities to achieve the objective.[3]

The goal of the framework is to enable SC system resilience. The design processes employed linear COG analysis methods, then non-linear approaches to modify critical factors and transform critical vulnerabilities. It includes a holistic and customized approach to planning, which not only shapes, but allows for shaping by the changing environment to enable resilience.

Accurately assessing and repairing critical vulnerabilities that exacerbate system perturbations is critical for a strategy oriented towards resilient and "smart" living. The strategy is applied to a chaotic and multi-domain environment. The overall aim of this article is to confirm COG concept utility by identifying the primary COG, which possesses the critical capabilities to influence non-linear human and environmental system perturbations. Resilience occurs when relevant systems re-order to become less vulnerable to shocks.

Understanding Nonlinear Science, Dynamical Systems and Resilience

A systems perspective to understanding interdependent yet diverse environments is contained in decades of academic and military assessments (Figure 1). Revised COG analysis draws on systems theory and uses it to link critical factors to the center of gravity. Critical factors consist of critical capabilities, critical requirements and critical vulnerabilities.

Figure 1: JP 2-01.3

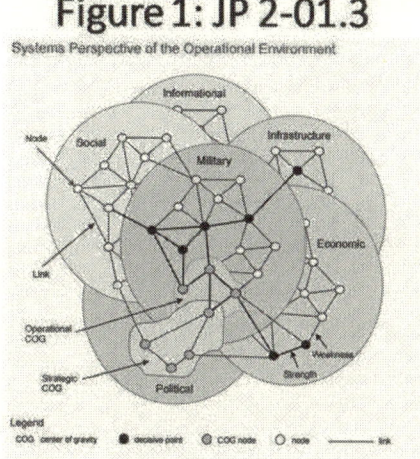

Systems Perspective of the Operational Environment

The majority of the systems present in the world are nonlinear in nature. Nonlinear science has origins in mathematics, general systems theory, cybernetics, fractal geometry and meteorology.[4] Network centric warfare borrowed concepts from chaos theory to describe an international system prone to exponential changes or "butterfly effect". Chaos theory describes certain nonlinear dynamical systems as having a sensitivity to changes in initial conditions. Nonlinear means that due to feedback or multiplicative effects between the components, the whole becomes something greater than the mere sum of its individual parts. Dynamical means the system changes over time.[5]

Dr. Mark Galeotti uses the term nonlinear war in his book "Hybrid War or Gibridnaya Voina Getting Russia's non-linear military challenge right". He states there are two separate kinds of intertwined nonlinear war. One aspect involves political destabilization and the other a hope of dividing, demoralizing and distracting the West. These aspects overlap heavily as two sides of a wider form of nonlinear war.[6]

Nonlinear system resilience initially decreases the formation of malign networks. If malign networks are already present in the system, resilience compels such networks to adopt incentive structures leading toward a high fitness landscape. In evolutionary biology, fitness or adaptive landscapes represent the relationship between individual and reproductive success. High fitness is typically represented by mountain ranges (figure 1). An evolving population climbs uphill until a local optimum is reached.

Resilience is a term used in ecology, social sciences, engineering and the military. In all cases, the term emphasizes the ability of a system to cope with disturbances, adapt, and re-organize into a stable state. Coping refers to degrees of success and increased stability when presented with disturbances. Similarly, the term thriving, whether physical or psychological, reflects decreased reactivity to stressors, faster recovery or consistently higher level of functioning. After an adverse system perturbation, at least four potential consequences occur (Figure 2). Conceptions of thriving involve desensitization and enhanced recovery potential. Recent approaches involve urban resilience to chronic stresses and acute shocks. Some examples of chronic stresses and acute shocks are high unemployment, natural disasters and terrorist attacks. The urban system is a system of systems and requires a coherent and comprehensive approach to reach an adaptive state. A March 2017 RAND assessment discusses a counter-terrorism strategy centered on the historical resilience of American society. The author asserts understanding how terrorism works fosters a psychologically more resilient and less vulnerable mindset.[7] This is one specific example of coping, re-organizing and adapting to stressors.

Figure 2: Four potential consequences Resilience and Thriving: Issues, Models and Linkages

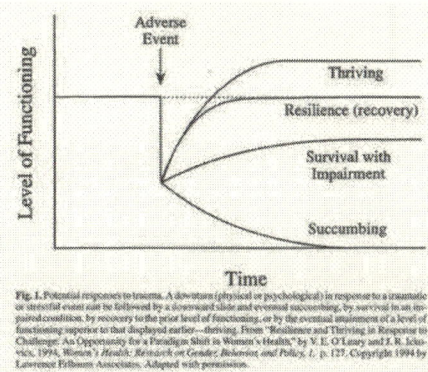

In the dynamic systems view, the overall goal of urban resilience is to move the city system from a local minimum, to a location that is closer to optimal. To reach this state, reorganization of what currently exists must occur. The term "resilience" in this case reflects the process of establishing resilient behavior to reach a thriving status and optimal position within the fitness landscape (Figure 3).

Figure 3: Fitness Landscape Illustration

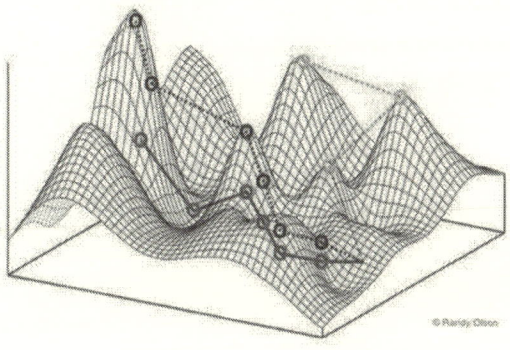

This article uses the term "complex evolving system", in lieu of the more widespread "complex adaptive system" based on the influence of human interactions. Complex evolving systems "work together to create new order and coherence, to sustain the organization and to ensure its survival, particularly when its environment or social ecosystem is changing fast."[8] Cities exhibit a high number of complex systems characteristics (Figure 4).

Figure 4: Complex System Characteristics

- **Memory:** Complex systems are dynamical systems that change over time. Prior states may have influence over present states.
- **Emergent properties:** Larger phenomena arise through interactions among smaller or simpler entities. The larger entities exhibit properties the smaller entities do not.
- **Multiplicity:** Dynamic networks have many local interactions and a smaller number of inter-area connections and dense local connectivity with fewer projections between regions.
- **Openness:** Systems dissipate energy and are frequently far from energetic equilibrium.
- **Relationships:** Nonlinear and feedback oriented (circular causality) meaning a small perturbation may cause a large effect e.g. the "butterfly effect", proportional effect or no effect at all. Additionally, negative and positive effects of an elements behavior feedback altering the element itself.
- **Yield Cascading Failures:** Strong coupling among system components means failure in one or more components leads to both cascading failures and catastrophic effects on the ability of the entire system to function properly.

City as a Complex Evolving System

A 2015 *Small Wars Journal* article entitled "City as a System Analytical Framework: A Structured Analytical Approach to Understanding and Acting in Urban Environments" identifies cities of all sizes present a variety of challenges. These challenges include information saturation, unique terrain, and diversity of controllers.[9] The same article identifies "Environmental Centers of Gravity" or E-COGs as the nodes and/ or flows most critical to a problem system. This article assesses environmental and cognitive considerations as being related to the primary COG. Data-rich online social media platforms are "Cognitive COGs" or C-COGs which overlap domains and city systems. The "weaponization of information" necessitates cognitive resilience within the information environment as well.

This section uses of variety of cities as short case studies to highlight the above challenges and aids in the development of resilience solutions. These challenges or factors personalize in the physical, cyberspace and information environments by residents who are part of groups, organizations and populations. The aforementioned article describes unique terrain with the concept of "edgelessness' meaning cities no longer end at their administrative edges or political boundaries. Concepts of interdependence and resilience have no physical boundary and depend on the mutual support of all relevant systems and subsystems.

Another crucial factor is the influence of human populations, as the center of gravity for information activities, unique or contested terrain, and diversity of controllers. Ukraine, Kiev, and the War in Donbass illustrates a fusion of the four above factors resulting in bifurcation or split from mono-stable to multi-stable states. Kiev is more resilient than the eastern oblasts, which demonstrates multiplicity. As the hub, Kiev has more dense interactions, but fewer axons or connections to the Donbass region.

Recent assessments by the General Staff of the Russian Federation's Armed Forces concluded "the protest potential of the population"[10] has a high probability to turn a once thriving state into a "web of chaos". These assessments are based on lessons learned from the Arab Spring. This theory personifies non-linear escalation and fluctuating fitness landscapes, but also justifies consolidation of control in Russia and Turkey. Moscow and Istanbul are the 11th and 7th largest cities proper in the world by population.[11] Their leaders exhibit an aversion to "western influence" through so-called "political warfare" resulting in regime change.

One Russian Federation assessments finds color revolutions and "exporting security" results in violence, poverty, social disasters, and total disregard for human rights. Western intervention is the system perturbation that exacerbated the existing grievances or perturbations in Ukraine. This phenomenon escalated non-linearly into chaotic states.[12] The post 9/11 Global Transaction Strategy (GTS) included the concept of exporting security as preventive war strategy to remove rogue regimes who threaten globalization.[13]

In summary, when perturbations affect the totality of city challenges it results in unpredictable and chaotic states. This is a lesson learned from on-going operations in Afghanistan and Iraq, which has resulted in co-evolution of complex systems and physically emerging states. The extremist proto-state referred to as "Daesh" exhibits complex system characteristics and city centric challenges. Ramadi, Mosul, Aleppo, al-Raqqa and Dabiq are cities of varying sizes and have proven to be centers of gravity for various populations, organizations, groups and ideologies. The city as a center of gravity is not limited to the specific regions and has implications for international systems as well. This phenomenon involves 21stcentury irregular warfare as a state of persistent conflict or perpetual war. Pre-emptive use of military force in conjunction with stateless, disenfranchised, and identity driven populations account for dense interactions. These interactions often result in system(s) perturbations that lead to the escalating nonlinearity and chaos.

The city system is the wielder of a high fitness landscape. A large part of resilience involves coping with conflict enabling conditions before they escalate into chaos and total war. Those conditions include internal and external political interference and environmental stressors. Resilience is not limited to the human domain and is enabled by regulated autonomous systems too.

COG Analysis Methods Overview and Application

What disturbances destabilize complex evolving systems and what enables resilience to destabilization and chaos?

The answer lies in the SC COG analysis for enabling relevant populations. In 1996, Dr. Joe Strange developed a concept to link factors to the center of gravity. His critical factors concept became United States Joint Doctrine in 2002.[14] COG analysis consists of critical factors analysis, which includes critical capabilities, requirements and vulnerabilities of the COG. This section applies three existing COG analysis methods and one emergent method to the SC system to demonstrate holistic application and evolution of the concept. This application expands the enemy centric focus, similar to recent Australian Defense Force's approaches involving addressing non-adversarial threats preventing mission accomplishment.[15] The Australian Defense Forces have also modified the definition of the COG focused on capability to achieve a desired end state or specific objective.

A modern definition of COG uses logic to define what a COG is or is not. Logically: A (primary entity) + B (capability to achieve the objective) = COG.[16]

The COG is not a source of power as previously defined; it is the possessor and wielder of that power. The SC COG uses or consumes supporting resources to accomplish the objective; a tangible physical agent that must perform the actions. Relevant organizations and actors who draw power from the city have interrelated requirements. These include controlling information, terrain and populations and result in the multi-layering and overlapping of critical factors. Next, this method takes concepts from mathematics like exploring system behavior and stability. Similar to mathematical methods COG and critical factors analysis reveals hidden structure and patterns in underlying dynamics that may not be apparent. Defeat, stability and response options also develop from this type of analysis. Promoting or "targeting" resilience is intangible, but targeting individuals, organizations, and systems compelled to enable resilience is not.

COG Analysis Method 1: Forward or Linear

"Let's Fix or Kill the Center of Gravity Concept" by Colonel (Retired) Dale C. Eikmeir describes COG analysis within Dr. Strange's framework of three critical factors, which can be targets for indirect attacks.[17] The below factors are analyzed in a linear way, which involves identifying the COG and associated critical factors.

Critical capability: primary abilities that merit a COG, identified in the context of a given scenario.

Critical requirement: essential conditions, resources, and means for a critical capability.

Critical vulnerability: critical requirements or components thereof that are deficient or vulnerable to neutralization, interdiction, or attack in a manner achieving decisive results.

COG Analysis Method 2: Inside Out

The second method applied conducts COG analysis from the inside out.[18] According to this method, beginning with the COG is erroneous because of a non-definitive method to determine it. There is also no safeguard against picking the wrong COG. A re-iteration that the process does not have to occur in a sequential manner emphasizes an earlier assessment by Col Eikmeir to identify objectives, then critical factors. Identifying the objective and "working to the right of the critical capabilities" (CC-CR-CV) is the "inside out method".

COG Analysis Method 3: Hybrid Threat 6 Step

The third approach applies a new method for hybrid threat COG analysis.[19] It accounts for the amorphous nature of hybrid threat adversaries. The six-step analytical process outlined below was verified against the center of gravity analysis for a SC as an adaptive system of systems.

- Identify Observed Modalities
- Identify Adversary's Assessed Objectives and Limitations—Ends
- Identify the Critical Capabilities—Ways
- Identify the COG—Modality of Principal Use
- Identify the Critical Requirements—Means
- Identify the Critical Vulnerabilities

Combination COG Analysis Method and Framework Development

The following two-part method emerged from a variety of critical factors analyses of a known COG and objectives. First, the linear method based on familiarity, then an inside-out and nonlinear approach by identifying factors and re-aligning them to the appropriate category (Figures 5 and 6).

Figure 5 General COG Analysis Method 4: Emergent Linear, and Reverse

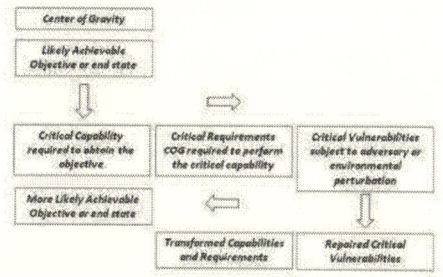

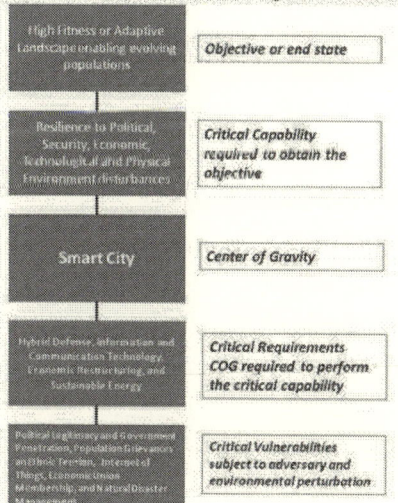

Figure 6 Specific COG Analysis Method 4: Emergent Linear and Reverse

The detailed list of critical vulnerabilities became the focal point for repairing and resilience framework development. Once again, a SC is one that utilizes information and communication technology (ICT) to meet the demands of the market and incentive structures. Incentive structures were highlighted for repair, as things that motivate an individual to perform an action or promote cooperation or competition within a larger structure. ICT-generated data guides the incentive structures, relevant functions and connects objects and environments to form the Internet of Things (IoT) as a SC and resilience enabler.

Key concepts involving unified communications and communities are crucial to making critical vulnerabilities resilient to environmental disturbances. The below findings are the focal points for part two of the framework development.

The main effort or modality of principle use to establish a high 21st century fitness landscape for human and intelligent agent populations is the urban system of systems.

Urban or City COGs link to national and international knowledge economy and high fitness landscape objectives.

Urban COGs establish the foundation for the identification and selection of incentive structures.

Critical Factors to SC resilience objectives are: state sovereignty and government penetration, super empowered groups and coalitions, legitimate use of physical force (monopoly on violence), economic integration, and globally connected high-speed communications.

Whole of Society Resilience Analytical Framework (Ways, Means and Ends)

Critical Capabilities or Ways (Verbs or Ability to): RECIPE

- **R**estructure economic and energy sectors through growth, innovation cooperation and free trade
- **E**nable government transparency, penetration, and population access to essential services

- **C**onnect, secure and standardize ICT and large data set architecture with embedded fail safes, and alternate function systems (primary, alternate, contingency and emergency)
- **I**nter-organize institutions, maker culture, and spaces to optimize national security and rule of law
- **P**lace make, enable e-participation and deliver narratives through mutual aid networks in the information environment
- **E**xtend smart living through artificial general intelligence (AGI)[20] life cycle management and artificial neural networks

Critical Requirements or Means (Nouns):

Urban Informatics (people, ideas and technology)

- Government
- Personal
- Network of sensors

Urban Design (built environment)

- Super empowered administrative network
- Global trade network access and creation of resources
- Mobility and transportation (e.g. Barcelona superblocks)
- Agriculture
- Sustainable, renewable, and smart energy
- Heat effects mitigation

Urban Protection (multi-domain)

- Information and critical infrastructure protection
- Enhanced medical and rehabilitation services and outreach (substance and mental health)
- Infectious disease tracking, prediction and outbreak containment
- Ethical surveillance and policing

- Enhanced multinational civil-military forward engagement and positioning
- Complex Intelligence Preparation of the Battlefield/Battlespace with agent-based models (ABMs)[21]
- Target centric warfare as "war control"
- Cyber security and deterrence, human in the loop contingencies and electromagnetic spectrum protection
- Improved collective, artificial and all-source intelligence approaches and sharing
- Decentralized mission command systems and combined arms integration
- Joint and combined arms forces and sustainment
- Multination counter-proliferation policies
- Flood, earthquake and storm effects mitigation and response

Urban Partnerships (inter-organization and multi-national)

- Public, private, and maker cooperation
- Local, national and international resilience shaping
- Digital inclusion of all demographics

Smart Living in Smart Cities (Ends)

- Community awareness and education
- Mass collaboration
- High fitness landscape
- Inclusive incentive structures
- Quality of life and well-being management

Conclusion

In conclusion, hybrid and parallel resilience is critical to minimizing disturbances and developing effective coping strategies in the contexts of future conflict and adaptability. Identifying and transforming critical vulnerabilities that exacerbate system perturbations facilitates a strategy oriented towards resilient or "smart" living. Organizational and technological adaptation are ways to reduce the effects of instability and complexity in dynamic systems. The SC Resilience Framework facilitates the objective of the smart city system to preform actions enabling human and intelligent agent populations towards high fitness. Smart Cities + Smart Power = Smart Living.

The views expressed in this article are based on the author's assessment and do not reflect official policy of the US Army or Booz Allen Hamilton.

End Notes and References

[1]   Gian Gentile, David E. Johnson, Lisa Saum-Manning, Raphael S. Cohen, Shara Williams, Carrie Lee, Michael Shurkin, Brenna Allen, Sarah Soliman, James L. Doty III, "Reimagining the Character of Urban Operations for the U.S. Army", The RAND Corporation (2017).

[2]   Anthony H. Cordesman, "Afghanistan, Iraq, Syria, and Yemen: Is Decisive Force an Option?" CSIS (4 April 2017). Accessed on 20 April 2017 at: https://csis-prod.s3.amazonaws.com/ s3fspublic/publication/170404_War_Use_Decisive_Force. pdf?365r7YdicB5HDUHnEox7c9M_4N5swDKh.

[3]   COL (Retired) Dale C. Eikmeier "Let's Fix or Kill the Center of Gravity Concept", *Joint Force Quarterly* 83 (1 October 2016).

[4]   Dr. Sean T. Lawson "Nonlinear Science and Warfare" Chaos, complexity and the U.S. military in the information age" (2014).

[5]   Geoff Boeing "Visual Analysis of Nonlinear Dynamical Systems: Chaos, Fractals, Self-Similarity and the Limits of Prediction" (7 September 2016). Accessed on 15 April 2017: http://www.mdpi. com/2079-8954/4/4/37/htm.

[6]   Dr. Mark Galeotti "Hybrid War or Gibridnaya Voina Getting Russia's non-linear military challenge right", *Mayak Intelligence* (2016).

[7]   Brian Michael Jenkins "Taking the 'Terror' Out of Terrorism Requires Outsmarting Fear", *The RAND Blog* (16 March 2017).

[8]   Dr. Eve Mitleton-Kelly, "Complex Systems and Evolutionary Perspectives on Organizations" The Application of Complexity Theory to Organizations. London School of Economics, Chapter 2 Accessed on 17 April 2017: https://www.researchgate.net/profile/Eve_Mitleton-Kelly/publication/38959106_Complex_Systems_And_Evolutionary_Perspectives_Of_Organisations_The_Application_of/links/00b4952939abe2f538000000.pdf?origin=publication_list.

[9]   Mark Lomedico and Elizabeth M. Bartels, "City As a System Analytical Framework: A Structured Analytical Approach to Understanding and Acting in Urban Environments," *Small Wars Journal* (4 August 2015).

[10]   General of the Army Valery Gerasimov, Chief of the General Staff of the Russian Federation Armed Forces "The Value of Science Is in the Foresight" English Version, *Military Review* (January-February 2016).

[11]   "List of cities proper by population" accessed on 26 April at: https://en.wikipedia.org/wiki/List_of_cities_proper_by_population.

[12]   "Comments by Russian President Vladimir Putin to the UN General Assembly", *Military Review* (January-February 2016). Editor's note: This is the official transcript of a speech given by Russian President Vladimir Putin 28 September 2015 to the UN General Assembly as released by the office of the Russian president.

[13]   Dr. Sean T. Lawson "Nonlinear Science and Warfare: Chaos, complexity and the U.S. military in the information age" (2014).

[14]   LTCs Jan L. Rueschhoff and Jonathan P. Dunne "Centers of Gravity from the Inside Out", *Joint Force Quarterly*, Issue 60 (1st Quarter 2011).

[15]   Timothy R. Heath, "Chinese Political and Military Thinking Regarding Taiwan and the East and South China Seas", The RAND Corporation (13 April 2017).

[16] COL (Retired) Dale C. Eikmeier "Let's Fix or Kill the Center of
      Gravity Concept", *Joint Force Quarterly* 83, 4th Quarter 2016 (1
      October 2016).

[17] COL (Retired) Dale C. Eikmeier "Let's Fix or Kill the Center of
      Gravity Concept", *Joint Force Quarterly* 83, 4th Quarter 2016 (1
      October 2016).

[18] LTCs Jan L. Rueschhoff and Jonathan P. Dunne "Centers of
      Gravity from the Inside Out", *Joint Force Quarterly*, Issue 60 (1st
      Quarter 2011).

[19] LTC Michael D. Reilly "Hybrid Threat COG Analysis: Taking
      a Fresh Look at ISIL", *Joint Force Quarterly*, Issue 84 (1st Quarter
      2017).

[20] Luke Muehlhauser "What is AGI", *MIRI*, 11 August 2013.

[21] Majors Tom Pike and Eddie Brown, "Complex IPB," *Small Wars
      Journal* (24 March 2016).

Chapter 43

Complex Cyber Terrain in Hyper-Connected Urban Areas

Mike Matson

First Published 7 July 2017

Summary

The cyberspace domain of the future will most forcefully assert itself in urban areas. These urban areas will vary greatly in population density and spatial distribution, level of integration between systems, and the formality of systems. Within every urban area (UA) will exist complex physical cyber terrain and complex virtual cyber terrain.

The number of connected devices, sensors, and tags in a UA will be staggering. The most significant systems in hyper-connected UAs will be the millions of personal area networks, and corresponding millions of discrete artificial intelligence programs. The adaptation of artificial intelligence in future networks introduces a new and potentially powerful actor in the cyberspace and land domains commanders will have to interact with to succeed in urban operations—the city itself.

One Size Does Not Fit All

Megacities and dense urban areas of 2050 will not be not monolithic constructs, nor will the cyberspace domain within them. The level of integration within a UA and the formality of the computer systems will fluctuate between and within UAs. At urban cores, cyber infrastructure may be both highly integrated between systems, and highly formal. This means multiple, centrally designed and deployed networks put in place by city planners to effectively manage the various services in a city. Systems may become both less integrated and less formal the farther out from the urban core, but that is not a given, meaning every UA will fluctuate not only in a physical sense, but a virtual sense, block by block.

In highly integrated UAs, highly formal systems may stretch deep into the suburbs. Whereas in developing countries, as rural populations move to cities, informal population centers often build up on lines of communication stretching out from the urban core. These areas will likely experience less integrated systems linked to the urban core but may still be highly integrated at the local level, creating islands of highly integrated systems within otherwise low integration areas. And the systems may be more informal, creating a significant mishmash of hardware and software to create jerry-rigged solutions to hyper-local problems.

The most critical dynamic in these UAs will be the population. Just as the Internet of Things (IoT) and Internet of Service (IoS) will continue to evolve to support people and services, the population will become hyper-connected at the individual level, becoming an Internet of People (IoP): "People becoming a part of ubiquitous intelligence networks having potential to seamlessly connect, interact and exchange information about themselves and their social context and environment."[1]

The combination of completely integrated people and systems in UAs is what will define future hyper-connected UAs, which are constantly changing in both space and time. These hyper-connected UAs will have complex cyber terrain and this terrain will cross into the other warfighting domains.

Complex Cyber Terrain within an Urban Area

The Cyberspace domain is manmade and that is what makes the domain fundamentally different from its predecessors. Cyberspace is malleable where other domains are not.[2] Most discussions of the cyberspace domain focus on the software, and not the hardware of the Internet. The software is generally considered a more significant aspect of the domain.[3] As a result, the physical aspect of the domain has not received a great deal of focus, because of claims it is inherently too complex to effectively visualize. The problem is, "…although the cyber domain is a human construct, the complexity of cyber infrastructure, together with the speed and global reach of cyber action, frustrates the ability to visualize cyber-space in a coherent way."[4]

Within the framework of multi-domain battle, however, the cyberspace domain has its own complex *physical* terrain within the land domain, and operations within hyper-connected UAs will need to take this physical cyber terrain into consideration. Nowhere else is complex physical cyber terrain more evident than in UAs.

What does complex physical cyber terrain look like today, and what it might look like in 2050? A great primer on complex physical cyber terrain in urban areas is Ingrid Burrington's 2016 book, *Networks of New York: An Illustrated Field Guide to Urban Internet Infrastructure*. In it she takes the reader on a tour of the complex physical cyber terrain of a megacity. She focuses on below ground, ground level, and above ground systems. Three major pieces of terrain stand out in importance.

Fiber Optic Cable

The Internet primarily moves over fiber optic cable. While wireless access to the Internet will be ubiquitous in UAs by 2050, and there will be multiple technologies to move data over the last mile between fiber and endpoint, the basic construct will likely remain that the vast bulk of data ultimately will move between systems via fiber optic cable.

Where is fiber optic cable in UAs? It is right under your feet. Fiber optic cable often is laid in UAs on top of prior services like phone and electricity, making cable easy to find and access. If you know the code, a person can read the utility markings, manhole and access covers, and scars in the pavement to see where fiber cable is laid even without maps or diagrams.[5][6]

Another key piece of physical terrain related to fiber optic cable unique to coastal cities is submarine landing points, and submarine termination points. The vast majority of all Internet traffic flows over submarine cables between continents. Submarine landing points are where cables cross from the maritime to land domains. Termination points may be several miles away where the cable enters the local network at a carrier hotel or data center. These are both important pieces of infrastructure in coastal cities.

Carrier Hotels and Data Centers

A termination point is a good pivot to discuss the largest individual pieces of complex physical cyber terrain in a UA. These are carrier hotels and data centers. Carrier hotels and data centers are the nerve centers of a UA. A carrier hotel, also known as Internet exchanges, are where different commercial networks on the Internet interact. Carrier hotels and data centers can fill an entire building. "Racks and racks of switching equipment and cables run through these buildings."[7] Very often they may be clustered where fiber optic cable is laid in the densest amounts, such as lower Manhattan.[8]

Data centers may go by different names, but the purpose is the same. Large numbers of servers are located in the same location and provide remote processing or storage capability for consumers. Those consumers can be governments, private companies, and individuals. Data centers are the key to cloud infrastructure, and the disruption of processing and storage activity in a data center could have impacts well beyond the local area.[9] There could be dozens or even hundreds of data centers of various levels of military importance in any particular

UA which may need to be seized, destroyed, or defended in order to facilitate operations within the cyberspace domain.

Ubiquitous Sensor Networks

Burrington's book does a good job of sampling what will eventually evolve into ubiquitous sensor networks (USNs). She identifies a variety of camera and radio frequency ID (RFID) sensor networks below ground, at ground level, and above ground, which provide sensor data to larger systems.[10] These systems are in their infancy when compared to what is planned for the future. USNs are a major driver of the IoT for industry and government.

There are three main elements to an USN, which are sensors, tags, and communication/processing capacity.[11] From a complex physical cyber terrain perspective, the physical devices of interest are the sensors and tags. (The data from the sensors flows over networks, ultimately via fiber optic able, to processing and storage at data centers already discussed.)

USNs have three primary applications: detecting, tracking, and monitoring. Some examples include:

- *Detection*—Detect abnormalities in systems, identification of intruders / CCTV etc.
- *Tracking*—Supply chain management via RFIDs, tracking vehicles, and tracking people, etc.
- *Monitoring*—Health monitoring, environmental monitoring, recording rates of degradation of infrastructure like bridges and roads.[12]

USN's paired smart software are the foundation of "smart cities." A smart city is essentially a hyper-connected urban area which functions in an intelligent way by integrating all its infrastructures and services into a cohesive whole and uses intelligent devices for monitoring and control.[13]

Why are USN's important complex physical cyber infrastructure? First, "sensing is at the heart of smart infrastructures, which can monitor themselves and act on their own intelligently."[14] Future Industrial Control Systems (ICS), Supervisory Control and Data Acquisition (SCADA) networks, Intelligent Transport Networks, and other smart systems will rely on remote sensing to operate.

The second reason is the sheer number of sensors which are going to be employed. PlanIT Valley is a conceptual city in Portugal, designed to be a smart city testbed with a targeted population of 250,000. The planners' intent is to place 100 million sensors in the city, or roughly 444 sensors per person.[15] In a single UA of 2 million people, one quarter the size of a megacity, that would equate to 888 *million* sensors connected to the Internet, not counting any other type of Internet infrastructure.[16]

USN platforms represent the key physical infrastructure required to create a smart city environment.[17] The volume of these connected devices blanketing a city will make them an attractive target for cyber operations. Seizing control of them in large numbers can be used for cyber effects operations, as the massive IoT-enabled DDOS attacks of the Mirai malware aptly demonstrated in late 2016. Or by taking them off-line, it can deny an enemy vital intelligence.

Remaining Key Physical Terrain

One attribute of the future cyber domain will be ubiquity. Cyber will be everywhere and so pervasive that in the future "cyber is no longer cyber."[18] As everything is plugged into the Internet and conforms to a TCP/IP protocol, physical infrastructure related to mobile communications also becomes complex physical cyber terrain, such as cellular towers, and mobile base stations, along with "classic" telephone switching stations and satellite ground stations.

The volume of mundane connected devices within a UA will be staggering. Within a UA, there will be blue space (ours), red space (theirs) and gray space (neutral). All three of these spaces have significant surface and deep web portions, and some level of dark web.[19] The physical devices in the surface web and deep web will reach into the millions of individual connected devices. Each home will have a network with any number of connected devices. Each building will have its own network hardware in addition to the networks of its residents. Each business may have hundreds or thousands of connected devices.

Personal Area Networks

Interacting with these static devices embedded within a UA will be Personal Area Networks (PAN). A PAN "is a personal, short distance area wireless network, typically extending 10 meters in all directions, for interconnecting devices centered around [an individual.]"[20] Individuals today may have upwards of four to five personal devices interconnected upon their body such as a phone, smart watch, fitness tracker, GPS tracker, or Internet-enabled medical device. These devices are already designed to interact with their environment, such as phones syncing to cars for hands free driving, or apps granting reward points for walking into a particular store.

PANs will likely become vastly more complex by 2050. They will begin to grow around a person from shortly after birth. Wearable technology, technology embedded in clothing, and technology embedded within the body are all being explored. Interaction with the environment via augmented reality is likely to be ubiquitous. The PAN will move with the person, syncing with its owners' home base, and virtual smart assistants, the future decedents of Siri and Alexa, will travel with an individual wherever they go on their virtual shoulder. Interacting often on a machine to machine (M2M) level without the owner's awareness, PANs and their Artificial Intelligence (AI) assistants form the basis for the evolution of Sentient Tools.

Sentient Tools will be aware of their surroundings and able to make sense of and adapt to them. But more than that, the tools will have a social awareness of the people using them.[21] In a hyper-connected UA, these PAN's will interact on a constant basis with each other and the millions of devices within a UA as individuals move through it. PANs therefore have obvious intelligence and operational value.[22]

Complex Virtual Cyber Terrain

Just as UAs have complex physical cyber terrain, they will have complex virtual cyber terrain. There will be more systems, with greater complexity, and with incalculable amounts of data generated on a minute-to-minute basis. Increasing data volume will drive the evolution of complex virtual cyber terrain and the most significant complex virtual cyber terrain faced in 2050 will be AI programs.

AI programs are the next logical step in computer programming. Future UAs will be overlaid with tens of thousands if not hundreds of thousands of discrete AI programs, sentient tools, machine learning systems and possibly autonomic computing. Autonomic computing for example, involves systems which are self-configuring, self-healing, self-optimizing, and provide self-protection.[23][24]

As computer systems become more complex, the ability for individuals to manage the systems will decrease to the point AI programs will be tasked to self-optimize to most effectively execute their defined objectives. For smart cities to function, AI becomes a necessity. These systems will come from different vendors, be individually configured, and operate on systems large and small. Each AI program, through purpose and configuration, will become unique. The end result will be UAs in 2050 saturated with hundreds of thousands of AI-run systems, each slightly different then the next.

Running the Numbers

To add it all up, and using some admittedly *very* broad estimates for illustration purposes, for every one million people living in in a hyper-connected UA in 2050 there could be:

- 1,000,000 AI-supported PANs. Each PAN has 5-10 devices in their immediate network, for a total of 5-10 million mobile connected devices, supported by AI systems, moving around and interacting with the UA on a constant basis with a social awareness of their environment.
- Between home and work, another 10-30 IoT connected devices per person, for a total of 10,000,000 to 30,000,000 additional connected devices in a UA, not counting USN networks.

USN networks, while allowing for wide variances in density, formality, and connectedness of the networks UA to UA, averaging between 50-500 sensors and tags per person, for a total of 50,000,000 to 500,000,000 sensors or tags.

AI programs and sentient tools big and small on a ratio of 1-50 to 1-100 per connected devices, not counting PANs or USNs, for a total of 100,000 (10,000,000 devices at 1-100 ratio) to 600,000 (30,000,000 devices at 1-50 ratio) additional AI programs per 1 million people.

This means any given UA of a million people could have five to ten million devices directly linked to individuals, with another 10 to 30 million additional static connected devices, and 50 million to half a billion sensors and tags. And all of those devices interacting with a million PAN AIs and 100-600 thousand additional AI systems, some of which will be working together to run the essential services in the UA.

Extend those numbers to a UA half the size of a megacity, five million people, scaled to the high end of connectedness and formality of systems, and you get a hyperconnected UA with billions of connected devices and millions of AI programs—five million socially aware sentient tools alone directly linked to individuals. The UA will be blanketed with fiber optic cable, and the densest concentrations will be identifiable by having clusters of carrier hotels and data centers in the same geographic area.

Enter the City

A hyper-connected UA in 2050 will have networks of millions of sensors, which will allow the UA to perform the equivalent of seeing, hearing, touching, smelling and even tasting its environment. It will be operating through the individual and collective effort of hundreds or thousands of AI systems, reacting to sensory input from vast USN networks, and in conjunction with and on the behalf of PANs moving through its systems.

This massive level of connectedness will turn UAs from static pieces of concrete and steel into large-scale entities which can sense and react to what is happening within it. UAs may become independent actors in their own right operating on a M2M level. What if a city can take actions which are self-optimizing, self-healing, and self-protecting, to counter activities which are disrupting the UA? In essence, what happens when the city starts reacting to military operations autonomously to heal or even "defend" itself?[25]

This does not suggest UAs will develop an artificial general intelligence (AGI). But the massive numbers of AI systems in a UA by 2050, linked to USN networks, and managed via distributed data centers, means UAs will likely have capacity to autonomously react as those systems attempt to continue to execute their functions to the best of their ability in the face of military operations.

And these UAs, constantly interacting with PANs on an M2M level, will also attempt to interact directly with military personnel and equipment in unforeseen ways. These consequences cut across warfighting domains, as both complex physical cyber terrain and complex virtual cyber terrain play a part in a UAs ability to react.

To conclude, some broad hypothetical questions are presented for consideration if hyper-connected UAs with significant complex cyber terrain become "independent actors" within the cyberspace and land domains during military operations:

- How does a commander address a UA's immune system response by AI systems detecting and reacting to military operations within the UA?
- How does a commander shield blue force "smart" military equipment and networks from disruptive M2M communications and millions of interactive PANs?
- Can a commander "recruit" a hyper-connected UA to operate in conjunction with blue forces?

Notes

[1]   Jose Hernandez-Munoz, Jesus Bernat Vercher, Luis Munoz, Jose Galache, Mirko Presser, Luis A. Hernandez Gomez, and Jan Petterson, *Smart Cities at the Forefront of the Future Internet*, LNCS 6656, Pages 447-462, 449.

[2]   Martin Libicki, *Cyberspace is Not a Warfighting Domain*, I/S: A Journal of Law and Policy for the Information Society. (2012) Vol 8:2. Page 324.

[3]   Mad Scientist Conference 2016, *The 2050 Cyber Army Technical Report*, (7 November 2016) Page 5.

[4]   *The US Army Landcyber White Paper, 2018-2030*, Army Cyber Command (9 September 2013) Page 7. Drawn from Mad Scientist Conference 2016, *The 2050 Cyber Army Technical Report*, (7 November 2016) Page 18.

[5]   Ingrid Burrington, *Networks of New York: An Illustrated Guide to Urban Internet Infrastructure*, Melville House, Brooklyn, NY. 2016. Pages 20-21.

[6]   Having physical access to an important fiber optic cable in a UA has obvious advantages. It can be tapped and monitored for intelligence. Data transmission can be throttled or blocked to choke off UAs from sensor networks, either virtually or via physical means. And propaganda, disinformation, corrupted data, and other cyber effects operations can be inserted into data streams via MITM attacks.

[7] Ibid, Page 64.

[8] Ibid, Page 65.

[9] Conversely data centers in other locations can and will impact the functionality of a local UA.

[10] Ibid, Pages 88-92.

[11] *Ubiquitous Sensor Networks (USN)*, ITU-T Technology Watch Briefing Report Series, No. 4 (February 2008) Page 1.

[12] Ibid, Pages 5-6.

[13] Gerhard P. Hancke, Bruno de Carvalho e Silva, Gerhard P. Hancke Jr., *The Role of Advanced Sensing in Smart Cities*, Sensors. (2013) Vol 13. Page 394.

[14] Ibid, Page 394.

[15] Ibid, Page 397.

[16] While USNs would likely not scale up on a strict 1-1 ratio, it is a good exercise to illustrate how quickly USN numbers can reach staggering proportions in a UA.

[17] Jose Hernandez-Munoz, et all, Page 450.

[18] Mad Scientist Conference 2016, *The 2050 Cyber Army Technical Report*, (7 November 2016) Page 6.

[19] Ibid, Page 19.

[20] *Ubiquitous Sensor Networks (USN)*, ITU-T Technology Watch Briefing Report Series, No. 4. (February 2008) Page 3.

[21] Brian David Johnson, Frost and Sullivan, *Science Fiction and the Coming Age of Sentient Tools*, Computer, IEEE Computer Society (June 2016), Page 95.

[22] For additional reading, *Using the IoT to Gain and Maintain Situational Awareness in UDE and Megacities* by Alfred C. Crane, *Bringing Big Data to War in Megacities* by Robert Dixon, and *Flocking Phones & Drones* by Alex Bittermand and Richard Carlo, all touch on interesting aspects of tapping into the intelligence and operational potential of what are identified here as PANs.

[23] Stefan Polard, *Autonomous systems and Artificial Life*, Ubiquitous Computing Smart Devices, Smart Environments and Smart interaction (2009) Pages 317-341.

[24] For example, imagine every personal home network having a router with a firewall with limited autonomic capabilities. A new piece of malware hits the firewall and is stopped by heuristic programming. Then, like trees which secrete chemicals to warn other trees of attacks, the wireless network disseminates binary samples with snort signatures of the malware to all nearby wireless networks. This snort signature is passed across the entire UA, wireless network to wireless network. And unlike trees which take days or weeks to warn and have other trees prepare their defenses, this happens 50-100 times a day at the speed of light, moving like virtual waves across vast areas of UAs.

[25] For example, an intelligent transportation network (ITN) notices massive abnormalities in normal traffic flows. A military commander may be trying to keep a particular main supply route clear, but the ITN begins adjusting traffic lights, reroutes self-driving cars, and sends out text alerts to citizens to identify detours, attempting to "fix" the traffic problem and steer people back onto the route the commander is attempting to keep clear.

Chapter 44

Cyber Operational Considerations in Dense Urban Terrain

Paul Maxwell, Andrew Hall and Daniel Bennett

First Published 12 July 2017

Introduction

Thirtieth Corps began its attack on the city of Metropolis and its 12 million inhabitants. The Corps planners had done their homework on urban operations and had studied many historical predecessors such as Stalingrad and Hue. Initially the attack proceeded well. Over time however, enemy indirect fire accuracy seemed to defy expectations given a lack of detected observers. Patrols were increasingly ambushed and leaders were targeted at an abnormal frequency. Raids failed to produce the desired results as targets were seldom found where they were expected. It seemed that the opponent knew their every move before they were executed. It soon became clear that the enemy had more capability than our intelligence sources briefed. The attack on the dense urban area stalled without success.

Scenarios like the one described are possible given our current training models and doctrine. Military operations are likely to occur in

Dense Urban Terrain (DUT) similar to Metropolis due to demographic changes of modern society. DUT is a sub-set of Military Operations in Urban Terrain (MOUT) in which there is a corpus of knowledge. As described in the Army's Field Manual, FM 3-06, *Urban Operations*, the operational characteristics of this environment that the military should account for include physical, social, economic, and demographic factors. Many of these factors have been investigated and documented in the field manual and training products. Factors that have not been thoroughly discussed are the cyber characteristics of DUT and the impacts of those factors on military operations whether they are offensive, defensive, stability, or civil support. As the military analyses DUT and writes its doctrine on how to conduct operations and how to train in these environments, it is important to consider how cyber elements may influence the mission.

The urban areas in which military forces fight will certainly vary. They will range from low tech emerging cities to high tech smart cities. The structures, transport patterns, infrastructure, and footprints will be different. Despite these differences, they will possess a multitude of sensors connected by networks that can be leveraged for offensive or defensive purposes. Many of these sensors will be in the Internet of Things (IOT) devices that are exponentially growing in number. These devices can be connected together to provide useful functions to government officials, citizens, and military personnel [ZaB14]. Even the most technically limited cities are inundated with networked sensors in the form of mobile phones and the cyber operational potential of other cities only grows beyond that to varying degrees.

For the purposes of this work, the term cyber includes computer network operations and electronic warfare. Included in this analysis are the pervasive sensors, various network technologies, electro-magnetic spectrum issues, and the ability of modern artificial intelligence to analyze the digital mountains of data produced daily. Some of the threats and opportunities discussed currently exist and some are on the horizon and will become operational in five to ten years. Additionally, the conditions under which the operations are conducted will affect the impact of these systems. High intensity operations in DUT with evacuated populations will be less affected by some of these cyber considerations while low intensity operations will be more affected.

Technological Landscape of Dense Urban Terrain

Sensors

The rapid and cyclic advancement of technology has resulted in a proliferation of inexpensive yet capable sensors throughout the globe. These can have many forms and purposes. They can be commercially installed systems with a dedicated function to personally owned sensors that are general purpose in nature. Regardless of their intended use, they provide a rich palette of military options for those who wish to use them.

Cameras are everywhere, from the traditional surveillance cameras for security purposes to the ubiquitous cameras found in mobile devices and the growing population of unmanned aerial vehicles. There is little room for something to go unobserved by a camera in a city. It is estimated that there are close to a million cameras deployed in cities such as London and Beijing [ZhC15]. This does not even include cameras within homes that exist in computers, tablets, phones, smart televisions, security systems, etc.

Complementing the cameras are microphones. These sensors are frequently found in cell phones and other mobile devices. Increasingly, they are found in items such as surveillance cameras, toys, and even watches. Many of these devices are 'always on', such as the Amazon Alexa, listening for acoustic events and potentially recording all that they can sense to include nearby conversations.

Another common sensor is the accelerometer. These devices are capable of measuring movement in two and three dimensions. They are embedded in mobile devices to assist with navigation, orientation, and sometimes even for protection of the device in case they fall. Accelerometers are increasingly found in 'wearables' of all types too such as fitness trackers.

Magnetometers are in widespread use as well. These devices sense magnetic fields such as the earth's natural field or those resulting from the presence of ferrous objects. Typical applications include navigation (compasses) and counting/sensing objects such as vehicles. These devices are found in mobile devices, traffic management applications, and underneath our roadways.

Finally, there are numerous types of sensors connected to our urban infrastructure that measure things such as pressure in pipes, valve states (open/closed), temperatures, and volumes. These sensors are often connected to Supervisory Control and Data Acquisition (SCADA) devices to provide remote control over our water, electrical, and transportation infrastructure.

Networks

All of these sensors would be somewhat insignificant though were it not for the networks that connect them and allow them to share their data. The most well-known are the internet and cellular networks. DUT environments are often blanketed by both networks. Even emerging cities with poor internet penetration are frequently well covered by cellular networks. As discussed in the next section, even the network itself can be used as a sensor for use in military operations.

Other communications protocols can often be harnessed into Mobile Ad-hoc Networks (MANETs) or dedicated mesh networks thus allowing systems to share data. Technologies such as Bluetooth, Near-Field Communications (NFC), IEEE 802.15.4 (Zigbee), IPv6 Low-power wireless Personal Area Network (6LowPAN), and cognitive radios provide backbone capability to establish a sensor network.

With a network established, the power of these numerous sensors can be utilized. Whether it is through a deliberate design or surreptitious hacking of others' devices, the data from these sensors can help a military force to accomplish its mission or contribute to its failure. The sensors and the connective tissue of the networks are continually present in DUT and therefore a factor that must be considered in the planning of urban operations.

Impact of Technology on Operations in Dense Urban Terrain

Maneuver and Intelligence

Tracking. In military operations of all types tracking friendly and enemy units is useful. Such information can assist with coordination, fire control, identification, and targeting. Traditionally, militaries accomplish this with methods such as networked GPS devices, imagery, radars, and direction finding. In DUT environments, these methods may be limited or ineffective. However, cyber enabled devices can replace or supplement traditional methods.

An important feature of many of these cyber enabled sensors is their ability to track personnel and/or vehicles. Mobile devices, Wi-Fi, RFID, camera-based systems (e.g., vehicle plate recognition systems), and more support this type of intelligence gathering for those who wish to know [MiC13], [PaQ13]. This tracking can be low resolution tracking with only the ability to sense one or more objects or high resolution with the ability to identify and track specific targets. Tracking of this nature can be used for purposes such as intelligence gathering, targeting, and triggering fires. One could imagine using this type of tracking capability for applications such as geo-fencing [NaS13]. Geo-fences can establish areas that generate alerts when attacking forces enter them or when specific targets leave them.

An obvious tracking technology is based on video cameras. As previously discussed, cameras are everywhere in DUT environments. Whether it is securing a facility, providing public security, observing streets for traffic conditions, or taking selfies, the cameras are constantly capturing data. Deliberately configured or subsumed via cyber offensive operations, these video-based systems such as the third-generation surveillance systems in [Rat10] or the systems in [VaV05] and [BeR11] can detect, recognize, and track multiple objects. Their method for achieving this varies by system but all rely on distributed cameras, processing power (edge or centralized), and communications networks. Some systems [ZhC15] propose using under-utilized licensed frequencies such as UHF to communicate. Another system described in [AjB15] allows for users to query its surveillance database for events, generate alerts, and even predict future events. When connected to modern signal processing algorithms and artificial intelligence systems, this video data can provide valuable intelligence. This type of sensor network can allow for persistent identification and tracking of forces within the city. The ability to conceal operations or achieve tactical surprise may not exist in DUT environments.

Improved signal processing algorithms and cheaper processing power is enabling various tracking techniques based on electro-magnetic radiation. One such set of algorithms uses Wi-Fi for tracking movement. Research such as that done in [GoY15], [YaZ16], and [SoG16] demonstrate how Wi-Fi signals can be used to detect motion of human targets. Attributes of the Wi-Fi signals such as the Received Signal Strength, Time of Flight, phase of the signals, and channel state information are all used to detect movement. These systems have limited range and capability but given the widespread availability of Wi-Fi nodes in DUT environments, this technology could be adapted to provide early warning of opposing forces or indications movements by the populace. The work in [CoP14] used Wi-Fi signals as passive radar to detect and track moving vehicles at ranges up to 50m.

Other work in this area tracks targets but is more protocol agnostic and also supplements the inputs with other data types. The research in [SaW16] relies on a combination of signal analysis from wireless nodes and data from inertial measurement units (IMUs) or accelerometers. This system allows indoor navigation in what is usually a GPS denied region. Similarly, research using cell phones and the signals received from many sources (e.g., Wi-Fi, Bluetooth, 4G LTE, GPS, NFC) showed that large spaces could be radio frequency mapped in a crowd source technique thus allowing for navigation in GPS denied areas. Forces using this technology can navigate better inside the DUT environment where traditional navigation means are not as effective.

Data from devices connecting to Wi-Fi nodes can also provide a method for tracking individual devices. As shown in [AbB14], devices can be tracked passively by using data from connection logs in Wi-Fi access points. As devices interact with these access points, information about the device, such as it unique MAC address is logged. An ISR program could access these logs and use the data to track traffic flow in an area or even a particular device.

This type of tracking has also been shown to be feasible for Bluetooth devices. Using the information contained in these devices as they search to connect to other devices, movements of groups or individual devices can be mapped [StL11]. These low power sensors are common in many mobile devices and wearables thus creating a large population of data points.

Magnetometers provide another means of tracking targets. It is common for magnetic based systems to be embedded in roadways for traffic control. These sensors normally trigger traffic signals or count the number of vehicles passing a particular point to help transportation engineers improve traffic flows. If this data is shared via a wifi network then it is possible to track and with appropriate processing identify vehicles [KoO13]. Magnetic sensors may also be placed on the sides of roadways. The work of [WaZ15] showed how these sensors can count vehicles passing. This type of traffic flow data could help operations by identifying slow-go areas during intelligence preparation of the battlefield (IPB) or tracking convoy operations of opposing forces.

Due to a lack of line of sight (LOS) in DUT, radar systems would not frequently be incorporated into the Intelligence, Surveillance, and Reconnaissance (ISR) plan. Traditionally, these systems are employed in areas with clear LOS to allow their full tracking capability. FM 3-06 recommends only employing them on the peripheries of urban areas. However, enhancements in signal processing algorithms is making it possible for radars to work in Non-Line of Sight (NLOS) environments [ZhZ16] showed how airborne radars (carried by heliostats) could track multiple targets in an urban environment using new processing algorithms. Additionally, dismounted personnel were tracked in a NLOS urban environment using X-band radars and new signal processing techniques. As computing power is improved and signal processing algorithms become more powerful, these systems will continue to break new ground.

Microphones when connected to additional processing power (Acoustic Processing Units) [HoN13] can detect acoustic events using the plethora of available sensors in DUT. These systems would detect an event (e.g., explosion, vehicle ignition), tag it with some metadata, and then forward it to a centralized server for additional processing. Devices such as these can monitor traffic density, approximate the number of people in a given space, and even identify and track specific vehicle types. Additionally, sound files from these devices have demonstrated the ability to identify which route a vehicle (or person) has travelled and in which direction [ScP13]. Even more simply, these devices can record the sounds around them to include voice communication and then forward those conversations to remote nodes for analysis. In this type of environment, every sound can be heard, recorded, and analyzed.

Finally, cellular phones or other devices that connect to cellular networks provide a rich tracking capability. Each device provides an identifier to the cell nodes that it connects even if the device is not actively transmitting. This information is readily available in access logs for the cell nodes and can be used to track movements of the devices [BeC13], [RuS12]. This can help with targeting individuals. At a minimum, this technology should lead to a force protection consideration for those leaders who possess these devices.

Event Detection. Often it is desirable in military operations to detect when certain events occur. These events could be things such as perimeter violations, detection of a target in an area of interest, or the occurrence of detonations. On the current battlefield there already exists tools such as acoustic sniper detection/location devices and the unattended ground sensor. However, many of these were designed for and work best in non-DUT environments where back-ground noise is limited and wave propagation models are simpler. The good news is that the density of networked sensors in DUT enables events of these types and more to be detected more easily than in other environments.

One scenario is to use the IMUs and compasses built into mobile devices to detect vehicle movement or even the occurrence of detonations (e.g., indirect fire, bombs, IEDs). [ReD13] showed that these sensors can detect and report the location and other data about earthquakes. With modified software, this could be extended to detecting large vehicle (e.g., tanks, IFVs) movement or other events that result in significant ground disturbance. A single or group of mobile devices could sense a passing vehicle through the vibrations their IMU detects and then forward that data to a central server with location and direction of travel.

Other work such as [KnP07] has demonstrated how blast events could be detected using microphones and signal processing algorithms. Once a microphone detects a blast, it adds location, time, and other metadata to an information file that is then sent to a server for further processing. Techniques such as this could be used to assist with determination of weapon accuracy and perhaps even allow for adjustment of indirect fires without an observer. Blasts could be pin-pointed to a location and compared against the target data to determine how to adjust subsequent rounds.

Movement. It is easy to envision how attacks (cyber or otherwise) on a city's infrastructure can impact the civilian populace and therefore hinder military operations. FM 3-06 discusses considerations for protecting or attacking these systems. However, not as well considered is how cyber enabled devices can also assist with military operations in DUT by influencing movement. Attacks on infrastructure control systems can augment movement by providing concealment. Additionally, they can detect or create congested movement corridors that have an effect on current operations. The bottom line is that a city's critical infrastructure must be considered during operational planning.

Critical infrastructure is often controlled via devices known as Supervisory Control and Data Acquisition (SCADA) devices. These systems provide remote, intelligent control over things such as our electrical grid, the water and gas distribution networks, and transportation systems. These systems exist in many places and with the development of the "smart city" concept, their numbers are sure to grow. As shown in the attack on the Ukraine's electrical grid, these systems can be vulnerable to cyber operations. A criminal, military, or other user with access can use these systems to the advantage of an operation.

Deliberate use of these systems could provide counter-mobility effects or assist with the mobility of units for an operation.

As mentioned, the electrical grid contains SCADA devices. These devices can open and close switches to control power at the sub-station-level and below. In some cases, as discussed in [HiV11], this control can be narrowed down to a particular neighborhood or block. Couple this with an increasing number of devices known as "demand response controllers" and you have the ability to target an increasingly narrow geographic area. This ability could allow an operator to turn-off power to areas of their choosing. This could help offensive operations by creating concealment through the elimination of electrical light sources or hurt a defensive operation by severing electronic-based C2.

Along these same lines is the water distribution network. This network consists of control stations containing networked sensors with SCADA controllers [UKY16]. These controllers are connected to valves that turn the water on and off. Similar to the electrical power scenario, an operator could use these SCADA controllers and sensors to deny water to select areas, create dangerous over-pressure areas, or even create mass leakages that undermine the above ground infrastructure.

Lastly, the transportation network's connectivity could be used to influence military movement. Traffic signals are increasingly monitored and controlled remotely. They also have increasingly powerful capabilities [Cisco][Surtrac]. The purpose is normally to alleviate traffic problems and provide data to assist with future traffic engineering. Instead, an operator could command these systems to cause congestion along a maneuver corridor or utilize the monitoring capabilities to understand movement patterns in the area as part of intelligence preparation of the battlefield.

Communications

Planning for military communications normally involves a variety of considerations (e.g., band allocations, emissions, line of sight) and covers technologies ranging from radio frequency to satellite to wired. This planning helps to ensure that friendly forces can communicate effectively and that we can detect, deny, and destroy enemy communications sources. However, the combination of new technologies and the characteristics of DUT environments should force the consideration of other aspects.

Cognitive Radios. There is a growing research and commercial interest in cognitive radios. These devices use intelligent algorithms to sense the radio frequency environment for the purpose of providing reliable communications. These devices offer the possibility of creating communications networks using bands of frequencies that are currently restricted. The techniques vary but the general idea is that the radio communicates on empty/under-utilized frequencies and has the ability to cede the frequencies to higher priority devices upon detection of congestion. This means that a sensor network could be developed and emplaced that uses un-used television frequencies or FAA frequencies reserved for airports where none exist [JoN13].

This frequency flexibility can be useful not only in the commercial world to set- up inexpensive sensor and control networks without purchasing a license for a frequency band but also in the military domain. Frequency policies vary from nation to nation and thus production of devices and who can own them and transmit on them is controlled. The ability for the military to use radios that can alter the frequency range in which it operates could help decongest existing bands and improve communications [Elm13], [AkL06].

On the other hand, an adversary with this technology could create sensor or C2 networks in non-traditional bands thus making them hard to detect. Additionally, once identified, they technology is difficult to jam due to its sensing and intelligent channel switching. In the noisy RF environment of DUT, creating networks using this technology could make it difficult for military forces to find the enemy 'needle in a haystack' if you will.

Electro-magnetic Models. In the planning phases of operations, simulation tools are often used to plan communication node locations and to define the operational limits of the nodes for the forces involved. These tools rely upon signal propagation models to predict how well a signal will be received based on a selected location. Many of these models are line of sight (LOS) based and do not model well in areas with heavy NLOS sections and the related challenges faced due to multipath signals. Additionally, many of our military C2 systems rely upon adequate reception of signals to provide reliable data (e.g., GPS). Current systems do not reliably handle the NLOS DUT environment. Finally, the RF spectrum of DUT locations has not been well mapped for the vast array of urban environments that exist. What this spectrum looks like and how it will affect military communications is not well known.

There is a dearth of research on the effectiveness of military communications systems in DUT. How signals will propagate and the ability of systems to effectively communicate is not well characterized. One study has shown that the most common path-loss models do not accurately capture the realities of the environment [Xin15] from city to city. This is especially true in outdoor-to-indoor or indoor-to-indoor communications. Other work exploring low power transmitters such as those found in sensor networks describes the inadequacy of the models used for those devices [AlC16]. The authors propose the development of new algorithms and models to make better predictions on transmitter and receiver positioning. However, given the ever-growing pervasiveness of emitting devices within an urban environment and the terrain that an urban environment presents to RF signals the ability to accurately model signal propagation, particularly deterministically, will be a fairly intractable problem for the foreseeable future.

DUT environments can be expected to have a very crowded RF spectrum. The number of transmitters is immense and includes things such as television, radio, Wi-Fi, cellular, Bluetooth, emergency services, airport and weather radars, and IOT devices. How all of these systems will impact military operations and systems is not well known. The authors of [AlT15] conducted a study to map the RF spectrum in an urban location. As expected, some bands are heavily occupied and thus jamming a system (e.g., cognitive radio network) in this region could impact many bystander systems. Additionally, they found there were many open bands in restricted ranges that could be utilized by intelligent cognitive radios. Much potential exists in the use of cognitive radios in that they can sense the environment in real time and then have the flexibility to react appropriately given that environment. However, given the uncertainty of knowing this environment ahead of time it can be very difficult to plan and coordinate the communications aspect of an operation in advance from a capacity and capability perspective.

Finally, the structures in many DUT locations create what are known as "urban canyons" where LOS dependent systems such as GPS receivers do not function well. Given the increasing reliance on GPS signals for navigation, C2, and precision weapon control access to these signals and the quality of the data therein is vital. As with many of the challenges mentioned, increasing computational power coupled with better algorithms can help. Work done by [WaG14] suggests that coupling 3-D models of DUT environments with signal processing algorithms can result in improved GPS location data in urban canyons.

Mesh and Other Networks. As previously discussed, DUT environments are flush with network devices. They are engineered to work on purpose-built networks for specific uses. Despite this, they are not limited to just that purpose. Ad-hoc mesh networks could be established either willingly or using malicious code to create C2 or sensor networks for an adversary. These networks can be dynamic and resilient in the face of changing device density and operational conditions.

One must also consider the use of designed networks for operational needs. There are numerous "apps" and other software on mobile devices that create communications platforms that can perform as C2 nodes. Some of these apps even provide end-to-end encryption capabilities that provide an unsophisticated opponent communications security on par with the most technologically advanced nations. The effectiveness of these non-traditional networks has been demonstrated in public movements such as the Arab Spring where masses of people were assembled and directed via social media and other applications. Military operations in DUT must consider how to monitor and when necessary utilize these means of communications to ensure operational success.

Conclusions and Future Work

Dense Urban Terrain presents numerous challenges and opportunities to military forces due its cyber characteristics. The volume of networked devices and communications platforms offers both offensive and defensive opportunities and challenges. The intelligence and command and control capabilities that these devices offer is unparalleled in other terrain. As discussed, these devices can impact maneuver, movement, and targeting as well. Without deliberate planning by operational staffs and appropriate action, it will be difficult to conceal operations and protect high value assets. It is necessary for the military to investigate these technologies more closely, to develop techniques for mitigating/ utilizing them, and to create training environments where they can be used. Given the likelihood of conducting future operations in a DUT zone, it is imperative that we prepare adequately.

The preparation for this environment of course includes continuing work on the cyber security of our networks and critical infrastructure. Many of the issues discussed can be mitigated or taken advantage of through thorough knowledge of their cyber security and electronic properties. Training should incorporate scenarios where IOT and mobile device sensors are used offensively or defensively to alter the operation's outcome. Just as we learned to camouflage personnel and equipment to protect against visual detection and radars, troops need to learn how to camouflage operations from these networked sensors. Intelligence personnel need to learn about the data offered by these sensors and how to acquire that data. This can improve their IPB and their targeting. Electronic warfare units need to understand the evolving spectrum they face and the nature of the devices they will attempt to surveil or jam. Finally, continued research needs to be done to improve signal propagation models and signal processing algorithms so that planning tools and the use GPS devices within an urban environment can be improved.

The views of the authors are their own and do not reflect the views of the United States Military Academy, the United States Army, or the United States Government.

References

Abedi, N., Bhaskar, A., and Chung, E., "Tracking spatio-temporal movement of human in terms of space utilization using Media-Access-Control address data", *Applied Geography*, Vol. 51, 2014., pp. 72-81.

Ajiboye, S. et. al., "Hierarchical video surveillance architecture: a chassis for video big data analytics and exploration", *SPIE/IS&T Electronic Imaging.* International Society for Optics and Photonics, 2015, pp. 94070K1-94070K10.

Akyildiz, I., et al., "NeXt generation/dynamic spectrum access/cognitive radio wireless networks: A survey", *Computer Networks*, Vol. 50, Iss. 13, 15 September 2006, pp. 2127-2159.

Al-Hourani, A., et al., "Spectrum occupancy measurements for different urban environments", *2015 European Conference on Networks and Communications (EuCNC)*, 29 June-2 July 2015, p. 6.

Alwajeeh, T., et al., "Efficient Method for Associating Radio Propagation Models with Spatial Partitioning for Smart City Applications", *ICC '16 Proceedings of the International Conference on Internet of things and Cloud Computing*, No. 8, Cambridge, United Kingdom, March 22-23, 2016, p. 7.

Bekhor, S., Cohen, Y., and Solomon, C., "Evaluating long-distance travel patterns in Israel by tracking cellular phone positions", *Journal of Advanced Transportation*, Vol. 47, 2013, pp. 435-446.

Benfold, B. and Reid, I., "Stable multi-target tracking in real-time surveillance video", *2011 IEEE Conference on Computer Vision and Pattern Recognition (CVPR)*, 20-25 June 2011, p. 8.

Bottero, M., Chiara, B., Deflorio, F., "Wireless Sensor Networks for Traffic Monitoring in a Logistic Centre", *Transportation*

Research Part C: Emerging Technologies, Vol. 26, January 2013, pp. 99–12.

Cisco, *Smart Traffic Management*, Available at: http://www.cisco.com/c/en_in/about/knowledge-network/smart-traffic.html, [Accessed 10 Nov 16].

Colone, F., et al., "WiFi-Based Passive ISAR for High-Resolution Cross-Range Profiling of Moving Targets", *IEEE Transactions on Geoscience and Remote Sensing*, Vol. 52, Iss. 6, June 2014, pp. 3486-3501.

Elmasry, G., "The Progress of Tactical Radios from Legacy Systems to Cognitive Radios", *IEEE Communications Magazine*, Vol. 51, Issue 10, Oct. 2013, pp. 50-56.

Gong, L., et al., "Wifi-based Real-time Calibration-free Passive Human Motion Detection", *Sensors*, Vol. 15, 21 December 2015, pp. 32213-32229.

Gustafsson, M., et al., "Extraction of Human Micro-Doppler Signature in an Urban Environment Using a "Sensing-Behind-the-Corner" Radar", *IEEE Geoscience and Remote Sensing Letters*, Vol. 13, No. 2, February 2016, pp. 187-191.

Higgins, N., et al., "Distributed Power System Automation with IEC 61850, IEC 61499, and Intelligent Control", *IEEE Transactions on Systems, Man, And Cybernetics—Part C: Applications And Reviews*, Vol. 41, No. 1, January 2011, pp. 81-92.

Hollosi, D., et al., "Enhancing Wireless Sensor Networks with Acoustic Sensing Technology: Use Cases, Applications & Experiments", *2013 IEEE International Conference on Green Computing and Communications (GreenCom), and IEEE Internet of Things and IEEE Cyber, Physical and Social Computing (iThings/CPSCom)*, 20-23 Aug. 2013, pp. 335-342.

Joshi, G., Nam, S., and Kim, S., "Cognitive Radio Wireless Sensor Networks: Applications, Challenges and Research Trends", *Sensors*, Vol. 13, No. 9, 2013, pp. 11196-11228.

Knobler, R., and Plummer, T., "Time Difference of Arrival Blast Localization Using a Network of Disposable Sensors", *Sensors, and Command, Control, Communications, and Intelligence (C3I)*

Technologies for Homeland Security and Homeland Defense VI, ed. Edward M. Carapezza, Vol. 6538, 2007, p. 11.

Kostakos, V., Ojala, T., and Juntunen, T., "Traffic in the Smart City: Exploring City-Wide Sensing for Traffic Control Center Augmentation", *IEEE Internet Computing*, Vol. 17, Iss. 6, Nov.-Dec. 2013, pp. 22-29.

Michael, K, and Clarke, R., "Location and Tracking of Mobile Devices: Uberveillance Stalks the Streets", *Computer Law & Security Review*, Vol. 29, 2013, pp. 216- 228.

Mirowski, P., et al., "SignalSLAM: Simultaneous localization and mapping with mixed WiFi, Bluetooth, LTE and magnetic signals", *2013 International Conference on Indoor Positioning and Indoor Navigation (IPIN)*, 28-31 Oct. 2013, p. 10.

Namiot, D., and Sneps-Sneppe, M., "Geofence and Network Proximity", *Internet of Things, Smart Spaces, and Next Generation Networking*. Springer, Berlin Heidelberg, 2013, pp. 117-127.

Pan, Gang, et al. "Trace Analysis and Mining for Smart Cities: Issues, Methods, and Applications," *IEEE Communications Magazine*, Vol. 51, No. 6, 2013, pp. 120- 126.

Raty, T., "Survey on Contemporary Remote Surveillance Systems for Public Safety", *IEEE Transactions on Systems, Man, and Cybernetics, Part C (Applications and Reviews)*, Vol. 40, Iss. 5, September 2010, pp. 493-515.

Reilly, J., et al., "Mobile Phones as Seismologic Sensors: Automating Data Extraction for the iShake System", *IEEE Transactions on Automation Science and Engineering*, Vol. 10, Iss. 2, April 2013, pp. 242-251.

Rubio, A., Sanchez, A., and Frias-Martinez, E., "Adaptive Non-parametric Identification of Dense Areas Using Cell Phone Records for Urban Analysis", *Engineering Applications of Artificial Intelligence*, Vol. 26, Iss. 1, January 2013, pp. 551-563.

Savic, V., Wymeersch, H., and Larsson, E., "Target Tracking in Confined Environments with Uncertain Sensor Positions", *IEEE Transactions on Vehicular Technology*, Vol. 65, Iss. 2, February 2016, pp. 870-882.

Schuller, B., et al., "Acoustic Geo-Sensing: Recognising Cyclists' Route, Route Direction, and Route Progress from Cell-Phone Audio", *2013 IEEE International Conference on Acoustics, Speech and Signal Processing (ICASSP)*, 26-31 May 2013, p. 5.

Soldovieri, F., and Gennarelli, G., "Exploitation of Ubiquitous Wi-Fi Devices as Building Blocks for Improvised Motion Detection Systems", *Sensors*, Vol. 16, No. 307, 27 February 2016, p. 13.

Stange, H., et al., "Analytical Workflow of Monitoring Human Mobility in Big Event Settings using Bluetooth", *ISA '11 Proceedings of the 3rd ACM SIGSPATIAL International Workshop on Indoor Spatial Awareness*, Chicago, IL, 1 November 2011, pp. 51-58.

Surtrac, "Smart Traffic light", Available at: https://www.surtrac.net/, [Accessed 8 November 2016]. University of Kentucky, "Water Distribution System Toolkit", Available at: http://www.uky.edu/WDST/SCADA.html, [Accessed on 2 November 2016].

Valera, M., and Velastin, S.A., "Intelligent Distributed Surveillance Systems: a Review", *IEE Proceedings—Vision, Image and Signal Processing*, Vol. 152, Iss. 2, 8 April 2005, pp. 192-204.

Wang, L., Groves, P., and Ziebart, M., "Smartphone Shadow Matching for Better Cross-street GNSS Positioning in Urban Environments", *The Journal of Navigation*, Vol. 68, 2015, pp. 411-433.

Wang, Q., et al., "Analysis and Experiments of Vehicle Detection with Magnetic Sensors in Urban Environments", *2015 IEEE International Conference on Cyber Technology in Automation, Control, and Intelligent Systems (CYBER)*, Shenyang, China, 8-12 June 2015, pp. 71-75.

Xing, Qian. *"Peer-to-peer Urban Channel Characterization for Military UHF Band,"* Diss. 2015, p. 137.

Yahui, W., and Xiaoran, G., "The Study of Location Technology Based on Wireless Sensor Networks in Smart City", *2016 12th IEEE International Conference on Control and Automation (ICCA)*, Kathmandu, Nepal, 1-3 June 2016, pp. 848-853.

Zanella, A., et al., "Internet of Things for Smart Cities", *IEEE Internet of Things Journal*, Vol. 1, Iss. 1, February 2014, pp. 22-32.

Zhang, T., et al., "The Design and Implementation of a Wireless Video Surveillance System", *Proceedings of the 21ˢᵗ Annual International Conference on Mobile Computing and Networking*, pp. 426-438.

Zhou, M., Zhang, J., and Papandreou-Suppappola, A., "Multiple Target Tracking in Urban Environments", *IEEE Transactions on Signal Processing*, Vol. 64, Iss. 5, March 1, 2016, pp. 1270-1279.

Chapter 45

A Flexible Data-Centric Approach for Modeling and Analyzing Hyper Connected Megacities

K. Selçuk Candan, Shade T. Shutters and Christian Fortunato

First Published 14 July 2017

The hyper-connected megacity epitomizes the multi-domain environment. As global centers of trade, communications, and migration, it is broadly recognized that megacities—or more generally Dense Urban Areas (DUA)—will emerge at the epicenter of future events necessitating military intervention. The often-picturesque skyline of the megacity belies the interconnected complexity of the systems and people that function within the cities themselves. DUAs extend vertically from outer space where satellites that enable navigation and communications reside downward though urban valleys underground where subways operate, and horizontally across the city from the waterways that support trade to distinct cultural centers to the hinterlands that sustain the city. Urban systems crisscross hundreds of kilometers of sprawl and are further linked to systems that cross land, oceans, space, and airways. The interconnected nature of these systems means that second and third order effects to a change in a system can have drastic, unintended consequences to the system as a whole. In multi-domain operations the breadth scale and scope of the interconnected complexity can have a significant impact on a commander's decision-making process.

Military discussions of urban operations often conjure images of quagmires of urban combat. Though this historical perspective is arguably accurate, these images frame operations in a kinetic perspective. Future military operations in urban areas will be defined by data. Understanding data in terms of the urban operational environment and acting upon the data seamlessly across military domains enables exploitation of the situation and Operating Environment. To enable this capability, a flexible data-centric approach for modeling and analyzing hyper connected megacities is needed.

Commanders, analysts, and operators need a capability that provides a meaningful level of understanding to enable decision making, shaping the situation, and exploiting the Operating Environment. Though capabilities must be developed to support situational understanding and decision making for DUAs, there are several interrelated problems that inhibit the effective development of a multi-model monitoring or decision support capability for DUAs:

- Dense Urban Areas, though similar, requires a multi-model approach.
- Given the wide variety of available models, identification of the appropriate model(s) to answer a specific question is a daunting assignment.
- Integration of multiple models is hampered by inconsistent measures between models; spatial resolution, temporal scale, units of measure, data requirements, and variables.
- Data for use by the modeling capability must be identified, extracted from its native format, aligned with the appropriate dictionary, and cleaned.
- Current visualization methods do not reflect the multidimensional nature of DUA, nor do they adequately enable an operator to understand second and third order effects.

To address these issues and to effectively understand interconnected complexity of Dense Urban Areas an open adaptive framework of integrated modeling capabilities is needed. The framework should enable users to query the modeling framework in order to select the best models for the specific operational question, create an instance of a modeling system for a specific question, tie models to the appropriate datasets, provide operational norms for factors being used in the models, and create an aggregated view of the data interpreted within the models for the operator using the visualization framework.

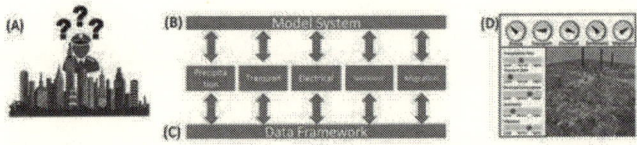

Figure 1. Conceptual Modeling framework depicting (A) the operational question, (B) an instantiation of the modeling framework, (C) the appropriate data for the model sets, and (D) the visualized data.

A cornerstone of developing an integrated DUA modeling capability is the use of a high-level environment, or framework, that links together different sophisticated computational models so that the output of one sub-model or process can provide input to another. This structuring of models in a single framework creates an adaptive framework capable of evolving to add greater capabilities over time. An open source framework enables the modeling and simulation community to develop models and analytical capabilities that are specifically designed for integration into the framework. The Framework should enable workflows that automatically process and aggregate numerical and graphical outputs to web based graphical dashboards. The use of workflows in this manner allows the models to operate in high speed computing environments while the interface to the models can function on browser enabled and bandwidth limited devices.

In conjunction with the framework a common modeling ontology is required. An ontology establishes a common language to describe and evaluate models. This allows a homogeneous description of model coming from different communities using an established and defined set of criteria. An example ontology is listed in the following graphic (Figure 2).

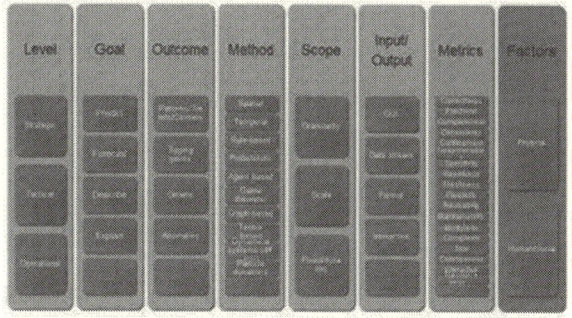

*Figure 2. An ontology used to describe, evaluate,
and compare computational models.*

Most importantly, an ontology enables an operator to evaluate, compare or contrast the models to support a specific purpose. When fully integrated into a modeling framework the ontology supports structured, operator defined queries, which configure the modeling framework. For example, given a question such as "Which models can be used to discover important figures in a religious organization given their Tweets in the last 6 months in Jakarta and help describe their network" the information in the framework enables the identification and comparison of candidate models across their critical dimensions, depicted as green circles in the following graphic (Figure 3).

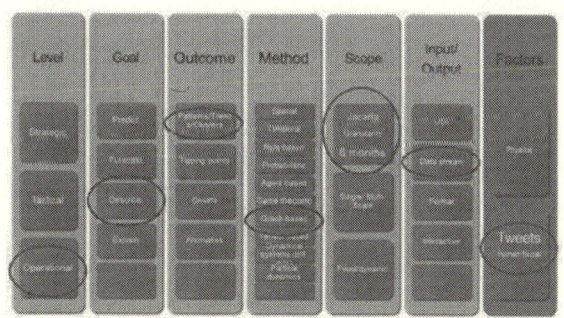

*Figure 3. The application of the modeling ontology to the
specific query, which models can be used to discover important
figures in a religious organization given their Tweets in the last
6 months in Jakarta and help describe their network.*

Further, when an ontology is used in this manner and as part of a modeling framework an instantiation of a modeling system can be created to specifically address the question being asked. Essentially, the ontology and framework interact to enable the most appropriate set of models to address a specific question.

In conjunction with the modeling framework and ontology, a data framework should be implemented to provide data sources to the models on demand into an open source data storage architecture. This could be achieved with data profiling and mining techniques to automatically discover and integrate data sources for DUAs. While in general the process cannot be fully automated, machine learning algorithms and similar technologies, would reduce user involvement to only when it is needed to guarantee the desired level of quality for the data. Once a new source is brought into the data framework, historical and static data can be stored in a central repository. Data, once collected, can then be analyzed determine relationships and establish operational norms. Once quantified continuous evaluation of data provides an indicator of trends toward abnormal behavior.

Development of advanced visualization capabilities should focus operators on relevant data through the creation of simplistic, user centric visualization concepts yet utilize minimal bandwidth to enable operation on limited bandwidth networks. The visualization framework should focus on representing large inter-related datasets that are typical to DUAs. A key attribute in developing situational understanding through visualization is providing the tools to understand the relationships between data, from the current situation though predictive analysis and inclusive of second and third order effects within the DUA.

A flexible data-centric approach to understanding megacities provides critical capabilities in the hyper-connected urban multi-domain environment. First and foremost, the approach enables users to define specific questions that need answered based upon an ontology, connects the appropriate models and data to a visualization system, and provides graphical and numerical data tailored to answer the specific question posed to the framework. Second, the hosting of the modeling framework on a high-speed computing platform and serving of the visualization system to any network connected browser enabled device means a standard synchronize view of the Operating Environment is potentially accessible at the tactical and strategic level of all services. Finally, the approach creates an open, extensible structure, using a defined set of architects to integrate additional data and modeling capabilities as needed.

Chapter 46

On a Modern Form of Terrorism: Small-Scale and Self-Contained

Kyle R. Brady

First Published 13 November 2017

The recent vehicle-based terror attacks in London[1] and Stockholm[2] have been noted as much for their devastation and chaos[3] as for its low-tech approach to terrorism.[4] At the core, these attacks are predicated upon a very simple premise: drive a regular civilian passenger vehicle through crowds of people in a very public, high-profile, and undefended area—colliding with as many individuals as possible—with some form of knife-based or small-arms attack afterward, if desired. As devastating and chaotic as these are, this is not a new form of attack.[5]

The problem, however, is that this form of attack is so simple and effective. These attacks can be executed with very little planning, no training, no funding, and no preparation, which makes them quick, easy, and deadly. Given the simple and self-contained nature of these attacks, there is very little law enforcement, the intelligence community, or even the military can do: when a future terror actor decides to undertake this effort, they simply don't raise any red flags that would trigger various forms of government surveillance or contact.

Moreover, these forms of attack are extraordinarily difficult[6]—if not possible—to prevent.[7] Cities cannot simply wall off all roadways in order to ensure vehicles don't become weaponized and employed against either people or buildings. Governments cannot easily install security features around every public space and security gates in every driveway entrance. Law enforcement agencies cannot place officers and agents in every location that may experience a vehicle-based attack. There is no easy form of protection[8] against these kinds of attacks.

One attempt to address this small-scale and self-contained form of modern terrorism is through what is known as Countering Violent Extremism (CVE): an integrated approach to terrorism that includes attempting to prevent individuals, in the early stages of radicalization, from undertaking a path to terrorism. These efforts, however, are both new and as-yet largely unsuccessful,[9] in part because the pathways and motivations to terrorism are many. Since terrorists have no universal set of motivations, personal characteristics, demographics, birthplace, backgrounds, or behaviors, it is extraordinarily difficult and costly to target allegedly at-risk individuals in a way that is comprehensive, effective, and on-budget. The end result, then, is that terrorists are most often met on the battlefield they choose.

There will always be disaffected members of society who desire to make their voices heard and the modern prevalence of terrorism—as well as the messaging, strategy, and tactics of most terror attacks—have ensured that this method of individual expression is considered viable. For the most desperate, the most dedicated, or the most disturbed, terrorism—in all its forms—presents a curiously plausible option. Now that terrorism is no longer understood as requiring formal affiliation or field training, the decision to employ terror to meet a goal has become that much easier. A major consequence of this confluence is that small-scale and self-contained attacks will become increasingly common: as more such attacks occur, they will garner media attention, they will become more interesting to certain individuals, and more attacks will occur. It has become a self-feeding cycle.

Short of locking down cities in attempt to prevent all forms of attack, there would seem to be only three options to address this modern form of terrorism: acceptance, indifference, or diversion.

The most basic response to the evolution of urban terrorism is simply to accept that it can happen, may happen, and, over a long enough timescale, will happen. Although this requires no extra resources or efforts, it is quite clearly a response that cannot be tolerated. No society should have to accept the possibility that attacks can, may, and will occur—at any time, in any place, and involving any persons—as this places an undue burden of existential fear on citizens and residents. A pervasive fear of harm or death is not conducive to a productive or content society.

Indifference to these attacks, as experienced by the attackers and those who may be inspired by them, is a choice worth exploring. Since the success of a terror attack, by very definition, can be measured as much by the second- or third-order public fear created as by the actual casualties of the attack, perhaps new media response structures should be put in place. If the media does not cover small-scale terror attacks, then perhaps the self-feeding cycle of this type of terrorism can be broken by refusing to provide attention to actors and inspiration to others. Although not a new concept,[10] it remains largely unapplied and unexplored, despite its potential to achieve very real and very successful results.

A third option, diversion, presents interesting possibilities as a fusion of a variety of counter- and anti-terrorism concepts. If assumptions are made that small-scale terrorism cannot be prevented, that such attacks cannot be tolerated, and that current CVE practices are insufficient, then perhaps an effort should be made to divert the focus of attacks. Instead of terror actors targeting random groups of people unaffiliated with their complaints or concerns, efforts should be made to guide acts of terrorism toward targets more in-line with their goals: if there is a grievance against government, let the government suffer the attack. By encouraging terrorists—through media campaigns, carefully crafted responses to attacks on the public, and more—to more selectively target their actions, the public no longer suffers. Moreover, if the fundamental components of terrorism—wanton violence and widespread fear—are negated, then terrorism becomes asymmetric warfare and the problem produces a solution, as warfare is a subject modern governments know very well how to address.

Governments need a better plan for addressing terrorism, since current efforts are not working and attacks will not cease on their own. Moreover, terrorism cannot be prevented by diplomatic or military efforts: terrorism is sourced in the disaffection of an individual and this individual need not live abroad. The actual strategies and tactics of terror actors will continue to evolve alongside technology, media coverage, and the inspiration of others, which inherently requires that solutions focus on either the sources or consequences of terrorism, rather than the means. However, in an age when terrorism is undertaken for seemingly endless reasons, focusing on mitigating the consequences of terrorism—if only at the level of small-scale and self-contained attacks—would appear to be a worthy effort.

Opinions expressed here are directly and expressly the author's own; they do not represent—unless stated—his employers (past, present, or future) or associated/affiliated institutions.

Notes

[1] Eshe Nleson, "Four people are dead and 29 are injured in a terror incident outside Britain's parliament." *Quartz*. 22 March 2017, https://qz.com/939302/police-shot-an-attacker-outside-britains-parliament-after-a-car-attack-injured-several-people-nearby/.

[2] "Stockholm lorry rams crowds, killing 'at least four people.'" *BBC News*. 7 April 2017, http://www.bbc.com/news/world-europe-39531108.

[3] Aamna Mohdin, "Is there any way to combat the rise of low-tech terror?" *Quartz*. 24 March 2017, https://qz.com/940370/uk-parliament-attack-is-there-any-way-to-combat-the-rise-of-low-tech-terror/.

Small Wars Journal

[4]   Aamna Mohdin, "The Stockholm Attack Is a Stark Reminder We Have No Way to Fight Low-Tech Terror." *Defense One*. 7 April 2017, https://www.defenseone.com/threats/2017/04/stockholm-attack-stark-reminder-we-have-no-way-fight-low-tech-terror/136834/.

[5]   Referenced to a *Washington Post* article; the original article link is broken.

[6]   Jack Moore, "After London, Nice and Berlin Vehicle Attacks, What can Cities do to Prevent Moore? *Newsweek*. 23 March 2017, http://www.newsweek.com/after-london-nice-and-berlin-what-can-cities-do-prevent-car-ramming-attacks-572692.

[7]   Adam Taylor, "It's nearly impossible to stop terrorists from using trucks as weapons. Here's what cities are trying." *The Washington Post*. 8 April 2017, https://www.washingtonpost.com/news/worldviews/wp/2017/04/08/its-nearly-impossible-to-stop-terrorists-from-using-trucks-as-weapons-heres-what-cities-are-trying-anyway/?utm_term=.4e37353c9253.

[8]   Tommy Daniel, "Concrete Barriers: A False Counterinsurgency Idol." Modern War Institute. 23 March 2017, https://mwi.usma.edu/concrete-barriers-false-counterinsurgency-idol/.

[9]   Candace Rondeaux and Bethany L. McGann, "Fight Against Violent Extremism Suffers Research Gaps: Study Highlights 'Blindspots,' Suggests Where to Look Next." United States Institute of Peace. 1 March 2017, https://www.usip.org/node/101036.

[10]   "The Symbiotic Relationship between Western Media and Terrorism." Carnegie Council for Ethics in International Affairs. 24 May 2016, https://www.carnegiecouncil.org/publications/ethics_online/0117.

Chapter 47

Preparing General Purpose Forces for Combat in Megacities: How Conventional Units Can Best Train for Fighting in Dense Urban Terrain

Adam Scher

First Published 15 May 2018

Team live fires in a shoot-house normally represent a basic task that is one of the key building blocks of the Army's room-clearing battle drill. For the paratroopers of 1-508th Parachute Infantry Regiment (PIR), this basic task became complex when the battalion executed its most recent live fires and dense urban area training by employing innovative mission command technology in a chemical environment while wearing gas masks and protective suits. While 1-508th PIR is surely not the first organization to conduct live fires or train for operations in a chemically contaminated environment, our training serves as a clear example of how conventional forces can prepare themselves to operate and win in megacities under extreme environmental conditions.

Some urban warfare scholars are clamoring for the Army to establish urban specific fighting formations. MAJ John Spencer, Deputy Director of the Modern War Institute at West Point, outlines in several opinion pieces the need for a 5,000 soldier unit[1] consisting of cyber warriors, aviators, mechanized and airborne infantry, engineers, and a myriad other enablers. These units would focus on indirect fires, information operations, and combat service support that is committed to rapidly deploying, innovating on a grand scale, and employing advanced technologies not normally fielded to conventional forces. Major Spencer identifies megacities as a future battlefield the US military would be foolish to ignore, and he is also absolutely right "that megacities will require major changes"[2] to today's fighting vehicles, weapons, and equipment. Every aspect of the "shoot, move, and communicate" framework is challenged by the urban environment. Current systems will have to be modified, new capabilities and technologies implemented." Additionally, he recognizes that the lack of dense urban training facilities[3] limits the Army's ability to train for megacity warfare. His detractors that argue these three points either ignore general trends in migration and economic development or fail to truly appreciate the complexity of dense urban terrain and what it means to the warfighter. While I concur with MAJ Spencer's holistic diagnosis of the problem, I fear his cure, centered on the establishment of an entirely new unit, is impractical and in some ways fails to appreciate the bureaucratic challenges associated with creating, and perhaps more importantly, maintaining such a specialized unit. Further, I think the energy and effort aimed at trying to build such a particular solution reduces readiness in other combat formations and could serve to reduce grassroots-level creativity at the lowest tactical levels.

I do not disagree that an urban operations school would pay great dividends, and I do not even necessarily disagree that modified organization and unit structure could be part of a long-term future solution. Today's battalion and brigade commanders, leading men and women into harm's way, can't wait for an ideal solution to be produced from the top-down. Instead, this generation of battalion and brigade commanders that spent their junior officer years in Baghdad, Kabul, Mosul, and Kandahar must find ways to address the challenges of megacities without the luxury of 'wish-list' novelty equipment, or dedicated schooling and training for combat in dense urban areas.

It is only within the last forty to fifty years that militaries began developing formalized doctrine for fighting inside urban centers with civilians on the battlefield that aimed at preserving critical infrastructure and protecting the civilian population. Many of those writing doctrine before the US invasions of Afghanistan and Iraq correctly identified that general purpose forces increasingly would find themselves operating in urban areas, not only to defeat an entrenched enemy, but also to preserve delivery of services, protect critical infrastructure, and secure a disaffected population.

The current fights in Iraq, Syria, and Afghanistan, exemplified by battles for cities like Mosul and Raqqa, highlighted the importance of operating in subterranean and urban terrain. Numerous media reports confirmed that coalition forces fighting to liberate Mosul discovered extensive tunnel networks. "This infrastructure allowed Islamic State fighters to creep quickly into position, then ambush advance troops from concealed locations. One commander recounted driving a tank into Eastern Mosul. He watched as dozens of Islamic State fighters quickly slipped from the street to the tunnels.[4] These fortified positions seemingly had significant tactical importance to the Islamic State and were riddled with booby-traps that injured and killed coalition forces, severely reducing the speed and tempo of clearing operations. "It's like we are fighting two wars in two cities," Col. Falah al-Obaidi of the Iraqi counterterror forces told The Washington Post.[5] "There's the war on the streets and there is a whole city underground where they are hiding. Now it's hard to consider an area liberated, because though we control the surface, ISIS will appear from under the ground, like rats." Despite recent success against ISIS, fighting a near-peer enemy in megacities like Lagos, Los Angeles, or Sao Paolo would present greater and more dangerous risks to friendly forces that can only be avoided through innovations in our mission command architecture, our operating philosophies, and our tactics techniques and procedures. Army Chief of Staff General Mark Milley[6] "has characterized recent and current urban operations, including fighting in Aleppo in Syria, and Fallujah and Mosul in Iraq as 'previews' of future conflict. Those fights, while bloody, costly and destructive, hardly reach the scale of a megacity—Mosul is not equal to a neighborhood in Seoul." Conventional forces must adapt in real time to this current reality; waiting for these 'previews' to become 'primetime' is a recipe for disaster for the conventional ground forces training for close combat.

Today's new challenge for military thinkers is addressing the problems associated with extremely dense urban centers and their underground facilities that include transit tunnels, bunkers and other below-ground hardened facilities. According to MAJ Spencer, "a new unit would serve as the primary learning organization for the Army and the vanguard of development of planning and doctrine for fighting in megacities."[7] Unfortunately, current battalion and brigade commanders do not have the time to wait for this proposed sea change to Army organizational structure. Even if such a unit could be trained, equipped, and organized starting today, any dividends from their existence is three to five years away at best. Worse, what would be the opportunity cost of designing such a tailored urban-only unit? Commanders in all other formations would feel confident embracing many of the counterarguments MAJ Spencer goes to great lengths to discredit about how the US Army can avoid fighting in megacities. In fact, the urban unit actually proves this point for leaders of the more traditional non-urban units who could presumably justify not training for megacities precisely because they aren't designated, educated, trained, or equipped like the specialized formations MAJ Spencer envisions. This would work to actually reduce the Army's overall preparedness to fight in dense urban areas. A more comprehensive solution comes not from over-specialization, but from empowering our pre-existing combat formations with the facilities, direction, and mission command equipment to fight and win no matter the terrain.

To enhance the lethality and improve the combat readiness of our conventional formation right now, 1-508th PIR Battalion Commander, LTC Robert McChrystal, began the fielding of an integrated tactical network.[8] Paratroopers from one company and the battalion staff employed the Android Tactical Assault Kit (ATAK) End User Device (EUD) and the Tactical Scalable Manet (TSM) waveform radio during a Joint Forcible Entry (JFE) culminating exercise at Fort Bragg in the summer of 2017. The enhanced mission command capabilities with data, voice, and chat proved extremely effective and spurred fielding to the entire battalion less than two weeks prior to the next major training event. During successful missions at the Joint Readiness Training Center (JRTC) at Fort Polk, Louisiana, as part of direct action rotation 18-01 in October 2017, it became apparent to the 1-508th team, the opposing force elements, and many other leaders throughout the Army that the 1-508th employment of the integrated tactical network made them exponentially more flexible and lethal when compared to similar formations operating under similar enemy and terrain conditions at JRTC. Upon return to Fort Bragg and following a review of the literature focused on growing threats facing militaries operating in megacities, LTC McChrystal searched for the next collective training opportunity that would allow his battalion to implement this network in subsurface and other dense urban environments.

With the help of the Asymmetric Warfare Group at Fort A.P. Hill, 1-508th PIR created and tested its standard operating procedures for military operations urban terrain (MOUT) for the 21st century during a comprehensive two-week training program in March 2018. The training plan focused on an operating environment which is increasingly characterized by rapid urbanization, sweeping information technology development, weapons of mass destruction, the privatization of violence, and the growing capabilities of America's near-peer adversaries to disrupt the US Military's mission command networks. While the dangers of such terrain, especially if chemically or biologically contaminated, are well documented, the mission command technology, doctrine, and training facilities to prepare conventional forces for such combat have not kept pace with the growing threat.

1-508 Paratroopers Execute Battle Drill 6 Live Fire in MOPP4

1-508 Paratroopers Enter a Tunnel System

1-508 Paratroopers Clear Rooms in a Simulated Chemical Lab

MOUT 2.0, as dubbed by 1-508th, is focused on fighting a uniformed enemy among the sub-surfaces and skyscrapers in dense urban areas. This type of terrain degrades communication and navigation systems that rely on line of sight connections to satellite or other antenna networks.

Fighting in such a harsh and unfamiliar environment ensures that the attacker remains at a disadvantage. 1-508th PIR is training to fight and win under these conditions by executing the live fire training noted above and through the implementation of an integrated tactical network of End User Devices (EUD) operating the Android Tactical Assault Kit (ATAK)[9] and Tactical Scalable Manet (TSM) waveform radios that enable mission command over voice, chat, and data communication in the most unforgiving of environmental conditions. These advanced waveform radios and secure but unclassified Android Galaxy smartphones are optimizing friendly unit tracking, voice and text communications, and creating a survivable tactical network for general purpose battalions.[10] What makes this network unique is how it seamlessly integrates existing sensors like full-motion video drones, infrared cameras, and other ground sensors already employed to combat units. Furthermore, the secure but unclassified nature of the system allows for coalition partner integration and with the use of a cross-domain solution, other army 'secret-level' programs have access to the entire common operating picture managed by local servers at the battalion level. Most importantly the network EUDs are intuitive and employed at the team leader level without the need for lengthy training or instruction manuals to make the system accessible to general purpose forces.

Beyond the ease of use and implementation, the integrated tactical network is survivable and resilient. The TSM waveform employs software driven correction for multipath fading, known as barraging, which increase end receipt signal and reduces the probability of jamming.[11] Furthermore, barraging allows for all radios to broadcast simultaneously, something key to overcoming the hazards of dense urban terrain both underground and in multi-story buildings. Major General Gallagher, Director of Networks, Services and Strategy, recently explained the Army's focus on multiband radios that can incorporate innovative anti-jam solutions, multipath networks, and dynamic spectrum reallocation based on near-peer threats in dense urban terrain.[12] Paratroopers of the 1-508th are refuting the notion that specialized urban units need futuristic equipment and proving that "short-term solutions can be as simple as replacing old server stacks with new ones one-third the size, replacing bulky metal antennas with inflatable ones, or loading new software on an off-the-shelf Android phone."[13] These types of bottom-up doctrinal, material, facility, and training advances risk being ignored if today's military leaders are left waiting for MAJ Spencer's transformation of combat units and centralized schooling.

Navigating the current and future risks associated with the contemporary operating environment will require a creative employment and fielding of resources, human capital, and an updated enterprise of mission command equipment to plan and implement realistic training opportunities to further enhance doctrine, tactics, techniques, procedures and equipment that already reside in conventional units. The AWG and the integrated tactical network enabled such training to 1-508th PIR.

Many other units across the Army are experimenting and innovating with underground and megacity operations. Training these together, doing so with an integrated tactical network, and operating under chemically contaminated conditions represent 1-508th's small contribution to this conversation. This ongoing discussion is critically important because the previous two decades of war in Afghanistan, Iraq, and Syria created ground forces capable of sustained small-scale urban combat focused on the precision targeting of individuals that has left close combat formations ill-prepared to endure the challenges presented by megacities. Secretary of Defense Jim Mattis underscored this point in a memo outlining his vision for enhancing the lethality of ground combat units.[14] "These formations have historically accounted for almost 90 percent of our casualties and yet our personnel policies, advances in training methods, and equipment have not kept pace with changes in available technology, human factors science, and talent management best practices."[15] Establishing a single, urban-only, unit doesn't address the broader concerns conveyed by the Secretary of Defense about America's military entire close-combat enterprise. The innovation and creativity required to improve the military's ground combat forces readiness, lethality, survivability, and resiliency in chemically contaminated dense urban terrain already exists in our current formations and should be enabled, encouraged, and resourced appropriately to empower today's tactical leaders to exercise true mission command in a megacity combat environment.

The views expressed are those of the author and do not reflect the official position of the 82ⁿᵈ Airborne Division, United States Army, or Department of Defense.

Notes

[1]   John Spencer, "What an Army Megacities Unit Would Look Like." Modern War Institute. 8 March 2017, https://mwi.usma. edu/army-megacities-unit-look-like/.

[2]   Ibid.

[3]   John Spencer, "The Army Needs an Urban Warfare School and It Needs It Soon." Modern War Institute. 5 April 2017, https://mwi. usma.edu/army-needs-urban-warfare-school-needs-soon/.

[4]   Amanda Erickson, "The Islamic State has tunnels everywhere. It's making ISIS much harder to defeat." *The Washington Post.* 14 April 2017, https://www.washingtonpost.com/news/worldviews/ wp/2017/04/14/the-islamic-state-has-tunnels-everywhere-its-making-them-much-harder-to-defeat/?utm_term=.fb97e0160224.

[5]   Ibid.

[6]   Todd South, "The future battlefield: Army, Marines prepare for 'massive' fight in megacities." *Military Times.* 6 March 2018, https:// www.militarytimes.com/news/your-army/2018/03/06/the-future-battlefield-army-marines-prepare-for-massive-fight-in-megacities/.

[7]   John Spencer, "It's Time to Create a Megacities Combat Unit." Modern War Institute. 31 January 2017, https://mwi.usma.edu/ time-create-megacities-combat-unit/.

[8]   Sean Kimmons, "Team tasked with modernizing Army network discusses way forward with industry." U.S. Army. 8 February 2018, https://www.army.mil/article/200371/ team_tasked_with_modernizing_army_network_discusses_way _forward_with_industry.

Small Wars Journal

[9]   Android Windows Tactical Assault Kit (ATAK). For Official Use Only Site (FOUO). Nd, https://atakmap.com.

[10]   Connie Lee, "Army Official Outlines Plans for Future Tactical Network." *National Defense Magazine.* 27 March 2018, http://www.nationaldefensemagazine.org/articles/2018/3/27/army-official-outlines-potential-future-capabilities-for-network.

[11]   TSM™ WAVEFORM. Nd, https://www.trellisware.com/waveforms/tsm-waveform/.

[12]   Sydney F. Freeberg, Jr., "Army Patches Its Network For Near Term." *Breaking Defense.* 20 March 2018, https://breakingdefense.com/2018/03/army-patches-its-network-for-near-term/.

[13]   Ibid.

[14]   Matthew Cox, "Mattis Wants Ground Combat Units to Be More Lethal in the Close Fight." Military.com. 23 February 2018, https://www.military.com/daily-news/2018/02/23/mattis-wants-ground-combat-units-be-more-lethal-close-fight.html.

[15]   Ibid.

Chapter 48

The Tricky Business of Counting the Costs of Armed Conflict in Cities

Robert Muggah

First Published 23 May 2018

Paraphrasing the Greek dramatist Aeschylus, in war, terrorism and crime, truth is the first casualty. While a proper accounting of the human toll of organized violence is critical to achieving justice and stability, it is a tricky endeavor. Part of the problem is that there are few people or institutions actually keeping track of the dead. In some of the most conflict-, terrorist- and crime-prone countries and cities, there may be no data collection systems in place at all.

It is difficult, then, to appreciate the full scale of violent deaths around the world, much less in cities. According to one estimate,[1] at least 99,000 people died violently in armed conflicts in 2016 (the most recent year for which data is available), a significant decline from the estimated 143,000 people killed in 2014. This compares [2] to an estimated 34,000 deaths terrorist-related killings in 2016 [3] in contrast to over 43,000 in 2014.[4] Notwithstanding debates over what counts as a conflict- or terrorist-related death, the biggest killer of all is intentionally homicide: 385,000 victims in 2016, slightly higher than the 375,000 murders in 2014.[5]

Most forms of contemporary organized violence are concentrating in urban areas. The reason is obvious: the world is undergoing a process of hyper-urbanization. In the 1950s, less than 30% of the world lived in a city: today, the proportion is over 55%. More than 68% by 2050,[6] at least 416 new million urban dwellers in India, 255 million in China and another 189 million in Nigeria. Meanwhile, the rural population is reaching its peak and will contract over the coming decades. It is not just people migrating to cities—warfare is moving into urban spaces as well.[7]

Killings arising during armed conflicts, terrorist acts and violent crimes are not evenly distributed among the world's cities. Rather, they tend to be hyper-concentrated in specific geographic areas. In the case of warfare and terrorism, they are overwhelmingly concentrated in cities of the Middle East, North Africa [8] and Central and South Asia. Although homicidal violence is more widespread, it is clustered in large and medium-sized cities across Latin America,[9] the Caribbean parts of southern and central Africa. Not surprisingly, the chances of being killed in Damascus, Kabul or San Salvador are literally hundreds of times higher than New York, Oslo or Tokyo.

Twenty-first century urban warfare can be highly destructive, as the cases of Aleppo, Kunduz. Mosul and Sana'a illustrate. The fact that war and terrorism is increasingly concentrated in urban settings of the Middle East, North Africa and Central Asia is not lost on militaries [10] and humanitarian agencies [11] around the world. And for good reason: armed conflicts in Afghanistan, Iraq, Syria, and Yemen accounted for two thirds of all reported violent conflict deaths over the past decade, most of them occurring in large and medium-sized cities. Urban populations in cities across Somalia and South Sudan are also routinely subjected to airstrikes, artillery and small arms fire.

Urban warfare is hardly new. Nor is it confined to mega-cities in the Middle East, North Africa or Central and South Asia. Throughout the Middle Ages hundreds of large, medium and small cities [12] around the world experienced armed conflicts of varying intensity, including siege warfare. During the nineteenth and twentieth centuries, [13] cities were targets of aerial bombing, from nuclear bombs and chemical weapons to precision-guided cruise missiles and drone strikes. Some cities collapsed entirely in the wake of devastating attacks, while others bounced back [14] with remarkable speed. While generating untold misery, urban warfare was largely neglected [15] by military historians and theorists until comparatively recently.

Warfare is urbanizing because the planet is urbanizing. Most of the world's cities are coastal and increasingly inter-linked through global supply chains and digital communications systems. These characteristics—some old and others new—are shaping the strategies of armies [16] and guerrilla and militia groups.[17] Some military theorists are predicting that [18] future wars will be waged in coastal and connected cities, requiring shifts in doctrine and tactics. While western militaries have traditionally been reluctant to get involved [19] in the messy business of city fighting, the central importance of cities in the functioning of nation states and global capital and commodity flows means that "multi-spectrum" urban engagements are unavoidable.[20]

Contemporary urban warfare comes in many shapes and sizes. Depending on whether it occurs in Donetsk, Grozny, Monrovia, or Raqqa, urban conflicts range from full-scale assaults on critical infrastructure to pitched street-battles between factions. The largest urban conflict since the Second World War occurred in Mosul in 2016,[21] a city of 1.2 million civilians. It was epic in scale, involving over 100,000 Iraqi-led coalition troops against between 3,000 and 5,000 ISIS fighters. Cities are sponges that soak up troops. They are not easily pacified through aerial precision attacks alone. Armies must contend with a complex maze of built-up areas and subterranean defense systems.

In spite of international norms regulating the use of force and protection of civilians, the urbanization of warfare has vast implications for population wellbeing. Take the case of population displacement. During a single battle in Fallujah [22] between November and December 2014, the US launched 540 airstrikes, expended 14,000 artillery and mortar shells used 300 per cent more rounds than anticipated. Anywhere between 60,000 and 80,000 [23] of the city's roughly one million residents fled. Civilians who can afford to flee do so, while those who cannot seek sanctuary in cities. The UN claims [24] that roughly 75 per cent of today's 65 million refugees and internally displaced people live in cities. The proportion may be higher still in some countries: estimated 90% of Syrian refugees live in cities,[25] as opposed to organized camps or rural areas.

Urban warfare is deadly for combatants and civilians alike. This is because military operations in cities typically entail close-range combat, involve the use of explosive weaponry [26] and encounter obstacles when it comes to evacuating wounded soldiers. Due in part to the dense population of cities and the periodic (and illegal) targeting of hospitals and schools,[27] urban warfare often results in comparatively high civilian casualties, especially among women and children.[28] Recent studies of conflict deaths in Iraq and Syria [29] between 2014 and 2017 found that over 70 per cent of all killings occurred in cities. Moreover, civilian deaths increased five-fold [30] when offensives occurred in urban areas.

Generating a comparative global assessment of conflict deaths in cities is exceedingly difficult. One of the biggest challenges is logistical [31]—how to count the dead? National and municipal vital registration systems routinely collapse during armed conflicts. Instead, researchers rely on periodic household surveys (called verbal autopsies), human rights organizations and media outlets. What they often find is that the violent death count is just the tip of the mortality iceberg. Wars also result in massive numbers of non-violent deaths, or so-called excess mortality,[32] due to starvation, illness and disease. These excess deaths can be an order of magnitude higher than the number of civilians killed immediately by bullets, rockets and mines.

These logistical challenges explain why there are so few estimates of violent casualties arising from armed conflicts, including cities. Take the case of the Uppsala Conflict Database Program (UCDP)[33] that records conflict deaths by counting incidents reported in the public domain (Table 1). After adjusting the absolute numbers of conflict deaths relative to the total population per country, they established national prevalence rates per 100,000 people between 2010 and 2016. While in some war-affected countries the rates are high, the overall conflict death rates in conflict zones are far lower than expected. For example, the average conflict death rate is sky-high in Syria but comparatively lower in places like Afghanistan, Iraq, Libya, South Sudan, Chad and Yemen.

Table 1: Top 25 most conflict-affected countries – absolute and per 100,000 (2010-2016)

Ranking	Country	Conflict deaths 2010-16	Rate average 2010-16
1	Syrian Arab Republic	250507	184.0
2	Afghanistan	77749	34.4
3	Iraq	40822	16.4
4	Somalia	11881	13.1
5	Libya	4204	9.6
6	Yemen	15201	8.3
7	South Sudan	4149	5.2
8	Israel	1818	3.3
9	Sudan	7614	3.0
10	Ukraine	5913	1.9
11	Pakistan	18561	1.5
12	Central African Republic	440	1.4
13	Mali	1471	1.3
14	Nigeria	14520	1.2
15	Turkey	5362	1.0
16	Myanmar	2783	0.8
17	Cameroon	1216	0.8
18	Rwanda	536	0.7
19	Uganda	1549	0.6
20	Lebanon	202	0.5
21	Democratic Republic of the Congo	2355	0.5
22	Algeria	1209	0.5
23	Philippines	2947	0.4
24	Azerbaijan	284	0.4
25	Colombia	1250	0.4

Source: Uppsala Conflict Database Program (UCDP)

A separate effort to measure conflict deaths in cities comes from the Peace Research Institute in Oslo (PRIO). PRIO generated a dataset on the number of "conflict events" resulting in death in capitals and other major cities from 1960-2014. While based on a comparatively small sample of lethal events, the so-called Urban Social Disorder Database [34](Table 2) provides a very conservative estimate of killings arising during various types of warfare and social unrest from over 89 countries. While some war-affected cities like Mogadishu, Baghdad, Kabul and Sana'a register comparatively high prevalence of killing (per 100,000), most cities exhibit still comparatively low conflict death rates when compared to, say, equivalent rates for terrorism and homicide.

Not surprisingly, micro-level data collected by national data collection observatories such as the Syria Network for Human Rights or Iraq Body Count suggest that Uppsala and PRIO are dramatically under-counting conflict deaths. For example, monthly reports [35] released by the Syria Network for Human Rights [36] estimate that 2,019 civilians were killed in Damascus and its suburbs and another 1,512 in Raqqa in 2017 alone. Meanwhile, Iraq Body Count [37] estimates that at least 300 civilians were killed by conflict-related violence in Baghdad, 125 in Kirkuk, 90 in Anbar in 2017. Unfortunately, few comparable entities exist in other war zones such as Afghanistan, South Sudan or Yemen.

Table 2: Top 25 most conflict-affected cities (2014) – absolute and per 100,000

Ranking	City	Country	Events 2014	Rate per 100,000
1	Mogadishu	Somalia	15	7.02
2	Baghdad	Iraq	12	1.81
3	Kabul	Afghanistan	8	1.73
4	Sanaa	Yemen	8	2.70
5	Karachi	Pakistan	7	0.42
6	Bangkok	Thailand	6	0.65
7	Cairo	Egypt	4	0.21
8	Tripoli	Libya	4	3.55
9	Nairobi	Kenya	3	0.77
10	Caracas	Venezuela	3	1.03
11	Beirut	Lebanon	2	0.90
12	Abuja	Nigeria	2	0.82
13	Islamabad	Pakistan	2	1.47
14	Rio De Janeiro	Brazil	2	0.16
15	Ndjamena	Chad	2	1.59
16	Istanbul	Turkey	1	0.07
17	Amman	Jordan	1	0.87
18	Khartoum	Sudan	1	0.19
19	Antananarivo	Madagascar	1	0.38
20	Kuala Lumpur	Malaysia	1	0.15
21	Johannesburg	South Africa	1	0.11
22	Damascus	Syria	0	0.00
23	Conakry	Guinea	0	0.00
24	Dhaka	Bangladesh	0	0.00
25	Kigali	Rwanda	0	0.00

Source: PRIO

Table 3: Top 20 most terrorist prone cities - absolute and per 100,000 (2016 or latest year)

Ranking	City name	Country name	Absolute	Rate
1	Mosul	Iraq	2132	125.8
2	Gamboru Ngala	Nigeria	327	125.8
3	Fallujah	Iraq	357	110.6
4	Ramadi	Iraq	365	98.8
5	Kunduz	Afghanistan	220	72.2
6	Deir ez-Zor	Syrian Arab Republic	202	48.8
7	Taizz	Yemen	314	45.2
8	Mukalla	Yemen	118	32.5
9	Baghdad	Iraq	2075	31.2
10	Tall	Iraq	68	26.8
11	Aden	Yemen	229	26.0
12	Benghazi	Libya	190	25.5
13	Quetta	Pakistan	237	21.4
14	Mogadishu	Somalia	368	17.2
15	Nice	France	87	16.7
16	Kirkuk	Iraq	107	16.5
17	Aleppo	Syrian Arab Republic	557	15.6
18	Tartus	Syrian Arab Republic	80	13.4
19	Hillah	Iraq	62	12.2
20	Maiduguri	Nigeria	85	11.7
21	Barna	Nigeria	31	10.3
22	Baqubah	Iraq	43	10.1
23	Kabul	Afghanistan	430	9.3
24	Ikorodu	Nigeria	56	7.9
25	Samarra	Iraq	27	7.8

Source: Global Terrorism Database

Another form of organized violence affecting city residents in war zones (and outside of them) is terrorism. Estimating the numbers of people killed due to terrorism, like casualties of armed conflict, is fraught with difficulties. One reason is that there is no universal definition of terrorism nor agreement on what constitutes a terrorist act or who is a terrorist. What counts as terrorism is intensely political: governments and non-government bodies routinely attribute deaths in war zones to either (or both) terrorism or armed conflict.

As in the case of conflict-related deaths, the vast majority of terrorist-related killings [38] over the past decade are concentrated in the Middle East and North Africa and Central and South Asia. Many of these countries are not just war-affected, but also suffer high levels of terrorism owing to weak security institutions. A review of more than 2,100 of the world's most populous cities underlined how terrorism is highly concentrated. In 2016, cities across Iraq, Syria, Somalia and Afghanistan featured among the most violent (Table 3).[39] Taking a longer view, from 2010 to 2016, the list expands slightly to include cities from Nigeria and Pakistan (Table 4).[40]

Table 4: Top 20 most terrorist prone cities – absolute and per 100,000 (2010-2016)

Ranking	City name	Country name	Number of killings 2010-2016
1	Baghdad	Iraq	10,655
2	Mosul	Iraq	3,976
3	Mogadishu	Somalia	1,966
4	Ramadi	Iraq	1,896
5	Maiduguri	Nigeria	1,740
6	Karachi	Pakistan	1,666
7	Aleppo	Syrian Arab Republic	1,561
8	Fallujah	Iraq	1,522
9	Quetta	Pakistan	1,343
10	Kabul	Afghanistan	1,312
11	Damascus	Syrian Arab Republic	1,014
12	Peshawar	Pakistan	986
13	Baqubah	Iraq	932
14	Sanaa	Yemen	928
15	Benghazi	Libya	900
16	Kirkuk	Iraq	852
17	Badush	Iraq	678
18	Kunduz	Afghanistan	671
19	Aden	Yemen	638
20	Homs	Syrian Arab Republic	615
21	Taizz	Yemen	607
22	Kano	Nigeria	605
23	Taji	Iraq	580
24	Samarra	Iraq	555
25	Kandahar	Afghanistan	553

Source: Global Terrorism Database

Perhaps most surprising is the fact that urban residents around the world are much more at risk of being killed as result of intentional homicide than either terrorist violence or warfare. Drawing on the Homicide Monitor,[41] it is possible to track murder rates for more than 225 countries and territories from 2010 to 2017 (Table 5)[42]; in addition, the top 25 cities for homicide for 2016 or 2017 (latest year available) are depicted (Table 6)[43]. Although homicidal violence is steadily declining [44] in most parts of the world, it still presents a real threat to urban dwellers in Latin America, the Caribbean and Southern and Central Africa. Indeed, 46 of the 50 most violent cities [45] are concentrated in the Americas. This is not to trivialize the real dangers and destruction associated with urban warfare and terrorism, but rather to put them in perspective.

Table 5: Top 25 most homicidal cities per 100,000 (2010-2017)

Ranking	City	Country name	Average 2010-17
1	San Pedro Sula	Honduras	135.06
2	Guarenas-Guatire	Venezuela	125.45
3	Maturín	Venezuela	113.86
4	San Salvador	El Salvador	111.55
5	Acapulco de Juarez	Mexico	107.97
6	Ciudad Guayana	Venezuela	99.14
7	Caracas	Venezuela	91.45
8	Valencia	Venezuela	89.86
9	Guatemala	Guatemala	82.74
10	Choloma	Honduras	81.93
11	Ciudad Bolívar	Venezuela	79.82
12	Cumaná	Venezuela	79.58
13	Camacari	Brazil	77.15
14	Distrito Central	Honduras	74.25
15	Ananindeua	Brazil	72.63
16	Maracay	Venezuela	72.13
17	Mossoró	Brazil	71.70
18	Palmira	Colombia	71.52
19	Chilpancingo De Los Bravo	Mexico	71.10
20	Cali	Colombia	70.09
21	Barinas	Venezuela	68.97
22	Caucaia	Brazil	67.87
23	Marabá	Brazil	67.63
24	San Miguel	El Salvador	67.45
25	Puerto Ordaz	Venezuela	65.36

Source: HomicideMonitor

Table 6: Top 25 most homicidal cities per 100,000 (2016 or latest year)

Ranking	City	Country name	Latest	Year
1	Guarenas-Guatire	Venezuela	125.45	2016
2	Maturín	Venezuela	113.86	2016
3	Ciudad Guayana	Venezuela	99.14	2016
4	Acapulco de Juárez	Mexico	97.70	2017
5	Chilpancingo De Los Bravo	Mexico	97.05	2017
6	Caucaia (city in Brazil)	Brazil	96.80	2017
7	Los Cabos	Mexico	96.57	2017
8	San Salvador	El Salvador	95.70	2017
9	Caracas	Venezuela	92.90	2016
10	Tijuana	Mexico	91.23	2017
11	Valencia	Venezuela	89.86	2016
12	Choloma	Honduras	86.45	2017
13	Mossoró	Brazil	84.20	2017
14	Ciudad Bolívar	Venezuela	79.82	2016
15	Ananindeua	Brazil	79.60	2017
16	Cumaná	Venezuela	79.58	2016
17	Camacari	Brazil	79.40	2016
18	Fortaleza	Brazil	75.30	2017
19	Guatemala	Guatemala	75.11	2017
20	Maracay	Venezuela	72.13	2016
21	Natal	Brazil	70.30	2017
22	La Paz	Mexico	69.08	2017
23	Barinas	Venezuela	68.97	2016
24	Paulista	Brazil	67.90	2017
25	San Miguel	El Salvador	66.94	2017

Source: HomicideMonitor

Developing a standard methodology for documenting and tracking the organized violence (e.g. deaths, injuries, and related violence, including rape, sexual assaults, and displacement) generated by armed conflicts in cities is essential to understanding the wider dynamics of urban warfare and urban terrorism. This essay offers a preliminary attempt to start the process, while also signaling critical knowledge gaps.

Notes

[1] Claire Mc Evoy and Gergely Hideg, *Global Violent Deaths 2017: Time to Decide*. Small Arms Survey; http://www.smallarmssurvey.org/fileadmin/docs/U-Reports/SAS-Report-GVD2017.pdf.

[2] *Global Terrorism Database* (GTD), University of Maryland, National Consortium for the Study of Terrorism and Response to Terrorism (START); https://www.start.umd.edu/gtd/.

[3] GTD 2016 Overview; https://www.start.umd.edu/pubs/START_GTD_OverviewTerrorism2016_August2017.pdf.

[4] Ibid.

[5] Small Arms Survey, Note 1.

[6] *2018 Revision of World Urbanization Prospects*, United Nations, https://www.un.org/development/desa/publications/2018-revision-of-world-urbanization-prospects.html.

[7] *War in Cities*. Geneva: International Committee of the Red Cross (ICRC); https://www.icrc.org/en/war-in-cities.

[8] "Middle East Conflicts Spur Disastrous New Trends for Region," *Human Rights Watch*, 18 January 2018; https://www.hrw.org/news/2018/01/18/middle-east-conflicts-spur-disastrous-new-trends-region.

[9] "Shining light on Latin America's homicide epidemic," *The Economist*, 5 April 2018; https://www.economist.com/briefing/2018/04/05/shining-light-on-latin-americas-homicide-epidemic.

[10] David Kilcullen, "Urban Combat: 'Cities Are Sponges That Soak Up Troops'," *The Cipher Brief*, 22 October 2017; https://www.thecipherbrief.com/urban-combat-cities-are-sponges-that-soak-up-troops.

[11] Peter Maurer, "War in Cities: What is at Stake?" Geneva: International Committee of the Red Cross (ICRC); https://www.icrc.org/en/document/war-cities-what-stake-0.

[12] "List Of Sieges," *Wikipedia*; https://en.wikipedia.org/wiki/List_of_sieges.

[13] Alastair Gee, "Aerial bombing: Turns out, it almost never works," *IDEAS.TED.COM*, 17 November 2014; https://ideas.ted.com/the-warfare-tactic-that-crushed-cities-but-not-spirits/.

[14] Adria Mourby, "Where are the world's most war-damaged cities?" *The Guardian*, 17 December 2015; https://www.theguardian.com/cities/2015/dec/17/where-world-most-war-damaged-city.

[15] Michael Evans, "City Without Joy: Urban Military Operations into the 21st Century." Australian Defence College, *Occasional Paper No. 2* (2007);

[16] *"Joint Urban Operations," Joint Publication 3-06*. Washington, DC: Department of Defense, 20 November 2013; http://www.jcs.mil/Portals/36/Documents/Doctrine/pubs/jp3_06.pdf.

[17] David Kilcullen, "The Future of War?: Expect to see urban, connected, irregular 'zombie' conflicts." *Foreign Policy*, 5 February

2014; http://foreignpolicy.com/2014/02/05/the-future-of-war-expect-to-see-urban-connected-irregular-zombie-conflicts/.

[18] David Kilcullen, "A future of coastal, connected cities." *TEDxSydney 2014* at YouTube, 26 May 2014; https://www.youtube.com/watch?v=_AD4c2R1i1w.

[19] Michael Evans, "City Without Joy: Urban Military Operations into the 21st Century." Note 15.

[20] Ibid.

[21] Tim Lister, Mohammed Tawfeeq and Angela Dewan, "Iraqi forces fight ISIS on Mosul streets," *CNN*, 4 November 2016; https://edition.cnn.com/2016/11/03/middleeast/mosul-offensive-iraq-troops-in/index.html.

[22] Michael Evans, "City Without Joy: Urban Military Operations into the 21st Century." Note 15.

[23] Annie Slemrod, "The failure in Fallujah: And how lessons must be learnt for Mosul." *IRIN News*, 28 June 2016; https://www.irinnews.org/analysis/2016/06/28/failure-fallujah.

[24] "Global Trends: Forced Displacement in 2016," UNHCR; http://www.unhcr.org/globaltrends2016/.

[25] Filippo Grandi, "Syria has changed the way we respond to refugees. Here's how," *World Economic Forum*, 18 May 2017; https://www.weforum.org/agenda/2017/05/syria-changed-our-response-to-refugees/.

[26] Michael Talhami and Mark Zeitoun, "The impact of explosive weapons on urban services: Direct and reverberating effects across space and time." *International Review of the Red Cross (IRRC)*, No. 901, 11 April 2017; https://www.icrc.org/en/international-review/article/impact-explosive-weapons-urban-services-direct-and-reverberating.

[27] "Life in War Zones Remains Grim, with Cities Turned into Death Traps, Civilian Suffering 'Pushed to the Limits', Secretary-General Tells Security Council," Security Council, 7951st Meeting (AM) (SC/12841). New York: United Nations, 25 May 2017; https://www.un.org/press/en/2017/sc12841.doc.htm.

[28] Guha-Sapir, Debarati et al, "Patterns of civilian and child deaths due to war-related violence in Syria: a comparative analysis from the Violation Documentation Center dataset, 2011–16." *The Lancet (Global Health)*, Vol. 6, Issue 1, 6 December 2017; https://doi.org/10.1016/S2214-109X(17)30469-2 /https://www.thelancet.com/journals/langlo/article/PIIS2214-109X(17)30469-2/fulltext.

[29] Stephanie Nebehay, "Urban Warfare Takes Heavy Civilian Toll in Syria, Iraq, Yemen: ICRC." *U.S. News & World Report* (via Reuters), 14 June 2017; https://www.usnews.com/news/world/articles/2017-06-14/urban-warfare-takes-heavy-civilian-toll-in-syria-iraq-yemen-icrc.

[30] *I saw my city die: A special report of the International Committee of the Red Cross.* Geneva; ICRC, n.d.; http://redcross.michiko.design.

[31] Robert Muggah, "Counting Conflict Deaths: Options for SDG 16.1 (Sustainable Development Goal 16). Rio de Janeiro: Igarapé Institute, October 2015; https://igarape.org.br/wp-content/uploads/2015/10/counting-conflict-deaths-muggah-2015.pdf.

[32] Colin D. Mathers and Dejan Loncar, "Updated projections of global mortality and burden of disease, 2002-2030: data sources, methods and results" *Evidence and Information for Policy Working Paper.* World Health Organization, October 2005; http://www.who.int/healthinfo/statistics/bodprojectionspaper.pdf.

[33] *Uppsala Conflict Database Program (UCDP).* Uppsala, Sweden: Uppsala University; http://ucdp.uu.se.

[34] *Urban Social Disorder v2.* Oslo: Peace Research Institute Oslo (PRIO); https://www.prio.org/Data/Armed-Conflict/Urban-Social-Disorder/.

[35] "10,204 Civilians Killed in Syria in 2017: Including 569 Civilians in December. *Syrian Network for Human Rights*, 1 January 2017; http://sn4hr.org/blog/2018/01/01/50220/.

[36] Ibid.

[37] "Documented civilian deaths form violence." *Iraq Body Count*, 2003-2018; https://www.iraqbodycount.org/database/.

[38]   Dave Mosher and Skye Gould, "How likely are foreign terrorists to kill Americans? The odds may surprise you." *Business Insider UK*, 1 February 2017; http://uk.businessinsider.com/death-risk-statistics-terrorism-disease-accidents-2017-1?r=US&IR=T.

[39]   *Global Terrorism Database* (GTD).

[40]   Ibid. (GTD).

[41]   *Homicide Monitor*, Rio de Janeiro: Igarapé Institute; http://homicide.igarape.org.br.

[42]   Ibid.

[43]   Ibid.

[44]   Carlos J. Vilalta, "Global Trends and Projections of Homicidal Violence: 2000 to 2030." *Homicide Monitor*, Rio de Janeiro: Igarapé Institute, 26 November 2015; https://igarape.org.br/en/homicide-dispatch-2/.

[45]   "Revisiting the world's most violent cities." *The Economist*, 30 March 2016; https://www.economist.com/graphic-detail/2016/03/30/revisiting-the-worlds-most-violent-cities.

Chapter 49

Surrounded, Yet Unaware: Achieving Isolation in Future Urban Terrain

Ryan Orsini

First Published 30 May 2018

Future operating environments project a rapid increase of contested urban space and technological connectedness providing a convergence of threat capability for tactical commanders to negotiate. This article identifies future complications in achieving physical and psychological isolation, which both historically and doctrinally are so essential to successfully achieving military objectives in urban terrain. Furthermore, this article outlines tactical leader application of a new urban operational framework to understand and achieve both physical and psychological isolation in this future environment.

The Urban Terrain Focus

David Kilcullen's *Out of the Mountains* identified four key worldwide megatrends—urbanization, population growth, littoralization, and connectedness—that will place overwhelming demands on scarce city and country resources, thereby increasing the likelihood and difficulty of conflict in urban areas.[1] In this future environment, US ground forces are likely to see employment across and below the threshold of armed conflict from humanitarian disaster relief and peace support to great power conflict. This likelihood is reflected in US Army Chief of Staff GEN Milley's 2016 AUSA Conference statement "In the future, I can say with very high degrees of confidence, the American Army is probably going to be fighting in urban areas."[2]

Multi-Domain Battle Concept codifies these conclusions. The December 2017 concept identified a future operating environment (OE) featuring staples of urban terrain: accelerating information technology; hybrid threats synchronizing conventional, irregular, criminal, and terrorist cells; increasing urban terrain convolution and global network collection.[3] Ground forces must prepare for this latent convergence of threat, complexity, and connectedness.

Our Focus Must be on Achieving Isolation in Urban Terrain

History and doctrine both point to isolation as the decisive operational effect in urban terrain. Lou DiMarco's *Concrete Hell* is a study of modern urban warfare. DiMarco writes that across the spectrum of conflict "the history of urban conflict makes plain that when the enemy is isolated then success follows."[4] *Concrete Hell* identifies the German Army's inability to isolate Soviet forces across the Volga as ultimately decisive in their loss of momentum and resulting entrapment. Further, he points to the Allies' isolation of Aachen as essential to city seizure while outnumbered 3:1. He attributes US success at Hue came only after the isolation of enemy elements from northern sanctuary and the innovative use of lethal mobile protective firepower with non-lethal TTPs such as CS gas to physically isolate one urban objective after another. Finally, DiMarco reports the success of French 10th Para Division's Quadrillage system in Algiers and 3rd ACR's clear, hold, and build strategy in Ramadi due to isolating threat groups from support physically and psychologically in stability operations.

These historical examples and future concepts of war ground the importance of isolation in current ground force doctrine. US Army and Marine Corps December 2017 joint publication ATP 3-06/MCTP 12-10B *Urban Operations* labels isolation as essential across the spectrum of Unified Land Operations. In the offense isolation disrupts the advantages of the urban defense labels and manipulates combatant maneuver.[5] Furthermore, in the defense "failure to prevent isolation of the urban area rapidly leads to the failure of the entire urban defense. Its importance cannot be overstated."[6]

Future war will stress the ability of leaders at all echelons to operate detached and create these isolative effects at increasingly lower echelons. The Multi-Domain Battle Concept describes a changing battlespace whereby strategic, operational, and tactical levels of war are compressed due to converging adversary capabilities that shorten commanders' decision cycles.[7] Unit leaders must be prepared to create these small effect windows on their own because they may find themselves operating with degraded capabilities without secured flanks.[8] Thus in future urban terrain leaders at all echelons must focus resources on creating pockets of isolation, regardless of objective size, to control the absolutely essential and be successful.

Defining the Problem and Components of the Solution

Isolation is "...a tactical mission task that requires a unit to seal off—both physically and psychologically—an enemy from sources of support, deny the enemy freedom of movement, and prevent the isolated enemy force from having contact with other enemy forces."[9] As a result, isolation is a two-part task, physical and psychological, that must adapt to the dynamics of both urban terrain and future conflict. As a result, we arrive at the following problem statement: how do ground leaders achieve isolation in urban terrain given increasingly complex OEs which creates a convergence of physical and psychological threat capability across the spectrum of conflict?

As the Army's Multi-Domain Battle Concept explains, components of this solution will include force posture, resilient formations, and convergence. Tactical formations will need proficiency in wide ranges of force posture to include forward deterrent presence, sustainable expeditionary capacity, and compatibility with partner forces. They will require resilience to operate interchangeably across domains and survive persistent enemy detection and contact. Finally, tactical units must be able to converge capabilities creating windows of advantage by synchronizing scarce resources in time, space, and purpose to overwhelm a threat.[10]

Achieving Physical Isolation for Tactical Leaders

The Challenge of Physical Isolation in Urban Terrain

Physical isolation begins with a fundamental understanding of urban terrain's ultimate physical challenge: the ubiquity of unfamiliar subsurface, intrasurface, and supersurface structures. From conventional subway and skyscraper to unconventional urban rubble and congested alleyways, the pervasiveness of four dimensional (4D) features makes terrain analysis difficult. Future conflict presents contested airspace and cyberspace domains. This includes threat air capability and reduced friendly access to satellite technology like GPS and image intelligence, thereby limiting many of the tools historically leveraged to overcome the urban terrain's challenges. Together this limits a tactical unit's operational reach resulting in compartmentalized efforts, canalized movement, attrited combat power, and degraded command and control (C2).

In this physical environment advantage goes to the actor that can best disaggregate, disperse, and re-aggregate repeatedly in synchronized force within the urban terrain. Disaggregation provides tactical units flexibility moving over complex terrain minimizing the problem of canalization. Dispersion provides the ability to control only the essential and bypass threats countering attrition. Finally re-aggregation gives the ability to synchronize efforts mitigating compartmentalization and C2 degradation. Given the ubiquity of urban terrain, operations will only be effective through an iterative process from urban objective to urban objective. Units spread across great distances must quickly orient, consolidate, and attack to limit susceptibility to emerging threats within the urban terrain. This requires cycles of disaggregation, dispersion, and re-aggregation.

New Operational Framework for Urban Terrain: The Breach Mindset

> **OPERATIONALIZING THE BREACH MINDSET OPERATIONAL FRAMEWORK IN URBAN TERRAIN**
> NON-COURSE OF ACTION SPECIFIC (OFFENSE/DEFENSE/STABILITY) KEY TASK #1
>
> Continually be ready to breach—assess and set conditions in multiple domains with adapted SOSRA MINFOR (physical)

Facing these emergent urban challenges and opportunities, formations require a new operational framework. These are cognitive tools used to visualize and direct the allocation of combat power.[11] A new operational framework to achieve isolation is the breach mindset. Urban terrain's complexities form a seemingly endless cumulative obstacle offering threats both continuously and precipitously over time. To overcome this obstacle, tactical units must be able to prioritize and control only the essential and quickly disaggregate, disperse, and re-aggregate to mass effects and gain isolation. As a result, we must continually breach or be ready to breach. The minimum force guideline is a vital piece of the commander's intent. Fortunately, these are tactics our fighting force knows. In the breach mindset, leaders use the doctrinal acronym SOSRA (suppress, obscure, secure, reduce, assault) to iteratively evaluate minimum force. This sets conditions against the 4D and multi-domain threat wherever they find themselves in the spectrum of conflict: in the offense, defense, or stability. Tactical leaders use the SOSRA minimum force mental model to set isolative conditions prior to clearing a room, initiating an engagement area, or starting a street level engagement in a crowded market. This drives troops to consolidate based on situation and requirement, rather than organic structure or hardened courses of action. Each objective has a minimum force requirement to set conditions for attack initiation. As long as the tactical conditions are set the ground tactical plan begins in an iterative process as more objectives are seized and new resources arrive.

Creating Windows of Physical Isolation

Leaders can enable this urban operational framework through certain tactics, techniques, and procedures (TTPs) focused on infiltration, exfiltration, communications and enablers to create small windows of physical isolation. First, effective graphical control measures such as assembly area, axis of advance, attack position, assault position, and direction of attack enables disciplined initiative in the movement and assembly of men, weapons, and equipment (MWE) as units disaggregate, disperse, and re-aggregate within urban terrain through iterative urban objectives. Units can designate critical points to re-aggregate in successive infiltration and exfiltration movements around their decentralized movement. Critically, these control measures nest with anticipated friendly, enemy, or civilian reactions to physical isolation to account for the iterative processes in both the offense and defense.[12] Finally, formations employ flexibility in infiltration and exfiltration through task organization or cross training to create a mobility or counter-mobility advantage to create or deny surface, intra-surface, and subsurface avenues of approach.[13]

Effective communications planning also enables the breach mindset. Units create redundant communications with planned internal retransmission nodes as well as predictable leader placement at designated critical points guiding MWE. Furthermore, leaders achieve effective communications with a shared operating graphic ready for the expansive urban landscape. Overlay techniques such as the British military's DOT map combine a simple letter and color scheme to quickly orient a force over a wide area, expanding understanding across a large area where an American-style grid reference graphic is insufficient. Finally, units utilize graduated response matrices such as those detailed in the US Army ATP 3-39.33 Civil Disturbance to provide a decentralized collective escalation of force based on crowd threat assessment, giving more tactical options for physical isolation given collateral damage risk.

Finally, leaders must carefully manage their enablers within the breach mindset. Urban conflict consistently requires combined arms integration from echeloned ground and aerial fires. This creates redundant sensor to shooter capabilities needed for adequate suppression and maneuver.[14] This requires proficiency in a training environment. Ground units without organic armor such as Army IBCTs can seek interoperability opportunities with local armored National Guard elements. Similarly, units should seek out opportunities with short range air defense artillery elements and cyber-electromagnetic activities teams to prepare for ground force multi-domain capability. Furthermore, future conflict particularly with competitive powers will bring partner nation operations possibly on shared encrypted communications. This force integration requires thorough rehearsals over shared communications platforms using easily translatable pro-words. A leader's plan must be simply planned and well-rehearsed to allow combined small units to meet on a third successive urban objective and quickly establish a SORSA-based minimum force to achieve physical isolation.

OPERATIONALIZING THE BREACH MINDSET OPERATIONAL FRAMEWORK IN URBAN TERRAIN
NON-COURSE OF ACTION SPECIFIC (OFFENSE/DEFENSE/STABILITY) KEY TASK #2
Use flexible control measures to facilitate iterative disaggregation, dispersion and aggregation of MWE (physical)

In future four-dimensional urban terrain competitive in multiple domains the physical advantage goes to the actor that can best disaggregate, disperse, and re-aggregate repeatedly in synchronized force. Tactical leaders can optimize their physical isolative effect against this converged urban obstacle and creative windows of advantage by leveraging a new urban operational framework focusing on a shared breach mindset.

Achieving Psychological Isolation for Tactical Leaders

The Challenge of Psychological Isolation in Urban Terrain

Psychological isolation begins with the recognition of urban terrain's ultimate psychological challenge: ground forces lack the technical combat power and authorities necessary to effectively shape the speed of human interaction due to internet technology (IT) proliferation as well as competitors' cyberspace domain proficiency. IT proliferation benefits both general consumer and competitor alike with communication devices that outpace ground force capability in terms of weight, range, bandwidth, speed, innovation rate, encryption, and price per unit. IT proliferation connects information with the power of social groups to streamline both slow, large scale movements and fast, small scale action. This presents a powerful incentive to manipulate the information a community absorbs—influencing the information's distribution and content to serve an actor's own interests. Thus, if the dominant effect in future urban terrain is isolation and the physical advantage belongs to can best repeated disaggregation, dispersion, and re-aggregation cycles, then the psychological advantage goes to the actor that can manipulate information.[15]

However, ground forces lack the technical combat power and authorities necessary to manipulate information. Through enablers, ground forces have the capacity to jam utilities or combatant communications. However, these resources are scarce and can result in excessive damage to city systems for limited tactical gain. As a result, the tactical unit's ability to psychologically isolate in an era of pervasive connectivity is likely limited to the seconds of organic suppression and obscuration on the urban objective. This provides ample opportunity for competitor psychological connection supporting C2 and information operations before, during, and after contact. This gap is in part due to task organization. The current ground force is still modeled after Air-Land Battle, not yet Multi Domain Battle.[16] By placing fire supporters and air space coordinators down to the platoon level our ground forces can lethally synchronize ground and air-delivered fires. However, with information and civil affairs coordinators at the brigade level, our attempts at psychological isolation fail due to lack of contextual understanding and centralized decision making. As a result, ground forces in Iraq and Afghanistan continually ceded psychological momentum to our adversary. This negative trend will likely continue until tactical units at the battalion and below are prepared and authorized to effectively act within the information domain.

Furthermore, ground forces find themselves in OEs with competitors that are doctrinally and materially equipped to manipulate information in the cyber domain. Unlike our ground force, these potential adversaries long recognized its debilitating psychological effect across the conflict spectrum. The Russian Gerasimov Doctrine and the Chinese 2025 Strategic Plan outline efforts to achieve social control through the cyber domain.[17] Russia's 2014 Ukraine intervention featured synchronized ground maneuver with a larger cyber campaign of disinformation, economic manipulation, and intimidation effectively fixing Ukrainian forces at the tactical level.[18] The Russian NotPetya cyber-attack in June 2017 crippled Ukrainian critical infrastructure, select corporations, and private citizens' computers in mass.[19] Our competitors, both near-peer and irregular, consistently show proficiency, intent, and low-risk threshold to achieve local social control and psychological isolation by manipulating information. This is a staggering discrepancy in the focus, authorities, and capability to manipulate information between our ground force and potential adversaries.

Remaining Competitive by Understanding Information Manipulation

Faced with IT proliferation and a competitive information cyber domain with limited and restricted organic multi-domain capability, tactical units must first put a renewed emphasis on understanding the information environment to maximize the available isolative effect. While outgunned psychologically, ground force understanding of information manipulation is the first irreplaceable step to remain competitive in the information environment and flexible enough to create needed windows of isolation advantage.

Understanding information manipulation requires analysis of how an interconnected community finds, consumes, and reacts to information. In this new competitive information environment, the typical PMESII-ASCOPE crosswalk of civilian analysis is insufficient. However, Wardle and Derakhsan's Information Disorder framework is such an analytic tool. They stratify information into three types known as mis-information, dis-information, and mal-information. Dis-information is false and deliberately distributed to cause harm to an intended target. Mis-information is false but created with unknowing intent. Finally, mal-information is true, but deliberately distributed to cause harm to an intended target. By distinguishing between true and false as well as harmful and peaceful we can understand the influence and reaction of competitors in the environment.[20] This framework also allows tactical leaders to look critically at our own balance of information distribution efforts.

Wardle and Derakhsan also analyze the three elements of information: the agent who creates and distributes, the message which has particularly formatted information, and the interpreter who receives, interprets and takes action. This framework provides an intimate understanding of emotional responses, cultural identity, and existing world view that are so powerful in creating or manipulating information.[21] However it also provides tactical leaders awareness of important transmission mechanisms such as key mediums, vulnerabilities, and effects. This analysis reveals important pockets of resistance and vulnerability in the ground or cyber domain such as a leader or idea that has magnified effect within the community for subsequent tactical targeting to disrupt, destroy, or bypass.

This requirement to understand information networks is fundamental to remain competitive in the urban IO environment given limited organic capability. Since we can no longer prevent information manipulation, we must get better at harnessing its energy and understanding its tendencies. Ongoing information manipulation within the OE is the psychological obstacle that we continually breach, knowingly or unknowingly, in urban terrain from direct action to peace support operations. By understanding local contexts of information manipulation, leaders can achieve two critical effects. First, they can anticipate overly impactful resources and ideas either vulnerable to or under the influence of competitors to direct scarce psychological resources against, thereby demoralizing the enemy. Instead of reacting to the destruction of a community's shipping infrastructure from cyber-attack, we can preposition and reorient forces to deter its occurrence. Second, this understanding can shape higher headquarters' willingness to release assets and approve effects as targets are refined decreasing risk to macro city systems. For example, instead of knocking out a neighborhood's electricity, we can temporarily prevent its access to a particular YouTube channel, disrupting information manipulation. As a result, units are in better position to quickly identify information effects within the urban terrain's system and disrupt competitors' multi-domain actions.

> **OPERATIONALIZING THE BREACH MINDSET OPERATIONAL FRAMEWORK IN URBAN TERRAIN**
> NON-COURSE OF ACTION SPECIFIC (OFFENSE/DEFENSE/STABILITY) KEY TASK #3
>
> Remain competitive in the IO environment by understanding the manipulation of information (psychological)

Creating Windows of Psychological Isolation

Armed with an understanding of local information manipulation, leaders can execute targeted psychological disruption and exploitation supporting urban terrain's breach mindset operational framework. These windows of psychological isolation are not limited to ground, air, and cyber domains. Rather, tactical units match organic capability—platoon leaders, blocking positions, or host nation partners—to best harness the desired effect. These efforts are decentralized to tactical units, synchronized as technical triggers complementing the tactical maneuver, and tailored to the tempo of the conflict. Our psychological disruption and exploitation can help set conditions to achieve or prevent isolation in urban terrain.

Psychological disruption supports the typical "suppression" of the breach mindset's SOSRA minimum force requirement to simplify the complex tactical problem at hand. This suppression should focus on the key elements of competitor infiltration, exfiltration, communications, and enablers to best compliment physical isolation. For instance, leaders can achieve psychological disruption over infiltration and exfiltration by directing civilians over known mediums along advantageous dispersal routes to lower collateral damage. Leaders psychologically disrupt communications by denying identified key mediums of support such as important social media channels during tactical operations or intermittently over time. Finally, units can psychologically disrupt competitor enablers denying access to important support nodes—such as an NGO or neighborhood—by leveraging local engagement or proper positioning of blocking positions and traffic control points to seal them off.

OPERATIONALIZING THE BREACH MINDSET OPERATIONAL FRAMEWORK IN URBAN TERRAIN
NON-COURSE OF ACTION SPECIFIC (OFFENSE/DEFENSE/STABILITY) KEY TASK #4

Utilize decentralized mal-information and dis-information to enable suppression and assault (psychological)

Psychological exploitation supports the breach mindset's SOSRA "assault" minimum force requirement to intensify the effect and enable future operations. Units utilize targeted mal-information and dis-information to achieve psychological exploitation in both the ground and cyber domains. Mal-information is relayed over known powerful information mediums and nested with an understanding of key cultural ideas, harnessing the truth in real time to support ground maneuver. For example, units can release tailored battle damage assessments and discovered cultural norm violations by competitors. Mal-information is especially important during stability and peace support phases due to its impact on important local and regional public opinion. Tactical units utilize targeted dis-information to disguise friendly efforts or cause confusion within critical competitor nodes when there is military necessity for surprise. Enabled by an understanding of information manipulation, units can overcome IT proliferation and mitigate competitor cyber proficiency, setting conditions to achieve or disrupt psychological isolation through targeted use of mal- and dis-information.

Facing Tomorrow's Problem Today

Future urban conflict presents a convergence of threat capability that tactical leaders must negotiate. War never waits for militaries to be ready and the next one will be no different. Future urban conflict will require not just high proficiency in combined arms maneuver the across the conflict spectrum. It will require proficiency and authorizations across domains including space and cyber to include information manipulation—at echelons below brigade. Until the ground force generates a framework for employing needed capabilities to combat these changes, tactical leaders will require a renewed operational framework—the breach mindset—to achieve or prevent physical and psychological isolation in urban terrain.

The views expressed in this article are those of the author and do not reflect the official policy or position of the Department of the Army, Department of Defense, or the US Government.

Bibliography

Stefan J., Banach. "Virtual War—A Revolution in Human Affairs." *Small Wars Journal.* February 2, 2018. http://smallwarsjournal. com/jrnl/art/virtual-war-revolution-human-affairs (accessed May 16, 2018).

Berzins, Janis. "Russia's New Generation Warfare in Ukraine." National Defense Academy of Latvia Center for Strategic and Strategic Research. April 2014. http://www.naa.mil.lv/~/media/NAA/ AZPC/Publikacijas/PP%2002-2014.ashx_(accessed May 16, 2018).

DiMarco, Louis. *Concrete Hell: Urban Warfare from Stalingrad to Iraq.* Oxford: Osprey Group, 2012.

Kilcullen, David. *Out of the Mountains: The Coming Age of the Urban Guerrilla*. New York: Oxford University Press, 2013.

Maxwell, David. "David Maxwell on Unconventional Warfare." *The Security Studies Podcast*. Podcast audio, November 7, 2016. https://itunes.apple.com/us/podcast/the-security-studies-podcast/id1110393903?mt=2.

Perkins, David. "Multi-Domain Battle." US Army TRADOC. October 7, 2017. https://www.youtube.com/watch?v=nfOgPayfATo&index=9&list=PLiX4QSJW9_Q9-evZSvunqY3dMrcgSCJII (accessed May 16, 2018).

Tan, Michelle. "Army Chief: Soldiers Must Be Ready To Fight in Megacities." *Defense News*. October 5, 2016. https://www.defensenews.com/digital-show-dailies/ausa/2016/10/05/army-chief-soldiers-must-be-ready-to-fight-in-megacities/ (accessed May 16, 2018).

U.S. Army. *Doctrine Primer*. Department of the Army. ADP 1-01. Washington, D.C.: Government Printing Office, 2014), 4-8.

U.S. Army. *Multi-Domain Battle: Evolution of Combined Arms for the 21st Century*. Department of the Army. Washington, D.C.: Government Printing Office, 2017.

U.S. Army. *Terms and Military Symbols*. Department of the Army. ADRP 1-02. Washington, D.C.: Government Printing Office, 2016.

U.S. Army. *Urban Operations*. Department of the Army. ATP 3-06. Washington, D.C.: Government Printing Office, 2017.

Volz, Dustin and Young, Sarah. "White House Blames Russia for Reckless NotPetya Cyber Attack." *Reuters Cyber Risk*. February 15, 2018. https://www.reuters.com/article/us-britain-russia-cyber-usa/white-house-blames-russia-for-reckless-notpetya-cyber-attack-idUSKCN1FZ2UJ (accessed May 16, 2018).

Wardle, Claire and Hossein Derakhsan. "Information Disorder." Council of Europe. October 2017. https://rm.coe.int/information-disorder-toward-an-interdisciplinary-framework-for-researc/168076277c_(accessed May 16, 2018).

Small Wars Journal

End Notes

[1] David Kilcullen, *Out of the Mountains: The Coming Age of the Urban Guerrilla* (New York: Oxford University Press, 2013), 25.

[2] Michelle Tan, "Army Chief: Soldiers Must Be Ready To Fight in Megacities," *Defense News*, October 5, 2016, https://www.defensenews.com/digital-show-dailies/ausa/2016/10/05/army-chief-soldiers-must-be-ready-to-fight-in-megacities/__(accessed May 16, 2018), in paragraph 9.

[3] U.S. Army, *Multi-Domain Battle: Evolution of Combined Arms for the 21st Century* (Washington, D.C.: Government Printing Office, 2017), 5.

[4] Louis DiMarco, *Concrete Hell: Urban Warfare from Stalingrad to Iraq* (Oxford: Osprey Group, 2012), 7.

[5] U.S. Army, *Urban Operations*, ATP 3-06 (Washington, D.C.: Government Printing Office, 2017), 4-14.

[6] U.S. Army, *Urban Operations*, ATP 3-06 (Washington, D.C.: Government Printing Office, 2017), 5-7.

[7] *Multi-Domain Battle: Evolution of Combined Arms for the 21st Century*, 8.

[8] Ibid, 35.

[9] U.S. Army, *Terms and Military Symbols*, ADRP 1-02 Washington, D.C.: Government Printing Office, 2017), 1-33.

[10] *Multi-Domain Battle: Evolution of Combined Arms for the 21st Century*, 23-25.

[11] U.S. Army, *Doctrine* Primer, ADP 1-01 (Washington, D.C.: Government Printing Office, 2014), 4-8.

[12] *Urban Operations*, 5-7.

[13] Ibid, 5-8.

[14] *Urban Operations*, 4-15.

[15] David Maxwell, "David Maxwell on Unconventional Warfare," *The Security Studies Podcast*, Podcast audio, November 7, 2016, https://itunes.apple.com/us/podcast/the-security-studies-podcast/id1110393903?mt=2.

[16] David Perkins, "Multi-Domain Battle," *US Army TRADOC*, October 7, 2017, https://www.youtube.com/watch?v=nfOgPayfATo&index=9&list=PLiX4QSJW9_Q9-evZSvunqY3dMrcgSCJII (accessed May 16, 2018), 9:00.

[17] Stefan Banach, "Virtual War—A Revolution in Human Affairs," *Small Wars Journal*, February 2, 2018, http://smallwarsjournal.com/jrnl/art/virtual-war-revolution-human-affairs (accessed May 16, 2018), in paragraph 16.

[18] Janis Berzins, "Russia's New Generation Warfare in Ukraine," National Defense Academy of Latvia Center for Strategic and Strategic Research, April, 2014, http://www.naa.mil.lv/~/media/NAA/AZPC/Publikacijas/PP%2002-2014.ashx (accessed May 16, 2018), 4.

[19] Dustin Volz and Sarah Young, "White House Blames Russia for Reckless NotPetya Cyber Attack," *Reuters Cyber Risk*, February 15, 2018, https://www.reuters.com/article/us-britain-russia-cyber-usa/white-house-blames-russia-for-reckless-notpetya-cyber-attack-idUSKCN1FZ2UJ (accessed May 16, 2018).

[20] Claire Wardle and Hossein Derakhsan, "Information Disorder," Council of Europe, October 2017, https://rm.coe.int/information-disorder-toward-an-interdisciplinary-framework-for-researc/168076277c (accessed May 16, 2018), 21-22.

[21] Ibid, 23-29.

Postscript

Cities in the Crossfire:
The Global Rise of Urban Violence

Margarita Konaev

Washington, District of Columbia

June 2018

The locus of violence is shifting to cities.[1] Over the last five years alone, cities such as Mosul, Aleppo, and Raqqa were largely destroyed in high-intensity urban warfare between conventional state military forces and powerful non-state groups. ISIS-linked terrorist groups and lone wolf attackers, as well as groups like Boko Haram and Al-Shabaab have orchestrated sophisticated, mass-casualties urban terrorism campaigns across major European and African cities. Even historically rural insurgencies like the Taliban and the Kurdish Workers' Party (PKK) in Turkey have shifted their strategy from rural guerilla warfare to urban-based operations and attacks.[2] Meanwhile in Latin America and the Caribbean, urban violence related to organized crime and drug trafficking has at times been as deadly as war-time violence in some conflict-affected countries.[3]

The rise in urban violence and conflict, then, is a global phenomenon.

Insurgent groups, terrorists, criminal gangs, narco-traffickers, and transnational organized crime syndicates differ a great deal in their motives, goals, capabilities, and tactics. But it is not a coincidence that these different violent actors are increasingly choosing to target and fight in cities.

For one, whether their motives are political, ideological, religious, or economic, cities offer violent groups an array of lucrative, high-visibility soft targets—airports, metro stations, shopping malls, hotels, concert halls, restaurants, and religious sites—all endowed with practical and symbolic importance. Asymmetric warfare is constantly evolving in response to emerging technologies, and advances in surveillance techniques and aerial detection capabilities have also made the classic rural guerilla warfare settings of dense jungles and remote mountain hideouts far less safe for violent non-state groups.[4] In cities, however, these militants can more easily blend into the local civilian population and use the city's complex and dense terrain for cover and concealment.

At the most basic level, however, this global rise in urban violence and conflict is fueled by rapid urbanization and population growth, rising inequality, and increasingly unstable political conditions in developing countries. Cities such as Lagos, Johannesburg, Kinshasa, and Karachi have grown and expanded in an unprecedented rate. But national economies and governments have not kept up with the growing demand for public services and infrastructure. In many such areas, urban poverty, youth unemployment, social and economic marginalization, poor governance and weak rule of law have opened a space for violent non-state actors to compete for political power and patronage, and for criminal networks to gain ground, enabling the flow of illicit drugs, arms, and money.[5]

As different forms of violence increasingly collide in cities, governments and security forces are struggling to keep up. Police forces, typically the first line of defense against rising rates of urban violence, are often underfunded, understaffed, and can quickly become overwhelmed when faced with well-equipped and zealous adversaries. And in countries plagued by transnational organized crime and drug trafficking, such as Brazil, El Salvador, Honduras, and Mexico, they also tend to be crippled by corruption and inefficiency, and have a dark record of human rights abuses.

At the same time, most conventional state militaries are simply not trained, organized, or equipped to operate in cities. Even technologically advanced and highly professionalized militaries such as those of the United States and leading NATO countries still encounter serious challenges in urban warfare, including the movement and maneuver of large forces and heavy equipment, the ability to use firepower and employ precision weapons effectively, collect intelligence, and communicate between and within units. The legal and moral imperatives to protect civilians caught in the crossfire and to minimize damage to critical urban infrastructure can also create difficult tradeoffs for commanders with respect to resource allocation, targeting decisions, and limitations on fire support to friendly forces.[6]

Moreover, the presence of the media in urban conflict zones and the ubiquitous, Internet-enabled access to social media effectively reduce the ability of state forces to control the information environment and shape public opinion. Negative media coverage then, especially of civilian deaths, can erode domestic and international support for the forces on the ground, which can hurt morale, lead to lapses in discipline, and undermine the mission as a whole. Taken together, it is unsurprising that the consensus among military decision-makers has remained largely unchanged since nearly 2,500 years ago, the ancient Chinese military strategist Sun Tzu urged to avoid urban warfare unless absolutely necessary, as a last resort.[7]

Looking to the future, however, there is little doubt that high intensity urban warfare, terrorism, crime and drug-related lethal violence, as well as social and political unrest will increasingly intersect, combine, and overlap in cities, posing a great risk to the lives and livelihoods of civilians. Because the nature and scope of urban violence and conflict varies significantly across different cities, countries, and regions, policy solutions must remain highly responsive to local context and conditions. Nonetheless, a common thread running through the different policy options is the need for time-sensitive, comprehensive, and multi-sectoral approaches.

First, with respect to timing, protracted social or political conflicts tend to follow a determinable cycle, and each phase of the conflict presents an opportunity for a particular type of intervention. Considering the destructive impact of urban conflict, a strong emphasis on preventive measures and the development and deployment of early-warning systems is critical.[8] The fall of Mosul, for example, was preceded by months of ISIS terrorist attacks targeting the Iraqi Army troops, and federal and local police forces in the city. At such critical junctures, a localized, focused response providing kinetic and non-kinetic support to urban security forces and an enhanced counterterrorism posture may help avert a full-scale war.

Second, the root causes of violence in urban areas are multifaceted, complex, and effectively immune to unidimensional solutions. Despite this, countries suffering from high rates of urban violence linked to organized crime and drug-trafficking, such as Brazil and Mexico, are increasingly using heavily armed military units to pacify restive neighborhoods and slums where the gangs and cartels have taken control.[9] In doing so, they repeatedly discover that a myopic focus on the military and security dimensions can and often does backfire.[10] In fact, human rights groups and researchers have documented an increase in violence in areas in Mexico where the military was sent to fight the cartels.[11]

In contrast, lessons from Medellín in Colombia, once one of the world's most violent cities, illustrate the potential of holistic strategies attuned to local needs in the marginalized urban slums. In addition to increased security and police presence aimed at dismantling the violent drug cartels, the local city government substantially increased investment in public services in the poorer areas of the city, including changes to transportation networks and infrastructure aimed at integrating these areas into the broader urban society, thereby increasing opportunities for education and employment. Although criminal gangs still engage in extortion, car theft, and drug trafficking, homicide rates in Medellín have declined enormously and there has been a marked improvement in certain socioeconomic conditions for the city's poor communities.[12]

In closing, multifaceted challenges call for timely, comprehensive and coordinated responses from states, international organizations, NGOs, and civil society. The political, financial, bureaucratic, and socio-cultural obstacles to effective policy interventions designed to prevent, contain, reduce, and recover from urban violence and conflict are substantial. But they are not insurmountable.

Ultimately, the primary takeaway is fairly straightforward: as the world's urban population continues to grow, the future of global security will be determined by what happens in cities.

Notes

[1] OECD. *States of Fragility 2016: Understanding Violence.* Paris: The Organisation for Economic Co-operation and Development (OECD Publishing), 2016: 51 http://dx.doi. org/10.1787/9789264267213-en.

[2] Margarita Konaev and Burak Kadercan. "Old Dogs, New Tricks: Urban Warfare in Turkey's War with the PKK." *War on the Rocks.* 3 January 2018, https://warontherocks.com/2018/01/ old-dogs-new-tricks-urban-warfare-turkeys-war-pkk/.

[3] Christopher Woody, "These were the 50 most violent cities in the world in 2017." *Business Insider.* 6 March 2018, http://www. businessinsider.com/most-violent-cities-in-the-world-2018-3.

[4] David Kilcullen, "Urban Combat: Cities Are Sponges That Soak Up Troops." *The Cipher Brief.* 22 October 2017, https://www.thecipherbrief.com /urban-combat-cities-are-sponges-that-soak-up-troops.

[5] Clionadh Raleigh, "Urban Violence Patterns Across African States." *International Studies Review.* Vol. 17, Issue 1, 1 March 2015: 90-106, https://doi.org/10.1111/misr.12206.

Small Wars Journal

[6]   Headquarters, Department of the Army. "Urban Operations." ATP 3-06 / MCTP 12-10B, 7 December 2017, https://fas.org/irp/doddir/army/atp3_06.pdf.

[7]   Sun Tzu, *The Art of War*, Samuel B Griffith, trans. Oxford: Oxford University Press, 1971.

[8]   Antônio Sampaio, "Before and after urban warfare: Conflict prevention and transitions in cities." *International Review of the Red Cross*. Vol. 98, Iss. 901, April 2016: 71-95, https://www.cambridge.org/core/journals/international-review-of-the-red-cross/article/div-classtitlebefore-and-after-urban-warfare-conflict-prevention-and-transitions-in-citiesdiv/9CAA6C6AAAD7ED15C2DAEA2822734D7E.

[9]   Vanda Felbab-Brown, "Bringing the State to the Slum: Confronting Organized Crime and Urban Violence in Latin America: Lessons for Law Enforcement and Policymakers." *Brookings*. 5 December 2011, https://www.brookings.edu/research/bringing-the-state-to-the-slum-confronting-organized-crime-and-urban-violence-in-latin-america/.

[10]   David Pion-Berlin and Miguel Carreras, "Armed Force, Police and Crime-fighting in Latin America," *Journal of Politics in Latin America*. Vol. 9, No.3, 2017, p. 3-26, https://journals.sub.uni-hamburg.de/giga/jpla/article/view/1072.

[11]   Human Rights Watch, *Neither Rights Nor Security: Killings, Torture, and Disappearances in Mexico's "War on Drugs."* 9 November 2011, https://www.hrw.org/report/2011/11/09/neither-rights-nor-security/killings-torture-and-disappearances-mexicos-war-drugs#page and Valeria Espinosa and Donald B. Rubin, "Did the Military Intervention in the Mexican Drug War Increase Violence?" *The American Statistician*. Vol. 69, Issue 1, 2015: 17-27, DOI: 10.1080/00031305.2014.965796

[12]   Caroline Doyle, "Explaining Patterns of Urban Violence in Medellin, Colombia." *Laws*. Vol. 5, Issue 1:3, https://doi.org/10.3390/laws5010003.

Afterword

Urban Operations: Meeting Challenges, Seizing Opportunities, Improving the Approach

Russell W. Glenn

Williamsburg, Virginia

July 2018

The breadth of topics covered by the previous essays makes clear the scope and nature of urban operations opportunities and challenges. Views of undertakings in the world's most densely populated regions unfortunately tend to over-focus on the latter to the neglect of the former. Similarly, it has historically been the physical infrastructure—buildings; streets; bridges; power, water, and waste disposal facilities; and more—rather than the population that stakes first claim on attentions as armed forces ready for missions in such terrain. These are mistakes. Virtually every individual in a city is a potential source of information: a two-eyed, two-eared "sensor" in militaryspeak, albeit one who needs to be convinced of the value they could offer to fellow urban residents and themselves. They are often also sources of other support. Ultimately, they are all but inevitably the reason a coalition deploys to a given city.

In this regard, I often find it valuable to return to a construct originated by colleague and co-author Jamison Jo Medby nearly two decades ago. Her "continuum of relative interests" modified the long-oversimplified assessment of a population's consisting of but three primary groups when viewed from the perspective of a combatant or other authority: adversaries, allies, and neutrals. Her addition of two more categories sacrifices little of the traditional depiction's simplicity while adding much valuable nuance, a richness that grows as one allows the mind to explore the intricacies of the continuum's implications. (See figure.)

Adversary-Obstacle-Neutral-Accomplice-Ally

The continuum of relative interests[1]

The addition of "obstacle"—individuals or groups predisposed to assisting those competing with allies—and "accomplice"—others inclined to favor friendly authorities with their support—more clearly implies not a five-point spectrum but rather one with infinite gradations of potential collaboration. The operational implications, intelligence implications in particular, readily become evident during reflection. Among them:

- It is in opposing parties' interests to move individuals and groups toward their respective end of the continuum: to the right for allies, to the left for those in opposition. (Though the figure is linear, the concept also applies when there are multiple adversary, ally, or other interests competing for popular support.)
- We and our coalition partners should no more spend significant (if any) resources on trying to win over those at the extreme adversary end any more than a politician would waste efforts attempting to convince diehard members of an opposition party to cast a vote in his favor.
- Rather, the coalition's aid and services are better focused on individuals and collectives providing reasonable potential of

moving along the continuum in a direction favorable to the provider's objectives. Allies would therefore commit resources to factions falling somewhere to the right of "adversaries" in efforts to move them yet further in that direction.

- Yet those providing such resources are ill-advised to neglect others already favoring their "camp." An accomplice town or individual ally seeing a village with obstacle or neutral leanings benefiting from ally expenditures while getting none might logically see the wisdom of slipping leftward to reap such rewards.

- Considering a group of any sort as being of uniform persuasion makes no more sense than did the old model of adversary-neutral-ally. Urban areas are hyper-complex. It is largely their populations that makes them so. Virtually any organization will include individuals occupying various locations along the continuum. Recognizing this opens doors to undermining competitors from within or moving groups in a favorable direction via influencing potentially willing and particularly persuasive individuals within. Sun Tzu's advice regarding the wisdom of disrupting alliances pertains with citizen groups just as it does an enemy.

The essentiality of expanding a coalition

Partners will be essential to all but the most transient of successes during urban undertakings. Security operations in densely populated areas demand a comprehensive approach (also at times referred to as an inter-organizational approach). This brings together not only a single nation's military and other federal government resources, but also those of multinational federal representatives (including host-nation representatives in the case of international deployments), local and broader regional authorities (formal and informal), nongovernmental and inter-governmental organizations (NGOs and IGOs, respectively), and commercial private sector capabilities as appropriate.[2] This melding of assets is nowhere more vital than in the world's most populous urban areas where the number of coalition participants needed will be large and varied.

Essential though they are, expanding the number of operational partners complicates efforts to persuade members of an urban population. Consistent behaviors and messaging will be fundamental to successful inducement. Yet orchestrating (or at least loosely coordinating) coalition partners' actions and communications in the spirit of consistency is no easy task. Partners they might be, but objectives are far more likely similar than shared. Cooperation is often an expedient with a diminishing lifespan, particularly when success seems within reach.

Communications are sure to be further complicated by incompatible radio and other hardware. Cell phones seem the obvious solution, but a moment's thought reminds us that war and other disasters can render cellular coverage inoperable. Even when operational, chances are good that there will be need for secure communications whether or not a contingency features foes. Intercepting a call detailing the location of scarce necessities such as food or medicine would be a coup for criminal groups or others desperate for access. Language can present unforeseen and possibly tragic communication problems even when parties share a common tongue. Major General James Delk, field commander during the 1992 Los Angeles riots, related how two Compton police officers were fired on when they responded to a domestic dispute complaint. Helping the slightly wounded comrade escape further injury, his partner shouted "cover me" to the United States Marine Corps squad accompanying them on the call, intending that the military men be poised at the ready should the shooter attempt to engage a second time. The marines immediately opened suppressing fire, their over two hundred rounds fortunately not hitting the mother, father, or three children within as they sought to prevent any further gunfire from the house.[3] Same English phrase; quite different meanings. It is, however, the local expertise and other capabilities extant in such heterogeneous coalitions that offer advantages less varied organizations could never replicate.

The consequences of such misunderstandings reverberate more quickly in urban settings than elsewhere. The logic of the "butterfly effect" oft cited in conjunction with complexity theory is easier to envision in this environment. It asserts that small actions within a sensitive system can have disproportionately large consequences. The example frequently cited is one of a butterfly flapping its wings on one continent setting in motion a series of effects that results in severe weather on another. An urban area's population density and many means of communications make it easy to comprehend how such a phenomenon could come to be in that environment. Yet we need to recognize the danger in thinking this model applies only *internally* to a city system. Urban areas are systems in and of themselves. They are also subsystems, parts of larger local and often broader regional, national, and even worldwide systems. A coalition's actions have repercussions not only *within* an urban area, therefore, but potentially far *beyond* in addition. The transportation and economic effects of the September 11, 2001 attacks on New York and Washington, D.C. provide obvious examples. Tokyo provides another. Consider the possible knock-on effects of a major manmade or natural disaster within and beyond given that the megacity is government center for one of the world's most wealthy nations, home to some 30% of its population, place of employment for one of every ten workers in the country, and host to 80% of foreign companies in Japan.[4] The risk of far-reaching implications disruptive of coalition objectives are also apparent in the inadvertent 1999 bombing of the Chinese embassy in Belgrade by North Atlantic Treaty Organization coalition forces. Concentrations of traditional and social media in urban areas means even far less prominent activities can reverberate rapidly, widely, and influentially. In no other environment will the ripples from a decision by one of General Krulak's "strategic corporals" attain such reach at such speed.

Further implications

The above, no less than the many chapters preceding this, present those operating in urban areas with myriad hard truths...and no few opportunities to accompany them. The compartmented nature of urban environments and ubiquitous cover and concealment provided by structures suggests even organizations hesitant when it comes to working with the military will find it wise to cooperate to at least a minimal extent. Ensuring military forces know the whereabouts of their personnel will be crucial. Failure to do so exposes them to injury or death as unintentional victims during combat operations. It would be naïve to believe that these groups' leadership would not bear significant responsibility for such tragedies. This limited-extent participation benefits all parties in other ways as well. The scale of aid needed during and after urban disasters will exceed the capabilities of any one organization. Such was true in 2014 during Operation Protective Edge fighting in Gaza's densely populated terrain.[5] The International Committee of the Red Cross (ICRC) acted as an intermediary and supplemental aid provider for suffering Palestinians. Gazans in need dialed "101" (the equivalent of 911 in the U.S.) to connect with the Palestinian Red Crescent Society (PRCS). When the PRCS was unable to meet demand, it contacted local representatives of the ICRC who then turned to the Israel Defense Forces' Coordinator of Government Activities in the Territories, parent organization of that responsible for liaison between Palestinians and Israel Defense Forces (IDF) forces in these cases: the Civil Liaison Administration (CLA). CLA in turn coordinated with relevant IDF tactical units to reduce risk during PRCS or ICRC aid provider movement in the combat theater. Such coordination could unfortunately take up to twenty-four hours, however, possibly rendering mute the called-for assistance.

Practicing such coordination prior to hostilities is obviously desirable. Doing affords opportunities to establish mutually-agreeable procedures in addition to working out potential sources of friction and shortcuts. Coordination is considerably enhanced when aid providers agree to having a qualified third party take on responsibility for the provider-combatant interface, thus reducing the number of separate providers a combatant has to deal with separately and leaving it to the third party to deal with varying levels of individual provider administrative talent. Israeli representatives found the United Nations Relief and Works Agency (UNRWA) notably capable in this regard during Operation Protective Edge while some other organizations foundered.

Orchestrating coalition activities will be further hindered by limited line-of-sight (LOS); dispersion; inability to determine the location of friendly forces, enemy, and noncombatants; and inconsistent communications thanks to those LOS challenges; incompatible hardware; aforementioned language differences, and signals interference due to a plethora of transmitters. Mission command, "the practice of assigning a subordinate commander a mission without specifying how the mission is to be achieved," will prove beneficial, even essential, under these conditions.[6] Relevant characteristics include:

- A commander clearly articulating both mission and intent for his subordinates
- That commander individually adapting guidance given to subordinates based on (1) the subordinate's past performance, (2) commander evaluation of individual expertise, (3) the junior leader's experience relevant to the challenges at hand, and (4) the leader's familiarity with the subordinate, among other factors. Thus a long-trusted and proven junior familiar with a mission's implications and a senior's expectations will tend to receive less detailed guidance than one leading a unit recently attached and with whom the senior is thus less familiar.
- The senior checking on his subordinates to the extent necessary to ensure performance within the constraints of the mission and intent, then providing any further guidance deemed necessary without defaulting to overly detailed direction or centralized oversight.
- Subordinates also have responsibilities, responsibilities beyond merely executing the mission. Less senior leaders must keep

their commander informed to the extent feasible, thereby assisting him or her to gage whether the subordinate's efforts are as needed and determine how to most effectively allocate always-limited resources.

- Further, a subordinate's responsibilities also include understanding that seniors should check on those led. Such interactions are opportunities not only for the senior to confirm his command is on track, but also for subordinates to ask for additional guidance or resources should conditions demand. (Interestingly, this element has often proved poorly understood by junior leaders in both the United States and Australia, who tend to assume mission command is "fire and forget," i.e., that their seniors should simply provide mission and intent, then leave subordinates alone.)

These several points should make it apparent that mission command requires trust, insightful leaders, perceptive subordinates, and considerable practice. This is all the truer as commanders will frequently find it difficult to move quickly between unit locations in urban areas' compartmented terrain. Now the standard for Western militaries worldwide (albeit one practiced with mixed effectiveness), mission command is also familiar to better-led civilian organizations, to include the New York City police and fire departments. The larger the city, the greater the likelihood that this bounded decentralization will prove helpful to achieving coalition objectives. It is in these urban areas that one can find dramatic differences from neighborhood to neighborhood, differences that require fine-grained judgments impossible with more centralized oversight, judgments men and women intimately familiar with conditions on the street are therefore best able to make. Equipping leaders at these lower echelons with clear guidance and the confidence to exercise personal judgment within its bounds sets the stage for seizing opportunities otherwise more apt to be overlooked.

Seizing these opportunities will take many forms. Some cases will allow setting the conditions for persevering in combat; others will promote translating combat-won successes into lasting victories.

Looking beyond battlefield success should be a part of every commander's intent. Thus staff officers planning for urban operations need to recognize the importance of securing key resource nodes that might lie outside an urban area's limits, e.g., distant dams and reservoirs distant that nonetheless provide city residents with liquid sustenance. Properly designed intents mean each echelon would understand that some buildings, persons, or infrastructure have importance of beyond local or even national significance. Port management facilities, cellular company headquarters, or political leaders might join the more recently familiar religious sites and dictator statues as key terrain, perhaps not in the tactical sense but rather in the service of strategic objectives. Our butterfly effect discussion reminds us that second and higher order consequences will come to bear. The platoon leader securing a distribution point for generator fuel and equitably providing its product to a community addresses the immediate need of providing heat, light, and power in the aftermath of combat operations that have rendered central power distribution inoperable. He or she at the same time militates against the inevitable rumors of coalition member atrocities.

Well-guided, mission command-savvy leaders and units will likewise be best able to detect variations in routine during patrols, spotting variations from what they have come to know is the routine pulse of their neighborhoods. The captain, colonel, general, or NGO leader wanting to gage the extent of urban fragility or consequences of a spike in potential violence would be wise to rely on these junior soldier, police, aid provider, or others' assessments from the sharp end.

Final thoughts

"The future is urban." An oft cited and valid observation. We cannot allow it to cause our overlooking the reality that the present is already urban. Yet, as United States Army Pacific commander General Robert B. Brown observed, America's is a military designed for combat in open terrain.[7] The tactical expertise gained through years of operations in Iraqi cities and Afghan towns is already dissipating. Lessons from those countries, from studying Israel's operations in Gaza, and insights regarding recovery efforts after domestic disasters in New Orleans, New York, and Houston provide repeated reminders that urban operations anywhere along the spectrum of conflict are not business as usual. Nevertheless, repeated calls for a more comprehensive approach to these undertakings have largely gone unheeded. There are exceptions. Terrorism Early Warning Groups (TEWs) or their equivalents as established in Los Angeles and elsewhere have long brought together federal, state, local, and private enterprises in more or less formal preparation for contingencies.[8] Complementing these sometimes other-than-military led initiatives are more recent partnerships such as those between the United States Military Academy, U.S. Army Asymmetric Warfare Group, and New York Army National Guard with New York City authorities. The Michigan Army National Guard has recently initiated similar contacts with city of Detroit, state, Canadian, and other relevant organizations to foster better mutual understanding of mutual capabilities and potential ways of cooperating that might be brought to bear in times of distress. Early writings on the emerging concept of Multi-Domain Operations refer to the necessity of more extensively bringing non-traditional partners into the operational fold. Other intra- and inter-service efforts similarly reflect understanding that the time for demonstrating similar initiative is at hand.

But these initiatives currently lack the centralized oversight required to achieve synergy and avoid wasteful redundancy. (Such oversight, however, should provide only sufficient supervision to promote efficiency while not inducing officious suffocation. Mission command can flourish in bureaucratic as well as operational environments.) Service and joint doctrine and concepts lag requirements. As these impact training, influence force structure, advise acquisition, inform intelligence collection, underlie planning, enlighten modeling and simulation, and suggest what partners are needed to address operational needs, the time is at hand to redress the shortfall, in particular with respect to heretofore virtually ignored operational and strategic level considerations. These readiness tools must address combat challenges. Yet, as noted, major urban combat operations remain fortunate rarity. Assistance rendered during and after domestic and international urban disasters is a far more frequent occurrence. Preparing for combat operations while ignoring activities essential to recovery in their aftermath or those in which combat is absent addresses but a fraction of requirements. The above authors provide the evidence: Readiness for urban combat is a necessary but not sufficient condition. Their essays tell us much of what our preparations must encompass. Those writings also provide a foundation for understanding demands and opportunities spanning the entire spectrum of conflict.

Notes

[1] Jamison Jo Medby and Russell W. Glenn, *Street Smart: Intelligence Preparation of the Battlefield for Urban Operations*, Santa Monica, CA: RAND, 2002, 90-102.

[2] Examples of informal authorities are neighborhood associations, volunteer societies, unions, gangs and other organized criminal enterprises, and religious groups.

[3] James Delk (Major General, California Army National Guard), "MOUT: A Domestic Case Study – The 1992 Los Angeles Riots," in The City's Many Faces: Proceedings of the RAND Arroyo Center-Marine Corps Warfighting Lab-J8 Urban Working Urban Working Group Conference on Joint Urban Operations, ed. Russell W. Glenn, Santa Monica, CA: RAND, 2000, 135.

[4] Russell W. Glenn, et al., *Where none have gone before: Operational and Strategic Perspectives on Multi-Domain Operations in Megacities - Proceedings of the "Multi-Domain Battle in Megacities" Conference*, April 3-4, 2018, Fort Hamilton, New York, Fort Eustis, VA: U.S. Army Training and Doctrine Command, (July 15, 2018), 8-9.

[5] Russell W. Glenn, Short War in a Perpetual Conflict: Implications of Israel's 2014 Operation Protective Edge for the Australian Army, Canberra, Australia: Australian Army, 2016, 87-91.

[6] This definition and several of the points addressed later in this paragraph can be found in Russell W. Glenn, "Mission Command Overview," in *Trust and Leadership: The Australian Army Approach to Mission Command* (tentative title), ed. Russell W. Glenn, Annapolis, MD: Naval Institute Press, to be published in 2019; or Russell W. Glenn, et al., *Where none have gone before: Operational and Strategic Perspectives on Multi-Domain Operations in Megacities - Proceedings of the "Multi-Domain Battle in Megacities" Conference*, April 3-4, 2018, Fort Hamilton, New York, Fort Eustis, VA: U.S. Army Training and Doctrine Command, (July 15, 2018), 25-26.

[7] Observation by General Robert B. Brown during the G2 U.S. Training and Doctrine Command – United States Army Pacific – Australian Army "Multi-Domain Battle in Megacities" conference, April 3-4, 2018. See Russell W. Glenn, et al., *Where none have gone before: Operational and Strategic Perspectives on Multi-Domain Operations in Megacities - Proceedings of the "Multi-Domain Battle in Megacities" Conference*, April 3-4, 2018, Fort Hamilton, New York, Fort Eustis, VA: U.S. Army Training and Doctrine Command, (July 15, 2018), 21.

[8] See John P. Sullivan and Alain Bauer (Eds.), *Terrorism Early Warning: 10 Years of Achievement in Fighting Terrorism and Crime*. Los Angeles: Los Angeles County Sheriff's Department, October 2008.

Recommended Reading

The following doctrinal publications provide useful context to the articles in this anthology. Readers may find them as a useful adjunct or introduction to the discussion of urban warfare and urban operations in this collection. —*The Editors*

Marine Corps Warfighting Publication 3-35.3, *Military Operations on Urban Terrain (MOUT)*. Washington, D.C.: Headquarters U.S. Marine Corps, 26 April 1998, http://www.marines.mil/Portals/59/MCWP%20 3-35.3.pdf. Superseded by the new designation MCRP 12-10B.1, *Military Operations on Urban Terrain (MOUT)*. Washington, D.C.: Headquarters U.S. Marine Corps, 2 May 2016, https://www.marines. mil/Portals/59/Publications/MCRP%2012-10B.1%20(Formerly%20 MCWP%203-35.3).pdf?ver=2016-06-27-101305-967).

FM 3-06, *Urban Operations*. Washington, D.C.: Headquarters U.S. Army, 26 October 2006, https://fas.org/irp/doddir/army/fm3-06.pdf.

ATTP 3-06.11 (FM 3-06.11), *Combined Arms Operations in Urban Terrain*. Washington, D.C.: Headquarters U.S. Army, June 2011, https://www. globalsecurity.org/military//library/policy/army/attp/attp3-06-11.pdf.

Joint Publication 3-06, *Joint Urban Operations*. Washington, D.C.: The Joint Chiefs of Staff, 20 November 2013, http://www.jcs.mil/ Portals/36/Documents/Doctrine/pubs/jp3_06.pdf.

Selected References

William G. Adamson, "Megacities and the US Army." *Parameters*. Vol. 45, No. 1, Spring 2015: 45-54, http://www. strategicstudiesinstitute.army.mil/pubs/Parameters/Issues/ Spring_2015/7_AdamsonWilliam_Megacities%20and%20 the%20US%20Army.pdf.

John Amble and John W. Spencer, "Prepare the Army for Future Urban Battlefield." *Army*. June 2018: 14-15, https://www.ausa.org/ articles/prepare-army-future-urban-battlefield.

John Antal, *City Fights: Selected Histories of Urban Combat from World War II to Vietnam*. New York: Presidio Press, 2003: 1-464.

Kate Ascher, *The Works: Anatomy of a City*. New York: Penguin Books, 2005: 1-240.

Jo Beall, Tom Goodfellow, and Dennis Rodgers, *Cities, Conflict and State Failure*. Working Paper No. 85, Cities and Fragile States, Crisis States Working Paper Series No. 2, London: Crisis States Research Centre, London School of Economics and Political Science, January 2011: 1-33, http://eprints.lse.ac.uk/39766/1/ Cities%2C_conflict_and_state_fragility_wp852%28author% 29.pdf.

Antony Beevor, *Stalingrad: The Fateful Siege: 1942-1943*. New York: Penguin, 1999: 1-528.

Antony Beevor, "Antony Beevor on how Germany and Britain are learning the art of urban warfare," *The Sunday Times* (of London). 15 July 2018, https://www.thetimes.co.uk/article/

Small Wars Journal

antony-beevor-on-how-germany-and-britain-are-learning-the-art-of-urban-warfare-nbnfkbnzc.

David Betz, "Peering into the past and Future of Urban Warfare in Israel." *War on the Rocks*. 17 December 2015, https://warontherocks.com/2015/12/peering-into-the-past-and-future-of-urban-warfare-in-israel/.

Adrian T. Bogart III, *Block by Block: Civic Action in the Battle of Baghdad*. JSOU Report 0708, November, Hurlbert Field: Joint Special Operations University, 2007, http://jsou.libguides.com/ld.php?content_id=2876967

Louise Bosetti, Hannah Cooper, and John de Boer, "Peacekeeping in Cities: Is the UN Prepared?" United Nations University. 12 April 2016, https://cpr.unu.edu/peacekeeping-in-cities-is-the-un-prepared.html.

Henri Boshoff, Anneli Botha and Martin Schönteich, *Fear in the City: Urban Terrorism in South Africa. Monograph 63*, Pretoria: Institute of Security Studies, September 2001, https://oldsite.issafrica.org/publications/monographs/monograph-63-fear-in-the-city-urban-terrorism-in-south-africa-henri-boshoff-anneli-botha-and-martin-schonteich.

Charles Bowden, *Murder City: Ciudad Juarez and the Global Economy's New Killing Fields*, New York: Nation Books, 2010: 1-354.

Mark Bowden, *Black Hawk Down: A Story of Modern War*. New York: Atlantic Monthly Press, 1999: 1-386.

Mark Bowden, *Hue 1968: A Turning Point of the American War in Vietnam*. New York: Atlantic Monthly Press, 2017: 1-608.

Christopher O. Bowers, "Future Megacity Operations—Lessons from Sadr City." *Military Review*. Vol. 95, No. 3, May-June, 2015: 8-16, https://usacac.army.mil/sites/default/files/publications/MilitaryReview_20150630_art001.pdf. 17 December

Pablo Brum, *The Robin Hood Guerrillas: The Epic Journey of Uruguay's Tupamaros*. Seattle, WA: CreateSpace, 2014: 1-404.

Robert J. Bunker and John P. Sullivan, "Integrating feral cities and third phase cartels/third generation gangs research: the rise of criminal (narco) city networks and BlackFor." *Small Wars & Insurgencies*. Vol. 22, No. 5, November 2011: 764-786.

Robert J. Bunker, *The Emergence of Feral and Criminal Cities: U.S. Military Implications in a Time of Austerity*. Land Warfare Paper 99W. Arlington, VA: Association of the United States Army, April 2014: 1-14, http://scholarship.claremont.edu/cgi/viewcontent.cgi?article=1556&context=cgu_fac_pub.

Manuel Castells, *The Informational City: Economic Restructuring and Urban Development*. Hoboken, NJ: Wiley-Blackwell, 1992: 1-416.

Manuel Castells, *Communication Power*. New York: Oxford University Press, 2013: 1-624.

Manuel Castells, *Networks of Outrage and Hope; Social Movements in the Internet Age* (Second Edition). Cambridge: Polity, 2015: 1-328.

Gary Cecchine, *The U.S. Military Response to the 2010 Haiti Earthquake: Considerations for Army Leaders*. RR-304-A. Washington, DC: The Arroyo Center, The RAND Corporation, 2013: 1-115, https://www.rand.org/pubs/research_reports/RR304.html.

Diane E. Chido, *Alternate Governance Structures in Megacities: Threats or Opportunities?* Carlisle, PA: Strategic Studies Institute, U.S. Army War College, 7 November 2016: 1-75, https://ssi.armywarcollege.edu/pubs/display.cfm?pubID=1335.

John M. Collins, Military Geography for Professionals and the Public. Washington, DC: National Defense University, 1998: 1-437.

Martin Coward, *Urbicide: The Politics of Urban Destruction*. New York: Routledge, 2008: 1-176.

Mike Davis, *City of Quartz: Excavating the Future of Los Angeles*. New York: Vintage, 1992: 1-462.

Mike Davis, *Planet of Slums*, Brooklyn: Verso, 2006: 1-228.

Michael C. Desch, *Soldiers in Cities: Military Operations On Urban Terrain*. Carlisle, PA: Strategic Studies Institute (SSI), U.S. Army War College, October 2001: 1-174, http://www.strategicstudiesinstitute.army.mil/pdffiles/pub294.pdf.

David P. Dilegge and Matthew Van Konynenburg, "A View from the Wolves' Den: The Chechens and Urban Operations." Robert

J. Bunker. Ed., *Non-State Threats and Future Wars*, London: Frank Cass, 2003: 171-184.

Louis A. DiMarco, *Concrete Hell: Urban Warfare from Stalingrad to Iraq*. Oxford, UK: Osprey, 2012: 1-320.

Robert Dixon, "Bringing Big Data to War in Mega-Cities." *War on the Rocks*. 19 January 2016, http://warontherocks.com/2016/01/bringing-big-data-to-operations-in-mega-cities/.

Richard Dobbs, "Prime Numbers: Megacities." *Foreign Policy*. 16 August 2010, http://foreignpolicy.com/2010/08/16/megacities/.

Sean J.A. Edwards, *Mars Unmasked: The Changing Face of Urban Operations*. Santa Monica, CA: The Arroyo Center, The RAND Corporation, 2000: 1-125, https://www.rand.org/pubs/monograph_reports/MR1173.html.

Michael Evans, *City Without Joy: Urban Military Operations into the 21st Century*. Australian Defence College Occasional Paper No. 2. 20 October 2007: 1-69, http://www.defence.gov.au/ADC/publications/Occasional/PublcnsOccasional_310310_CitywithoutJoy.pdf.

Michael Evans, "War and the City in the New Urban Century." *Quadrant Online*, 1 January 2009, https://quadrant.org.au/magazine/2009/01-02/war-and-the-city-in-the-new-urban-century/.

Michael Evans, "The Case Against Megacities." *Parameters*. Vol. 45, No. 1, Spring 2015: 33-46, https://ssi.armywarcollege.edu/pubs/parameters/Issues/Spring_2015/6_EvansMichael_The%20Case%20against%20Megacities.pdf.

Michael Evans, "Future war in cities: Urbanization's challenge to strategic studies in the 21st century." *International Review of the Red Cross*. Vol. 98, Iss. 901, April 2016: 37-51, https://www.cambridge.org/core/journals/international-review-of-the-red-cross/article/future-war-in-cities-urbanizations-challenge-to-strategic-studies-in-the-21st-century/D1999E08103B58ECB46D25B9F42C049A.

C. Christine Fair, *Urban Battle Fields of South Asia: Lessons Learned from Sri Lanka, India, and Pakistan*. Santa Monica, CA: The

Arroyo Center, The RAND Corporation, 2004: 1-172, https://www.rand.org/content/dam/rand/pubs/monographs/2004/RAND_MG210.pdf.

David N. Farrell and Megan Ward, *Megacities and DUAs in 2025 and Beyond: Final Report*. U.S. Army TRADOC G-2 Mad Scientist Megacities and Dense Urban Areas Initiative: Data Collection and Analysis. Hampton, VA: MITRE, 2016: 1-94, https://community.apan.org/wg/tradoc-g2/mad-scientist/m/mdua/170021.

Kevin M. Felix and Frederick D. Wong, "The Case for Megacities." *Parameters*. Spring 2015, Vol. 45, No. 1: 19-32, https://ssi.armywarcollege.edu/pubs/parameters/Issues/Spring_2015/Parameters_Spring%202015%20v45n1.pdf.

Amos C. Fox, "The Reemergence of the Siege: An Assessment of Trends in Modern Land Warfare." *Landpower Essay*, No. 18-2. Arlington, VA: Association of the United States Army, Institute of Land Warfare. June 2018, https://www.ausa.org/sites/default/files/LPE-18-2-The-Reemergence-of-the-Siege-An-Assessment-of-Trends-in-Modern-Land-Warfare.pdf.

Daveed Gartenstein-Ross, "The Westgate Mall Attack and the Future of Terrorism." *Georgetown Journal of International Affairs*. 23 September 2013, https://www.georgetownjournalofinternationalaffairs.org/online-edition/the-westgate-mall-attack-and-the-future-of-terrorism-by-daveed-gartenstein-ross.

Gian Gentile ct. al., *Reimagining the Character of Urban Operations for the U.S. Army*. RR-1602-A. Santa Monica, CA: The Arroyo Center, The RAND Corporation, 2017: 1-214, https://www.rand.org/content/dam/rand/pubs/research_reports/RR1600/RR1602/RAND_RR1602.pdf.

Scott Gerwher and Russell W. Glenn, *The Art of Darkness: Deception and Urban Operations*. MR-1132-A. Santa Monica, CA: The Arroyo Center, The RAND Corporation, 2000: 1-81, https://www.rand.org/pubs/monograph_reports/MR1132.html.

Small Wars Journal

Scott Gerwher and Russell W. Glenn, *Unweaving the Web: Deception and Adaptation in Future Urban Operations*. MR-1495-A. Santa Monica, CA: The Arroyo Center, The RAND Corporation, 2003: 1-92, https://www.rand.org/pubs/monograph_reports/MR1495.html.

David M. Glantz with Jonathan House, *Armageddon in Stalingrad, September-November 1942*. Lawrence, KS: University of Kansas Press, 2009: 1-920.

David M. Glantz and Jonathan M. House, *Stalingrad*. Lawrence, KS: University of Kansas Press, 2017: 1-650.

Russell W. Glenn, *Combat in Hell: A Consideration of Constrained Urban Warfare*. MR-780-A/DARPA. Santa Monica, CA: The RAND Corporation, 1996: 1-67, https://www.rand.org/pubs/monograph_reports/MR780.html.

Russell W. Glenn, *Marching Under Darkening Skies: The American Military and the Impending Urban Operations Threat*. MR-1007-A. Santa Monica, CA: The RAND Corporation, 1998; 1-43, https://www.rand.org/pubs/monograph_reports/MR1007.html.

Russell W. Glenn, et. al., *Denying the Widow-Maker: Summary of Proceedings of the RAND-DBBL Conference on Military Operations on Urbanized Terrain*. CF-143-A. Santa Monica, CA: The Arroyo Center, the RAND Corporation, 1998: 1-177, https://www.rand.org/pubs/conf_proceedings/CF143.html.

Russell W. Glenn, *"...We Band of Brothers:" The Call for Joint Urban Operations Doctrine*. Santa Monica, CA: The Arroyo Center, the RAND Corporation, 1999: 1-81, https://www.rand.org/pubs/documented_briefings/DB270.html.

Russell W. Glenn, ed., *The City's Many Faces: Proceedings of the RAND Arroyo-MCWL-J8 UWG Urban Operations Conference, April 13-14, 1999*. CF-148-A. Santa Monica, CA: The RAND Corporation, 2000: 1-692, https://www.rand.org/pubs/conf_proceedings/CF148.html.

Russell W. Glenn, ed., *Capital Preservation: Preparing for Urban Operations in the Twenty-First Century: Proceedings of the*

RAND Arroyo-TRADOC-MCWL-OSD Urban Operations Conference, March 22-23, 2000. CF-162-A. Santa Monica, CA: The Arroyo Center, The RAND Corporation, 2001: 1-638, https://www.rand.org/pubs/conf_proceedings/CF162. html.

Russell W. Glenn, *An Attack on Duffer's Downtown.* P-8058-1, Santa Monica, CA: The RAND Corporation, 2001, https://www. rand.org/pubs/papers/P8058-1.html.

Russell W. Glenn, et. al., *Honing the Keys to the City: Refining the United States Marine Corps Reconnaissance Force for Urban Ground Combat Operations.* MR-1628-USMC Santa Monica, CA: The RAND Corporation, 2003: 1-130, https://www.rand.org/ pubs/monograph_reports/MR1628.html.

Russell W. Glenn, *Managing Complexity During Military Urban Operations: Visualizing the Elephant.* DB-430-A. Santa Monica, CA: The Arroyo Center, the RAND Corporation, January 2004: 1-54, https://www.rand.org/content/dam/rand/ pubs/documented_briefings/2005/DB430.pdf.

Russell W. Glenn, *Urban Combat Service Support Operations: The Shoulders of Atlas.* MR-1717-A. Santa Monica, CA: The Arroyo Center, the RAND Corporation, 2004: 1-160, https://www. rand.org/pubs/monograph_reports/MR1717.html.

Russell W. Glenn and Gina Kingston, *Urban Battle Command in the Twenty-First Century.* MG-181-A. Santa Monica, CA: The Arroyo Center, the RAND Corporation, 2005: 1-136, https:// www.rand.org/pubs/monographs/MG181.html.

Kendall D. Gott, *Breaking the Mold: Tanks in the Cities.* Fort Leavenworth, KS: Combat Studies Institute Press, 2006: 1-132, https://www. armyupress.army.mil/Portals/7/Primer-on-Urban-Operation/ Documents/Breaking-the-Mold.pdf.

Stephen Graham, ed., *Cities, War, and Terrorism: Towards an Urban Geopolitics.* Oxford, UK: Blackwell, 2004: 1-385.

Stephen Graham, *Cities Under Siege: The New Military Urbanism,* New York: Verso, 2011: 1-432.

Stephen Graham, *Vertical: The City from Satellites to Bunkers*. London: Verso, 2018: 1-402.

Lester Grau and Jacob W. Kipp, "Urban Combat: Confronting the Specter." Vol. 89, No. 3, *Military Review*. July-August 1991: 9-17, http://cgsc.contentdm.oclc.org/utils/getfile/collection/p124201coll1/id/314/filename/315.pdf.

Abraham Guillen, ed., *Philosophy of the Urban Guerrilla: The Revolutionary Writings of Abraham Guillen*. Donald C. Hodges, trans. New York: William and Morrow, 1973: 1-305.

Ihsan Gunduz, *The Islamic State of Iraq and al-Sham and Its Urban Warfare Tactics*. Fort Leavenworth, KS: Foreign Military Studies Office, 18 April 2018: 1-16; https://community.apan.org/wg/tradoc-g2/fmso/w/o-e-watch-mobile-edition-v1/23861/20170418-gunduz---the-islamic-state-of-iraq-and-al-sham-and-its-urban-warfare-tactics/

Jaideep Gupte with Steve Commins, *Cities, Violence and Order: the Challenges and Complex Taxonomy of Security Provision in Cities of Tomorrow*. IDS Evidence Report 175. Brighton, UK: Institute of Development Studies, University of Sussex. 26 February 2016, http://www.ids.ac.uk/publication/cities-violence-and-order-the-challenges-and-complex-taxonomy-of-security-provision-in-cities-of-tomorrow.chi.

Jaideep Gupte, "'These streets are ours': Mumbai's urban form and security in the vernacular." *Peacebuilding*. Vol. 5, Issue 2, pp. 203-217, 2017. DOI: 10.1080/21647259.2016.1277022.

Robert F. Hahn II and Bonnie Jezior, "Urban Warfare and the Urban Warfighter of 2025," *Parameters*. Vol. 29, No. 2, Summer 1999: 74-86, http://smallwarsjournal.com/documents/urban2025.pdf.

Marc Harris et. al. (Megacities Concept Team), *Megacities and the United States Army: Preparing for a Complex and Uncertain Future*. Washington, DC: Chief of Staff of the Army, Strategic Studies Group, June 2014: 1-28, https://www.army.mil/e2/c/downloads/351235.pdf.

Headquarters Department of the Army, *FM 3-06 Urban Operations*, 26 October 2006: 1-314, https://www.globalsecurity.org/military/library/policy/army/fm/3-06/fm3-06_2006.pdf.

Headquarters Department of the Army, *ATTP 3-06.11 Combined Operations in Urban Terrain*. Washington, DC: 10 June 2011: 1-284, https://www.globalsecurity.org/military/library/policy/army/attp/attp3-06-11.pdf.

Alice Hills, *Future War in Cities: Rethinking a Liberal Dilemma*. New York: Routledge, 2004: 1-320.

Alice Hills, *Policing Post-Conflict Cities*. London: Zed, 2009: 1-244.

Donald L. Horowitz, *The Deadly Ethnic Riot*. Berkeley, CA: University of California Press, 2003: 1-605.

International Committee of the Red Cross, *War in Cities*. Vol. 98, Iss. 901, April 2016: 1-396, https://www.icrc.org/en/international-review/war-in-cities.

Anthony James Joes, *Urban Guerrilla Warfare*. Lexington, KY: University of Kentucky Press, 2007: 1-232.

David E. Johnson, M. Wade Markel and Brian Shannon, *The 2008 Battle of Sadr City: Reimagining Urban Combat*. Santa Monica, CA: The Arroyo Center, The RAND Corporation, 2013: 1-165, https://www.rand.org/content/dam/rand/pubs/research_reports/RR100/RR160/RAND_RR160.pdf.

Joint Chiefs of Staff, *JP 3-06 Joint Urban Operations*. Washington, DC: Department of Defense 20, November 2013: 1-161, http://www.jcs.mil/Portals/36/Documents/Doctrine/pubs/jp3_06.pdf.

Parag Khanna, "Beyond City Limits." *Foreign Policy*. October/September 2010, http://www.foreignpolicy.com/articles/2010/08/16/beyond_city_limits.

Farhad Khosrokhavar, "The jihadogenous urban structure." *Open Democracy/Open Movements*. 9 June 2018, https://opendemocracy.net/farhad-khosrokhavar/jihadogenous-urban-structure.

David Kilcullen, *Out of the Mountains: The Coming Age of the Urban Guerrilla*. New York: Oxford University Press, 2013: 1-352.

David Kilcullen, "Westgate mall attacks: urban areas are the battleground of the 21st century." *The Guardian*. 27 September 2013, https://www.theguardian.com/world/2013/sep/27/westgate-mall-attacks-al-qaida.

David Kilcullen, *The Australian Army in the urban networked littoral*. Army Research Paper, no. 2. Russell, ACT: Directorate of Future Land Warfare, Department of Defence (Australia), 2014: 1-43.

David Kilcullen, "Urban Combat: 'Cities Are Sponges That Soak Up Troops.'" *The Cipher Brief*. 22 October 2017, https://www.thecipherbrief.com/urban-combat-cities-are-sponges-that-soak-up-troops.

Charles Knight and Katja Theodorakis, "The Battle of Marawi, one year on." *The Strategist* (Australian Security Policy Institute). 24 October 2018, https://www.aspistrategist.org.au/the-battle-of-marawi-one-year-on/.

Margarita Konaev and John Spencer, "The Era of Urban Warfare is Already Here." *E-Notes*, Foreign Policy Research Institute (FPRI). 21 March 2018, https://www.fpri.org/article/2018/03/the-era-of-urban-warfare-is-already-here/

Joel Lawton and Lori Shields, *Mad Scientist: Megacities and Dense Urban Areas in 2025 and Beyond*. Fort Eustis, VA: Training and Doctrine Command (TRADOC) G-2, August 2016: 1-372, https://www.scribd.com/document/322095824/Megacities-Compendium.

P.H. Liotta and James F. Miskel, *The Real Population Bomb: Megacities, Global Security and The Map of the Future*. Dulles, VA: Potomac Books, 2012: 1-264.

Richard S. Lowry, *New Dawn: The Battles for Fallujah*. New York: Savas Beatie, 2010: 1-312.

Peter A. Lupsa, "On Theories of Urban Violence." *Urban Affairs Review*. Vol. 4, Issue 3, March 1969: 273-296, https://doi.org/10.1177/107808746900400302.

Carlos Marighella, *Mini-Manual of the Urban Guerilla*. 1969, https:// www.marxists.org/archive/marighella-carlos/1969/06/ minimanual-urban-guerrilla/index.htm.

Marine Corps Intelligence Activity, Urban Warfare Study: City Case Studies Compilation. Quantico, VA: Marine Corps Intelligence Activity, April 1999: 1-47.

Dayton McCarthy, *The Worst of Both Worlds: An analysis of urban littoral combat*. Australian Army Occasional Paper, Conflict Theory and Strategy 002, Canberra: Commonwealth of Australia, April 2018, https://www.army.gov.au/sites/g/files/net1846/f/ publications/the_worst_of_both_worlds.pdf.

Jamison Jo Medby and Russell W. Glenn, *Streetmart: Intelligence Preparation of the Battlefield for Urban Operations*. MR-1287-A. Santa Monica, CA: The Arroyo Center, The RAND Corporation, 2002: 1-165, http://www.rand.org/pubs/ monograph_reports/MR1287.html.

Doug Miller and George Hazel, *Megacity Challenges: A Stakeholder Perspective*. Munich: Siemens AG, 2006: 1-11, https:// www.siemens.com/press/pool/en/events/megacities/ media_mrc_globe_170107_d_1431329.pdf.

Wesley A. Morbe, *Seven Times Around A City: The Evolution of Israeli Operational Art in Urban Operations*. Fort Leavenwoth, KS: U.S. Army Command and General Staff College, 2006: 1-87, http://www.dtic.mil/dtic/tr/fulltext/u2/1022147.pdf.

Robert Muggah, "The Fragile City Arrives." *E-International Relations*. 23 November 2013, http://www.e-ir.info/2013/11/23/ the-fragile-city-arrives/.

Robert Muggah, "Fixing Fragile Cities: Solutions for Urban Violence and Poverty." *Foreign Affairs*. 15 January 2015, https://www.foreignaffairs.com/articles/africa/2015-01-15/ fixing-fragile-cities.

Robert Muggah and Katherine Aguirre, "Terrorists want to destroy our cities. We can't let them." *World Economic Fourm*. 13 December 2016, https://www.weforum.org/agenda/2016/12/ terrorists-want-to-destroy-our-cities-we-can-t-let-them/.

North Atlantic Treaty Organization (NATO), Research and Technology Organization, *Urban Operations in the Year 2020*. RTO-TR-071 AC/323(SAS-030)TP/35. Cedex, France: April 2003: 1-140, https://www.sto.nato.int/publications/.../RTO-TR-071/TR-071-$$ALL.pdf.

Richard Norton, "Feral Cities." *Naval War College Review*, Vol. 56, No. 4, Autumn 2003: 97-106, www.nwc.navy.mil/press/Review/2003/Autumn/pdfs/art6-a03.pdf.

Richard Norton, "Feral Cities: Problems Today, Battlefields Tomorrow?" *Marine Corps University Journal*. Vol. 1, No. 1, Spring 2010: 1-77, https://www.marines.mil/LinkClick.aspx?fileticket=1UK5Eeer_jw%3D&portalid=59.

Raymond Odierno and Michael O'Hanlon, "The Future of Securing Global Cities." *The National Interest*. 22 March 2016, http://nationalinterest.org/feature/securing-global-cities-15563.

Olga Oliker, *Russia's Chechen Wars 1994-2000: Lessons from Urban Combat*. MR-1289-A. Santa Monica, CA: The RAND Corporation, 2001: 1-121, https://www.rand.org/pubs/monograph_reports/MR1289.html.

Ralph Peters, "Our Soldiers, Their Cities." *Parameters*. Vol. 26, No. 1, Spring 1996: 43-50, http://strategicstudiesinstitute.army.mil/pubs/parameters/articles/96spring/peters.htm.

Ralph Peters, "The Human Terrain of Urban Operations." *Parameters*. Vol. 40, No. 1, Spring 2010: 4-12, http://www.carlisle.army.mil/USAWC/parameters/Articles/00spring/peters.htm.

Alvaro de Souza Pinheiro, *Irregular Warfare: Brazil's fight Against Urban Criminal Guerrillas*. JSOU Report 09-8, September, Hurlburt Field: Joint Special Operations University, 2009, http://jsou.libguides.com/ld.php?content_id=2876949

Robert Postings, "A Guide to the Islamic State's Way of Urban Warfare." West Point, NY: Modern War Institute, 9 July 2018, https://mwi.usma.edu/guide-islamic-states-way-urban-warfare/.

Daphné Richemond-Barak, *Underground Warfare*, New York: Oxford University Press, 2018.

John Robb, "The Coming Urban Terror: Systems disruption, networked gangs, and bioweapons." *City Journal*. Summer 2007, https://www.city-journal.org/html/coming-urban-terror-13026.html.

William G. Robertson and Lawrence A. Yates, Eds., *Block by Block: The Challenges of Urban Operations*. Ft. Leavenworth, KS: US Army Command and General Staff College Press, 2003: 1-463.

Antônio Sampaio, "Before and after urban warfare: Conflict prevention and transitions in cities." *International Review of the Red Cross*. Vol. 98, Iss. 901, April 2016: 71-95, https://www.cambridge.org/core/journals/international-review-of-the-red-cross/article/div-classtitlebefore-and-after-urban-warfare-conflict-prevention-and-transitions-in-citiesdiv/9CAA6C6AAAD7ED15C2DAEA2822734D7E.

Antônio Sampaio, "The New Frontlines Are in the Slums." *Foreign Policy*, 3 July 2018, https://foreignpolicy.com/2018/07/03/the-new-frontlines-are-in-the-slums/.

Saskia Sassen, *The Global City: New York, London, Tokyo*. Princeton University Press, 2001: 1-480, https://www.opendemocracy.net/article/the-new-wars-and-cities-after-mumbai-0.

Saskia Sassen, *The Global City* and *Cities in a World Economy*. Thousand Oaks, CA: Sage Publications, 2018: 1-440.

John C. Scharfen and Michael J. Deane, "Soviet Tactical Doctrine for Urban Warfare." Menlo Park, CA: Stanford Research Institute, Report SSC-TN-2625-16, http://www.dtic.mil/dtic/tr/fulltext/u2/a022998.pdf.

John Spencer, "The Most Effective Weapon on the Modern Battlefield is Concrete." Modern War Institute. 14 November 2016, https://mwi.usma.edu/effective-weapon-modern-battlefield-concrete/.

John Spencer, "It's Time to Create a Megacities Combat Unit." Modern War Institute. 31 January 2017, https://mwi.usma.edu/time-create-megacities-combat-unit/.

John Spencer, "What an Army Megacities Unit Would Look Like." Modern War Institute. 8 March 2017, https://mwi.usma.edu/army-megacities-unit-look-like/.

John Spencer, "The Army Needs an Urban Warfare School and It Needs It Soon." Modern War Institute. 5 April 2017, https://mwi.usma.edu/army-needs-urban-warfare-school-needs-soon/.

John Spencer, "How drone swarms could change urban warfare." *C4ISRNET*, 11 December 2017, https://www.c4isrnet.com/opinion/the-compass/net-defense-blogs/2017/12/11/how-drone-swarms-could-change-urban-warfare-commentary/.

John Spencer, "Getting Beyond Door Kicking: Four Tasks for Urban Warriors." Modern War Institute. 18 September 2018, https://mwi.usma.edu/getting-beyond-door-kicking-four-tasks-urban-warriors/.

John Spencer. "MWI Podcast: War Goes To The City, With David Kilcullen." Modern Warfare Institute. 14 November 2018, https://mwi.usma.edu/mwi-podcast-war-goes-city-david-kilcullen/.

Roger J. Spiller, *Sharp Corners: Urban Operations at Century's End*. Fort Leavenworth, Kansas Command and General Staff College, 2001: 1-156, https://usacac.army.mil/cac2/cgsc/carl/download/csipubs/SharpCorners.pdf.

David Stanford, Mike Jackson, and Sam Ruppert, "MWI Battlefield Assessment on the Siege of Sarajevo." Modern Warfare Institute. 5 December 2015, https://mwi.usma.edu/mwi-battlefield-assessment-siege-sarajevo/.

John P. Sullivan, "Critical Pathways: Responding to the 1992 Los Angeles Riot." *Journal of California Law Enforcement*. Vol. 30, No. 1, 1996: 14-18, https://www.academia.edu/1117334/Critical_Pathways_Responding_to_the_1992_Los_Angeles_Riot.

John P. Sullivan, "The Urban Imperative: War, Terrorism, and Insecurity in Megacities." *Stratfor*. 13 February 2018, https://worldview.stratfor.com/horizons/fellows/dr-john-p-sullivan/13022018-urban-imperative-war-terrorism-and-insecurity-megacities.

John P. Sullivan, "Urban Warfighting and Classic Siege." *Stratfor*. 20 March 2018, https://worldview.stratfor.com/horizons/fellows/dr-john-p-sullivan/20032018-urban-warfighting-and-classic-siege.

John P. Sullivan, "Policing Urban Conflict: Urban Siege, Terrorism and Insecurity." *Stratfor*. 19 April 2018, https://worldview.stratfor.com/horizons/fellows/dr-john-p-sullivan/30042018-policing-urban-conflict-urban-siege-terrorism-and-insecurity.

John P. Sullivan, "Protecting the Populace: Humanitarian Considerations in Urban Operations." *Stratfor*. 2 June 2018, https://www.stratfor.com/horizons/fellows/dr-john-p-sullivan/26062018-protecting-populace-humanitarian-considerations-urban-operations.

John P. Sullivan, "New Wars in the City: Global Cities – Global Slums." *Stratfor*. 4 July 2018, https://www.stratfor.com/horizons/fellows/dr-john-p-sullivan/04072018-new-wars-city-global-cities-global-slums.

John P. Sullivan and Alain Bauer, Eds., *Terrorism Early Warning: 10 Years of Achievement in Fighting Terrorism and Crime*. Los Angeles: Los Angeles County Sheriff's Department, October 2008, https://www.academia.edu/1115115/Terrorism_Early_Warning_10_Years_of_Achievement_in_Fighting_Terrorism_and_Crime.

John P. Sullivan, Hal Kempfer, and Jamison Jo Medby, "Understanding Consequences in Urban Operations." *On Point*. 2005. Available at https://www.oodaloop.com/wp-content/uploads/2015/03/Understanding-Consequences-in-Urban-Operations.pdf.

John P. Sullivan and Adam Elkus, "Preventing Another Mumbai: Building a Police Operational Art." *CTC Sentinel*. Vol. 2, No. 6, June 2009: 1-3, https://www.ctc.usma.edu/posts/preventing-another-mumbai-building-a-police-operational-art.

John P. Sullivan and Adam Elkus, "Police Operational Art for a Five-Dimensional Operational Space." *Small Wars Journal*. 23 July 2009, https://smallwarsjournal.com/jrnl/art/police-operational-art-for-a-five-dimensional-operational-space.

John P. Sullivan and Adam Elkus, "Global cities–global gangs." *OpenDemocracy*. 2 December 2009, http://www.opendemocracy.net/opensecurity/john-p-sullivan-adam-elkus/global-cities---global-gangs.

Jennifer Taw and Bruce Hoffman, *The Urbanization of Insurgency: Potential Challenges to U.S. Army Operations*. Santa Monica: RAND Corporation, 1994, https://www.rand.org/pubs/monograph_reports/MR398.html.

Urbano, *Fighting in the Streets: A Manual of Urban Guerilla Warfare*. Fort Lee, NJ: Barricade Books, 1992: 1-129.

Alec Wahlman, *Storming the City: U.S. Military Performance in Urban Warfare from World War II to Vietnam*. Denton, TX: University of North Texas Press, 2015: 1-400.

Bing West, "Urban Warfare, Then and Now. *The Atlantic*. 30 June 2017, https://www.theatlantic.com/international/archive/2017/06/urban-warfare-hue-mosul/532173/.

Phil Williams and Werner Selle, *Military Contingencies in Megacities and Sub-Megacities*. Carlisle, PA: Strategic Studies Institute, U.S. Army War College, 9 December 2016: 1-165, https://ssi.armywarcollege.edu/pubs/display.cfm?pubID=1328.

Notes on Contributors

The biographies of the contributors were current at the time of the first publication of their articles. This has been done to place them in historical context. The biographies of the editors and those contributors providing new material for this anthology are current as of November 2018.

Editors

Dr. Robert J. Bunker is an Adjunct Research Professor, Strategic Studies Institute, US Army War College and an Instructor, Safe Communities Institute (SCI), Sol Price School of Public Policy, University of Southern California. Dr. Bunker has hundreds of publications including *Studies in Gangs and Cartels*, with John Sullivan (Routledge, 2013), *Red Teams and Counterterrorism Training*, with Stephen Sloan (University of Oklahoma, 2011), and edited works, including *Global Criminal and Sovereign Free Economies and the Demise of the Western Democracies: Dark Renaissance* (Routledge, 2014), co-edited with Pamela Ligouri Bunker; *Criminal Insurgencies in Mexico and the Americas: The Gangs and Cartels Wage War* (Routledge, 2012); *Narcos Over the Border: Gangs, Cartels and Mercenaries* (Routledge, 2011); *Criminal-States and Criminal-Soldiers* (Routledge, 2008); *Networks, Terrorism and Global Insurgency* (Routledge, 2005); and *Non-State Threats and Future Wars* (Routledge, 2002).

Dave Dilegge is a retired USMCR Intelligence and Counterintelligence / HUMINT officer. He is also a former USMC civilian intelligence analyst and worked several years in the private sector. He served with the 1st Marine Division during Operation Desert Storm. In 1999 he was the recipient of the National Military Intelligence Association's Colonel Donald G. Cook Award for his work in supporting USMC and DoD urban operations analysis, wargaming and experimentation. He is currently a Director at the Small Wars Foundation and is Editor-in-Chief of *Small Wars Journal*. He is a member of the Marine Corps Association, Military Writers Guild, Warlord Loop, Veterans of Foreign Wars, National Rifle Association, Sons of Italy, and Tau Kappa Epsilon. His son David is an Infantry Sergeant currently serving in the Army's 1st Infantry Division (Mechanized).

Dr. Alma Keshavarz is a *Small Wars Journal—El Centro* Associate. She received her PhD in Political Science at Claremont Graduate University. Her dissertation focused on hybrid warfare applied to the Islamic State, Russia, and Iran's Islamic Revolutionary Guard Corps. She received her MPP from Pepperdine's School of Public Policy with a master's thesis focused on United States interests and policy towards Russia. She also holds a BA in Political Science and English from University of California, Davis. She has held various research intern and associate positions and has served as a graduate assistant at Pepperdine University. Her research interests include non-state actors, specifically Hezbollah, cyber security and warfare, and national security strategy with a regional focus on Middle East politics, specifically Iran, Lebanon, Yemen, and Syria. She is fluent in Spanish and Farsi.

Dr. John P. Sullivan is a Senior Fellow, *Small Wars Journal—El Centro* and served as a lieutenant with the Los Angeles Sheriff's Department; specializing in emergency operations, transit policing, counterterrorism and intelligence. He is an Instructor in the Safe Communities Institute (SCI), Sol Price School of Public Policy, University of Southern California, Global Fellow at Stratfor, an adjunct researcher at the VORTEX Research Group, Bogotá, Colombia, Member of the

Urban Violence Research Network, Member of the California Gang Investigators Association, and Member of the Scientific Advisory Board of the Global Observatory of Transnational Criminal Networks. He completed the CREATE Executive Program in Counter-Terrorism at the University of Southern California and holds a Bachelor of Arts in Government form the College of William and Mary, a Master of Arts in Urban Affairs and Policy Analysis from the New School for Social Research, and a PhD, doctorate in Information and Knowledge Society, from the Open University of Catalonia (Universitat Oberta de Catalunya) in Barcelona. His doctoral thesis was 'Mexico's Drug War: Cartels, Gangs, Sovereignty and the Network State." His current research focus is the impact of transnational organized crime on sovereignty in Mexico and other countries.

Contributors

Luke Allison holds a M.A. in International Security from the University of Denver and a B.A. in Communication Studies from Loyola University New Orleans. He received additional training in Political Psychology at Stanford University. He contributes at The Center for Warfare and Neuropsychological Studies.

Gary Anderson is a retired Marine Corps officer. He recently left the State Department after a year-long tour in Iraq as a Senior Governance Advisor with a Provincial Reconstruction Team.

Dr. Chris Arney is a professor of mathematics and network science researcher at the United States Military Academy at West Point NY. He is a former Military Intelligence officer in the Army and a program manager for the Army Research Office.

Michael Bailey is a Strategic Planner with the Joint Program Executive Office for Chemical and Biological Defense. He is a Microbiologist and served as a fellow on the Chief of Staff of the Army's Strategic Studies Group.

Elizabeth M. Bartels is a senior associate at Caerus Associates, leading efforts to develop and test concepts and tools to better understand urban operational environments. Prior to joining Caerus, Ellie led teams in designing educational and analytical strategic wargames at the National Defense University. She holds an SM in Comparative Political Science from MIT and an AB in Political Science and Near Eastern Languages and Civilization from the University of Chicago. You can follow her on Twitter here: https://twitter.com/elliebartels.

Dr. Daniel Bennett was commissioned a distinguished military graduate in 1994 from the Colorado School of Mines as a Signal Officer. He has a B.S. in Engineering (Electrical Specialty), and an M.S. and Ph.D. in Electrical Engineering. His most recent operational experience was as the Cyberspace Operations Infrastructure and Special Projects lead for the Commander of the Cyber National Mission Force, U.S. Cyber Command. He is currently assigned as the Chief of Research of the Army Cyber Institute at West Point.

A.J. Besik is an Armor officer in the U.S. Army Reserves and assigned as the secretary of the General Staff for the 100th Division. He is a veteran of deployments to Iraq and Afghanistan and a graduate of the U.S. Army Command & General Staff College's School of Advanced Military Studies. He is currently attending the University of Louisville's Brandeis Law School.

Kyle R. Brady is a security-oriented academic with a primary interest in contextualizing security concerns, which he currently explores as a postgraduate student at King's College London in the Department of War Studies. He also holds a Masters in Homeland Security from Pennsylvania State University with foci on terrorism, public administration, and emergency management, as well as a Bachelors in Political Science from San Jose State University with interests in international relations and political theory. All of Kyle's work can be found online through https://site.kyle-brady.com; he can be reached by email at brady.k@gmail.com or kyle.brady@kcl.ac.uk, on *Twitter* as @KyleBradyOnline, or on Facebook as /KyleBradyOnline; and he occasionally blogs at https://site.kyle-brady.com/blog/.

Eddie Brown is a Military Intelligence officer in the US Army. He is a SAMS graduate and has served as an intelligence planner for multiple tactical and operational military units.

Michael L. Burgoyne, U.S. Army, is a Foreign Area Officer currently serving as the Assistant Army Attaché in Mexico City. LTC Burgoyne deployed in support of Operation Iraqi Freedom as a Squadron Logistics Officer in 2003 and again in 2005 as Commander, C Troop, 3d Squadron, 7th Cavalry. He is the co-author of *The Defense of Jisr al-Doreaa*, a tactical primer on counterinsurgency. He holds a B.A. from the University of Arizona and a M.A. in Security Studies from Georgetown University.

Alex Calvo, a guest professor at Nagoya University (Japan), focuses on security and defence policy, international law, and military history, in the Indian-Pacific Ocean Region. A member of Taiwan's South China Sea Think-Tank and CIMSEC (The Center for International Maritime Security), he tweets at Alex__Calvo and his work can be found at https://nagoya-u.academia.edu/AlexCalvo.

Chuck Campbell is the founder and President of Edgewise Technologies LLC. He provides systems engineering, software development, and management support services to the modeling and simulation industry, concentrated on simplifying architectures, extending terrain capabilities, and automating behaviors. With over 25 years' synthetic natural environment (SNE) experience, Mr. Campbell remains actively involved in efforts for terrain generation, representation, and runtime services. He has been directly involved in designing, developing, and managing SNE components on several programs of record, but has focused primarily on SNE research for the last decade.

Dr. K. Selçuk Candan is a professor of computer science and engineering at Arizona State University and the director of ASU's Center for Assured and Scalable Data Engineering (CASCADE). His primary research interest is in the area of management and analysis of non-traditional, heterogeneous, and imprecise (such as multimedia, web, and scientific) data.

Sean M. Castilla is an Armor Officer currently serving in Headquarters, Department of the Army staff as part of the Joint Chiefs of Staff/Office of the Secretary of Defense Internship. Previous assignments include the 1st Cavalry Division, Special Operations Command Africa, and the 101st Airborne Division. He holds a M.P.M in Policy Management from Georgetown University, an M.A. in International Relations from St. Mary's University, San Antonio, and a B.A. Psychology from the University of Texas, Austin.

Dr. Kathryn Coronges is the Executive Director of the Network Science Institute at Northeastern University. Prior to this, she was a Program Manager at Army Research Office where she ran two portfolios of high risk, high impact research to support US Army's basic science investments in Social and Cognitive Networks and Social Informatics; and an Assistant Professor in the Department of Behavioral Sciences and Leadership at the United States Military Academy. Her research has focused on social structures and dynamics of teams and communities and their impacts on communication patterns, behaviors and performance.

Alfred C. Crane currently works at the Army Capabilities Integration Center, Concepts and Learning Directorate, Science & Technology, Research and Accelerated Capabilities Development Division as a Spiral Developments Analyst. Mr. Crane has worked for the Army as a civilian since April of 1997. He has served as an Instructional Systems Specialist for the US Army Military Police School, Military Analyst for the Army Training Support Center and Army Futures Center, and Spiral Developments Analyst for the Army Capabilities Integration Center.

Mr. Crane also served in the United States Marine Corps Reserve from 1990-1996. He holds a Master's Degree in Education (Teaching History) from Jacksonville State University and a Bachelor's Degree in History from Christopher Newport University. His hobbies include wargaming, painting miniatures, historical re-enacting, collecting toys and militaria, as well as historical and science-fiction books and movies. He also created and manages two Facebook forums (The Video Alternative and The Video Alternative Part 2) devoted to movies, books, music and gaming.

Dr. Geoffrey Demarest is a researcher in the US Army's Foreign Military Studies Office at Ft. Leavenworth, Kansas. He holds a JD and a PhD in International Studies from the University of Denver, and a PhD in Geography from the University of Kansas. He is a graduate of the US Army War College at Carlisle Barracks, Pennsylvania, and of the School of the Americas at Ft. Benning, Georgia. Demarest's latest book is titled *Winning Insurgent War*.

Kirby Dennis is an Infantry officer recently assigned to the 10th Mountain Division at Fort Drum, NY. He is also a member of the Council on Foreign Relations.

Robert Dixon is a resident student at the US Army War College and a member of the Carlisle Scholars Program. He is an Alumni of the Chief of Staff of the Army's Strategic Studies Group. Prior to that assignment he commanded 31st Engineer Battalion (OSUT) at Ft. Leonard Wood, MO from 2011-2013 and is proud to have worked with some of the finest and most professional Drill Sergeants in the Army.

Adam Elkus is a PhD student in Computational Social Science at George Mason University. He has published articles on defense, international security, and technology at *Small Wars Journal*, CTOVision, *The Atlantic*, the West Point Combating Terrorism Center's *Sentinel*, and *Foreign Policy*.

Dr. Christopher Flaherty has a Ph.D. in Economic Relations from the University of Melbourne with a focus on networking. Following this, he pursued a career in defence and security research in the Australian Department of Defence. Christopher has been based in London since 2008. A Senior Research Associate of the Terrorism Research Center (TRC), he regularly contributes to its' current publications. He is also the co-primary author of *Body Cavity Bombers: The New Martyrs* (iUniverse, 2013). Two essays of his from 2003 and 2010 were reprinted in the TRC book—*Fifth Dimensional Operations* (iUniverse, 2014). He is the author of *Australian Manoeuvrist Strategy* (Seaview Press, 1996). Christopher has been an active contributor on security, terrorism early warning, and related international intelligence issues, including tactics, techniques and procedures analysis, published in the TRC report 'Dangerous Minds' (2012). He has a long-term involvement in the development of a 'Scripted Agent Based Microsimulation Project', at the University of Wollongong (NSW, Australia).

Christian Fortunato is a Systems Engineer with ASU Research Enterprise (ASURE) where he leads ASURE's megacities research. Prior to ASURE, Christian developed innovative ISR solutions for the Department of Defense by applying his military experience with tactical ground and strategic airborne surveillance systems. Christian holds a bachelors in geography and Master of Advanced Studies in Geographic Information Systems from Arizona State University.

Dr. Russell W. Glenn since retirement from the U.S. Army has completed numerous studies on urban operations, irregular warfare, conflict in southern Lebanon and Gaza, and other topics while in the think tank community and with the Australian National University. He is author/editor of the forthcoming *Trust and Leadership: The Australian Army Approach to Mission Command* due out in autumn 2019.

Dr. Andrew O. Hall was commissioned in 1991 from the United States Military Academy as an Infantry Officer. He has a BS in Computer Science, a MS in Applied Mathematics, and a Ph.D. in Management

Science. He previously served as the Chief of the Military Personnel Structure and Plans Division in the Army G-1 where he was instrumental in the establishment of the Cyber Branch and is currently assigned as the Director of the Army Cyber Institute at West Point.

Marc Harris is a Signal Officer and Fellow in the Chief of Staff of the Army's Strategic Studies Group.

William Hedges Command Sergeant Major (Ret), USA, is a liaison officer for the Intelligence & Information Warfare Directorate and the US Army's Intelligence Center of Excellence (ICoE), and additionally serves as a Science & Technology analyst for ICoE's Requirements Determination Directorate. A career intelligence analyst, Mr. Hedges has been posted to multiple senior intelligence analyst positions to include stints with: Field Station Berlin; the Central American Joint Intelligence Team (CAJIT-DIA); the Multi-national Force and Observers (Sinai); the Defense Intelligence Agency/CJCS-J-2; Task Force 134, Camp Cropper (Iraq); and the 501st Military Intelligence Brigade, INSCOM (South Korea). In his final assignment, he served as the Command Sergeant Major and Commandant of the Army's Intelligence Center's Noncommissioned Officer Academy. Prior to his present position, Mr. Hedges served as the program manager, course manager, and master instructor for ICoE's Analytic Tradecraft program. His primary research areas are human domain-human dimension convergence, as a primary nexus towards producing future generations of master intelligence analysts. Mr. Hedges holds a B.S. degree in Political Science and is also a graduate of the Defense Intelligence Agency's National Intelligence University.

Daniel Hendrex is a Cavalryman and Fellow in the Chief of Staff of the Army's Strategic Studies Group.

Wes Herche is a research scientist with the Global Security Initiative at Arizona State University, with an additional appointment of senior sustainability scientist in the Global Institute of Sustainability. He holds a bachelor's in geography from Southern Illinois University, an MBA from Thunderbird School of Global Management, and is currently completing a doctorate in sustainability science. His research focuses on energy security and policy. Wes was previously an intelligence analyst with the U.S. National Geospatial Intelligence Agency.

Dr. Frank G. Hoffman is a Senior Research Fellow at the Center for Strategic Research at National Defense University (NDU).

James Howcroft serves as the Director of the Program on Terrorism and Security Studies at the George C. Marshall Center. Professor Howcroft retired as a Colonel after 30 years as an Intelligence Officer in the United States Marine Corps. He served in a wide range of Marine Corps tactical and operational intelligence billets, from Infantry Battalion up to the Marine Expeditionary Force level. His combat tours include duty with the 2nd Marine Division in Operation Desert Storm and tours of duty as the Assistant Chief of Staff for Intelligence (G2) with both the 1st Marine Division and then the 1st Marine Expeditionary Force in Iraq. While in the Marine Corps, Colonel Howcroft was trained and served as a Marine Corps Foreign Area Officer. His Foreign Area Officer service includes two tours of duty as a military attaché at the American Embassy in Moscow, Russia. He was also the first permanent US Defense Attaché in Tbilisi, Georgia. The Commandant of the Marine Corps has nominated him for inclusion in the Defense Intelligence Agency's Attaché Hall of Fame in recognition for his contributions while in Moscow and Tbilisi. His military decorations include the Defense Superior Service Medal, the Legion of Merit with Combat "V", and the Bronze Star Medal with Combat "V". While in the Marine Corps, Colonel Howcroft served as the Marine Corps Commandant's Chair on the Marshall Center Faculty from 2004 to 2008. For the five years prior to rejoining the Marshall Center in 2014, Professor Howcroft was a Course Director for the United States European and Africa Commands' Expeditionary Intelligence Training Program, teaching intelligence collection and analysis to thousands of US, European and African partners engaged in Combat, Counterterrorist, Counterinsurgency and

Peace Support Operations around the world. Professor Howcroft's professional education includes a Master of Arts in National Security and Strategic Studies from the US Naval War College and a Master of Science in Strategic Intelligence from the US Defense Intelligence College. He is a graduate of the US Army Russian Institute and Duke University. Professor Howcroft has authored a number of articles on intelligence and operational cultural issues and is a frequent contributor to *Small Wars Journal*.

Dr. Danielle L. Ippolito Ph.D., is a Research Physiologist and Task Area Manager for the US Army Center for Environmental Health Research (USACEHR). She is a biomedical researcher with nearly 10 years of Army experience in clinical and laboratory research environments at Fort Detrick and Madigan Army Medical Center (Joint-Base Lewis McChord). She uses an integrative systems biology approach to develop medical diagnostics and decision aids that protect Warfighters from chemical threats in hostile operational environments.

Kris Karafa is a former U.S. Army Special Forces officer who currently works at the global engineering and construction firm Bechtel. He is also a member of the Council on Foreign Relations.

Dr. David Kilcullen is a former army officer, diplomat and policy advisor for the Australian and United States governments. He has served in counterrorism and counterinsurgency roles in the Middle East, South and Southeast Asia, Africa and Europe. Dr. Kilcullen has also made significant contributions to urban studies, including urban modeling and simulation, public safety and emergency management. His books *The Accidental Guerrilla* and *Counterinsurgency* are used by policy-makers, the military, intelligence and development agencies worldwide. His third book, *Out of the Mountains* (2013) examines conflict in the connected, coastal cities of the future, while his 2015 essay, *Blood Year: Terror and the Islamic State* was published as a full-length book in 2016 by Oxford University Press. He is currently completing a book on hybrid and asymmetric conflict.

Erin King is a staff member of the Global Security Initiative at Arizona State University where she is completing a bachelor's in sociology and a certification in homeland security. Her research interests include a broad spectrum of security issues. Erin previously served as a counterterrorism intelligence intern in Israel with TAM-C Solutions.

David Knapp is the Associate Division Chief for Science and Technology in the Battlefield Environment Division at Army Research Laboratory (ARL). He supports the laboratory's new Atmospheric Science Center by leading efforts to develop new and strengthen current research collaborations in the areas of atmospheric sensing, characterization, and modeling for the Army's future battlefield needs. He recently completed a 10-year stint as chief of the Division's Atmospheric Modeling Branch, providing technical leadership to scientists and engineers focused on developing, validating, and fielding innovative atmospheric prediction capabilities tailored for all Army battlefield operational scales. Mr. Knapp has been with ARL for over 20 years in different research capacities related to battlefield weather forecasting. He retired from the Air Force Reserves in 2003 after serving a combined 22 years of active and reserve duty as a weather officer in a variety of operational forecasting, research, and leadership positions. He has extensive experience focused on applied research addressing specific Army weather capability gaps, with additional expertise in aviation weather research topics. Mr. Knapp received his B.S. in Meteorology from the University of Utah in 1981 and his M.S. in Meteorology in 1988 from North Carolina State University.

Dr. Margarita Konaev is a non-resident fellow at the Modern War Institute at the United States Military Academy, West Point and a post-doctoral fellow in the Center for Strategic Studies at the Fletcher School of Law and Diplomacy at Tufts University. Her research examines the impact of population growth and urbanization on the changing character and conduct of armed conflict, as well as the consequences for civilians living in cities at war. From a regional standpoint, her work focuses on the Middle East, Russia, and Eurasia. Dr. Konaev's research has been published by Conflict Management and Peace Science, and her writing on urban warfare has appeared in a variety of policy outlets, including the Bulletin of Atomic Scientists and War on the Rocks. Previously, she was a pre-doctoral fellow at the University of Pennsylvania's Perry World House. Dr. Konaev holds a Ph.D. in Political Science from the University of Notre Dame, an M.A. in Conflict Resolution from Georgetown University, and a B.A. from Brandeis University.

Mark Lomedico is an associate at Caerus Associates working on assessing and understanding cities. Prior to joining Caerus, Mark was an intelligence officer with the U.S. Army. His assignments included: signals intelligence platoon leader, military intelligence company executive officer (forward deployed to RC-East, Afghanistan), and assistant battalion intelligence officer, most recently with 4th Brigade Combat Team (Currahee), 101st Airborne Division (Air Assault). Before serving in the Army, Mark attended Middlebury College's Summer Arabic Language Program and American University in Cairo's Arabic Language Institute. He holds a BA in Political Science from the University of Vermont.

Dennis A. Lowe currently serves as an Armor platoon leader in the 1-66 AR BN. He graduated from the United States Military Academy in 2012 with a Bachelor of Science degree in International Relations.

Michael A. Marra is a veteran of conflicts in Somalia, Bosnia, Haiti, Liberia, and served in major operations including Desert Shield, Storm and Calm, Operation Enduring Freedom and Operation Iraqi Freedom as a commander, staff officer and aviator. He is on the faculty at the US Army War College in the Department of Military Strategy, Planning and Operations.

Mike Matson is a writer in Louisville, Kentucky, and has a deep interest in national security and cyber matters. His fictional writing primarily focuses on military and intelligence-oriented science fiction. In addition to Louisville, Kentucky, and Washington, DC, he has lived, studied, and worked in Brussels, Belgium, and Tallinn, Estonia. He holds a B.A. in International Studies from The American University and a M.S. in Strategic Intelligence from the National Intelligence University, both in Washington, DC. He can be found on *Twitter* at @Mike40245.

Dr. Paul Maxwell is the Cyber Fellow of Computer Engineering at the Army Cyber Institute and an Associate Professor in the department of Electrical Engineering and Computer Science at West Point. He served 24 years in the Army as an Armor officer. His military assignments include Battalion Executive/Operations Officer, Brigade Logistics Officer, Company Commander, Scout Platoon Leader, Company Executive Officer, and Mechanized Infantry Platoon Leader. He is a member of the Institute of Electrical and Electronics Engineers (IEEE) and is a CISSP. His research interests include programmable logic, computer architecture, robotics, robustness, and cyber policy.

Nicholas Melin is part of the Army Corps of Engineers and Fellow in the Chief of Staff of the Army's Strategic Studies Group.

Victor R. Morris is an irregular warfare and counter-improvised-explosive device instructor at the Joint Multinational Readiness Center (JMRC) in Germany, where he has conducted partnered training in sixteen European nations, to include Ukraine, and with four NATO centers of excellence and NATO Joint Warfare Center. A civilian contractor and former combat arms U.S. Army officer, he has experience in both capacities in Iraq and Afghanistan.

Dr. Dawn A. Morrison is a researcher working for the U.S. Army Corps of Engineer (USACE), Engineer Research and Development Center, Construction Engineering Research Laboratory (ERDC-CERL) in Champaign, Illinois. Her research focuses on analyzing and modeling how human populations interact with the built environment. She earned both a M.A. and Ph.D. in Human Geography from the University of Illinois, Urbana-Champaign, and a B.A. in History and Geography from the University of Chicago, The College.

Dr. Robert Muggah oversees research at the Igarapé Institute, a think and do tank working at the interface of security and development. He is also research director of the SecDev Foundation, a cyber-analytics group. He is a fellow at the Graduate Institute in Geneva, the University of Oxford and the University of San Diego. Before that he directed research at the Small Arms Survey (2000-2011). Robert works with the UN and World Bank, among others, in over 30 countries. He was recently named one of the top 100 most influential people in violence reduction and between 2014-2016 he delivered talks at TED Global, the Web Summit and the World Economic Forum in Davos, Abu Dhabi, Medellin and Geneva. He is the founder and executive editor of *Stability Journal*, and serves on the editorial board of several academic journals. Robert is also affiliated with the World Economic Forum Global Agenda Council on Fragility, the Global Initiative Against Transnational Organized Crime, the Know Violence in Childhood Initiative, and other international networks. He earned his PhD from the University of Oxford.

Natalie Myers has served as a community planner with the U.S. Army Corps of Engineers at the construction Engineering Research Laboratory (ERDC-CERL) since 2003. She is currently a member of the Land Management Research Team. Prior to this, Ms. Myers served within the Water Resources Research Team. As part of a diverse area in natural resources, Ms. Myers works to protect environmental, economic, and social resources for future generations. Her technical expertise is in developing geospatial models in support of visualization of patterns, relationships, and trends. Her work has significantly contributed to the Sustainable Installations Regional Resource Assessment (SIRRA)—a spatially-based installation sustainability support tool; the Strategic Sustainability Assessment (SSA)—a resource projection model for regions surrounding military installations; and the Cultural Reasoning and Ethnographic analysis for the Tactical Environment (CREATE)—a knowledge frameworks for infusing socio-cultural theory into Civil Affairs practices. Each project empowers the U.S. military and their adjacent communities to act co-operatively toward a desirable future. For her efforts, Natalie was awarded the Department of the Army Achievement Award for Civilian Service. Ms. Myers received a bachelor's of arts in both urban planning and environmental design from Ball State University and a Master of regional planning from the University of Illinois. Ms. Myers has been inducted into the American Institute of Certified Planners (AICP) and serves in a variety of outreach opportunities such contributing to installation sustainability workshops and representing the Construction Engineering Research Laboratory at professional conferences.

Ryan Orsini is an infantry company commander in 1ˢᵗ Brigade, 82ⁿᵈ Airborne Division, pending assignment to Georgetown University for advanced schooling. CPT Orsini has previously served in 1ˢᵗ Brigade, 101ˢᵗ Airborne Division (AASLT), and has three operational deployments in support of Operation Enduring Freedom, Freedom Sentinel, and Joint Guardian.

Gustav A. Otto is the Distinguished Chair of Defense Intelligence, and DIA Representative to the Army Combined Arms Center & Army University. A career human and counterintelligence officer and veteran of eight deployments in and out of uniform. A graduate of National War College, Gus instructs and advises faculty, and students on issues spanning intelligence, national security and leadership, across government, academic and industry.

Dr. Rebecca Patterson, Lieutenant Colonel U.S. Army and PhD is an Associate Professor at the National Defense University and author of *The Challenge of Nation-Building: Implementing Effective Innovation in the U.S. Army from World War II to the Iraq War* (Rowland & Littlefield, 2014). She is also a member of the Council on Foreign Relations.

Michael Peck is a defense and national security writer. He can be found on *Twitter* and *Facebook*.

Richard Peeke serves as the Chief, Innovation Branch at HQ TRADOC, US Army Capabilities Integration Center, Science & Technology, Research and Accelerated Capabilities Division. His recent assignments include Graduate Research Student as part of the US Army Advanced Civil Schooling Program at The College of William & Mary Materials Science & Engineering—Nanomaterials & Imaging Lab; Special Operations Liaison Officer / Embedded Planner with the NSOCC / Special Operations Joint Task Force deployed to Afghanistan; Chief, Incident Analysis Branch, US Army, Joint Task Force-Civil Support Chemical, Biological, Radiological and Nuclear Response Operations; and Deputy Commander North Carolina Army National Guard, 42nd Civil Support Team North Carolina Area Weapons of Mass Destruction Response Operations. LTC Peeke holds a Master of Science, Applied Science—Materials Science and Engineering from the College of William and Mary and a Bachelor of Science in Biology/ Biological Sciences, General from the US Air Force Academy.

Dr. William G. Pierce retired after thirty years of active duty as an officer in the Army Corps of Engineers. He is on the faculty at the US Army War College in the Department of Military Strategy, Planning and Operations. His current role in the department is the Director of the Advanced Strategic Art Program (ASAP), a position he has held for eight years.

Tom Pike is a Strategic Intelligence officer in the US Army. He has studied Complex Adaptive System applications to analysis for the past 8 years, initiated and contributed to the Inter-Agency Agent Based Modeling efforts, and served as a representative to the Defense Intelligence Socio-Cultural Capabilities Council.

Frank Prautzsch is the President of Velocity Technology Partners LLC, being recognized as a technology and business leader known for exposing or crafting innovative technology solutions for the DoD, SOF, DHS and Intelligence community. His focus is upon innovation and not invention. His waking moments are spent in the process of identifying and contriving use cases for global commercial technologies that the government is unaware of, or at best has yet to assume a use case for that could support their needs. Prior to his own consulting program, Mr. Prautzsch served as the Sr. VP for Government Programs for ORBCOMM, the Director of the Raytheon Rapid Initiatives Group (RIG), and Director of Army Requirements for Hughes Space and Communications Company While on active duty in the US Army, Mr. Prautzsch held a variety of Command, Staff, and Engineering positions. He served on numerous Joint Task Force, Army, and contingency missions across all operational environments and was instrumental in defining many of the Army's MILSATCOM concepts of operations and doctrine used today. He was the Secretary of the Army's selection to Lead the DoD MILSATCOM Architecture under the DoD Space Architect. During this process, he was instrumental in formulating a $42B investment plan for wideband, protected and narrowband communications for the Nation. Mr. Prautzsch holds a Bachelor of Science in Engineering from the United States Military Academy at West Point, is a distinguished graduate of the Marine Corps Signal Advanced Course, Army Airborne School, Ranger School, and Command and General Staff College. He attended Raytheon's University of Chicago Business Development School and is Six Sigma qualified. He also holds a Master of Science Degree from Naval Postgraduate School in Monterey, California with a degree in Systems Technology (C3) and Space.

Dr. Robb Randall leads the Army Research Laboratory's (ARL) Atmospheric Science Center, the Battlefield Environment Division's entity managing and coordinating ARL's open campus initiative, bringing together government, industry, and academia for the mission of advancing atmospheric science and its application to critical defense technologies through a collaborative, innovative research ecosystem. He is also Chief (A) of the Atmospheric Dynamics Branch. Dr. Randall recently retired from the Air Force after 28+ years. During his career he serve in Special Operations, Operational Weather Squadron, as a FOA Military Deputy Director and Division Chief, Advisor to the Iraqi Air Force, and Air Force Institute of Technology Professor. Before his retirement he served as the Commander, 16th Weather Squadron. The 16th Weather Squadron functions as the Air Force's center of excellence for atmospheric model development, implementation, and visualization. As Commander, he executed a worldwide weather support mission that delivered advanced terrestrial and space environmental intelligence tools to Joint warfighters, national agencies, and allied nations for planning and execution of full-spectrum military operations in addition to providing meteorological support to DoD research and development, acquisition, testing and sustainment. Dr. Randall received a B.S. in Meteorology from the University of Oklahoma in 1995, M.S. in Meteorology from the Air Force Institute of Technology in 2002 and Ph.D. from the University of Arizona in 2007.

Dr. Mark Read is a Colonel in the U.S. Army, and serves as the Deputy Head of the Department of Geography and Environmental Engineering at the U.S. Military Academy, West Point. A career infantry officer, Mark has served in a wide variety of assignments in the U.S, Europe, and the Middle East. He holds a BS in Environmental Engineering from West Point, and a MS and PhD in Geography from The Pennsylvania State University.

Dr. Amy Krakowka Richmond is an associate professor of Geography in the Department of Geography and Environmental Engineering at the United States Military Academy at West Point NY. She applies her skills to understanding the interactions between environmental resources and human populations. Her current research on Sub-Saharan Africa develops an interdisciplinary framework to investigate the relationship between environmental processes and human wellbeing that can be adapted to any geographic location.

Richard Russo is an intelligence analyst and Fellow in the Chief of Staff of the Army's Strategic Studies Group.

Adam Scher is the battalion executive officer of 1-508th Parachute Infantry Regiment. Major Scher graduated the United States Military

Academy in 2004 and Columbia University's School of International and Public Affairs in 2013. He previously served as an Assistant Professor of American Politics in the Department of Social Sciences at West Point and has deployed to both Afghanistan and Iraq as a platoon leader, company commander, and battalion and brigade staff officer. He is published in *The Washington Post*, *The Hill*, *Military Review*, *Task and Purpose*, was a guest contributor to *Tom Rick's Best Defense*, and completed a *TEDx* talk on leadership.

David Shunk is a retired USAF Colonel, B-52G pilot, and Desert Storm combat veteran whose last military assignment was as the B-2 Vice Wing Commander of the 509th Bomb Wing, Whitman AFB, MO. Currently, he is a researcher/writer and DA civilian working in Army Capabilities Integration Center (ARCIC), Future Warfare Division, Fort Eustis, Virginia. He has a National Security Strategy MS from the National War College.

Dr. Shade T. Shutters is a research scientist with the Global Security Initiative at Arizona State University, with additional faculty appointments in the Center of Social Dynamics and Complexity, Center on the Future of War, and the Center for Policy Informatics. He holds a bachelor's in finance from Indiana University, a doctorate in theoretical ecology from Arizona State University, and completed a post-doc in applied economics at the University of Vigo, Spain. His research is focused on the dynamics of urban systems and the networks both within and between cities.

Matthew Simonson a second-year doctoral student in Network Science at Northeastern University. His research focuses on using network and data science tools in conjunction with traditional qualitative methods to predict outbreaks of ethnic and political mass violence.

John Spencer is a retired U.S. Army infantry major currently serving as Chair of Urban Warfare Studies at the Modern War Institute at West Point. He served over twenty-five years in the Army to include two combat deployments to Iraq. Considered an expert on urban warfare, his writing has appeared in the *New York Times*, *Wall Street Journal*, *Politico*, *Foreign Policy*, and many other publications. He holds a master of policy management degree from Georgetown University.

Jim Staley leads the Army Weather Proponent Office (AWPO) at the U.S. Army Intelligence Center of Excellence, Ft Huachuca AZ. Since inception in 2008, the AWPO is responsible for investigating and processing Army-unique weather support requirements utilizing the DoD's Joint Capabilities Integration and Development System (JCIDS). The AWPO also identifies and disseminates Army weather support doctrine. Additionally, the AWPO interfaces with the Army-wide weather Research and Development community to incorporate Army weather requirements into collective R&D efforts. Mr. Staley has extensive experience focused on tactical Army and Special Operations weather support to world-wide DoD missions. During his career he led weather support to Joint Special Operations forces, conventional Army units at multiple levels, and to the Air Force Special Operations Command. In 2007 Mr. Staley retired from the U.S. Air Force after 23 years of service. Mr. Staley received his B.S. in Geophysics from Boise State University in 1984, and his M.S. in Atmospheric Science from Colorado State University in 1990.

Colin Tansey is a Major in the U.S. Army, and serves as the assistant course director for Physical Geography (EV203) in the Department of Geography and Environmental Engineering at the U.S. Military Academy, West Point. A career military intelligence officer, Colin has served in a wide variety of assignments in the U.S, Europe, and the Middle East. He holds a BA in Anthropology from California State University, San Bernardino, and a MA in Security Studies (Europe and Eurasia) from the Naval Postgraduate School.

Darryl Ward has 30 combined years of experience in Military Intelligence with the U.S. Army, civil service, and as a government contractor. He is retired from the U.S. Army and currently serving as an MCR contractor within the TRADOC G27 OPFOR Program Management Directorate supporting the U.S. Army Quality Assurance Program. He holds a BS in Education from the University of Arkansas and an MA in Health Business Administration from Webster University.

Jon Watkins is the founder and Chief Operating Officer of Dignitas Technologies LLC. He has 25 years of applied experience related to modeling and simulation applications, with a specific focus on terrain databases, database generation, terrain services, dynamic terrain, and entity-level movement control algorithms. Mr. Watkins has worked with the modeling and simulation terrain formats and/or services for many Army simulation systems (such as SIMNET, ModSAF/OTB, CCTT, JSIMS/WARSIM, OneSAF, Common Driver Trainer). Mr. Watkins presently supports a wide range of constructive and virtual programs, including major programs and research efforts related to Synthetic Natural Environments, terrain representations, terrain reasoning, weather/ocean, and simulation and training.

Dr. Peter W. Wielhouwer is in the Command and Operations Group for JFCOM / J9 with General Dynamics Advanced Information Systems.

Dr. Richard L. Wolfel is an associate professor of Geography and the Chair of Cross Cultural Competence in the Center for Languages, Cultures and Regional Studies at the US Military Academy, West Point. Rick is a social and political geography with strong research interests in urban geography, nationalism, social movements and migration with a regional interest in Post-Soviet Landscapes. He holds a BSED in American History and Geography from West Chester University, a MA in Urban Geography from the University of Cincinnati and a PhD in Geography from Indiana University.

Colin D. Wood has 6 years of military service in the U.S. Army, and served in combat in Iraq. He is currently a Federal Pathways Intern conducting research in international relations for the U.S. Army

Corps of Engineers (USACE), Engineer Research and Development Center Construction Engineering Research Laboratory (ERDC-CERL). Additionally, he is an Atlantic Council Veterans Take Point Initiative Thought Leadership Fellow and is pursuing his M.A. in International Relations: U.S. Foreign Policy and National Security at American University's School of International Service. He holds a B.A. in International Studies from the University of North Texas and is a former National Science Foundation Research Experience for Undergraduates (NSF-REU) Fellow, and a Department of Homeland Security, Homeland Security Science, Technology, Engineering, and Mathematics (DHS, HS-STEM) Intern.

Made in the USA
Monee, IL
27 March 2020